Bullying in North American Schools

Forty-two states have now passed statutes mandating that schools have a bullying policy in place, a remarkable increase since the first edition of *Bullying in American Schools* was published in 2004. Although these statutes vary in their requirements, most school districts realize that bullying behavior has to be addressed through targeted prevention and intervention program. This book provides an exciting compilation of research on bullying in school-aged youth by a representative group of researchers, including developmental, social, counseling, school, and clinical psychologists. Its social–ecological perspective illustrates the complexity of bullying behaviors and offers suggestions for databased decision-making to intervene and reduce those behaviors. The book provides empirical guidance for schools as they develop bullying prevention and intervention programs or evaluate existing programs.

Key Features

Ecological Perspective—The book is organized by a social–ecological perspective in which bullying is examined across multiple contexts including individual characteristics, peer and family influences, and classroom dynamics. An introductory chapter explains the tenets of the social–ecological framework and how each chapter exemplifies this perspective.

Empirical Research—Chapters include basic research data on bullying and victimization from samples in the United States and Canada. Evaluation data for existing programs are also presented.

Implications for Practice—Service providers (teachers, school psychologists, counsellors, school administrators, school social workers, psychotherapists in private practice) will learn the practical implications of various types of programs and how to choose and implement one that fits their school ecology.

Expertise—Chapter authors, all of whom are leaders in the area of bullying research in the United States and Canada, were selected on the basis of the following criteria: 1) they have an active bullying research program within North American schools, 2) their theoretical framework is social–ecological, and 3) their findings have practical implications for school service providers as well as for future research.

Dorothy L. Espelage is Professor in the Child Development Division of the Educational Psychology department at the University of Illinois at Urbana-Champaign.

Susan M. Swearer is Associate Professor of School Psychology at the University of Nebraska-Lincoln.

Bullying in North American Schools

Second Edition

Edited by

Dorothy L. Espelage and Susan M. Swearer

Routledge
Taylor & Francis Group

NEW YORK AND LONDON

KH

First published 2004
by Lawrence Erlbaum Associates, Inc.

This edition published 2011
by Routledge
270 Madison Avenue, New York, NY 10016

Simultaneously published in the UK
by Routledge
2 Park Square, Milton Park, Abingdon, Oxon OX14 4RN

Routledge is an imprint of the Taylor & Francis Group, an informa business

Typeset in Minion by EvS Communication Networx, Inc.
Printed and bound in the United States of America on acid-free paper by Edwards Brothers, Inc.

Library of Congress Cataloging-in-Publication Data
Bullying in North American schools / Dorothy L. Espelage & Susan M. Swearer, [editors]. — 2nd ed.
p. cm.
Includes bibliographical references and index.
1. Bullying in schools—United States—Prevention. 2. Bullying in schools—United States—Psychological aspects. I. Espelage, Dorothy L. (Dorothy Lynn) II. Swearer, Susan M.
LB3013.32.B85 2010
371.5'8—dc22
2010014442

ISBN13: 978–0–415–80654–1 (hbk)
ISBN13: 978–0–415–80655–8 (pbk)
ISBN13: 978–0–203–84289–8 (ebk)

9/2/11

I dedicate this book to my dear colleague and friend—Sue Swearer—who shares my passion to create safer schools for students.

Dorothy L. Espelage

As a member of the mutual admiration society, I would like to dedicate this book to Dorothy Espelage, colleague and friend extraordinaire. I'm looking forward to the next decade of collaboration and friendship!

Susan M. Swearer

CONTENTS

LIST OF CONTRIBUTORS

Barbara Ball, Safeplace, Austin, Texas

Christopher D. Bell is an Assistant Professor in the Psychology Department at Augusta State University. In addition to his research on bullying intervention and prevention programs, he also studies the factors related to adjustment to university. He maintains a part-time practice at Walton Rehabilitation Health System working with individuals who are adjusting to chronic illness and traumatic brain injury.

Eric C. Brown is a Research Scientist with the Social Development Research Group, School of Social Work, University of Washington and is the Principal Investigator of the school-randomized trial of *Steps to Respect: A School Bullying Prevention Program*. His research interests include evaluating community- and school-based prevention programs and policies, and the application of advanced quantitative methods and designs in these evaluations.

Diane Carlson Jones, PhD, is a Professor of Educational Psychology at the University of Washington in Seattle, WA. She specializes in the social–emotional development of adolescents with an emphasis on gender issues.

Allison Champion, MA, is a graduate student in School Psychology at the University of Nebraska-Lincoln. Her research interests include promoting positive school and classroom environments, promoting student satisfaction with school, and consulting with teachers and parents to problem solve.

Henian Chen, M.D., Ph.D., until recently was a Research Scientist in the Division of Biostatistics at New York State Psychiatric Institute; Assistant Professor in Psychiatry at Columbia University Medical Center, New York; and a Co-Investigator of the Children in the Community (CIC) Study, an ongoing longitudinal study of child psychopathology. Dr. Chen is currently Senior Biostatistician at Winthrop University Hospital and Associate Professor of Preventive Medicine at Stony Brook University Medical School, and continues to collaborate on the CIC study.

Patricia Cohen, PhD, is a Research Scientist in the Division of Epidemiology at New York State Psychiatric Institute, and Professor of Epidemiology in Psychiatry at Columbia University Medical Center, New York. She is Principal Investigator of the Children in the Community Study, an ongoing study of child psychopathology, and a widely recognized expert on statistical and design issues in the behavioral sciences.

Adam Collins, MA, is a second-year doctoral student in the School Psychology Program at the University of Nebraska-Lincoln. He has co-authored two chapters on bullying and is the site developer for the Bully Research Network (brnet.unl.edu). His research interests are in the area of gender differences among youth who cyber-bully and the long-term repercussions of cyberbullying.

Thomas N. Crawford, PhD, is a Research Scientist in the Division of Epidemiology at New York State Psychiatric Institute, and Assistant Clinical Professor in Psychiatry at Columbia University Medical Center, New York. He is a Co-Investigator on the Children in the Community Study, an ongoing longitudinal study of child psychopathology.

Michelle K. Demaray is an Associate Professor in the Psychology Department at Northern Illinois University. She conducts research on bullying and victimization in schools, perceived social support, and Attention-Deficit/Hyperactivity Disorder.

Beth Doll, PhD, is Professor in the School Psychology Program at the University of Nebraska-Lincoln. Her research addresses school mental health practices that enhance the well-being of students in naturally occurring communities, with particular attention to classrooms and playgrounds.

Renae D. Duncan, PhD, is Chair of the Department of Psychology at Murray State University. She earned her PhD in clinical psychology from Florida State University. She also served a post-doctoral fellowship at the National Crime Victims Research and Treatment Center in Charleston, South Carolina.

Leihua V. Edstrom, PhD, studied implementation factors in school-based prevention outcomes while at Committee for Children. She currently serves as a school psychologist in Bellevue, WA, with interests in prevention, consultation, and cultural and linguistic influences on learning.

Dorothy L. Espelage is Professor in the Child Development Division of the Educational Psychology department at the University of Illinois at Urbana-Champaign.

Richard A. Fabes, PhD, is the Dee and John Whiteman Distinguished Professor of Child Development at Arizona State University. He is also the Director of the School of Social and Family Dynamics, as well as the Co-Director of The Lives of Girls and Boys: Initiatives on Gender Development and Relationships. He studies girls' and boys' peer relations, social competence, and school success during the preschool and elementary school years.

Kate Fernandez is a Data Collection Manager at the Social Development Research Group, School of Social Work, University of Washington, and specializes in multimodal collection of data from various populations related to preventive interventions.

Melanie A. Freedman works at The Children's Hospital of Philadelphia, and The University of Pennsylvania School of Medicine.

Karin S. Frey, PhD, is Research Associate Professor of Educational Psychology at the University of Washington. Her work in school-based prevention focuses on the influence of teacher and peer factors in bullying, retaliation, and socially responsible behavior.

Carla Garrity, PhD, is an author with Creating Caring Communities, creators of the Bully-Proofing Your School Program, and a child psychologist in independent practice with The Neuro-Developmental Center in Denver, Colorado.

Scott D. Gest is an Associate Professor in the Department of Human Development and Family Studies at The Pennsylvania State University. His research focuses on youths' peer relationships and school adjustment in middle childhood and adolescence. His featured project with Professor Philip Rodkin of the University of Illinois investigates how teachers can better manage classroom social dynamics to improve student learning and adjustment.

Sherri Gosney, MS, is a doctoral student in the School of Social and Family Dynamics at Arizona State University. She studies the links between children's regulatory abilities, their experiences with teachers, and school success in preschool and the early elementary years.

Kevin P. Haggerty is the Assistant Director of Social Development Research Group, School of Social Work, University of Washington. He specializes in the development and implementation of prevention programs at the community, school, and family levels. He is the Principal Investigator of the Family Connections study.

Laura D. Hanish, PhD, is an Associate Professor in the School of Social and Family Dynamics at Arizona State University. She is Co-Director of The Lives of Girls and Boys: Initiatives on Gender Development and Relationships. She studies girls' and boys' peer relations, problem behaviors, and school success during the preschool and elementary school years.

Koren Hanson is a Data Manager at the Social Development Research Group, School of Social Work, University of Washington, and works on a variety of studies examining family-, school-, and community-based prevention programs and policies.

Patricia H. Hawley received her PhD from the University of California Riverside in 1994 and she spent her postdoctoral years at the Max Planck Institute in Berlin, Germany, and Yale University. She specializes in evolution and social development, with her research focusing on the role of social dominance in interpersonal relationships and personality development. Her provocative views on aggression and social competence are published in multiple book chapters, journal articles, and in her edited volume, *Aggression and Adaptation: The Bright Side to Bad Behavior* (2007, Erlbaum).

Alison Hill, PhD, is currently a Senior Research Associate in the Center for Spoken Language Understanding at Oregon Health Sciences University, where she studies the early social and emotional development of young children at risk.

Miriam K. Hirschstein, PhD, is Director of Evaluation at the Center on Infant Mental Health and Development at the University of Washington. Her work focuses on classroom-based practices to promote children's social–emotional development.

Melissa Holt is a Research Associate at the Crimes Against Children Research Center. She has extensive experience researching youth violence, with an emphasis on the intersection between bullying and victimization and perpetration outside the school environment. Further, she has explored how multiple victimization affects psychological functioning, and which factors promote resilience among victimized youth.

Arthur M. Horne is a Distinguished Research Professor and Dean of the College of Education at the University of Georgia. He has conducted extensive research on understanding and reducing violence and aggression in children, families, and schools and is fortunate to have experienced little of the topic in his life.

Shelley Hymel is a Professor in the Faculty of Education at the University of British Columbia, whose research focuses on social and emotional learning and development. Currently, she serves on the executive teams for the Human Early Learning Partnership, an interdisciplinary research unit aimed at optimizing children's development, and PREVNet, a National Centre of Excellence New Initiative, focused on "Promoting Relationships and Eliminating Violence," and is a regional hub director for the Canadian Prevention Science Knowledge Cluster, funded by the Social Sciences and Humanities Research Council of Canada. She has published extensively in the area of social development and peer relations both nationally and internationally and works regularly with children and youth experiencing social difficulties and with schools and school districts that want to address the social side of learning.

Kathryn Jens, PhD, is an author, trainer, and researcher with Creating Caring Communities, creators of the Bully-Proofing Your School Program, and a School Psychologist with the Cherry Creek School District in Greenwood Village, Colorado.

Jeffrey G. Johnson, PhD, is a Research Scientist in the Division of Epidemiology at New York State Psychiatric Institute, and Associate Professor in Psychiatry at Columbia University Medical Center, New York. He is a Co-Investigator of the Children in the Community Study, an ongoing longitudinal study of child psychopathology.

Kristin Jones, M.A., is a doctoral student in the School Psychology Program at the University of Nebraska-Lincoln. Her research interests include school mental health services and the role that administrators and teachers play in the delivery of school-wide practices that promote students' socio-emotional competence.

Stephanie Kasen, PhD, is a Research Scientist in the Division of Epidemiology at New York State Psychiatric Institute, and Associate Clinical Professor in Psychiatry at Columbia University Medical Center, New York. She is a Co-Principal Investigator of the Children in the Community (CIC) Study, an ongoing longitudinal study of child psychopathology, and Principal Investigator of the Suicide Transmission across Three Generations Study, which is based on the CIC cohort, their parents, and their offspring.

Melissa Keyes is retired and living in Madison, WI.

Brian Koenig, MS, is the President of K12 Associates in Middleton, Wisconsin. He has been a trainer, speaker, and consultant since 1983 and has worked with more than 100 districts to prevent antisocial behaviors at school.

Stephen S. Leff, PhD, works at The Children's Hospital of Philadelphia, and University of Pennsylvania School of Medicine.

Susan P. Limber, PhD, MLS, is the Dan Olweus Distinguished Professor within the Institute on Family and Neighborhood Life at Clemson University, where she also is a professor in the Department of Psychology.

Sabina M. Low, PhD, is an Assistant Professor of Clinical Psychology at Wichita State University. She primarily draws from ecological models to study the overlap and prevention of bullying and dating violence. Additional interests include family and parenting interventions, and family-peer linkages in the development of health-risk behaviors.

Christine K. Malecki is an Associate Professor in the Psychology Department at Northern Illinois University where she is the Director of the School Psychology Program. Her research program includes the study of elements of response to intervention, including curriculum-based measurement, social support, and peer victimization.

Carol Lynn Martin, PhD, is a Cowden Distinguished Professor in the School of Social and Family Dynamics at Arizona State University. She is the Executive Director of The Lives of Girls and Boys: Initiatives on Gender Development and Relationships. She studies gender development, peer relations, and school success in young children.

Suzanne Martin, Principal at Martin Research Consulting, earned a PhD in Educational Psychology and an MS in Marketing from the University of Arizona. She has over 15 years experience actively conducting all aspects of the research process with a specific expertise in youth. She also spent time as a postdoctoral fellow at the Annenberg Public Policy Center at the University of Pennsylvania, working with behavior change expert, Dr. Martin Fishbein, conducting research on teens, sex and the media.

Patricia McDougall is an Associate Professor and Associate Dean at St. Thomas More College, University of Saskatchewan. Her primary area of research involves the study of social relationships in childhood and adolescence with a focus on bullying, peer status, and friendships.

Julie P. MacEvoy, Lynch School of Education, Boston College.

Anthony D. Pellegrini is a Professor in the Department of Educational Psychology at the University of Minnesota, Twin Cities Campus. His teaching and research interests include observational research methods, children's peer relations, the role of play in development, and social contextual influences on classroom achievement.

Amy Plog, PhD, is Director of Research for Creating Caring Communities, creators of the Bully-Proofing Your School Program, and a psychologist with the Cherry Creek School District in Greenwood Village, Colorado.

William Porter, PhD, is Director of Creating Caring Communities, creators of the Bully-Proofing Your School Program.

Thomas J. Power works at The Children's Hospital of Philadelphia, and The University of Pennsylvania School of Medicine.

Katherine A. Raczynski is the project director of the Healthy Teens project, a seven-year study investigating adolescent social development. She has worked with teachers, parents, and students to reduce bullying and aggression in middle and high schools, and is pursuing a PhD in Educational Psychology at the University of Georgia.

Kisha Haye Radliff, PhD, is an Assistant Professor at The Ohio State University in the School Psychology Program. She teaches courses on mental health in the school, counseling theory and techniques, social–emotional assessment, and the biological basis of behaviors. Her research interests include exploring mental health issues and how they affect the academic experience and examining bullying and aggression among children and adolescents.

Jacklyn Ratliff received her MA from the University of Kansas in 2008. She is presently a graduate student in the Social Psychology Program at the University of Kansas. Her research broadly focuses on aggression while specifically looking at the role stereotyping plays in perceptions of aggressive people and behaviors.

Philip C. Rodkin is an Associate Professor of Child Development in the Departments of Educational Psychology and Psychology at the University of Illinois at Urbana-Champaign. His interests include children's personality and social development, with a focus on peer relationships in childhood and adolescence. His featured project with Professor Scott Gest of the Pennsylvania State University investigates how teachers can better manage classroom social dynamics to improve student learning and adjustment.

Chad A. Rose is a doctoral candidate in the Department of Special Education at the University of Illinois at Urbana-Champaign. He has spent the past four years investigating bullying among students with disabilities on a federally funded grant entitled *Middle School Bullying and Sexual Violence: Measurement Issues and Etiological Models*. His research interests include examining perpetration and victimization among marginalized student populations and investigating multi-tiered approaches to bully prevention.

Lisa H. Rosen is a Postdoctoral Fellow in the School of Behavioral and Brain Sciences, at The University of Texas at Dallas.

Barri Rosenbluth, LCSW, directs SafePlace's Expect Respect Program in Austin, Texas. Expect Respect provides school-based counseling and support groups for vulnerable youth, mobilizes teen leaders, educates students, teachers and parents and engages the entire community in building healthy teen relationships. Ms. Rosenbluth has over 20 years of experience in developing sexual violence prevention programs and curricula.

Brian H. Smith is a Research Scientist at the non-profit Committee for Children. He earned his PhD at the Social Development Research Group at the University of Washington. His research interests include the development and evaluation of bullying prevention and social emotional learning interventions.

Samuel Song, PhD, is Assistant Professor of School Psychology at Seattle University. Interested in social justice issues and population-based school mental health, his research examines school bullying interventions that work in low-resource schools and communities.

Kathryn N. Stump received her MS from Pennsylvania State University in 2007. She is currently a doctoral student in the Developmental Psychology Program at University of Kansas. Her research focuses on power in peer relations and, specifically, the role that social power plays in dyadic friendship dynamics.

Susan M. Swearer, PhD is an Associate Professor of School Psychology at the University of Nebraska-Lincoln (UNL) and a supervising psychologist in the Child and Adolescent Therapy Clinic at UNL. She has been studying the relationship between internalizing processes and bullying behaviors for over a decade. She is also the co-author of the book, *Bullying Prevention and Intervention: Realistic Strategies for Schools* (2009, Guilford Press Publishers).

Marion K. Underwood is the Ashbel Smith Professor of Psychological Sciences at the School of Behavioral and Brain Sciences, The University of Texas at Dallas.

Tracy Vaillancourt is a Canada Research Chair in Children's Mental Health and Violence Prevention at the University of Ottawa where she is cross-appointed as an Associate Professor in the Faculty of Education and School of Psychology. She is also an Adjunct Associate Professor in the Department of Psychology, Neuroscience, and Behaviour and a core member of the Offord Centre for Child Studies at McMaster University. Her research examines the links between aggression/bullying and children's mental health functioning, with a focus on social neuroscience. She is funded by the Social Sciences and Humanities Research Council of Canada, the Canadian Institutes for Health Research, the Canadian Foundation for Innovation and the Canada Research Chairs Program.

Linda Anne Valle, Centers for Disease Control and Prevention.

Mark J. Van Ryzin, PhD, Research Associate, Oregon Social Learning Center, was awarded a PhD in Educational Psychology by the University of Minnesota in 2008. His primary research interests are social, motivational, and developmental processes in adolescence, particularly in the educational context.

Cixin Wang, MA, is a fourth-year doctoral student in the Department of Educational Psychology at the University of Nebraska-Lincoln. She received her MS degree in Child

Development, and her MA degree in Educational Psychology. Her research interests include bullying, peer victimization, depression, and anxiety.

Daniel J. Whitaker, Georgia State University.

Jennifer L. Whitford is a licensed psychologist employed at the Charlie Norwood VA Medical Center in Augusta, GA. Her clinical work focuses on the treatment of traumatic brain injury, chronic pain and other medical conditions. Her dissertation evaluated the efficacy of a multiple family intervention for first time juvenile offenders and has resulted in continued collaboration and friendships with the Bully Busters research team.

Michele Ybarra, PhD, is President and Research Director for Internet Solutions for Kids, a non-profit research organization focused on leveraging technology to promote healthy youth development. She is internationally known for her work in Internet harassment and associated psychosocial characteristics, and is on the forefront of technology-based intervention program development.

ACKNOWLEDGMENTS

Dorothy L. Espelage: I would like to thank my editorial team at the University of Illinois, Urbana-Champaign: John Elliott, Nicole Patterson, and Chad Rose. And my undergraduate research assistants who also participated in making this book happen: Allie Fish, Amanda Mangian, Amanda Ramirez, Brittany Glenn, Christina Lee, Dan Frost, Daria Jammal, Dominique Malebranche, Emily McDevitt, Joo Eun Park, Justin Steffen, Lindsay Taylor, Melvin Tillman, Michelle Miernicki, and Olga Lopez. Also, I would like to acknowledge Ray Musleh's endless patience, daily encouragement, and support.

Susan M. Swearer: I would like to thank Dr. Marjorie Kostelnik, Dean of the College of Education and Human Sciences at the University of Nebraska-Lincoln. Behind every successful faculty member is a supportive Dean, and for her unwavering support, I am truly grateful. I am also fortunate to have a great group of graduate students in the Target Bullying Research Project who helped with this second edition: Jami Givens, Cixin Wang, Adam Collins, Brandi Berry, and Paige Lembeck. Thank you for your hard work, dedication, and tenacity! Last, but definitely not least, I would like to thank my husband, Dr. Scott Napolitano, and our two daughters, Catherine and Alexandra, for their never-ending support, encouragement, and patience as "mom writes."

Introduction

1

EXPANDING THE SOCIAL–ECOLOGICAL FRAMEWORK OF BULLYING AMONG YOUTH

Lessons Learned from the Past and Directions for the Future

SUSAN M. SWEARER AND DOROTHY L. ESPELAGE

Broad problems require broad hypotheses.

(Morse & Allport, 1952)

In 1952, an article was published in the *Journal of Psychology* that sought to unearth the causes of anti-Semitism (Morse & Allport, 1952). What the authors found was that the variables related to anti-Semitism included physical behaviors (i.e., discriminatory actions), verbal behavior (i.e., derogatory comments), and affective states (i.e., feelings of aversion). The authors also concluded that no one factor could be delineated as the only cause of anti-Semitism. The complexities of behaviors that comprise discrimination have been studied for over 60 years. When the first edition of this book was published in 2004, we argued that bullying had to be studied across individual, peer, family, school, community, and cultural contexts (see Figure 1.1). Like discrimination, bullying is a complex phenomenon, with multiple causal factors and multiple outcomes.

We and other authors (Espelage & Swearer, 2010; Garbarino & deLara, 2002; Newman, Horne, & Bartolomucci, 2000; Orpinas & Horne, 2006; Swearer & Doll, 2001; Swearer et al., 2006) have continued to frame bullying among school-aged youth from this social ecological perspective. Drawing a parallel to discriminatory behavior, research on bullying has established that bully perpetration includes physical and verbal behavior within an affective framework (i.e., the intent to harm) (Olweus, 1993; Swearer, Espelage, Vailliancourt, & Hymel, 2010). Bullying comprises a complex set of antecedents, behaviors, and consequences. The reasons why children and adolescents bully one another are complex, multiply-determined, and differentially reinforced. In the next section we will explicate these factors and frame the content for the second edition of *Bullying in North American Schools*.

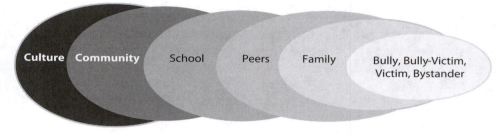

Figure 1.1 An expanded social–ecological framework of bullying among youth.

EQUIFINALITY OF BULLYING BEHAVIORS

In the mid-1900s, Ludwig von Bertalanffy, an Austrian biologist, developed a theory known as General System Theory (GST; von Bertalanffy, 1969) that posited that the same result may be achieved via many different paths. This concept is termed "equifinality." Applied to the study of human behavior, equifinality refers to the fact that many different early experiences can lead to similar outcomes. In other words, there are many different early experiences that can lead to the same end result. Specific to the study of bullying behaviors, equifinality suggests that there are many different factors that can result in the bullying phenomenon.

Much has been written about the reciprocal interplay among the individual, family, peer group, school, community, and cultural influences on human behavior. Motivated by the writings of Uri Bronfenbrenner (1979), research on bullying and peer victimization has been influenced by the reality that human behavior is multiply-determined and multiply-influenced (Astor, Meyer, & Pitner, 2001; Espelage & Swearer, 2009; Espelage & Swearer, 2010; Swearer et al., 2006). Take for example the following scenario:

> A child (we'll call her Sarah) who is impulsive and who has a hostile attributional style lives in a family with a father who is a biologist who works in private industry and a mother who is a homemaker. Sarah's mother is very concerned about her daughter's social status and she wants her to have all the advantages that she didn't have growing up. Sarah goes to school in a middle-class community with a high emphasis on athletics. She is one of the star athletes, playing soccer, softball, and club swimming. In the community in which Sarah lives, athletics are highly valued and the girls on her soccer team enjoy high social status. The girls all have Facebook accounts, cell phones, and are typical adolescents, spending about four hours per day on their computers and cell phones. A new girl (we'll call her Beth) who is also a star athlete moves into the community. Sarah and her friends end up being relationally aggressive to Beth. As they tell the story, she "deserved" the bullying since her family bought the largest house in this community and she had an "attitude." What they failed to mention was that Beth tried out for the soccer team and was awarded a starting position over one of Sarah's friends, who had been on the team for three years. Sarah and her friend organized a Facebook campaign against Beth, who was devastated when she found out that her "friends" on the soccer team were spreading rumors that she was a lesbian. Her parents didn't understand what happened since Beth was always well liked and had been a star athlete and student throughout junior high and in to her high school years.

If we change any variable in this example, the end result is that the bullying might not have happened. As the complexity of this example illustrates, the principle of equifinality can be applied to bullying behavior. There are no simple explanations for bullying—it is often the result of complex psychological and social interactions.

OVERVIEW OF *BULLYING IN NORTH AMERICAN SCHOOLS*

The second edition of this book is an exciting compilation of research conducted across North America by a representative group of psychological researchers, including developmental psychologists, social psychologists, counseling psychologists, school psychologists, and clinical psychologists who are studying bullying among school-aged youth. Thus, the contributors in this volume bring both research and clinical perspectives to the phenomena of bullying and peer victimization. As such, this book provides support for the complexity of bullying behaviors and offers suggestions for using databased decision-making to intervene and reduce bullying among school-aged youth. Given the complexity of bullying, it is our aim that this book will provide guidance for researchers, school personnel, parents, and students as they develop prevention and intervention programming to put an end to bullying in our nation's schools. In the sections that follow, we will outline the chapters that comprise this exciting second edition of *Bullying in North American Schools*.

INDIVIDUAL CHARACTERISTICS ASSOCIATED WITH BULLYING

In this section, the chapters unearth individual factors that are associated with bullying among school-aged youth. As the example of Sarah and Beth illustrate, individual personality characteristics are part of the equifinality in resultant bullying behaviors. Swearer, Collins, Radliff, and Wang in their chapter "Internalizing Problems in Students Involved in Bullying and Victimization" review and demonstrate the important role of internalizing behaviors among bullies, victims, and bully-victims. They present data collected on a longitudinal sample of 5th through 9th graders and suggest that bullying prevention should include not only primary prevention approaches, but also more targeted one-on-one mental health treatment for bullies, victims, and bully-victims. These factors are further explicated in Vaillancourt, Hymel, and McDougall's chapter "Why does being Bullied Hurt so Much?: Insights from Neuroscience" where they argue that being bullied causes significant social pain, which, over time, alters brain functioning. These insights from neuroscience have been notably missing from the bullying literature and Vaillancourt and colleagues make this important link. In addition to understanding these individual personality and neurological characteristics among youth involved in bullying and victimization, Rose reviews the literature on bullying among students with disabilities in his chapter "Bullying among Students with Disabilities: Impact and Implications," and argues that interventions must target at-risk subgroups of students. Whole-school anti-bullying initiatives may not effectively address bullying by or toward students who are in special education.

Two chapters in this section deal with a growing concern for parents and educators—cyberbullying or technologically based aggression. Ybarra, Espelage, and Martin in their chapter "Unwanted Sexual and Harassing Experiences: From School to Text

Messaging" examine the intersection of youth sexual and relational/physical harassment at school and through text messaging. Of children and adolescents between 10 and 18 years of age, 23% of youth reported some type of harassment both at school and via text messaging. Findings suggest that harassment both inside and outside of school may affect school safety perceptions. Underwood and Rosen in their literature review of gender differences in bullying and cyberbullying, "Gender and Bullying: Moving Beyond Mean Differences to Consider Conceptions of Bullying, Processes by which Bullying Unfolds, and Cyberbullying," encourage the field to more carefully consider boys' and girls' experiences in the development of prevention programs. More specifically, girls who are often victims of bullying experience bullying in the form of sexual harassment and these authors urge scholars to call these experiences sexual harassment rather than bullying. They also urge scholars and educators to consider the different peer victimization experiences in school and in cyberspace for boys and girls.

PEER CHARACTERISTICS ASSOCIATED WITH BULLYING

The idea that similarities are more salient than differences in peer group membership is called the *homophily hypothesis* (Kandel, 1978) and has been empirically linked to bullying by both boys and girls (Espelage, Holt, & Henkel, 2003). Espelage and colleagues demonstrated that students tended to affiliate with other students who perpetrated bullying at similar frequencies and students who hung out in bullying peer groups increased in their amount of self-reported bullying over the course of a school year. Certainly individual characteristics are influenced by the peer group and the chapters in this section illustrate the complexity of the role of peers in bullying and victimization.

Hawley, Stump, and Ratliff in their chapter "Sidestepping the Jingle Fallacy: Bullying, Aggression, and the Importance of Knowing the Difference" remind readers that "the jingle fallacy," which was coined in the early 1900s by educational researcher Edward L. Thorndike to illustrate the danger of referring to two different psychological constructs using the same label (i.e., "bullying" and "aggression"), may be a factor in understanding the function that bullying holds in peer groups. These authors draw from self-determination theory and resource control theory to understand the function that bullying and aggression serve in the peer group. Pellegrini and Van Ryzin in their chapter "Part of the Problem *and* Part of the Solution: The Role of Peers in Bullying, Dominance, and Victimization during the Transition from Primary School to Secondary School" demonstrate in greater detail the powerful role of peers over the transition from elementary to middle school. These authors provide some important guidance in how positive peer relations can be promoted in educational interventions, such as peer mentoring. Rodkin and Gest in their chapter "Teaching Practices, Classroom Peer Ecologies, and Bullying Behaviors among Schoolchildren" propose a peer ecological approach to understanding bullying among school-aged youth. This model examines social structures in the classroom setting and examines the influence of teacher–student interactions. Collectively, these chapters set the stage for examining bullying in the contexts in which these behaviors occur.

CLASSROOM CHARACTERISTICS ASSOCIATED WITH BULLYING

A discussion of gender differences in bullying and peer victimization experiences continues in the chapter entitled "Girls, Boys, and Bullying in Preschool: The Role of Gender in the Development of Bullying" by Hanish, Hill, Gosney, Fabes, and Martin who review the empirical data on the prevalence of bullying among preschool children. Their data suggest that preschool children who are exposed to aggressive youth are at risk for engaging in aggression themselves. This effect appears to be most relevant for boys in preschool, given the tendency for preschoolers to play in gender-segregated groups. This chapter includes a discussion of a population—preschoolers—that are often not included in bully investigations and also includes data from several studies that employ cutting-edge observational methods.

Doll, Song, Champion, and Jones in their chapter "Classroom Ecologies that Support or Discourage Bullying" consider the ways in which classrooms and teachers encourage or inhibit bullying behaviors. In their chapter, we learn that classrooms with positive teacher–student relationships have less bullying and peer aggression than classrooms where the teacher–student relations are strained. Individual students and peers also play a role in minimizing bullying in the classroom. We learn in this chapter how classrooms can promote self-determination in individual students and how peers who are bystanders can be encouraged to contribute to the development of prosocial behaviors. Teachers are encouraged to have consistently reinforced rules and routines, and to maintain open dialogue with students. In the chapter "Teachers' Attitudes Toward Bullying" Holt, Keyes, and Koenig tackle the important function of school culture and explicate the link between school personnel attitudes and school culture. Specifically, equity, hostile climate, openness to diversity, and willingness to intervene are school climate factors connected to bullying among school-aged youth. Importantly, these authors discuss that school culture varies by school.

SCHOOL AND FAMILY CHARACTERISTICS ASSOCIATED WITH BULLYING

Because school culture varies by individual schools and school climate is created by staff and student attitudes, it logically follows that school and family characteristics are linked to bullying and victimization. As the example of Sarah and Beth illustrates, school and family contexts are important influences on bullying and peer victimization. In the chapter "School Climate and Change in Personality Disorder Symptom Trajectories Related to Bullying: A Prospective Study," Kasen, Johnson, Chen, Crawford, and Cohen take the reader from classroom-level understanding of bullying to the school-level. Through a complex longitudinal study of the impact of school climate on the intersection of personality and bullying, these authors discuss the importance of minimizing the levels of teacher–student conflict and the importance of this interaction on school climate. Demaray and Malecki explicate this interaction in their chapter "The Role of Social Support in the Lives of Students Involved in Bullying" by reviewing the importance of adult and peer social support. They conclude that students who are bullied perceive less social support from peers and students who perpetrate bullying perceive less social support from parents and teachers. The role of social support is an important contextual factor in bullying prevention and intervention programming.

Leff, Freedman, MacEnvoy, and Power in their chapter "Considerations when Measuring Outcomes to Assess for the Effectiveness of Bullying- and Aggression-Prevention Programs in Schools" use their years of experiences in the Philadelphia public schools to encourage researchers to use community partnership-based methods to study bullying behaviors. Their methodologies for studying bullying behaviors are clearly linked to the conclusions drawn in the literature and the complexity of designing studies from a partnership-based approach will strengthen the literature base. In the chapter "Family Relationships of Bullies and Victims," Duncan reviews what is known about the families of bullies, victims, and bully-victims. Her review of the literature highlights the areas of research that are still understudied. It is also clear from her chapter that familial characteristics such as parenting practices, abuse, and sibling aggression are significant predictors of bullying involvement. This work suggests that bullying prevention programs need to consider how to modify these risk factors. Studying bullying across school and family contexts is vital, yet most of the bullying prevention and intervention programs do not take into account the role of family, community, or culture.

EFFECTIVE BULLYING PREVENTION AND INTERVENTION PROGRAMS

When we present workshops to teachers and parents about bullying prevention and intervention, we are fond of saying, "It's not the program, it's the people." It is people who will help stop bullying in our schools and communities. Programs are sufficient for changing behavior, but caring, dedicated people are necessary in order to stop bullying behavior. Additionally, we suggest that school personnel consider adopting bullying prevention and intervention strategies that have an evidence-base. There are over 300 published violence prevention programs geared toward schools, however, less than a quarter of these programs are empirically validated (Howard, Flora, & Griffin, 1999). In this final section of the book, the chapters present programs that have an evidence base and that have been implemented in school settings for over a decade. As such, these programs have addressed real-world implementation issues and have a solid database on which to examine their effectiveness.

Low, Smith, Brown, Fernandez, Hanson, and Haggerty in their chapter "Design and Analysis of a Randomized Controlled Trial of Steps to Respect: A School-Based Bullying Prevention Program" describe the *Steps to Respect: A Bullying Prevention Program* that was developed by the Committee for Children in Seattle, Washington. They report data on their school-randomized program evaluation. One compelling finding was that school staff underestimate the extent of bullying among students and they overestimate students' willingness to intervene and student confidence in the ability of staff to effectively intervene. These results have direct implications for bullying prevention and intervention programming. Several of the chapters discuss bullying prevention programs that focus on teacher training. Frey, Carlson Jones, Hirschstein, and Edstrom present results in their chapter "Teacher Support of Bullying Prevention: The Good, the Bad, and the Promising" from their evaluation of teaching coaching aspects of the *Steps to Respect* program (StR; Committee for Children, 2001). These authors highlight the efficacy of teacher interventions on reducing bullying in classrooms through empathy scaffolding, brief individual coaching sessions with students involved in bullying situations, and emotion regulation. *The Bully Busters* prevention program (Newman et al., 2000) is discussed in the chapter "Bully Busters: A Resource for Schools and Parents to Prevent and Respond to Bullying" by Horne, Bell, Raczynski, and Whitford. *Bully Busters* is a program directed at increasing knowledge, efficacy, and competence of teachers to prevent bullying in their classrooms. The components of both the elementary and the middle school versions of *Bully Busters* are discussed and evaluation data are presented.

Several chapters discuss bullying prevention programs that target the entire school community through comprehensive whole-school approaches. Plog, Garrity, Jens, and Porter discuss in detail *Bully-Proofing Your School* (Garrity, Jens, Porter, Sager, & Short-Camilli, 1994, 2004) in their chapter "Bully-Proofing Your School: Overview of the Program, Outcome Research, and Questions that Remain about how Best to Implement Effective Bullying Prevention in Schools." Limber summarizes the components of the *Olweus Bullying Prevention Program* (Olweus, 1993) in her chapter "Implementation of the Olweus Bullying Prevention Program in American Schools: Lessons Learned From the Field." Both of these programs focus on staff training and student instruction with the goal of shifting school-level and classroom-level attitudes and behaviors from bullying to prosocial interactions. In the chapter "Integrating Strategies for Bullying, Sexual Harassment, and Dating Violence Prevention: The Expect Respect Elementary School Project," Rosenbluth, Whitaker, Valle, and Ball describe the *Expect Respect Elementary School Project* in Austin, Texas. This program is unique in that it links bullying prevention to dating violence prevention, recognizing the connection between bullying, sexual harassment, and dating violence. This chapter also illustrates the importance of developing school district and state policies regarding harassment and bullying. The authors note that in order to address these problematic behaviors, integrated, multilevel, and youth-led approaches need to be promoted.

TRANSLATING RESEARCH INTO PRACTICE: IMPLICATIONS FOR BULLYING PREVENTION AND INTERVENTION PROGRAMMING

The value of research is its applicability. Our work in bullying and peer victimization is only as important as it positively impacts the lives of youth, families, and schools that are impacted by these behaviors. We hope that this book continues to help advance the link between research and practice as we seek to understand the dynamics surrounding bullying behaviors. Each chapter in the book ends with a section, "Translating research into practice: Implications for bullying prevention and intervention programs." As noted in the beginning of this chapter, not only do "broad problems require broad hypotheses," but also large problems are complex, multiply-determined, and differentially reinforced. The solutions to stopping bullying behaviors must be framed from a social ecological perspective if we are to have any hope of truly stopping bullying in North American schools.

REFERENCES

Astor, R.A., Meyer, H.A., & Pitner, R.O. (2001). Elementary and middle school students' perceptions of safety: An examination of violence-prone school sub-contexts. *The Elementary School Journal, 101*, 511–528.

Bertalanffy, L. von (1969). *General system theory.* New York: George Braziller.

Bronfenbrenner, U. (1979). *The ecology of human development: Experiments by nature and design.* Cambridge, MA: Harvard University Press.

Committee for Children (2010). Steps to respect: A Bullying prevention program. Retrieved from www.cfchildren.org/programs/str/overview.

Espelage, D.L., & Swearer, S.M. (2009). Contributions of three social theories to understanding bullying perpetration and victimization among school-aged youth. In M.J. Harris (Ed.), *Bullying, rejection, and peer victimization: A social cognitive neuroscience perspective* (pp. 151–170). New York, NY: Springer Publishing Company.

Espelage, D.L., & Swearer, S.M. (2010). A social-ecological model for bullying prevention and intervention: Understanding the impact of adults in the social ecology of youngsters. In S.R. Jimerson, S.M. Swearer, & D.L. Espelage (Eds.), *Handbook of bullying in schools: An international perspective*, (pp. 61–72). New York, NY: Routledge.

Espelage, D.L., Holt, M.K., & Henkel, R.R. (2003). Examination of peer group contextual effects on aggression during early adolescence. *Child Development, 74*, 205–220.

Garbarino, J., & deLara, E. (2002). *And words can hurt forever: How to protect adolescents from bullying, harassment, and emotional violence.* New York, NY: The Free Press.

Garrity, C., Jens, K., Porter, W., Sager, N., & Short-Camilli. C. (1994). *Bully-Proofing Your School: Administrators guide to staff development in elementary schools* (3rd ed.). Longmont, CO: Sopris West.

Garrity, C., Jens, K., Porter, W., Sager, N., & Short-Camilli. C. (2004). *Bully-Proofing Your School: A comprehensive approach for elementary schools* (3rd ed). Longmont, CO: Sopris West.

Howard, K.A., Flora, J., & Griffin, M. (1999). Violence-prevention programs in schools: State of the science and implications for future research. *Applied & Preventive Psychology, 8*, 197–215.

Kandel, D.B. (1978). Homophily, selection, and socialization in adolescent friendships. *American Journal of Sociology, 84*, 427–436.

Morse, N.C., & Allport, F.H. (1952). The causation of anti-Semitism: An investigation of seven hypotheses. *The Journal of Psychology, 34*, 197–233.

Newman, D.A., Horne, A.M., & Bartolomucci, C.L. (2000). *Bully busters: A teacher's manual for helping bullies, victims, and bystanders.* Champaign, IL: Research Press.

Olweus, D. (1993). *Bullying at school.* Oxford, UK: Blackwell.

Swearer, S.M. & Doll, B. (2001). Bullying in schools: An ecological framework. *Journal of Emotional Abuse, 2*, 7–23.

Swearer, S.M., Espelage, D.L., Vaillancourt, T., & Hymel, S. (2010). What can be done about school bullying?: Linking research to educational practice. *Educational Researcher, 39*, 38–47.

Swearer, S.M., Peugh, J., Espelage, D.L., Siebecker, A.B., Kingsbury, W.L., & Bevins, K.S. (2006). A social-ecological model for bullying prevention and intervention in early adolescents. In M. Furlong, & S. Jimerson (Eds.), *Handbook of school violence and school safety* (pp. 257–273). Mahwah, NJ: Lawrence Erlbaum Associates, Inc.

Part I
Individual Characteristics Associated With Bullying

2

GENDER AND BULLYING

Moving Beyond Mean Differences to Consider Conceptions
of Bullying, Processes by which Bullying Unfolds, and Cyberbullying

MARION K. UNDERWOOD AND LISA H. ROSEN

Girls as well as boys engage in bullying behavior. Bullying has been described as a gendered phenomenon (Rodkin & Berger, 2008) and a relationship problem (Pepler, Jiang, Craig, & Connolly, 2008). Understanding what these characterizations really means requires investigating how gender influences every aspect of bullying relationships: how children understand bullying, contexts in which children bully, forms that bullying might take, processes by which bullying may unfold, and whether and how children feel empowered to respond or even to intervene. Examining how gender influences bullying requires careful thinking about gender differences in frequency of bullying behaviors, but also moving beyond these mean differences to consider other ways in which gender might have an effect on the complex phenomenon of bullying (Espelage, Mebane, & Swearer, 2004). This chapter will briefly examine the empirical evidence for gender differences in children's conceptions of bullying and the scant evidence for gender differences in the processes by which bullying unfolds, and then focus in some detail on gender differences in bullying through electronic communication. Cyberbullying is an important context in which to examine gender and bullying because gender differences in physical size and strength are less relevant, so this context may be especially important for girls, and because the vast majority of youth communicate with peers electronically. The chapter will conclude with commentary on the implications of the research on gender and bullying for the design of gender sensitive prevention and intervention programs.

This chapter will focus on bullying specifically, defined as, "a specific type of aggression in which (1) the behavior is intended to harm or disturb; (2) the behavior occurs repeatedly over time; and (3) there is an imbalance of power, with a more powerful person or group attacking a less powerful one" (Nansel et al., 2001, p. 2094; see also Olweus, 1978). Research on the broader phenomenon of aggression will be consulted only as it pertains specifically to issues related to gender and bullying. Because a comprehensive review of these enormous literatures is beyond the scope of this chapter, this review will be selective in focusing on the most recent evidence and studies that highlight social processes in bullying. This discussion will feature studies with U.S. samples, but given the complexities of gender and bullying and the sparse evidence on some issues, will also consult research with international samples.

Moving beyond consideration of mean gender differences in bullying requires carefully considering where gender differences do and do not exist. For a large, nationally representative United States sample, Nansel et al. (2001) found that boys reported perpetrating and being victimized by bullying more than girls. When specific forms of victimization were examined, boys reported experiencing more physical bullying than girls, and girls reported more bullying by rumors and sexual comments. In another U.S. study, 4th and 5th graders responded to a survey about "Who bullies whom?" (Rodkin & Berger, 2008). Boys were more likely to be bullies and bully-victims, and girls were more likely to be victims. In a study of developmental trajectories for bullying from ages 10 to 17 with a large Canadian sample (Pepler et al., 2008), the high and moderate bullying trajectory groups included more boys than girls, and the trajectory group for low involvement included more girls than boys.

One reason why boys might be found to be higher on perpetrating bullying than girls is that the definitions of bullying provided include both physical and social aggression but do not differentiate between them (Nansel et al., 2001; Pepler et al., 2008). A wealth of evidence documents that boys are higher on physical and direct aggression than girls (Dodge, Coie, & Lynam, 2006; Card, Stucky, Sawalani, & Little, 2008). However, gender differences are less clear for social aggression. Competing terms have been used to describe aggression that hurts others by disputing friendships or social status: indirect aggression, social aggression, and relational aggression. These constructs overlap; there is currently no consensus as to which is best, and empirical evidence does not clearly support their differentiation (Archer & Coyne, 2005). This discussion will use the term social aggression because this construct includes both direct and indirect forms of relationship harm, and verbal and non-verbal social exclusion (Underwood, 2003). A recent, large meta-analysis found the gender difference in social aggression so small as to be trivial (Card et al., 2008). The "gender oversimplification" of social aggression has likely been fueled by popular media (Swearer, 2008, p. 612), as well as by gender stereotypes that portray girls as catty and manipulative—stereotypes that children seem to understand as early as preschool (Giles & Heyman, 2005). Bullying is a subset of the broader phenomenon of aggression because criteria for bullying include chronicity and a power imbalance (Nansel et al., 2001; Olweus, 1978). Still, the fact that bullying is broadly defined as including both physical and social aggression may explain why boys are characterized as higher on perpetrating bullying; boys are clearly higher on physical aggression but gender differences in social aggression seem small if they exist at all.

GENDER AND CHILDREN'S CONCEPTIONS OF BULLYING

Though researchers use a precise definition of bullying, children themselves may conceive of this phenomenon differently and conceptions of bullying may differ for girls and boys. In a study with a large sample of children from 14 different Asian and European countries, children were shown 25 cartoons of stick figures depicting social encounters with simple captions, and were asked to sort the cartoons as to whether the situation did or did not constitute various terms for bullying behaviors in each native language

(Smith, Cowie, Olafsson, & Liefooghe, 2002). Overall, boys and girls had very similar conceptions of what was and was not bullying, and six types of terms referring to bullying emerged: bullying of all types, verbal and physical; verbal only; social exclusion; physical only; and mostly physical. Young children (8-year-olds) primarily distinguished between aggressive and non-aggressive behaviors but 14-year-olds made distinctions between physical bullying, verbal bullying, and social exclusion.

Another study examined whether gender differences in conceptions of bullying emerge when 8–18-year-old children were asked to provide their own definition (Vaillancourt et al., 2008). Interestingly, both boys' and girls' definitions rarely included the three criteria of the research definition: intentionality (1.7%), chronicity (6%), and power imbalance (25%). Girls in this study were more likely than boys to mention social aggression in their definitions of bullying, especially during middle childhood. These results strongly suggest that social aggression is more common in girls' conceptions of bullying and that understanding the phenomenon of bullying for both gender groups requires consideration of both subtle and overt forms.

GENDER AND THE SOCIAL PROCESSES BY WHICH BULLYING UNFOLDS

If bullying is indeed a gendered, relationship phenomenon, then it is important to understand whether the social processes involved in bullying differ for girls and boys. Because many studies have relied on surveys to study bullying (see Nansel et al., 2001, Pepler et al., 2008, and many others), our knowledge of social processes in bullying is scant. However, existing work provides some interesting clues.

Girls and boys seem likely to play different roles in the group process of bullying. According to self- and peer-reports, Finnish girls are more likely to assume the roles of defender and outsider, whereas boys are more likely to play the roles of bully, reinforcer, and assistant (Salmivalli, Lagerspetz, Bjorkqvist, Osterman, & Kaukiainen, 1996). Similarly, a U.S. study found that according to self-reports, girls are more often classified in an uninvolved cluster for bullying, whereas boys are more likely to be classified in bully, victim, and bully-victim groups (Espelage & Holt, 2007). A naturalistic, observational study of peer intervention in playground bullying found that girls were more likely to intervene in bullying when the bully and victim were female, and boys were more likely to intervene when the bully and victim were male (Hawkins, Pepler, & Craig, 2001). Girls and boys were equally likely to intervene and their interventions were equally effective. Girls and boys used physical aggression to intervene at similar rates (19% and 22%, respectively), but girls' attempts were more likely to involve verbal assertion than were boys' interventions (48% and 19%, respectively).

Girls' bullying may take more subtle forms and even be associated with social power, as suggested by Salmivalli et al. (1996), "Maybe the female bullies are socially and verbally smart children who can choose their words and amuse the others by verbally directly or indirectly attacking their victims" (p. 13). In support of this hypothesis, a Canadian study found that compared to boys identified as bullies, girl bullies were more socially and less physically aggressive, reported greater friendship intimacy, and were rated by peers as more attractive (Vaillancourt, Hymel, & McDougall, 2003). If girls' bullying is more likely to be verbal or social and less likely to be physical, then an important context for examining gender and bullying is electronic communication, where bullying must be conveyed by verbal communication.

GENDER AND CYBERBULLYING

A generation of children and adolescents are now growing up in a digital world. Over 90% of adolescents use the Internet, with current estimates ranging from 93% to 97% of American adolescents being online (Lenhart, Madden, Macgill, & Smith, 2007; UCLA Center for Communication Policy, 2003). The majority of adolescents report using the Internet on a daily basis and are able to access the Internet both at home and at school (Lenhart et al., 2007; UCLA Center for Communication Policy, 2003). Four out of five adolescents have a mobile device, and many are able to text message, use the Internet, and take digital pictures with their phones (CTIA, 2008; Rogers, Taylor, Cunning, Jones, & Taylor, 2006). The frequency with which adolescents use the Internet and cell phones has increased over the past five years (CTIA, 2008; Lenhart et al., 2007). This expanding ability to communicate with others via the Internet and cell phones has the potential to be extremely advantageous to youth, creating opportunities to foster greater feelings of connectedness (David-Ferdon & Hertz, 2007). However, the proliferation of these technologies may also be associated with growing risks to youth. Notably, cyberspace may become a burgeoning venue for bullying peers (Kowalski & Limber, 2007).

Bullying others through electronic media is a fairly new phenomenon, and researchers have pointed to the lack of scholarly attention devoted to studying technologically assisted bullying and have called for more empirical research in this area (Jerome & Segal, 2003; Kowalski, Limber, & Agatston, 2008; Patchin & Hinduja, 2006). An increasing number of researchers from different disciplines have begun to examine these issues using diverse methods. Many terms have been used to refer to bullying through electronic channels including cyberbullying, electronic bullying, e-bullying, online harassment, Internet bullying, and online social cruelty (Hinduja & Patchin, 2009). There are almost as many definitions of bullying online as there are of terms to refer to the phenomenon, and there is no consistent definition as of yet (David-Ferdon & Hertz, 2007; Hertz & David-Ferdon, 2008; Wolak, Mitchell, & Finkelhor, 2007; Vandebosch & Van Cleemput, 2008). Here, we use the term "cyberbullying" and define this construct as "willful and repeated harm inflicted through the use of computers, cell phones, and other electronic devices" (Hinduja & Patchin, 2009, p. 5). However, given the limited work in this area and the many different conceptualizations, we include studies in our review that more broadly look at aggressive behavior perpetrated with technology, even when this behavior may not meet the criteria of our definition of cyberbullying.

Cyberbullying includes many different types of behaviors and can occur through different technological mediums (Hinduja & Patchin, 2009; Kowalski et al., 2008; Shariff, 2008; Smith, Mahdavi, Carvalho, & Tippett, 2006). Cyberbullies may use behaviors that are either direct (e.g., threatening someone online) or indirect (e.g., spreading rumors online) in nature (Chibbaro, 2007). Many behaviors that bullies use in the school setting may also be applied to cyber environments including ignoring, exclusion, name-calling, rumor spreading, and physical threats (Hinduja & Patchin, 2007; Kowalski et al., 2008). Cyber environments also allow for the introduction of a new set of hostile behaviors such as outing and trickery, masquerading, happy slapping, and picture or video clip bullying (Bauman, 2007; Burgess-Proctor, Patchin, & Hinduja, 2009; Hinduja & Patchin, 2009; Kowalski et al., 2008; Shariff, 2008; Smith et al., 2006). Outing and trickery refers to convincing a target to reveal personal information and then sharing this private information with others electronically. Masquerading, also known as impersonation, involves the bully pretending to be the victim and then sending messages to others that seem to come from the target and/or changing information the target has posted about him or herself online. Happy slapping entails digitally recording an instance of physical aggression and then electronically sharing this episode with others. Bullies may also alter pictures and/or video clips of their victims and then post these for others to see in the hopes of embarrassing the victim. Cyberbullying behaviors can occur through many different communication modalities including instant messenger, email, text message, social networking sites, chat rooms, blogs, voting and rating websites (e.g., Hot or Not), websites built to embarrass another, and online gaming sites (Bauman, 2007; Hinduja & Patchin, 2009; Kowalski et al., 2008; Smith et al., 2006).

Cyberbullying differs from traditional bullying in many important respects. Given youths' wide access to the Internet and cell phones, cyberbullying can take place outside of the school setting and can occur anywhere at all times; thus, the potential omnipresence of cyberbullying may result in victims feeling more vulnerable (Hinduja & Patchin, 2009; Kowalski & Limber, 2007; Slonje & Smith, 2008). Cyberbullies can maintain a sense of anonymity by using pseudonyms in online environments. This sense of anonymity coupled with a lack of face-to-face contact may lead to greater feelings of disinhibition among cyberbullies as compared to traditional bullies (Hinduja & Patchin, 2008; Shariff, 2008; Slonje & Smith, 2008). In fact, 31% of adolescents report they have said something over instant messenger that they would not have shared in a face-to-face context (Lenhart, Madden, & Hitlin, 2005). Further, cyberbullies have the potential to reach a very wide audience; cyber attacks can be easily shared with many in a very short time or posted in a public forum (Hinduja & Patchin, 2009; Kowalski & Limber, 2007; Shariff, 2008; Slonje & Smith, 2008).

Given these differences between cyberbullying and traditional bullying, an important question is whether the gender differences seen in traditional bullying also hold for bullying in cyber environments. Some researchers have suggested that girls may be more likely to engage in cyberbullying than traditional forms of bullying (Hinduja & Patchin, 2009; Kowalski & Limber, 2007). Girls often have strong verbal abilities and may be adept at delivering attacks through electronic text. Further, girls may feel more disinhibited interacting with others through online media as compared to face-to-face encounters (Hinduja & Patchin, 2009). In considering whether boys and girls cyberbully at equivalent rates, it is important to remember that many forms of cyberbullying resemble social aggression rather than physical aggression (e.g., online exclusion and spreading of rumors; Hinduja & Patchin, 2009; Smith et al., 2008). As described above, a recent meta-analysis (Card et al., 2008) suggests no strong gender differences in social aggression. However, this meta-analysis did suggest that boys are more physically aggressive than girls, and some forms of cyberbullying involve physical aggression (e.g., happy slapping, threats of physical harm). We will present findings from the extant literature on gender and cyberbullying. We focus first on children's descriptions of cyberbullying, then report the results of surveys examining mean level gender differences in cyberbullying, and finally present the limited work examining gender differences in the types of cyberbullying behaviors employed by girls and boys.

Gender differences exist in the way adolescents perceive cyberbullying. In focus groups on cyberbullying with middle and high school students, girls were more likely than boys to acknowledge that cyberbullying was a problem facing students in their schools (Agatston, Kowalski, & Limber, 2007). Adolescents also mentioned that their responses to cyberbullying would depend on the gender of the perpetrator. One adolescent participant said:

> It depends on if it's a guy or a girl or how mean they are. Some people are just going to do it anyway. Girls are harder to stand up to. Cause like guys can be like 'stop bothering me.' I'm not afraid that a guy is going to hit me, but girls are like catty. They get back at you in a more subtle way.
>
> (Kowalski et al., 2008, p. 79).

Boys reported a greater willingness to confront perpetrators of cyberbullying than did girls.

Studies examining the frequency of cyberbullying by gender have yielded mixed results (Berkman Center for Internet & Society at Harvard University, 2008; Hertz & David-Ferdon, 2008; Kowalski et al., 2008). Estimates of the frequency of bullying as well as estimates of gender differences vary from study to study. This is likely the result of researchers conceptualizing cyberbullying along different lines and using diverse methods to study this phenomenon. The vast majority of the extant research has examined cyberbullying with surveys that are administered online, by phone, or in the classroom. However, researchers often ask about cyberbullying in different ways through their questionnaires. Some researchers may simply ask participants if they have experienced cyberbullying either as a perpetrator or victim. Alternatively, other researchers may ask respondents if they have perpetrated or been victim of specific cyberbullying behaviors such as online threats or online rumors (Vandebosch & Van Cleemput, 2008). Studies differ along other important dimensions, such as whether researchers inquire about cyberbullying within a specific time frame as well as key characteristics of the sample (e.g., age of respondent; Kowalski et al., 2008). These differences in definition and methodology likely account for the discrepant findings in the cyberbullying literature regarding frequency and gender.

Some studies have found that boys are more likely than girls to cyberbully others. The First Youth Internet Safety Survey was a nationally representative phone survey in which children and adolescents between the ages of 10 and 17 were interviewed (Finkelhor, Mitchell, & Wolak, 2000; Mitchell, Finkelhor, & Wolak, 2003). As part of this larger study, youth were asked about experiences with online harassment. More cyberbullies were reported to be boys (54%) than girls (20%). The gender of the perpetrator was unknown for 26% of the episodes. Similarly, a survey of Canadian middle-school students found that boys were more likely to perpetrate cyberbullying than were girls; 22% of boys reported cyberbullying others as compared to 12% of girls (Li, 2006).

However, the majority of the extant research suggests that girls are involved in cyberbullying both as perpetrators and as victims at rates that are equal to or higher than that of their male counterparts (Hertz & David-Ferdon, 2008; Hinduja & Patchin, 2009; Kowalski et al., 2008). In a study of 5th, 8th, and 11th grade students, boys and girls were equally likely to report spreading lies about peers through email or instant messaging (Williams & Guerra, 2007). Likewise, a survey of adolescents found that gender was not a significant predictor of involvement in cyberbullying (Raskauskas & Stoltz, 2007). In addition, an online study of youth found no significant gender differences in the frequency with which boys and girls engaged in cyberbullying (Hinduja & Patchin, 2008). These researchers also specifically examined serious cyberbullying, which they assessed with the following two items regarding online behavior: "threatened someone with physical harm" or "made other kids scared of them" (Hinduja & Patchin, 2008, p. 139). No significant gender differences were found for serious cyberbullying offending.

An investigation by Kowalski and colleagues (2008) found that girls might be more likely than boys to perpetrate cyberbullying. More girls (13%) than boys (9%) reported cyberbullying others at least once in the past two months. However, different findings emerged when chronicity of cyberbullying was examined. Boys were more likely than girls to admit cyberbullying others on a weekly basis. Similar findings emerged from the Second Youth Internet Safety Survey (Ybarra & Mitchell, 2007). In interviews, youth were asked to specify the number of times they cyberbullied others in the past year. Participants were assigned to categories on the basis of this information to specify the regularity with which they cyberbullied others. Those who rarely cyberbullied others were assigned to the category of limited perpetrators, and those who often cyberbullied others were assigned to the category of frequent perpetrators. Although girls were significantly more likely to be classified as limited perpetrators, boys were more likely to be classified as frequent perpetrators.

As is the case for perpetration of cyberbullying, studies that have examined gender differences in victimization by cyberbullying have also yielded mixed results. Some studies have found that girls and boys are equally likely to be victims of cyberbullying (Finkelhor et al., 2000; Hinduja & Patchin, 2008; Li, 2006; Mitchell et al., 2003; Patchin & Hinduja, 2006). However, other research including the Pew Internet & American Life Project Parents and Teens Survey find that girls are more likely to be targeted by cyberbullying than are boys (Lenhart, 2007). In this large survey of online adolescents, 38% of girls and 26% of boys reported being the target of cyberbullying.

Future research is needed to move beyond examining mean level gender differences in cyberbullying and to consider the methods and mechanisms through which adolescent girls and boys aggress and are victimized online. Initial research suggests that boys may be more likely to hack into others' systems and engage in online name-calling (Dehue, Bolman, & Vollink, 2008). Girls, on the other hand, may be more likely than boys to gossip in cyberspace, and in turn may also more frequently be the subject of online rumors (Dehue et al., 2008; Lenhart, 2007). Research on traditional bullying has found that boys are more likely than girls to engage in physical aggression (Card et al., 2008); cyberbullying research should specifically examine forms of physical aggression such as threats of harm and happy slapping to determine if these gender differences hold in cyberspace. Initial evidence for gender differences in physical forms of cyberbullying comes from examining emotional responses to cyberbullying. Hinduja and Patchin (2009) found that girls are more likely to feel frustrated whereas boys are more likely to feel scared following cyberbullying, and they suggest that this difference may result from boys being subject to more online physical threats.

In terms of mediums used to cyberbully, girls more often report being bullied through email and text messages than do boys (Dehue et al., 2008; Hinduja & Patchin, 2008; Smith et al., 2006). Future research is needed to study gender differences in how cyberbullying unfolds. Girls and boys have different online footprints: boys are more likely to play games online and to post videos to video sharing websites, and girls are more likely to have a blog and use instant messaging (Lenhart, Madden, and Hitlin, 2005; Lenhart et al., 2007). These different activities that online girls and boys gravitate toward may be the mediums through which they are likely to aggress against their peers. Additional research will allow for firmer conclusions to be drawn regarding gender differences in bullying in the new arena of cyber space.

TRANSLATING RESEARCH INTO PRACTICE: IMPLICATIONS FOR BULLYING PREVENTION AND INTERVENTION PROGRAMS

To be maximally effective, bullying prevention and intervention programs must include programming for both girls and boys and must address non-physical forms of aggression. Whether at school on the playground or in cyberspace, the numbers of girls who engage in and are victimized by bullying are non-trivial and prevention and intervention programs must be designed with girls' as well as boys' needs in mind. Adults, school policies, and even peer interveners must convey the strong message that social aggression and cyberbullying in addition to physical aggression will not be tolerated. Adults need to be sensitive to the fact that bullies may enjoy high status related to their bullying behavior, perhaps especially girl bullies, who are likely to be socially aggressive, enjoy high levels of friendship intimacy, and to be viewed by peers as attractive (Vaillancourt et al., 2003). Further research is needed to test the interesting conjecture that social aggression may result when a socially intelligent bully manipulates a group with weak friendship bonds and engages them in excluding others as a means of joining and strengthening their group bonds (Garandeau & Cillessen, 2006). This hypothesis should be tested for boys as well as girls. High status youth prone to bullying should be actively engaged in prevention and intervention programs and encouraged to be positive leaders, and, to the extent possible, the social climate must be changed so these youth do not enjoy advantages as a result of their manipulating others. All youth should be challenged to consider what type of friends they want to have, what type of friend they want to be, that they could be the next victim, and that if they stand by and watch any form of bullying behavior, they are contributing to a group climate in which no one can trust anyone else. Intervention programs should harness girls' natural proclivities toward being defenders (Salmivalli et al., 1996) and relationship strengths such as empathy (Underwood, 2003).

In intervening to reduce bullying with both genders, it is important to remember that at least for girls victimized by boys, bullying often takes the form of sexual harassment (Shute, Owens, & Slee, 2008). In a U.S. study with high school students, the correlation between bullying and sexual harassment was strong ($r = .56$), and sexual harassment was more strongly related to mental health problems than was bullying (Gruber & Fineran, 2008). The ways in which girls and boys bully and are victimized at school by peers are clearly related to the sex-gender system, in other words, "patriarchy matters" (Brown, Chesney-Lind, & Stein, 2007). Considering sexual harassment to be just another form of bullying may trivialize this experience for girls and deny them access to important legal remedies.

Similarly, viewing girls' social aggression as just another form of bullying ignores that girls, like many groups with less status or physical power, may resort to subtle forms of aggression because they lack the power to assert themselves forthrightly (LaFrance, 2002). Conceiving of girls' social aggression as bullying neglects the possibility that social aggression may express "girls' need to have more control in their lives, to feel important, to be visible, to be taken seriously, to have an effect" (Brown et al., 2007, p. 1268). Gender sensitive intervention and prevention programs must consider how our patriarchal culture limits possibilities for both girls and boys and provide both gender groups with constructive paths toward social ascendancy in their interactions at school, in their homes and neighborhoods, and in their electronic communication.

REFERENCES

Agatston, P.W., Kowalski, R., & Limber, S. (2007). Students' perspectives on cyberbullying. *Journal of Adolescent Health, 41,* 59–60.

Archer, J. & Coyne, S.M. (2005). An integrated review of indirect, relational, and social aggression. *Personality and Social Psychology Review, 9,* 212–230.

Bauman, S. (2007, November). Cyberbullying: A virtual menace. Paper presented at the National Coalition against Bullying National Conference, Melbourne, Australia. Retrieved May 10, 2009 from www.ncab.org. au/Assets/Files/Bauman,%20S.%20Cyberbullying%20the%20virtual%20menace.pdf.

Berkman Center for Internet & Society at Harvard University (2008). Enhancing child safety & online technologies: Final report of the Internet Safety Technical Task Force to the Multi-State Working Group on Social Networking of State Attorneys General of the United States. Retrieved May 10, 2009, from http://cyber.law. harvard.edu/sites/cyber.law.harvard.edu/files/ISTTF_Final_Report.pdf.

Brown, L.M., Chesney-Lind, M., & Stein, N. (2007). Patriarchy matters: Toward a gendered theory of teen violence and victimization. *Violence Against Women, 13,* 1249–1273.

Burgess-Proctor, A., Patchin, J.W., & Hinduja, S. (2009). Cyberbullying and online harassment: Reconceptualizing the victimization of adolescent girls. In V. Garcia and J. Clifford (Eds.), *Female crime victims: Reality reconsidered.* Upper Saddle River, NJ: Prentice Hall.

Card, N.A., Stucky, B.D., Sawalani, G.M., & Little, T.D. (2008). Direct and indirect aggression during childhood and adolescence: A meta-analytic review of gender differences, intercorrelations, and relations to maladjustment. *Child Development, 79,* 1185–1229.

Chibbaro, J.S. (2007). School counselors and the cyberbully: Interventions and implications. *Professional School Counseling, 11,* 65–68.

CTIA (2008). Teenagers: A generation unplugged—A national survey by CTIA—The Wireless Association and Harris Interactive. Retrieved May 10, 2009, from www.ctia.org/advocacy/research/index.cfm/AID/11483.

David-Ferdon, C., & Hertz, M.F. (2007). Electronic media, violence, and adolescents: An emerging public health problem. *Journal of Adolescent Health, 41,* 1–5.

Dehue, F., Bolman, C., & Vollink, T. (2008). Cyberbullying: Youngsters' experiences and parental perception. *CyberPsychology & Behavior, 11,* 217–223.

Dodge, K.A., Coie, J.D., & Lynam, D. (2006). Aggression and antisocial behavior in youth. In W. Damon (Series Ed.) & N. Eisenberg (Vol. Ed.), *Handbook of Child Psychology, Vol. 3* (pp. 719–788). Hoboken, NJ: Wiley.

Espelage, D.L., & Holt, M.K. (2007). Dating violence and sexual harassment across the bully-victim continuum among middle and high school students. *Journal of Youth and Adolescence, 36,* 799–811.

Espelage, D.L., Mebane, S.E., & Swearer, S.M. (2004). Gender differences in bullying: Moving beyond mean level differences. In D.L. Espelage & S.M. Swearer (Eds.), *Bullying in American Schools: A Social-Ecological Perspective on Prevention and Intervention* (pp. 15–35). Mahwah, NJ: Lawrence Erlbaum.

Finkelhor, D., Mitchell, K.J., & Wolak, J. (2000). *Online victimization: A report on the nation's youth.* Retrieved May 10, 2009, www.missingkids.com/en_US/publications/NC62.pdf.

Garandeau, C.F., & Cillessen, A.H.N. (2006). From indirect to invisible aggression: A conceptual view on bullying and peer group manipulation. *Aggression and Violent Behavior, 11,* 641–654.

Giles, J.W., & Heyman, G.D. (2005). Young children's beliefs about the relationship between gender and aggressive behavior. *Child Development, 76,* 107–121.

Gruber, J.E., & Fineran, S. (2008). Comparing the impact of bullying and sexual harassment victimization on the mental and physical health of adolescents. *Sex Roles, 59,* 1–13.

Hawkins, D.L., Pepler, D.J, & Craig, W.M. (2001). Naturalistic observations of peer intervention in bullying. *Social Development, 10,* 512–527.

Hertz, M.F., & David-Ferdon, C. (2008). Electronic media and youth violence: A CDC issue brief for educators and caregivers. Retrieved May 10, 2009, www.cdc.gov/violenceprevention/pdf/EA-brief-a.pdf.

Hinduja, S., & Patchin, J.W. (2007). Offline consequences of online victimization: School violence and delinquency. *Journal of School Violence, 6,* 89–112.

Hinduja, S., & Patchin, J. W. (2008). Cyberbullying: An exploratory analysis of factors related to offending and victimization. *Deviant Behavior, 29,* 129–156.

Hinduja, S., & Patchin, J. W. (2009). *Bullying beyond the schoolyard: Preventing and responding to cyberbullying.* Thousand Oaks, CA: Sage Publications.

Jerome, L., & Segal, A. (2003). Bullying by Internet. *Journal of the American Academy of Child & Adolescent Psychiatry, 42,* 751.

Kowalski, R.M., & Limber, S.P. (2007). Electronic bullying among middle school students. *Journal of Adolescent Health, 41,* 22–30.

Kowalski, R.M., Limber, S.P., & Agatston, P.W. (2008). *Cyberbullying: Bullying in the digital age.* Malden, MA: Blackwell Publishing.

LaFrance, M. (2002). Smile boycotts and other body politics. *Feminism & Psychology, 12*, 319–323.

Lenhart, A. (2007). *Cyberbullying.* Retrieved May 10, 2009, from www.pewinternet.org/Reports/2007/Cyber-bullying.aspx.

Lenhart, A., Madden, M., & Hitlin, P. (2005). *Teens and technology: Youth are leading the transition to a fully wired and mobile nation.* Retrieved May 10, 2009, from www.pewinternet.org/Reports/2005/Teens-and-Technology.aspx.

Lenhart, A., Madden, M., Macgill, A.R., & Smith, A. (2007). *Teens and social media* (Pew Internet & American Life Project report). Retrieved May 10, 2009, from www.pewinternet.org/PPF/r/230/report_display.asp.

Li, Q. (2006). Cyberbullying in schools: A research of gender differences. *School Psychology International, 27*, 157–170.

Mitchell, K.J., Finkelhor, D., & Wolak, J. (2003). Victimization of youths on the Internet. *Journal of Aggression, Maltreatment, and Trauma, 8*, 1–39.

Nansel, T.J., Overpeck, M., Pilla, R.S., Ruan, W.J., Simons-Morton, B., & Scheidt, P. (2001). Bullying behaviors among U.S. youth: Prevalence and associate with psychological adjustment. *Journal of the American Medical Association, 285*, 2094–2100.

Olweus, D. (1978). *Aggression in the schools: Bullies and whipping boys.* Washington, DC: Hemisphere Publishing Corporation.

Patchin, J.W., & Hinduja, S. (2006). Bullies move beyond the schoolyard: A preliminary look at cyberbullying. *Youth Violence and Juvenile Justice, 4*, 123–147.

Pepler, D., Jiang, D. Craig, W., & Connolly, J. (2008). Developmental trajectories of bullying and associated factors. *Child Development, 79*, 325–338.

Raskauskas, J., & Stoltz, A.D. (2007). Involvement in traditional and electronic bullying among adolescents. *Developmental Psychology, 43*, 564–575.

Rodkin, P.C., & Berger, C. (2008). Who bullies whom? Social status symmetries by victim gender. *International Journal of Behavioral Development, 32*, 473–485.

Rogers, M., Taylor, C.B., Cunning, D., Jones, M., & Taylor, K. (2006). Parental restrictions on adolescent Internet use. *Pediatrics, 118*, 1804–1805.

Salmivalli, C., Lagerspetz, K., Bjorkqvist, K., Osterman, K., & Kaukiainen, A. (1996). Bullying as a group process: Participant roles and their relations to social status within the group. *Aggressive Behavior, 22*, 1–15.

Shariff, S. (2008). *Cyberbullying: Issues and solutions for the school, the classroom and the home.* Abingdon, Oxfordshire, UK: Routledge.

Shute, R., Owens, L., & Slee, P. (2008). Everyday victimization of adolescent girls by boys: Sexual harassment, bullying, or aggression? *Sex Roles, 58*, 477–489.

Slonje, R., & Smith, P. K. (2008). Cyberbullying: Another main type of bullying? *Scandinavian Journal of Psychology, 49*, 147–154.

Smith, P.K., Coie, H., Olafsson, R.F., & Liefooghe, A.P.D. (2002). Definitions of bullying: A comparison of terms used, and age and gender differences, in a fourteen-country international comparison. *Child Development, 73*, 1119–1133.

Smith, P., Mahdavi, J., Carvalho, M., & Tippet, N. (2006). An investigation into cyberbullying, its forms, awareness and impact, and the relationship between age and gender in cyberbullying. A Report to the anti-Bullying Alliance. Retrieved May 10, 2009, from www.anti-bullyingalliance.org/.

Smith, P.K., Mahdavi, J., Carvalho, M., Fisher, S., Russell, S., & Tippett, N. (2008). Cyberbullying: Its nature and impact in secondary school pupils. *Journal of Child Psychology and Psychiatry, 49*, 376–385.

Swearer. S.M. (2008). Relational aggression: Not just a female issue. *Journal of School Psychology, 46*, 611–616.

UCLA Center for Communication Policy (2003). *The UCLA Internet report—Surveying the digital future.* Retrieved May 10, 2009, from www.digitalcenter.org/pdf/InternetReportYearThree.pdf.

Underwood, M.K. (2003). *Social aggression among girls.* New York, NY: Guilford.

Vaillancourt, T., Hymel, S., & McDougall, P. (2003). Bullying is power: Implications for school-based intervention strategies. *Journal of Applied School Psychology, 19*, 157–176.

Vaillancourt, T, McDougall, P., Hymel, S., Krygsman, A., Miller, J., Stiver, K., & Davis, C. (2008). Bullying: Are researchers and children/youth talking about the same thing? *International Journal of Behavioral Development, 32*, 486–495.

Vandebosch, H., & Van Cleemput, K. (2008). Defining cyberbullying: A qualitative research into the perceptions of youngsters. *CyberPsychology & Behavior, 11*, 499–503.

Williams, K.R., & Guerra, N.G. (2007). Prevalence and predictors of Internet bullying. *Journal of Adolescent Health, 41*, 14–21.

Wolak, J., Mitchell, K.J., & Finkelhor, D. (2007). Does online harassment constitute bullying? An exploration of online harassment by known peers and online-only contacts. *Journal of Adolescent Health, 41*, 51–58.

Ybarra, M., & Mitchell, K.J. (2007). Prevalence and frequency of Internet harassment instigation: Implications for adolescent health. *Journal of Adolescent Health, 41*, 189–195.

3

WHY DOES BEING BULLIED HURT SO MUCH?

Insights from Neuroscience

TRACY VAILLANCOURT, SHELLEY HYMEL, AND PATRICIA MCDOUGALL

> It is my belief that if we face our problems honestly and without regard to, or fear of, difficulty, the theoretical psychology of the future will catch up with, and eventually surpass, common sense.
>
> (Harry Harlow, 1953; cited in Blum, 2002, 89)

With a plethora of theoretical and empirical writing dedicated to the study of bullying in childhood and adolescence (including this volume), it is clear that we have faced our problems in earnest, yet it remains difficult to evaluate whether we have, as Harlow advised, faced the problem of bullying honestly. For decades, schoolyard bullying has been considered by many to be a normal part of childhood, a "rite of passage" that can help to "toughen kids up" or "build character." At the same time, common sense, often born out of personal experience, tells us that being rejected, shunned, ostracized, or bullied hurts. It hurts so much that some bullied youth take their life (Marr & Fields, 2000) or consider suicide as a way of ending their suffering (e.g., Bonanno & Hymel, 2010; Carney, 2000; Kaltiala-Heino, Rimpela, Marttunen, Rimpela, & Rantanen, 1999; Kim, Koh, & Leventhal, 2005).

Recent research on the effects of peer victimization and rejection strongly confirms intuition, documenting the negative correlates and consequences of bullying, especially for those who are victimized (see Card, Isaacs & Hodges, 2007; Hawker & Boulton, 2000). Children and youth who are bullied by peers, relative to non-victimized youth, report lower self-esteem and self-worth (e.g., Austin & Joseph, 1996; Kokkinos & Panayiotou, 2004; Rigby & Slee, 1993); are more lonely and socially withdrawn (Boivin, Hymel & Bukowski, 1995; Boulton & Underwood, 1992; Espelage & Holt, 2001; Graham, & Juvonen, 1998; Juvonen, Nishina & Graham, 2000; Storch, Brassard, & Masia-Warner, 2003), and are more anxious and depressed (Espelage & Holt, 2001; Graham, & Juvonen, 1998; Kaltiala-Heino et al., 1999; Kim et al., 2005; Vaillancourt et al., 2008; van der Wal, De Wit & Hirasing, 2003). Bullied children and youth also report more headaches, stomachaches and the like (e.g., Gruber & Fineran, 2007), which may reflect stress-related illness (Rigby, 1999). What is more, longitudinal research strongly suggests that this inventory of ills is the result of being abused and not a precipitator of poor treatment by peers (Arseneault et al., 2006; Kim et al., 2005; Sourander, Helstela, Helenius, & Piha, 2000).

In this chapter, we argue that bullying and related experiences such as peer rejection and ostracism interferes with that which is instinctually human—the quest to find a social place within the peer group and to fulfill a fundamental need to belong. In making this case, we consider historical events in the fields of medicine and psychology as well as evolutionary accounts, and delve into the work of neuroscientists, drawing a connection between physical and social pain.

THE NEED TO BELONG

Humans are highly social beings, and the need to belong is a fundamental human motivator (Baumiester & Leary, 1995). Attachment theorists (e.g., Bowlby, 1969/1997, 1973, 1988) have long argued that infants are born with a fundamental drive to form emotional bonds with others. Recent evidence from neuroscience suggests that humans are "wired" for social interaction and interpersonal connections (see Goleman, 2006). Accordingly, it is not surprising that peer rejection and victimization have a significant negative impact. Indeed, even being rejected by a deplorable, loathed group such as the Ku Klux Klan is perceived as hurtful to people who are not part of, nor condone, such a group (Gonsalkorale & Williams, 2007).

Seminal studies with non-human primates by Harry Harlow have demonstrated that social ties are not just a luxury, but rather are essential for optimal development (see Suomi, 1997 for a review). Indeed, despite Freud's (1905/1953) argument concerning the sustenance role of mothers in relation to infant attachment (e.g., mothers are needed primarily for physical survival), Harlow's studies showed how infant rhesus monkeys separated from their birth-mothers preferred a cloth surrogate over a wire-mesh mother that provided them with milk. More importantly, Harlow's work demonstrated that optimal development was the result of healthy mother–infant attachment and healthy relations with peers. In a series of studies in which infant monkeys were isolated from birth from either mothers or peers or both, Harlow demonstrated that juvenile monkeys thrived when they were raised among both family and peers, but not when isolated from either during infancy, especially not when isolated from peers (Harlow & Harlow, 1962; Suomi & Harlow, 1975). Specifically, monkeys raised without a mother but who were caged with several other infant monkeys had a difficult time during infancy but seemed to behave more normally by one year of age, although some behavioral difficulties persisted (Suomi, 1997). In contrast, peer-isolated monkeys behaved poorly when re-introduced to the group. They were atypically shy, asocial, and hyper-aggressive, and the longer they were isolated from peers, the worse their adjustment. Taken together, these studies underscore the importance of interpersonal relationships for optimal development, especially peer relationships. Indeed, although parent–child attachment was important, for Harlow's monkeys peer relationships were critical in order to flourish (Blum, 2002).

Among humans, for whom experimental studies of social deprivation would be unethical, evidence concerning the need for love, affection, acceptance, and affiliation for the promotion of well-being comes from the many blunders made in an attempt to *improve* children's health and welfare. For example, from the latter part of the 19th century into the early 20th century, close to 100% of infants admitted to foundling homes died before their first birthday (Chapin, 1915; Hrdy, 1999). Initially, these appalling statistics were attributed to "incomplete knowledge of nutrition" (Bakwin, 1942), but with improved nutrition, came increased concern for infection. To guard against the spread of "hospitalism," a term coined to describe repeated infections infants contracted while under hospital or foundling care, most mid-20th-century hospitals adopted strict sterilization procedures. Infants were isolated in small cubicle rooms. Masked and hooded attending nurses and physicians handled infants as infrequently as possible and moved "about cautiously so as not to stir up bacteria" (p. 31). Parent visits were forbidden. Although these hygienic practices were successful in reducing infant deaths, the mortality rate remained curiously high (still over 35% in the late 1930s). It took a long time for someone to question "whether the measures used to prevent infection may not be harmful to the child" (p. 31).

Similarly, in keeping with the zeitgeist of that time concerning the innocuous effects of social deprivation on development, famed pediatrician Arnold Gesell strongly opposed the adoption of young babies from institutions (Blum, 2002). In fact, he counseled prospective parents against early adoption, urging them to wait until the child matured in order to verify their true quality (i.e., presence or absence of mental defects). It had not occurred to Gesell, despite protests from his Yale colleague, Milton Seen, that the depraved environment of the institutions may in effect be contributing to the mental defects (Blum, 2002). Even this brief snapshot of history clearly documents the fact that experiences which interfere with the development of positive and healthy relationships are singularly damaging.

In the 1980s, over 65,000 Romanian children were placed in orphanages where they spent up to 20 hours per day unattended in their cribs, a result of an incredible caregiver-to-child ratio of 10:1 for infants and 20:1 for children over three years (Ames & Carter, 1992). The deleterious effect of early relationship deprivation on social, emotional, cognitive, physical, and brain functioning are well documented (e.g., Ames, 1997; Rutter, 1998), and mirror in many ways those documented among socially deprived non-human primates (Suomi, 1997). For example, adopted children showed insecure patterns of attachment (Chisholm, 1998), more eating problems, medical problems, and stereotyped behavior problems (Fisher, Ames, Chisholm, & Savoie, 1997). They were also more impulsive than typical developing controls, had social deficits and issues with attention, as well as mild neurocognitive impairments, which may be attributable to documented brain differences (e.g., Chugani et al., 2001). Specifically, when compared to normal adults, children adopted from Romanian orphanages showed decreased metabolism in the orbital frontal gyrus, the infralimbic prefrontal cortex, the amygdala and head of hippocampus, the lateral temporal cortex, and the brain stem (Chugani et al., 2001), the same brain regions that relate to social functioning and emotional regulation.

Studies of early social deprivation, as well as studies of the detrimental effects of bullying, rejection, and ostracism, point to the fact that humans are hard-wired to belong (Goleman, 2006). Humans need to belong in their families, their romantic unions, and in their peer group. When children are bullied, the chance of meeting the need to feel a sense of belonging in the peer group is dangerously thwarted. Perhaps even more damaging is the fact that some will internalize these experiences (Graham & Juvonen, 1998). They blame themselves, believe they are at fault, and think that their poor treatment will be long lasting such that their future prospects for belonging look extremely grim.

Vicarious experience is similarly threatening. This need to belong is so ingrained that a human's 'ostracism detection system' (Kerr & Levine, 2008; Spoor & Williams,

2007) becomes activated even when a person witnesses another individual being ostra-cized (Wesselmann, Bagg & Williams, 2009). The ostracism detection system is fast and crude—biased in favor of over-detecting ostracism. At the slightest sign of ostracism, the pain system quickly calls the individual's attention to the exclusion so that "pre-emptive coping can forestall or avoid permanent expulsion" (Wesselmann et al., 2009). Of particular interest are recent studies in the area of neuroscience that provide further empirical support for the assertion that the need to belong is hard-wired. As shown in the review of literature that follows, these studies have demonstrated that the pain associated with physical injury is akin to the pain associated with loss and rejection (social pain), both activating similar brain regions. Making these links is important because, as Vaillancourt et al. (2010) suggest, understanding the biological underpin-nings of peer relations helps legitimize the plight of peer-abused children and youth, thus encouraging policy-makers and practitioners to prioritize the reduction of school bullying. Indeed, it is difficult to ignore the plight of victimized youth when confronted with evidence that such negative experience is associated with physiological changes that place the individual at risk of a host of cognitive, physical health, and mental health issues (see Vaillancourt et al., 2008, 2009, 2010).

SOCIAL PAIN IS AKIN TO PHYSICAL PAIN: INSIGHTS FROM NEUROSCIENCE

> Criticism may not be agreeable, but it is necessary. It fulfills the same function as pain in the human body. It calls attention to an unhealthy state of things.
>
> Sir Winston Churchill (1874–1965)

As Churchill pointed out, pain serves an important function. It calls attention to the issue and motivates the person to find a swift solution. Given the discomfort and dis-tress associated with physical pain, it is not surprising that much is known about the neurological underpinnings of this uncomfortable state (Price, 2000). However, recent neuroimaging studies have shown that parts of the cortical physical pain network are also activated when a person is socially excluded (Lieberman & Eisenberger, 2009, p. 890; Price, 2000). Before describing these studies, a brief overview of the brain regions associated with physical and affective pain is provided.

The cortical physical pain network involves a number of different brain regions, including the dorsal anterior cingulate cortex (dACC), the insula and somatosensory cortex, with subcortical contributions from the periaqueductal gray and thalamus. The dACC has been shown to be involved in the unpleasantness associated with physical pain (Rainville, Duncan, Price, Carrier, & Bushnell, 1997; Sawamoto et al., 2000), and the insula is involved with negative affect and visceral pain (e.g., Aziz, Schnitzler, & Enck, 2000; Lane, Fink, Chau, & Dolan, 1997). The periaqueductal gray is involved in pain processing and attachment behaviors (Bandler & Shipley, 1994; Dunckley et al., 2005), and the right ventral prefrontal cortex (RVPFC) has been linked with the regula-tion of distress associated with physical pain and negative emotional experiences (e.g., Hariri, Bookheimer, & Mazziott., 2000). Less is known about the role of the amygdala in social pain processing (Eisenberger, 2006), although it appears to play a central role in processing facial displays of affect (Fitzgerald, Angstadt, Jelsone, Nathan, & Phan,

2006; Morris et al. 1996; Whalen et al., 1998) and in particular, those signaling threat (see Calder, Lawrence, & Young, 2001 for review).

In a landmark study published in *Science* in 2003, Eisenberger, Lieberman and Williams (2003) asked the question "Does rejection hurt?" Using functional magnetic resonance imaging (fMRI), a technique used to study the operational organization of the human brain (Logothetis, Pauls, Augath, Trinath, Oeltermann, 2001), Eisenberger et al. found that adult participants who were socially excluded from a cyberball tossing game while having the neural activity of their brain measured, showed activation of the dACC, insula and RVPFC. Furthermore, the greater the social pain (i.e., the more participants felt rejected, excluded, meaningless, and invisible), the more the dACC was activated. In a similar study, social rejection (assessed using the cyberball social exclusion task) was again found to be related to greater activation of the dACC (Eisenberger, Gable & Lieberman, 2007). In this study of 42 healthy adults, the periaqueductal gray and amygdala were also activated when individuals believed they were rejected.

Burklund, Eisenberger and Lieberman (2007) also report evidence that the dACC is sensitive to cues of social rejection. In this study, 21 adults were scanned while watching brief video clips of facial expressions demonstrating disapproval, anger and disgust; some of the very looks that characterize acts of indirect or relational victimization (see Archer & Coyne, 2005 for review). Greater dACC, right ventrolateral prefrontal cortex, and right dorsolateral prefrontal cortex activation were found among individuals high on rejection sensitivity but only in response to disapproving expressions. Given that the stimuli consisted of video clips depicting negative emotions, it is not unexpected that there was also significant activity in bilateral amygdala.

These fMRI studies provide converging support for the role the dACC plays in the experience of social rejection. But why? Somerville, Heatherton and Kelley (2006) suggest that the reason the dACC was activated in response to perceived social exclusion was because of its role in detecting *cognitive conflict* (participants likely expected to be *included* in the game), and not due to its role in processing social rejection (Somerville et al., 2006). The anterior cingulate cortex (ACC) is thought to act as a neural "alarm system" and the dACC, in particular, is believed to act as a conflict monitor. Pulling cognitive conflict and social pain apart by using a task in which participants made social judgments and received bogus feedback that was either positive or negative (peer rejection) or consistent or inconsistent with their expectation (cognitive conflict), Somerville et al. found that dACC was indeed sensitive to expectancy violations that were independent of social rejection. The ventral ACC (vACC), in contrast, responded specifically to rejection, a finding supported in another recent study by Onoda et al. (2009).

The teenage brain also reacts to social pain as if the individual was being physically injured. Masten et al. (2009) found that, like socially excluded adults, 13-year-olds showed increased activation of the right ventral prefrontal cortex and insula when they were being excluded from a virtual ball tossing game. These rejected teens (n=23) also showed increased activation of the ventral striatum, a brain structure implicated in reward processing and emotion regulation (e.g., McClure, Berns, and Montague, 2003; Rodriguez, Aron, and Poldrack, 2006). Moreover, similar to rejected adults, teens who showed the greatest activation in the insula also reported being most distressed by the social exclusion. Brain activation in response to social exclusion was not identical in adults and teens, however. Specifically, the dACC was found to be activated in response to exclusion for adults (e.g., Eisenberger et al., 2003), but not for teens. Additionally, teens and adults also differed in terms of the activation of the subgenual portion of the

ACC (subACC) in response to inclusion, a region that tends to be associated with positive emotion processing such as social acceptance (Somerville et al., 2006), as well as depression (Chen et al., 2008; Keedwell et al., 2009). The reasons for these differences are not yet clear. More work is needed to understand how the teen (and child) brain differs from the adult brain with regard to processing negative emotions and events.

Taken together, these studies suggest that physical pain and social pain share similar neural structures. Further evidence for the overlap of these two types of pain comes from studies demonstrating the negative effects of low social support on health and wellness, as well as tolerance of pain. For example, Brown, Sheffield, Leary, and Robinson (2003) have shown that social support moderates the effects of physical pain—participants who were alone reported more pain in a cold-pressor task than those who were accompanied by a friend or supportive stranger. Also, studies have documented the positive effects of social support on pain. Supported individuals reported less back pain (Hoogendoorn, van Poppel, Bongers, Koes, & Bouter, 2000), labour pain (Chalmers, Wolman, Nikodem, Gulmezoglu, & Hofmeyer, 1995; Kennell, Klaus, McGrath, Robertson, & Hinkley, 1991), and cancer pain (Zaza & Baine, 2002) than those without adequate social support (see Eisenberger & Lieberman, 2004 for a review). In fact, it is now widely recognized that loneliness and isolation are bad for a person's health (Cohen, 2004; Edwards, Hershberger, Russell, & Market, 2001; Uchino, Cacioppo, & Kiecolt-Glaser, 1996).

With respect to bullying, Vaillancourt and colleagues (2008, 2010) have argued that the stress of being bullied by peers likely disrupts the immune system, which is what is driving the association between poor health and peer victimization (e.g., Gruber & Fineran, 2007; Rigby, 1999). Knack and Vaillancourt (2010) and Knack, Jensen-Campbell and Baum (in press) recently reported that cortisol, a hormone that indicates elevated stress and that has been linked to peer victimization (Kliewer, 2006; Vaillancourt et al., 2008), moderated the link between peer victimization and physical health. Bullied teens in these studies reported poorer health, especially if they had altered neuroendocrine functioning (assessed via cortisol).

Studies have also shown that social and physical pain can be regulated in a similar manner. For example, recent experimental research by DeWall and colleagues showed that participants assigned to an acetaminophen condition (e.g., Tylenol™), a well-known analgesic for physical pain, also reported less hurt feelings after two weeks of consumption than those in the placebo condition (cited in DeWall, Pond, & Deckerman, 2011).

Why would the two pain systems overlap? Panksepp (1998) proposed an evolutionary hypothesis for the overlap. Specifically, he noted that opiate-based drugs which ease the physical pain of injury also reduce separation distress signals across many species (see also Nelson & Panksepp, 1998). In light of these findings, Panksepp argued that the system involved in separation distress (social pain) likely "piggybacked" onto the physical pain system in order to increase survival among mammalian species (Eisenberger & Lieberman, 2004). Given the length of immaturity of human infants, and the vulnerability associated with social separation during infancy, a warning system was needed to motivate attachment. Historically, maintaining proximity to a caregiver has been inextricably linked to survival (Hrdy, 1999). Thus, a system that monitors distance from a caregiver should enhance survival and be selected for. Beyond infancy, social acceptance has also been linked to survival. Being socially accepted meant having access to shelter, food, security, and mates, all of which increased the chances of surviving and procreating (Baumeister & Leary, 1995; McDonald & Leary, 2005).

TRANSLATING RESEARCH INTO PRACTICE: IMPLICATIONS FOR BULLYING PREVENTION AND INTERVENTION PROGRAMS

As highlighted in this review, we have, as recently as this past century, made enormous errors in judgment concerning the importance of interpersonal relationships and the fundamental need to belong. As noted, educated men decided that isolation was needed to help promote health in infants with a resulting near perfect mortality rate. We suspect a similar error in judgment is being made concerning bullying. In contrast to suggestions that bullying is "normal" and can "build character," common sense and an indisputable body of evidence have shown that being victimized by peers causes harm (Card et al., 2007; Hawker & Boulton, 2000). Not surprisingly, bullied children and youth are unhappy at school, like it less, and feel less safe when they are there (Slee & Rigby, 1993; Spriggs, Iannotti, Nansel, & Haynie, 2007; Vaillancourt, Brittain, Bennett, Arnocky, McDougall et al., 2010). And yet, the calls for a response are often ignored because schools have traditionally prioritized academic achievement over emotional well-being, despite increasing evidence for the importance of social and emotional learning for both academic and life success (Greenberg et al., 2003; Hymel, Schonert-Reichl, & Miller, 2006; Zins, Weissberg, Wang, and Walberg, 2004).

The neuroimaging research reviewed herein suggests that we have evolved to feel social pain in a manner similar to how we feel physical pain—both types of pain seem to share a common neural basis that acts as an alarm system for threat. Although physical pain and social pain overlap, there are likely differences between the two that have yet to be studied. For example, studies show that people can relive and re-experience social pain more easily than physical pain and the emotions they feel are more intense and painful (Chen et al., 2008). It seems that physical pain is often short lived whereas social pain can last a life time.

What are the implications of this? It has been suggested that being frequently victimized by peers alters brain functioning in the ACC, insula, and RVPFC, which in turn increases sensitivity to future victimization and pain (Knack, Gomez & Jensen-Campbell, 2011). The nature of bullying, characterized by *repeated* abuse by one or more persons who hold more power than their victim (Olweus, 1993), implies a constantly ramping up the social pain system. Given the fact that the brain is a "use it or lose it" organ, it may be problematic if the social neural alarm system is continually activated because such activation could result in efficiency and dominance of a network that is now extremely sensitive to threat. Being bullied is difficult enough without adding the extra burden of interpreting even ambiguous social exchanges as threatening. This type of hypervigilance to social rejection has been noted in the depression literature in that depressed individuals hold negative schemas or attributions that lead to negative cognitive biases (e.g., Beck, 1967), that is, people who are depressed tend to have biased attributions and notice threat in situations where others, presented with similar information, do not.

More generally, the significance of having rejection, ostracism, and loss feels so terrible that it motivates a person to avoid it. Over the course of human evolution, avoiding rejection from the group increased chances of surviving, prospering, and procreating. Even in modern times, being socially marginalized is linked to morbidity and mortality (see Baumeister & Leary, 1995; McDougall, Hymel, Vaillancourt, & Mercer, 2001). As reviewed above, victimized children and youth experience poorer physical and mental health. They fantasize about killing themselves more than non-bullied children, and also attempt to take their life more often than their non-victimized peers (Brunstein Klomek, Marrocco, Kleinman, Schonfeld, & Gould, 2008). In this chapter, we have demonstrated how recent research in neuroscience suggests that, rather than "building character," peer victimization can cause significant social pain which can jeopardize the individual's capacity for effective functioning. Our next challenge is to find ways to effectively alleviate that pain. In the words of one 17-year-old girl who had been victimized by peers during her school years, "In conclusion, there is no conclusion to what children who are bullied live with. They take it home with them at night. It lives inside them and eats away at them. It never ends. So neither should our struggle to end it."

REFERENCES

Arsenault, L., Walsh, E., Trzesniewski, K., Newcombe, R., Caspi, A., & Moffitt, T.E. (2006). Bullying victimization uniquely contributes to adjustment problems in young children: A nationally representative cohort study. *Pediatrics, 118*, 130–138.

Ames, E.W. 1997. The development of Romanian orphanage children adopted into Canada. In Final Report to Human Resources Development, Canada.

Ames, E.W., and Carter, M. 1992. Development of Romanian orphanage children adopted to Canada. *Canadian Psychology, 33*, 503.

Archer, J., & Coyne, S.M. (2005). An integrated review of indirect, relational, and social aggression. *Personality and Social Psychology Review, 9*, 212–230.

Austin, S., & Joseph, S. (1996). Assessment of bully/victim problems in 8–11 year-olds. *British Journal of Educational Psychology, 66*, 447–456.

Aziz, Q., Schnitzler, A., & Enck, P. (2000). Functional neuroimaging of visceral sensation. *Journal of Clinical Neurophysiology, 17*, 604–612.

Bakwin, H. (1942). Loneliness in infants. *Archives of Pediatrics & Adolescent Medicine, 63*, 30–40.

Bandler, R., & Shipley, M.T. (1994). Columnar organization in the midbrain periaqueductal gray: Modules for emotional expression? *Trends in Neurosciences, 17*, 379–389.

Baumeister, R.F. & Leary, M.R. (1995). The need to belong: Desire for interpersonal attachments as a fundamental human motivation. *Psychological Bulletin, 117*, 497–529.

Beck, A.T. (1967). *Depression: Causes and treatment*. Pennsylvania: University of Pennsylvania Press.

Blum, D. (2002). *Love at Goon Park: Harry Harlow and the science of affection*. Cambridge, MA: Perseus.

Boivin, M., Hymel, S., & Bukowski, W.M. (1995). The roles of social withdrawal, peer rejection, and victimization by peers in predicting loneliness and depressed mood in childhood. *Development and Psychopathology, 7*, 765–785.

Bonanno, R., & Hymel, S. (2010). Beyond hurt feelings: Investigating why some victims of bullying are at greater risk for suicidal ideation. *Merrill-Palmer Quarterly, 56*, 320–440.

Boulton, M. J., & Underwood, K. (1992). Bully/victim problems among middle school children. *British Journal of Educational Psychology, 62*, 73–87.

Bowlby, J. (1969/1997). *Attachment and loss, Vol. 1: Attachment*. London: Pimlico.

Bowlby, J. (1973). *Attachment and loss, Vol. 2: Separation*. New York, NY: Basic Books.

Bowlby, J. (1988). *A secure base: Parent-child attachment and healthy human development*. London: Routledge.

Brown, J.L., Sheffield, D., Leary, M.R., & Robinson, M.E. (2003). Social support and experimental pain. *Psychosomatic Medicine, 65*, 276–283.

Brunstein Klomek, A., Marrocco, F., Kleinman, M., Schonfeld, I. S., & Gould, M.S. (2008). Bullying, depression, and suicidality in adolescents. *Journal of the American Academy of Child and Adolescent Psychiatry, 46*, 40–49.

Burklund, L., Eisenberger, N.I., & Lieberman, M.D. (2007). The face of rejection: Rejection sensitivity moderates dorsal anterior cingulate activity to disapproving facial expressions. *Social Neuroscience, 2*, 238–253.

Calder, A.J., Lawrence, A.D., & Young, A.W. (2001). Neuropsychology of fear and loathing. *Nature Reviews, 2*, 352–363.

Card, N.A., Isaacs, J., & Hodges, E.V.E. (2007). Correlates of school victimization: Implications for prevention and intervention. In J.E. Zins, M.J. Elias, & C.A. Maher (Eds.), *Bullying, victimization, and peer harassment: A handbook of prevention and intervention* (pp. 339–366). New York, NY: The Haworth Press.

Carney, J.V. (2000). Bullied to death: perceptions of peer abuse and suicidal behaviour during adolescence. *School Psychology International, 21*, 213–223.

Chalmers, B., Wolman, W.L., Nikodem, V.C., Gulmezoglu, A.M., & Hofmeyer, G.J. (1995). Companionship in labour: Do the personality characteristics of labour supporters influence their effectiveness? *Curationis, 18,* 77–80.

Chapin, H.D. (1915). A plea for accurate statistics in infants' institutions. *Journal of the American Pediatric Society, 27,* 180.

Chen, Z., Williams, K.D., Fitness, J., & Newton, N.C. (2008). When hurt will not heal: Exploring the capacity to relive social and physical pain. *Psychological Science, 19,* 789–795.

Chisholm, K. (1998). A three-year follow-up of attachment and indiscriminate friendliness in children adopted from Romanian orphanages. *Child Development, 69,* 1092–1106.

Chugani, H.T., Behen, M.E., Muzik, O., Juhasz, C., Nagy, F., & Chugani, D.C. (2001). Local brain functional activity following early deprivation: A study of postinstitutionalized Romanian orphans. *NeuroImage, 14,* 1290–1301.

Cohen, S. (2004). Social relationships and health. *American Psychologist, 59,* 676–684.

DeWall, C.N., Pond, R., & Deckerman, T. (2011). Acetaminophen dulls psychological pain. In L.A. Jensen-Campbell & G. MacDonald (Eds.), *Social pain: Neuropsychological and health implications of loss and exclusion* (pp. 123–140). Washington, DC: American Psychological Association.

Dunckley, P., Wise, R.G., Fairhurst, M., Hobden, P., Aziz, Q., Chang, L., & Tracey, I. (2005). A comparison of visceral and somatic pain processing in the human brainstem using functional magnetic resonance imaging. *The Journal of Neuroscience, 25,* 7333–7341.

Edwards, K.J., Hershberger, P.J., Russell, R.K., & Markert, R.J. (2001). Stress, negative social exchange, and health symptoms in university students. *Journal of American College Health, 50,* 75–79.

Eisenberger, N.I. (2006). Identifying the neural correlates underlying social pain: Implications for developmental processes. *Human Development, 49,* 273–293.

Eisenberger, N.I., Gable, S.L., & Lieberman, M.D. (2007). Functional magnetic resonance imaging responses related to differences in real-world social experience. *Emotion, 7,* 745–754.

Eisenberger, N.I., & Lieberman, M.D. (2004). Why rejection hurts: a common neural alarm system for physical and social pain. *TRENDS in Cognitive Sciences, 8,* 294–300.

Eisenberger, N.I., Lieberman, M.D., & Williams, K.D. (2003). Does rejection hurt: An fMRI study of social exclusion. *Science, 302,* 290–292.

Espelage, D.L., & Holt, M.K. (2001). Bullying and victimization during early adolescence: Peer influences and psychosocial correlates. *Journal of Emotional Abuse, 2,* 123–142.

Fisher, L., Ames, E.W., Chisholm, K., & Savoie, L. (1997). Problems reported by parents of Romanian orphans adopted to British Columbia. *International Journal of Behavioral Development, 20,* 67–82.

Fitzgerald, D.A., Angstadt, M., Jelsone, L.M., Nathan, P.J., & Phan, K.L. (2006). Beyond threat: Amygdala reactivity across multiple expressions of facial affect. *NeuroImage, 30,* 1441–1448.

Freud, S. (1953). *Three essays on the theory of sexuality. Standard edition, VII.* 1905. London: Hogarth (pp. 125–245).

Graham, S., & Juvonen, J. (1998). Self-blame and peer victimization in middle school: An attributional analysis. *Developmental Psychology, 34,* 587–599.

Greenberg, M.T., Weissberg, R.P., O'Brien, M.U., Zins, J.E., Fredericks, L., Resnik, H., et al. (2003). Enhancing school-based prevention and youth development through coordinated social, emotional, and academic learning. *American Psychologist, 58,* 466–474.

Goleman, D. (2006). *Social intelligence: The new science of human relationships.* New York, NY: Bantam.

Gonsalkorale, K., & Williams, K. (2007). The KKK won't let me play: ostracism even by a despised outgroup hurts. *European Journal of Social Psychology, 37,* 1176–1186.

Gruber, J.E., & Fineran, S. (2007). The impact of bullying and sexual harassment on middle and high school girls. *Violence against Women, 13,* 627–643.

Hariri, A.R., Bookheimer, S.Y., & Mazziotta, J.C. (2000) Modulating emotional responses: effects of a neocortical network on the limbic system. *Neuroreport, 11,* 43–48.

Harlow, H.F., & Harlow, M. (1962). Social deprivation in monkeys. *Scientific American, 207,* 136–146.

Hawker, D.S.J., & Boulton, M.J. (2000). Twenty years' research on peer victimization and psychosocial maladjustment: A meta-analytic review of cross-sectional studies. *Journal of child Psychology and Psychiatry, 41,* 441–455.

Hoogendoorn, W.E., van Poppel, M.N.M., Bongers, P.M., Koes, B.W., & Bouter, L.M. (2000). Systematic review of psychosocial factors at work and private life as risk factors for back pain. *Spine, 25,* 2114–2125.

Hrdy, S.B. (1999). *Mother nature: Maternal Instincts and how they shape the human species.* New York, NY: Ballantine Books.

Hymel, S., Schonert-Reichl, K.A., & Miller, L.D. (2006). Reading, 'riting, 'rithmetic and relationships: Considering the social side of education. *Exceptionality Education Canada, 16,* 149–192.

Juvonen, J., Nishina, A., & Graham, S. (2000). Peer harassment, psychological adjustment, and school functioning in early adolescence. *Journal of Educational Psychology, 92,* 349–359.

Kaltiala-Heino, R., Rimpela, M., Marttunen, M., Rimpela, A., & Rantanen, P. (1999). Bullying, depression, and suicidal ideation in Finnish adolescents: School survey. *British Medical Journal, 319,* 348–351.

Keedwell, P., Drapier, D., Surguladze , S., Giampietro, V., Brammer, M., & Phillips, M. (2009). Neural markers of symptomatic improvement during antidepressant therapy in severe depression: subgenual cingulate and visual cortical responses to sad, but not happy, facial stimuli are correlated with changes in symptom score. *Journal of Psychopharmacology, 23,* 775–788.

Kennell, J., Klaus, M., McGrath, S., Robertson, S., & Hinkley, C. (1991). Continuous emotional support during labor in U.S. hospital: A randomized control trial. *Journal of the American Medical Association, 265,* 2197–2201.

Kerr, N.I., & Levine, J.M. (2008). The detection of social exclusion: Evolution and beyond. *Group Dynamics: Theory, Research, and Practice, 12,* 39–52.

Kim, Y., Koh, Y., & Leventhal, B. (2005). School bullying and suicidal risk in Korean middle school students. *Pediatrics, 115,* 357–363.

Kliewer, W. (2006). Violence exposure and cortisol responses in urban youth. *International Journal of Behavioral Medicine, 13,* 109–120.

Knack, J., Gomez, H.L., & Jensen-Campbell, L.A. (2011). Bullying and its long-term health implications. In L.A. Jensen-Campbell and G. MacDonald (Eds.), *Social pain: Neuropsychological and health implications of loss and exclusion* (pp. 215–236). Washington, DC: American Psychological Association.

Knack, J., Jensen-Campbell, L.A., & Baum, A. (in press). Worse than sticks and stones? Bullying is associated with altered HPA axis functioning and poorer health. *Brain and Cognition.*

Knack, J., & Vaillancourt, T. (2010). *Morning cortisol levels moderate the link between peer victimization and physical health.* Paper presented at the biennial meeting of the International Society for the Study of Behavioural Development, Lusaka, Zambia.

Kokkinos, C., & Panayiotou, G. (2004). Predicting bullying and victimization among early adolescents: Associations with disruptive behavior disorders. *Aggressive Behavior, 30,* 520–553.

Lane R.D., Fink, G.R., Chau, P.M. & Dolan R.J. (1997). Neural activation during selective attention to subjective emotional responses. *Neuroreport, 8,* 3969–3972.

Lieberman, M., & Eisenberger, N.(2009). Pains and pleasures of social life. *Science, 323,* 890–891.

Logothetis, N.K., Pauls, J., Augath, M., Trinath, T., Oeltermann, A. (2001). Neurophysiological investigation of the basis of fMRI signal. *Nature, 412,* 150–157.

Marr, N., & Fields, T. (2000). *Bullycide: Death at playtime.* Wantage, Oxford, UK: Wessex Press.

Masten, C.L., Eisenberger, N.I., Borofsky, L.A., Pfeifer, J.H., McNealy, K., Mazziotta, J.C., & Dapretto, M. (2009). Neural correlates of social exclusion during adolescence: Understanding the distress of peer rejection. *Scan, 4,* 143–157.

McClure, S., Berns, G., & Montague, P. (2003). Temporal prediction errors in a passive learning task activate human striatum. *Neuron, 38,* 339–346.

McDonald, G., & Leary, M.R. (2005). Why does social exclusion hurt? The relationship between social and physical pain. *Psychological Bulletin, 31,* 202–223.

McDougall, P, Hymel, S., Vaillancourt, T., & Mercer, L. (2001). The consequences of childhood peer rejection. In M.Leary (Ed.), *Interpersonal rejection* (pp. 213–247). New York, NY: Oxford University Press.

Morris, J.S., Frith, C.D., Perrett, D.I., Rowland, D., Young, A.W., Calder, A.J., & Dolan, R.J. (1996). A differential neural response in the human amygdala to fearful and happy facial expressions. *Nature, 383,* 812–815.

Nelson, E.E., & Panksepp, J. (1998). Brain substrates of infant-mother attachment: Contributions of opioids, oxytocin, and norepinephrine. *Neuroscience and Biobehavioral Reviews, 22,* 437–452.

Olweus, D. (1993). Victimization by peers: Antecedents and long-term outcomes. In K.H. Rubin and J.B. Asendorf (Eds.), *Social withdrawal, inhibition, and shyness in childhood* (pp. 315–341). Hillsdale, NJ: Lawrence Erlbaum.

Onoda, K., Okamoto, Y., Nakashima, K., Nittono, H., Ura, M., & Yamawaki, S. (2009). Decreased ventral anterior cingulate cortex activity is associated with reduced social pain during emotional support. *Social Neuroscience, 4,* 443–454.

Panksepp, J. (1998). *Affective neuroscience.* New York, NY: Oxford University Press.

Price D.D. (2000). Psychological and neural mechanisms of the affective dimension of pain. *Science, 288,* 1769–1772.

Rainville, P., Duncan, G.H., Price, D.D., Carrier, B., & Bushnell, M.D. (1997). Pain affect encoded in human anterior cingulate but not somatosensory cortex. *Science, 277,* 968–971.

Rigby, K. (1999). Peer victimisation at school and the health of secondary school students. *British Journal of Educational Psychology, 69,* 95–104.

Rigby, K., & Slee, P.T. (1993). Dimensions of interpersonal relation among Australian children and implications for psychological well-being. *The Journal of Social Psychology, 133,* 33–42.

Rodriguez, P.F., Aron, A.R., & Poldrack, R.A. (2006). Ventral–striatal/nucleus–accumbens sensitivity to prediction errors during classification learning. *Human Brain Mapping 27,* 306 –313.

Roland, E. (2002). Bullying, depressive symptoms and suicidal thoughts. *Educational Research, 44,* 55–67.

Rutter, M. 1998. Developmental catch-up, and deficit, following adoption after severe global early privation. English and Romanian Adoptees (ERA) Study Team. *Journal of Child Psychology and Psychiatry, 39,* 465–476.

Sawamoto, N., Honda, M., Okada, T., Hanakawa, T., Kanda, M., Fukuyama, H., Konishi, J., & Shibasaki, H. (2000). Expectation of pain enhances responses to nonpainful somatosensory stimulation in the anterior cingulate cortex and parietal operculum/posterior insula: an event-related functional magnetic resonance imaging study. *The Journal of Neuroscience, 20,* 7438–7445.

Slee, P.T., & Rigby, K. (1993). Australian school children's self appraisal of interpersonal relations: The bullying experience. *Child Psychiatry and Human Development, 23,* 273–282.

Somerville, L.H., Heatherton, T.F., & Kelley, W.M. (2006). Anterior cingulate cortex responds differentially to expectancy violation and social rejection. *Nature Neuroscience, 9,* 1007–1008.

Sourander, A., Helstela, L., Helenius, H., & Piha, J. (2000). Persistence of bullying from childhood to adolescence: A longitudinal 8-year follow-up study. *Child Abuse and Neglect, 24,* 873–881.

Spoor, J. & Williams, K.D. (2007). The evolution of an ostrasicism detection system. In J.P. Forgas, M.Hselton, & W. von Hippel (Eds.), *The evolution of the social mind: Evolutionary psychology and social cognition* (pp. 279–292). New York, NY: Psychology Press.

Spriggs, A.L., Iannotti, R.J., Nansel, T.R., & Haynie, D.L. (2007). Adolescent bullying involvement and perceived family, peer and school relations: Commonalities and differences across race/ethnicity. *Journal of Adolescent Health, 41,* 283–293.

Storch, A., Brassard, M.R., & Masia-Warner, C.L. (2003). The relationship of peer victimization to social anxiety and loneliness in adolescence. *Child Study Journal, 33,* 1–18.

Suomi, S.J. (1997). Early determinants of behaviour: evidence from primate studies. *British Medical Bulletin, 53,* 170–184.

Suomi, S.J., & Harlow, H.F. (1975). The role and reason of peer relationships in rhesus monkeys. In M. Lewis, & L.A. Rosenblum (Eds.), *Friendship and peer relations* (pp. 153–186). New York, NY: Wiley.

Uchino, B.N. Cacioppo, J.T., & Kiecolt-Glaser, J.K. (1996). The relationship between social support and physiological processes: A review with emphasis on underlying mechanisms and implications for health. *Psychological Bulletin, 119,* 488–531.

Vaillancourt, T., deCatanzaro, D., Duku, E., Muir, C. (2009). Androgen dynamics in the context of children's peer relations: An examination of the links between testosterone and peer-victimization. *Aggressive Behavior, 35,* 103–113.

Vaillancourt, T., Clinton, J., McDougall, P., Schmidt, L., & Hymel, S. (2010). The neurobiology of peer victimization and rejection. In S.R. Jimerson, S.M. Swearer, & D.L. Espelage (Eds.), *The Handbook of Bullying in Schools: An International Perspective* (pp. 293–304). New York, NY: Routledge.

Vaillancourt, T., Duku, E, deCatanzaro, D., MacMillan, H., Muir, C., & Schmidt, L.A. (2008). Variation in hypothalamic-pituitary-adrenal axis activity among bullied and non-bullied children. *Aggressive Behavior, 34,* 294–305.

Vaillancourt, T., Brittain, H., Bennett, L., Arnocky, S., McDougall, P., Hymel, S., Short, K., Sunderani, S., Scott, C., Mackenzie, M., & Cunningham, L. (2010). Places to avoid: population-based study of student reports of unsafe and high bullying areas at school. *Canadian Journal of School Psychology, 25,* 40–54.

van der Wal, M.F., de Wit, C.A.M., & Hirasing, R.A. (2003). Psychosocial health among young victims and offenders of direct and indirect bullying. *Pediatrics, 111,* 1312–1317.

Wesselmann, E.D., Bagg, D., & Williams, K.D. (2009). "I feel your pain": The effects of observing ostracism on the ostracism detection system. *Journal of Experimental Social Psychology, 45,* 1308–1311.

Whalen, P.J., Rauch, S.L., Etcoff, N.L., McInerney, S.C., Lee, M.B., & Jenike, M.A. (1998). Masked presentations of emotional facial expressions modulate amygdala activity without explicit knowledge. *The Journal of Neuroscience, 18,* 411–418.

Zaza, C., & Baine, N. (2002). Cancer pain and psychosocial factors: A critical review of the literature. *Journal of Pain and Symptom Management, 24,* 526–542.

Zins, J.E., Weissberg, R.P., Wang, M.C., & Walberg, H. J. (Eds.). (2004). *Building academic success on social and emotional learning: What does the research say?* New York, NY: Teachers College Press.

4

BULLYING AMONG STUDENTS WITH DISABILITIES
Impact and Implications

CHAD A. ROSE

Bullying has emerged as one of the most fundamental problems facing our nation's schools to date (Espelage & Swearer, 2003). Since 1999, state legislators have taken a keen interest in this issue, and a majority of the nation's states have enacted legislation that prohibits bullying and harassment, and have taken measures to report policies, programs, and procedures to students and parents (Swearer, Espelage, & Napolitano, 2009). In addition to adopting specific policies regarding bullying, schools are often encouraged to adopt research-supported programs that focus on reducing perpetration and victimization through teacher awareness, social skill development, and curricular instruction (Rose, Espelage, & Monda-Amaya, 2009). While increased state mandates are a critical first step in reducing bullying, many of the programs and policies neglect to provide targeted approaches for addressing marginalized student populations.

When the continuum of the bullying dynamic is considered (i.e., bullies, victims, bully-victims, bystanders), evidence suggests that it involves the overwhelming major-ity of the nation's student population (Espelage, Bosworth, & Simon, 2000). However, conventional research has investigated this phenomenon in a whole-school context by comparing students based on general demographic descriptors (e.g., school, age, gen-der, race). Unfortunately, the statistics and implications from these studies may sig-nificantly underestimate the prevalence of bullying within certain subpopulations of students (Rose, Monda-Amaya, & Espelage, in press). For example, the National Center for Educational Statistics documented that 28% of adolescents reported being victim-ized within a six month period prior to being surveyed (Dinkes, Cataldi, Kena, & Baum, 2006), while several studies involving students with disabilities have yielded victimiza-tion rates in excess of 50% (*see* Dawkins, 1996; Doren, Bullis, & Benz, 1996; Little, 2002; O'Moore & Hillery, 1989; Whitney, Smith, & Thompson, 1994). Therefore, consideration must be given to the bullying dynamic as it relates to students with disabilities.

Understanding this discrepancy involves attending to several variables that may place students with disabilities at a greater risk for involvement in bullying as both the victims and the perpetrators. While Whitney and colleagues stated, "Often just being different in a noticeable way can be a risk factor for being a victim" (1994, p. 213), careful consideration must be given to the factors that contribute to this "difference" for students with disabilities. Broadly defined, students with disabilities include those who receive special education services for academic, behavioral, physical, or functional performance. Generally, these students have an Individualized Education Plan (IEP), but this definition may include students with 504 plans or those who have been diagnosed via the Diagnostic and Statistical Manual of Mental Disorders (DSM-IV; American Psychiatric Association, 2000). This chapter will focus on bullying among students with disabilities as it relates to the discrepancies between students without disabilities, the severity of the disability, classroom placement and instruction, and disability characteristics that may place students with disabilities at a greater risk for being bullied.

VICTIMIZATION OF AND PERPETRATION BY STUDENTS WITH DISABILITIES

The "social hierarchy extant in our system of education, in which bullying and victimization are generally considered a social ritual, a typical part of adolescent experience, or even a student's rite of passage" (Rose et al., 2010, p. 1) may prove to be more detrimental for students with disabilities. While evidence suggests that special education status does not directly predict victimization among primary-aged students (Woods & Wolke, 2004), preschool-aged victims may be characterized as having preexisting internalizing problems (Arseneault et al., 2006). These internalizing problems may be exacerbated by the early development of group dynamics where students migrate into social clusters based on social, physical, or environmental similarities (Perren & Alsaker, 2006). The development of these early social clusters may exclude students with disabilities, because evidence suggests that students with disabilities are regarded as unpopular and have fewer close friendships than students without disabilities (see Baker & Donelly, 2001; Davis, Howell, & Cooke, 2002; Martlew & Hodson, 1991; Nabuzoka & Smith, 1993; Whitney et al., 1994), thereby placing them at a greater risk for victimization.

Although special education status may not serve as a predictor for victimization at the primary level, as students' progress through their educational careers, the discrepancy between students with and without disabilities becomes increasingly more evident. Contextually, special education status may not be a direct predictor during the early stages of education because students may not be able to cognitively identify the differences, the disability may not be noticeable, or the disability may yet to have been identified (Langevin, Bortnick, Hammer, & Wiebe, 1998; Monks, Smith, & Sweetenham, 2005). Presumably, once these differences have been established within a social context, disability status emerges as a potential predictor for involvement within the bullying dynamic. This broad assumption is grounded in the majority of the extant literature that explicitly identifies adolescents with disabilities as being victimized significantly more often than their general education peers (Rose et al., 2010).

It is important to recall that when general and special education are viewed as a dichotomy (i.e., presence or absence of a disability), research suggests that students with disabilities are victimized significantly more than students without disabilities. For example, typical estimates suggest that approximately 20% to 30% of the student population have experienced bullying either through victimization or perpetration (Rose et al., 2010). Conversely, several reports suggest that students with disabilities, without consideration for disability labels, are victimized at least twice as much as their general education peers (Kaukiainen et al., 2002; Monchy, Pijl, & Zandberg, 2004; Nabuzoka & Smith, 1993). More specifically, by making the dichotomous distinction between general and special education, Rose, Espelage, Aragon, & Elliott (2010) found in a large-scale sample of middle school students (n = 1009) that students with disabilities reported significantly higher rates of victimization when compared to their general education peers.

Additionally, significant differences between students with and without disabilities are not necessarily isolated to victimization. At the present time, a growing number of research reports are beginning to investigate the bullying behaviors of students with disabilities. While approximately 13% of the American school population exhibits bullying characteristics (Nansel et al., 2001), several research reports suggest that students with disabilities are identified as bullies twice as often as students without (Dawkins, 1996; Kumpulainen, Räsänen, & Puura, 2001; Rose et al., 2009; Woods & Wolke, 2004). However, escalated victimization rates among students with disabilities may lead to increased bullying rates, because victimized students may develop aggressive characteristics to combat victimization (Kumpulainen et al., 2001; O'Moore & Hillery, 1989; Van Cleave & Davis, 2006).

Unfortunately, bullying and overt aggression may be interpreted in a similar manner even though the terms are distinctly different. For example, Rose and colleagues (2010) found that students with and without disabilities reported similar rates of bullying behaviors, but students with disabilities reported significantly higher rates of fighting behaviors. Interestingly, students without disabilities who reported being victimized also reported higher levels of bullying behaviors, while students with disabilities who reported being victimized reported higher levels of fighting behaviors. These findings suggest that victimization may lead to more aggressive behaviors in students with disabilities, but not necessarily more bullying behaviors (Rose et al., 2010).

The distinction between students with and without disabilities, in reality, is more complex than a simple dichotomous approach. While the term "disability" is used to refer to a large subgroup of students, in actuality, disability status falls upon a continuum. More specifically, the federal government has identified 13 disabilities categories that maintain different eligibility criteria (Smith, 2007). However, eligibility criteria may differ from state to state, and each disability maintains a range of severity. This range of severity leads to a range of supports and instructional placements for students with disabilities. Therefore, it becomes necessary to explore the discrepancy in bully involvement for students with and without disabilities in terms of class placement (i.e., inclusive classrooms, segregated settings), the severity and overt nature of the disability, and the specific disability characteristics.

CLASS PLACEMENT'S INFLUENCE ON BULLY PERPETRATION AND VICTIMIZATION

One of the central issues currently facing students with disabilities is access to the general curricula. The 1997 amendments of the Individuals with Disabilities Education Act (IDEA, 1997) escalated the initiative to increase access for students with disabilities by requiring participation and progress in the general curriculum. More specifically, the Individualized Education Plan (IEP) must include statements regarding how the disabilities affect participation in the general curriculum, annual measurable goals geared toward increasing the participation in the general curriculum, and program modifications (e.g., services, adaptations, supports) necessary to achieve these goals (Agran, Alper, & Wehmeyer, 2002). More recently, the revisions of IDEA, now referred to as the Individuals with Disabilities Education Improvement Act (IDEIA, 2004), placed a strong emphasis on improving the educational outcomes for students with disabilities through evidence-based practices. These provisions allow school districts to use up to 15% of their federal budget for early intervening services, which include extra academic and behavioral supports in general education classrooms (Yell, Shriner, & Katsiyannis, 2006). However, all of the provisions to IDEA or IDEIA to date have allowed for the continuum of services for students with disabilities (e.g., inclusion, self-contained classrooms, and segregated schools) as long as the placement is justified by the student's least restrictive environment (Smith, 2007).

The continuum of services available for students with disabilities may be necessary for some students to be successful either functionally or academically. These additional services, however, provide a fundamental difference between students with and without disabilities, because they often include alternative classroom placements, overt academic accommodations, or increased personnel support. Although this chapter is not explicitly about class placement per se, it is necessary to explore how this difference could potentially serve as a predictor for increased perpetration and victimization. Traditionally, class placement is broadly defined in terms of inclusive or segregated settings. Inclusive services represents a philosophy of education that is geared toward including all students in the general education classroom with the purposes of providing a meaningful, challenging, and appropriate curriculum for everyone (Salend, 2008). In contrast, segregated settings (e.g., pullout programs) are provided outside the general education classroom for purposes of providing specific academic instruction or behavioral supports (Smith, 2007). While these two approaches are distinctly different, students with disabilities may be subjected to multiple variations of each defined by their least restrictive environment. Based on the ambiguity of the definitions and the general assumption that all students with disabilities require some level of academic or behavioral supports, this chapter will consider inclusive services where the student receives a majority of their core academic instruction in a general education classroom.

In general, students and teachers consistently rank students with disabilities as frequent victims of bullying (Nabuzoka, 2003; Nabuzoka & Smith, 1993; Sabornie, 1994). When consideration is given to class placement, rates of victimization often vary between students in inclusive settings and students in more restrictive placements. This variation could be attributed to educational practices, classroom structure, or the severity of the disability (Rose et al., 2010). For example, Whitney and colleagues (1994) investigated the victimization rates of 93 students with disabilities in an inclusive setting and their demographically matched peers and determined that the students with disabilities were victimized significantly more than their general education classmates. Similarly, O'Moore and Hillery (1989) explored the victimization rates of students with disabilities in inclusive and restrictive settings and compared them to their general education peers. The researchers reported that students in self-contained settings were victimized significantly more than their peers with disabilities in inclusive settings and their general education counterparts. These findings are supported by current literature that has documented that students in segregated settings are victimized by their peers twice as often as any other subgroup of students (Martlew & Hodson, 1991; Morrison, Furlong, & Smith, 1994; Sabornie, 1994).

Similar to victimization, class placement could also serve as a predictor of bullying perpetration. Although current research is limited regarding bullying among students with disabilities in inclusive and restrictive settings, foundational research suggests that perpetration follows the same pattern as victimization (O'Moore & Hillery, 1989; Rose et al., 2010). For example, in a large-scale middle school sample, Rose and colleagues (2009) determined that students with disabilities in a more restrictive environment engaged in more bullying and fighting behaviors than students with disabilities in inclusive settings and their general education peers. Whitney, Nabuzoka, and Smith (1992) also suggested that students with disabilities who were victimized in inclusive environments tended to exhibit bullying behaviors when moved to a more restrictive environment. Unfortunately, as previously stated, bullying and aggressive behaviors could be interpreted synonymously, and this distinction will be discussed further in the disabilities characteristics section.

Although current research suggests that students with disabilities are victims and perpetrators more often than their general education peers, inclusive practices could serve as a preventative factor for the victimization of and perpetration by students with disabilities. The preventative characteristics of inclusive settings could be attributed to positive behavior modeling, acquisition of social skills, increased social and academic development (Brown et al., 1989), increased acceptance, reduction in negative stereotypes (Martlew & Hodson, 1991), and increased participation in classroom activities (Sabornie, 1994). However, it should be noted that not all of the existent literature has documented the discrepancy between victimization rates among students in inclusive and restrictive settings (Reiter & Lapidot-Lefler, 2007; Rose et al., 2009), indicating that inclusion does not always maintain these preventative characteristics. For example, if students are not fully integrated into peer groups, inclusion may maintain or exacerbate victimization and perpetration (Martlew & Hodson, 1991). This lack of integration could hinder the development of a protective peer base (Morrison et al., 1994; Whitney et al., 1994) and limit students' opportunities to learn, practice, and validate social skills (Mishna, 2003). Thus, ineffective inclusive practices could be detrimental for students with disabilities in regards to involvement in bullying as perpetrators and victims.

DISABILITY TYPE AND SEVERITY

Given the Least Restrictive Environment mandate (i.e., continuum of placements) for students with disabilities, the discrepancy between perpetration and victimization among students in inclusive or restrictive settings could partially be explained by the disability type and severity. For example, current educational trends and national mandates are placing a strong emphasis on Response to Intervention (RtI; Batsche et al., 2006) and Positive Behavior Supports (PBS; Bambara & Kern, 2005), defined by a multitiered framework for providing academic interventions and behavioral accommodations for all students. Based on this framework, as a student's academic or behavioral needs increase the level of support also increases. Therefore, once a student's needs exceed pre-set criterion, their supports and classroom placement become more individualized in order to provide the most appropriate curriculum. Often, the restrictiveness of this placement, which is based on the severity of the student's disability, causes the student to be removed from the general education classroom for an extended period of time.

Based on the aforementioned framework, with the general assumption that students have been placed in their Least Restrictive Environment, an argument can be made that the discrepancy in victimization and perpetration rates among students in inclusive and self-contained settings may more likely be due to the severity of the disability as opposed to the actual classroom placement. Therefore, attention must be paid to the overall severity and overt nature of the disability. For example, Dawkins (1996) investigated the difference between victimization rates of students with observable and unobservable disabilities. The researchers documented that 50% of the students with observable disabilities reported being victimized at least once during the current term, with 30% victimized on a regular basis. Conversely, 21% of students with unobservable disabilities reported being victimized at least once during the current term, and 14% on a regular basis. Therefore, students with unobservable disabilities reported victimization rates similar to the United States average, where students with observable disabilities reported significantly higher victimization rates.

While empirical research supports the Dawkins' study, it is important to note that visibility of disabilities also fall upon a continuum. For example, Whitney and colleagues (1994) noted that students with mild to moderate learning difficulties were two to three times more likely to be victimized, whereas students with physical disabilities and hearing impairments were two to four times more likely to be victimized than their general education peers. Similarly, students with language impairments (Davis et al., 2002; Knox & Conti-Ramsden, 2003; Sweeting & West, 2001) and psychiatric disorders (Unnever & Cornell, 2003; Van Cleave & Davis, 2006) reported being victimized 20% more, and students with emotional/behavioral disorder (EBD; Monchy et al., 2004; Van Cleave & Davis, 2006) reported being victimized 30% more than students without disabilities. Additionally, recent reports suggest that students with Asperger's syndrome or autistic traits are victimized as much as, if not more than, any other subgroup of students (Bejerot & Mörtberg, 2009; Little, 2002). Interestingly, all of the aforementioned disability labels account for a significant proportion of students who are educated in self-contained settings.

While evidence suggests that the observable nature and severity of a disability predicts escalated victimization, bully perpetration follows a much different pattern. Presumably, the social nature of bullying, which is reinforced by peers and peer groups, dictates the difference between victimization and perpetration among students with disabilities (Rose et al., 2009). For example, students with high-incidence disabilities (e.g, learning disabilities, EBD) engage in bullying behaviors twice as often as the United States average (Kaukiainen et al., 2002; Whitney et al., 1994). Additionally, students with EBD demonstrate the highest level of bully perpetration when compared to any other subgroup of students (Monchy et al., 2004; Van Cleave & Davis, 2006). However, students with low-incidence disabilities (e.g., severe cognitive disabilities) report much lower rates of perpetration when compared to students with high-incidence disabilities and students without disabilities (Sheard, Clegg, Standen, & Cromby, 2001). This discrepancy may be attributed to minimal interaction opportunities with chronically aged peer groups, social skills development, and cognitive understanding of bully perpetration. While these factors could be limited for all students with disabilities, students with high incidence disabilities have a higher likelihood of being included within the typical school structure (Giangreco, Hurley, & Suter, 2009).

DISABILITY CHARACTERISTICS

Although educational setting and severity of the disability may serve as predictors for victimization and perpetration, it is necessary to explore the disability characteristics that may place students with disabilities at a greater risk for involvement in bullying.

Reiter and Lapidot-Lefler (2007) found that "being a victim was correlated with emotional problems and interpersonal problems" (p. 179). More importantly, the concept of bullying is complex, based on the social interplay between perpetration and victimization, and can only be understood in relations among individuals, families, peer groups, schools, communities, and cultures (Espelage & Swearer, 2009; Swearer & Espelage, 2004). However, students with disabilities often struggle with these social relationships because they often lack age-appropriate social skills (see Baker & Donelly, 2001; Doren et al., 1996; Kaukiainen et al., 2002; Llewellyn, 2000; Woods & Wolke, 2004).

Based on the general lack of social skills combined with the social nature of bullying, several hypotheses have been developed to explain the escalated rates of victimization among students with disabilities. According to Sabornie (1994), victims of bullying may be too passive, exhibit timid responses, misread non-verbal communication, or misinterpret non-threatening cues. This passivity may reinforce the bullying and misinterpretation may incite aggressive responses from peers. Additionally, students with disabilities may be at greater risk for victimization because they lack the appropriate socializing behaviors that help them avoid being victimized (Nabuzoka, 2003). This lack of socializing behaviors may also lead to the victim's inability to develop close friendships, rejection from classroom peers, and the perception that they are dependent on adult assistance (Baker & Donelly, 2001; Llewellyn, 2000; Martlew & Hodson, 1991; Morrison et al., 1994; Nabuzoka & Smith, 1993). Conversely, research suggests that when students with disabilities possess age-appropriate social skills with a positive self-concept, exhibit academic independence, maintain quality relationships, and participate in school and classroom activities, they are less likely to be targets of bullying (Flynt & Morton, 2004; Kumpulainen et al., 1998; Martlew & Hodson, 1991; Mishna, 2003; Whitney et al., 1994).

With respect to perpetration, Rose and colleagues (2010) argue, "bullying perpetration by students with disabilities is often a learned behavior, possibly a reaction to prolonged victimization, or an overall lack of social skills" (p. 36). While a lack of social skills may cause students with disabilities to have greater difficultly with assertion and self-control (Mayer & Leone, 2007), they may also misread social communication (Withney et al., 1994), misinterpret social stimuli, or act too aggressively toward the wrong peers (Sabornie, 1994). Additionally, lack of social skills may also lead students with disabilities to misinterpret rough and tumble play as a physical attack and thus respond inappropriately with aggressive behavior (Nabuzoka & Smith, 1999). Although perpetration may be a learned behavior, below average social skills may also indicate that students with disabilities who engage in bully perpetration could have social information-processing deficits (Crick & Dodge, 1994; Crick & Dodge, 1996; Dodge et al., 2003).

If bully perpetration is a reaction to prolonged periods of victimization, a distinction must be made between overt aggression (e.g., fighting) and actual bullying behaviors. This distinction must be made because bullying is a social construct and, as stated above, many students with disabilities who are involved in bullying display a general lack of social skills. For example, Rose and colleagues (2010) determined that students with disabilities who are victimized tend to fight, while students without disabilities who are victimized tend to bully. The work of Björkqvist (2001) and Björkqvist, Österman, and Kaukiainen (1992) suggests that students maintain distinct developmental patterns, and many of these patterns hinge on development of social skills. More specifically, they theorize that aggression is more direct during the early stages of development, becoming more indirect with age (i.e., physical, verbal, indirect). For students without disabilities, these developmental patterns are achieved at an age-appropriate rate, allowing them to process social information and effectively engage in social behaviors. Therefore, students without disabilities maintain the social skills necessary to engage in more indirect forms of bullying (Rose et al., 2010). However, students with disabilities often have delayed social skills (Baker & Donelly, 2001; Doren et al., 1996; Kaukiainen et al., 2002; Llewellyn, 2000; Woods & Wolke, 2004), placing them in the earlier stages of Björkqvist and colleagues' (1992, 2001) developmental trajectory. Therefore, the behaviors displayed by students with disabilities in response to victimization may be more appropriately defined as overt aggression as opposed to bullying.

CONCLUSION

This chapter examined bully perpetration and victimization as it relates to students with disabilities. While disability is a broad term used to describe 13 subcategories of students, it becomes evident that both bullying and disabilities fall upon continuums. Therefore, the interplay between disability status and participation in bullying becomes exponentially complex and must be examined longitudinally. Although complexity is an issue, the social nature of bullying and the lack of social skills among students with disabilities who are perpetrators or victims remain central to preventing bullying among this population.

Although current research in the field of bullying among students with disabilities is limited, evidence suggests that they are victims and perpetrators of bullying more often than their general education counterparts. However, several questions arise when exploring the bullying phenomena among this population of students. Most importantly, do the predictive and preventative factors of involvement in bullying differ for students with and without disabilities? Evidence suggests that class placement, disability severity and visibility, and disability characteristics play an integral role in predicting victimization and perpetration. Unfortunately, the extent to which the relationship among these factors' ability to predict victimization and perpetration remains untested. Therefore, future research is critical in the field of bullying among students with disabilities.

Future research should consider predictive and preventative factors for students with disabilities. In doing so, research should attempt to examine specific disability categories and characteristics that may predispose students to victimization and perpetration. Further, social skills programs should be incorporated into students with disabilities curricula to determine if a lack of social skills predicts bully involvement or if being bullied inhibits the development of appropriate social skills. Finally, intervention studies should be conducted to address appropriate strategies or programs for decreasing victimization, bullying, and fighting among students who receive special education services. Overall, the aforementioned lines of research will provide the foundational knowledge needed to address bullying among students with disabilities.

TRANSLATING RESEARCH INTO PRACTICE: IMPLICATIONS FOR BULLYING PREVENTION AND INTERVENTION PROGRAMS

Prevention policies and programs are necessary for decreasing bullying among the nation's youth. However, many of these programs are based on a whole-school approach, with intent on addressing bullying among the entire school population (Rose et al., 2009; Rose et al., 2010). However, current research suggests that students with disabilities are at greater risk for involvement in bullying as both victims and perpetrators (Rose et al., 2009) and may not be effectively treated via a whole-school program. Based on the current push for the multilevel support structures of PBS and RtI, anti-bullying campaigns should include school-wide support programs in tandem with interventions for at-risk subgroups of students. This type of comprehensive program will provide supports for the entire student population, specific subgroups of students, and individuals who are chronic victims or perpetrators.

REFERENCES

Agran, M., Alper, S., & Wehmeyer, M. (2002). Access to the general curriculum for students with significant disabilities: What it means to teachers. *Education and Training in Mental Retardation and Developmental Disabilities, 37*, 123–133.

American Psychiatric Association. (2000). *Diagnostic and statistical manual of mental disorders* (4th ed., text revision). Washington, DC: Author.

Arseneault, L., Walsh, E., Trzesniewski, K., Newcombe, R., Caspi, A., & Moffitt, T.E. (2006). Bullying victimization uniquely contributes to adjustment problems in young children: A nationally representative cohort study. *Pediatrics, 118*, 130–138.

Baker, K., & Donelly, M. (2001). The social experiences of children with disabilities and the influence of environment: A framework for intervention. *Disability & Society, 16*, 71–85.

Bambara, L.M., & Kern, L. (2005). *Individualized supports for students with problem behaviors: Designing positive behavior plans.* New York, NY: The Guilford Press.

Batsche, G., Elliott, J., Garden, J.L., Grimes, J., Kovaleski, J.F., Prasse, D., et al. (2006). *Response to intervention: Policy considerations and implementation.* Alexandria, VA: National Association of State Directors of Special Education, Inc.

Bejerot, S., & Mörtberg, E. (2009). Do autistic traits play a role in the bullying of obsessive-compulsive disorder and social phobia sufferers? *Psychopathology, 42*, 170–176.

Björkqvist, K. (2001). Different name, same issue. *Social Development, 10*, 272–274.

Björkqvist, K., Österman, K., & Kaukiainen, A. (1992). The development of direct and indirect aggressive strategies in males and females. In K. Björkqvist & P. Niemelä (Eds.), *Of mice and women: Aspects of female aggression* (pp. 51–64). San Diego, CA: Academic Press.

Brown, L., Long, E., Udvari-Solner, A., Schwarz, P., Van Deventer, P., Ahlgren, C., et al. (1989). Should students with severe intellectual disabilities be based in regular or in special education classrooms in home schools? *The Journal of the Association for Persons with Severe Handicaps, 14*, 8–13.

Crick, N.R., & Dodge, K.A. (1994). A review and reformulation of social information-processing mechanisms in children's social adjustment. *Psychological Bulletin, 115*, 74–101.

Crick, N.R., & Dodge, K.A. (1996). Social information-processing mechanisms in reactive and proactive aggression. *Child Development, 67*, 993–1002.

Davis, S., Howell, P., & Cooke, F. (2002). Sociodynamic relationships between children who stutter and their non-stuttering classmates. *Journal of Child Psychology and Psychiatry, 43*, 939–947.

Dawkins, J.L. (1996). Bullying, physical disability and the pediatric patient. *Developmental Medicine & Child Neurology, 38*, 603–612.

Dinkes, R., Cataldi, E.F., Kena, G., & Baum, K. (2006). *Indicators of school crime and safety: 2006.* Washington, DC: Government Printing Office.

Dodge, K.A., Lansford, J.E., Burks, V.S., Bates, J.E., Pettit, G.S., Fontaine, R., et al. (2003). Peer rejection and social information-processing factors in the development of aggressive behavior problems in children. *Child Development, 74*, 374–393.

Doren, B., Bullis, M., & Benz, M.R. (1996). Predictors of victimization experiences of adolescents with disabilities in transition. *Exceptional Children, 63*, 7–18.

Espelage, D.L., & Swearer, S.M. (2003). Research on school bullying and victimization: What have we learned and where do we go from here? *School Psychology Review, 32*, 365–383.

Espelage, D.L., & Swearer, S.M. (2009). Contributions of three social theories to understanding bullying perpetration and victimization among school-aged youth. In M.J. Harris (Ed.), *Bullying, rejection, and peer victimization: A social cognitive neuroscience perspective* (pp. 151–170). New York, NY: Springer

Espelage, D.L., Bosworth, K., & Simon, T.R. (2000). Examining the social context of bullying behaviors in early adolescence. *Journal of Counseling and Development, 78,* 326–333.

Flynt, S.W., & Morton, R.C. (2004). Bullying and children with disabilities. *Journal of Instructional Psychology, 31,* 330–333.

Giangreco, M.F., Hurley, S.M., & Suter, J.C. (2009). Special education personnel utilization and general class placement of students with disabilities: Ranges and ratios. *Intellectual and Developmental Disabilities, 47,* 53–56.

Individuals with Disabilities Education Act (IDEA) (1997). 20 USC § 1401 et seq.

Individuals with Disabilities Education Improvement Act (IDEIA) (2004). HR 1350, 108th Congress.

Kaukiainen, A., Salmivalli, C., Lagerspetz, K., Tamminen, M., Vauras, M., Mäki, H., et al. (2002). Learning difficulties, social intelligence, and self-concept: Connections to bully-victim problems. *Scandinavian Journal of Psychology, 43,* 269–278.

Knox, E., & Conti-Ramsden, G. (2003). Bullying risks of 11-year-old children with specific language impairment (SLI): Does school placement matter? *International Journal of Language & Communication Disorders, 38,* 1–12.

Kumpulainen, K., Räsänen, E., & Puura, K. (2001). Psychiatric disorders and the use of mental health services among children involved in bullying. *Aggressive Behavior, 27,* 102–110.

Kumpulainen, K., Räsänen, E., Henttonen, I., Almqvist, F., Kresanov, K., Linna, S.-L., et al. (1998). Bullying and psychiatric symptoms among elementary school-age children. *Child Abuse & Neglect, 22,* 705–717.

Langevin, M., Bortnick, K., Hammer, T., & Wiebe, E. (1998). Teasing/bullying experienced by children who stutter: Toward development of a questionnaire. *Contemporary Issues in Communication Science and Disorders, 25,* 12–24.

Little, L. (2002). Middle-class mothers' perceptions of peer and sibling victimization among children with Asperger's Syndrome and nonverbal learning disorders. *Issues in Comprehensive Pediatric Nursing, 25,* 43–57.

Llewellyn, A. (2000). Perceptions of mainstreaming: A systems approach. *Developmental Medicine & Child Neurology, 42,* 106–115.

Martlew, M., & Hodson, J. (1991). Children with mild learning difficulties in an integrated and in a special school: Comparisons of behaviour, teasing, and teachers' attitudes. *The British Journal of Educational Psychology, 61,* 355–372.

Mayer, M.J., & Leone, P.E. (2007). School violence and disruption revisited: Equity and safety in the school house. *Focus on Exceptional Children, 40,* 1–28.

Mishna, F. (2003). Learning disabilities and bullying: Double jeopardy. *Journal of Learning Disabilities, 36,* 336–347.

Monchy, M.D., Pijl, S.J., & Zandberg, T. (2004). Discrepancies in judging social inclusion and bullying of pupils with behaviour problems. *European Journal of Special Needs Education, 19,* 317–330.

Monks, C.P., Smith, P.K., & Swettenham, J. (2005). Psychological correlates of peer victimisation in preschool: Social cognitive skills, executive function and attachment profiles. *Aggressive Behavior, 31,* 571–588.

Morrison, G.M., Furlong, M.J., & Smith, G. (1994). Factors associated with the experience of school violence among general education, leadership class, opportunity class, and special day class pupils [electronic version]. *Education & Treatment of Children, 17,* 356–369.

Nabuzoka, D. (2003). Teacher ratings and peer nominations of bullying and other behaviour of children with and without learning difficulties. *Educational Psychology, 23,* 307–321.

Nabuzoka, D., & Smith, P.K. (1993). Sociometric status and social behaviour of children with and without learning difficulties. *Journal of Child Psychology and Psychiatry, 34,* 1435–1448.

Nabuzoka, D., & Smith, P.K. (1999). Distinguishing serious and playful fighting by children with learning disabilities and nondisabled children. *Journal of Child Psychology and Psychiatry, 40,* 883–890.

Nansel, T.R., Overpeck, M., Pilla, R.S., Ruan, W.J., Simons-Morton, B., & Scheidt, P. (2001). Bullying behaviors among U.S. youth: Prevalence and association with psychosocial adjustment. *The Journal of the American Medical Association, 285,* 2094–2100.

O'Moore, A.M., & Hillery, B. (1989). Bullying in Dublin schools. *The Irish Journal of Psychology, 10,* 426–441.

Perren, S., & Alsaker, F. (2006). Social behavior and peer relationships of victims, bully-victims, and bullies in kindergarten. *Journal of Child Psychology and Psychiatry, 47,* 45–57.

Reiter, S. & Lapidot-Lefler, N. (2007). Bullying among special education students with intellectual disabilities: Differences in social adjustment and social skills. *Intellectual and Developmental Disabilities, 3,* 174–181.

Rose, C.A., Espelage, D.L., & Monda-Amaya, L.E. (2009). Bullying and victimisation rates among students in general and special education: A comparative analysis. *Educational Psychology, 29,* 761–776.

Rose, C.A., Monda-Amaya, L.E., & Espelage, D.L. (2010). Bullying perpetration and victimization in special education: A review of the literature. Remedial and Special Education. Advance online publication. doi: 10.1177/0741932510361247.

Rose, C.A., Espelage, D.L., Aragon, S.R., & Elliott, J. (2010). *Bullying and victimization among students in special education and general education curricula.* Manuscript submitted for publication.

Sabornie, E.J. (1994). Social-affective characteristics in early adolescents identified as learning disabled and nondisabled. *Learning Disability Quarterly, 17,* 268–279.

Salend, S.J. (2008). *Creating Inclusive classrooms: Effective and reflective practices* (6th ed.). Upper Saddle River, NJ: Pearson.

Sheard, C., Clegg, J., Standen, P., & Cromby, J. (2001). Bullying and people with severe intellectual disability. *Journal of Intellectual Disability Research, 45,* 407–415.

Smith, D.D. (2007). *Introduction to special education: Making a difference* (6th ed.). Boston, MA: Pearson.

Swearer, S.M., & Espelage, D.L. (2004). Introduction: A social-ecological framework of bullying among youth. In D.L. Espelage, & S.M. Swearer (Eds.), *Bullying in American schools* (pp. 1–11). Mahwah, NJ: Lawrence Erlbaum Associates.

Swearer, S.M., Espelage, D.L., & Napolitano, S.A. (2009). *Bullying prevention and intervention: Realistic strategies for schools.* New York, NY: The Guilford Press, Inc.

Sweeting, H., & West, P. (2001). Being different: Correlates of the experience of teasing and bullying at age 11 [electronic version]. *Research Papers in Education, 16,* 225–246. Online: http://eprints.gla.ac.uk/archive/00002724/.

Unnever, J.D., & Cornell, D.G. (2003). Bullying, self-control, and ADHD. *Journal of Interpersonal Violence, 18,* 129–147.

Van Cleave, J., & Davis, M.M. (2006). Bullying and peer victimization among children with special health care needs. *Pediatrics, 118,* 1212–1219.

Whitney, I., Nabuzoka, D., & Smith, P.K. (1992). Bullying in schools: Mainstream and special needs. *Support for Learning, 7,* 3–7.

Whitney, I., Smith, P.K., & Thompson, D. (1994). Bullying and children with special educational needs. In P.K. Smith & S. Sharp (Eds.), *School bullying: Insights and perspectives* (pp. 213–240). London: Routledge.

Woods, S., & Wolke, D. (2004). Direct and relational bullying among primary school children and academic achievement. *Journal of School Psychology, 42,* 135–155.

Yell, M.L., Shriner, J.G., Katsiyannis, A. (2006). Individuals with Disabilities Education Improvement Act of 2004 and IDEA regulations of 2006: Implications for educators, administrators and teacher trainers. *Focus on Exceptional Children, 39,* 1–24.

5

INTERNALIZING PROBLEMS IN STUDENTS INVOLVED IN BULLYING AND VICTIMIZATION

SUSAN M. SWEARER, ADAM COLLINS, KISHA HAYE RADLIFF, AND CIXIN WANG

Misery is…

Misery is when you go to school and bullies pick on you.
Misery is when you share with someone, but they don't share with you.
Misery is when friends become bullies.
Misery is when you go to school and kids threaten you by
telling you that they will get you after school.
Misery is when you are at breakfast recess and kids push you around for no reason.
Misery is when people invite everyone but you to play tag and football.

(Written by a 10-year-old depressed and anxious male bully-victim)

In this chapter, we will review the literature on internalizing problems in youth who are involved in bullying. Involvement in bullying occurs along a continuum (i.e., the bully–victim continuum), meaning that students can participate in multiple roles, including bullying others, being bullied, both bullying others and being bullied, witnessing bullying, and no involvement in bullying (Espelage & Swearer, 2003; Swearer, Siebecker, Johnsen-Frerichs, & Wang, 2010). It is clear that involvement in bullying is not defined by static and fixed roles in individuals. It is also evident that students involved in the bully–victim continuum experience greater levels of internalizing problems compared to students who are not involved in bullying (Craig, 1998; Swearer et al., 2010; Swearer, Song, Cary, Eagle, & Mickelson, 2001). The goal of this chapter is to examine the relation between internalizing problems and the bully–victim continuum, to present longitudinal data on this dynamic, and to provide suggestions for effective mental health interventions for youth involved in bullying. It is our contention that parents, students, teachers, and mental health professionals must work in tandem in order to derail the destructive cycle of bullying and mental health problems (Swearer, Espelage, & Napolitano, 2009).

INTERNALIZING ISSUES AND INVOLVEMENT
IN BULLYING AND VICTIMIZATION

Depression and the Bully–Victim Continuum

Youth who experience depressive symptoms typically report feelings of sadness, anger, worthlessness, and hopelessness. How might these feelings be connected to bullying and victimization? As the opening poem, "Misery is..." illustrated, students who are bullied often feel hopeless about themselves and their situation.

The prevalence of depressive disorders among children and adolescents vary depending upon age, sex, and appear to be increasing. Prevalence rates range from 1% to 2% in children and from 1% to 7% in adolescents (see Avenevoli, Knight, Kessler, & Merikangas, 2008). The affect of depressed youth can be characterized as sad, depressed, irritable, and/or angry (Friedberg & McClure, 2002). Youth with depression display a negative cognitive style, marked by negative perceptions of themselves, the world, and their future (Beck, Rush, Shaw, & Emery, 1979). Additionally, youth with depression typically experience problems in their interpersonal relationships and may experience decreased interest in activities. They may also experience distorted thinking and poor problem-solving skills (Friedberg & McClure, 2002), as well as loss of appetite, insomnia, psychomotor agitation, fatigue, and suicidal ideation (APA). Thus, symptoms of depression are related to both inter- and intrapersonal functioning.

Researchers and clinicians have identified a significant association between depression and being bullied (Callaghan & Joseph, 1995; Swearer et al., 2001) and with bullying others (Craig, 1998; Kaltiala-Heino, Rimpela, Rantanen, & Rimpela, 2000; Kumpulainen, Räsänen, & Puura, 2001). Research suggests that all participants in the bully–victim continuum, regardless of role (i.e., victim, bully-victim, or bully) are likely to experience symptoms of depression (Austin & Joseph, 1996), with bully-victims endorsing the highest levels of depression (Haynie et al., 2001; Swearer et al., 2001). Kumpulainen and colleagues (2001) found higher rates of depressive disorders among bully-victims compared to victims, bullies, and controls. Specifically, they found that 18% of bully-victims, 13% of bullies, and 10% of victims were diagnosed with a depressive disorder.

There are dire consequences associated with depression and bullying. Findings from an analysis of school shootings over the past three decades indicated that 79% of the attackers had a history of suicide attempts or suicidal thoughts and 61% had a history of serious depression (Vossekuil, Fein, Reddy, Borum, & Modzeleski, 2002). Over two-thirds of the attackers were victimized prior to the school shootings. Kaltiala-Heino, Rimpela, Marttunen, Rimpela, and Rantanen (1999) assessed the relation between involvement in bullying, depression, and suicidal ideation among adolescents aged 14 to 16. After controlling for age and gender, results indicated that bully-victims endorsed the highest risk for depression, followed by victims and then bullies. Bully-victims were the most at-risk group for suicidal ideation, followed by bullies and then victims. The high frequency of suicidal ideation among youth involved in bullying is not surprising, given that, by definition, bullying is a repeated behavior over time. Those individuals experiencing bullying are likely to feel hopeless as a result of the bullying (Haye, 2005).

Depressed children often view their future as hopeless (Kazdin, Rodgers, & Colbus, 1986; Weisz, Sweeney, Profitt, & Carr, 1993). Kazdin and colleagues (1986) have defined hopelessness as negative expectations toward oneself and the future. Over the past two decades, researchers have evaluated the role of hopelessness as it relates to depression.

Known as the Hopelessness Theory of Depression, Abramson, Metalsky, and Alloy (1989) have championed *hopelessness depression* as a subtype of depression. According to their research, individuals are more likely to experience feelings of hopelessness if they have an attribution style that (1) attributes negative events to stable and global causes, (2) catastrophizes the consequences of negative events, or (3) attributes negative events to self-characteristics. This study as well as others (Brozina & Abela, 2006; Kazdin, French, Unis, Esveldt-Dawson, & Sherick, 1983) suggests that hopelessness likely precedes depression.

Individuals may also experience hopelessness and depression because of the level of control they believe they have in their environment. When individuals do not believe they can influence their environment, they may "give up" trying to change their environment, resulting in feelings of helplessness, hopelessness, and depression (Abramson et al., 1989). The attributions individuals make toward either positive or negative events has also been shown to correlate with depressive symptoms. More specifically, individuals who attribute negative events to internal, stable, and global factors and attribute positive events to external, specific, and unstable factors are at-risk for future depressive symptoms (Dodge, 1993).

Although there is a limited body of research on the topic of the bully–victim continuum and hopelessness, Gibb and Alloy (2006) recently examined the mediating role of attribution style between verbal victimization and depression. In the study, 415 4th- and 5th-grade students were administered a modified version of the Childhood Trauma Questionnaire-Emotional Abuse subscale, the Revised Children's Attributional Style Questionnaire, and the Children's Depression Inventory. The researchers concluded that attributional style partially mediated the connection between verbal victimization and depressive symptoms. Specifically, verbal victimization (negative events) correlated with developing a negative attributional style, which created a vulnerability to depression. In addition, they found that depressive symptoms may increase the occurrence of negative attribution styles and verbal victimization, suggesting a cyclical pattern. These depressive symptoms can then lead to other adaptive problems for a student. Errors in information processing, for example, may lead the student to focus on negative events while effectively ignoring the positive (Stark, Napolitano, Swearer, Schmidt, Jaramillo, & Hoyle, 1996).

Anxiety and the Bully–Victim Continuum

Anxiety disorders are the most common psychiatric disorder diagnosed in children and adolescents (Anderson, 1994; Beidel, 1991; Costello & Angold, 1995). Estimated prevalence rates of anxiety disorder have been reported to range between 5.8% and 17.7% (Silverman & Kurtines, 2001) and between 2% and 4% (Costello, Mustillo, Erkani, Keeler, & Angold, 2003; Ford, Goodman, & Meltzer, 2003) for children and adolescents. Anxiety can be debilitating for youth and can negatively impact friendship-making skills, school attendance, and school performance. Research has repeatedly shown that individuals who are victimized typically experience social anxiety (Gladstone, Parker, & Malhi, 2006; Huphrey, Storch, & Geffken, 2007; La Greca & Harrison, 2005; Storch, Zelman, Sweeney, Danner, & Dove, 2002). There are three responses to anxiety that can be present individually or in combination: (1) motoric responses (e.g., isolation), (2) physiological responses (e.g., sweating), and (3) subjective responses (e.g., fearful thoughts) (Wicks-Nelson & Israel, 1991). Among school-aged youth, this can be expressed in several ways.

For example, the victim of bullying may manifest his or her anxiety by skipping classes shared with the perpetrator to avoid potential conflict and harassment.

There are also common comorbid behavioral or psychological problems associated with individuals who suffer from anxiety. The most common co-occurring problems with anxiety are depression (Lewinsohn, Zinbarg, Seeley, Lewinsohn, & Sack, 1997), an inability to establish or maintain satisfying relationships (Chipuer, 2001; Cacioppo et al. 2000), loneliness (Galanaki & Vassilopoulou, 2007; Crick & Ladd, 1993), low self-worth (Grills & Ollendick, 2002), and school refusal behaviors (Heyne & Rollings, 2002; Kearney, Eisen, & Silverman, 1995). In a recent study, Starr and Davila (2008) examined the correlates of depression and anxiety and found that while many correlates were common to both depression and anxiety, social anxiety was shown to have a greater correlation with peer variables (e.g., social competence, communication in friendships).

Bullying has been characterized as a peer relationship problem (Pepler, Graig, & O'Connell, 2010) and given the peer difficulties that students with anxiety experience, it is particularly important to understand the experience of anxiety among students who are involved in the bully–victim continuum. Gazelle (2008) examined the differences in children who are both anxious and social isolates. These children typically want to play with their peers, but are unable to do so due to either shyness or social anxiety. In a diverse sample of 688 3rd graders, children's degree of anxious solitude (e.g., watching other kids play, but not joining in), agreeableness (e.g., being good at sharing with other kids), attention-seeking-immaturity (e.g., trying to get attention of other kids in ways that are considered annoying), and externalizing behaviors (e.g., starting fights) were assessed. Results showed several different subgroups of anxious solitary children. The first group of children, coined, "agreeable anxious solitary," were less excluded and victimized and perceived by peers as more likable than the other subgroups. In contrast, a second group, coined "attention-seeking-immature anxious solitary," had much different outcomes. Specifically, children in this group experienced higher levels of rejection, exclusion, and victimization. The variability of peer responses in children with anxiety with isolating behaviors demonstrates the complexity of peer relationships problems among anxious youth.

While the correlation between anxiety and victimization has been well documented, less is known regarding the directionality of these phenomena. Recent research on anxiety and victimization has focused on the cause and effect between these two variables. Research has shown that students who exhibit anxious behaviors as well as other internalizing behaviors (e.g., withdrawal, shyness) are often victimized (Gladstone et al., 2006; Hodges & Perry, 1999). It has been hypothesized that anxiety is maintained or results from victimization. Because bullying typically takes place in a student's social milieu, anxiety involving social situations may be even more likely to occur among victimized youth (Craig & Pepler, 1995). Thus, students who are victimized might avoid school and social situations.

The effects of victimization and anxiety can often last beyond the school year in which it occurs. Sourander and colleagues (2007) examined the outcomes of males who bullied or were bullied in childhood and long-term effects were found for both groups. The longitudinal study followed an original population of 2,540 boys born in 1981 and used parent, teacher, and self-reports to determine bully-victim status and psychiatric disorders. Being classified as a bully was predictive of future substance abuse, depression, and anxiety. Those boys classified as bully-victims were prone to antisocial personality disorder and anxiety disorders. Finally, those boys classified as victims were more likely to be diagnosed with an anxiety disorder. Regardless of a boy's status on the bully–victim continuum, involvement in bullying was associated with anxiety.

In a similar study with younger children, Snyder and colleagues (2003) examined the relations between victimization and teacher and parent reported variables (e.g., antisocial behavior, depressive behavior) during kindergarten and 1st grade. The results for the boys in the study revealed an association between aggressive behavior and chronic victimization. Boys who responded to chronic victimization with antisocial behavior saw a reduction in victimization in the short term. However, in the long term, these boys were more likely to continue being victimized and to receive higher teacher-reported antisocial behavior. This suggests that there may be a link between aggressive behavior and persistent victimization.

Some researchers have found that childhood victimization can have effects that last for years, in some cases into adulthood. In a retrospective study by Roth and colleagues (Roth, Coles, & Heimberg, 2002), adults who reported victimization during childhood had higher levels of trait anxiety, social anxiety, worry, and anxiety sensitivity. Other forms of anxiety have been correlated with childhood victimization as well. Gladstone and colleagues (2006) found that adults were more likely to suffer from social phobia and agoraphobia and have greater levels of state anxiety if they had experienced childhood bullying. Thus, even though victimization decreases with age (Byrne, 1994; Salmivalli, Lappalainen, & Lagerspetz, 1998), the effects of victimization on symptoms of anxiety still persist into adulthood (Gladstone et al., 2006; Olweus, 1993; Roth et al., 2002).

Aggression, Anxiety, and the Bully–Victim Continuum

The relationship between aggression and anxiety has both empirical and theoretical foundations. One assertion is that students who are anxious are more aggressive. The findings from Snyder and colleagues (2003) support this claim. In addition, Kashani, Dueser, and Reid (1991) found similar results between anxiety and physical and verbal aggression. In both studies, children compensated for apparent weaknesses by behaving aggressively. An explanation for this behavior can be explained by the correlation between anxiety and false interpretations. Research has shown that children who have a high level of social anxiety misinterpret ambiguous situations in a negative fashion (Barrett, Rapee, Dadds, & Ryan, 1996; Miers, Blöte, Bögels, & Westenberg, 2008). In addition, children with anxiety have been shown to discount positive social events (Vassilopoulos & Banerjee, 2008). In combination, these two cognitive distortions may perpetuate and maintain an anxious child's aggressive, maladaptive behaviors.

Another explanation linking aggression and anxiety is that anxiety mediates aggressive responses. According to this argument, anxious youth are less likely to be aggressive and more likely to display increased caution or inhibition. Support for the mediating effects of anxiety on aggression has been shown across various studies, many examining the variable of behavioral inhibition (Mick & Telch, 1998; Schwartz, Snidman, & Kagan, 1999; van Ameringen Mancini, & Oakman, 1998). To better understand the role of behavioral inhibition in anxiety, Gladstone, Parker, Mitchell, Wilhelm, and Malhi (2005) examined the relation between early childhood inhibited temperament and lifetime anxiety disorders. They found that individuals reporting higher levels of childhood behavioral inhibition were more likely to meet criteria for an anxiety disorder.

Many questions remain about the associations among anger, aggression, anxiety and the bully–victim continuum. The correlation between anxiety and bully-victims and victims has been well documented. However, the relation between anxiety and youth who perpetrate bullying is still debated. Ivarsson, Broberg, Arvidsson, and Gillberg (2005) found that bullies were more likely to experience externalizing behaviors (e.g., delinquency, aggression) than internalizing behaviors. However, other studies have found that bully perpetrators do experience elevated levels of anxiety (Duncan, 1999; Kaltiala-Heino et al., 2000). Given that there are several anxiety disorders that can be diagnosed in youth, an interesting question for further study is whether there are different anxiety disorders associated with different types of involvement in the bully–victim continuum?

As previously discussed, research has found an association between negative psychological outcomes for students involved in bullying, such as depression (Austin & Joseph, 1996; Bosworth, Espelage, & Simon, 1999; Craig, 1998; Haynie et al., 2001), and anxiety (Craig, 1998; Rigby, 2003; Sourander et al., 2007; Swearer et al., 2001). However, few longitudinal studies have explored the developmental relations among aggression, depression, and anxiety in the bullying dynamic. Given the dearth of empirical literature in this area, we were interested in examining the following research questions:

1. Does previous bully–victim status (bully, victim, bully-victim, and not involved) predict depression, anxiety, physical and relational aggression?
2. What are the developmental trajectories of depression, anxiety, physical and relational aggression?
3. Does initial status in aggression, depression, and anxiety predict changes in those variables?

METHOD

Participants

Participants for this study were recruited as part of a larger longitudinal investigation examining school experiences in the United States, Japan, Korea, Australia, and Canada. Data were gathered in the fall of 2005 (Time 1), spring of 2005 (Time 2), and the fall of 2006 (Time 3). The sample included 1,173 students (53% female and 47% male) in the 5th through 9th grades at Time 1, 1,112 students at Time 2, and 995 students in the 6th through 10th grades at Time 3 from nine Midwestern schools (i.e., four elementary schools, three middle schools, and two high schools). The attrition rate was 5.0% from Time 1 to Time 2 and 10.4% from Time 2 to Time 3. Students' attrition from the study was mostly due to students moving to a different school and absence from class at the time of assessment. The age range of the participants across all time points was 10 to 16 at Time 1 ($M = 12.20$, $SD = 1.29$), 10 to 16 at Time 2 ($M = 12.57$, $SD = 1.27$), and 10 to 17 at Time 3 ($M = 13.11$, $SD = 1.29$). Most students self-identified as European-American (82.8%), with the remaining identifying as African American (7.4%), Hispanic (5.6%), Asian American (2.5%), Asian (0.9%), Native American (0.4%), and Other (0.5%) in the fall of 2005.

Measures

The Children's Depression Inventory-Short (CDI-S; Kovacs, 1992). The CDI-S is a ten-item measure comprising a subset of the original CDI items, designed as a screening measure for children 7 to 17 years of age. Participants are asked to rate the severity of each item on a three-point scale from 0 through 2 during the two weeks prior to testing, with higher scores indicating more severe symptoms. Items on the CDI-S are summed to reach a total depressive symptoms score. The CDI-S yields scores with high reliability with alpha reliability coefficients of .83 (Houghton, Cowley, Houghton, & Kelleher, 2003), and .84 (Frerichs, 2009). At least one study indicated a significant positive correlation between the CDI and CDI-S ($r = .91$; Houghton et al., 2003). In the current study, the internal consistency reliability for the CDI-S using coefficient alpha was .84 at Time 1, .87 at Time 2, and .85 at Time 3, suggesting that this measure yields scores with high internal consistency.

The Multidimensional Scale for Children-10 (MASC-10; March, 1997). The Multidimensional Scale for Children is a self-report measure designed to assess symptoms of anxiety in children ages 8 to 19 years. Individuals are asked to rate the severity of each item based upon a four-point Likert-type scale from "Never true about me" to "Often true about me." The MASC has demonstrated satisfactory to excellent test–retest reliability with a coefficient alpha of .83. The MASC-10 scores have demonstrated satisfactory internal reliability with a coefficient alpha of .67 for females and .68 for males and test–retest reliability with a coefficient alpha of .82 (March, 1997). In the current study, the internal consistency reliability for the MASC-10 using coefficient alpha was .76 at Time 1, .80 at Time 2, and .81 at Time 3, suggesting good internal consistency of the measure's scores.

The Children's Social Behavior Scale (CSBS; Crick & Grotpeter, 1995). The Children's Social Behavior Scale is a 15-item self-report measure used to assess how often children engage in various aggressive and prosocial behaviors on a five-point Likert-type scale from "Never" to "All the time." Responses to items are summed to reach total scores. The CSBS consists of 15 items and six subscales (Relational Aggression, Physical Aggression, Prosocial Behavior, Verbal Aggression, Inclusion, and Loneliness). The subscales have shown acceptable internal consistency, ranging from .66 to .82 (Crick & Grotpeter, 1995). In the current study, the internal consistency reliability for Physical Aggression subscale using coefficient alpha was .80 at Time 1, .80 at Time 2, and .81 at Time 3. The internal consistency reliability for Relational Aggression subscale was .83 at Time 1, .83 at Time 2, and .85 at Time 3, suggesting good internal consistency of scores.

RESULTS

Prediction of Physical and Relational Aggression

ANOVA results showed that Time 1, Time 2, and Time 3 bully–victim status predicted Time 3 physical aggression, $F(4, 925) = 2.88$, $p < .05$, $F(4, 925) = 6.43$, $p < .001$, $F(4, 925) = 18.995$, $p < .001$, respectively. Time 1 and Time 2 bully–victim status predicted Time 2 physical aggression, $F(4, 1060) = 4.40$, $p < .01$, $F(4, 1060) = 18.90$, $p < .001$, respectively. Time 2 and Time 3 (not Time 1) bully–victim status predicted Time 3 relational aggression, $F(4, 911) = 3.44$, $p < .01$, $F(4, 910) = 20.47$, $p < .001$, respectively. Time 1 and Time 2 bully–victim status predicted Time 2 relational aggression, $F(4, 1055) = 4.32$, $p < .01$, $F(4, 910) = 8.97$, $p < .001$, respectively. Post hoc analysis indicated that students who previously or currently bullied others engaged in significantly more physical and relational aggression than students who were victims or not involved in bullying ($ps < .05$).

Prediction of Depression and Anxiety

Time 1 and Time 3 (not Time 2) bully–victim status predicted Time 3 depression, $F(4, 910) = 3.72$, $p < .01$, $F(4, 910) = 12.41$, $p < .001$, respectively. Time 2 (not Time 1) bully–victim status predicted Time 2 depression, $F(4, 1054) = 4.45$, $p < .001$ Time 1, Time 2 and Time 3 bully–victim status predicted Time 3 anxiety, $F(4, 900) = 2.59$, $p < .05$, $F(4, 900) = 4.88$, $p < .001$, $F(4, 900) = 6.62$, $p < .001$, respectively. Time 1 and Time 2 bully–victim status predicted Time 2 anxiety, $F(4, 1051) = 3.84$, $p < .01$, $F(4, 1051) = 12.08$, $p < .001$, respectively. Post hoc analysis showed that bully-victims and victims (previous and/or current) were significantly more depressed and more anxious than both the bullies and the students who were not involved in bullying ($ps < .05$).

Relationship between Initial Status and Change in Aggression, Depression, and Anxiety

An associative latent growth curve model (Little, Bovaird & Slegers, 2006) was developed to model the initial status at the first time point and behavior change over time using Mplus software. Residual variances were allowed to correlate between variables at the same time points. The model depicted in Figure 5.1 represents the data well, $\chi^2(12) = 16.99$, $p = .15$; CFI = .99; RMSEA = .02, $p = .998$. The covariance and variance estimates for initial status and change constructs are listed in Table 5.1. The model shows that the initial status of physical aggression correlates negatively with change in physical aggression and relational aggression, and correlates positively with depression, anxiety, and relational aggression at the initial time point. Relational aggression at the initial time point correlates negatively with change in physical aggression and relational aggression, and correlates positively with depression at the initial time point. Depression at the initial time point correlates negatively with change of depression. Anxiety at the initial time point correlates negatively with change of anxiety and depression (Table 5.1).

The results were consistent with previous studies, which have found a relation between depression, anxiety, aggression and bully–victim continuum, not only concur-

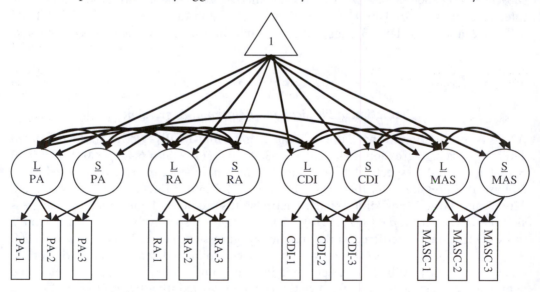

Figure 5.1 The final associative level and shape model.

Table 5.1 Correlations (Off-diagonal Elements) and Variance Estimates (Diagonal Elements) for Initial Status and Change Constructs

	Initial Status/Level				Change/Shape			
	PA	RA	CDI	MASC	PA	RA	CDI	MASC
L_PA	1.76 *							
L_RA	2.47 *	6.11 *						
L_CDI	0.52 *	1.56 *	7.55 *					
L_MASC	−0.94 *	−0.82	5.11 *	23.68 *				
S_PA	−0.44 *	−0.55 *	−0.15	0.07	0.37 *			
S_RA	−0.64 *	−1.36 *	−0.38	−0.02	0.45 *	0.78 *		
S_CDI	−0.14	−0.31	−1.83 *	−1.00 *	0.14	0.21	1.36 *	
S_MASC	0.00	0.38	−0.83	−4.70 *	0.19	0.07	0.75 *	5.12 *

Note: PA = Physical aggression score measured by The Children's Social Behavior Scale (Crick & Grotpeter, 1995). RA = Relational aggression score measured by The Children's Social Behavior Scale (Crick & Grotpeter, 1995). CDI = Depression score measured by Children's Depression Inventory- Short (Kovacs, 1992). MASC = Anxiety score measured by Multidimensional Scale for Children- Short (March, 1997). L= Initial Status/Level. S= Change/Shape.
All non-included paths were not statistically significant at the $p < .05$ level. Residual errors and residual correlations between errors at the same time point are not shown.

rently (Craig, 1998; Snyder et al., 2003; Swearer et al., 2001, 2010) but also longitudinally (Gladstone et al., 2006; Olweus, 1993; Roth et al., 2002). Students who scored higher on aggression, depression, and anxiety at Time 1 were at increased risk for continuously experiencing internalizing and externalizing problems compared with peers who had lower scores at Time 1.

TRANSLATING RESEARCH INTO PRACTICE: IMPLICATIONS FOR BULLYING PREVENTION AND INTERVENTION PROGRAMS

The experiences of bully perpetration and victimization have a long-term negative impact on externalizing and internalizing symptoms for students across the bully–victim continuum. Given the empirical connection between bullying and mental health difficulties, bullying prevention and intervention should include treatment for concomitant mental health issues. The complexity among bully perpetrators and the students who are victimized suggests that a "one size fits all" approach is likely to fail. Thus, one mechanism for effective intervention is individual treatment for those affected by bullying behaviors.

Working Individually with Students Who Bully Others

Given our findings linking bully–victim status to depression and anxiety over time, it is clearly important to consider working individually with the students who are involved in bullying (Doll & Swearer, 2006). Interventions to help students change their behavior can powerfully reduce bullying in schools. The *Bullying Intervention Program* (BIP; Swearer & Givens, 2006) is an individual cognitive–behavioral intervention for use with students who bully others. The guiding premise behind BIP is twofold. First, we are guided by the reality that the social–cognitive perceptions of students involved in bullying interactions are as critical as are the aggressive behaviors, because the perceptions and cognitions of the participants serve to underlie, perpetuate, and escalate bullying interactions (Doll & Swearer, 2006; Swearer & Cary, 2003). Second, research suggests that homogenous group interventions are not helpful for aggressive youth and, in fact, may be damaging (Dishion, McCord, & Poulin, 1999). Based on these two principles, the BIP was developed as a mechanism for school counselors and school psychologists to work directly with students who bully others.

The BIP is an alternative to in-school suspension for bullying behaviors. When a student is referred for bullying behaviors, the typical protocol is that the student is sent to in-school suspension. In BIP, parents are given a choice: in-school suspension or the BIP. In order to participate in BIP, active parental consent and student assent are obtained. Then, the BIP is scheduled according to the same policies and procedures that the school uses to schedule in-school suspension.

The BIP is a three-hour one-on-one cognitive–behavioral intervention session with a masters-level student-therapist under the supervision of a licensed psychologist. There are three components to the BIP: (1) assessment, (2) psychoeducation, and (3) feedback. The assessment component consists of widely used measures to assess experiences with bullying, depression, anxiety, cognitive distortions, school climate, and self-concept. The psychoeducation component lasts about two hours and consists of the student-therapist presenting an engaging and youth-friendly PowerPoint presentation about bullying behaviors. The presentation is followed by a short quiz to assess for understanding. This is followed by several worksheet activities about bullying behavior that are used from Bully Busters (Newman, Horne, & Bartolomucci, 2001). Finally, the student-therapist and the referred student watch a video about bullying. The session ends with a debriefing component where the referred student talks about his or her experiences with bullying and impressions of BIP. Based on the assessment data and the interactions with the referred student, a bullying intervention treatment report is written. Recommendations are based on the data collected. The treatment report is reviewed with the parents, student, and school personnel during a face-to-face solution-oriented meeting.

Suggested Interventions for Depression

Individuals along the bully–victim continuum experiencing depression would likely benefit from a therapeutic component that includes increasing positive views of the future. Abramson et al. (1989) suggested two therapeutic approaches to treating hopelessness depression: (1) a direct approach to treating hopelessness including reattribution training, and (2) an indirect treatment approach including a modification of the environment that induces hopefulness through pleasant-events scheduling. Both problem-solving training and cognitive restructuring have been suggested as intervention strategies for hopelessness (Stark, Sander, Yancy, Bronik, & Hoke, 2000); thus, targeting the individual's attributions or behaviors that contribute to the hopelessness are therapeutic approaches that can be utilized as a component of bullying-intervention programs.

Group treatments for depression have also been found to be effective. Clarke, Rohde, Lewinsohn, Hops, and Seely (1999) conducted a study that examined the effectiveness of a cognitive–behavioral group intervention for adolescents with depression in comparison to a wait-list group. The study consisted of two treatment groups that utilized the same adolescent group format, while one also included a parent component, and a control group. The group intervention for the adolescents included teaching specific skills to increase pleasurable activities, techniques to control depressive thoughts, relaxation, and skills to improve social interaction. Both group treatment interventions were found to be effective in reducing the adolescents' level of depression both at the end of treatment and at a two-year follow-up. This study replicated the short- and long-term effects of an earlier study by Lewinsohn, Clarke, Hops, and Andrews (1990). Group treatment may be useful for victims and bully-victims who are depressed. However, previous research suggests that group interventions are not useful for aggressive youth (Dishion et al., 1999); therefore, group approaches should be used cautiously with bullies.

In order to identify and implement appropriate and efficacious interventions for bullying and victimization, the status a student endorses along the bully–victim continuum must be considered. Students who both are bullied and bully others (bully-victims) have been reported to be the most at-risk for depression (Kaltiala-Heino et al., 1999; Kumpulainen et al., 2001; Swearer et al., 2001). Interventions for bully-victims need to address the internalizing symptomatology, as well as the aggressive (i.e., bullying) behaviors (Kaltiala-Heino et al., 1999). A treatment manual such as *Taking Action: A Workbook for Overcoming Depression* (Stark, Kendall, McCarthy, Stafford, Barron, & Thomeer, 1996) in combination with the *Keeping Your Cool: The Anger Management Workbook* (Nelson & Fitch, 1996) can be a useful strategy for working with bully-victims who are experiencing depressive symptomatology.

Suggested Interventions for Anxiety

Interventions targeted for individuals experiencing victimization should be appropriate to the characteristics the victim displays. A passive victim is likely to express symptoms of depression and would benefit from a therapeutic intervention addressing the development of increased self-esteem (Carney & Merrell, 2001) and alternative coping skills (Batsche, 1997). Depression might be a reflection of the victim's coping style (Craig, 1998). Therefore, utilizing bullying interventions that teach alternative coping methods, such as assertiveness training, could help in reducing continued victimization (Smith, Shu, & Madsen, 2001). A provocative victim is more likely to benefit from an intervention aimed at reducing his or her level of aggression (Batsche, 1997). This approach should teach students skills that can be used in place of the aggressive behaviors (i.e., aggression replacement training).

It is also important to distinguish between depressive and anxious symptoms when intervening with students along the bully–victim continuum. Lonigan, Carey, and Finch (1994) conducted a study that examined self-reported depression and anxiety among 233 inpatient children aged 6 to 17, who were diagnosed with either an anxiety disorder or a depressive disorder. The authors reported that although there was some overlap between self-reports of depression and anxiety, there were characteristics that distinguished between children diagnosed with depression and those diagnosed with anxiety. Children who were diagnosed with a depressive disorder reported less satisfaction with themselves and more difficulties with loss of interest and motivation than anxious children. Anxious children endorsed more distress about the future, their happiness, and how others respond to them. It is important that interventions address the different needs of individuals possessing depressive or anxious symptomatology.

Currently, there are no interventions that have been designed to specifically target children who are both involved in victimization and display symptoms of anxiety.

However, two recent studies were found that evaluated an intervention that targeted or included victims of bullying and assessed anxiety. Furthermore, general strategies from the literature on anxiety can be applied to this population. It is often important to include peers in the treatment of socially anxious children in order to provide practice as well as naturalistic exposure opportunities. Peer relations research showing greater improvement for treatments including non-problematic peers versus those that have not (Bierman & Furman, 1984) provide further support for these proposals.

Fox and Boulton (2003) developed a Social Skills Training (SST) program specifically for victims of bullying. There were two intervention groups and two wait-list groups across four schools with a total of 28 participants (treatment group mean age of 9.5 years, control group mean age of 9.8 years). Participants were chosen from a larger study and had to meet the following selection criteria: chronic victim of bullying, demonstrated problems with social skills, and not being a bully-victim. The youth were taught to use social problem-solving skills and relaxation skills, increase positive thoughts, how to change non-verbal behaviors, and introduced to different verbal strategies. Findings revealed a significant increase in global self-worth for youth in the treatment group, gains that were maintained at three-month follow-up. No significant effects were found for the other psychosocial variables, though trends were found for a decrease in reported symptoms of anxiety and depression.

A recent study by DeRosier and Marcus (2005) examined a program called the Social Skills Group Intervention (S.S.GRIN; DeRosier, 2002), a school-based group social-skills training program that targets children who experience poor relationships. The program includes cognitive-behavioral strategies and social learning to help children develop appropriate social skills and healthy peer relationships. The study included 749 children from 11 different schools; 274 of the youth were identified as having significant problems with peers (specifically experiencing peer rejection, victimization, or social anxiety) and were randomly assigned to a treatment or control group. Children in the treatment group demonstrated significant improvement across several areas, including lower social anxiety, increased self-esteem, greater self-efficacy in social situations, and fewer antisocial relationships. One-year follow-up data demonstrated treatment maintenance with continued reports of lower levels of social anxiety and depression and higher self-efficacy. While no immediate changes were seen in peers' negative views of these children, data at one-year follow-up revealed that peers rated these youth as more likable and less aggressive. Interestingly, almost a fourth of the children in the study were identified as highly aggressive youth and these individuals demonstrated the strongest treatment effects. This suggests that social skills training programs that include both cognitive and behavioral components might be effective for all individuals involved in bullying who express symptoms of anxiety.

Specific treatments for generalized as well as social anxiety have been developed and empirically supported for children and may be applicable to victims of bullying who display these characteristics. For example, the Coping Cat (cf. Kendall, Kane, Howard, & Siqueland, 1990) is an empirically supported treatment developed for children with generalized anxiety. Similarly, treatment manuals are available for working with children who have social anxiety, such as *Cognitive-Behavioral Group Treatment for Social Phobia in Adolescents* (cf. Albano, Marten, Holt, Heimberg, & Barlow, 1995) or *Social Effectiveness Therapy for Children* (cf. Beidel, Turner, & Morris, 1996; 1999). These approaches are generally designed for individual or small group treatment, but could also be utilized by school counselors. Likewise, components of these interventions could be incorporated into larger school-based efforts to provide children with anxiety reduction skills.

Similarly, it seems that most children can benefit from learning strategies used in the treatment of anxiety. Relaxation training teaches children a skill that could be applied at any point when they might feel tense or anxious. For example, children can be taught to relax muscle groups in order to release tension from their body (i.e., progressive muscle relaxation). In addition, breathing retraining exercises can be taught to reduce anxiety and calm the child during times of stress. Scripts for these procedures are available and can be used to teach progressive muscle relaxation and breathing retraining skills that help the child feel more relaxed in anxiety-producing situations. Younger children may benefit from scripts that include imagery (e.g., pretend you are squeezing a lemon to illustrate muscle relaxation) or facilitate appropriate practice of the skill (e.g., placing a plastic cup on the stomach to demonstrate diaphragmatic breathing). Anxiety management strategies can be taught individually or in small groups to maximize cooperation and minimize disruption.

Summary

Bullying prevention and intervention strategies developed at the school-wide level have demonstrated limited empirical support and effectiveness, particularly in the United States (Tofti, Farrington, & Baldry, 2008). Current work needs to continue in the development of prevention and intervention for youth involved in bullying at the individual levels and it is important that these interventions include components that address comorbid mental health issues. Future research is needed to determine which treatment strategies are most successful (either alone or in combination) to respond effectively to psychological precursors and/or consequences of bullying.

REFERENCES

Abramson, L.Y., Metalsky, G.I., & Alloy, L.B. (1989). Hopelessness depression: A theory-based subtype of depression. *Psychological Review, 96,* 358–372.

Albano, A.M., Marten, P.A., Holt, C.S., Heimberg, R.G., & Barlow, D.H. (1995). Cognitive-behavioral group treatment for social phobia in adolescents: A preliminary study. *The Journal of Nervous and Mental Disease, 183,* 649–656.

Anderson, J.C. (1994). Epedemiological issues. In T.H. Ollendick, N.J. King, & W. Yule (Eds.), *International handbook of phobic and anxiety disorders in children and adolescents* (pp. 43–65). New York, NY: Plenum Press.

Austin, S., & Joseph, S. (1996). Assessment of bully/victim problems in 8 to 11 year-olds. *British Journal of Educational Psychology, 66,* 447–456.

Avenevoli, S., Knight, E., Kessler, R.C., & Merikangas, K.R. (2008). Epidemiology of depression in children and adolescents. In J.R.Z. Abela & B.L. Hankin (Eds.), *Handbook of depression in children and adolescents* (pp. 6–32). New York, NY: Guilford.

Barrett, P., Rapee, R., Dadds, M., & Ryan, S. (1996). Family enhancement of cognitive style in anxious and aggressive children. *Journal of Abnormal Child Psychology, 24,* 187–203.

Batsche, G.M. (1997). Bullying. In G.G. Bear, K.M. Minke, & A. Thomas (Eds.), *Children's Needs II: Development, problems, and alternatives* (pp. 171–179). Bethesda, MD: National Association of School Psychologists.

Beck, A.T., Rush, A.J., Shaw, B.F., & Emery, G. (1979). *Cognitive therapy of depression.* New York, NY: Guilford.

Beidel, D. (1991). Social phobia and overanxious disorder in school-age children. *Journal of the American Academy of Child & Adolescent Psychiatry, 30,* 545–552.

Beidel, D.C., Turner, S.M., & Morris, T.L. (1996). *Social effectiveness therapy for children: A treatment manual.* Unpublished manuscript, Medical University of South Carolina.

Beidel, D.C., Turner, S.M., & Morris, T.L. (1999). Psychopathology of childhood social phobia. *Journal of the American Academy of Child and Adolescent Psychiatry, 38,* 643–650.

Bierman, K.L., & Furman, W. (1984). The effects of social-skills training and peer involvement on the social adjustment of preadolescents. *Child Development, 55,* 151–162.

Bosworth, K., Espelage, D., & Simon, T. (1999). Factors associated with bullying behavior in middle school students. *The Journal of Early Adolescence, 19,* 341–362.

Brozina, K., & Abela, J. (2006). Symptoms of depression and anxiety in children: Specificity of the hopelessness theory. *Journal of Clinical Child and Adolescent Psychology, 35,* 515–527.

Byrne, B. (1994). *Coping with bullying in schools.* New York, NY: Cassell Villiers House.

Cacioppo, J., Ernst, J., Burleson, M., McClintock, M., Malarkey, W., Hawkley, L., et al. (2000). Lonely traits and concomitant physiological processes: The MacArthur social neuroscience studies. *International Journal of Psychophysiology, 35,* 143–154.

Callagan, S. & Joseph, S. (1995). Self-concept and peer victimization among school children. *Personality and Individual Differences, 18,* 161–163.

Carney, A.G., & Merrell, K.W. (2001). Bullying in schools: Perspectives on understanding and preventing an international problem. *School Psychology International, 22,* 364–382.

Chipuer, H. (2001). Dyadic attachments and community connectedness: Links with youths' loneliness experiences. *Journal of Community Psychology, 29,* 429–446.

Clarke, G., Rohde, P., Lewinsohn, P., Hops, H., & Seely, J. (1999). Cognitive-behavioral treatment of adolescent depression: Efficacy of acute group treatment and booster session. *Journal of the American Academy of Child and Adolescent Psychiatry, 38,* 272–280.

Costello, E.J., & Angold, A. (1995). Epidemiology. In J. March (Ed.), *Anxiety disorders in children and adolescents* (pp. 109–124). New York, NY: Guilford.

Costello, E.J., Mustillo, S., Erkanli, A., Keeler, G., & Angold, A. (2003). Prevalence and development of psychiatric disorders in childhood and adolescence. *Archives of General Psychiatry 60,* 837–844.

Craig, W.M. (1998). The relationship among bullying, victimization, depression, anxiety, and aggression in elementary school children. *Personality and Individual Differences, 24,* 123–130.

Craig, W.M., & Pepler, D.J. (1995). Peer processes in bullying and victimization: A naturalistic study. *Exceptionality Education in Canada, 4,* 81–95.

Crick, N.R., & Grotpeter, J.K. (1995). Relational aggression, gender, and social-psychological adjustment. *Child Development, 66,* 710–722.

Crick, N.R., & Ladd, G.W. (1993). Children's perceptions of their peer experiences: Attributions, loneliness, social anxiety, and social avoidance. *Developmental Psychology, 29,* 244–254.

DeRosier, M.E. (2002). *Group interventions and exercises for enhancing children's communication, cooperation, and confidence.* Sarasota, FL: Professional Resources Press.

DeRosier, M.E., & Marcus, S.R. (2005). Building friendships and combating bullying: Effectiveness of S.S.GRIN at one-year follow-up. *Journal of Clinical Child and Adolescent Psychology, 34,* 140–150.

Dishion, T.J., McCord, J., & Poulin, F. (1999). When interventions harm: Peer groups and problem behavior. *American Psychologist, 54,* 755–764.

Dodge, K. (1993). Social-cognitive mechanisms in the development of conduct disorder and depression. *Annual Review of Psychology, 44,* 559–584.

Doll, B., & Swearer, S. (2006). Cognitive-behavioral interventions for participants in bullying and coercion. In R. Mennuti, A. Freeman, & R. Christner (Eds.), *Cognitive behavioral interventions in educational settings: A handbook for practice* (pp. 183–201). New York, NY: Brunner-Routledge.

Duncan, R.D. (1999). Peer and sibling aggression: An investigation of intra- and extrafamilial bullying. *Journal of Interpersonal Violence, 14,* 871–886.

Espelage, D., & Swearer, S. (2003). Research on school bullying and victimization: What have we learned and where do we go from here? *School Psychology Review, 32,* 365–383.

Ford, T., Goodman, R., & Meltzer, H. (2003). The British child and adolescent mental health survey 1999: The prevalence of DSM-IV disorders. *Journal of the American Academy of Child and Adolescent Psychiatry 42,* 1203–1211.

Fox, C.L., & Boulton, M.J. (2003). Evaluating the effectiveness of a social skills training (SST) programme for victims of bullying. *Educational Research, 45,* 231–247.

Frerichs, L.J. (2009). *Sad and alone: Social and psychological correlates of relational victimization in preadolescence. Unpublished doctoral dissertation.* University of Nebraska-Lincoln, Lincoln, NE.

Friedberg, R.D., & McClure, J.M. (2002). *Clinical practice of cognitive therapy with children and adolescents: The nuts and bolts.* New York, NY: Guilford.

Galanaki, E., & Vassilopoulou, H. (2007). Teachers and children's loneliness: A review of the literature and educational implications. *European Journal of Psychology of Education, 22,* 455–475.

Gazelle, H. (2008). Behavioral profiles of anxious solitary children and heterogeneity in peer relations. *Developmental Psychology, 44*, 1604–1624.

Gibb, B., & Alloy, L. (2006). A prospective test of the hopelessness theory of depression in children. *Journal of Clinical Child and Adolescent Psychology, 35*, 264–274.

Gladstone, G., Parker, G., & Malhi, G. (2006). Do bullied children become anxious and depressed adults? A cross-sectional investigation of the correlates of bullying and anxious depression. *Journal of Nervous and Mental Disease, 194*, 201–208.

Gladstone, G., Parker, G., Mitchell, P., Wilhelm, K., & Malhi, G. (2005). Relationship between self-reported childhood behavioral inhibition and lifetime anxiety disorders in a clinical sample. *Depression and Anxiety, 22*, 103–113.

Grills, A.E., & Ollendick, T.H. (2002). Peer victimization, global self-worth, and anxiety in middle school children. *Journal of Clinical Child and Adolescent Psychology, 31*, 59–68.

Haye, K. (2005). *An exploratory look at the relationship between bully/victim status, locus of control, and hopelessness: A moderator model.* Unpublished doctoral dissertation, Department of Educational Psychology, University of Nebraska-Lincoln, Lincoln, Nebraska.

Haynie, D., Nansel, T., Eitel, P., Crump, A., Saylor, K., Yu, K., et al. (2001). Bullies, victims, and bully/victims: Distinct groups of at-risk youth. *Journal of Early Adolescence, 21*, 29–49.

Heyne, D., & Rollings, S. (2002). *School refusal.* Malden, MA: Blackwell.

Hodges, E., & Perry, D. (1999). Personal and interpersonal antecedents and consequences of victimization by peers. *Journal of Personality and Social Psychology, 76*, 677–685.

Houghton, F., Cowley, H., Houghton, S., & Kelleher, K. (2003). The Children's Depression Inventory short form (CDI-S) in an Irish context. *Irish Journal of Psychology, 24*, 193–198.

Huphrey, J., Storch, E., & Geffken, G. (2007). Peer victimization in children with attention-deficit hyperactivity disorder. *Journal of Child Health Care, 11*, 248–260.

Ivarsson, T., Broberg, A., Arvidsson, T., & Gillberg, C. (2005). Bullying in adolescence: Psychiatric problems in victims and bullies as measured by the Youth Self Report (YSR) and the Depression Self-Rating Scale (DSRS). *Nordic Journal of Psychiatry, 59*, 365–373.

Kaltiala-Heino, R., Rimpela, M., Rantanen, P., & Rimpela, A. (2000). Bullying at school: An indicator of adolescents at risk for mental disorders. *Journal of Adolescence, 23*, 661–674.

Kaltiala-Heino, R., Rimpela, M., Marttunen, M., Rimpela, A., & Rantanen, P. (1999). Bullying, depression, and suicidal ideation in Finnish adolescents: School survey. *British Medical Journal, 319*, 348–351.

Kashani, J.H., Deuser, W., & Reid, J.C. (1991). Aggression and anxiety: A new look at an old notion. *Journal of the American Academy of Child and Adolescent Psychiatry, 30*, 218–223.

Kazdin, A.E., Rodgers, A., & Colbus, D. (1986). The hopelessness scale for children: Psychometric characteristics and concurrent validity. *Journal of Consulting and Clinical Psychology, 54*, 241–245.

Kazdin, A.E., French, N.H., Unis, A.S., Esveldt-Dawson, K., & Sherick, R.B. (1983). Hopelessness, depression, and suicidal intent among psychiatrically disturbed inpatient children. *Journal of Consulting and Clinical Psychology, 51*, 504–510.

Kearney, C.A., Eisen, A.R., & Silverman, W.K. (1995). The legend and myth of school phobia. *School Psychology Quarterly, 10*, 65–85.

Kendall, P.C., Kane, M., Howard, B., & Siqueland, L. (1990). Cognitive-behavioral treatment of anxious children: Treatment manual. Available from the author, Department of Psychology, Temple University, Philadelphia, PA.

Kovacs, M. (1992). *Children's Depression Inventory.* Pittsburgh, PA: Western Psychiatric Institute and Clinic.

Kumpulainen, K., Räsänen, E., & Puura, K. (2001). Psychiatric disorders and the use of mental health services among children involved in bullying. *Aggressive Behavior, 27*, 102–110.

La Greca, A., & Harrison, H. (2005). Adolescent peer relations, friendships, and romantic relationships: Do they predict social anxiety and depression? *Journal of Clinical Child and Adolescent Psychology, 34*, 49–61.

Lewinsohn, P.M., Clarke, G.N., Hops, H., & Andrews, J. (1990). Cognitive-behavioral treatment for depressed adolescents. *Behavior Therapy, 21*, 385–401.

Lewinsohn, P.M., Zinbarg, R., Seeley, J.R., Lewinsohn, M., & Sack, W.H. (1997). Lifetime comorbidity among anxiety disorders and between anxiety disorders and other mental disorders in adolescents. *Journal of Anxiety Disorders, 11*, 377–394.

Little, T., Bovaird, J., & Slegers, D. (2006). Methods for the analysis of change. In D. Mroczek & T. Little (Eds.), *Handbook of personality development* (pp. 181–211). Mahwah, NJ: Lawrence Erlbaum Associates Publishers.

Lonigan, C.J., Carey, M.P., & Finch, A.J., Jr. (1994). Anxiety and depression in children and adolescents: Negative affectivity and the utility of self-reports. *Journal of Consulting and Clinical Psychology, 62*, 1000–1008.

March, J. (1997). *Anxiety disorders in children and adolescents.* New York, NY: Guilford Press.

Mick, M.A., & Telch, M.J. (1998). Social anxiety and history of behavioral inhibition in young adults. *Journal of Anxiety Disorders, 12*, 1–20.

Miers, A., Blöte, A., Bögels, S., & Westenberg, P. (2008). Interpretation bias and social anxiety in adolescents. *Journal of Anxiety Disorders, 22*, 1462–1471.

Nelson, W.M., III, & Fitch, A.J., Jr. (1996). *Keeping your cool: The anger management workbook* (Parts 1 and 2). Ardmore, PA: Workbook Publishing.

Newman, D., Horne, A., & Bartolomucci, C. (2001). Bully busters: A teacher's manual for helping bullies, victims, and bystanders: Book review. *Social Work with Groups, 24*, 197–201.

Olweus, D. (1993). Bully/victim problems among schoolchildren: Long-term consequences and an effective intervention program. In S. Hodgins (Ed.), *Mental disorders and crime.* Newbury Park, CA: Sage.

Pepler, D., Craig, W., & O'Connell, P. (2010). Peer processes in bullying: Informing prevention and intervention strategies. In S.R. Jimerson, S.M. Swearer & D.L. Espelage (Eds.), *Handbook of bullying in schools: An international perspective* (pp. 469–479). New York, NY: Routledge.

Rigby, K. (2003). Consequences of bullying in schools. *The Canadian Journal of Psychiatry, 48*, 583–590.

Roth, D.A., Coles, M.E., & Heimberg, R.G. (2002). The relationship between memories for childhood teasing and anxiety and depression in adulthood. *Journal of Anxiety Disorders, 16*, 149–164.

Salmivalli, C., Lappalainen, M., & Lagerspetz, K.M.J. (1998). Stability and change of behavior in connection with bullying in schools: A two-year follow-up. *Aggressive Behavior, 24*, 205–218.

Schwartz, C.E., Snidman, V., & Kagan, J. (1999). Adolescent social anxiety as an outcome of inhibited temperament in childhood. *Journal of the American Academy of Child and Adolescent Psychiatry, 38*, 1008–1015.

Silverman, W., & Kurtines, W. (2001). Anxiety disorders. In J. Hughes, A.M. La Greca, & J. Conoley (Eds.), *Handbook of psychological services for children and adolescents* (pp. 225–244). New York, NY: Oxford University Press.

Smith, P.K., Shu, S., & Madsen, K. (2001). Characteristics of victims of school bullying: Developmental changes in coping strategies and skills. In J. Juvonen & S. Graham (Eds.), *Peer harassment in school: The plight of the vulnerable and victimized* (pp. 332–352). New York, NY: Guilford Press.

Snyder, J., Brooker, M., Patrick, M., Snyder, A., Schrepferman, L., & Stoolmiller, M. (2003). Observed peer victimization during early elementary school: Continuity, growth, and relation to risk for child antisocial and depressive behavior. *Child Development, 74*, 1881–1898.

Sourander, A., Jensen, P., Rönning, J., Niemelä, S., Helenius, H., Sillanmäki, L., et al. (2007). What is the early adulthood outcome of boys who bully or are bullied in childhood? The Finnish 'From a Boy to a Man' study. *Pediatrics, 120*, 397–404.

Stark, K., Kendall, P.C., McCarthy, M., Stafford, M., Barron, R., & Thomeer, M. (1996). *Taking action: A workbook for overcoming depression.* Ardmore, PA: Workbook Publishing

Stark, K.D., Napolitano, S., Swearer, S., Schmidt, K., Jaramillo, D., & Hoyle, J. (1996). Issues in the treatment of depression. *Applied & Preventive Psychology, 5*, 59–83.

Stark, K.D., Sander, J.B., Yancy, M.G., Bronik, M.D., & Hoke, J.A. (2000). Treatment of depression in childhood and adolescence: Cognitive-behavioral procedures for the individual and family. In P.C. Kendall (Ed.), *Child and adolescent therapy: Cognitive-behavioral procedures* (pp. 173–234). New York, NY: The Guilford Press.

Starr, L., & Davila, J. (2008). Differentiating interpersonal correlates of depressive symptoms and social anxiety in adolescence: Implications for models of comorbidity. *Journal of Clinical Child and Adolescent Psychology, 37*, 337–349.

Storch, E., Zelman, E., Sweeney, M., Danner, G., & Dove, S. (2002). Overt and relational victimization and psychosocial adjustment in minority preadolescents. *Child Study Journal, 32*, 73–80.

Swearer, S.M., & Cary, P.T. (2003). Perceptions and attitudes toward bullying in middle school youth: A developmental examination across the bully/victim continuum. *Journal of Applied School Psychology, 19*, 63–79.

Swearer, S.M. & Givens, J.E. (2006, March). *Designing an Alternative to Suspension for Middle School Bullies.* Paper presented at the annual convention of the National Association of School Psychologists, Anaheim, CA.

Swearer, S.M., Espelage, D.L., & Napolitano, S.A. (2009). *Bullying prevention and intervention: Realistic strategies for schools.* New York, NY: Guilford Press.

Swearer, S.M., Siebecker, A.B., Johnsen-Frerichs, L.A., & Wang, C. (2010). Assessment of bullying/victimization: The problem of comparability across studies and across methodologies. In S. Jimmerson, S. Swearer, & D.L. Espelage (Eds.), *Handbook of bullying in schools: An international perspective* (305–327). New York, NY: Taylor & Francis.

Swearer, S.M., Song, S.Y., Cary, P.T., Eagle, J.W., & Mickelson, W.T. (2001). Psychosocial correlates in bullying and victimization: The relationship between depression, anxiety, and bully/victim status. *Journal of Emotional Abuse, 2*, 95–121.

Ttofi, M.M., Farrington, D.P., & Baldry, A.C. (2008). Effectiveness of programmes to reduce school bullying: A systematic review. The Swedish National Council for Crime Prevention. Retrieved January 9, 2009, from www.bra.se/extra/faq/?module_instance=2&action=question_show&id=474&category_id=9.

Van Ameringen, M., Mancini, C., & Oakman, J.M. (1998). The relationship of behavioral inhibition and shyness to anxiety disorder. *Journal of Nervous and Mental Disease, 186,* 425–431.

Vassilopoulos, S., & Banerjee, R. (2008). Interpretations and judgments regarding positive and negative social scenarios in childhood social anxiety. *Behaviour Research and Therapy, 46,* 870–876.

Vossekuil, B., Fein, R.A., Reddy, M., Borum, R., & Modzeleski, W. (2002). *The final report and findings of the Safe School Initiative: Implications for the prevention of school attacks in the United States.* Washington, DC: U.S. Secret Service and U.S. Department of Education.

Weisz, J.R., Sweeney, L., Proffitt, V., & Carr, T. (1993). Control-related beliefs and self-reported depressive symptoms in late childhood. *Journal of Abnormal Psychology, 102,* 411–418.

Wicks-Nelson, R., & Israel, A.C. (1991). *Behavior disorders of childhood.* New Jersey: Simon and Schuster.

6

UNWANTED SEXUAL AND HARASSING EXPERIENCES
From School to Text Messaging

MICHELE YBARRA, DOROTHY L. ESPELAGE, AND SUZANNE MARTIN

Text messaging plays an important role in peer groups and is an integral component of social interaction (Lenhart, Arafeh, Smith, & Macgill, 2008). An estimated 36% of youth between 12 and 17 years of age use cell phone text messaging as a daily means of communication (Lenhart et al., 2008). As Danah Boyd (2007), an expert on technology's influence on youth social networks, explains, "Teens know who is on what [text messaging] plan, who can be called after 7PM ... who is over their texting for the month, etc. It's part of their mental model of their social network and knowing this is a core exchange of friendship" (p. 3). Additionally, text messaging is used as a tool to heighten popularity among peers and to facilitate dating relationships (Boyd, 2007). Text messaging might be used as a tool to engage in harassment and verbal/relational aggression (e.g., social exclusion, rumor spreading) in order to achieve the goals of popularity attainment and desired dating relationships, coupled with the social nature of bullying behaviors (Espelage, Bosworth, & Simon, 2000). Aggression through text messaging could also be a continuation of peer aggression or victimization that has occurred at school. While many youth encounter bullying and harassment at some point in their educational career (Kann et al., 1995), the spillover of peer victimization at school to text messaging outside the confines of the educational environment may create a world for some youth where peer victimization and/or bullying feels inescapable.

Over 15% of children and adolescents report being bullied "sometimes" or more frequently in the last year (Due et al., 2005; Nansel et al., 2001). Considering the continuum of the bully dynamic (i.e., bully, victim, bully-victim, bystander), evidence suggests that involvement may include the majority of the nation's student population (Espelage et al., 2000). Unfortunately, involvement as a bully, victim, bully-victim, or bystander is associated with concerning psychosocial problems such as depression, anxiety, and anger problems (Fox & Boulton, 2005; Hawker & Boulton, 2000; Juvoven, Nishina, & Graham, 2000; Kaltiala-Heino, Rimpelä, Rantanen, & Rimpelä, 2000; Nansel, Haynie, & Simons-Morton, 2003; Sourander, Helstelä, Helenius, & Piha, 2000).

In addition to peer aggression and bullying, sexual harassment also appears to be widespread in schools: an estimated 50% of students reporting non-physical sexual harassment and 32% of students reporting physical sexual harassment "occasionally" or "often" over the last year (AAUW, 2001). Concurrent psychosocial problems associated with victims of sexual harassment (AAUW, 2001; Fineran, 2002) are similar to those noted for students targeted by bullying. Both are adolescent health issues of great importance, and may be exacerbated by harassment via text messaging.

At school, victimization often occurs in public spaces, sometimes in front of adults and school personnel who do not intervene (Astor, Meyer, & Behre, 1999). This lack of intervention in public domains can serve to normalize aggression and maintain the common societal view that bullying and harassment are typical adolescent experiences (Dawkins, 1996; Thompson, Whitney, & Smith, 1994; Walker, Ramsey, & Gresham, 2004). It is possible that this tacit approval of bullying generally leads to adolescents harassing and bullying in private through text messaging. Schools therefore might serve as "training grounds" for the transfer of harassment across contexts and environments (Stein, 1995, 1999, 2005).

Although little is known about text messaging-based aggression, recent research highlights the psychosocial problems associated with harassment and unwanted sexual solicitation of youth on the Internet (Finkelhor, Mitchell, & Wolak, 2000; Wolak, Mitchell, & Finkelhor, 2006; Ybarra, Espelage, & Mitchell, 2007). Emerging evidence suggests that being a victim of Internet harassment can affect problem behavior at school. In a national survey of 1,588 youth between the ages of 10 and 15 years, Ybarra, Diener-West, and Leaf (2007) report that one-third of youth who were harassed online were also being bullied at school. Whether or not youth were also harassed at school, youth bullied online were significantly more likely to report two or more detentions or suspensions, to skip school in the previous year, and were eight times more likely than youth not harassed online to concurrently report carrying a weapon to school in the past 30 days. For some youth, technology-based harassment may affect their self-appraised safety at school. Given the "always-on" aspect of text messaging (i.e., cell phone and the ability to text-message is always within the adolescent's reach) and current literature regarding Internet-based peer harassment, it is imperative that more research examines the impact of cell phone-based harassment on psychosocial concerns among youth.

OVERLAPS AMONG SEXUAL, PHYSICAL, AND RELATIONAL AGGRESSION

Beyond understanding how text messaging-based aggression relates to school-based aggression, this chapter is also focused on the associations among sexual, physical, and relational forms of aggression at school and via text-messaging. Indeed, little is known about the overlaps in experiences of bullying and sexual harassment in schools. Given the commonality in psychosocial correlates for victims of bullying and sexual harassment, however, it seems likely that there is overlap in the representation of youth who are being targeted. Espelage and Holt (2007) recently found that students who were victims or bully-victims reported the highest rate of peer sexual harassment victimization compared to all other youth. Similar patterns were noted for youth who were victims of Internet harassment and unwanted sexual solicitation (Ybarra et al., , 2007). Importantly, Espelage and Holt (2007) found that anxiety/depression levels were highest for victims of bullying who concurrently reported the highest levels of sexual harassment victimization, suggesting that an overlap in sexual aggression and bullying may portend internalizing problems for some youth.

GAP IN LITERATURE

With the emergence of text messaging use among young people and the mental health problems associated with both school-based and Internet-based harassment experiences, examining harassment within newly emerging technologies, specifically text messaging, is of utmost importance. Given recent reports of an overlap in victims of sexual and relational/physical harassment at school and online, it also appears important to further investigate whether these experiences extend to text messaging harassment specifically, as well as across environments generally. Based upon previous findings, we hypothesize overlaps in victims of bullying and sexual harassment (Espelage & Holt, 2007; Ybarra et al., 2007) both within and across text messaging and school environments. We further posit associations between text messaging-based harassment and school behavior problems (Ybarra et al., 2007), and anticipate youth who report harassment across environments to report the greatest level of distress.

METHODS

A secondary data analysis of a national sample of youth surveyed online was used for this study. Data were collected between November 15, 2006 and November 27, 2006 as part of Harris Interactive's Youth Query, which is a monthly omnibus survey of children and adolescents living in the United States. The research methodology was conducted in accordance with the ethical standards as stated in the Declaration of Helsinki; the secondary data analysis was reviewed and approved by the University of Illinois at Urbana-Champaign Institutional Review Board.

Data Source Sampling Method

The sample was obtained from the Harris Poll OnLine (HPOL) opt-in panel, which includes over four million members (Harris Interactive, 2006) and is the largest of its kind in the world. Panel participants are recruited through over 100 different sources. Diverse methods are leveraged to identify and recruit potential panelists, including co-registration offers on partners' websites, targeted emails sent by online partners to their audiences, graphical and text banner placement on partners' websites, trade show presentations, targeted postal mail invitations, TV advertisements, member referrals, and telephone recruitment of targeted populations. Respondents 8 through 12 years of age were recruited through an initial email contact with their parents who then could forward the survey link to their child. Respondents older than 13 years were recruited directly or through an initial email contact with their parents.

Methods in Data Collection

Email invitations were sent to randomly identified youth respondents and read: "What's this survey about? All about you: Tell us what makes you who you are! Share your thoughts on everything from the world." Invitations to randomly identified parents read: "What's this survey about? All about teens: We want to know what makes teens who they are. We'd like to hear their thoughts on everything from the world around them to the people they hang out with." When youth participants clicked on the survey invitation email, they were taken to the secure survey website. They then completed an eligibil-ity questionnaire, which confirmed that their age was in the target range (8–18 years) and stratification goals were yet unmet (goals varied based upon source; youth recruited directly were stratified on age, sex, and race; youth recruited through their parents were stratified on the age of child and race of parent). Eligible youth were then invited to take part in the self-administered online survey. Participants were told that the survey would take approximately 20 minutes to complete and that the information would be aggre-gated, void of personally identifiable information. The survey response rate was 8.4%. A total of 90% of youth who started the survey completed the survey. Additional details of the survey methodology can be found elsewhere (Harris Interactive, 2007).

Identifying the Analytical Sample

Due to their potential sensitivity, questions related to sexual harassment were asked only of respondents 10 years of age and older. Of the 1,240 youth that completed the survey, 210 youth were less than 10 years of age and therefore dropped from the sample. Additionally, to be included in the current study, respondents had to: (1) be attending a public or private grade school or high school; (2) have sent and received text mes-sages in the past year; and (3) have provided "valid" responses (i.e., not "don't know" or "refused") for at least 85% of the variables analyzed. Of the 1,030 youth in the valid age range, 49 did not report attending a public or private school, 381 did not have a cell phone, 209 had a cell phone but did not send and receive text messages, and 57 had fewer than 85% valid data. Thus, the final analytical sample included 334 youth. As shown in Table 6.1, the 1,030 youth 10–18 years of age in the survey were similar to the general population of 10–18-year-olds in the U.S. Among these youth, those owning cell phones and meeting the criteria for the analytical sample ($n = 344$) were older and more likely to be African American.

Measures

Cell ownership. Youth were asked to indicate which of the three following statements was applicable: (1) "I have a cell phone and send and receive text messages"; (2) "I have a cell phone, but do not send or receive text messages"; or (3) "I do not have a cell phone." The current sample was restricted to youth who responded positively to the first item response option.

Text messaging-based harassment. Relational and sexual harassment were assessed using the following question: "During the last year did someone do the following things to you?" Relational harassment was defined by: (1) "Someone sent me a text message that said rude or mean things" (33%); or (2) "Someone spread rumors about me, whether they were true or not, over text messaging" (20%). Sexual harassment was defined by: (1) "Someone sent a text message that was sexual in any way that I did not want to receive" (17%); or (2) "Someone sent a picture text message that was sexual in any way that I did not want to receive" (8%).

School-based harassment. Relational harassment was indicated for youth who reported that in the last year they: (1) "Had been verbally harassed at school (e.g., called names)" (30%), or (2) "Had mean rumors or lies spread about them at school" (24%). Physical harassment was indicated for those who responded positively about being: (1) "Physi-cally harassed at school (pushed, shoved, etc)" (17%); or (2) "Physically assaulted at school

Table 6.1   Comparison of Sample Demographic Characteristics with the General Population

	US Population (CPS Data, 2006)	Unweighted sample of 10–18-year-olds (*n* = 1,030)	Unweighted analytical sample of 8–18-year-olds attending school* (*n* = 334)	Weighted analytical sample of 8–18-year-olds attending school * (*n* = 334)
Sex				
Male	51%	50%	47%	47%
Female	49%	50%	53%	53%
Age				
10 years old	11%	9%	4%	6%
11 years old	11%	11%	4%	3%
12 years old	11%	12%	9%	7%
13 years old	11%	8%	8%	11%
14 years old	11 %	10%	13%	16%
15 years old	11%	14%	19%	18%
16 years old	12%	14%	19%	17%
17 years old	12%	15%	21%	17%
18 years old	11%	7%	3%	4%
Race/Ethnicity**				
Hispanic	18%	17%	18%	25%
Black/AA	15%	17%	23%	19%
White and all other	67%	67%	59%	56%
Urbanicity***				
Urban	28%	31%	38%	36%
Suburban	48%	40%	41%	48%
Rural	23%	27%	21%	16%
Missing (enter %)	1.0%	2%	0%	0%

*   Excludes 68 participants attending college or university, 27 participants home schooled, 15 missing school data, 575 youth not 'at risk' for text messaging-based victimization because they did not send and receive text messages, and 11 participants who did not provide responsive answers to at least 85% of the variables analyzed.
**   Categories are based upon CPS definition (2006)
***   Youth in the sample were asked where their school was located, not where their house was located.

(punched, kicked, injured with a weapon, etc)" (9%). Sexual harassment was indicated if the youth responded positively that they had been "sexually harassed at school (someone made sexual remarks or touched your body when you did not want to be touched)" (5%).

Personal well-being at school. Youth were asked: "Overall, how safe do you feel when you are at school?" Answers were captured on a four-point Likert scale (1 (Not at all safe) to 4 (Very safe)) and dichotomized to reflect youth who felt "not at all safe" or "not very safe" with those who felt "somewhat safe" and "very safe."

Data Analysis

Missing data were imputed, which affected less than 3% of cases. Census-based weighting to account for non-participation was applied to the data (Bureau of Labor Statistics and Bureau of the Census, 2006) according to sex, age, race, urbanicity, parent education, and region for youth 10–17 years of age and sex, race, education, and region for youth 18 years of age. Associations between categorical variables were estimated using logistic regression and were not correlated because correlation matrices underestimate the true associations between categorical variables. Furthermore, the use of the statistical program Stata (StataCorp, 2006) for conducting logistical regression allows for the incorporation of a weighting variable in logistic regression, but it does not do so for correlation analyses. Finally, multivariate logistic regression was used to estimate the odds of feeling unsafe at school given reports of harassment via text messaging and in school, while taking into account differences in demographic characteristics and intensity of text messaging use.

RESULTS

Reported percentages are weighted as described above; 'n's are reflective of the actual number in the sample (StataCorp, 2006). Sixty percent of survey respondents reported being targeted by harassment of some kind either at school or via text messaging in the past year. Thirty-eight percent of youth reported relational harassment and 18% reported sexual harassment via text messaging at least once in the past year. By comparison, 38% of youth reported relational harassment, 19% reported physical harassment, and 5% reported sexual harassment at school.

Overlap between Text Messaging-based and School-based Harassment Experiences

Moderate overlap in harassment at school and via text messaging was observed: 23% reported harassment both via text messaging and at school, whereas 18% of all youth reported harassment via text messaging only and 19% reported harassment at school only. Less than half of all youth (40%) reported no type of harassment in the past year.

Overlap in Sexual, Verbal, and Physical Harassment Experiences

Across environments, 19% of youth reported both sexual harassment and physical/relational harassment. One percent of youth reported sexual harassment only, whereas 39% reported physical/relational harassment only. Table 6.2 shows the magnitudes of association for sexual, verbal, and physical harassment across environments.

Association between Harassment and Personal Well-being at School

Eleven percent ($n = 22$) of all youth reported feeling not very or not at all safe in general when at school. Text messaging-based harassment was associated with fivefold increased odds of reporting feeling unsafe at school (OR: 4.7, $p < .01$). School harassment was associated with a marginally significant trend noted for feeling unsafe at school (OR: 3.2, $p < .10$). As shown in Table 6.3, neither association was explained by concurrent harassment in the other environment respectively, or underlying differences in sex, age, race, urbanicity, and text messaging usage.

It is possible that youth who were harassed *both* at school and via text messaging were at risk for heightened concern regarding their safety at school. Twenty-four percent of

Table 6.2   Overlap between School-based and Text Messaging-based Harassment Types among School-attending Youth Ages 10–18 Years (*n* = 334)

		School-based			Text messaging-based	
		Sexual harassment	Physical harassment	Relational harassment	Sexual harassment	Relational harassment
		Odds ratio	Odds ratio	Odds ratio	Odds ratio	Odds ratio
School-based	Sexual harassment	1				
	Physical harassment	5.2*	1			
	Relational harassment	4.6	14.0***	1		
Text messaging-based	Sexual harassment	6.1*	2.6*	2.0	1	
	Relational harassment	5.6**	2.8**	2.2*	14.8***	1

*   p<.05
**   p<.01
*** p<.001

youth reporting harassment at both school and via text messaging sometime in the last year also reported feeling unsafe at school in the past month compared to 13% of youth harassed in only one of those environments over the last year (OR = 2.2, p = 0.36).

TRANSLATING RESEARCH INTO PRACTICE: IMPLICATIONS FOR BULLYING PREVENTION AND INTERVENTION PROGRAMS

Among youth 10 to 18 years of age attending public or private school who send and receive text messages, a large minority report receiving harassing text messages in the last year: 38% report receiving a relational harassment text message and 18% report a sexual harassment text message at least once. Consistent with emerging research examining the links between Internet and school-based harassment (Ybarra et al., 2007), only moderate overlap in text messaging-based and school-based harassment is observed among text messaging users. Almost one in four youth (23%) who use text messaging report being harassed both via text messaging and at school, whereas 37% report harassment in one environment but not the other.

It is possible that different dynamics are driving harassment at school versus harassment via text messaging. At the simplest level, students who are targets in person might have different personality characteristics than those who are targets via text messaging. For example, victims of school bullying are often characterized as more insecure, anxious, and quiet than their peers (Olweus, 1995) and tend to have fewer friends (Paul & Cillessen, 2003). It is plausible that targets of text messaging-based harassment have more social power in school or have personality characteristics that buffer them from experiencing harassment at school. Furthermore, bullying and sexual harassment perpetration in school is often reinforced and maintained by peer groups (Espelage, Holt,

Table 6.3   Relative Odds of Feeling Unsafe at School given Reports of Harassment at School or via Text Messaging among School-attending Youth Ages 10–18 Years (*n* = 334)

Personal characteristics	Felt unsafe at school in "overall"	
	AOR (95% CI)	p-value
Harassment in the past year		
Text-based (any)	5.6 (1.9, 16.1)	0.002
School-based (any)	2.8 (0.9, 8.6)	0.07
Demographic characteristics		
Male	0.3 (0.09, 0.2)	0.04
Age	1.0 (0.8, 1.3)	0.80
Race		
White	1.0 (Reference)	
Black / African American	4.1 (1.2, 13.6)	0.02
Mixed	0.4 (0.06, 3.0)	0.40
All other	4.4 (0.9, 20.9)	0.07
Hispanic	1.6 (0.5, 5.3)	0.48
Urbanicity		
Urban setting	1.0 (Reference)	
Suburban setting	1.9 (0.6, 6.1)	0.28
Rural setting	0.2 (0.02, 2.0)	0.17
Average # of text messages sent and received/day	1.0 (1.0, 1.0)	0.47

AOR: Adjusted odds ratio. All estimates are adjusted for all other characteristics listed in the model

& Henkel, 2003) and ignored by teachers and administrators (Hoover & Hazler, 1994). Technology might thus provide a forum for different types of perpetrators to emerge who do not necessarily have social clout in the school setting. This different type of perpetrator may bring about a new group of victims. It is also possible that text messaging-based harassment could be in retaliation for some harassment that was perpetrated in school. Perhaps, then, similar to Internet harassment (Ybarra & Mitchell, 2004; Ybarra, Mitchell, Wolak, & Finkelhor, 2006), victims in one environment are instigators in another.

Overlap in Sexual and Relational/Physical Harassment

Findings suggest that youth who are sexually harassed are most likely being targeted by other types of harassment as well. Youth reporting sexual harassment at school are five times more likely to also report physical harassment at school with similar but non-significant trends noted for overlaps in sexual and relational harassment at school. Even more striking, youth reporting sexual harassment via text are almost 15 times more likely to also report relational harassment via text. This finding suggests that text-messaging harassment might include a tremendous amount of sexual overtone. It may also be that sexual harassment is a marker for greater vulnerability to peer harassment generally. Future studies should examine how the content of harassment varies across these contexts. Given that text messaging does not involve physical proximity, relational and sexual aspects may be more salient.

Associations between Text Messaging-based Harassment and Personal Well-being at School

Youth who are targeted by text messaging-based harassment are six times more likely to feel unsafe at school even after the concurrence of school-based harassment and the amount of text messaging are accounted for. These findings are consistent with Ybarra and colleagues (2007), who report that youth targeted by Internet-based harassment are more likely to also report bringing a weapon to school in the past 30 days, among other concerning school behavior problems. These perceptions of feeling unsafe might be attributable to hyper-vigilance resulting from the harassment, which youth might see as unpredictable or uncontrollable. It also is possible that youth are concerned that the harassing text messages will be discovered by classmates, subsequently leading to harassment at school as well. Another possibility is that there is a third, underlying factor that differentiates youth who are harassed via text messaging from those who are not, which may explain why they are more likely to feel unsafe at school even when compared to peers who are only harassed at school. The current data suggest a complex picture about how harassment outside of school may be affecting behaviors and functioning inside the school. Further research is needed before any conclusions can be made.

Limitations

The current findings should be interpreted within the following limitations. First, although the data were weighted to reflect the general youth population, it is important to recognize sample bias introduced by membership in the Harris Poll OnLine. Second, the harassment items are not sensitive to variations in the severity of messages received or the sender/origin of the message. Moreover, online harassment was not included in the survey but would have certainly added helpful context. Third, data were collected cross-sectionally, precluding temporal inferences. Fourth, data are not available to determine the perpetrator of the harassment. It is possible that the aggression is not coming from a peer, but rather from an adult. Finally, because this is a new field, measures are still being developed and refined. Additionally, it is possible that youth endorsed the school-based victimization experiences less frequently because they referred to experiences (e.g., "being sexually harassed") as opposed to behaviors (e.g., "being asked to talk about sex when you don't want to"). It is also plausible that the reliance on single items may be measuring the constructs too narrowly.

Implications

Sixty percent of youth who send and receive text messages in our sample report being targeted by some kind of harassment either at school or via text messaging in the past year; 34% report being targeted both at school and via text messaging. Perhaps helping to explain these high percentages, Smith (2007) argues that while aggression is deemed socially deviant by scholars and clinicians across disciplines, it is not necessarily developmentally deviant. Indeed, there is strong empirical support for developmental theories of youth using bullying and relational aggression to establish dominance in peer groups, to increase popularity among peers, and to increase the likelihood of dating among middle school students (Smith, 2007). Rodkin and Wilson (2007) hypothesize that perhaps the reason why many of the school bullying prevention programs are ineffective (Smith, Schneider, Smith, & Ananiadou, 2004) is partially because these programs ignore the possibility that aggression is adaptive and plays an important role in improving the social status of children. If true, then an area of concern for the emerging technology and victimization literature is a replication of this misconception. Therefore, if we continue to refer to youth aggression as maladaptive, then we miss the opportunity to understand how prevention efforts can work within the social nature of bullying to prevent it.

Conclusion

Even if the harassment is not occurring on school grounds or even necessarily by peers, the current data suggest that harassment may be related to a youth's appraisal of safety at school. Furthermore, significant overlap between youth who are sexually harassed and physically/verbally harassed is observed whether it occurs at school, via text messaging, or both. This suggests that youth who report sexual harassment may be in particular need of intervention and support. Professionals working with children and adolescents, especially those working in the schools, should be aware of the possible linkages between problems at school and harassment via text messaging for some youth. With the adoption of newer communication technologies that represent additional environments through which bullying and aggression may be expressed, integrated prevention programs that focus globally on aggression rather than specific types and in specific environments are warranted. Researchers need to focus on identifying concrete harm-reduction strategies that will improve the likelihood of positive communication.

REFERENCES

American Association of University Women Educational Foundation (AAUW). (2001). *Hostile hallways: Sexual harassment and bullying in schools.* Washington, DC: Harris/Scholastic Research.

Astor, R.A., Meyer, H.A., & Behre, W.J. (1999). Unowned places and times: Maps and interviews about violence in high schools. *American Educational Research Journal, 36,* 3–42.

Boyd, D. (2007, November). Gluttonous texting. Apophenia: Making connections where none previously existed. Retrieved May 1, 2009, from http://www.zephoria.org/thoughts/archives/2007/11/16/gluttonous_text.html.

Bureau of Labor Statistics & Bureau of the Census. (2006, July 5). Current population survey. Retrieved May 1, 2009, from www.census.gov/cps/.

Dawkins, J.L. (1996). Bullying, physical disability and the pediatric patient. *Developmental Medicine & Child Neurology, 38,* 603–612.

Due, P., Holstein, B.E., Lynch, J., Diderichsen, F., Gabhain, S.N., Scheidt, P., et al. (2005). Bullying and symptoms among school-aged children: International comparative cross sectional study in 28 countries. *European Journal of Public Health, 15,* 128–132.

Espelage, D.L., & Holt, M.K. (2007). Dating violence & sexual harassment across the bully-victim continuum among middle and high school students. *Journal of Youth and Adolescence, 36,* 799–811.

Espelage, D.L., Bosworth, K., & Simon, T.R. (2000). Examining the social context of bullying behaviors in early adolescence. *Journal of Counseling and Development, 78,* 326–333.

Espelage, D.L., Holt, M.K., & Henkel, R. (2003). Examination of peer-group contextual effects on aggression during early adolescence. *Child Development, 74,* 205–220.

Fineran, S. (2002). Sexual harassment between same-sex peers: Intersection of mental health, homophobia, and sexual violence in schools. *Social Work, 47,* 65–74.

Finkelhor, D., Mitchell, K.J., & Wolak, J. (2000). *Online victimization: A report on the nation's youth.* Alexandria, VA: National Center for Missing & Exploited Children.

Fox, C.L., & Boulton, M.J. (2005). The social skills problems of victims of bullying: Self, peer and teacher perceptions. *British Journal of Educational Psychology, 75,* 313–328.

Harris Interactive (2006, July). Online methodology. Retrieved May 1, 2009, from www.harrisinteractive.com/partner/methodology.asp.

Harris Interactive (2007, March). November 2006 youth query methodology report. Retrieved May 1, 2009, from www.isolutions4kids.org/youthquery.

Hawker, D.S., & Boulton, M.J. (2000). Twenty years' research on peer victimization and psychosocial malad-justment: A meta-analytic review of cross-sectional studies. *Journal of Child Psychological Psychiatry, 41,* 441–455.

Hoover, J.H., & Hazler, R.J. (1994). Bullies and victims. *Elementary School Guidance and Counseling, 25,* 212–220.

Juvonen, J., Nishina, A., & Graham, S. (2000). Self-views versus peer perceptions of victim status among early adolescents. In J. Juvonen & S. Graham (Eds.), *Peer harassment in schools: The plight of the vulnerable and victimized* (pp. 105–124). New York, NY: The Guilford Press.

Kaltiala-Heino, R., Rimpelä, M., Rantanen, P., & Rimpelä, A. (2000). Bullying at school: An indicator of adolescents at risk for mental disorders. *Journal of Adolescence, 23,* 661–674.

Kann, K.L., Warren, C.W., Harris, W.A., Collins, J., Douglas, K.A., & Collins, M.E. (1995). *Youth risk behavior surveillance.* Atlanta, GA: Centers for Disease Control and Prevention.

Lenhart, A., Arafeh, S., Smith, A., & Macgill, A.R. (2008). *Writing, technology, and teens.* Washington, DC: The National Commission on Writing, Pew Internet and American Life Project.

Nansel, T.R., Haynie, D.L., & Simons-Morton, B.G. (2003). The association of bullying and victimization with middle school adjustment. *Journal of Applied School Psychology, 19,* 45–61.

Nansel, T.R., Overpeck, M., Pilla, R.S., Ruan, W.J., Simons-Morton, B., & Scheidt, P. (2001). Bullying behaviors among U.S. youth: Prevalence and association with psychosocial adjustment. *The Journal of the American Medical Association, 285,* 2094–2100.

Olweus, D. (1995). Bullying or peer abuse in school: Intervention and prevention. In G. Davies, & S. Lloyd-Bostock (Eds.), *Psychology, law, and criminal justice: International developments in research and practice* (pp. 248–266). Oxford, UK: Walter De Gruyter.

Paul, J.J., & Cillessen, A.H.N. (2003). Dynamics and peer victimization in early adolescence: Results from a four-year longitudinal study. *Journal of Applied School Psychology, 19,* 25–43.

Rodkin, P.C., & Wilson, T. (2007). Aggression and adaptation: Psychological record, educational promise. In P. Hawley, T.D. Little, & P.C. Rodkin (Eds.). *Aggression and adaptation: The bright side to bad behavior* (pp. 233–265). Mahwah, NJ: Erlbaum.

Smith, J.D., Schneider, B.H., Smith, P.K., & Ananiadou, K. (2004). The effectiveness of whole-school antibullying programs: A synthesis of evaluation research. *School Psychology Review, 33,* 547–560.

Smith, P.K. (2007) Why has aggression been thought of as maladaptive? In P. Hawley, T.D. Little, & P.C. Rodkin (Eds.), *Aggression and adaptation: The bright side to bad behavior* (pp. 85–106). Mahwah, NJ: Erlbaum.

Sourander, A., Helstelä, L., Helenius, H., & Piha, J. (2000). Persistence of bullying from childhood to adolescence: A longitudinal 8-year follow-up study. *Child Abuse & Neglect, 24,* 873–881.

StataCorp. (2006). *Stata Statistical Software: Release 9.* College Station, TX: StataCorp LP.

Stein, N. (1995). Sexual harassment in K-12 schools: The public performance of gendered violence. *Harvard Educational Review, 65,* 145–162.

Stein, N. (1999). *Classrooms and courtrooms: Facing sexual harassment in K-12 schools.* New York, NY: Teacher's College Press.

Stein, N. (2005). A rising pandemic of sexual violence in elementary and secondary schools: Locating a secret problem. *Duke Journal of Gender Law and Policy, 12,* 33–52.

Thompson, D., Whitney, I., & Smith, P.K. (1994). Bullying of children with special needs in mainstream schools. *Support for Learning, 9,* 103–106.

Walker, H.M., Ramsey, E., & Gresham, F. M. (2004). *Antisocial behavior in school: Evidence-based practices* (2nd ed.). Belmont, CA: Thomson & Wadsworth.

Wolak, J., Mitchell, K.J., & Finkelhor, D. (2006). *Online victimization of youth: 5 years later.* Alexandria, VA: National Center for Missing & Exploited Children.

Ybarra, M.L., & Mitchell, K.J. (2004). Youth engaging in online harassment: Associations with caregiver-child relationships, Internet use, and personal characteristics. *Journal of Adolescence, 27,* 319–336.

Ybarra, M.L., Diener-West, M., & Leaf, P. (2007). Examining the overlap in Internet harassment and school bullying: Implications for school intervention. *Journal of Adolescent Health, 41,* S42–S52.

Ybarra, M.L., Espelage, D.L., & Mitchell, K.J. (2007). The co-occurrence of internet harassment and unwanted sexual solicitation victimization and perpetration: Associations with psychosocial indicators. *Journal of Adolescent Health, 41,* S31–S41.

Ybarra, M.L., Mitchell, K.J., Wolak, J., & Finkelhor, D. (2006). Examining characteristics and associated distress related to Internet harassment: Findings from the Second Youth Internet Safety Survey. *Pediatrics, 118,* e.1169–e1177.

Part II
Peer Characteristics Associated With Bullying

7

TEACHING PRACTICES, CLASSROOM PEER ECOLOGIES, AND BULLYING BEHAVIORS AMONG SCHOOLCHILDREN

PHILIP C. RODKIN AND SCOTT D. GEST

We are slowly coming to realize that all education is group work. Education of children and adults, education in families and schools never deals with the individual on the one hand and the subject to be taught on the other. It is common knowledge that the success of a teacher of French depends as much on the social atmosphere he (or she) creates as on his (or her) mastering the French language or the laws of learning. Probably in no country have the schools been as much aware of the importance of group management for education as in the United States. Still, the psychologist who has spent an immense amount of time studying learning curves has left the problems of social management in education almost entirely to practitioners, who is forced to base their procedures on the primitive method of trial and error, or upon a peculiar mix of philosophy and instinct.

(Lewin, 1943, p. 115)

Kurt Lewin, among the greatest of 20th century scholars of social development, analyzed every educational setting from the perspective of the child as a potential opportunity and challenge, as a motivating or inhibiting social current. In the epigraph above, Lewin portrays that current as a *social atmosphere* critical to student success. How might teachers, he asks, direct the social atmosphere of their classrooms toward learning and away from disruption? The situation Lewin describes still holds true today: educational practitioners who strive to cultivate a positive social atmosphere rely as much on "trial and error" or "philosophy and instinct" as on scientifically evaluated practices. A goal of our current research is to help change this state of affairs by developing new ways of thinking about and practicing "social management in education."

In this chapter, we summarize the origins of the framework that guides our current research, then we review theories and practices that have informed that framework. Our current research focuses primarily on elementary classrooms and so we refer primarily to classrooms and individual teachers throughout, but many aspects of our framework could be applied to middle or junior high schools and to the collective teaching faculty in those settings.

TEACHING PRACTICES, PEER ECOLOGIES AND YOUTH OUTCOMES

We approach the problem of social management in education through a developmental–contextual perspective on peer ecologies. In doing so, we have found it useful to attempt to integrate decades of theorizing about classroom social management (e.g., Farmer, Farmer, Estell, & Hutchins, 2007; Gronlund, 1959) with social network modeling procedures that map dynamic social structures and interpersonal connections among students (Gest, Davidson, Rulison, Moody, & Welsh, 2007; Hanish & Rodkin, 2007). In our own empirical research, we have examined how classroom peer ecologies relate to aggression and bullying, achievement, and school relatedness, and we have begun to explore teacher practices that may shape peer ecologies toward healthy, quality classroom environments. Two questions guide this work:

1. *What features of classroom peer ecologies are associated with positive youth outcomes?* We focus on two aspects of the peer ecology. *Social status* dynamics involve the prominence of status hierarchies and the behavioral correlates of acceptance and popularity. *Social network* dynamics include the overall tight-knittedness of the classroom and the distinctiveness and behavioral basis of children's peer group affiliations.
2. *What teaching practices are associated with positive classroom peer ecologies and youth outcomes?* We consider broad dimensions of classroom quality that are assessed by existing measures together with specific network-related teaching practices that may have particular relevance to how peer ecologies take shape and stabilize over the school year.

Lewin (1943) understood that teachers had the opportunity and the responsibility to optimize children's peer ecologies. Early studies of *sociometry,* or the science of the measurement of social relationships, focused creatively on how to quantify properties of peer social ecologies, relate these properties to educational success and failure, and build up a truly *social,* action-oriented theory of child social development (Rappaport, 1979). Unfortunately, the theoretical and applied ambitions of this early work did not yield a rigorous literature. Computational limitations precluded large-scale research on quantitative variations in the features of classroom peer ecologies; and logistical and political challenges (e.g., consent and assent procedures) made it difficult for practitioners to integrate sociometry into routine practice. By the 1960s, as attention turned to Sputnik and Piaget and away from child social development, and as the field of social network analysis fell into a "dark age" (Freeman, 2004), theory and measurement on classroom social systems declined.

But the pendulum is shifting. There is renewed emphasis on the variety of children's interpersonal relationships, with particular attention to group influence and social power, and to the implications of these dynamics for classroom management (Farmer, 2000). There is exciting potential in a new generation of social network methodologies to advance measurement and theory of classroom social settings (e.g., Espelage, Green, & Wasserman, 2007; Hanish, Martin, Fabes, & Barcelo, 2008; Veenstra et. al, 2007). The time is right for acquiring the concepts and quantitative tools necessary for the developmental, contextual framing of children's academic and social life in school (Hanish & Rodkin, 2007).

We find it useful to distinguish between four aspects of an educational setting such as

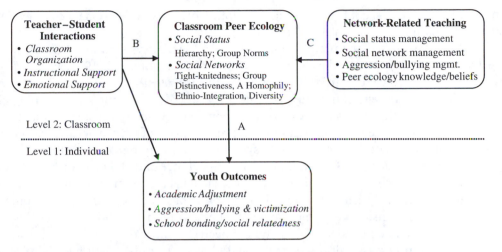

Figure 7.1 Conceptual model of teaching practices, classroom peer ecologies, and youth outcomes.

the classroom: (1) general aspects of teacher–student interaction; (2) aspects of teaching that focus specifically on the peer social network; (3) structural features and dynamics of the peer ecology; and (4) the youth outcomes of concern to practitioners. The inter-relations among these are illustrated in Figure 7.1. We view the classroom peer ecology, comprising social status and social network features, as proximal determinants of youth outcomes (Path A). In turn, classroom peer ecologies are shaped partly by general teaching practices (Path B) and partly by network-related teaching practices (Path C). Teacher practices may also affect youth outcomes directly (Path D), above and beyond the effects that may be mediated via the peer ecology (Path BàA).

What characterizes a classroom peer ecology that promotes positive youth outcomes? Our view is that peer ecologies characterized by more egalitarian (vs. highly stratified) status hierarchies, strong group norms in support of academic achievement and proso-cial behavior, tightly knit positive social ties, little aggression-based homophily (i.e., social clustering of aggressive students), and diverse, ethnically integrated peer relation-ships will foster greater academic adjustment, less aggression and peer victimization, and deeper feelings of school relatedness (Path A). We also believe that indicators of class-room teaching quality will predict improved youth outcomes in part due to their positive impact on the peer ecology (Path BàA). Finally, we expect that teachers who demonstrate more intentional management of social status and social networks, who actively address aggression and bullying, and who have more accurate knowledge of the peer ecology in their classroom will have a more positive peer ecology (Path CàA), even after taking account of overall teaching quality. In these cases, we are interested in whether youth succeed in the core developmental tasks of school adjustment: rule-abiding (as opposed to aggressive-disruptive) conduct, academic achievement, and positive peer relationships (Masten et. al, 1995). We are interested in youth behaviors and subjective experiences that may mediate the links between teaching practices and these core tasks.

FEATURES OF PEER ECOLOGIES

The peer ecology framework (Rodkin, 2004; Rodkin & Fischer, 2003; Rodkin & Hodges, 2003; Rodkin & Karimpour, 2008; Rodkin & Roisman, 2010) builds upon Lewin's (1943) and Bronfenbrenner's (1944, 1979, 1996) description of multileveled social ecologies. We take three main lessons from Bronfenbrenner's work.

The first lesson is that microsystems are critical. Microsystems are "the ultimate mechanism through which development occurs" (Bronfenbrenner, 1996, p. xv). Peer microsystems involve children interacting with, influencing, and socializing one another. More distal environmental systems are also part of a child's total ecological environment, but the effects of these distal systems are typically weaker, mediated by the microsystem (as Lewin assumed in his representations of *psychological space*), and more difficult to detect than for proximal systems (e.g., Swearer et al., 2006).

In Bronfenbrenner's (1979) formulation, the importance of distal environmental systems was not primarily in terms of direct, unmediated influence on individual behavior, but rather as settings which, when linked to other settings, show enduring developmental growth across transitions of time and place. The classroom (or school) peer ecology is thus a microsystem, embedded within and connected to more distal ecological systems (e.g., family, community, culture, occupational), but a naturally existing social unit in and of itself.

The second lesson, as Lewin intimates in the epigraph, is that poorly regulated peer ecologies endanger developmental growth. Bronfenbrenner (1979) was clear that peer microsystems were prone to problem behavior. In the context of the setting of day care (see also Rodkin & Roisman, 2010), Hypothesis 23 of *The Ecology of Human Development* is that:

> Children who from an early age are cared for in group settings for most of the day are more likely to engage in egocentric, aggressive, and antisocial behavior both during the preschool years and through later childhood into adolescence. The observed effect is particularly marked for boys. It is mediated through the children's peer group and is most likely to occur in societies that encourage the expression of individualism, aggression, and independence in children's groups, especially by boys.(p. 203)

Mesosystemic processes document that the developmental sequelae of accumulated peer group process within educational settings often narrows future life opportunities:

> [T]he school has become over the past two decades … one of the most potent breeding grounds of alienation in American society … [underlying] … the progressive decline observed in achievement test scores … rising rates of homicide, suicide, drug use, and delinquency for children of school age. (p. 231)

Bronfenbrenner (1979, p. 284) even finds that peer group processes hinder resilience in his discussion of macrosystemic forces in Elder's (1975) *Children of the Great Depression*:

> [I]ncreased exposure to peer group influences, as an indirect effect of growing up in the Depression from early childhood, may have contributed to the impaired educational, vocational, and psychological development exhibited by the adult males.

Thus, guiding children toward a positive social atmosphere is no small feat and may have short- and long-term developmental effects for the child. The nature of this guidance by teachers and other school professionals is what Lewin (1943) wrote was being left to "trial and error."

To analyze the role of teachers in peer social ecologies, we take a third lesson from Bronfenbrenner, namely that looking within settings is at least as critical as looking across settings. According to Bronfenbrenner (1979, chs. 3–5), the critical elements of a setting include the intentional, durable, molar activities that occur within it, its dyadic and social network structure, and the roles and status relations operating within the setting. For example, teachers are not themselves part of the peer ecology (as teachers are not "peers"), but teachers play a critical, unique role in the classroom microsystem, acting as bridging agents to other settings and other adults that impact the child's development. Our expectation is that teachers impact and can be impacted by the peer ecologies of their classrooms as they attempt to guide students toward learning and successful adjustment.

The peer ecological approach that we adopt complements similar socio-ecological approaches to bullying by Swearer, Espelage, and colleagues (Swearer & Espelage, 2004; Swearer et al., 2006). The main theoretical distinction is possibly that while the Swearer and Espelage model situate bullying "across individual, family, peer, school, and community contexts" (Swearer & Espelage, 2004, p. 1), the peer ecological model outlined here concentrates on the molar activities (e.g., child bullying, teacher emotional support), interpersonal roles, and social structures within the microsystemic setting of the elementary classroom. In particular, we focus on aggression and bullying behaviors along two dimensions of classroom peer ecologies: (1) a vertical dimension of *social status*, representing power and dominance relations among children; and (2) a horizontal dimension of *social networks*, representing patterns of positive (e.g., friendships, affiliations) and negative (e.g., antipathies, bully-victim) peer relationships.

To understand these features of the peer ecology, it is important to understand how information about peer ecologies is collected. All measures of the peer ecology described in this chapter are built upon children's reports of their relationships with or sentiments toward other specific children in the setting. For example, a child may be asked to identify all of her friends in the classroom (or school); or to identify classmates whom she "likes most" or "likes least." In addition, there are substantial differences in peer group identification procedures depending upon whether peer groups are constructed out of friendship versus affiliative nominations (i.e., "who is your friend?" as opposed to "who do you hang out together a lot with?") and whether children provide self-reports of their own relationships, or in addition give multi-informant reports of relationships in which they are not personally involved (Gest, Moody, & Rulison, 2007; Rodkin & Ahn, 2009). Once measurement issues are settled, when all (or nearly all) children in a setting provide responses to sociometric questions, the result is a dataset that summarizes a complex social network of peer relationships (or sentiments). The field of social network analysis (Wasserman & Faust, 1994) provides sophisticated means of quantifying different features of these networks for developmental analysis (see Cillessen & Borch, 2008).

Social Status

The vertical structure of peer ecologies is social status. Social status includes components of *likeability* and *popularity* that are differentially related to children's academic and behavioral adjustment (Cillessen & Mayeux, 2007). Being widely liked (i.e., named as "liked most") is related to prosocial behavior, but Rodkin, Farmer, Pearl, and Van Acker (2000) found that some children who are *perceived by classmates* to be popular fit a "model" profile (cool, athletic, leaders, cooperative, studious, not shy, and non-aggressive) while others fit a "tough" profile (cool, athletic, and antisocial). Being considered a friend by many peers is yet another operationalization of social status. Just as individual children within a classroom can differ in social status, individual class-rooms can differ in how social status is organized. Specifically, classrooms can vary in the salience of *status hierarchies* and in *group norms* that are reflected in the behavioral correlates of high social status.

Status hierarchies and structural embeddedness. Social status is concentrated among a few youth in highly stratified classrooms but is more equally distributed in egalitarian classrooms. For example, Figure 7.2 illustrates friendship nominations among a group of children (Gest et al., 2007). In Figure 7.2a, each youth (circles) receives either three or four nominations (arrows directed at the youth), with the limited variability suggesting an egalitarian structure. In contrast, in Figure 7.2b the number of friendship nomina-tions received ranges from one to five, suggesting a more pronounced status hierarchy. It has long been thought that egalitarian or democratic peer ecologies are superior to those in which social capital is held by just a few (e.g., Sherif, 1956). For example, pro-moting egalitarian, democratic peer relationships is a focus of jigsaw and cooperative learning interventions (e.g., Aronson, Blaney, Stephin, Sikes & Snapp, 1978). Conversely, the Olweus (1993) definition of bullying requires a physical or psychological power (i.e., social status) differential between bullies and the children whom they harass.

The construct of *structural embeddedness* (Granovetter, 1985; Moody & White, 2003) is a promising candidate for examining the impact of classroom status hierarchies on bullying and victimization. Granovetter (1985) frames the problem of embeddedness using undersocialized and oversocialized conceptions of human action in economics. The undersocialized conception is a rational-actor model, with no role for social struc-ture and influence; the oversocialized conception is a socialist-structural model where, due to cultural and economic class norms and constraints, individual actors have few choices to make. There is an inherent analogy to education (see also Akerloff & Kranton, 2002; Coleman, 1961; Frank et. al, 2008), where the undersocialized conception is akin to the individual student "learning French" in a vacuum devoid of social context and relations, and the oversocialized conception is akin to deficit models where children are given up on, "with little hope of effecting a lasting, significant improvement" due to wholesale problems in their "immediate environments" (Bronfenbrenner, 1979, p. 290). Granovetter (1985, p. 490) introduces embeddedness to emphasize the "role of concrete personal relations and structures (or 'networks') of such relations in generating trust and discouraging malfeasance." Moody and White (2003) quantify embeddedness as one aspect of social solidarity or cohesion, constructing an algorithm to index highly embedded actors who are highly connected in the social network from less embedded actors who operate in near-isolation from the network. In a study described below by Ahn, Garandeau, and Rodkin (2010), we explore the implications of classroom-level embeddedness for group norms pertaining to bullying and peer victimization.

(a) Egalitarian   (b) Hierarchical

Figure 7.2 Status hierarchies: (a) egalitarian, (b) hierarchical peer ecologies.

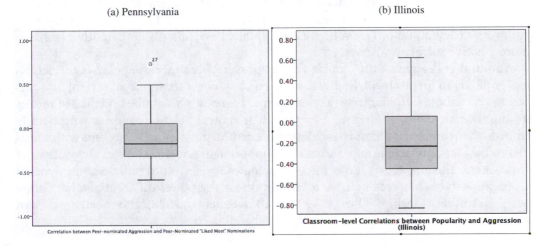

(a) Pennsylvania   (b) Illinois

Figure 7.3 Group norms. Note the broad range of within-classroom correlations between peer-rated aggression and being "liked most" in (a) Pennsylvania and (b) Illinois.

Group norms. Just as an individual's social status can be associated with either proso-cial or aggressive behavior (Rodkin et al., 2000), the norms of a peer ecology can be directed toward or away from bullying. In non-school youth settings, aggression is pop-ular in some groups but not in others (Wright, Giammarino & Parad, 1986), and the same appears to be true in school classrooms. Figure 7.3a illustrates the distribution of within-classroom correlations between teacher-rated aggression and peer nominations as "liked most" for 36 elementary classrooms in a small community in central Pennsyl-vania studied by Gest. Most classrooms have a negative correlation suggesting a norm against aggression, yet the correlations show wide variation, ranging from strongly neg-ative to moderately positive. Rodkin found a similarly large range of classroom-level norms regarding aggression in classrooms from small cities in Illinois (for details see Ahn et al., 2010; Rodkin, Wilson, & Ahn, 2007). This is significant as children in class-rooms where aggression is normative tend to become more aggressive themselves, even in future years (Dmitrieva, Steinberg, & Belsky, 2007; Thomas, Bierman, & Conduct Problems Prevention Research Group, 2006). Moreover, the social dynamics entailed in bully–victim relationships vary depending on whether interpersonal aggression occurs in the context of rejection by—or support from—children with high social status (Berger & Rodkin, 2009; Rodkin, Farmer, Pearl, & Van Acker, 2006).

A demonstration of the relationship between classroom social hierarchies and group norms favoring aggression was provided in our recent study of 42 classrooms nested within nine elementary schools in Midwest U.S. (Ahn et al., 2010). Although embeddedness can be calculated at the actor (or individual child) level, the construct also has meaning at the level of the setting (or classroom): classrooms vary accord-ing to whether they contain many or few embeddedness levels. Embeddedness lev-els ranged from two to eight across the 42 classrooms studied by Ahn and colleagues (2010). Following Moody and White's (2003) use of embeddedness to illustrate group hierarchy, Ahn and colleagues (2010) reasoned that classrooms with greater levels of embeddedness (e.g., eight) would be more hierarchical and less egalitarian than class-rooms with fewer embeddedness levels (e.g., two) because great variation exists within highly embedded classrooms with respect to children's integration in the classroom social network. Conversely, older experimental studies suggest that social networks with egalitarian structures have better group performance and morale across different age groups (Lewin, Lippitt, & White, 1939; Lippitt, 1939; Shaw, 1954), in other words, a more positive social atmosphere.

Ahn and colleagues (2010) found that aggressors were more popular (and victims less popular) in hierarchical, highly embedded classrooms than in egalitarian, low-embedded classrooms. In hierarchical classrooms, aggression might be an efficient means for highly embedded children to maintain their central position, and for peripherally embedded members to attempt to achieve more central positions. Classrooms with social hierarchies tend to have group norms that support aggressors and reject the victims of harassment. In sum, social status in peer ecologies is relevant to bully–victim dynamics because status hierarchies are a precondition for the power differentials that define bully–victim relationships (Olweus, 1993; Rodkin & Berger, 2008), and social norms can either inhibit or reinforce bullying behavior when it occurs.

Social Networks

Classrooms that are similar in the prominence of status hierarchies and in group norms can nonetheless differ in their social network dynamics. Classroom *social networks* have multiple types of social ties that can provide each child with a niche and social support (e.g., friendships, liking, "hanging around together"), but also with experiences of mutual dislike or enmity (Card & Hodges, 2007; Kindermann & Gest, 2009). Classroom social network dynamics can be described in terms of the overall tight-knittedness of the classroom and the distinctiveness and behavioral basis of subgroups. When students in a classroom come from diverse ethnic and racial backgrounds, classroom social networks can also be characterized by the degree of integrated social relationships as opposed to splits based on race and ethnicity.

Tight-knittedness. Tight-knittedness can be quantified in terms of the density, reciprocity, and transitivity of positive and negative social ties. For example, the two groups of seven individuals illustrated in Figure 7.4 differ strongly in tight-knittedness. The less tight-knit network in Figure 7.4b has a density of .45 (19 out of 42 possible friendship ties exist) compared to a density of .86 (36 out of 42 possible ties exist) for the more tight-knit network in Figure 7.4a. The two networks differ in the proportion of reciprocated friendship nominations (i.e., 15 out of 21 = .71 in Figure 7.4a vs. 4 out of 15 = .27 in Figure 7.4b). In the more tight-knit Figure 7.4a, friendship ties are also more transitive (i.e., if AB and BC are friends, then AC are friends). It has long been thought that tight-knit classrooms, with rich ties between children and many positive social relations, lead to better academic and behavioral outcomes, but rarely has this notion been put to empirical test (Roseth, Johnson, & Johnson, 2008). In the Ahn and colleagues (2010) study

(a) Tight-knit   (b) Loose-knit

Figure 7.4 Tight-knittedness: (a) tightly knit peer ecology, (b) loosely knit peer ecology.

(a) Highly distinct

(b) Not very distinct

Figure 7.5 Distinctiveness of subgroups: (a) highly distinctive peer subgroups, (b) not very distinctive peer subgroups.

showing that bullies were most popular in highly embedded, hierarchical classrooms, effects were strongest in classrooms that were also dense, possibly because pathways of communication and influence to transmit behavioral norms are numerous and varied in these classroom social networks.

Subgroup distinctiveness. Subgroups of peers deserve special mention as a unit of social structure. These informal social groups are typically segregated by gender (Gest et al., 2007) and sometimes ethnicity (Garandeau, Wilson, & Rodkin, 2010; Rodkin et al., 2007), and are the most immediate context of children's perceptions and behaviors. Subgroups can be identified in virtually all peer settings containing more than a few youth, but there are variations in the extent to which these subgroups or cliques represent distinct, non-overlapping social worlds. For example, Figure 7.5 illustrates friendship patterns among subgroups of girls within the same classroom whom peers identified as "hanging around together a lot." In Figure 7.5a, there was only one instance of a friendship bridging these subgroups, which are easily distinguished. In contrast, it is difficult to discern the two groups in Figure 7.5b because friendships are virtually as common between as within the two groups. Traditionally, educational researchers have interpreted highly distinct subgroups as representing "fault lines" in the classroom social fabric that should be minimized (Gronlund, 1959), and more general perspectives on social networks indicate that ties between otherwise disconnected groups can be valuable (Granovetter, 1972), but this issue has not been studied extensively outside the context of ethnic segregation.

Homophily and behavioral bases of subgroups. Classrooms vary in the degree to which relationships are organized around key behaviors such as achievement or aggression (Cairns, Cairns, Neckermann, Gest & Gariépy, 1988; Farmer, Estell, Bishop, O'Neal, & Cairns, 2003). The predominant behaviors within a subgroup affect the individual outcomes of its members for diverse behaviors including aggression (Cairns et al., 1988; Ellis & Zarbatany, 2007; Espelage, Holt & Henkel, 2003; Rodkin et al., 2006), deviant behavior (Fergusson, Vitaro, Wanner, & Brendgen, 2007), and academic engagement and motivation (Ellis & Zarbatany, 2007; Kindermann, 2007; Ryan, 2001). There is broad consensus that when subgroups coalesce around aggression and bullying behaviors, there can be serious threats to classroom behavior management (Farmer, 2000; Gronlund, 1959) and group dynamics of bullying (Salmavalli, 2001). At the same time, aggressive children engage their peer ecology at higher rates than non-aggressive children, and interact with aggressive and non-aggressive children alike (Farmer et al., 2002; Pepler, Craig, & Roberts, 1998).

Ethnic integration and diversity. The integrated elementary school stands as one of our proudest and most hard-won achievements. Yet true integration calls for more than just a diverse collection of children in the same building, but also for *social* integration. An ideal scenario is when children value peers who have positive cross-ethnic relationships and limited negative cross-ethnic relationships. Children with integrated social relationships may be particularly well adjusted, with high social status and reputations as leaders (Kawabata & Crick, 2008; Lease & Blake, 2005). Moreover, diverse schools may offer psychological benefits to students including increased feelings of safety and social satisfaction, and less bullying and loneliness (Juvonen, Nishina, & Graham, 2006).

TEACHER INFLUENCE ON THE PEER ECOLOGY

Teachers play a central role in the organization of educational settings and in doing so they constrain the peer ecologies that develop within them. We distinguish between teacher influence on peer ecologies that derives from general patterns of *teacher–student interactions* and teachers' direct efforts to understand and exert influence on peer ecologies. As illustrated in Figure 7.1, we believe that general teacher–student interactions may be related to a broad range of youth outcomes, partly through their impact on the peer ecology (Path B→A), but perhaps primarily through direct processes (Path D). In contrast, teachers' explicit attempts to understand and influence the peer ecology, which we call network-related teaching, affect youth outcomes primarily through their impact on the peer ecology (Path C→A).

General Teacher–Student Interactions

Recent approaches to assessing general classroom quality are based on the premise that observable teacher–student interactions are the key proximal influence on youth outcomes, in contrast to more distal factors such as teacher characteristics (e.g., experience) or classroom features (e.g., curriculum). For example, the Classroom Assessment Scoring System (CLASS; Pianta, La Paro, & Hamre, 2006) assesses three broad dimensions that represent a best-practices synthesis of important qualities of teacher–student interaction. *Classroom Organization* refers to "the organization and management of students' behavior, time and attention" (Pianta et al., 2006, p. 3): it encompasses monitoring, preventing and redirecting student behavior; establishing clear and efficient routines; and facilitating varied and effective learning activities. *Instructional Support* entails leading instructional discussions focused on higher-order thinking, providing feedback that extends student learning, and facilitating and encouraging new vocabulary and grammar. Finally, *Emotional Support* is defined by: a positive emotional connection with students; the absence of anger, hostility or aggression toward students; responsivity to student needs; and regard for student perspectives. Studies of elementary classrooms indicate that patterns of Instructional and Emotional Support predict improved academic outcomes (Hamre & Pianta, 2001; Pianta, Belsky, Vandergrift, Houts, & Morrison, 2008). However, studies have not generally tested whether associations with youth outcomes might be mediated by changes in the peer ecology (i.e., Path B→A). General patterns of teacher–student interaction may affect student outcomes—including bullying and peer harassment—in part through the peer ecology.

TRANSLATING RESEARCH INTO PRACTICE WITH NETWORK-RELATED TEACHING: IMPLICATIONS FOR BULLYING PREVENTION AND INTERVENTION PROGRAMS

Examining bullying in schools from an ecological framework is directly linked to intervention and practice (Pepler, Craig, & O'Connell, 2001). The notion that teachers can and should set out to shape the peer ecology of their classrooms was at the heart of mid-century sociometric research (Gronlund, 1959). This theme was picked up with experimental rigor with the evaluation of cooperative learning techniques such as the jigsaw classroom (Aronson et al., 1978), which is based on a theory of contact that deals directly with peer ecologies via *equal social status between groups* and *subgroup interconnections* due to shared goals (Allport, 1954; Sherif, 1956). Recent efforts to shape the peer ecology have been in the context of systematic, school-wide interventions (e.g., Battistich, Schaps, Watson, & Solomon, 1996). Farmer proposes three categories of network-based teaching strategies that may have particular relevance for the peer ecology (Path C): social status management; social network management; and active management of aggression and bullying (Farmer et al., 2007). We also consider the potential importance of teachers' knowledge and beliefs about the peer ecology in their classroom.

Social status management. Classroom social status patterns can be altered with judicious teacher involvement. Gronlund (1959) proposed that teachers should identify low-status children and make systematic efforts to assign them desirable classroom roles that provide public recognition and afford status. Cohen and Lotan (1995) conducted a field experiment in which teachers gave "status treatments" to students who were performing poorly by stressing their multiple abilities and publicly praising their performance during times of success: these status treatments led to more equal-status interaction between students as measured by sociometric tabulations of friendship. Farmer (2000) emphasizes the importance of teachers seeking to avoid extreme status hierarchies by providing opportunities and recognition for diverse curricular and extracurricular accomplishments, making special efforts to provide low-status students with opportunities to occupy leadership positions and to interact with higher-status classmates.

Social network management. Carefully constructed cooperative learning groups can increase classroom social integration, but other types of groupings may affect social networks in ways that teachers do not necessarily plan or anticipate. For example, patterns of friendship formation and dissolution over a school year are partly attributable to the composition of instructional reading groups; other types of groups arranged by teachers are likely to have similar effects (Hallinan & Smith, 1989). Teachers should recognize that their choices of when and how to organize classroom groups can be a powerful tool for managing disruptive behavior (e.g., diversifying the affiliation patterns of a disruptive clique) and promoting social integration.

Management of aggression and bullying. The management of aggression is a component of general behavior management, but this topic warrants special attention since aggression plays a salient role in social status and social network dynamics. Teachers vary widely in whether they acknowledge peer victimization and whether or not they intervene (Frey, Jones, Hirschstein, & Edstrom, this volume; Frey, Hirschstein, Edstrom, & Snell, 2009; Pellegrini, 2002). Children use a wide range of aggressive behaviors (physical, verbal, relational) to jockey for power over one another and to establish and maintain status in prominent cliques. Key issues in managing these dynamics are monitoring students during informal periods of the day, responding to the variety of aggressive strategies that youth use, implementing clear and consistent social consequences when incidents arise (Farmer, 2000; Farmer et al., 2007), changing normative student beliefs that support bullying, and addressing children's social-emotional skills (Frey et al., 2009; Zins, Elias, & Maher, 2007). For example, in a field experimental evaluation of the Steps to Respect program to reduce school bullying in 3rd to 5th grade classrooms, Frey and colleagues (2009) reported that successful teacher management strategies, such as removing social support for being a bystander to peer victimization, reduced bullying on the playground over a two-year period.

Social network knowledge. Teachers vary widely in their understanding of the peer ecology of their classrooms. Gest (2006) examined agreement between teachers and their 1st, 3rd, and 5th grade students on reports of friendship and peer group affiliations. Some teachers had only chance levels of agreement whereas others were closely in tune with peer reports. Pearl, Leung, Van Acker, Farmer, and Rodkin (2007) found that while teachers reliably identified the most popular and salient classroom groups, less popular groups were systematically overlooked.

Educators' relative lack of understanding of classroom peer ecologies can exacerbate peer aggression and bullying (Olweus, 1993; Mulvey & Cauffman, 2001). Teachers often seem unaware of aggression among their students, or are overwhelmed by its prevalence. Teachers who try to stamp out bullying without an appreciation of their classroom peer ecologies may invite resistance that worsens existing problems (McFarland, 2001). In the case of peer sexual harassment or boys who bully girls, the problem of teacher awareness is still more problematic (Berger & Rodkin, 2009; Orpinas & Horne, 2006; Pellegrini, 2002; Rodkin & Fischer, 2003). Teachers should be well informed about the social status and social network dynamics operating among their students for network-related teaching strategies to be maximally effective.

Beliefs and norms regarding aggression and bullying. Teachers vary in classroom management skills that help shape the structure and norms of peer ecologies. Chang (2003) found that when teachers were warm and caring, children were less rejecting of aggressive peers than when teachers had very negative beliefs about aggression. However, when teachers had negative beliefs about aggression, aggressive students perceived themselves as socially efficacious. Chang's (2003) findings suggest that teachers' best efforts at quashing aggression can unwittingly open the way for alternative authority structures conducive to the emergence of high-status aggressors. Accurate understanding of a peer ecology is the platform from which intelligent decisions can be made about restructuring children's groups, encouraging feasible social relationships, and anticipating possible conflict (see also Frey et al., this volume).

Aside from Frey and colleagues (2009), field intervention work on bullying may be in a similar state to research on prejudice reduction, where Paluck and Green (2009, p. 357) conclude that very little research "supports internally valid inferences and externally valid generalization." Within this frame, some of the more promising techniques for teaching intergroup tolerance are methods based on social interdependence theory, such as jigsaw and other cooperative learning techniques, that consider the peer ecological structure of children's relationships. Cooperative goal structures, in which children help one another, share resources, and act in trustworthy ways, promote school achievement and positive peer relations (Roseth et al., 2008). A focus on how teachers can scaffold the emergence of a positive classroom peer ecology may increase the likelihood that cooperative goal structures can take hold. On this score, it is noteworthy that Granovetter's (1985) formulation of structural embeddedness concerned how *economic trust* is produced by specific, temporally ongoing relationships, as opposed to broad institutional arrangements or some generalized moral sense. The educational implication is that omnibus school policies (i.e., "institutional arrangements") and pronouncements (i.e., "generalized moral sense") are best complemented by an understanding of how knowledge and attitudes "penetrate irregularly and in differing degrees ... [through] the details of social structure" in educational life (Granovetter, 1985, pp. 491, 493), namely, peer social ecologies.

Socioemotional learning standards, which encourage children to develop self-awareness and self-management skills, use these skills to establish and maintain positive relationships, and demonstrate decision-making skills and responsible behaviors (O'Brien, Resnik, & Collaborative for Academic, Social, and Emotional Learning, 2009), are strong complements to the ecological approach adopted here (e.g., Zins et al., 2007). In some settings it is difficult for teachers to stay abreast of changing peer dynamics that are not typically apparent to adults (Berger, Karimpour, & Rodkin, 2008; Frey et al., this volume; Rodkin & Karimpour, 2008). We have found that teachers greatly appreciate feedback that is based upon social network data from the aggregate perspective of their students. Teachers and administrators tell us that it would be highly useful to have their student support personnel periodically conduct such assessments, as was done in years past, and as is done currently with socioemotional learning standards. Accordingly, as we identify key teaching practices and classroom social dynamics, we will disseminate these results not just to scholars, but also to teachers and school support personnel as a component of bullying-reduction activities throughout North American schools. To paraphrase the apt conclusions of Paluck and Green (2009, p. 359), future progress in research on bullying lies along the path that Lewin suggested over 60 years ago: "hypothesis generation through field observation, and intervention testing with parallel laboratory and field experiments." Lewin's path is the high road that leads away from the hapharzard mix of ideology and instinct that bedevils social management in education.

REFERENCES

Ahn, H-J., Garandeau, C.F., & Rodkin, P.C. (2010). Effects of classroom embeddedness and density on the social status of aggressive and victimized children. *Journal of Early Adolescence, 30*, 76–101.

Akerlof, G.A., & Kranton, R.E. (2002). Identity and schooling: Some lessons for the economics of education. *Journal of Economic Literature, 40*, 1167–1201.

Allport, G.A. (1954). *The nature of prejudice*. Garden City, NJ: Addison-Wesley.

Aronson, E., Blaney, N., Stephin, C., Sikes, J., & Snapp, M. (1978). *The jigsaw classroom*. Beverly Hills, CA: Sage.

Battistich, V., Schaps, E., Watson, M., & Solomon, D. (1996). Prevention effects of the Child Development Project: Early findings from an ongoing multisite demonstration trial. *Journal of Adolescent Research, 11*, 12–35.

Berger, C., & Rodkin, P.C. (2009). Male and female victims of male bullies: Social status differences by gender and informant source. *Sex Roles, 61*, 72–84.

Berger, C., Karimpour, R., & Rodkin, P.C. (2008). Bullies and victims at school: Perspectives and strategies for primary prevention. In T.W. Miller (Ed.), *School violence and primary prevention* (pp. 287–314). New York, NY: Springer.

Bronfenbrenner, U. (1944). A constant frame of reference for sociometric research: II. Experiment and inference. *Sociometry, 7*, 40–75.

Bronfenbrenner, U. (1979). *The ecology of human development: Experiments by nature and design*. Cambridge, MA: Harvard University Press.

Bronfenbrenner, U. (1996). Foreword. In R.B. Cairns, G.H. Elder Jr., & E.J. Costello (Eds.), *Developmental science* (pp. ix–xvii). New York, NY: Cambridge University Press.

Cairns, R.B., Cairns, B.D., Neckerman, H.J., Gest, S.D., & Gariépy, J-L. (1988). Social networks and aggressive behavior: Peer support or peer rejection? *Developmental Psychology, 24*, 815–823.

Card, N.A., & Hodges, E.V.E. (2007). Victimization within mutually antipathetic peer relationships. *Social Development, 16*, 479–496.

Chang, L. (2003). Variable effects of children's aggression, social withdrawal, and prosocial leadership as functions of teacher beliefs and behaviors. *Child Development, 74*, 535–548.

Cillessen, A.H.N., & Borch, C. (2008). Analyzing social networks in adolescence. In N. Card, J. Selig, & T.D. Little (Eds.), *Modeling dyadic and interdependent data in the developmental and behavioral sciences* (pp. 61–86). New York, NY: Routledge.

Cillessen, A.H.N., & Mayeux, L. (2007). Variations in the association between aggression and social status: Theoretical and empirical perspectives. In P.H. Hawley, T.D. Little, & P.C. Rodkin (Eds.), *Aggression and adaptation: The bright side to bad behavior* (pp. 135–156). Mahwah, NJ: Erlbaum.

Cohen, E.G., & Lotan, R.A. (1995). Producing equal-status interaction in the heterogeneous classroom. *American Educational Research Journal, 32*, 99–120.

Coleman, J.S. (1961). *The adolescent society: The social life of the teenager and its impact on education.* Glencoe, IL: Free Press.

Dmitrieva, J., Steinberg, L., & Belsky, J. (2007). Child-care history, classroom composition, and children's functioning in kindergarten. *Psychological Science, 18*, 1032–1039.

Elder, G.H., Jr. (1975). *Children of the Great Depression.* Chicago: University of Chicago Press.

Ellis, W., & Zarbatany, L. (2007). Peer group status as a moderator of group influence on children's deviant, aggressive, and prosocial behavior. *Child Development, 78*, 1240–1254.

Espelage, D.L., Green, H.D., Jr., & Wasserman, S. (2007). Statistical analysis of friendship patterns and bullying behaviors among youth. In P.C. Rodkin & L.D. Hanish (Eds.), *Social network analysis and children's peer relationships* (pp. 61–75). San Francisco: Jossey Bass.

Espelage, D.L., Holt, M.K., & Henkel, R.R. (2003). Examination of peer-group contextual effects on aggression during early adolescence. *Child Development, 74*, 205–220.

Farmer, T.W. (2000). Social dynamics of aggressive and disruptive behavior in school: Implications for behavior consultation. *Journal of Educational and Psychological Consultation, 11*, 299–322.

Farmer, T.W., Farmer, E.M.Z., Estell, D. & Hutchins, B.C. (2007). The developmental dynamics of aggression and the prevention of school violence. *Journal of Emotional and Behavioral Disorders, 15*, 197–208.

Farmer, T.W., Estell, D.B., Bishop, J.L., O'Neal, K., & Cairns, B.D. (2003). Rejected bullies or popular leaders? The social relations of aggressive subtypes of rural African American early adolescents. *Developmental Psychology, 39*, 992–1004.

Farmer, T.W., Leung, M.-C., Pearl, R., Rodkin, P.C., Cadwallader, T.W., & Van Acker, R. (2002). Deviant or diverse peer groups? The peer affiliations of aggressive elementary students. *Journal of Educational Psychology, 94*, 611–620.

Fergusson, D.M., Vitaro, F., Wanner, B., & Brendgen, M. (2007). Protective and compensatory factors mitigating the influence of deviant friends on delinquent behaviours during early adolescence. *Journal of Adolescence, 30*, 2–19.

Frank, K.A., Muller, C., Schiller, K.S., Riegle-Crub, C., Mueller, A.S., Crosnoe, R., & Pearson, J. (2008). The social dynamics of mathematics coursetaking in high school. *American Journal of Sociology, 113*, 1645–1696.

Freeman, L.C. (2004). *The development of social network analysis: A study in the sociology of science.* Vancouver, BC: Booksurge.

Frey, K.S., Hirschstein, M.K., Edstrom, L.V., & Snell, J.L. (2009). Observed reductions in school bullying, non-bullying aggression, and destructive bystander behavior: A longitudinal evaluation. *Journal of Educational Psychology, 101*, 466–481.

Frey, K.S., Jones, D.C., Hirschstein, M.K., & Edstrom, L.V. (this volume). Teacher support of bullying prevention: The good, the bad, and the promising. In D.L. Espelage & S. Swearer (Eds.), *Bullying in North American schools* (2nd ed.). New York, NY: Routledge.

Garandeau, C.F., Wilson, T., & Rodkin, P.C. (2010). The popularity of elementary school bullies in gender and racial context. In S.R. Jimerson, S.M. Swearer, & D.L. Espelage (Eds.), *The handbook of bullying in schools: An international perspective* (pp. 119–136). New York, NY: Routledge.

Gest, S.D. (2006). Teacher reports of children's friendships and social groups: Agreement with peer reports and implications for studying peer similarity. *Social Development, 15*, 248–259.

Gest, S.D., Moody, J., & Rulison, K.L. (2007). Density or distinction? The roles of data structure and group detection methods in describing adolescent peer groups. *Journal of Social Structure.* Online: www.cmu.edu/joss/content/articles/volume8/GestMoody/.

Gest, S.D., Davidson, A.J., Rulison, K.L., Moody, J., & Welsh, J.A. (2007). Features of groups and status hierarchies in girls' and boys' early adolescent peer networks. In P.C. Rodkin & L.D. Hanish (Eds.), *Social network analysis and children's peer relationships* (pp. 43–60). San Francisco: Jossey Bass.

Granovetter, M.S. (1972). The strength of weak ties. *American Journal of Sociology, 78*, 1360–1380.

Granovetter, M.S. (1985). Economic action and social structure: The problem of embeddedness. *American Journal of Sociology, 91*, 485–510.

Gronlund, N.E. (1959). *Sociometry in the classroom*. New York, NY: Harper & Brothers.

Hallinan, M.T., & Smith, S.S. (1989). Classroom characteristics and student friendship cliques. *Social Forces, 67*, 898–919.

Hamre, B.K., & Pianta, R.C. (2001). Early teacher-child relationships and the trajectory of children's school outcomes through eighth grade. *Child Development, 72*, 625–638.

Hanish, L.D., & Rodkin, P.C. (2007). Bridging children's social development and social network analysis. In P.C. Rodkin & L.D. Hanish (Eds.), *Social network analysis and children's peer relationships* (pp. 1–8). San Francisco: Jossey-Bass.

Hanish, L.D., Martin, C.L., Fabes, R.A., & Barcelo, H. (2008). The breadth of peer relationships among preschoolers: An application of the Q-connectivity method to externalizing behavior. *Child Development, 79*, 1119–1136.

Juvonen, J., Nishina, A., & Graham, S. (2006). Ethnic diversity and perceptions of safety in urban middle schools. *Psychological Science, 17*, 393–400.

Kawabata, Y., & Crick, N.R. (2008). The role of cross-racial/ethnic friendships in social adjustment. *Developmental Psychology, 44*, 1177–1183.

Kindermann, T. (2007). Effects of naturally existing peer groups on changes in academic engagement in a cohort of sixth graders. *Child Development, 78*, 1186–1203.

Kindermann, T., & Gest, S.D. (2009). Assessment of the peer group: Identifying naturally occurring social networks and capturing their effects. In K. Rubin, W. Bukowski, & B. Laursen (Eds.), *Handbook of peer interactions, relationships and groups* (pp. 100–118). New York, NY: Guilford.

Lease, A.M., & Blake, J.J. (2005). A comparison of majority-race children with and without a minority-race friend. *Social Development, 14*, 20–41.

Lewin, K. (1943). Psychology and the process of group living. *Journal of Social Psychology, 17*, 113–131.

Lewin, K., Lippitt, R., & White, R.K. (1939). Patterns of aggressive behavior in experimentally created "social climates." *Journal of Social Psychology, 10*, 271–299.

Lippitt, R. (1939). Field theory and experiment in social psychology: Autocratic and democratic group atmospheres. *American Journal of Sociology, 45*, 26–49.

McFarland, D.A. (2001). Student resistance: How the formal and informal organization of classrooms facilitate everyday forms of student defiance. *American Journal of Sociology, 107*, 612–678.

Masten, A.S., Coatswork, D., Neeman, J., Gest, S.D., Tellegen, A., & Garmezy, N. (1995). The structure and coherence of competence from childhood through adolescence. *Child Development, 66*, 1635–1659.

Moody, J., & White, D.R. (2003). Structural cohesion and embeddedness: A hierarchical concept of social groups. *American Sociological Review, 68*, 103–127.

Mulvey, E.P., & Cauffman, E. (2001). The inherent limits of predicting school violence. *American Psychologist, 56*, 797–802.

O'Brien, M.U., Resnik, H., & the Collaborative for Academic, Social, and Emotional Learning (2009). The Illinois Social and Emotional Learning (SEL) Standards: Leading the way for school and student success. *Illinois Principals Association: A Practitioner's Bulletin, 16*(7).

Olweus, D. (1993). *Bullying at school: What we know and what we can do*. Oxford, UK: Blackwell.

Orpinas, P., & Horne, A. M. (2006). *Bullying prevention: Creating a positive school climate and developing social competence*. Washington DC: American Psychological Association.

Paluck, E.L., & Green, D.P. (2009). Prejudice reduction: What works? A review and assessment of research and practice. *Annual Review of Psychology, 60*, 339–367.

Pearl, R., Leung, M-C., Van Acker, R., Farmer, T.W., & Rodkin, P.C. (2007). Fourth- and fifth-grade teachers' awareness of their classrooms' social networks. *Elementary School Journal, 108*, 25–39.

Pellegrini, A.D. (2002). Bullying, victimization, and sexual harassment during the transition to middle school. *Educational Psychologist, 37*, 151–163.

Pepler, D.J., Craig, W.M., & O'Connell, P. (2001). Understanding bullying from a dynamic systems perspective. In P.K. Smith (Ed.)., *Blackwell handbook of social development* (pp. 440–452). Cambridge, UK: Blackwell.

Pepler, D.J., Craig, W.M., & Roberts, W.L. (1998). Observations of aggressive and nonaggressive children on the school playground. *Merrill-Palmer Quarterly, 44*, 55–76.

Pianta, R.C., La Paro, K.M., & Hamre, B.K. (2006). *The Classroom Assessment Scoring System (CLASS)*. Brookes Publishing.

Pianta, R.C., Belsky, J., Vandergrift, R.H., Houts, R., & Morrison, F.J. (2008). Classroom effects on children's achievement trajectories in elementary school. *American Education Research Journal, 45*, 365–397.

Rappaport, J. (1977). *Community psychology: Values, research, and action*. New York, NY: Holt, Rinehart, & Winston.

Rodkin, P.C. (2004). Peer ecologies of aggression and bullying. In D.L. Espelage & S.M. Swearer (Eds.), *Bullying in American schools: A social-ecological perspective on prevention and intervention* (pp. 87–106). Mahwah, NJ: Erlbaum.

Rodkin, P.C., & Ahn, H-J. (2009). Social networks derived from affiliations and friendships, multi-informant and self-reports: Stability, concordance, placement of aggressive and unpopular children, and centrality. *Social Development, 18*, 556–576.

Rodkin, P.C., & Berger, C. (2008). Who bullies whom? Social status asymmetries by victim gender. *International Journal of Behavioral Development, 32*, 473–485.

Rodkin, P.C., & Fischer, K. (2003). Sexual harassment and the cultures of childhood: Developmental, domestic violence, and legal perspectives. *Journal of Applied School Psychology, 19*, 177–196.

Rodkin, P.C., & Hodges, E.V.E. (2003). Bullies and victims in the peer ecology: Four questions for psychologists and school professionals. *School Psychology Review, 32*, 384–400.

Rodkin, P.C., & Karimpour, R. (2008). What's a hidden bully? In S. Hymel, S. Swearer, & P. Gillette (Eds.), *Bullying at school and online*. Retrieved November 14, 2008, from www.education.com/reference/article/Ref_What_s_Hidden_Bully/.

Rodkin, P.C., & Roisman, G.I. (2010). Antecedents and correlates of the popular-aggressive phenomenon in elementary school. *Child Development, 81*, 837–850

Rodkin, P.C., Wilson, T., & Ahn, H.-J. (2007). Social integration between African American and European American children in majority Black, majority White, and multicultural elementary classrooms. In P.C. Rodkin & L.D. Hanish (Eds.), *Social network analysis and children's peer relationships* (pp. 25–42). San Francisco: Jossey-Bass.

Rodkin, P.C., Farmer, T.W., Pearl, R., & Van Acker, R. (2000). Heterogeneity of popular boys: Antisocial and prosocial configurations. *Developmental Psychology, 36*, 14–24.

Rodkin, P.C., Farmer, T.W., Pearl, R., & Van Acker, R. (2006). They're cool: Social status and peer group supports for aggressive boys and girls. *Social Development, 15*, 175–204.

Roseth, C.J., Johnson, D.W., & Johnson, R.T. (2008). Promoting early adolescents' achievement and peer relationships: The effects of cooperative, competitive, and individualistic goal structures. *Psychological Bulletin, 134*, 223–246.

Ryan, A.M. (2001). The peer group as a context for the development of young adolescent motivation and achievement. *Child Development, 72*, 1135–1150.

Salmivalli, C. (2001). Group view on victimization: Empirical findings and their implications. In J. Juvonen & S. Graham (Eds.), *Peer harassment in school: The plight of the vulnerable and the victimized* (pp. 398–419). New York, NY: Guilford.

Shaw, M.E. (1954). Some effects of problem complexity upon problem solution efficiency in different communication nets. *Journal of Experimental Psychology, 48*, 211–217.

Sherif, M. (1956). Experiments in group conflict. *Scientific American, 195*, 54–58.

Swearer, S.M., & Espelage, D.L. (2004). Introduction: A social-ecological framework of bullying among youth. In D.L. Espelage & S.M. Swearer (Eds.), *Bullying in American schools: A social-ecological perspective on prevention and intervention* (pp. 1–12). Mahwah, NJ: Erlbaum.

Swearer, S.M., Peugh, J., Espelage, D.L., Siebecker, A.B., Kingsbury, W.L., Bevins, K.S. (2006). A socioecological model for bullying prevention and intervention in early adolescence: An exploratory examination. In S.R. Jimerson & M.J. Furlong (Eds.), *The handbook of school violence and school safety: From research to practice* (pp. 257–273). Mahwah, NJ: Erlbaum.

Thomas, D.E., Bierman, K.L., & the Conduct Problems Prevention Research Group (2006). The impact of classroom aggression on the development of aggressive behavior problems in children. *Development and Psychopathology, 18*, 471–487.

Veenstra, R., Lindenberg, S., Zijlstra, B.J.H., De Winter, A.F., Verhulst, F.C., & Ormel, J. (2007). The dyadic nature of bullying and victimization: Testing a dual-perspective theory. *Child Development, 78*, 1843–1854.

Wasserman, S., & Faust, K. (1994). *Social network analysis: Methods and applications.* New York, NY: Cambridge University Press.

Wright, J.C., Giammarino, M., & Parad, H.W. (1986). Social status in small groups: Individual-group similarity and the social "misfit." *Journal of Personality and Social Psychology, 50*, 523–536.

Zins, J.E., Elias, M.J., & Maher, C.A. (Eds.). (2007). *Bullying, victimization, and peer harassment: A handbook of prevention and intervention.* New York, NY: Haworth Press.

8

PART OF THE PROBLEM *AND* PART OF THE SOLUTION

The Role of Peers in Bullying, Dominance, and Victimization during the Transition from Primary School to Secondary School

ANTHONY D. PELLEGRINI AND MARK J. VAN RYZIN

Aggression and bullying in school have become widely recognized as important empirical and policy issues in recent decades and have been studied at a variety of ages, from kindergarten through high school (Boldizar, Perry, & Perry, 1989; Hodges, Malone, & Perry, 1997; Kochenderfer & Ladd, 1996; Ladd, Kochenderfer, & Coleman, 1997; Olweus, 1993a, 1993b; Pellegrini, Bartini, & Brooks, 1999; Pellegrini & Long, 2002). Bullying is characterized by youths purposefully "victimizing" their peers via physical, verbal, or indirect aggression (Boulton & Smith, 1994; Espelage, Bosworth, & Simon, 2000; Smith & Sharp, 1994). Bullying is also typified by a power differential where aggressors are more powerful than their targets (Olweus, 1993a, 1993b).

Early adolescence is especially important for the study of bullying because the transition to adolescence and middle school witnesses an initial increase in aggression and bullying within the more general context of age-related decline (Smith, Madsen, & Moody, 1999). The influence of peers during this time period is complex and involves a number of developmental issues. For example, during early adolescence, aggression is viewed less negatively by peers relative to earlier periods in development (Bukowski, Sippola, & Newcomb, 2000; Graham & Juvonen, 1998; Moffitt, 1993; Pellegrini et al., 1999). This may reflect adolescents' interest in bullies as representing a challenge to adult values (Moffitt, 1993), given that such challenges are a core feature of adolescence as youth explore their own identity and strive to attain autonomy from the family unit (Steinberg, 1990).

Physical development during this period supports the use of aggression instrumentally in the pursuit of social dominance (Dunbar, 1988; Pellegrini, 2008). Rapid changes in body size lead to the reorganization of social dominance hierarchies, especially among boys (Pellegrini & Bartini, 2001). Bigger and stronger boys become more dominant than their smaller peers, and their dominance status, in turn, is related to their attractiveness to opposite-sex peers (Bukowski et al., 2000; Pellegrini & Bartini, 2001; Pellegrini & Long, 2003). This becomes particularly important as youth enter puberty (Connolly, Goldberg, Pepler, & Craig, 1999).

Adolescents are also faced with significant changes in the nature of the school environment as they move from smaller, more personal primary schools with well-established social groups to larger, less socially supportive secondary schools (Feldlaufer, Midgley, & Eccles, 1988; Midgley, Feldlaufer, & Eccles, 1989). During such transitions, aggression is often used deliberately to establish status with new peers (Pellegrini, 2002; Pellegrini & Long, 2002; Strayer & Noel, 1986). In this regard, bullying is a dimension of *proactive* aggression and distinct from reactive aggression, which occurs in response to social provocation (Dodge & Coie, 1987). More specifically, most bullies use aggression in a calculating way. They direct it at a specific target (e.g., someone they know has few allies) and they use it to achieve a specific end (e.g., a show of strength).

In contrast to proactive aggression, reactive aggression is an angry or defensive outburst in response to a real or perceived threat (Dodge, 1991; Dodge & Coie, 1987). Perry, Perry, and Kennedy (1992) labeled reactive aggressive children as "ineffectual aggressors" and hypothesized that their inability to regulate emotions during peer interaction results in a chronic escalation of relatively minor conflicts into high-intensity aggressive episodes that alienate peers. The tendency of these children to reward their aggressors with exaggerated emotional responses serves to encourage further victimization (Perry, Williard, & Perry, 1990).

Although the two types of aggression (i.e., proactive and reactive) have been found to be highly correlated, research has confirmed their status as distinct constructs (Crick & Dodge, 1996; Dodge & Coie, 1987; Poulin & Boivin, 2000; Vitaro, Brendgen, & Tremblay, 2002). In particular, the two constructs have divergent consequences, especially with regards to victimization. For example, reactive aggression has been linked to negative social status and increased peer victimization, while proactive aggression has not (Poulin & Boivin, 2000; Price & Dodge, 1989; Schwartz et al., 1998). Indeed, in our own data, we found that proactive aggression leads to *reduced* victimization over time; we also found a reciprocal relationship between reactive aggression and victimization, in which reactive aggression leads to increased victimization, while victimization in turn leads to increased reactive aggression (Van Ryzin & Pellegrini, in preparation). Our scope in this chapter includes both the bullies (i.e., proactive aggressive children) and their victims (i.e., often, but not always, reactive aggressive children), and we will discuss how peer factors both contribute to bullying and mitigate its impact.

BULLYING AS A STRATEGY TO GAIN STATUS WITH PEERS

Dominance status is achieved as a result of a series of agonistic and reconciliation interchanges between individuals (deWaal, 1986; Pellegrini & Bartini, 2001; Strayer, 1980). As discussed above, individuals who are able to use agonistic strategies effectively should be dominant and have higher status (e.g., more attention from same-sex and opposite-sex peers). Dominant individuals use both aggression and prosocial behavior in agonistic encounters with their peers. Aggressive strategies are often used in the initial phases of the formation of dominance relationships, such as when individuals enter a new school (Pellegrini & Bartini, 2001). Individuals who are able to use agonistic strategies more effectively should be more dominant (Hawley, 1999; Hawley & Little, 1999). After the initial transition, more prosocial and cooperative strategies are used to consolidate status and reconcile with former peers (Ljungberg, Westlund, & Forsberg, 1999; Pellegrini & Bartini, 2001).

Once dominance hierarchies are stabilized, they serve the important function of reducing overall levels of aggression within a group (Dunbar, 1988; Vaughn, 1999; Vaughn & Santos, 2007). Dominant and subordinate individuals alike benefit by avoiding the costs of unmitigated aggression (Hawley & Little, 1999; Pellegrini, 2008). Use of aggression by dominant individuals is costly because, as their status is already established, they have little to gain relative to what they may lose (e.g., injury, social sanction). Similarly, subordinate individuals' use of aggression has high costs (e.g., likelihood of being defeated) relative to possible gains.

This description is consistent with our data as youth made the transition from one school to another school (Pellegrini & Long, 2002). In this multimethod, multi-informant, longitudinal study, we followed youth from the last year of primary school (5th grade) across the first two years of middle school (6th and 7th grades). Children were extensively observed across the entire school day and we asked about their own as well as their peers' bullying, victimization, dominance, and heterosexual relationships. These assessments were also collected from teachers. Our results demonstrated that bullying increased from 5th to 6th grade and then decreased from 6th to 7th grade. Correspondingly, dominance dropped from 5th to 6th grade and increased in 7th grade. This result is consistent with dominance theory to the extent that we found increases in aggression as youth moved into a new school and thus tried to establish dominance. A decrease in dominance at the transition and a subsequent increase following the transition again is consistent with dominance theory. Once dominance was established, however, aggression in the form of bullying decreased and was no longer used to maintain dominance.

Dominance was directly and formally tested in this study by examining the degree to which bullying mediated the association between dominance during primary school and dominance during middle school. Our data supported a hypothesis of mediation; that is, we found that in early phases of group formation in middle school, dominance is expressed through bullying and other agonistic strategies, while after the dominance hierarchy is stabilized, dominance is expressed through more prosocial and cooperative means. In sum, these results confirm that bullying is a form of aggression used by individuals to achieve dominance status (Pellegrini & Bartini, 2001; Sutton, Smith, & Swettenham, 1999).

That the transition to middle school witnesses an initial increase in bullying, in the more general context of age-related decline of bullying (Smith, Madsen, & Moody, 1999), provides further support for the dominance hypothesis. Specifically, a large body of research suggests that there is a monotonic decrease in bullying, victimization, and aggression as youth get older (see Pellegrini, 2002, for a review). These decreases have been reported in a series of large-scale investigations, often with nationally representative samples, and include countries in Western Europe and North America (Pellegrini, 2002).

These monotonic decreases during early adolescence, however, are evident only when youth do not change schools. When same-age youth do change schools, there is an initial increase at this transition point, followed by a decrease. More specifically, in the case where youths 10 to 14 years of age change schools, there is an initial increase in reported bullying and victimization. Within a year, the downward trend resumes. This decrease reflects re-established dominance relationships. As discussed above, dominance hierarchies, once stabilized, serve to reduce in-group aggression (Dunbar, 1988; Vaughn, 1999). Thus, bullying and dominance should not be conflated; although bullying may be applied in the establishment of dominance, the dominance hierarchy itself tends to *reduce* overall levels of aggression.

SEX DIFFERENCES IN AGGRESSION

Paralleling research on younger children (Boulton & Smith, 1994), proactive aggression and bullying are more frequent among adolescent boys than girls. Indeed, boys tend to use and endorse aggression, especially physical aggression, with other boys to establish and maintain dominance (Maccoby, 1998). Correspondingly, girls' attitudes toward bullying are more negative than those of boys (Crick & Werner, 1998; Maccoby, 1998; Pellegrini, 2002).

While girls are less likely than boys to endorse bullying, and especially physical aggression, they do engage in bullying and aggression of a different nature. Specifically, girls often engage in relational (Crick & Grotpeter, 1995) or indirect aggression (Bjorkqvist, 1994). Relational aggression is characterized by attacks on opponents' social relationships. That is, rather than confronting an opponent directly, as in a physical fight, one child may say something nasty about another child to a third party with the intent of damaging the child's social standing. While these strategies seem to be proactive in the sense that they are a deliberate attempt to accomplish some goal, they do not seem to be dominance strategies per se. In fact, female groups do not tend to be organized according to dominance hierarchies in the same sense as boys' groups (Maccoby, 1998). Rather, indirect aggression seems to fit well with sexual selection theory (Archer, 2004; Campbell, 1999). Sexual selection theory, as originally proposed by Darwin (1871) and extended by Trivers (1972), suggests that males and females use different strategies to attract mates. Males, being physically bigger, stronger, and more physically active, compete with each other, often using physical aggression to gain status, as expressed in dominance hierarchies. High status ensures access to females. Females, on the other hand, are smaller and more concerned with protecting themselves and their future offspring. Thus, they choose dominant mates and, when they are aggressive against their peers, do so indirectly. This indirectness minimizes direct confrontation and possible harm. It has been further proposed, though not empirically validated, that girls may use relational aggression to form coalitions and alliances against rival girls so as to attain social goals.

VICTIMIZATION AND PEER AFFILIATION

As discussed above, reactive aggressive children are often singled out as victims. These children often suffer from some form of behavioral disregulation, and their inappropriate or hyperactive behavior makes them an easy target for proactive aggressive children (Burk et al., 2008; Egan & Perry, 1998; Hodges, Boivin, Vitaro, & Bukowski, 1999; Hodges & Perry, 1999; Pope & Bierman, 1999; Salmivalli & Helteenvuori, 2007; Schwartz, McFadyen-Ketchum, Dodge, Pettit, & Bates, 1999; Toblin, Schwartz, Gorman, & Abou-ezzeddine, 2007). Research has also established that chronic victimization by peers can lead to increased levels of behavioral disregulation and reactive aggression over time (Hanish & Guerra, 2002; Hodges & Perry, 1999; Schwartz et al., 1998; Snyder et al., 2003), thus creating a "vicious cycle" for victimized children (Van Ryzin & Pellegrini, in preparation). The stress of repeated victimization and the marginalization of these children within the peer group limits their opportunities to affiliate and socialize, resulting in fewer friendships and lower levels of social skill; these factors, in turn, create increased risk for further victimization (Egan & Perry, 1998; Hodges et al., 1999;

Schwartz et al., 1999). Over the long term, victimized children are at risk for a range of behavioral, academic, and socio-emotional problems, including depression, anxiety, social withdrawal, and attention and self-regulatory problems (Boivin, Hymel, & Bukowski, 1995; Boivin, Hymel, & Hodges, 2001; Perry, Perry, & Kennedy, 1992; Rigby, 2001; Schwartz et al., 1998).

Often these issues can be exacerbated by the structure and culture of middle and junior high schools, especially in the United States, which do not support the formation of new social groupings among students. Instead, the transition to secondary school often includes more whole-class instruction, increased ability grouping and public evaluations, and a greater emphasis on grades and competition rather than cooperation (Eccles, Midgley, & Adler, 1984; Eccles et al., 1993). As a result, students transitioning to secondary school experience a reduced perception of social support and fewer opportunities for interaction and affiliation with peers (Feldlaufer et al., 1988). These changes come at a time when the peer group is taking on increased importance for youth (Simmons & Blyth, 1987).

Our research examined changes in peer affiliation as youth made the transition from primary through the first two years of middle school (Pellegrini & Long, 2002). Affiliation can be defined in terms of the number of friends youths have as well as individuals' popularity. We find that the number of affiliations for youths decreased, at least initially with the transition from primary to middle school, but it began to recover by the second year of middle school (in the 7th grade). It is likely the case that students' affiliations decreased because they were entering a new and much larger social institution with a more fractured, competitive social environment. The schools did make some effort to foster informal interaction among peers, but they were seemingly slow to take effect. For example, the weekly free time (called "Coke Breaks") typically occurred during the final hour of classes on Friday afternoons. Students went to a central gathering place, purchased a soft drink, and then went back to their homerooms and interacted with their peers. More concentrated mechanisms may be needed during the first year of middle school to foster more varied and closer relationships within these larger social networks during the school day.

Peer affiliation is particularly relevant to the study of victimization because dimensions of peer affiliation, such as reciprocal friendships, can serve to minimize victimization (Hodges et al., 1999; Hodges et al., 1997; Hodges & Perry, 1999; Pellegrini et al., 1999; Pellegrini & Long, 2002; Schwartz et al., 1999). Generally, higher numbers of friends, particularly close friends, seem to protect individuals from victimization. Youth who have friends, especially friends who are strong and popular, seem to be less attractive targets of bullying. In this model, friends serve as "protectors" for more vulnerable students. In addition, social support from close friends may buffer the negative effects of victimization on adjustment (Prinstein, Boergers, & Vernberg, 2001).

Being generally popular with peers also seems to reduce victimization. In fact, our research has indicated that popularity is a more robust buffer than the number of reciprocal friend nominations (Pellegrini et al., 1999; Pellegrini & Long, 2002). Specifically, we found that the number of "liked most" nominations, relative to the number of reciprocal friends, was a robust negative predictor of victimization across the middle school years (Pellegrini & Long, 2002). We also found that having a number of affiliates, relative to close friends, seems to protect against bullying because being liked by a number of peers represents the number of possible social sanctions or retaliation against bullies. If a child victimizes an individual who is liked by a large number of peers, he or she runs the very real risk of retaliation, public sanction, and peer disapproval. That bullies are concerned with social status among their peers would suggest that they would not target peers with allies or other social affiliations.

TRANSLATING RESEARCH INTO PRACTICE: IMPLICATIONS FOR BULLYING PREVENTION AND INTERVENTION PROGRAMS

In this chapter we examined bullying and victimization during a particularly important period. Early adolescence merits attention because it is a period where disruptions in peer affiliations afford opportunities for peer victimization and increased use of aggression, possibly to establish peer status. Consistent with this proposition, we found that bullying is used as a strategy to achieve dominance status during the transition to secondary school.

A path toward the reduction of bullying may include educational interventions that provide new opportunities for peer affiliation or the development of friendships. One example of such an intervention is peer tutoring, which can take place either within the classroom as part of daily learning activities or outside of class on a one-to-one basis (Maheady, Mallette, & Harper, 2006). Peer tutoring in the classroom often involves students working directly with each other to review current material, clarify concepts, and probe for understanding. Outside of class, peer tutoring can take place in study halls or in more formal after-school programs. Research has demonstrated that peer tutoring not only promotes higher levels of academic achievement, but also promotes improved peer relations (Kamps, Barbetta, Leonard, & Delquadri, 1994; McMaster, Fuchs, & Fuchs, 2006).

Another option is cooperative learning, which involves placing students in heterogeneous groups in situations of positive interdependence, in which individual goals are only realized in the context of group goals. Cooperative learning emphasizes teamwork, both group-level and individual accountability, face-to-face interaction within the group, use of interpersonal skills, and group reflection to encourage continuous improvement in group functioning. As with peer tutoring, there is evidence for positive effects of cooperative learning on both academic achievement and peer relations (Johnson, Johnson, & Holubec, 1984; Sharan & Shaulov, 1990; Slavin, 1977).

There are also programs that attempt to alter the nature of the school environment, particularly for incoming students, in order to encourage the development of friendships and buffer the transition to the secondary school environment. Some examples are the Child Development Project (Battistich, Solomon, Kim, Watson, & Schaps, 1995; Battistich et al., 1997), the Social Competence Program for Young Adolescents (Caplan et al., 1992), the Creating Lasting Connections Project (Johnson et al., 1996), and the Adolescent Transitions Project (Andrews, Soberman, & Dishion, 1995; see Greenberger, Domitrovich, & Bumbarger, 1999, for a review of related programs). Programs such as these, designed to increase opportunities for peer interaction and affiliation and to improve peer socialization skills, can be expected to have positive impacts on bullying. When implemented alongside classroom interventions such as peer tutoring and cooperative learning, the goal of reducing bullying can be achieved in the context of advancing academic achievement.

In the effort to reduce bullying, particular attention should be paid to reactive aggressive children, who may suffer from hostile attribution biases and hypervigilance to threat cues (Dodge, 1991). If an intervention targeting these students could reduce perceptual biases and provide some degree of social and self-regulatory skill, then they may be less likely to react aggressively to perceived threats; in turn, they may be able to overcome their rejected status and begin to develop friendship networks, which could protect them from on-going victimization. Dodge (1991) suggests that attachment difficulties may be present in reactively aggressive children, which implies that an on-going relationship with an adult mentor or school counselor may be particularly effective in reducing reactive aggression among these children.

REFERENCES

Andrews, D.W., Soberman, L.H., & Dishion, T.J. (1995). The Adolescent Transitions program for high-risk teens and their parents: Toward a school-based intervention. *Education and Treatment of Children, 18,* 478–498.

Archer, J. (2004). Sex differences in aggression in real-world settings: A meta-analytic review. *Review of General Psychology, 8,* 291–322.

Battistich, V., Solomon, D., Watson, M., & Schaps, E. (1997). Caring school communities. *Educational Psychologist, 32,* 137–151.

Battistich, V., Solomon, D., Kim, D., Watson, M., & Schaps, E. (1995). Schools as communities, poverty levels of student populations, and students' attitudes, motives, and performance: A multilevel analysis. *American Educational Research Journal, 32,* 627–658.

Bjorkqvist, K. (1994). Sex differences in physical, verbal, and indirect aggression: A review of recent research. *Sex Roles. 30,* 177–188.

Boivin, M., Hymel, S., & Bukowski, W.M. (1995). The roles of social withdrawal, peer rejection, and victimization by peers in predicting loneliness and depressed mood in children. *Development and Psychopathology, 7,* 765–786.

Boivin, M., Hymel, S., & Hodges, E.V.E. (2001). Toward a process view of peer rejection and harassment. In J. Juvonen & S. Graham (Eds.), *Peer harassment in school: The plight of the vulnerable and victimized* (pp. 265–289). New York, NY: Guilford.

Boldizar, J.P., Perry, D.G., & Perry, L.C. (1989). Outcome values and aggression. *Child Development, 60,* 571–579.

Boulton, M.J., & Smith, P.K. (1994). Bully/victim problems in middle school children: Stability, self-perceived competence, peer perceptions, and peer acceptance. *British Journal of Developmental Psychology, 12,* 315–329.

Bukowski, W.M., Sippola, L.A., & Newcomb, A.F. (2000). Variations in patterns of attraction to same-and other-sex peers-during early adolescence. *Developmental Psychology, 36,* 147–154.

Burk, L.R., Park, J., Armstrong, J.M., Klein, M.H., Goldsmith, H.H., Zahn-Waxler, C., & Essex, M.J. (2008). Identification of early child and family risk factors for aggressive victim status in first grade. *Journal of Abnormal Child Psychology, 36,* 513–526.

Campbell, A. (1999). Staying alive: Evolution, culture, and women's intrasexual aggression. *Behavioral and Brain Sciences, 22,* 203–252.

Caplan, M., Weissberg, R.P., Grober, J.S., Sivo, P.J., Grady, K., & Jacoby, C. (1992). Social competence promotion with inner-city and suburban young adolescents: Effects on school adjustment and alcohol use. *Journal of Consulting and Clinical Psychology 60,* 56–63.

Connolly, J., Goldberg. A., Pepler, D., & Craig, W.M. (1999). Development and significance of cross-sex activities in early adolescence. *Journal of Youth and Adolescence, 24,* 123–130.

Crick, N.R., & Dodge, K.A. (1996). Social information-processing mechanisms in reactive and proactive aggression. *Child Development, 67,* 993–1002.

Crick, N.R., & Grotpeter, J. (1995). Relational aggression, gender and social psychological adjustment. *Child Development, 66,* 710–727.

Crick, N.R., & Werner, N.E. (1998). Response decision processes in relational and overt aggression. *Child Development, 69,* 1630–1639.

Darwin, C. (1871). *The descent of man, and selection in relation to sex.* London: John Murray.

deWaal, F.B.M. (1986). The integration of dominance and social bonding in primates. *Journal of Theoretical Biology, 61,* 459–479.

Dodge, K.A. (1991). The structure and function of reactive and proactive aggression. In D. Pepler & K. Rubin (Eds.), *The development and treatment of childhood aggression* (pp. 201–218). Hillsdale, NJ: Erlbaum.

Dodge, K.A., & Coie, J.D. (1987). Social information processing factors in reactive and proactive aggression in children's peer groups. *Journal of Personality and Social Psychology, 53,* 1146–1158.

Dunbar, R.I.M. (1988). *Primate social systems.* Ithaca: Cornell University Press.

Eccles, J., Midgley, C., & Adler, T. (1984). Grade-related changes in the school environment: Effects of achievement motivation. In J.G. Nicholls (Ed.), *The development of achievement motivation* (pp. 283–331). Greenwich, CT: JAI Press.

Eccles, J.S., Wigfield, A., Midgley, C., Reuman, D., MacIver, D., & Feldlaufer, H. (1993). Negative effects of traditional middle schools on students' motivation. *The Elementary School Journal, 93,* 553–574.

Egan, S.K., & Perry, D.G. (1998). Does low self-esteem invite victimization? *Developmental Psychology, 34,* 299–309.

Espelage, D.L., Bosworth, K., & Simon, T.R. (2000). Examining the social context of bullying behaviors in early adolescence. *Journal of Counseling & Development, 78,* 326–333.

Feldlaufer, H., Midgley, C., & Eccles, J.S. (1988). Student, teacher, and observer perceptions of the classroom environment before and after the transition to junior high school. *Journal of Early Adolescence, 8,* 133–156.

Graham, S., & Juvonen, J. (1998). A social cognitive perspective on peer aggression and victimization. In R. Vasta (Ed.), *Annals of child development* (pp. 23–70). London: Jessica Kingsley Publishers.

Greenberger, M.T., Domitrovich, C., & Bumbarger, B. (1999). Preventing mental disorders in school-age children: A review of the effectiveness of prevention programs. Washington DC: Center for Mental Health Services (CMHS), U.S. Department of Health and Human Services.

Hanish, L.D., & Guerra, N.G. (2002). A longitudinal analysis of patterns of adjustment following peer victimization. *Development and Psychopathology, 14,* 69–89.

Hawley, P.H. (1999). The ontogenesis of social dominance: A strategy-based evolutionary perspective. *Developmental Review, 19,* 97–132.

Hawley, P.H., & Little, T.D. (1999). On winning some and losing some: A social relations approach to social dominance in toddlers. *Merrill–Palmer Quarterly, 45,* 185–214.

Hodges, E.V.E., & Perry, D.G. (1999). Personal and interpersonal antecedents and consequences of victimization by peers. *Journal of Personality and Social Psychology, 76,* 677–685.

Hodges, E.V.E., Malone, M.J., Jr., & Perry, D G. (1997). Individual risk and social risk as interacting determinants of victimization in the peer group. *Developmental Psychology, 33,* 1032–1039.

Hodges, E.V.E., Boivin, M., Vitaro, F., & Bukowski, W.M. (1999). The power of friendship: Protection against an escalating cycle of peer victimization. *Developmental Psychology, 35,* 94–101.

Johnson, D.W., Johnson, R.T., & Holubec, E.J. (1984). *Cooperation in the classroom.* Edina, MN: Interaction Book Company.

Johnson, K., Strader, T., Berbaum, M., Bryant, D., Bucholtz, G., Collins, D. & Noe, T. (1996). Reducing alcohol and other drug use by strengthening community, family, and youth resiliency: An evaluation of the Creating Lasting Connections Program. *Journal of Adolescent Research, 11,* 36–67.

Kamps, D.M., Barbetta, P.M., Leonard, B.R., & Delquadri, J. (1994). Classwide peer tutoring: An integration strategy to improve reading skills and promote peer interactions among students with autism and general education peers. *Journal of Applied Behavioral Analysis, 27,* 49–61.

Kochenderfer, B.J., & Ladd, G.W. (1996). Peer victimization: Manifestations and relations to school adjustment in kindergarten. *Journal of School Psychology, 34,* 267–283.

Ladd, G.W., Kochenderfer, B.J., & Coleman, C.C. (1997). Classroom peer acceptance, friendship, and victimization: Distinct relational systems that contribute uniquely to children's school adjustment. *Child Development, 68,* 1181–1197.

Ljungberg, T., Westlund, K., & Forsberg, A.J.L. (1999). Conflict resolution in 5-year-old boys. *Animal Behaviour, 58,* 1007–1016.

Maccoby, E.E. (1998). *The two sexes: Growing up apart, coming together.* Cambridge, MA: Harvard University Press.

Maheady, L., Mallette, B., & Harper, G.F. (2006). Four classwide peer tutoring models: Similarities, differences, and implications for research and practice. *Reading & Writing Quarterly, 22,* 65–89.

McMaster, K.L., Fuchs, D., & Fuchs, L.S. (2006). Research on peer-assisted learning strategies: The promise and limitations of peer-mediated instruction. *Reading & Writing Quarterly, 22,* 5–25.

Midgley, C., Feldlaufer, H., & Eccles, J.S. (1989). Student/teacher relations and attitudes toward mathematics before and after the transition to junior high school. *Child Development, 60,* 981–992.

Moffitt, T.E. (1993). Adolescent-limited and life-course-persistent anti-social behavior: A developmental taxonomy. *Psychological Review, 100,* 674–701.

Olweus, D. (1993a). *Bullying at school.* Cambridge, MA: Blackwell.

Olweus, D. (1993b). Victimization by peers. In K.H. Rubin & J. Asendorf (Eds.), *Social withdrawal, inhibition, and shyness in childhood* (pp. 315–341). Hillsdale, NJ: Erlbaum.

Pellegrini, A.D. (2002). Bullying and victimization in middle school: A dominance relations perspective. *Educational Psychologist, 37,* 151–163.

Pellegrini, A.D. (2008). The roles of aggressive and affiliative behaviors in resource control: A behavioral ecological perspective. *Developmental Review, 28,* 461–487.

Pellegrini, A.D., & Bartini, M. (2001). Dominance in early adolescent boys: Affiliative and aggressive dimensions and possible functions. *Merrill-Palmer Quarterly, 47,* 142–163.

Pellegrini. A.D., & Long, J. (2002). A longitudinal study of bullying, dominance, and victimization during the transition from primary to secondary school. *British Journal of Developmental Psychology, 20,* 259–280.

Pellegrini, A.D., & Long, J.D. (2003). A sexual selection theory longitudinal analysis of sexual segregation and integration in early adolescence. *Journal of Experimental Child Psychology, 85,* 257–278.

Pellegrini, A.D., Bartini, M., & Brooks, F. (1999). School bullies, victims, and aggressive victims: Factors relating top group affiliation and victimization in early adolescence. *Journal of Educational Psychology, 91,* 216–224.

Perry, D.G., Perry, L.C., & Kennedy, E. (1992). Conflict and the development of anti-social behavior. In C.U. Shantz & W.W. Hartup (Eds.), *Conflict in child and adolescent development* (pp. 301–329). New York, NY: Cambridge University Press.

Perry, D.G., Willard, J., & Perry, L. (1990). Peers' perceptions of consequences that victimized children provide aggressors. *Child Development, 61,* 1289–1309.

Pope, A.W., & Bierman, K.L. (1999). Predicting adolescent peer problems and antisocial activities: The relative roles of aggression and dysregulation. *Developmental Psychology, 35,* 335–346.

Poulin, F., & Boivin, M. (2000). Reactive and proactive aggression: Evidence of a two-factor model. *Psychological Assessment, 12,* 115–122.

Price, J.M., & Dodge, K.A. (1989). Reactive and proactive aggression in childhood: Relations to peer status and social context dimensions. *Journal of Abnormal Child Psychology, 17,* 455–471.

Prinstein, M.J., Boergers, J., & Vernberg, E.M. (2001). Overt and relational aggression in adolescents: Social-psychological adjustment of aggressors and victims. *Journal of Clinical Child Psychology, 30,* 479–491.

Rigby, K. (2001). Health consequences of bullying and its prevention in schools. In J. Juvonen & S. Graham (Eds.), *Peer harassment in school: The plight of the vulnerable and the victimized* (pp. 310–331). New York, NY: Guilford Press.

Salmivalli, C., & Helteenvuori, T. (2007). Reactive, but not proactive aggression predicts victimization among boys. *Aggressive Behavior, 33,* 198–206.

Schwartz, D., McFadyen-Ketchum, S.A., Dodge, K.A., Pettit, G.S., & Bates, J.E. (1998). Peer group victimization as a predictor of children's behavior problems at home and in school. *Development and Psychopathology, 10,* 87–99.

Schwartz, D., McFadyen-Ketchum, S.A., Dodge, K.A., Pettit, G.S., & Bates, J.E. (1999). Early behavior problems as a predictor of later peer group victimization: Moderators and mediators in the pathways of social risk. *Journal of Abnormal Child Psychology, 27,* 191–201.

Schwartz, D., Dodge, K.A., Coie, J.D., Hubbard, J.A., Cillessen, A.H.N., Lemerise, E.A., & Bateman, H. (1998). Social-cognitive and behavioral correlates of aggression and victimization in boys' play groups. *Journal of Abnormal Child Psychology, 26,* 431–440.

Sharan, S., & Shaulov, A. (1990). Cooperative learning, motivation to learn, and academic achievement. In S. Sharan (Ed.), *Cooperative learning: Theory and research* (pp. 173–202). New York, NY: Praeger.

Simmons, R.G., & Blyth, D. A. (1987). *Moving into adolescence: The impact of pubertal change and school context.* Hawthorn, NY: Aldine de Gruyter.

Slavin, R.E. (1977). Classroom rewards structure: An analytical and practical review. *Review of Educational Research, 47,* 633–650.

Smith, P.K., & Sharp, S. (1994). The problem of school bullying. In P.K. Smith & S. Sharp (Eds.), *School bullying* (pp. 1–19). London: Routledge.

Smith, P.K., Madsen, K.C., & Moody, J.C. (1999). What causes the age decline in reports of being bullied at school? Toward a developmental analysis of risks of being bullied. *Educational Research, 41,* 267–285.

Snyder, J., Brooker, M., Patrick, M.R., Snyder, A., Schrepferman, L., & Stoolmiller, M. (2003). Observed peer victimization during early elementary school: Continuity, growth, and relation to risk for child antisocial and depressive behavior. *Child Development, 74,* 1881–1898.

Steinberg, L. (1990). Autonomy, conflict, and harmony in the family relationship. In S.S. Feldman & G.R. Elliott (Eds.), *At the threshold: The developing adolescent* (pp. 255–276). Cambridge, MA: Harvard University Press.

Strayer, F. (1980). Social ecology of the preschool peer group. In W.A. Collins (Ed.), *The Minnesota symposia on child psychology: Development of cognition, affect, and social relations, Vol. 13* (pp. 165–196). Hillsdale, NJ: Erlbaurn.

Strayer, F.F., & Noel, J.M. (1986). The prosocial and antisocial functions of aggression: An ethological study of triadic conflict among young children. In C. Zahn-Waxler, E.M. Cummings, & R. Iannotti (Eds.), *Altruism and aggression* (pp. 107–131). New York, NY: Academic Press.

Sutton, J., Smith, P.K., & Swettenharn, J. (1999). Socially undesirable need not be incompetent: A response to Crick and Dodge. *Social Development, 8,* 132–134.

Toblin, R.L., Schwartz, D., Gorman, A.H., & Abou-ezzeddine, T. (2007). Social–cognitive and behavioral attributes of aggressive victims of bullying. *Journal of Applied Developmental Psychology, 26,* 329–346.

Trivers, R. (1972). Parental investment and sexual selection. In B. Campbell (Ed.), *Sexual selection and the descent of man* (pp. 136–179). Chicago: Aldine.

Van Ryzin, M.J., & Pellegrini, A.D. (in preparation). The reciprocal relationship between proactive and reactive aggression and victimization.

Vaughn, B.E. (1999). Power is knowledge (and vice versa): A commentary on "Winning some and losing some: A social relations approach to social dominance in toddler". *Merrill–Palmer Quarterly, 45,* 215–225.

Vaughn, B.E., & Santos, A.J. (2007). An evolutionary-ecological account of aggressive behavior and trait aggression in human children and adolescents. In P.H. Hawley, T.D. Little, and P.C. Rodkin (Eds.), *Aggression and adaptation: The bright side of bad behavior* (pp. 31–64). Mahwah, NJ: Erlbaum.

Vitaro, F., Brendgen, M., & Tremblay, R.E. (2002). Reactively and proactively aggressive children: Antecedent and subsequent characteristics. *Journal of Child Psychology and Psychiatry, 43,* 495–505.

9

SIDESTEPPING THE JINGLE FALLACY

Bullying, Aggression, and the Importance of Knowing the Difference

PATRICIA H. HAWLEY, KATHRYN N. STUMP, AND JACKLYN RATLIFF

Awareness of the "problem of the bully" goes back hundreds of years, references to which emerge in the literature as early as the late 1600s. These literary references, as such references generally do, shape public perceptions. Famously, for example, a deeply disenfranchised Mr. Bumble from *Oliver Twist* (Dickens, 1838/1846), a "hard hearted brute" who was so insensitive to tears that his "heart was waterproof," was characterized as having a "decided propensity for bullying" in which he "derived no inconsiderable pleasure from the exercise of petty cruelty; and, consequently, was (it is needless to say) a coward" (p. 208). Bullying as "petty tyranny" had long been seen as a problem in school contexts. Thus, not only are bullies aggressive, but they also have deep character flaws reflected in their tendency to prey on the weak, presumably stemming from a low self-concept. Now, of course, it is cliché to consider the bully a socially unskilled tyrant who pales in the face of real danger.

Perhaps somewhat startling, serious scientific inquiry into the causes, consequences, and group processes related to bullying has only emerged in the last decades, no doubt in response to the call to arms by Dan Olweus (Olweus, 1978), who took his lead loosely from the animal behavior literature of the 20th century (mobbing; Barrington, 1932; see also Pikas, 1975).[1] Olweus has guided the field in accepting the critical characteristics defining bullying as (1) negative actions intended to harm (i.e., aggression), (2) repeated acts over time, and (3) an existing power differential between the bully and the victim.

The literature has made clear that bullying is a pervasive and serious problem. Nearly one-third of American adolescents are involved in bullying, either as a bully, a victim, or both (Nansel et al., 2001). Deservingly, the topic has garnered a tremendous amount of attention in the psychological literature (878 peer-reviewed journal articles with *bully* or *bullying* in title since 1987). This literature (see other contributions this volume) has made clear that bullying is particularly bad for victims (anxiety, depression, and, in extreme cases, suicide; Espelage & Swearer, 2003) and, as a consequence, has been a topic of conversation among researchers, educational administration, and government agencies (e.g., Olweus, 1995; Swearer, Espelage, & Napolitano, 2009).

The goals of the present chapter are less to report consequences of bullying or derive viable solutions or evaluate present ones, but rather to shed a light of a different color on the problems of childhood aggression and bullying. First, we will explore the theoretical definitions and measurement models of aggression and bullying, and then describe the consequences of inadvertently blurring the two. Next, we will present an argument suggesting that, whereas aggression may be associated with the competent pursuit of human need fulfillment, bullying may not involve this same competent pursuit. We will cast this discussion in the parlance of Self Determination Theory (Deci & Ryan, 1985) and evoke arguments based on the evolution of human social development. We will close by discussing the possible ramifications of these arguments on intervention programs.

AGGRESSION VERSUS BULLYING

Olweus was clear at the outset: Aggression and bullying are different. Aggression typically is defined as a negative act that is specifically intended to harm a target (Coie & Dodge, 1998). For the greater part of the 20th century, researchers considered aggression to manifest exclusively in direct, physical forms (Coie & Dodge, 1998), consistent with the "male goals" of physical dominance and instrumentality (Ojanen, Grönroos, & Salmivali, 2005; Hawley, Little, & Card, 2008) leading to the conclusion that males are more aggressive than females (Maccoby & Jacklin, 1980). As is well known by now, researchers began identifying more subtle, social forms of aggression beginning in the late 1980s that are widely held to be more characteristic of females (Lagerspetz, Björkqvist, & Peltonen, 1988; Crick & Grotpeter, 1995; Galen & Underwood, 1997).

Important for our present purposes are the different functions of aggression: instrumental and reactive. Instrumental aggression, by definition, involves goal-directed behavior and, accordingly, tends to be well thought out, planned, and self-serving (Dodge, 1991; Little, Jones, Henrich, & Hawley, 2003). With its theoretical roots in social learning theory (Bandura, 1973), instrumental aggression occurs when external reinforcements elicit planful, deliberately aggressive behavior. In contrast, reactive aggression has its theoretical roots in the aggression–frustration hypothesis (Dollard, Miller, Doob, Mowrer, & Sears, 1939). Reactive aggression tends to be considered a "hot-headed" response to provocation or obstruction. Instrumental and reactive aggression can take overt (e.g., physical) or indirect (e.g., social) forms (Little et al., 2003).

Bullying is aggression, to be sure (see Olweus's first definitional point above). Olweus, however, stressed two additional criteria that cause bullying to stand apart from general aggression. The bullying must involve repeated acts and an imbalance of power. Olweus (2001) explicitly differentiates bullying from an argument between equals (e.g., "it is *not bullying* when two students of about the same strength or power argue or fight," p. 6) and additionally emphasizes the strength of the differential (e.g., "it is *difficult for the student being bullied to defend himself or herself,*" p. 6). Clearly, all bullying is aggression (regardless of form or function), but not all aggression is bullying. Thus, aggression is the super-ordinate category.

CONCEPTUAL DRIFT AND ITS VAGARIES

Due to the considerable influence of Olweus's work, researchers in psychological and educational settings tend to agree on the definition of bullying and that it is explicitly distinct from aggression. At the same time, however, many writers drift from their theoretical model (their definition of "bullying") when specifying their measurement model. That is, when measuring bullying, they fail to consider the repetitive nature or power differential aspects of the construct (Salmivalli & Peets, 2009 also make this point).[2] In other words, many authors measure aggression rather than bullying even though they set up the distinction at the outset. Often one finds that the measurement model is so vague that the reader cannot adequately judge. Alternatively, children are sometimes asked to identify peers who bully, but the particulars about the definition of "bullying" (versus aggression) are absent; that is, children are not asked to focus attention on those who repeatedly violate the weak. Thus, when children are asked, "Who is a bully?" or "Who bullies you?" they tend to answer in terms of who they find aggressive (Monks & Smith, 2006). Whereas some older children and adolescents reference power differentials in open-ended descriptions of bullies (20–35% of 10–18-year-olds), most do not (Vaillancourt et al., 2008). By the same token, less than 10% of children aged 8 to 18 years mention the repetitive nature of bullying (Vaillancourt et al., 2008), further suggesting that children are equating bullying with aggression. Additionally, and perhaps most frequently, we find many articles where "bullying" and "aggression" are simply used interchangeably.[3]

Are we just splitting hairs or is this issue consequential? We have good reason to believe that aggression and bullying, though overlapping, are actually distinct. This conclusion has been borne out of confirmatory factor analysis, for example, where bullying and aggression have only 25% shared variance (Pepler et al., 2008). Since the mid- to late 1980s, several researchers have identified socially central or socially well-integrated aggressive youth (e.g., Cairns, Cairns, Neckerman, Gest, & Gariépy, 1988; Hawley, 2002; Rodkin, Farmer, Pearl, & Van Acker, 2006). Bullies, however, tend to receive the fewest number of friendship nominations from their peers or be rejected by them (e.g., Parault, Davis, Pellegrini, 2007; Boulton & Smith, 1994; Salmivalli et al., 1996). For example, Salmivalli and colleagues (1996) examined the sociometric statuses of all bullying participants (e.g., bullies, assistants, reinforcers) and found both bullies and victims to be overwhelmingly placed in the sociometrically rejected category. Yet, in contrast, an important subset of aggressors garners *more* friendship nominations than the majority of their peers (Rodkin & Roisman, 2010; Hawley, Little, & Card, 2007; Bost, Vaughn, Washington, Cielinski, & Bradbard, 1998). Both bullies and aggressors, however, tend to draw many *liked least* nominations (Salmivalli et al., 1996; Hawley et al., 2007). Bullies and aggressors share the common outcome of being disliked by their peer groups, but some aggressors manage to attract many friends.

The Jingle Fallacy

At this point, we would like to interject an age-old cautionary tale. Common use of language is notoriously imprecise. This imprecision is an issue that has historically dogged lexical approaches to personality (e.g., Allport & Odbert, 1936), but is in no way limited to this domain. For example, often when we (the authors) talk about the high levels of "aggression" in youth with prosocial skills, several audience members assume we really mean "assertion" (i.e., *moving toward* rather than *moving against*). Certainly this is a commonly accepted use of the term "aggressive," and indeed might so be understood when aggression is used effectively rather than ineffectively (we return to this point below). And herein is the crux of the problem well understood by, for example, Jack

Block: "Psychologists have tended to be sloppy with words. We need to become more intimate with their meanings, denotatively and connotatively, because summary labels … quickly will control—often in unrecognized ways—the way we think" (Block, 1995, p. 211). This warning harkens back nearly a century, a fallacy referred to as the "the jingle fallacy" (see also Thorndike, 1904), a common error in which two different psychological constructs are labeled identically, and as a consequence are used (erroneously) interchangeably. We worry that this is the present state of affairs with much (though certainly not all) bullying research (see Hawley, Johnson, Mize, & McNamara, 2007 for a similar problem occurring in the peer-relations research).

The jingle of ambivalence toward aggression. As psychological researchers, we tend to display a considerable amount of ambivalence toward aggression, possibly because aggression can be used in ways that support the goals of the group. Sears's prosocial aggression (1961; "aggression used in a socially approved way for purposes that are acceptable to the moral standards of the group," p. 471) is a case in point (see also Dodge, 1991). Moreover, children are often gently socialized to stand up for their rights when warranted, and if put under duress, to lash out on their own behalf, or on the behalf of a friend or a weaker peer. Bullying, it seems all authors would agree to date, is never justified.

Aggression versus Bullying: A Question of Proximal Function

An important question thus is: *What are the key distinctions between aggression and bullying that can lead to different social outcomes?* We believe that part of the answer lies in the function of the behavior, or, as described above, what the behavior is *for*. Little and colleagues (2003) found important differences in developmental outcomes associated with reactive versus instrumental aggression, such that reactive aggression is associated with hostility and frustration whereas instrumental aggression tends to be associated with social influence (see also Dodge, 1991). This pattern of differential associations with reactive versus instrumental aggression have been found elsewhere with reactive aggression correlating with peer rejection and externalizing symptoms and instrumental aggression correlating with delinquency and, in some instances, leadership skills (Poulin & Boivin, 2000; Vitaro, Gendreau, Tremblay, & Oligny, 1998). Thus, in general, we might expect to find instrumental aggression associated with various competencies (see also Suttonn et al., 1999b; Hawley, 1999, 2002).

A case has been made on exactly this point in our own lab. Namely, when aggression is performed in the service of resource control (i.e., social dominance), and is performed in a manner suggesting that it is strategic rather than impulsive (e.g., aggression balanced with prosocial behavior in the service of goal attainment), then it tends to be associated with positive attention from peers, high status, acceptance, and a litany of attributes that might be characterized as "skills" (e.g., Hawley, 2003; think CEO rather than criminal). It may be the case that the form of aggression is less important than its function for developmental outcomes (Little et al., 2003).

At the same time, however, some readers may find the current literature confusing. Specifically, some authors argue that strategic aggression may be associated with status, but not with acceptance (Ojanen et al., 2005; Cillessen & Mayeaux, 2004). Hawley and colleagues (2007), however, contend that aggression, status, and likeability can in fact go hand in hand. These seemingly divergent conclusions may simply be a function of the analytic method employed. When one looks at the relationships among variables in terms of correlations (i.e., a variable centered approach), the relationship between aggression and acceptance is equivocal (some authors find a negative correlation and others find no correlation). Researchers who look at *types* of youth (i.e., person-centered approach) who have both positive and negative characteristics clearly find a subset that is highly aggressive and yet who garner positive attention. Taken together, these conflicting findings highlight the importance of taking into consideration the analytic methods employed when drawing conclusions. (For an extended explication of person versus variable centered approaches and their ramifications, see Hawley et al., 2007, and, more recently, Rodkin & Roisman, 2010).

Other researchers have examined peer-regard outcomes from a standpoint of "perceived popularity," a construct associated with both leadership and aggression (Parkhurst & Hopmeyer, 1998). Ethnographic studies suggest that peer-perceived popularity may better typify power and influence in peer groups (Adler & Adler, 1995, 1998; Eder, 1985; Merten, 1997; but see Hawley et al., 2007). Unlike measures of acceptance, bullies and victims experience different patterns of perceived popularity; victims maintain low levels and bullies maintain high levels (Sijtsema, Veenstra, Lindenberg, & Salmivalli, 2009). These findings suggest that bullies are afforded and maintain power in group contexts.

Goals of acceptance or domination? Are bullies disliked but powerful? Perhaps domination is the goal of bullying (Pellegrini, 2002). Time and again the power differentiation between the reputed bully and their victim has been documented (e.g., Veenstra et al., 2007; Vaillancourt, Hymel, & McDougall, 2003). Others have made inroads by considering the social goals of bullies (e.g., Renshaw & Asher, 1983). Ojanen and colleagues (2005), for example, construed goals as either agentic (status, dominance, respect) or communal (intimacy, acceptance; see also a "goal framing approach" of Dijkstra, Lindenberg, & Veenstra, 2007). Generally, instrumentally aggressive children endorse agentic goals (presumably the raison d'être for their aggression; Crick & Dodge, 1994; Erdley & Asher, 1998), and agentic goals increase over time as children approach adolescence (Pellegrini & Long, 2002). Much of the work on bullying evoking "goals" concepts converges on the point that bullies pursue power, popularity, or domination[4] more so than non-bullying peers (e.g., Sijtsema et al., 2009; Vaillancourt et al., 2003; Veenstra et al., 2007), or that bullying is an "agonistic strategy used to obtain and maintain dominance" (Long & Pellegrini, 2003, p. 402).

It is difficult to reconcile the images of the rejected bully whose future "looks quite bleak" (Parault et al., 2007, p. 150) with the aggressive social dominant who attracts a great deal of positive attention (e.g., Hawley, 2003; Rodkin et al., 2006; Bost et al., 1998; Cairns et al., 1988). The former uninviting portrayal may apply more to children who are both bullies and victims of bullying (Holt & Espelage, 2007). Moreover, numerous victims of bullying tend to be passive, anxious, physically weak, and insecure (Olweus, 1978; Parault et al., 2007). It is not clear to the present authors that repeatedly victimizing the helpless and socially isolated is an effective path to social dominance in and of itself. This point will be discussed in more detail later.

Group Cohesion and Social Identity

Bukowski and Sippola (2001) suggested bullying may additionally serve group goals, and accordingly serve some cohesive function especially when group goals are blocked (e.g., when an individual pursues individual goals that are contrary to group goals). Given the power campaign in which bullies appear to be engaged, how then could bullying foster group cohesion? Additional answers may stem from classical concepts from social psychology. Founders of modern social psychology emphasized the role of the "in-group" (a group to which one sees him/herself as a part) on behavioral processes and self-identity (e.g., Allport, 1954; Sherif & Sherif, 1953; Tajfel & Turner, 1986). Namely, feelings of group membership affirm the existence of the self (Allport, 1954) or contribute to a positive sense of identity (Tajfel & Turner, 1986). Hostility and rejection toward "out group members" (those who are not part of one's in-group) serve to strengthen the sense of belonging of in-group members (Brown & Abrams, 1986). Such rejection can progress from mild verbal derogation (teasing under the guise of "friendly humor"[5]; Allport, 1954) to extreme forms, including physical attack. Anticipating the recent strides in indirect aggression, Allport (1954) understood the central role of rumor in that "rumor is found to enter into the pattern of violence at one or all … stages" (p. 63).

Modern instantiations of social identity theory (Tajfel & Turner, 1979, 1986) have established the minimal conditions necessary for individuals to favor the in-group at the expense of out-group members in order to establish or reestablish a positive in-group perception (i.e., the quest for positive distinctiveness; Tajfel & Turner, 1986). Tajfel famously showed that schoolboys could be randomly assigned to groups (e.g., based on a contrived tendency to over- or underestimate dots), and participants still showed in-group favoritism based on this arbitrary categorization (e.g., Tajfel, 1970). Under these minimal conditions, personal identity gives way to social identity.

Bullying has long been found to be a social process (O'Connell, Pepler, & Craig, 1999; Olweus, 1991; Salmivalli et al., 1996; Swearer et al., 2009) and indeed the bullying episode has been shown to be more likely to continue when there is an audience implicitly or explicitly supporting the bullying act (O'Connell et al., 1999). Sometimes the reasons why children bully escape us and appear to have little more value than to make onlookers laugh (Salmivalli, 2009, personal communication; Adler & Adler, 1995). In fact, close attention to the social psychological research gives the chilling impression that even slight offense *need not* precede the victimizing of an out-group member. Merely being anxious or physically weak could very well do the trick. In contrast to proclivities of those working in the developmental domain, considerations of "personality" or "social skills" or "theory of mind" generally do not influence social psychological models. However, the degree of identification with the in-group does; that is, those who identify with the in-group especially strongly are at heightened risk for prejudicial behavior (Tajfel & Turner, 1979; Branscombe & Wann, 1994).

Implications for intervention. Interventionists might do well to be mindful of social identity processes. Recent work, for example, makes the point that taking the perspective of another can induce a social identity threat (e.g., undermining of positive feelings associated with one's social identity) and, accordingly, challenges our inherent motivation to achieve *identity distinctiveness* (i.e., the motive to maintain a sense of differentiation from others; Brewer, 1991). Thus, there appears to be an intrinsic bias against empathizing with out-group members (Tarrant, Dazeley, & Cottom, 2009), especially if the individual identifies highly with the in-group. Previous work has demonstrated a positive effect of perspective-taking on views of out-group members (e.g., Galinsky & Moskowitz, 2000). This of course is good news to interventionists wishing to target perspective-taking skills to mitigate victimization of others. However, more recent work suggests that this positive effect may be due to "low identifiers," that is, those who do not strongly identify with the in-group (see Tarrant et al., 2009). Individuals who strongly identify with the in-group are *less likely* to adopt the perspective of out-group members than are low identifiers, and yet hold *more negative* attitudes toward the out-group if they do adopt another's perspective. This is all to suggest that social identity processes may hinder well-intended interventions attempting to encourage a socially central bully to adopt the perspective of his or her victim. Indeed, such attempts may back-fire. Instead, social identity processes may suggest that the most effective intervention efforts focus on peripheral group members (see, for example, Salmivalli, Kaukiainen, & Voeten, 2005; Swearer et al., 2009).

HUMAN NEEDS AND BALANCING "GETTING ALONG" WITH "GETTING AHEAD": DIFFERENTIATING BULLYING FROM AGGRESSION

Such discussion of social identity processes and group cohesion highlights the necessity of considering fundamental human needs and the roles they play in child and adolescent behavior. That is, the basic human need of "belongingness" (Baumeister & Leary, 1995) can drive much behavior for good or ill. Human needs have long been a part of psychological discourse (see Adler, 1924; Freud, 1930/1964; Maslow, 1971) and accordingly may well inform the discussion about the differences between bullying and aggression; namely, we wonder if aggression plays a role in healthy need fulfillment in a way that bullying does not. Again, we believe the distinction may lie in function and how function interfaces with human needs.

We will ground our discussion of aggression and human need fulfillment on self-determination theory (SDT; Deci & Ryan, 1985, 2000). SDT is a meta-theoretical perspective of adaptive functioning that emphasizes the evolution of the organism and its basic needs and need fulfillment. With its foundation in evolutionary theory, SDT acknowledges the essential role of self-interest in human functioning. Thus, because of its focus on the interest of the organism, SDT is somewhat at odds with more traditional, other-oriented theories of human functioning that place more importance on peaceful group relations than on individual success (see Stump, Ratliff, Wu, & Hawley, 2009, for extended discussion).

As its primary thesis, SDT recognizes that humans universally have three innate needs: autonomy, competence, and relatedness (Ryan, Kuhl, & Deci, 1997). Autonomy refers to the extent to which one perceives that his or her behaviors are caused by the self versus directed by others. Competence is derived from *effectance motivation* (White, 1959), the motivation for successful and accomplished interactions with one's environment. The need for competence is dependent upon skill, action, and ability to master one's environment. Relatedness, the third fundamental need, signifies a feeling of connectedness to others, and serves as a foundation for interpersonal relationships and group cohesion.

Insufficient need fulfillment can result in marked deficits in psychosocial functioning (Ryan, Deci, & Grolnick, 1995). When autonomy is suppressed, for example, individuals are likely to experience ill-being; extreme suppression levels may result in psychopathology such as depression and eating disorders (Ryan et al., 1995). One can certainly imagine that individuals who are repeatedly victimized by bullies may not be satisfying all of their fundamental human needs. Plotting alternative routes home from school to avoid bullies, for instance, illustrates a significant suppression of autonomy.

From our perspective, a socially competent and optimally functioning individual satisfies the three fundamental human needs within his or her social environment (see also

Buhrmester, 1996; Stump et al., 2009). Thus, we would contend that an individual who can display autonomy and effectiveness without alienating the broader group is successfully functioning in his or her context.[6] Social competence, in this evolutionary frame of reference, is somewhat at odds with conventional developmental psychological models of social competence. Developmentalists traditionally discuss social competence in terms of culturally valued skills and attributes such as displaying low levels of aggression, maintaining harmony in groups, being self-sacrificing, self-regulated, and garnering high levels of peer acceptance and low levels of peer rejection (Anderson & Messick, 1974; Coie & Dodge, 1998). Whereas these skills are certainly helpful in educational contexts in that they garner teacher and parent approval, they may not result in optimal functioning in a diverse range of cultures and contexts (Ogbu, 1981).

From our evolutionary view, social competence at least in part involves effective goal attainment (Hawley, 2002). As such, competence may not rule out aggression simply because the behavior—under circumscribed conditions—is socially censured. In developmental circles, aggression has been nearly unilaterally considered to be a predominant index of social incompetence, presumably because aggression had been thought to be strongly associated with deficits in information processing (i.e., socially unskilled; Crick & Dodge, 1994) and high levels of peer rejection (which are antithetical to acceptance; Coie & Dodge, 1998; Newcomb, Bukowski, & Pattee, 1993). Thus, from a needs perspective, the assumption has been that aggressive children sacrifice both their effectance and relatedness needs.

More recently, however, researchers have questioned this straightforward unilateral approach to aggression, particularly as it relates to social competence and needs satisfaction (see Bukowski, 2003; Hawley, 2003; Sutton, Smith, & Swettenham, 1999b, c; Vaughn & Santos, 2007; esp. Stump et al., 2009). Namely, authors postulate that certain aggressors, those who are adept at group manipulation, might have superior theory of mind skills, which would facilitate satisfying effectance needs (Sutton, Smith, & Swettenham, 1999a). Hawley (1999), in a revised theory of social dominance, suggested that effective resource control (i.e., social dominance) can involve aggressively pursuing goals while balancing aggression (not bullying per se) with prosociality or cooperation, thus promoting satisfaction of effectance and relatedness needs.

Can effective competitive behavior, such as in within group competition for resources, be "competent"? SDT does not seem to rule out the possibility, as long as such behavior, however "socially unacceptable," does not win wholesale group rejection and ostracism. Indeed, Bukowski (2003) traced the linguistic lineage of *"competence"* and discovered that it shares a common linguistic ancestry with *"compete,"* leading Bukowski to conclude "that being competent means that one is able to compete in the company of others" (p. 394). This definition is in line with White's (1959) contention that competence refers to "an organism's capacity to interact effectively with its environment" (p. 297), thus providing the foundation for competence needs in the SDT theoretic perspective.

From this line of thought, we can consider social competence to imply effective competition in social contexts. Effective competition undeniably involves an element of power striving (i.e., getting ahead), but it also requires maintaining positive relations in the group (i.e., getting along). Though competition is typically regarded to be less than socially desirable (though competition is sometimes denoted in the softer form of "agency needs"; Buhrmester, 1996), it lies at the root of resource control theory, an evolutionary perspective on human social dominance focusing on children's competitive strategies and success, and subsequent developmental outcomes.

Aggression versus Bullying: A Question of Ultimate (Evolutionary) Function

Resource control theory (RCT; Hawley, 1999) is primarily concerned with individual proximal adaptation to local circumstances, with group response as a secondary outcome of that adaptation process. *Resource control* (RC) in general refers to the degree to which individuals successfully access social, informational, or material resources (Hawley, 1999). Successful RC or competition in the presence of others results in social dominance, and she or he who controls resources wields power (Keltner, Gruenfeld, & Anderson, 2003).

Resource control strategies. According to RCT, there are two primary strategies (products of evolution) that humans use to control resources. Coercive strategies involve threats, manipulation, and instrumental aggression. These strategies are well discussed in the primate literature as methods of obtaining dominance (e.g. Alberts, Watts, & Altmann, 2003). Because they are associated with an aggressive sorting, they may be considered akin to aggressive domination. Setting RCT apart from other theories of social dominance (e.g., Krebs & Davies, 1997), however, are prosocial strategies of resource control (behaviors that serve to gain resources via cooperative means such as reciprocation; Charlesworth, 1996). That is, in the competitive arena, cooperation can be as effective as aggression.

Resource control subtypes. Resource control theory employs a person-centered, typological approach in which we classify individuals into "types," depending on their relative usage of prosocial and coercive strategies. "Bistrategic resource controllers" are those who employ high levels of both prosocial and coercive strategies, "prosocial controllers" predominately use prosocial strategies, "coercive controllers" predominately use coercive strategies, "noncontrollers" employ neither, and the remaining "typical controllers" display average levels of both strategies (see Hawley, 2003 for details).

When discussing the distinctions between aggression and bullying, the two most instructive types are coercive and bistrategic controllers because both display high levels of coercive behavior. Though they share this common behavioral thread, coercives and bistrategics experience disparate outcomes. Coercive controllers are better than average at goal attainment and power pursuit; that is, they "get ahead." Yet, they are hostile, unskilled, rejected by peers, and sustain low-quality friendships (Hawley, 2003, Hawley et al., 2007). Thus, they are not "getting along," and, as such, coercive concontrollers achieve their competence needs at the expense of relatedness needs. In contrast, bistrategic controllers are far more successful; they are not only very effective at resource control, but they also are well integrated into the social group in that they accumulate many *like most* nominations (but also *like least* nominations), are perceived to be popular, and attract more friendship nominations than the majority of their peers (Hawley, 2003; Hawley et al., 2007). This marked divergence in social reception already clearly emerges in preschool (Hawley, 2002). Thus, they do not seem to suffer the same social costs borne by the coercive controllers.

If aggression is associated with skills deficits, then how do bistrategics pull off the prosocial strategies and concomitant positive reception from the social group? Bistrategics do not seem to suffer the same skills deficits that the coercive controllers do (Hawley, 2003; Stump, Middleton, & Hawley, 2009). A traditionally trained developmentalist may predict that bistrategics have poor quality relationships because of their elevated level of *like least* nominations. This prediction has not been empirically supported; though friends of bistrategics report that their relationships are high in conflict, they also describe their friendships as close, fun, and high in companionship (Hawley et al., 2007). It seems that bistrategics are displaying an effective balance of "getting along and getting ahead" (though, not as effectively as prosocial controllers to be sure). As such, they appear to be meeting their competence and relatedness needs and, because they tend not to defer to the will of peers, also satisfy their autonomy needs.

Are Aggressive Social Dominants Bullies?

Bistrategics seem to be benefitting from their aggression as they are certainly powerful in their social contexts. This, of course, raises the question: Are bistrategics *bullies*? To address this question, we must first consider to whom bistrategics are aggressive. One might reasonably assume that bistrategics do not aggress against members of their "in group." In actuality, however, bistrategic controllers aggress against their very own friends, both relationally and overtly (Hawley et al., 2007). It is not clear, however, that they tend to repeatedly victimize low status others any more than they target their inner circle. Indeed, though bistrategics display the aggressive characteristic of bullies, we hesitate to assume—with the jingle fallacy firmly in mind—that they are indeed engaging in significant bullying behavior.

Low status, weak victims of bullies (Olweus, 1978) likely correspond to "non-controllers" in RCT parlance. And because non-controllers are unsuccessful in controlling resources, are not well socially integrated, and continuously defer to others (Hawley, 2003; Hawley & Little, 1999), they fail at meeting their basic needs from an SDT perspective. In contrast, bistrategics tend to be very instrumental and socially savvy individuals, making us believe that many of their interactions have some calculus behind them. Aggression and prosociality might be doled out with care; especially, perhaps toward others of similar rank with whom they come into competition and from whom there is much to be gained. What could they gain from a non-controller? Instead, we wonder whether coercive controllers might be bullies. They are powerful and share the same aggressive profile as bistrategics, but lack social intelligence (Hawley, 2003; Stump, Middleton, & Hawley, 2009). Their aggression, therefore, may not be as tactically employed as that of bistrategics and their victims may indeed be the lower status non-controllers.

Group level and dyadic investigations regarding bullies and victims and resource control types have not been conducted, thus the above conjectures about bistrategic and coercive controllers are purely speculative. At the same time, we have long held the minority view that some acts of aggression may facilitate the socially competent quest for human needs satisfaction (see Hawley, 2007; Stump et al., 2009, for extended arguments). Empirical and theoretical treatments of bullying, however, do not give us the impression that bullying fills the same role. As the bullying and aggression research progresses, we are more than willing to be proven wrong. Indeed, these are very interesting and important questions to pursue.

TRANSLATING RESEARCH INTO PRACTICE: IMPLICATIONS FOR BULLYING PREVENTION AND INTERVENTION PROGRAMS

As we are not skilled interventionists, we hesitate to analyze or suggest specific prevention and intervention programs that might reduce bullying in school contexts. Such issues are already in very capable hands (e.g., Swearer et al., 2009; Salmivalli et al., 2005).

Instead, in addition to the perspective from the framework of social psychology above, we find utility in discussing the implications of SDT and RCT for understanding the root causes of children's social behavior. If aggression can underlie need fulfillment and is not always predictive of poor social outcomes in children (as we see with bistrategics), then should we as child professionals strive to eradicate all aggression in all children? We are certainly not the first to raise this question; early childhood researchers openly wondered about girls' aggressive "executive skills" (e.g., Woolley, 1925).

In stark contrast, bullying—the repeated victimization of the defenseless—is extremely problematic in all school contexts. Accordingly, intervention programs should continue striving to minimize its occurrence and to ameliorate the problems associated with it. At the same time, we caution against committing the "jingle fallacy" by equating all acts of aggression with bullying. We understand that the terms may be used interchangeably in part because many interventionists and school personnel are committed to improving children's lives by minimizing all "negative" social behaviors that do not mesh well with values we tend to associate with "character." There is no denying that these are certainly difficult and complex issues, but we should not eschew the possibility that aggression, when balanced with prosociality, can play a role in the competent pursuit of human needs satisfaction.

NOTES

1. See also "mob psychology" where multiple youths with "delinquent egos" come together and do things they would not do singly (Redl &Wineman, 1951).
2. Though note the interesting discussion of late as to whether the power differential is necessary (e.g., Rodkin & Berger, 2008).
3. We hope that readers will forgive us for not providing explicit citations to identify the offenders. Now that readers have been appraised of the problem, we are sure they will have little trouble identifying potential confounds. In our perusal of the literature, however, we found clear connection between theoretical and measurement models in the bullying domain to be the exception rather than the rule (see, for example, the work of Pepler et al., 2008; Salmivalli, Lagerspetz, Bjorkqvist, Osterman, and Kaukianen, 1996; Sutton, Smith, & Swettenham, 1999b).
4. Here we wouldd like to interject once again about the wisdom of being cautious on use of language. As with the interchanging of "aggression" and "bullying," we see a similar situation developing with the term "dominance," which is being used interchangeably in the bullying literature to mean both domination and social dominance. Domination is one means to achieve social dominance (resource control and power), but it certainly is not the only means (Hawley, 1999). Though both concepts are legitimate targets of inquiry, the terms are not synonymous.
5. For an additional view on the paradoxical effects of teasing (in that it both strains and strengthens ties), see Keltner, Capps, Kring, Young, Randall, & Heerey, 2001.
6. By "without alienating the broader group," we do not mean that individuals must be adored by everyone (i.e., sociometrically popular; Coie, Dodge, & Coppotelli, 1982), but that individuals be accepted (i.e., receive numerous *like most* nominations), regardless of rejection (i.e., *like least* nominations).

REFERENCES

Adler, A. (1924). *The practice and theory of individual psychology.* Oxford, UK: Harcourt Brace.

Adler, P.A., & Adler, P. (1995). Dynamics of inclusion and exclusion in preadolescent cliques. *Social Psychology Quarterly, 58,* 145–162.

Adler, P.A., & Adler, P. (1998). *Peer power: Preadolescent culture and identity.* New Brunswick, NJ: Rutgers University Press.

Alberts, S.C., Watts, H.E., & Altmann, J. (2003). Queuing and queue-jumping: Long-term patterns of reproductive skew in male savannah baboons. *Papio cynocephalus. Animal Behaviour, 65,* 821–840.

Allport, G.W. (1954). *The nature of prejudice*. Oxford, UK: Addison-Wesley.

Allport, G.W., & Odbert, H.S. (1936). Trait names: A psycho-lexical study. *Psychological Monographs, 47*.

Anderson, S., & Messick, S. (1974). Social competency in young children. *Developmental Psychology, 10*, 282–293.

Bandura, A. (1973). *Aggression: A social learning analysis*. Oxford, UK: Prentice-Hall.

Barrington, R.E.D. (1932). Bullying amongst birds. *Nature, 129*, 395.

Baumeister, R., & Leary, M.R. (1995). The need to belong: Desire for interpersonal attachments as a fundamental human motivation. *Psychological Bulletin, 117*, 497–529.

Block, J. (1995). A contrarian view of the five-factor approach to personality description. *Psychological Bulletin, 117*, 187–215.

Bost, K.K., Vaughn, B.E., Washington, W.N., Cielinski, K.L., & Bradbard, M.R. (1998). Social competence, social support, and attachment: Demarcation of construct domains, measurement, and paths of influence for pre-school children attending head start. *Child Development, 69*, 192–218.

Boulton, M.J., & Smith, P.K. (1994). Bully/victim problems in middle-school children: Stability, self-perceived competence, peer perceptions and peer acceptance. *British Journal of Developmental Psychology, 12*, 315–329.

Branscombe, N.R., & Wann, D.L. (1994). Collective self-esteem consequences of outgroup derogation when a valued social identity is on trial. *European Journal of Social Psychology, 24*, 641–657

Brewer, M.B. (1991). The social self: On being the same and different at the same time. *Personality and Social Psychology Bulletin, 17*, 475–482.

Brown, R., & Abrams, D. (1986). The effects of intergroup similarity and goal interdependence on intergroup attitudes and task performance. *Journal of Experimental Social Psychology, 22*, 78–92.

Buhrmester, D. (1996). Need fulfillment, interpersonal competence, and the developmental contexts of early adolescent friendship. In W.M. Bukowski, A.F. Newcomb, & W.W. Hartup (Eds.), *The company they keep: Friendship in childhood and adolescence* (pp. 158–185). New York, NY: Cambridge University Press.

Bukowski, W.M. (2003). What does it mean to say that aggressive children are competent or incompetent? *Merrill-Palmer Quarterly. Special Issue: Aggression and Adaptive Functioning: The Bright Side to Bad Behavior, 49*, 390–400.

Bukowski, W.M., & Sippola, L.K. (2001). Groups, individuals, and victimization: A view of the peer system. In J. Juvonen & S. Graham (Eds.), *Peer harassment in school: The plight of the vulnerable and victimized* (pp. 355–377). New York, NY: Guilford Press.

Cairns, R.B., Cairns, B.D., Neckerman, H.J., Gest, S.D., & Gariépy, J. (1988). Social networks and aggressive behavior: Peer support or peer rejection? *Developmental Psychology, 24*, 815–823.

Charlesworth, W.R. (1996). Co-operation and competition: Contributions to an evolutionary and developmental model. *International Journal of Behavioral Development, 19*, 25–38.

Cillessen, A.H.N., & Mayeux, L. (2004). Sociometric status and peer group behavior: Previous findings and current directions. In J.B. Kupersmidt & K.A. Dodge (Eds.), *Children's peer relations: From development to intervention* (pp. 3–20). Washington, DC: American Psychological Association.

Coie, J.D., & Dodge, K.A. (1998). Aggression and antisocial behavior. In W. Damon & N. Eisenberg (Eds.), *Handbook of child psychology: Vol 3. Social, emotional, and personality development* (5th ed.) (pp. 779–862). Hoboken, NJ: John Wiley & Sons Inc.

Coie, J.D., Dodge, K.A., & Coppotelli, H. (1982). Dimensions and types of social status: A cross-age perspective. *Developmental Psychology, 18*, 557–570.

Crick, N.R., & Dodge, K.A. (1994). A review and reformulation of social information-processing mechanisms in children's social adjustment. *Psychological Bulletin, 115*, 74–101.

Crick, N.R., & Grotpeter, J.K. (1995). Relational aggression, gender, and social-psychological adjustment. *Child Development, 66*, 710–722.

Deci, E.L., & Ryan, R.M. (1985). *Intrinsic motivation and self-determination in human behavior*. New York, NY: Plenum.

Deci, E.L., & Ryan, R.M. (2000). The "what" and "why" of goal pursuits: Human needs and the self-determination of behavior. *Psychological Inquiry, 11*, 227–268.

Dickens, C. (1838/1846). *The adventures of Oliver Twist* (3rd ed.). London: Bradbury & Evans, Whitefriars.

Dijkstra, J.K., Lindenberg, S., & Veenstra, R. (2007). Same-gender and cross-gender peer acceptance and peer rejection and their relation to bullying and helping among preadolescents: Comparing predictions from gender-homophily and goal-framing approaches. *Developmental Psychology, 43*, 1377–1389.

Dodge, K.A. (1991). The structure and function of reactive and proactive aggression. In D.J. Pepler & K.H. Rubin (Eds.), *The development and treatment of childhood aggression* (pp. 201–218). Hillsdale, NJ: Lawrence Erlbaum Associates.

Dollard, J., Miller, N.E., Doob, L.W., Mowrer, O.H., & Sears, R.R. (1939). *Frustration and aggression*. New Haven, CT: Yale University Press.

Eder, D. (1985). The cycle of popularity: Interpersonal relations among female adolescents. *Sociology of Education, 58*, 154–165.

Erdley, C.A., & Asher, S.R. (1998). Linkages between children's beliefs about the legitimacy of aggression and their behavior. *Social Development, 7,* 321–339.

Espelage, D.L., & Swearer, S.M. (2003). Research on school bullying and victimization: What have we learned and where do we go from here? *School Psychology Review, 32*, 365–383.

Freud, S. (1930/1964). *Civilization and its discontents.* New York, NY: W.W. Norton.

Galen, B.R., & Underwood, M.K. (1997). A developmental investigation of social aggression among children. *Developmental Psychology, 33*, 589–600.

Galinsky, A.D., & Moskowitz, G.B. (2000). Perspective-taking: Decreasing stereotype expression, stereotype accessibility, and in-group favoritism. *Journal of Personality and Social Psychology, 78*, 708–724.

Hawley, P.H. (1999). The ontogenesis of social dominance: A strategy-based evolutionary perspective. *Developmental Review, 19,* 97–132.

Hawley, P.H. (2002). Social dominance and prosocial and coercive strategies of resource control in preschoolers. *International Journal of Behavioral Development, 26*, 167–176.

Hawley, P.H. (2003). Prosocial and coercive configurations of resource control in early adolescence: A case for the well-adapted Machiavellian. *Merrill-Palmer Quarterly. Special Issue: Aggression and Adaptive Functioning: The Bright Side to Bad Behavior, 49*, 279–309.

Hawley, P.H. (2007). Social dominance in childhood and adolescence: Why social competence and aggression may go hand in hand. In P.H. Hawley, T.D Little, & P. Rodkin (Eds.), *Aggression and adaptation: The bright side to bad behavior* (pp. 1–29). Hillsdale, NJ: Lawrence Erlbaum and Associates

Hawley, P.H., & Little, T.D. (1999). On winning some and losing some: A social relations approach to social dominance in toddlers. *Merrill-Palmer Quarterly, 45,* 185–214.

Hawley, P.H., Little, T.D., & Card, N.A. (2007). The allure of a mean friend: Relationship quality and processes of aggressive adolescents with prosocial skills. *International Journal of Behavioral Development, 31*, 170–180.

Hawley, P.H., Little, T.D., & Card, N.A. (2008). The myth of the alpha male: A new look at dominance-related beliefs and behaviors among adolescent males and females. *International Journal of Behavioral Development, 32*, 76–88.

Hawley, P.H., Johnson, S.E., Mize, J.A., & McNamara, K.A. (2007). Physical attractiveness in preschoolers: Relationships with power, status, aggression and social skills. *Journal of School Psychology, 45*, 499–521.

Holt, M.K., & Espelage, D.L. (2007). Perceived social support among bullies, victims, and bully-victims. *Journal of Youth and Adolescence, 36*, 984–994.

Keltner, D., Gruenfeld, D.H., & Anderson, C. (2003). Power, approach, and inhibition. *Psychological Review, 110*, 265–284.

Keltner, D., Capps, L., Kring, A.M., Young, R.C., & Heerey, E.A. (2001). Just teasing: A conceptual analysis and empirical review. *Psychological Bulletin, 127*, 229–248.

Krebs, J.R., & Davies, N.B. (Eds.). (1997). *Behavioral ecology: An evolutionary approach.* Oxford: Blackwell.

Lagerspetz, K.M., Björkqvist, K., & Peltonen, T. (1988). Is indirect aggression typical of females? Gender differences in aggressiveness in 11- to 12-year-old children. *Aggressive Behavior, 14*, 403–414.

Little, T.D., Jones, S.M., Henrich, C.C., & Hawley, P.H. (2003). Disentangling the "whys" from the "whats" of aggressive behaviour. *International Journal of Behavioral Development, 27*, 122–133.

Long, J.D., & Pellegrini, A.D. (2003). Studying change in dominance and bullying with linear mixed models. *School Psychology Review, 32*, 401–417.

Maccoby, E.E., & Jacklin, C.N. (1980). Sex differences in aggression: A rejoinder and reprise. *Child Development, 51*, 964–980.

Maslow, A.H. (1971). *The farther reaches of human nature.* Oxford, UK: Viking.

Merten, D.E. (1997). The meaning of meanness: Popularity, competition, and conflict among junior high school girls. *Sociology of Education, 70*, 175–191.

Monks, C.P., & Smith, P.K. (2006). Definitions of bullying: Age differences in understanding of the term, and the role of experience. *British Journal of Developmental Psychology, 24*, 801–821.

Nansel, T.R., Overpeck, M., Pilla, R.S., Ruan, W.J., Simons-Morton, B., & Scheidt, P. (2001). Bullying behaviors among U.S. youth: Prevalence and association with psychosocial adjustment. *JAMA: Journal of the American Medical Association, 285*, 2094–2100.

Newcomb, A.F., Bukowski, W.M., & Pattee, L. (1993). Children's peer relations: A meta-analytic review of popular, rejected, neglected, controversial, and average sociometric status. *Psychological Bulletin, 113*, 99–128.

O'Connell, P., Pepler, D., & Craig, W. (1999). Peer involvement in bullying: Insights and challenges for intervention. *Journal of Adolescence, 22*, 437–452.

Ogbu, J.U. (1981). Origins of human competence: A cultural-ecological perspective. *Child Development, 52*, 413–429.

Ojanen, T., Grönroos, M., & Salmivalli, C. (2005). An interpersonal circumplex model of children's social goals: Links with peer-reported behavior and sociometric status. *Developmental Psychology, 41*, 699–710

Olweus, D. (1978). *Aggression in the schools: Bullies and whipping boys*. Oxford, UK: Hemisphere.

Olweus, D. (1991). Bully/victim problems among schoolchildren: Basic facts and effects of a school based intervention program. In D.J. Pepler & K.H. Rubin (Eds.), *Earlscourt symposium on childhood aggression, Jun 1988, Toronto, Canada* (pp. 411–448). Hillsdale, NJ, England: Lawrence Erlbaum Associates, Inc.

Olweus, D. (1995). Bullying or peer abuse at school: Facts and interventions. *Current Directions in Psychological Science, 4*, 196–200.

Olweus, D. (2001). Peer harassment: A critical analysis and some important issues. In J. Juvonen & S. Graham (Eds.), *Peer harassment in school: The plight of the vulnerable and victimized* (pp. 3–20). New York, NY: Guilford.

Parault, S.J., Davis, H.A., & Pellegrini, A.D. (2007). The social contexts of bullying and victimization. *The Journal of Early Adolescence, 27*, 145–174.

Parkhurst, J.T., & Hopmeyer, A. (1998). Sociometric popularity and peer-perceived popularity: Two distinct dimensions of peer status. *Journal of Early Adolescence, 18*, 125–144.

Pellegrini, A.D. (2002). Bullying, victimization, and sexual harassment during the transition to middle school. *Educational Psychologist, 37*, 151–163.

Pellegrini, A.D., & Long, J.D. (2002). A longitudinal study of bullying, dominance, and victimization during the transition from primary school through secondary school. *British Journal of Developmental Psychology, 20*, 259–280.

Pepler, D.J., Jiang, D., Craig, W., & Connolly, J. (2008). Developmental trajectories of bullying and associated factors. *Child Development, 79*, 325–338.

Pikas, A. (1975). Treatment of mobbing in school: Principles for the results of the work of an anti-mobbing group. *Scandinavian Journal of Educational Research, 19*, 1–12.

Poulin, F., & Boivin, M. (2000). Reactive and proactive aggression: Evidence of a two- factor model. *Psychological Assessment, 12*, 115–122.

Redl, F., & Wineman, D. (1951). *Children who hate: The disorganization and breakdown of behavior controls*. New York, NY: Free Press.

Renshaw, P.D. & Asher, S.R. (1983). Children's goals and strategies for social interaction. *Merrill-Palmer Quarterly, 29*, 353–374.

Rodkin, P.C., & Berger, C. (2008). Who bullies whom? Social status asymmetries by victim gender. *International Journal of Behavioral Development, 32*, 473–485.

Rodkin, P.C. & Roisman, G.I. (2010). Antecedents and correlates of the popular-aggressive phenomenon in elementary school. *Child Development, 81*, 837–850.

Rodkin, P.C., Farmer, T.W., Pearl, R., & Van Acker, R. (2006). They're cool: Social status and peer group supports for aggressive boys and girls. *Social Development, 15*, 175–204.

Ryan, R.M., Deci, E.L., & Grolnick, W.S. (1995). Autonomy, relatedness, and the self: Their relation to development and psychopathology. In D. Cicchetti & D.J. Cohen (Eds.), *Developmental psychopathology: Vol. 1. Theory and methods* (pp. 618–655). New York, NY: Wiley.

Ryan, R.M., Kuhl, J., & Deci, E.L. (1997). Nature and autonomy: An organization view of social and neurobiological aspects of self-regulation in behavior and development. *Development and Psychopathology, 9*, 701–728.

Salmivalli, C., & Peets, K. (2009). Bullies, victims, and bully-victim relationships in middle childhood and early adolescence. In K.H. Rubin, W.M Bukowski, & B. Laursen (Eds.), *Handbook of peer interactions, relationships, and groups* (pp. 322–340). New York, NY: Guilford.

Salmivalli, C., Kaukiainen, A., & Voeten, M. (2005). Anti-bullying intervention: Implementation and outcome. *British Journal of Educational Psychology, 75*, 465–487.

Salmivalli, C., Lagerspetz, K., Bjorkqvist, K., Osterman, K., & Kaukiainen, A. (1996). Bullying as a group process: Participant roles and their relations to social status within the group. *Aggressive Behavior, 22*, 1–15.

Sears, R.R. (1961). Relation of early socialization experiences to aggression in middle childhood. *Journal of Abnormal and Social Psychology, 63*, 466–492.

Sherif, M., & Sherif, C.W. (1953). *Groups in harmony and tension: An integration of studies of intergroup relations*. Oxford, UK: Harper & Brothers.

Sijtsema, J.J., Veenstra, R., Lindenberg, S., & Salmivalli, C. (2009). Empirical test of bullies' status goals: Assessing direct goals, aggression, and prestige. *Aggressive Behavior, 35*, 57–67.

Stump, K.S., Middleton, J., & Hawley, P.H. (2009, April). Social dominance and social intelligence: A resource control theoretic perspective. Poster presented at the biennial meeting of the Society for Research in Child Development, Denver.

Stump, K.S., Ratliff, J.M., Wu, Y.P., & Hawley, P.H. (2009). Theories of social competence from the top-down to the bottom-up: A case for considering foundational human needs. In J.L. Matson (Ed.), *Practitioners guide to social behavior and social skills in children* (pp. 23–37). New York, NY: Springer.

Sutton, J., Smith, P.K., & Swettenham, J. (1999a). Bullying and "Theory of Mind": A critique of the "Social Skills Deficit" view of anti-social behavior. *Social Development, 8,* 117–127.

Sutton, J., Smith, P.K., & Swettenham, J. (1999b). Social cognition and bullying: Social inadequacy or skilled manipulation? *British Journal of Develomental Psychology, 17,* 435–450.

Sutton, J., Smith, P.K., & Swettenham, J. (1999c). Socially undesirable need not be incompetent: A response to Crick and Dodge. *Social Development, 8,* 132–134.

Swearer, S.M., Espelage, D.L., & Napolitano, S.A. (2009). *Bullying prevention & intervention: Realistic strategies for schools.* New York, NY: Guilford.

Tajfel, H. (1970). Experiments in intergroup discrimination. *Scientific American, 223,* 96- 102.

Tajfel, H., & Turner, J.C. (1986). An integrative theory of intergroup conflict. In S. Worchel & W. Austin (Eds.), *Psychology of intergroup relations* (pp. 2–24). Chicago: Nelson-Hall.

Tajfel, H., & Turner, J.C. (1979). An integrative theory of intergroup conflict. In W. Austin & S. Worchel (Eds.), *Psychology of intergroup relations* (pp. 94–109). Monterey: Books-Cole.

Tarrant, M., Dazeley, S., & Cottom (2009). Social categorization and empathy for outgroup members. *British Journal of Social Psychology, 48,* 427–446.

Thorndike, E.L. (1904). *An introduction to the theory of mental and social measurements.* New York, NY: Teachers College, Columbia University.

Vaillancourt, T., Hymel, S., & McDougall, P. (2003). Bullying is power: Implications for school-based intervention strategies. *Journal of Applied School Psychology, 19,* 157–176.

Vaillancourt, T., McDougall, P., Hymel, S., Krygsman, A., Miller, J., Stiver, K., & Davis, C. (2008). Bullying: Are researchers and children/youth talking about the same thing? *International Journal of Behavioral Development, 32,* 486–495.

Vaughn, B.E., & Santos, A.J. (2007). An evolutionary/ecological account of aggressive behavior and trait aggression in human children and adolescents. In P.H. Hawley, T.D. Little, & P.C. Rodkin (Eds.), *Aggression and adaptation: The bright side to bad behavior* (pp. 31–63). Mahwah, NJ: Lawrence Erlbaum Associates, Inc.

Veenstra, R., Lindenberg, S., Zijlstra, B.J.H., De Winter, A.F., Verhulst, F.C., & Ormel, J. (2007). The dyadic nature of bullying and victimization: Testing a dual-perspective theory. *Child Development, 78,* 1843–1854.

Vitaro, F., Gendreau, P.L., Tremblay, R.E., & Oligny, P. (1998). Reactive and proactive aggression differentially predict later conduct problems. *Journal of Child Psychology and Psychiatry, 39,* 377–385.

White, R.W. (1959). Motivation reconsidered: The concept of competence. *Psychological Review, 66,* 297–333.

Woolley, H.T. (1925). Agnes: A dominant personality in the making. *Pedagogical Seminary, 32,* 569–598.

Part III

Classroom Characteristics Associated With Bullying

10

TEACHERS' ATTITUDES TOWARD BULLYING

MELISSA HOLT, MELISSA KEYES, AND BRIAN KOENIG

Optimal youth development is in part a function of the multiple contexts in which youth are embedded, from their families to communities to schools (Bronfenbrenner, 1979; Cowen, 1991; Espelage & Swearer, 2010). These environments can offer opportunities for growth or can pose threats to positive youth development, and their influences operate in conjunction with each individual's characteristics. Schools represent a key environment, as they are a place where children and adolescents spend a significant amount of time (Duncan & Raudenbush, 1999). Researchers have recognized the crucial role of school characteristics relative to bullying rates, and have conducted studies linking broad attributes such as school size (Bowes et al., 2009), teacher–student ratios (Bradshaw, Sawyer, & O'Brennan, 2009), and school climate to bullying perpetration and victimization. More specifically, teachers themselves can exert substantial influence over youth development, helping to shape not only their academic growth but also their social skills.

Bullying investigations have relied heavily on student questionnaires or student behavior observations (e.g., Leff, Kupersmidt, Patterson, & Power, 1999; Stockdale, Hangaduambo, Duys, Larson, & Sarvela, 2002). Although assessing students offers a crucial lens through which to understand bullying dynamics, it is also important to ascertain school staff members' perspectives. School personnel have frequent interactions with students and are also often involved in bullying interventions (e.g., Newman, Horne, & Bartolomucci, 2000). Accordingly, it is critical that staff attitudes and behaviors are evaluated given their contribution to the pervasive school culture (Olweus, 1992), which in turn serves to promote or to discourage bullying. Unfortunately, few studies have addressed attitudes toward bullying maintained by adult members of the school community. As such, after reviewing background information on (1) the extent to which school staff recognizes the occurrence of bullying within their schools, and (2) relevant school climate issues, the chapter turns to a study of school personnels' attitudes affecting bullying. Finally, implications for bullying prevention and intervention programs are discussed.

DO TEACHERS RECOGNIZE THE EXTENT OF BULLYING?

The majority of studies have found that there are discrepancies between teacher and student reports of bullying perpetration and victimization (for an exception, see Alsaker & Valkanover, 2001). For instance, an analysis of responses from 120 Canadian elementary students and their teachers to the Olweus Bully/Victim Questionnaire revealed that there was only a small correlation between results from these two sources (Beran, 2006). Similar results emerged from a recent large-scale investigation of over 15,000 4th to 12th grade students and over 1,500 school staff members from a large public school district, in which participants completed web-based self-report surveys. Specifically, researchers asked students if they had been bullied two or more times within the past month, and also asked staff what percentage of students had been bullied two or more times within the past month. Results indicated that less than 10% of staff reported bullying frequency rates similar to those that students reported (Bradshaw, Sawyer, & O'Brennan, 2007).

For the most part, studies have found that teachers report lower prevalence rates of bullying behaviors compared to student report. For instance, in a study conducted across seven rural elementary schools in the United States, 739 students completed self-report measures of bullying and 37 teachers responded to parallel measures assessing bullying behaviors among children at their schools. Results indicated that teachers reported lower prevalence rates of bullying than students reported (Stockdale et al., 2002). Similarly, a British investigation found that staff ($n = 13$) at an inner-city secondary school believed that bullying occurred less frequently than students did; whereas 26% of students noted on a self-report measure that they had been bullied, staff believed that only 5% to 10% had been bullied (Pervin & Turner, 1994). In some cases, reporting rates differ by type of bullying involvement. For example, in a study of 2,713 Finnish boys, whereas youth reported more peer victimization than their teachers thought occurred, teachers reported higher levels of bullying perpetration by students than youth reported (Ronning et al., 2009).

There are a number of factors that potentially contribute to divergent bullying rates across informants. For instance, teachers in the United States might not have historically reported bullying because it was not brought into the media spotlight as a salient issue until a number of school shootings occurred in the U.S. in the 1990s. Until that point, teachers might have dismissed bullying behaviors as non-hurtful interactions or a "rite of passage." In addition, school personnel are at a disadvantage because they typically find out about bullying after the bullying has occurred. For example, students might not be willing to inform staff about their victimization experiences out of fear that the bully will find out they told someone and retaliate (Espelage & Asidao, 2001), or because they do not believe that reporting incidents will lead to effective resolutions. Furthermore, even when teachers recognize the extent of bullying, they might not always be willing to report it. For instance, teachers at the preschool level who emphasize socialization as part of the educational experience might be hesitant to report problems with bullying and victimization for fear that it will reflect negatively upon their classroom management skills (e.g., Alsaker & Valkanover, 2001).

Research has found that teachers endorse restricted working definitions of bullying (for an exception, see Naylor, Cowie, Cossin, de Bettencourt, & Lemme, 2006), providing an additional reason why divergent rates might emerge from teachers' and students' responses to questionnaires. For example, findings from a study of 138 British teachers (preschool/infant, junior, and secondary schools) suggested that although teachers were aware of physical and verbal manifestations of bullying, they were not as likely to include social exclusion in their bullying definitions (Boulton, 1997). Similarly, 116 Canadian teacher trainees surveyed were more likely to identify physical attacks as bullying than verbal encounters and typically rated social exclusion as less consistent with bullying than physical and verbal forms (Craig, Henderson, & Murphy, 2000). Furthermore, although researchers (e.g., Olweus, 2000) have set forth characteristics inherent in bullying (i.e., aggressive behavior, repetition, power imbalance) teachers do not always consider these factors. For instance, British teachers ($n = 71$) at a secondary school recognized that multiple types of bullying existed (e.g., physical, emotional) and understood the salience of power in bullying dynamics, but they did not mention repetition as a critical feature (Siann, Callaghan, & Lockhart, 1993). Similarly, whereas the majority of pre-service teachers in one American study noted that bullying could be either physical or psychological, the minority of these individuals identified other components of bullying, including its intentional and repetitive nature and the inherent power imbalance (Bauman & Del Rio, 2005). In sum, even if teachers observe episodes that are indeed manifestations of bullying (e.g., social exclusion), if these behaviors are not consistent with the teachers' definitions of bullying, teachers will not classify them as such when asked about bullying frequency within their schools.

There is also variability among teachers themselves in terms of how they define bullying (e.g., Lee, 2006). One reason for this might be that individual characteristics of staff influence their perceptions of bullying. For instance, teacher gender has been posited to influence perceptions of bullying, although findings in this area have been inconclusive (Borg & Falzon, 1989; Boulton, 1997). Whereas Borg and Falzon's (1989) investigation indicated that male teachers were more likely to rate bullying as serious, Boulton (1997) found that preschool through secondary school female teachers maintained more negative attitudes toward bullying behaviors. In addition, in one study teacher empathy was linked to views on bullying (Craig et al., 2000). Specifically, among the 116 Canadian teachers in training, greater teacher empathy was associated with an increased likelihood of identifying scenarios as bullying, an increased likelihood of intervention, and greater perceived seriousness of scenarios.

Student characteristics also can relate to staff identification of bullying involvement. In terms of bullying involvement generally, staff might be better able to identify bullying among younger rather than older children, due to the fact that bullying among younger children is more often physical in nature and therefore more visible (Pakaslahti & Keltikangas-Jarvinen, 2000). With respect to bullying perpetration, bullies with particular demographic characteristics appear to be more easily recognized. As such, staff might be more likely to classify an episode as bullying if it involves such youth. For example, in a study of elementary and middle school teachers, elementary school bullies were more likely to be identified than middle school bullies (Leff et al., 1999). It might be easier for school staff to identify bullies who demonstrate learning problems compared to those bullies who do not. For instance, in a study of 1,442 middle school students and their teachers, teacher and student reports of bullying perpetration matched most closely in cases in which students were identified as having learning problems (Wienke Totura, Green, Karver, & Gensten, 2009). Further, a child's social status also might influence the way in which the teacher perceives any aggressive acts, and therefore whether or not the teacher classifies a student as a bully (Nesdale & Pickering, 2006).

In terms of teachers' accuracy in identifying victimized youth, one qualitative study (Mishna, Pepler, & Wiener, 2006) found that the stereotypes staff hold about victimized children impact their ability to recognize that a child has been the target of bullying. For instance, there were instances of teachers expressing surprise that a youth had been bullied when they characterized the child as being able to assert him or herself, or when they viewed the child as being well adjusted. Further, another study found that there was greater concordance between teacher and student reports of peer victimization in cases in which teachers had also characterized the student as not being moody (Wienke Totura et al., 2009).

SCHOOL CLIMATE

As Swearer and Doll (2001) argue, bullying needs to be viewed from an ecological framework and, accordingly, is best understood as an "interaction between the individual and his or her peer group, school, family, and community" (p. 19). With respect to school personnel's role, it is necessary to understand not only physical characteristics of the school building that influence bullying (e.g., physical layout of playgrounds), but also teachers' contributions to the school environment. One way in which to evaluate this area is through an exploration of school climate. As described by Tagiuri (1968), school climate is the "total environmental quality within an organization" (cited in Anderson, 1982). One element of Tagiuri's taxonomy is the school's "culture," which consists of factors such as beliefs and values. Those beliefs or values are manifested in the frequency and quality of interactions between adults and students, students and students, and adults and adults.

Beliefs or values also become evident through attitudes that school staff convey. Attitudes directly and indirectly related to bullying are both important to consider. For instance, Hoover and Hazler (1994) note that when school personnel tolerate, ignore, or dismiss bullying behaviors, they are conveying their values about bullying, which victimized students then might internalize. Conversely, if school staff hold attitudes not supportive of bullying behavior, and these are translated into voicing their opinions and/or actively intervening in bullying episodes, the school culture as a whole becomes less tolerant of bullying. In addition, it is important to evaluate the extent to which school cultures tolerate students who differ from the norm. Research has documented that students who do not "fit in" (Hoover, Oliver, & Thomson, 1993), who are obese (Lagerspetz, 1982), who are in remedial education (Byrne, 1994), and who have developmental disabilities (Marini, Fairbairn, & Zuber, 2001) are more likely to be victimized by their peers. The attitudes school staff maintain toward students with such physical or academic challenges likely influence how youth treat such individuals.

Emerging research lends support to the notion that staff attitudes toward bullying impact their willingness to intervene in bullying episodes. For instance, elementary school teachers who believed that bullying is normative behavior were less likely to intervene than teachers who did not hold this belief and were also less likely to involve parents in dealing with bullying situations (Kochenderfer-Ladd & Pelletier, 2007). Similarly, among elementary through high school staff, staff who endorsed the statement that "bullying is a part of life that everyone has to go through" were more likely to also think that if they intervened it would make the bullying situation worse (Bradshaw et al., 2007, p. 375). Through developing a better sense of how school personnel's attitudes directly and indirectly influence bullying, more successful prevention and intervention programs can be developed.

STATE-WIDE STUDY ON SCHOOL STAFF ATTITUDES
TOWARD BULLYING

To enhance our understanding of ways in which American teachers' attitudes shape school climate and in turn potentially influence the occurrence of bullying, this investigation examined results gleaned from a survey administered to teachers and other staff (e.g., aides) in 18 Wisconsin schools. The central aim of this study was to explore school climate factors such as attitudes toward bullying, degree of overt hostility, attitudes toward diversity, and rule-setting policies. Moreover, the survey was designed to inform an intervention for pilot schools in Wisconsin; although understanding staff attitudes does not necessarily translate into understanding staff behaviors, evaluating attitudes is a necessary first component in designing effective interventions.

With respect to definitions framing this investigation, attitudes toward bullying were conceptualized as staff members' feelings toward teasing and their observations and value judgments of student behavior. Respect for diversity was viewed as teachers' feelings toward specific groups of students at their schools. Specifically, diversity in this context included differences in sex, race or ethnicity, sexual orientation, ability, socioeconomic status, and religion. Overt hostility was defined as observable actions or words that intimidate, humiliate, or otherwise hurt someone. Finally, the definition of equity was fairness and justice or impartiality; as noted by Bitters (1997) equity goes beyond equal educational opportunity.

Method

Participants. Participants were 797 teachers and paraprofessionals or aides from 18 Wisconsin schools. Schools ranged from elementary to high school and included both rural and suburban communities. The number of respondents per school ranged from 11 to 133 ($M = 44.28$, $SD = 36.78$). There were 605 females (76%), 181 males (23%), and 11 (< 1%) individuals not indicating their gender. Most participants were White (95.4%), followed by Asian (1%), Hispanic (0.6%), Mixed (0.3%), and Black (0.1%); 21 respondents did not denote their race (2.6%). With respect to academic background, teachers and paraprofessionals or aides reported the following educational experiences: HS GED (4%), some schooling beyond high school but no college degree (8%), technical or community college (4%), four-year college or university degree (11%), grade credits but no advanced degree (36%), master's degree (34%), doctorate degree (< 1%). Seventeen participants (2%) did not reveal their educational history. Data on staff ages or years of experience were not collected. Among teachers, participants taught a wide range of disciplines with the majority indicating that they were responsible for all subject areas.

Survey. Surveys were distributed to teachers and other staff as a part of a larger state-wide investigation on school climate and diversity.[1] Instructions indicated that respondents would be asked about "how people work and learn together" in the school. Staff members voluntarily filled out surveys and were assured confidentiality.

In addition to responding to demographic questions, staff answered 50 questions that were developed by a panel of experts in the field. These questions assessed: (1) school climate constructs including attitudes toward bullying (e.g., "Teasing doesn't hurt"); (2) degree of respect ("I often hear students saying disrespectful things"), (3) attitudes toward diversity (e.g., "School makes all kinds of students feel welcome"), (4) overt hostility (e.g., "Adults make jokes about race"), and (5) rule-setting (e.g., "Students help set rules") within their respective institutions. Some statements referred to the school in general (e.g., "In this school, staff are trained to intervene appropriately in student-to-student harassment") whereas other items inquired about individual teachers' beliefs and behaviors (e.g., "I tell people to stop if they're making a joke or stereotypic remark based on race"). Response options were: Strongly Disagree, Disagree, Agree, and Strongly Agree. To determine whether the questions represented distinct attitudinal constructs, these items were factor analyzed as part of the current study and findings from this analysis are presented in the Results section.

Results

Descriptive analyses. First, percentages of staff selecting each response value for items were computed to provide a general understanding of staff attitudes toward school climate factors. With respect to bullying, 27% of school staff either agreed or strongly agreed that "a little teasing doesn't hurt." In addition, the majority of respondents (57%) believed that students would *not* intervene if they saw another student being teased or bothered. Conversely, most staff (93%) reported that adults *would* stop students from making hurtful comments to one another and stated that they would personally tell individuals making jokes based on race to stop (74%). In terms of training, two-thirds (65%) of the participants noted that staff received training on how to intervene in student-to-student harassment.

Responses also revealed that on average, staff believed that their schools promote equity and acceptance of diversity. For instance, respondents indicated that steps toward multicultural education have been taken (74%), administrators supported staff in efforts to create harassment-free environments (92%), and students were asked to be involved in rule-setting and solving problems (76%). Furthermore, nearly all school staff (95%) responded that they would be accepting of gay, lesbian, and bisexual students. Interestingly, however, 26% of individuals surveyed noted that they had observed other teachers making fun of the way students talk, look or act (although these individuals could be commenting on the same teachers).

Factor analysis. Next, a principal axis factor analysis was conducted using the 28 questions about staff attitudes. Results indicated that four attitudinal constructs (factors) existed. Items were retained for a factor when they had factor loadings of .40 or above on that factor and loadings under .40 on other factors. Higher factor loadings indicate a stronger relationship between the item and the factor. The resulting factors were named: (1) *Equity* (eigenvalue = 4.26), which accounted for 15% of the variance and consisted of 11 items assessing issues related to equality (e.g., staff speak out in favor of equality) and rule-setting (e.g., students help set rules); (2) *Hostile Climate* (eigenvalue = 3.41), which accounted for 12% of the variance and was composed of ten items evaluating attitudes and behaviors consistent with a hostile environment (e.g., teachers joke about gay and lesbian students); (3) *Openness to Diversity* (eigenvalue = 7.01), which accounted for 7% of the variance and consisted of five items relating to acceptance of diverse students (e.g., students with disabilities often have talents); and (4) *Willingness to Intervene* (eigenvalue = 5.20), which accounted for 5% of the variance and included two questions inquiring about school staff willingness to stop people from making inappropriate jokes. Alpha coefficients for the final scales were .88 for Equity, .83 for Hostile Climate, .71 for Openness to Diversity, and .78 for Willingness to Intervene, indicating that questions on each scale were reflective of a single attitudinal construct. (For specific factor loadings, refer to Holt & Keyes, 2003).

Inter-scale correlations were examined to determine how attitudinal constructs were related and findings supported the factor structure. Greater perceptions of equity were associated with less hostile environments ($r = -.54$, $p < .01$), more openness to diversity ($r = .33$, $p < .01$), and more willingness to intervene in situations in which inappropriate joking is occurring ($r = .22$, $p < .01$). In addition, a greater openness to diversity was related to a less hostile environment ($r = -.32$, $p < .01$) and more willingness to intervene when hearing jokes of a racial or sexual nature ($r = -.35$, $p < .01$). Finally, ratings indicating more hostile environments were associated with less staff willingness to tell people to stop making inappropriate jokes ($r = .29$, $p < .01$).

Means and standard deviations of factors. Means and standard deviations were then calculated for each scale resulting from the factor analysis: Equity ($M = 1.92$, $SD = 0.45$), Hostile Climate ($M = 2.94$, $SD = 0.44$), Openness to Diversity ($M = 1.54$, $SD = 0.42$), and Willingness to Intervene ($M = 2.14$, $SD = 0.65$). In the case of Equity, Openness to Diversity, and Willingness to Intervene, mean values around '2' indicated that these values were thought to be promoted. With respect to Hostile Climate, a mean value close to '3' implies that respondents did not believe that their school environments were hostile. Overall, these mean values suggest that school staff described their schools as equitable, open to diversity, and welcoming. In addition, participants reported willingness to intervene in harassing situations.

One-way Analyses of Variance (ANOVAs) were then conducted to determine whether scale means differed by sex, school type, or schools (See Holt & Keyes, 2002 for a detailed ANOVA table). Results indicated that scale means did not differ for males and females. This suggested that male and female school personnel tended to maintain similar attitudes across these areas. However, mean differences existed across school types (i.e., elementary, middle, high school) on Equity and Willingness to Intervene. With respect to Equity, high school staff rated equity significantly higher than elementary and middle school staff ($p < .01$). High school staff therefore viewed their schools as more equitable. Perhaps high schools include students in rule setting more often than elementary or middle schools. Conversely, high school staff was significantly less willing to intervene when hearing inappropriate jokes than elementary school staff ($p < .01$). This might be because high school staff interpret the jokes as less harmful to their students than elementary school staff do, or perhaps they feel less comfortable intervening because the students are older. Finally, results indicated that individual schools differed across the four attitudinal factors, suggesting that members of the 18 schools maintained different attitudes influencing school climate. It is unclear why these differences emerged. Correlations between number of staff members in each school completing surveys and the scale factors were not significant, indicating that attitudes were not a function of the number of teachers responding to the survey in a given school. Given that additional potentially salient indicators about each school did not exist in the data set (e.g., location of school, total enrollment, total number of teachers in school), a more comprehensive evaluation of school-to-school differences was not possible.

Discussion

The central aim of this study was to evaluate school climate factors in 18 schools in the Midwest that potentially influence bullying frequency at these schools. Results indicated that four distinct attitudinal constructs were evident among staff: Equity, hostile climate, openness to diversity, and willingness to intervene. On average, the school personnel surveyed maintained positive attitudes toward their students, believed that respect for diversity existed, and were generally willing to intervene when they witnessed inappropriate racial or sexual joking or heard a student make hurtful comments to a peer. In fact, school staff reported that they were more willing to intervene in teasing episodes than students were. Given previous findings suggesting that students do not believe that teachers intervene enough (e.g., O'Moore, Kirkham, & Smith, 1998), it appears that perceptions of intervention frequency are subjective, and based on who the respondent is. With respect to educational preparation, results indicated that the majority of individuals surveyed had received training on how to intervene appropriately in student-to-student harassment, a finding that is somewhat discrepant from previous literature suggesting that teachers do not receive adequate training (e.g., Boulton, 1997). However, it should be noted that the extent and quality of their training was not measured in this study.

When comparing attitudes as a function of individual and school characteristics, a number of findings emerged. First, attitudes toward bullying did not differ for male and female staff. Previous findings on sex differences have been inconclusive, but these research endeavors have tended to focus on physical manifestations of bullying (e.g., Borg & Falzon, 1989; Boulton, 1997). As such, results from the current investigation suggest that males and females might be more likely to have similar attitudes when verbal rather than physical forms of bullying are under consideration. Second, attitudes differed across school types. Whereas high school staff perceived their educational environments to be more equitable than elementary and middle school staff, they were less likely to intervene in inappropriate joking episodes than elementary school staff. This supports previous literature suggesting that willingness to intervene declines as students become older (e.g., O'Moore et al., 1998). Perhaps teachers of older students feel less responsible for their students' interactions than teachers of younger students who might view part of their jobs as teaching appropriate socialization skills. Third, attitudes differed across schools. These school-to-school differences may reflect the reality that each school is its own unique community and, accordingly, has its own school climate (Anderson, 1982); the staff attitudes that contribute to this overall climate will similarly differ across these environments. For example, it might be that school size or the existence of programming to create positive school environments influences staff attitudes.

Findings provide a preliminary understanding of staff attitudes influencing their respective school climates. This investigation was limited in some respects, however. Data were collected from only one state, and therefore efforts should be made to collect similar data in states with different characteristics. In addition, this investigation did not address the extent to which staff attitudes were linked to bullying behaviors, and this is a crucial factor to understand. For example, in schools in which there are well-trained teachers who view bullying as problematic, are rates of bullying lower than in schools in which there are teachers who have less training and do not view bullying as problematic? Furthermore, this survey was somewhat restricted in its definition of bullying, in that it mainly focused on verbal manifestations of bullying such as teasing. However, it is important to note that although teasing constitutes only one aspect of bullying, it is the most commonly observed and experienced form (Hoover et al., 1994). Finally, this study did not explore how staff attitudes toward school climate variables relate to students' perceptions. Because the survey used in this investigation was also given to students, we will be able to address this issue in future papers.

In sum, this study contributes to the field by presenting valuable information on school staff attitudes that likely influence the occurrence of bullying. Results are critical in informing essential training for teachers and other school personnel. As will be discussed in the following section, findings were influential in the design of a pilot bullying intervention for three of the schools surveyed.

TRANSLATING RESEARCH INTO PRACTICE: IMPLICATIONS FOR BULLYING PREVENTION AND INTERVENTION PROGRAMS

The role of school personnel is salient in ecologically based interventions, which have empirical evidence supporting their effectiveness (Limber, 2004). Various approaches derived from this framework exist including the "Whole-school approach," which involves teachers, students, parents, and outside agencies (e.g., Olweus & Alsaker, 1991; Smith & Sharp, 1994) and the systemic thinking approach (e.g., Sawatzky, Eckert, & Ryan, 1993), which relies on teachers, students, parents, and communities. Such comprehensive programs are necessary if bullying is to be adequately addressed, given that if all levels of the social ecology are not modified, there likely will not be persistent behavioral changes among students. As noted by Siann and colleagues (1993), "Bullying should be regarded within a social context rather than from the point of view of individual pathology."

A critical step in any successful prevention or intervention program involving school staff is training about bullying. Broadly, pre-service and in-service training should include defining bullying and its signs, effects, and causes, highlighting preventive strategies, teaching skills for how to deal with bully and victim problems, and encouraging the development of school policy to counter bullying (O'Moore, 2000). It is particularly important that training highlights the range of behaviors consistent with bullying, given evidence, for instance, that pre-service teachers are less likely to view relational bullying as serious and less likely to intervene in relational bullying episodes (Bauman & Del Rio, 2006). In addition, all educational support personnel should be included in trainings, given that in many circumstances it will be staff other than teachers who observe bullying behaviors and are positioned to intervene.

Unfortunately, not enough school staff are involved in comprehensive pre-service training or in-service educational programs. For instance, of 138 United Kingdom secondary school teachers surveyed, 87% desired additional training on bullying (Boulton, 1997). Specifically, these teachers either agreed or strongly agreed with at least one of the following two statements: "I would appreciate more training in how to deal with bullying" and "I would appreciate more training in how to prevent bullying." Similarly, only 5% of the 44 teachers surveyed at seven Dublin schools reported that their training had adequately equipped them to deal with bullying (Byrne, 1994).

This perceived lack of training might be one reason teachers do not always intervene when witnessing bullying (e.g., Espelage & Asidao, 2001) and often do not speak to bullies about their inappropriate behaviors (e.g., O'Moore et al., 1998). Teachers who feel more confident about dealing with bullying, either as a result of training or personal characteristics, are indeed more likely to intervene (e.g., Bradshaw et al., 2007). It is important, however, that teachers intervene in effective ways. For instance, one study found that whereas most staff thought they effectively dealt with bullying episodes, this was in sharp contrast to student beliefs, who instead felt that teachers made situations worse as a result of their interventions (Bradshaw et al., 2007). Continued in-service training would ensure that teachers are equipped with strategies that are beneficial to the students involved. When effective strategies are implemented, bullying rates will decrease (Olweus, 1993). Given the critical role of teachers and other school staff in this process, it is important to involve these individuals as part of the intervention development process.

As such, next we turn to a specific intervention program developed as part of the study described above that includes significant school staff involvement.

Wisconsin Pilot Bullying Intervention Program

A pilot bullying intervention program "Keep it Safe" is currently underway in three Wisconsin schools. The purpose of the "Keep It Safe" project is to develop a process for change in schools that will prevent sexual harassment and assault when students become adolescents and adults. The process and activities are designed to address bullying and harassment among younger children and the adults who teach and parent them. Additionally, another goal is to improve school climate so that, ultimately, student achievement is increased.

This project was informed by findings from the survey described above. Specifically, schools use the survey as an initial assessment and planning tool. In this manner, schools are able to tailor the intervention based on survey results from their particular school. Initial work with staff includes a review of the survey data and identification of areas most in need of improvement. In addition, three focal components are addressed in all schools: (1) school environment, including processes and policies, (2) adult behaviors, including modeling and response to bullying, and (3) student skill development. Although only the adult behavior component will be discussed thoroughly here, a more detailed explanation of this intervention can be obtained from K12 Associates LLC (www.k12associates.com/).

A basic premise of the intervention is that evaluating staff attitudes allows for a better understanding of which behaviors should be targeted. As such, the attitudinal constructs described above (e.g., hostile climate, equity, openness to diversity) are reflected in intervention themes. First, ways in which adult behaviors can contribute to a hostile climate are addressed. For example, adult modeling is a critical component that can exacerbate bullying and harassment in schools. Teachers who tease students in inappropriate ways provide reinforcement of verbal harassment and bullying among students. Therefore as part of the intervention, adults receive training in how to serve as effective role models. In addition, teachers are provided with information about curriculum addressing the prevention of bullying, harassment, and assault. By directly exploring these issues in the classroom, teachers convey the message that bullying contributes to a hostile climate.

Second, educators are encouraged to consider their attitudes and behaviors related to equity. For example, through their actions adults might increase gender inequality by accepting sex-role stereotypes or assuming that girls are better students than boys. Adults also might encourage unhealthy competition by basing their instructional methods on hierarchical limitations (e.g., creating a hierarchy in which only the same few students are rewarded all the time) rather than modeling equity regardless of student characteristics. When this occurs, those who are "outsiders" or on the margins develop resentments, and those on the inside develop arrogance. Either way, bullying can develop because of the imbalance of perceived power. Teachers in the pilot schools have therefore been trained to promote cooperative work among students, with a focus on inclusiveness and equal treatment of all students.

A third intervention component highlights respect for diversity. Staff members attend a four-day training in the "Tribes" process that shows teachers how they can use inclusive activities and cooperative methods to create stronger positive relationships among students. Students learn that they are truly valued and can be successful because the teacher creates support and highlights how individual contributions from diverse students strengthens the community.

Thus far the intervention has had mixed results. Although teachers have welcomed information about new intervention strategies, they have sometimes not been willing to make changes in the ways in which they intervene in bullying. The educators who have been open to examining their own words and actions, however, have found the subsequent changes in student behavior to be dramatic.

SUMMARY

Despite the high frequency with which bullying occurs in American elementary, middle, and high schools, school personnel often report lower prevalence rates than students (e.g., Stockdale et al., 2002). One way to increase awareness among school staff is through pre-service and in-service training. A necessary component of this educational process is assessment. In particular, by evaluating school personnels' attitudes that influence school climate, researchers can develop a more thorough conceptualization of the environments in which youth are educated. For example, teachers might foster bullying by failing to promote respectful interactions among students, modeling disrespectful behaviors, declining to intervene in bullying episodes, or intervening ineffectively. Evaluations of staff attitudes and behaviors in individual schools will allow for the development of targeted intervention programs that address the unique school climates of the specific schools under consideration. In turn, school climates that are intolerant of bullying will emerge.

NOTE

1. Surveys for students and adults are available from K12 Associates. Phone: 608–232–7099. Email: info@k12associates.com.

REFERENCES

Alsaker, F.D., & Valkanover, S. (2001). Early diagnosis and prevention of victimization in kindergarten. In J. Juvonen & S. Graham (Eds.), *Peer Harassment in Schools: The Plight of the Vulnerable and Victimized* (pp. 175–195). New York, NY: The Guilford Press.

Anderson, C.A. (1982). The search for school climate: A review of the research. *Review of Educational Research, 52*, 368–420.

Bauman, S., & Del Rio, A. (2005). Knowledge and beliefs about bullying in schools: Comparing pre-service teachers in the United States and the United Kingdom. *School Psychology International, 26*, 428–442.

Bauman, S., & Del Rio, A. (2006). Preservice teachers' responses to bullying scenarios: Comparing physical, verbal, and relational bullying. *Journal of Educational Psychology, 98*, 219–231.

Beran, T.N. (2006). A construct validity study of bullying. *The Alberta Journal of Educational Research, 52,* 241–250.

Bitters, B.A. (1997). *Glossary of Terms for Working with Equity and Diversity.* Madison, WI: Wisconsin Department of Public Instruction.

Borg, M.G., & Falzon, J.M. (1989). Primary school teachers' perception of pupils' undesirable behaviours. *Educational Studies, 15,* 251–260.

Boulton, M.J. (1997). Teachers' views on bullying: definitions, attitudes, and ability to cope. *British Journal of Educational Psychology, 67,* 223–233.

Bowes, L., Arseneault, L., Maughan, B., Taylor, A., Caspi, A., & Moffitt, T.E. (2009). School, family, and neighborhood factors are associated with children's bullying involvement: A nationally representative longitudinal study. *Journal of the American Academy of Child and Adolescent Psychiatry, 48,* 545–553.

Bradshaw, C.P., Sawyer, A.L., & O'Brennan, L.M. (2007). Bullying and peer victimization at school: Perceptual differences between students and school staff. *School Psychology Review, 36,* 361–182.

Bradshaw, C.P., Sawyer, A.L., & O'Brennan, L.M. (2009). A social disorganization perspective on bullying-related attitudes and behaviors: The role of school context. *American Journal of Community Psychology, 43,* 204–220.

Bronfenbrenner, U. (1979). *The ecology of human development: experiments by nature and design.* Cambridge, MA: Harvard University Press.

Byrne, B. (1994). Bullies and victims in a school setting with reference to some Dublin schools. *The Irish Journal of Psychology, 15,* 574–586.

Cowen, E.L. (1991). In pursuit of wellness. *American Psychologist, 46,* 404–408.

Craig, W.M., Henderson, K., & Murphy, J.G. (2000). Prospective teachers' attitudes toward bullying and victimization. *School Psychology International, 21,* 5–21.

Duncan, G.J., & Raudenbush, S.W. (1999). Assessing the effects of context in studies of child and youth development. *Educational Psychologist 34,* 29–41.

Espelage, D.L., & Asidao, C.S. (2001). Conversations with middle school students about bullying and victimization: Should we be concerned? *Journal of Emotional Abuse, 2,* 49–62.

Espelage, D.L., & Swearer, S. (2010). A social-ecological model for bullying prevention and intervention. Understanding the impact of adults in the social ecology of youngsters. In S. Jimerson (Ed.), *Handbook of Bullying in Schools: An International Perspective* (pp. 61–72). London: Taylor & Francis.

Holt, M., & Keyes, M. (2003). Teachers' attitudes toward teasing and general school climate. In D. Espelage and S. Swearer (Eds.), *Bullying in American Schools: A Social-Ecological Perspective on Prevention and Intervention.* New Jersey: Lawrence Erlbaum.

Hoover, J.H., & Hazler, R.J. (1994). Bullies and victims. *Elementary School Guidance and Counseling, 25,* 212–220.

Hoover, J.H., Oliver, R., & Thomson, K. (1993). Perceived victimization by school bullies: New research and future direction. *Journal of Humanistic Education and Development, 32,* 76–84.

Kochenderfer-Ladd, B., & Pelletier, M.E. (2008). Teachers' views and beliefs about bullying: Influences on classroom management strategies and students' coping with peer victimization. *Journal of School Psychology, 46,* 431–453.

Lagerspetz, K.M. (1982). Group aggression among school children in three schools. *Scandinavian Journal of Psychology, 23,* 45–52.

Lee, C. (2006). Exploring teachers' definitions of bullying. *Emotional and Behavioral Difficulties, 11,* 61–75.

Leff, S.S., Kupersmidt, J.B., Patterson, C.J., & Power, T.J. (1999). Factors influencing teacher identification of peer bullies and victims. *School Psychology Review, 28,* 505–517.

Limber, S.P. (2004). Implementation of the Olweus Bullying Prevention Program: Lessons Learned from the Field. In D. Espelage & S. Swearer (Eds.) *Bullying in American Schools: A Social-Ecological Perspective on Prevention and Intervention* (pp. 351–363). Mahwah, NJ: Lawrence Erlbaum.

Marini, Z., Fairbairn, L., & Zuber, R. (2001). Peer harassment in individuals with developmental disabilities: Toward the development of a multidimensional bullying identification model. *Developmental Disabilities Bulletin, 29,* 170–195.

Mishna, F., Pepler, D., & Weiner, J. (2006). Factors associated with perceptions and responses to bullying situations by children, parents, teachers, and principals. *Victims and Offenders, 1,* 255–288.

Naylor, P., Cowie, H., Cossin, F., de Bettencourt, R., & Lemme, F. (2006). Teachers' and pupils' definitions of bullying. *British Journal of Educational Psychology, 76,* 553–576.

Nesdale, D., & Pickerin, K. (2006). Teachers' reactions to children's aggression. *Social Development, 15,* 109–127.

Newman, D.A., Horne, A.M., & Bartolomucci, C.L. (2000). *Bully busters: A teacher's manual for helping bullies, victims, and bystanders, grades 6-8.* Champaign, IL: Research Press.

Olweus, D. (1992). Bullying among schoolchildren: Intervention and prevention. In R.D. Peters, R.J. McMahon, & V.L. Quinsey (Eds.), *Aggression and Violence Throughout the Life Span* (pp. 100–125). London: Sage Publications.

Olweus, D. (1993). *Bullying at School: What We Know and What We Can Do.* Cambridge: Blackwell.

Olweus, D. (2000). Bullying. In Kazdin, Alan E. (Ed.), *Encyclopedia of psychology, Vol. 1.* (pp. 487–489). Washington, DC, New York, NY: American Psychological Association.

Olweus, D., & Alsaker, F.D. (1991). Assessing change in a cohort longitudinal study with hierarchical data. In D. Magnusson, L. Gergman, G. Rudinger, & B. Torestad (Eds.), *Problems and Methods in Longitudinal Research* (pp. 107–132). New York, NY: Cambridge University Press.

O'Moore, M. (2000). Critical issues for teacher training to counter bullying and victimization in Ireland. *Aggressive Behavior, 26,* 99–111.

O'Moore, M., Kirkham, C., & Smith, M. (1998). Bullying in schools and Ireland: A nationwide study. *Irish Educational Studies, 17,* 254–271.

Pakaslahti, L., & Keltikangas-Jarvinen, L. (2000). Comparison of peer, teacher, and self-assessments on adolescent direct and indirect aggression. *Educational Psychology, 20,* 177–190.

Pervin, K., & Turner, A. (1994). An investigation into staff and pupils' knowledge, attitudes, and beliefs about bullying in an inner city school. *Pastoral Care in Education, 12,* 16–22.

Ronning, J.A., Sourander, A., Kumpalainen, K., Tamminen, T., Niemela, S., Moilanen, I., Helenius, H., Piha, J., & Almqvist, F. (2009). Cross-information agreement about bullying and victimization among eight-year-olds: whose information best predicts psychiatric caseness 10–15 years later? *Social Psychiatry and Psychiatric Epidemiology, 44,* 15–22.

Sawatzky, D.D., Eckert, C., & Ryan, B.R. (1993). The use of family systems approaches by school counsellors. *Canadian Journal of Counselling, 27,* 113–122.

Siann, G., Callaghan, M., & Lockhart, R. (1993). Bullying: Teachers' views and school effects. *Educational Studies, 19,* 307–21.

Smith, P.K., & Sharp, S. (Eds.). (1994). *School Bullying: Insights and Perspectives.* London: Routledge.

Stockdale, M.S., Hangaduambo, S., Duys, D., Larson, K., & Sarvela, P.D. (2002). Rural elementary students', parents', and teachers' perceptions of bullying. *American Journal of Health Behavior, 26,* 266–277.

Swearer, S.M., & Doll, B. (2001). Bullying in schools: An ecological framework. *Journal of Emotional Abuse, 2,* 7–23.

Taguiri, R. (1968). The concept of organizational climate. In R. Tagiuir & G.H. Litwin (Eds.), *Organizational Climate: Exploration of a Concept.* Boston: Harvard University.

Wienke Totura, C.M., Green, A. E., Karver, M.S., & Gesten, E. L. (2009). Multiple informants in the assessment of psychological, behavioral, and academic correlates of bullying and victimization in middle school. *Journal of Adolescence, 32,* 193–211.

11

GIRLS, BOYS, AND BULLYING IN PRESCHOOL
The Role of Gender in the Development of Bullying[1]

LAURA D. HANISH, ALISON HILL, SHERRI GOSNEY,
RICHARD A. FABES, AND CAROL LYNN MARTIN

Before children enter elementary school, they are likely to be enrolled in preschool programs. Indeed, 57% of 3 to 5-year-old children were enrolled in center-based preschool programs in 2005, with percentage estimates considerably higher when only 4- to 5-year-old children were counted (U.S. Department of Education, 2007). Compared to elementary school classrooms, preschool programs typically structure more learning opportunities within the context of peer-based play activities than in teacher–child or teacher–group interactions (Power, 2000). Thus, perhaps more than at any other developmental period, the context of preschool is greatly embedded within and dependent upon children's peer interactions. Moreover, at this age, social developmental tasks (e.g., acquiring the skills necessary for developing and maintaining peer relationships, negotiating peer conflict, establishing effective means of communicating with peers) are key developmental milestones, and children become increasingly more engaged with peers and more sophisticated in their peer interactions over this developmental period (Fabes, Martin, & Hanish, 2009; Strayer & Santos, 1996). In other words, peer interactions and relationships figure prominently in preschoolers' lives (Harris, 1995).

As such, the social nature of young children's preschool experiences provides numerous opportunities for children to engage in aggressive behavior. This may be because social play brings children into greater contact with peers, which, in turn, creates more opportunities for a variety of interactions to take place, including aggressive interactions. Indeed, children who play more frequently with peers are also more likely to be aggressive toward their peers and victimized by their peers (Hanish, Ryan, Martin, & Fabes, 2005; Patterson, Littman, & Bricker, 1967). Peer interactions provide opportunities for affectively charged and conflicted situations to emerge, leading some children to respond to these situations with aggressive behaviors (Fabes & Eisenberg, 1992). These situations also provide opportunities for peers to influence and (sometimes) reinforce children's initial aggressive tendencies (Hanish, Martin, Fabes, Leonard, & Herzog, 2005; Olson, 1992; Snyder et al., 2008). It is not surprising then that we see the genesis of peer bullying behaviors—those that are characterized by aggressive, victimizing acts that are directed toward peers—at this time.

In this chapter, we explore how peer-directed aggression is manifested in preschool. We begin by providing a developmental perspective and explaining how bullying in early childhood must be conceptualized in light of normative developmental patterns of aggression and victimization. We then address the fact that, beginning in preschool, boys and girls experience peer-directed aggression differently. These gender differences not only play out in the preschool classroom, but they also forecast gender differences in boys' and girls' subsequent involvement in aggression and victimization in elementary school and beyond. Thus, we explore the role of gender in the ontogeny of bullying, considering how boys and girls differ in aggression and victimization, how the gendered nature of children's social lives may influence the promotion or inhibition of aggression, and how teachers influence these behaviors. We conclude by providing suggestions for intervention at this age. To illustrate ideas, we draw on a sample of 261 preschoolers (52% boys; M age = 52 months, SD = 5.2) drawn from 18 Head Start preschool classrooms in the urban southwest. Children in this sample were primarily Hispanic (74%). Data include preschool teachers' reports of children's aggressive behaviors in the spring semester as well as naturalistic observations of children's tendencies to play with male and female peers and their involvement with teachers. Observations were conducted multiple times per day for two to three days per week over the spring semester.

A DEVELOPMENTAL PERSPECTIVE ON BULLYING BEHAVIORS IN EARLY CHILDHOOD

Bullying is typically defined as unprovoked aggressive behavior that is persistently directed toward a weaker child with the intention to harm (Olweus, 1991). Although bullies can be readily identified among older children (Olweus, 1991; Salmivalli, Lappalainen, & Lagerspetz, 1998; Sutton & Smith, 1999), given this definition, the degree to which we can and should label young children as bullies is debated. Aggressive behaviors are relatively prevalent among young children, and it is difficult to differentiate the early emergence of more serious bullying behavior from normative developmental trends in the expression of aggressive behavior in early childhood (Coie & Dodge, 1998). For example, peer-directed aggression has been observed in infants as young as 12 months of age (Caplan, Vespo, Pedersen, & Hay, 1991), and by the time children reach preschool, peer-directed aggression is quite common (Alsaker & Valkanover, 2001; Kochenderfer & Ladd, 1996; Olson, 1992; Patterson et al., 1967). In fact, physically and verbally aggressive behaviors peak in frequency during early childhood and subsequently decline, making them more common among young children than at any other age in the lifespan (Cummings, Iannotti, & Zahn-Waxler, 1989). For instance, Crowther, Bond, and Rolf (1981) reported that, among boys, 16% of three-year-olds, 12% of four-year-olds, and 7% of five-year-olds aggressed against others at least several times per day (prevalence rates for girls were approximately half that of boys).

It is not surprising, then, that approximately 20% of kindergartners reported being victimized frequently by peers, rates that are considerably higher than those that are typically reported for older youth (Kochenderfer & Ladd, 1996). It is important to note, however, that, in early childhood, aggression and victimization tend to co-occur at relatively higher rates. In fact, in our work, we have reported relatively strong positive correlations between the two constructs (Hanish et al., 2004). This means that there is a substantial relation between young children's own propensity to aggress and the likelihood of being aggressed against; in early childhood, aggressors and victims are often, though not always, one and the same. This is different from what is typically seen among older youth, for whom victimization is correlated more strongly with anxiety, social withdrawal, and submissive behaviors than with aggressive behaviors (Boivin, Hymel, & Bukowski, 1995; Hanish & Guerra, 2000; Hawker & Boulton, 2000).

For all of the reasons discussed thus far, it is difficult to differentiate young children's aggressive acts that are distinctly bullying in nature (i.e., intentionally emitted with the goal of harming a weaker peer) from those that represent immature or undercontrolled aggressive responses to social situations. There are, however, significant individual differences in the level of aggressive behavior displayed among young children, with some exhibiting more frequent (i.e., several times per day and several days per week) or more intense (in terms of severity or potential for harm) aggression than others. Moreover, young children who display relatively high rates of peer-directed aggressive behaviors also tend to express a constellation of externalizing problems, including intense and poorly regulated anger and oppositional or disruptive behaviors (Eisenberg et al., 2001; Loeber, Keenan, Lahey, Green, & Thomas, 1993). Thus, we suggest defining preschoolers' aggressive behavior according to the frequency with which they aggress against their peers, particularly for those who fall outside the normative range of aggressiveness for this age group. This should be done, however, with gender differences in mind.

GENDER DIFFERENCES IN PRESCHOOLERS' INVOLVEMENT IN AGGRESSIVE BEHAVIORS

Boys and girls tend to emphasize different sets of skills and behaviors in their social interactions. Boys' interactions tend to be more forceful, active, and physical, whereas girls' are calmer, more harmonious, and more likely to be oriented toward relationships (Rose & Rudolph, 2006). Boys also tend to play further away from teachers and to emphasize peer-group rule orientations, whereas girls play closer to teachers and emphasize adult-based rule orientations (Maccoby, 1998). Not surprisingly, then, boys are more likely than girls to exhibit aggressive behaviors; additionally, when boys display aggression, they tend to utilize a wider repertoire of aggressive behaviors than do girls (Archer & Coyne, 2005; Card, Stucky, Sawalani, & Little, 2008; Tomada & Schneider, 1997). Boys often use overt behaviors to aggress against others, such as physical force (e.g., hitting or pushing) and physical threats, as well as name-calling and other forms of direct verbal harassment. Moreover, boys tend to use such behaviors at rates that greatly exceed those of girls (Card et al., 2008). However, boys also attack peers in social ways that are more indirect and that involve relationally aggressive behaviors (e.g., spreading rumors and social exclusion) (Monks, Smith, & Swettenham, 2005). This is an important point as these behaviors are often thought to be the domain of girls. And, although girls tend to use such social and relational forms of aggression as their predominant form of aggression, boys engage in such behaviors at nearly the same rate as do girls (Crick, Casas, & Nelson, 2002; Underwood, 2003).

Similar to the enactment of aggression, there are also gender differences in forms of victimization. Physical victimization is the most common form of victimization among preschool children, and boys are significantly more likely than girls to be victims of physical aggression (Crick, Casas, & Ku, 1999; Monks et al., 2005). Girls, in contrast, are more likely to experience relational than physical victimization, and they are more likely to be victims of relational aggression than boys (Crick et al., 1999; Monks et al., 2005; Putallaz et al., 2007). However, overall rates of victimization among preschool children tend to be similar for boys and girls (Monks et al., 2005), suggesting that although boys are more likely to direct aggression toward peers, both boys and girls are similarly at risk for being victimized.

Importantly, the gender differences in aggression and victimization that have been observed in preschool foreshadow gender differences in the patterns of aggression and victimization that emerge across childhood and into adulthood (Forgatch, Patterson, Degarmo, & Beldavs, 2009; Temcheff et al., 2008). Although the specific nature of aggressive behavior may change from one developmental period to another—for example, relational aggression in preschool may take the form of telling a peer that one no longer wants to be friends, whereas, in adolescence, the same behavior may manifest as turning others against a peer or spreading rumors—the roots of such later behaviors in boys and girls are evident in early childhood. Moreover, children who bully are also at an elevated risk for later diversifying their aggressive behaviors to more extreme forms of violence as well as to sexual harassment and dating aggression in early adolescence (Connolly, Pepler, Craig, & Taradash, 2000). As such, researchers have expressed concern that aggression in early childhood may set the stage for serious relationship problems in adulthood such as marital aggression and even abuse (Craig & Pepler, 2003). It is, therefore, important to understand how the gendered social context that characterizes most preschool peer relationships impacts girls' and boys' involvement in peer aggression and victimization.

THE GENDERED SOCIAL CONTEXT OF PRESCHOOLERS' PEER-DIRECTED AGGRESSION

To understand the gender differences in aggression and victimization, it is necessary to consider how the gendered social context that emerges in preschool influences aggressive interactions. From as early as age three, children demonstrate a clear preference for interacting with same-gender peers, with boys overwhelmingly directing their peer interactions to other boys and girls overwhelmingly directing their peer interactions to other girls (Fabes, Martin, & Hanish, 2003). Peer-directed aggressive behavior also follows a similar pattern in preschool; when children aggress against peers, both boys and girls target same-gender peers more often than other-gender peers (Ostrov & Keating, 2004; Pellegrini et al., 2007; Smith & Green, 1975). However, as children get older and as bullying behaviors become more established, children begin to direct their bullying toward both same- and other-gender peers (Veenstra et al., 2007). In fact, in middle childhood and preadolescence, research suggests that bullying between other-gender peers may occur at rates similar to same-gender bullying in middle childhood and preadolescence. For example, Olweus (1991) reported that 60% of 5th through 7th grade girls who reported being bullied said that they were bullied by boys, and 15–20% reported being bullied by both boys and girls. In a more recent study with 4th and 5th grade children, children named over twice as many boy–girl as boy–boy bully-victim dyads (Rodkin & Berger, 2008). Moreover, victimization begets more victimization, such that adolescents who are victimized by same-gender peers are also likely to be victimized by other-gender peers (Craig, Pepler, Connolly, & Henderson, 2001). In light of these findings, researchers are beginning to focus on how other-gender bullying and harassment differs from same-gender bullying in form and function (McMaster, Connolly, Pepler, & Craig, 2002), highlighting the need for further research on the early development of both same- and other-gender aggressive behaviors in preschool and on the need for early intervention to prevent these from developing.

In considering gender differences in the form of aggression that children exhibit and the play partners with whom they interact, our own data indicate that the gender composition of preschoolers' peer groups is related to boys' and girls' own tendencies to engage in gender-differentiated forms of aggression. For example, as is typically seen, boys in our sample were rated by teachers as more aggressive than girls, $t(259) = 3.99$, $p < .001$ (using the Aggression subscale of the Teacher Report Form of the Child Behavior Checklist, Achenbach, 1991, which taps primarily physically aggressive behaviors). To assess the contribution of peers' gender to this effect, we controlled for gender and correlated the proportion of time that children were observed to play with boys (out of all observed social interactions) with teachers' reports of children's aggression. Playing with boys was positively correlated with aggression above and beyond children's own gender, $r(258) = .16$, $p < .05$. Playing with boys was also positively correlated with victimization above and beyond children's own gender, $r(258) = .15$, $p < .05$, and this effect was slightly stronger for physical victimization, $r(258) = .15$, $p < .05$ than for relational or verbal victimization, $rs(258) = .12$ and $.11$, $ps < .10$. These findings speak to children's general tendencies to behave aggressively toward peers. Our observational data also suggest that playing with male peers tends to elicit aggressive behaviors in the context of the interaction. Specifically, aggression was likely to be observed when children played with boys, $r(261) = .18$, $p < .01$, particularly when the play involved a single male peer, $r(261) = .26$, $p < .001$; conversely, aggression was unlikely to be observed when children played with groups of girls, $r(261) = -.13$, $p < .05$ or groups of both boys and girls, $r(261) = -.21$, $p < .001$.

Male and female peer groups have the potential to be a powerful influence on young boys' and girls' behavior. For example, Fabes, Shepard, Guthrie, and Martin (1997) found that temperamental characteristics, such as arousability, moderated the relation between playing with male peers and tendencies to display aggressive behaviors for preschool boys. That is, arousable boys who played with other boys were particularly likely to exhibit aggressive tendencies. Moreover, Martin and Fabes (2001) demonstrated that such peer effects were dosage dependent, with the effects enhanced for boys who spent the most time engaged with same-gender peers. Thus, as boys spend more time in male-dominated peer groups, their interaction styles may stimulate greater aggression (Dishion, Bullock, & Granic, 2002).

The effects of peer socialization are not limited to boys, but they seem to operate somewhat differently for girls. In the Fabes et al. (1997) study, playing with female peers seemed to mitigate arousable girls' aggressive tendencies, and these effects were strongest for girls who spent the most time with other girls (Martin & Fabes, 2001) option. This is likely a function of girls' relatively lower tendencies to engage in aggression and dysregulated behaviors as compared to boys. However, when young girls do interact frequently with aggressive peers (whether male or female) they are also susceptible to socialization along aggressive lines (and, perhaps even more susceptible than are boys) (Hanish et al., 2005). Thus, as young children increasingly spend more time together, peer influence processes have the potential to shape gender differences in aggression by escalating or diminishing existing aggressive tendencies (Hay, 2007).

In addition, preschoolers' experiences with male and female peers can impact the beliefs and expectations that they develop about boys' and girls' aggressive behaviors, which may influence children's own aggressive behavior as well as their responses to peers' behaviors (Heyman & Dweck, 1998; Heyman & Gelman, 1999). For instance, similar to older children and adults, preschool boys and girls tend to believe that boys are more physically aggressive than girls and that girls are more relationally aggressive than boys (Giles & Heyman, 2005). This gender stereotype may then encourage boys and girls to display aggressive behaviors in stereotypical ways. At the same time, it may impact how children interpret and respond to other children's aggressive behaviors. In one study, for example, both boys and girls systematically misremembered that a physically aggressive character in a fictional story was male, when the aggressive character in the story was actually female (Giles & Heyman, 2005). Moreover, young children may react to boys' and girls' aggressive behaviors differently. In our work, preschool boys tended to react negatively to aggressive girls' negative behaviors but their reactions were more neutral in response to aggressive boys' negative behaviors (Hanish et al., 2007). Research with older children has also suggested a similar pattern of preferential responding to the aggressive and provocative behaviors emitted by same-gender peers compared to other-gender peers (Underwood, Schockner, & Hurley, 2001). Given that boys and girls perceive aggression differently depending on whether the aggressor is a same- or an other-gender peer (Pellegrini & Roseth, 2006), it is possible that such a response bias could potentially lead boys and girls to begin to act in ways that provoke the types of behaviors they expect from other-gender peers (Hay, Castle, & Davies, 2000; Olson, 1992).

THE ROLE OF TEACHERS

Boys' and girls' peer interactions in preschool do not occur in isolation; rather they occur in proximity to teachers and within a classroom context that is largely shaped by teachers. For example, in our own data, preschoolers were observed to directly interact with teachers 26% of the time. Moreover, when preschoolers were not directly interacting with teachers, teachers were within five feet of the children 41% of the time. Thus, preschoolers spend the majority of their time at school interacting directly with or playing in close proximity to a teacher. This is a particularly important point when preschoolers are aggressive toward one another. Because of the relatively low student–teacher ratios in preschool and because preschoolers are rarely out of visual or auditory range of teachers, preschool teachers are very much aware of and involved in preschoolers' aggression and victimization.

As research with older youth has shown, teachers' behaviors can impact on the overall level of aggression and victimization in a classroom (Henry et al., 2000). And, at the preschool level, we have demonstrated that there is significant variability across classrooms in the level of aggressive behaviors that boys and girls display (Hanish, Martin, Fabes, & Barcelo, 2008; Hanish et al., 2005). This is likely due, at least in part, to variations across teachers, particularly in the nature of their interactions and relationships with aggressive and victimized boys and girls (Coplan & Prakash, 2003; Dobbs, Arnold, & Doctoroff, 2004). That is, the ways in which preschool teachers manage boys' and girls' aggression behaviors and the nature and quality of the relationships that they form with these children are significant influences on the overall classroom environment, the quality of peer interactions, and children's own tendencies toward aggression.

Unfortunately, less is known about the quality of preschool teachers' interactions and relationships with victimized children, although, as we noted previously, aggressive and victimized children are often one and the same in preschool (Hanish et al., 2004).

Preschool Teachers' Management of Boys' and Girls' Aggressive Behaviors

Teachers react differently to boys' and girls' aggressive behavior (Dobbs et al., 2004; Justice, Cottone, Mashburn, & Rimm-Kaufman, 2008). Teachers are more likely to respond to boys' aggressive behaviors than to girls' aggressive behavior (Fagot & Hagan, 1985; Serbin, O'Leary, Kent, & Tonick, 1973). Moreover, when they do respond, they tend to utilize different response strategies with boys and girls. For instance, Ahn and Stifter (2006) examined teachers' reactions to young children's negative emotional expressions, including anger (which often co-occurs with aggression), and found that girls were more likely to receive physical comfort or distraction, whereas boys were more likely to be instructed on better ways to express their negative emotions. Additionally, Serbin and her colleagues (1973) observed that teachers used more loud reprimands when disciplining boys than with girls. Further, teachers are more likely to discipline girls using lower power strategies in which the misbehaved student is given an opportunity to correct their behavior, whereas, with boys, they are more likely to use higher power based on punishment and reward (Erden & Wolfgang, 2004). Our data provide further evidence for gender differences in the types of interactions experienced with teachers. In our sample, although it happened at a low rate for both genders, boys were proportionately more likely to be disciplined ($M = .06$, $SD = .08$) than were girls ($M = .03$, $SD = .04$), $t(258) = 4.55$, $p < .001$. These gender differences in the nature of teacher–child interactions may be due to the fact that boys are more likely than girls to use overt, and therefore highly salient, aggression strategies such as hitting, kicking or pushing.

Importantly, the ways in which teachers respond to children's aggressive behaviors can impact on whether aggressive and victimizing behaviors become more or less prominent in the classroom over the course of the school year. For instance, in one study, teachers who used authoritarian strategies—including interrupting play without explanation, reprimanding or punishing peer contact, or separating the children—to manage young children's negative peer interactions had students who exhibited fewer competent behaviors with peers and greater aggressive behaviors with peers (Howes, Hamilton, & Matheson, 1994). When such strategies are used more frequently with the most aggressive children (typically boys), there is the potential to exacerbate (rather than mitigate) aggressive and victimizing interactions in the classroom.

Preschool Teachers' Relationships with Aggressive Boys and Girls

Teachers often report having closer relationships (and, in some cases, more dependent relationships) with female students than they do with male students and more conflictual relationships with male students as compared to female students (Birch & Ladd, 1998; Howes, 2000; Koepke & Harkins, 2008). These gender differences are exaggerated for more aggressive children, particularly for boys, who tend to have the most negative and conflictual relationships with teachers (Justice et al., 2008; Koles, O'Connor, & McCartney, 2009). Importantly, the quality of children's relationships with a teacher can influence the quality of their peer relationships, concurrently and over time, with effects observed as early as toddlerhood (Howes, 2000; Howes et al., 1994). Among aggressive children, a positive relationship with the teacher can serve as a protective factor, whereas difficult relationships with teachers can exacerbate children's problem behaviors, leading to increased difficulties with peers over time (Ladd & Burgess, 2001). For instance, Hamre and Pianta (2001) found that among children who had behavior problems in kindergarten, those who were able to develop positive relationships with teachers had fewer discipline problems and more positive motivation through 8th grade than those with less supportive relationships with teachers. In contrast, conflict with a preschool teacher was found to predict hostile–aggressive behavior later in the school year, especially for boys (Ewing & Taylor, 2009). Similarly, a study of kindergarteners found evidence for a reciprocal relationship between children's aggression and conflict with teachers; children with high levels of aggression early in the school year had greater levels of conflict with their teacher mid-year, and exhibited increased aggression at the end of school year (Doumen et al., 2008). The effects of early conflict with teachers may have lasting effects.

Conflict with a preschool teacher has been linked to aggression and disruption in the 2nd grade (Howes, 2000), and children who had conflictual relationships with their kindergarten teacher exhibited faster rates of increase in aggressive behavior from kindergarten through 3rd grade than did their peers with less conflictual relationships. Preschool teachers, then, can have potentially large impacts on the types of behaviors that boys and girls exhibit with peers and the extent to which children escalate, maintain, or diminish the frequency of their aggressive interactions with peers.

Translating Research into Practice: Implications for Bullying Intervention Programs for Preschool Boys and Girls

The research findings presented here point to the importance of gender in structuring young children's social experiences in preschool, including their impact on the development of bullying. Because instances of bullying between boys and girls have potentially serious implications in adolescence and into adulthood as more extreme and serious behaviors may emerge (Ozer, Tschann, Pasch, & Flores, 2004; Shute, Owens, & Slee, 2008), one should be particularly concerned about the developmental trajectories for those bullies and victims who experience repeated involvement in aggressive interactions or bullying episodes over time. Early aggression forecasts later aggression (Cummings et al., 1989; Huesmann, Eron, Lefkowitz, & Walder, 1984), and intervention programs for aggression tend to be most successful when delivered early, before stable behavioral and interactional patterns have had a chance to firmly solidify (Coie & Dodge, 1998; Kazdin, 1985). Thus, anti-bullying classroom intervention strategies should begin in preschool. Moreover, they should include components that can proactively prevent these acts from occurring as well as those that provide teachers and peers with effective strategies to use when they witness or are involved in acts of aggression.

Preventive Strategies Oriented Toward Enhancing Boys' and Girls' Relationships and Social Skills

Preschool classroom interventions should begin with teachers, given their focus on children's social–emotional development and the primary role they play in structuring the preschool classroom and children's peer interactions. In addition, preschool children tend be more accepting of teacher direction compared to older children (Smith,

Cousins, & Stewart, 2005). Therefore, preschool teachers have the potential to have a strong positive influence on children's aggressive behavior; this is particularly true for children who exhibit problem behaviors at young ages—especially boys, who are at risk for experiencing conflicted relationships with teachers (Justice et al., 2008). Teachers should be mindful of creating positive relationships with even the most challenging students, as it will provide a classroom environment that minimizes aggression. With this as a basis, teachers may be able to guide peer interactions and to manage the aggressive and victimizing behaviors that sometimes occur among preschool boys and girls. Additionally, reducing victimization between boys and girls should promote more positive classroom environments that are less stressful for children and teachers, thereby improving the learning environment for all children.

With the developmental context of preschool in mind, teachers can use strategies to guide children's peer interactions; this can serve the dual purpose of helping children to navigate key developmental milestones as well as helping to prevent bullying (Seidman & French, 2004). In preschool, a key developmental task involves acquiring the skills necessary for developing and maintaining positive peer relationships. These skills include communication, conflict resolution, cooperative play, emotional expression, and other social skills (Crick & Dodge, 1994). Thus, as a first step, we recommend that preschool teachers create opportunities during the school day in which children may interact and communicate positively with one another. This can be done, for example, by pairing children together for cooperative activities (e.g., working together to complete a project). Teachers can also take advantage of naturally occurring peer interactions to help shape positive peer experiences. Key to doing this is teacher supervision, in which the teacher guides peer interactions using such strategies as helping children to initiate or maintain peer interactions, monitoring peer interactions for positive behaviors (which should be reinforced) and negative behaviors (which should be redirected), and explaining peers' behaviors (e.g., Howes et al., 1994).

This is particularly important for children who do not typically play together, such as for boys and girls. In support of this, research suggests that children with other-gender friends engage in more social play, express more positive affect with peers, and are more flexible when cooperating with peers than children without other-gender friends (Howes, 1988). This is likely because children with other-gender friends must flexibly use a wider repertoire of social skills. Indeed, gender-segregated peer groups promote gender-differentiated styles of communication, with boys and girls preferring to communicate in different ways (Leman, Ahmed, & Ozarow, 2005; McCloskey & Coleman, 1992; Miller, Danaher, & Forbes, 1986; Murphy & Faulkner, 2006). Thus, interacting with other-gender peers gives children access to different interactional and communicative styles (Howes, 1988). These interactions can provide opportunities for children to learn a broad range of effective communication skills and problem-solving strategies, which can improve the quality of children's interactions with same- and other-gender peers, siblings, and parents. To enhance children's development of a wide repertoire of social skills, teachers may reinforce boys and girls for interacting together (Serbin, Tonick, & Sternglanz, 1977). They may also scaffold other-gender play interactions by encouraging boys and girls to listen, take turns, and compromise, all of which may facilitate children's communication and problem-solving skills, helping children to interact more effectively with both same- and other-gender peers. In vivo rehearsal of these types of communication and social skills can help children to generalize skills and use them flexibly in different kinds of contexts (Lochman & Wells, 2002). Thus, by encouraging interactions between other-gender peers, teachers can facilitate positive, cooperative peer experiences and support boys' and girls' acquisition of social skills.

In and of itself, having a broad repertoire of social skills on which to draw diminishes children's risk for concurrent and future involvement in bullying as both the aggressor and the victim (Card, Isaacs, & Hodges, 2007). Additionally, children may begin to identify common interests with others who are not like themselves, forming the basis for friendships later in childhood and into adulthood. For example, research with elementary-age children has shown that those who have other-gender friends have better social skills and that these friendships are mutually rewarding (Gottman, 1986; Howes & Phillipsen, 1992). Setting the stage for such diverse friendships in preschool may improve children's social outcomes in elementary school and through adolescence. As prior research has shown, having friendships is an important deterrent of victimization, particularly when those friends are themselves socially skilled (Hodges, Boivin, Vitaro, & Bukowski, 1999). Thus, by specifically taking advantage of opportunities to enhance children's social skills, interactions, and relationships at a developmentally sensitive period, preschool teachers have the potential to help children develop a range of skills that can diminish bullying. Moreover, when this effort is complemented by parents' efforts at home, there is even greater potential for positive effects (Lochman & Wells, 2004).

Strategies for Limiting Aggressive Peer Interactions

Teaching boys and girls how to identify and respond to peer bullying attempts is also an important element of preschool interventions (Harrist & Bradley, 2003; Lamb, Bigler, Liben, & Green, 2007). Because boys and girls evaluate aggression differently, it is important to incorporate both physical and relational forms of aggression into their conceptualizations of the problem. For example, Giles and Heyman (2005) reported that preschool boys were more likely to judge acts of physical aggression such as hitting or kicking as more negative than acts of relational aggression (such as exclusion), whereas preschool girls viewed both relationally and physically aggressive as equally negative. Thus, if a child tells another child "You can't play with us," a girl may be more likely than a boy to judge that peer's behavior as intentionally mean.

By providing children with developmentally appropriate and effective strategies for responding to peers' aggressive acts, it may be possible to minimize the cascading negative effects that aggressive acts can have on peer relationships. For instance, children who respond to peer conflicts using assertive verbal objections (e.g., "I don't like that") are more socially competent and less likely to be involved in aggressive peer interactions over time than those who respond in aggressive and dysregulated ways (Eisenberg et al., 1999). This method of managing peer conflicts can be modeled or taught by teachers to assist children in acquiring the skill. Moreover, research shows that many children witness bullying episodes without intervening, suggesting that training bystanders may be an effective strategy for limiting aggression in the classroom (Salmivalli et al., 1998). Thus, children can learn to mitigate their own and others' involvement in aggressive interactions.

SUMMARY

In preschool, these types of intervention strategies may work best in concert with more long-term prevention strategies. We have summarized research demonstrating that simply being exposed to aggressive peers can lead to increased aggressive behaviors among preschool children (Hanish et al., 2005; Patterson et al., 1967), and as preschoolers increasingly play in gender-segregated groups, boys may be more likely to experience peer-directed aggression and less likely to experience prosocial acts from peers (Fabes et al., 2003; Martin & Fabes, 2001). Developmental Psychology in light of this research, a preventive approach must take into account how gender influences the social context of bullying. Prevention strategies may require more planning and classroom time, but they also have the greatest potential for impact by addressing bullying issues as well as the primary role of gender in preschoolers' peer interactions.

NOTES

1. This work was supported, in part, by funds from the National Institute of Child Health and Human Development (R01 HD45816), the Lives of Girls and Boys project, and from the T. Denny Sanford Foundation.

REFERENCES

Achenbach, T.M. (1991). *Integrative guide to the 1991 CBCL/4–18, YSR, and TRF profiles*. Burlington, VT: University of Vermont, Department of Psychology.

Ahn, H. J., & Stifter, C. (2006). Child care teachers' response to children's emotional expression. *Early Education and Development, 17*, 253–270.

Alsaker, F.D., & Valkanover, S. (2001). Early diagnosis and prevention of victimization in kindergarten. In J. Juvonen & S. Graham (Eds.), *Peer harassment in school: The plight of the vulnerable and victimized* (pp. 175–195). New York, NY: Guilford.

Archer, J., & Coyne, S.M. (2005). An integrated review of indirect, relational, and social aggression. *Personality and Social Psychology Review, 9*, 212.

Birch, S.H., & Ladd, G.W. (1998). Children's interpersonal behaviors and the teacher-child relationship. *Developmental Psychology, 34*, 934–946.

Boivin, M., Hymel, S., & Bukowski, W.M. (1995). The roles of social withdrawal, peer rejection, and victimization by peers in predicting loneliness and depressed mood in children. *Development and Psychopathology, 7*, 765–786.

Caplan, R.B., Vespo, J., Pedersen, J., & Hay, D.F. (1991). Conflict and its resolution in small groups of one- and two-year-olds. *Child Development, 62*, 1513–1524.

Card, N.A., Isaacs, J., & Hodges, E.V.E. (2007). Correlates of school victimization: Recommendations for intervention and prevention. In J.E. Zins, M.J. Elias, & C.A. Maher (Eds.), *Bullying, victimization, and peer harassment: A handbook of prevention and intervention* (pp. 339–366). New York, NY: Haworth Press.

Card, N.A., Stucky, B.D., Sawalani, G.M., & Little, T.D. (2008). Direct and indirect aggression during childhood and adolescence: A meta-analytic review of gender differences, intercorrelations, and relations to maladjustment. *Child Development, 79*, 1185–1229.

Coie, J.D., & Dodge, K.A. (1998). Aggression and antisocial behavior. In W. Damon & N. Eisenberg (Eds.), *Handbook of Child Psychology: Social, Emotional, and Personality Development* (5th ed.) (pp. 779–862). New York, NY: John Wiley & Sons.

Connolly, J., Pepler, D., Craig, W., & Taradash, A. (2000). Dating experiences of bullies in early adolescence. *Child Maltreatment, 5*, 299–310.

Coplan, R.J., & Prakash, K. (2003). Spending time with teacher: Characteristics of preschoolers who frequently elicit versus initiate interactions with teachers. *Early Childhood Research Quarterly, 18*, 143–158.

Craig, W.M., & Pepler, D.J. (2003). Identifying and targeting risk for involvement in bullying and victimization. *The Canadian Journal of Psychiatry, 48*, 577–582.

Craig, W.M., Pepler, D.J., Connolly, J., & Henderson, K. (2001). Developmental context of peer harassment in early adolescence. In J. Juvonen & S. Graham (Eds.), *Peer harassment in school: The plight of the vulnerable and victimized* (pp. 242–262). New York, NY: Guilford Press.

Crick, N.R., & Dodge, K.A. (1994). A review and reformulation of social information processing mechanisms in children's social adjustment. *Psychological Bulletin, 115*, 74–101.

Crick, N.R., Casas, J.F., & Ku, H. (1999). Relational and physical forms of peer victimization in preschool. *Developmental Psychology, 35*, 376–385.

Crick, N.R., Casas, J.F., & Nelson, D.A. (2002). Toward a more comprehensive understanding of peer maltreatment: Studies of relational victimization. *Current Directions in Psychological Science, 11*(3), 98.

Crowther, J.H., Bond, L.A., & Rolf, J.E. (1981). The incidence, prevalence, and severity of behavior disorders among preschool-aged children in day care. *Journal of Abnormal Child Psychology, 9*, 23–42.

Cummings, E.M., Iannotti, R.J., & Zahn-Waxler, C. (1989). Aggression between peers in early childhood: Individual continuity and developmental change. *Child Development, 60*, 887–895.

Dishion, T.J., Bullock, B.M., & Granic, I. (2002). Pragmatism in modeling peer influence: Dynamics, outcomes and change processes. *Development and Psychopathology, 14*, 969–981.

Dobbs, J., Arnold, D.H., & Doctoroff, G.L. (2004). Attention in the preschool classroom: The relationships among child gender, child misbehavior, and types of teacher attention. *Early Child Development and Care, 174*, 281–295.

Doumen, S., Verschueren, K., Buyse, E., Germeijs, V., Luyckx, K., & Soenens, B. (2008). Reciprocal relations between teacher-child conflict and aggressive behavior in kindergarten: A three-wave longitudinal study. *Journal of Child Clinical and Adolescent Psychology, 37*, 588–599.

Eisenberg, N., Cumberland, A., Spinrad, T.L., Fabes, R.A., Shepard, S.A., Reiser, M., et al. (2001). The relations of regulation and emotionality to children's externalizing and internalizing problem behavior. *Child Development, 72*, 1112–1134.

Eisenberg, N., Fabes, R.A., Murphy, B.C., Shepard, S.A., Guthrie, I.K., Mazsk, P., et al. (1999). Prediction of elementary school children's socially appropriate and problem behavior from anger reactions at age 4–6 years. *Journal of Applied Developmental Psychology, 20*, 119–142.

Erden, F., & Wolfgang, C. (2004). An exploration of the differences in prekindergarten, kindergarten, and first grade teachers' beliefs related to discipline when dealing with male and female students. *Early Child Development and Care, 174*, 3–11.

Ewing, A.R., & Taylor, A.R. (2009). The role of child gender and ethnicity in teacher-child relationship quality and children's behavioral adjustment in preschool. *Early Childhood Research Quarterly, 24*, 92–105.

Fabes, R.A., & Eisenberg, N. (1992). Young children's coping with interpersonal anger. *Child Development, 63*, 116–128.

Fabes, R.A., Martin, C.L., & Hanish, L.D. (2003). Young children's play qualities in same-, other-, and mixed-sex peer groups. *Child Development, 74*, 921–932.

Fabes, R.A., Martin, C.L., & Hanish, L.D. (2009). Children's behaviors and interactions with peers. In W.B.K. Rubin, & B. Larsen (Eds.), *Handbook of peer interactions, relationships, and groups* (pp. 45–62). New York, NY: Guilford.

Fabes, R.A., Shepard, S.A., Guthrie, I.K., & Martin, C.L. (1997). Roles of temperamental arousal and gender-segregated play in young children's social adjustment. *Developmental Psychology, 33*, 693–702.

Fagot, B.I., & Hagan, R. (1985). Aggression in toddlers: Responses to the assertive acts of boys and girls. *Sex Roles, 12*, 341–351.

Forgatch, M.S., Patterson, G.R., Degarmo, D.S., & Beldavs, Z.G. (2009). Testing the oregon delinquency model with 9-year follow-up of the oregon divorce study. *Development and Psychopathology, 21* 637–660.

Giles, J.W., & Heyman, G.D. (2005). Young children's beliefs about the relationship between gender and aggressive behavior. *Child Development, 76*, 107–121.

Gottman, J.M. (1986). The world of coordinated play: Same- and cross-sex friendship in young children. In J.M. Gottman & J.G. Parker (Eds.), *Conversations of friends: Speculations on affective development* (pp. 139–191). New York, NY: Cambridge University Press.

Hamre, B.K., & Pianta, R.C. (2001). Early teacher-child relationships and the trajectory of children's social outcomes through eighth grade. *Child Development, 72*, 625–638.

Hanish, L.D., & Guerra, N.G. (2000). Predictors of peer victimization among urban youth. *Social Development, 9*, 521–543.

Hanish, L.D., Martin, C.L., Fabes, R.A., & Barcelo, H. (2008). The breadth of peer relationships among preschoolers: An application of the Q-connectivity method to externalizing behavior. *Child Development, 79*, 1119–1136.

Hanish, L.D., Ryan, P., Martin, C.L., & Fabes, R.A. (2005). The social context of young children's peer victimization. *Social Development, 14*, 2–19.

Hanish, L.D., Martin, C.L., Fabes, R.A., Leonard, S., & Herzog, M. (2005). Exposure to externalizing peers in early childhood: Homophily and peer contagion processes. *Journal of Abnormal Child Psychology, 33*, 267–281.

Hanish, L.D., Eisenberg, N., Fabes, R.A., Spinrad, T.L., Ryan, P., & Schmidt, S. (2004). The expression and regulation of negative emotions: Risk factors for young children's peer victimization. *Development and Psychopathology, 16*, 335–353.

Harris, J.R. (1995). Where is the child's environment? A group socialization theory of development. *Psychological Review, 102*, 458–489.

Harrist, A.W., & Bradley, K.D. (2003). "You can't say you can't play": Intervening in the process of social exclusion in the kindergarten classroom. *Early Childhood Research Quarterly, 18*, 185–205.

Hawker, D.S.J., & Boulton, M.J. (2000). Twenty years' research on peer victimization and psychosocial maladjustment: A meta-analytic review of cross-sectional studies. *Journal of Child Psychology and Psychiatry, 41*, 441–455.

Hay, D.F. (2007). The gradual emergence of sex differences in aggression: Alternative hypotheses. *Psychological Medicine 37*, 1527–1537.

Hay, D.F., Castle, J., & Davies, L. (2000). Toddlers' use of force against familiar peers: A precursor of serious aggression? *Child Development, 71*, 457–467.

Henry, D., Guerra, N.G., Huesmann, R., Tolan, P.H., Van Acker, R., & Eron, L. (2000). Normative influences on aggression in urban elementary school classrooms. *American Journal of Community Psychology, 28*, 59–81.

Heyman, G.D., & Dweck, C.S. (1998). Children's thinking about traits: Implications for judgments of the self and others. *Child Development, 69*, 391–403.

Heyman, G.D., & Gelman, S.A. (1999). The use of trait labels in making psychological inferences. *Child Development, 70*, 604–619.

Hodges, E.V.E., Boivin, M., Vitaro, F., & Bukowski, W.M. (1999). The power of friendship: Protection against an escalating cycle of peer victimization. *Developmental Psychology, 35*, 94–101.

Howes, C. (1988). Same- and cross-sex friends: Implications for interaction and social skills. *Early Childhood Research Quarterly, 3*, 21–37.

Howes, C. (2000). Social-emotional classroom climate in child care, child-teacher relationships and children's second grade peer relations. *Social Development, 9*, 191–204.

Howes, C., & Phillipsen, L. (1992). Gender and friendship: Relationships within peer groups of young children. *Social Development, 1*, 230–230.

Howes, C., Hamilton, C.E., & Matheson, C.C. (1994). Children's relationships with peers: Differential associations with aspects of the teacher-child relationship. *Child Development, 65*, 253–263.

Huesmann, L.R., Eron, L.D., Lefkowitz, M.M., & Walder, L.O. (1984). Stability of aggression over time and generations. *Developmental Psychology, 20*, 1120–1134.

Justice, L.M., Cottone, E.A., Mashburn, A., & Rimm-Kaufman, S.E. (2008). Relationships between teachers and preschoolers who are at risk: Contribution of children's language skills, temperamentally based attributes, and gender. *Early Education and Development, 19*, 600–621.

Kazdin, A.E. (1985). *Treatment of antisocial behavior in children and adolescents.* Homeword, IL: Dorsey Press.

Kochenderfer, B., & Ladd, G.W. (1996). Peer victimization: Manifestations and relations to school adjustment in kindergarten. *Journal of School Psychology, 34*, 267–283.

Koepke, M.F., & Harkins, D.A. (2008). Conflict in the classroom: Gender Differences in the teacher-child relationship. *Early Education and Development, 19*, 843–864.

Koles, B., O'Connor, E., & McCartney, K. (2009). Teacher-child relationships in prekindergarten: The Influences of child and teacher characteristics. *Journal of Early Childhood Teacher Education, 30*, 3–21.

Ladd, G.W., & Burgess, K.B. (2001). Do relational risks and protective factors moderate the linkages between childhood aggression and early psychological and school adjustment? *Child Development, 72*, 1579–1601.

Lamb, L., Bigler, R.S., Liben, L.S., & Green, V. (2007). When children bully peers for sex "inappropriate" behavior: Theoretical and practical implications of anti-bullying interventions. Paper presented at the Biennial Meeting of the Society for Research in Child Development.

Leman, P.J., Ahmed, S., & Ozarow, L. (2005). Gender, gender relations, and the social dynamics of children's conversations. *Jean Piaget Society International Workshop, Sep 2003, Geneva, Switzerland, 41*, 64–74.

Lochman, J.E., & Wells, K.C. (2002). Contextual social-cognitive mediators and child outcome: A test of the theoretical model in the coping power program. *Development and Psychopathology, 14*, 945–967.

Lochman, J.E., & Wells, K.C. (2004). The coping power program for preadolescent aggressive boys and their parents: Outcome effects at the 1-year follow-up. *Journal of Consulting and Clinical Psychology, 72*, 571–578.

Loeber, R., Keenan, K., Lahey, B.B., Green, S.M., & Thomas, C. (1993). Evidence for developmentally based diagnoses of oppositional defiant disorder and conduct disorder. *Journal of Abnormal Child Psychology, 21*, 377–410.

Maccoby, E.E. (1998). *The two sexes: Growing up apart, coming together.* Cambridge, MA: Harvard University Press.

Martin, C.L., & Fabes, R.A. (2001). The stability and consequences of young children's same-sex peer interactions. *Developmental Psychology, 37*, 431–446.

McCloskey, L.A., & Coleman, L.M. (1992). Difference without dominance: Children's talk in mixed- and same-sex dyads. *Sex Roles, 27*, 241–257.

McMaster, L.E., Connolly, J., Pepler, D., & Craig, W.M. (2002). Peer to peer sexual harassment in early adolescence: A developmental perspective. *Development and Psychopathology, 14*, 91–105.

Miller, P.M., Danaher, D.L., & Forbes, D. (1986). Sex-related strategies for coping with interpersonal conflict in children aged five and seven. *Developmental psychology, 22*, 543.

Monks, C.P., Smith, P.K., & Swettenham, J. (2005). Psychological correlates of peer victimization in preschool: Social cognitive skills, executive function and attachment profiles. *Aggressive Behavior, 31*, 571–588.

Murphy, S.M., & Faulkner, D. (2006). Gender differences in verbal communication between popular and unpopular children during an interactive task. *Social Development, 15*, 82–108.

Olson, S.L. (1992). Development of conduct problems and peer rejection in preschool children: A social systems analysis. *Journal of Abnormal Child Psychology, 20*, 327–350.

Olweus, D. (1991). Bully/victim problems among schoolchildren: Basic facts and effects of a school based intervention program. In D.J. Pepler & K.H. Rubin (Eds.), *The development and treatment of childhood aggression* (pp. 411–448). Hillsdale, NJ: Lawrence Erlbaum Associates.

Ostrov, J.M., & Keating, C.F. (2004). Gender differences in preschool aggression during free play and structured interactions: An observational study. *Social Development, 13*, 255–277.

Ozer, E.J., Tschann, J.M., Pasch, L.A., & Flores, E. (2004). Violence perpetration across peer and partner relationships: Co-occurrence and longitudinal patterns among adolescents. *Journal of Adolescent Health, 34*, 64–71.

Patterson, G.R., Littman, R.A., & Bricker, W. (1967). Assertive behavior in children: A step toward a theory of aggression. *Monographs of the Society for Research in Child Development, 32 (5, Serial No. 113)*.

Pellegrini, A.D., & Roseth, C.J. (2006). Relational aggression and relationships in preschoolers: A discussion of methods, gender differences, and function. *Journal of Applied Developmental Psychology, 27*, 269–276.

Pellegrini, A.D., Roseth, C.J., Mliner, S., Bohn, C.M., Van Ryzin, M., Vance, N., et al. (2007). Social dominance in preschool classrooms. *Journal of Comparative Psychology, 121*, 54.

Power, T.G. (2000). *Play and exploration in children and animals*. Mahwah, NJ: Erlbaum.

Putallaz, M., Grimes, C.L., Foster, K.J., Kupersmidt, J.B., Coie, J.D., & Dearing, K. (2007). Overt and relational aggression and victimization: Multiple perspectives within the school setting. *Journal of School Psychology, 45*, 523–547.

Rodkin, P.C., & Berger, C. (2008). Who bullies whom? social status asymmetries by victim gender. *International Journal of Behavioral Development, 32*, 473–485.

Rose, A.J., & Rudolph, K.D. (2006). A review of sex differences in peer relationship processes: Potential trade-offs for the emotional and behavioral development of girls and boys. *Psychological Bulletin, 132*, 98–131.

Salmivalli, C., Lappalainen, M., & Lagerspetz, K.M.J. (1998). Stability and change of behavior in connection with bullying in schools: A two-year follow-up. *Aggressive Behavior, 24*, 205–218.

Seidman, E., & French, E.S. (2004). Developmental trajectories and ecological transitions: A two-step procedure to aid in the choice of prevention and promotion interventions. *Development and Psychopathology, 16*, 1141–1159.

Serbin, L.A., Tonick, I.J., & Sternglanz, S.H. (1977). Shaping cooperative cross-sex play. *Child Development, 48*, 924–929.

Serbin, L.A., O'Leary, K.D., Kent, R.N., & Tonick, I.J. (1973). A comparison of teacher response to the preacademic and problem behavior of boys and girls. *Child Development, 44*, 796–804.

Shute, R., Owens, L., & Slee, P. (2008). Everyday victimization of adolescent girls by boys: Sexual harassment, bullying or aggression? *Sex Roles, 58*, 477–489.

Smith, J.D., Cousins, J.B., & Stewart, R. (2005). Antibullying interventions in schools: Ingredients of effective programs. *Canadian Journal of Education, 28*, 739–762.

Smith, P.K., & Green, M. (1975). Aggressive behavior in English nurseries and play groups: Sex differences and response of adults. *Child Development, 46*, 211–214.

Snyder, J., Schrepferman, L., McEachern, A., Barner, S., Johnson, K., & Provines, J. (2008). Peer deviancy training and peer coercion: Dual processes associated with early-onset conduct problems. *Child Development, 79*, 252–268.

Strayer, F.F., & Santos, A.J. (1996). Affiliative structures in preschool peer groups. *Social Development, 5*, 117–130.

Sutton, J., & Smith, P.K. (1999). Bullying as a group process: An adaptation of the participant role approach. *Aggressive Behavior, 25*, 97–111.

Temcheff, C.E., Serbin, L.A., Martin-Storey, A., Stack, D.M., Hodgins, S., Ledingham, J., et al. (2008). Continuity and pathways from aggression in childhood to family violence in adulthood: A 30-year longitudinal study. *Journal of Family Violence, 23*, 231–242.

Tomada, G., & Schneider, B.H. (1997). Relational aggression, gender, and peer acceptance: Invariance across culture, stability over time, and concordance among informants. *Developmental Psychology, 33*, 601–609.

U.S. Department of Education. (2007). The Condition of Education 2007 (NCES 2007–064). Retrieved April 23, 2009, from http://nces.ed.gov/fastfacts/display.asp?id=78.

Underwood, M.K. (2003). *Social aggression among girls*. New York, NY: Guilford Press.

Underwood, M.K., Schockner, A.E., & Hurley, J.C. (2001). Children's responses to same- and other-gender peers: An experimental investigation with 8-, 10-, and 12-year-olds. *Developmental Psychology, 37*, 362–372.

Veenstra, R., Lindenberg, S., Zijlstra, B.J.H., De Winter, A.F., Verhulst, F.C., & Ormel, J. (2007). The dyadic nature of bullying and victimization: Testing a dual-perspective theory. *Child Development, 78*, 1843–1854.

12

CLASSROOM ECOLOGIES THAT SUPPORT
OR DISCOURAGE BULLYING

BETH DOLL, SAMUEL SONG, ALLISON CHAMPION, AND KRISTIN JONES

This chapter will describe the characteristics of elementary school classrooms that can foster or discourage peer bullying. Classrooms are important contexts for understanding bullying because most bullying interactions occur among classmates (Salmivalli et al., 1996). In particular, two features of classrooms are highly relevant to understanding bullying: (1) the quality of social relationships in the classroom; and (2) the support for students' autonomy and self-regulation. These environmental characteristics represent a social ecology that interacts with individual characteristics of the students to determine the nature and prevalence of peer bullying in any classroom. Thus, bullying could be diminished by introducing routines and practices that alter the classroom ecology so that it is less tolerant of bullying.

To explain the relation between these classroom characteristics and bullying, this chapter will borrow from the rich developmental evidence of ecological influences on peer aggression. Bullying will be described as an extreme form of peer aggression in which one student seeks to gain status or power by repeatedly harming and intimidating a vulnerable peer (Espelage & Swearer, 2003; Olweus, 1993). It differs from less extreme forms of peer aggression in the malevolent intent of the bullying student and in the strikingly unequal power between bullying and victimized students.

AGGRESSIVE INTERACTIONS AMONG CLASSMATES

Socially competent children routinely engage in aggressive interactions with peers, and these are not always detrimental (Pellegrini, 2007, 2008). For example, adolescent boys often engage in aggressive behaviors as a means to establish new relationships with peers (Farmer, Estell, Bishop, O'Neal, & Cairns, 2003; Pellegrini & Long, 2004) or to negotiate their place within the hierarchy of a peer group (Gini, 2006). The "jostling" or "rough and tumble play" that occurs between friends includes the same verbally and physically aggressive behaviors that comprise bullying but differs in that it is not intended to harm or dominate the other child (Pellegrini, 2002; Pellegrini & Bartini, 2001). Instead, rough and tumble play occurs within benign reciprocal interactions, where friends take turns jostling each other both for entertainment and to strengthen the friendship. If they recognize that their rough and tumble play is becoming hurtful, most children will cease the aggressive behavior.

In our earlier research, children in elementary school classrooms reported that they struggled with conflicts involving teasing, name-calling, bad arguments or physical fighting in approximately 8% of all recesses (Doll, Murphy, & Song, 2003). Most of these aggressive peer conflicts do not represent bullying. Classmates might have authentic disagreements about games to play, accidental injuries or jostling that has crossed the line into meanness. Aggressive peer interactions such as cheating or exploitation can also occur when children compete for classroom resources (Pellegrini, 1995). The majority of these authentic conflicts will occur among friends rather than non-friends (Grotpeter & Crick, 1996), and friends will work to reconcile these social "accidents" when they occur (Pellegrini, 2002). It is unresolved conflict, often occurring outside of friendships, that most worry children.

Children may resort to bullying or malicious intimidation to dominate weaker peers or to control other children. The peer's inability to defend against the aggression may be due to individual factors such as physical weakness or ineffective verbal skills, or ecological factors such as a lack of protective support from peers or school adults (Card & Hodges, 2008; Orpinas & Horne, 2006; Rodkin & Hodges, 2003, Song & Stoiber, 2008). Their helplessness in the face of these instances of aggression can leave the victimized children feeling discouraged and worried (Swearer, Song, & Cary, 2001).

Although they differ in their intent, all of these interactions are characterized by the behaviors of physical, verbal, or social aggression. When aggression is physical, it may be observed as behaviors of hitting, kicking, poking, pouncing, sneaking-up, picking-up, play fighting, chasing, holding, and pushing (Orpinas & Horne, 2006; Pellegrini, 1995). Verbal aggression such as teasing, taunting, picking on, and making fun of is more difficult to observe directly, especially when the taunt is soft-spoken or occurs outside the hearing of adults. The exclusion, rumor-spreading, and name-calling that comprise social aggression may occur outside the immediate notice of the victimized student.

To distinguish between jostling, aggressive conflict and malicious bullying, children must be able to detect and interpret the intention of the other child in the interaction. Because children are integral to the "kid society" that operates in their classrooms, they are frequently better than adults at judging whether an aggressive interaction is a form of jostling (and therefore appropriate behavior among friends), simple conflict or bullying. Being able to interpret and react appropriately to the intentions of other children during aggressive interactions influences children's vulnerability to bullying and intimidation. Children who are unable to defend against peers' aggressive acts become hypersensitive to these occurrences, are less adept at reacting to aggression, and become preoccupied with future aggressive threats (Asher & Coie, 1990).

These forms of peer aggression hint at the kinds of strategies that might reduce bullying incidents within a classroom. For example, reducing the frequency of all aggressive interactions would likely reduce the frequency of bullying interactions at the extreme of the continuum. Alternatively, pulling more children into the friendship networks of the classroom would increase the likelihood that aggressive peer interactions, when they occur, will be among friends and so easier to resolve. It might be possible to diminish the frequency with which aggressive interactions escalate into bullying by increasing the successful resolution of peer conflicts before these escalate. Finally, it might be possible to discourage intimidation by equalizing the distribution of power in a classroom or prompting classmates to more readily protect each other.

WHAT CHILDREN THINK

Our descriptions of classroom characteristics that discourage bullying were first drawn from developmental research that describes the emergence of social competence in children, (Doll, LeClair, & Kurien, 2009; Doll, Zucker, & Brehm, 2004; National Research Council/Institute of Medicine, 2004). This research consistently identifies two sets of classroom characteristics that support children's social competence: (1) the quality of social relationships that develop within the classroom including relationships among peers, between students and the teacher, and between the classroom and the students' families; and (2) the strength of human agency among students including their sense of self-efficacy, self-determination, and behavioral self-control. Then, in preparation for this chapter, we analyzed data from 344 3rd, 4th, and 5th grade students to relate their perceptions of these classroom characteristics with their worries about and perceptions of peer aggression (Doll & Spies, 2007; Spies et al., 2007). Students completed brief anonymous surveys describing their perceptions of each aspect of classroom relationships and human agency. Five additional items assessed the degree to which students' classmates: argued; made fun of one another; engaged in teasing and name-calling; hit, pushed, or shoved; and said bad things about one another. Eight items assessed the students' worries about peer aggression, including worries that classmates would do or say mean things to them, or disrupt their friendships with other students.

While children's perceptions of the prevalence of peer aggression were correlated with their worries about aggression ($r = .49$), the very modest correlation showed that these were distinct, albeit related indices of peer aggression. We conducted multiple regression analyses to describe the unique variance in peer aggression that was predicted by student perceptions of each characteristic of the classroom environment. The results suggested that students' perceptions of the aggression in their classroom and their worries about that aggression were related, to a differing degree, to four of the six characteristics of students' classrooms: the availability of peer friendships, classmates' behavioral self-control, the students' sense of self-determination, and the relationship between teachers and the students. Results were somewhat different for boys and for girls. For both genders, peer friendships and behavioral self-control among students in the classroom were related to the occurrence of aggression. In the perceptions of girls, the aggression was also related to the strength of their relationship with the classroom teacher, while boys perceived a relation between aggression and their own self-determination. Boys' worries about peer aggression were predicted principally by their peer friendships. In contrast, girls' worries about peer aggression were predicted by their peer friendships and their self-determination. Children's perceptions of the home–school relationships and of self-efficacy were correlated with their perceptions of aggression, but predicted less unique variance in peer aggression.

The remainder of this chapter will focus on the four characteristics of classrooms that students perceived to be most related to peer aggression (peer friendships, behavioral self control, teacher–student relationships, and self-determination). We will draw upon existing developmental research to suggest the mechanisms that might underlie these

classroom characteristics' relation to classroom bullying, while highlighting the ecological strategies to prevent or restrict bullying in school classrooms.

FOUR CLASSROOM CHARACTERISTICS RELATED TO BULLYING

Peer Friendships

Students with friends have someone to sit with on the bus, someone to play with at recess, someone to eat with at lunch, someone who chooses them for their team, and someone to talk to during free moments in a classroom. In part, this is because friendships shift students' social power. Having a friend in class makes it easier for students to enjoy daily activities in the classroom, easier to ask for assistance in times of stress, and much more likely that students will receive help when they ask (Cowie, 2004). Classrooms in which more students have friends show fewer conflicts, and those conflicts that do arise are less likely to escalate (Newman, Murray, & Lussier, 2001). Having a friend and having more friends have repeatedly been found to be protective factors against bullying (Bollmer, Milich, Harris, & Maras, 2005; Fox & Boulton, 2006; Schmidt & Bagwell, 2007). More-over, the type of friends can influence the protective effects of friendships. Specifically, friendships made with children who are able and willing to protect the victim provide better defenses against bullying than friendships with children who are themselves vic-timized (Hodges, Boivin, Vitaro, & Bukowski, 1999; Ladd, 2005; Pellegrini, Bartini, & Brooks, 1999).

Traditionally, schools have intervened with peer relationships one student at a time (Doll, 1996; Whitted & Dupper, 2005). However, a premise of this chapter is that a class-room's particular routines and practices have powerful influence over the degree to which all students in a class are included in effective friendships with their classmates. Friend-ships emerge within a classroom when children have frequent opportunities to have fun together (Doll et al., 2003). "Having fun" does not necessarily need to be divorced from learning or productive work. Instead, Rizzo (1989) suggests that schools create multiple roles for students to fill that, incidentally, prompt students into new interactions with each other. For example, an experienced 5th grade teacher explained that she always gave classroom chore assignments to two students at a time, so that they would have an opportunity to work together. A 4th grader, new to her school, figured out that a good way to make friends was to volunteer to clear the cafeteria after lunch, because at least two students were assigned to work together.

Further, cooperative learning strategies can facilitate friendships by providing chil-dren with opportunities to learn in non-competitive groups (Cowie, 2004). In coopera-tive learning classrooms, students work together in small groups to accomplish common tasks and group members are expected to contribute to the work of the group and the learning of each group member. Delivering instruction within these cooperative groups modifies the classroom organization and the academic and social behavior of students in the class (Hertz-Lazarowitz, 2001). Cooperative learning programs promote toler-ance among peers and create a tranquil classroom environment where students practice listening and communicating with each other (Harris, Hopkins, & Wordsworth, 2001). Other peer-support strategies include circle time in which students can discuss their concerns and difficulties in a safe environment, having students volunteer to "befriend" other students, or peer counseling in which students are trained to use active listening skills to support friends who are in distress (Cowie, 2004).

At recess, children are more likely to interact competently when multiple, attractive and developmentally appealing games are readily available (Doll, 1996; Leff, Power, Costigan, & Manz, 2003). A lack of developmentally appropriate games leads to boring recess periods that inadvertently foster aggression because, as one 5th grader explained, "fighting is a lot of fun." Still, it is not uncommon for schools to inadvertently limit recess games. For example, in one school, upper elementary students could only play soccer, and that game was located on a large field without marked goals or sidelines, because much of the other playground equipment was lost or on the roof of the school. In another 7th grade classroom, the number of suspensions and office visits dropped dramatically once the classroom teachers purchased simple games for the students to take outside at lunch recess (Doll et al., 2004).

A powerful protective factor may be the number of children in the classroom (non-friends and friends) who are willing to defend against bullying (Song, Siegel, Sogo, & Doll, 2009; Song & Sogo, 2010; Song & Stoiber, 2008). Peers may encourage, discourage, or maintain bullying within the classroom by acting as "assistants" who join in the bullying directly, "reinforcers" who come around to watch or laugh when witnessing bullying, "defenders" who try to make the others stop bullying, and "outsiders" who are unaware of the bullying (Ladd, 2005; Salmivalli, 2001; Salmivalli et al., 1996). The presence of large numbers of "defenders" in the peer group inhibits bullying while "assistants" and "reinforcers" can increase its prevalence.

Teacher–Student Relationships

Classrooms are safer places for students when the teacher is warm, engaged, responsive, and holds high expectations for students (Baker, Grant, & Morlock, 2008; Olweus & Limber, 1999; Pianta, 1999). The presence of caring and demanding teachers can improve students' sense of class membership, limit their feelings of helplessness, and reduce peer conflict in the room (Bru, Stephens, & Torsheim, 2002). On the face of it, the link between bullying and teacher–student relationships is easy to understand. When children believe that their teacher is caring and fair, they trust that teacher to protect them from victimization and intimidation in the classroom.

Teachers who are sensitive to their students respond swiftly and judiciously to bullying incidents thereby protecting students from bullying (Bauman & Del Rio, 2005; Olweus, 1993; Olweus & Limber, 1999; Whitted & Dupper, 2005). Their swift response demonstrates that bullying is unacceptable, contributing to an "anti-bullying climate" in the classroom and making it more likely that students will protect other students. Well-liked teachers are powerful models for students (Werner & Smith, 1992), and the values and expectations that they convey for courtesy and fairness are deeply embedded within the classroom's social ecology.

Teacher monitoring is an especially important protection against bullying. Bullying is frequently covert because when students bully, they try to keep the victimization outside the notice of supervising adults. Conflicts are less likely to occur if teachers can heed the early warning signs of conflict, such as voices getting louder, and tense physical reactions (Meese, 1997). When teachers are not alert to the possibility of bullying, it is easy for them to overlook softly spoken taunts or assaults that occur in the hidden corners of the classroom or playground.

A consistent finding is that school personnel including classroom teachers do not respond adequately to student reports of bullying (Boulton & Underwood, 1992;

Bradshaw, Sawyer, and O'Brennan, 2007; Hoover, Oliver, & Hazler, 1992). Either they fail to recognize bullying when it occurs, they fail to understand the importance of intervening to stop bullying, or they do not know how to intervene effectively (Hazler, Miller, Carney, & Green, 2001; Holt & Keyes, 2004; Kochenderfer-Ladd & Pelletier, 2008). In one study, playground supervisors intervened in only 4% of bullying conflicts (Craig & Pepler, 1997). Although the majority of teachers report that they consistently try to stop bullying in their schools, students reported that teachers usually do not intervene in bullying (Bauman & Del Rio, 2005; Bradshaw et al., 2007; Olweus, 1993; Pepler, Craig, Ziegler & Charach, 1994).

Many teachers only recognize physical bullying behavior and require empathy training before recognizing more subtle, hidden forms of intimidation (Craig, Henderson, & Murphy, 2000; Hazler et al., 2001). Other teachers acknowledge that bullying occurs in the classroom but minimize its importance or view bullying as a normal challenge that children must learn to confront. Still others believe that it is helpful to ignore bullying (Stephenson & Smith, 1989). Teachers do not always recognize bullying in indirect intimidation such as social exclusion, spreading rumors, and name-calling (Boulton, 1997). They sometimes choose not to intervene out of a misguided belief that the victim is responsible for overcoming the victimization (Olweus, 1993). In still other cases, victimized students deliberately hide the bullying from teachers and other adults because they fear retaliation from the bully or because they perceive teachers as uncaring, or unable to protect them (Pepler et al., 1994). About half of victims do not report being bullied to any adult, but when they do, they are more likely to tell parents than teachers (Fekkes, Pijpers, & Verloove-Vanhorick, 2005; Houndoumadi & Pataeraki, 2001).

Although research shows that teachers are still unaware of a large proportion of the bullying that occurs in their classrooms, some strides have been made in sensitizing teachers to the importance of intervening to prevent bullying. For example, in a study comparing U.S. and UK pre-service teachers, only 3.7% of teachers thought ignoring bullying was a valid strategy in 2005 compared to 25% in 1989 (Bauman & Del Rio, 2005; Stephenson & Smith, 1989). In addition, in a study with 2nd and 4th grade students, students who did ask adults for help with bullying reported reduced levels of revenge seeking and peer victimization compared to students who did not ask for help (Kochenderfer-Ladd & Pelletier, 2008). Some recent research also suggests that adults in schools are becoming more aware of indirect forms of bullying. In a recent study by Bradshaw and colleagues (2007), teachers and school staff reported witnessing indirect forms of victimization.

On the playground, adult supervision strategies that limit peer aggression may also limit bullying (Doll & Brehm, 2010). Savvy playground supervisors will distribute themselves across the playground to eliminate any hidden corners where students play unobserved; they will actively monitor and intervene to enforce playground rules against aggression promptly and consistently; and, they will interrupt potentially aggressive interactions early, before more serious rule violations can occur. "Active supervision" is an even more effective strategy to prevent playground aggression (Lewis, Sugai, & Colvin, 1998). In addition to enforcing playground rules, active supervisors move around their assigned zone of the playground, commenting on students' play, complimenting their positive social behaviors, participating occasionally in the play, and drawing isolated students into the games.

Behavioral Self-Control

Teachers can manage and reduce problem behaviors exhibited by one student or an entire class by manipulating behavioral antecedents and consequences. Unfortunately, studies show that teachers are unlikely to use their authority to interrupt or prevent bullying (Bradshaw et al., 2007; Olweus, 1993; Rodkin & Hodges, 2003). Further, strict external behavioral contingencies may not prepare students to control their behavior outside the presence of the adults who notice and cue it since children are less likely to internalize rules and prosocial traits that are generated and enforced by adults (Rodkin & Hodges, 2003). Consequently, increasing emphasis is being placed on self-management strategies that include students in developing school and classroom rules, empower students to change or maintain their own behavior, and so promote independence and behavioral competence in monitored and non-monitored school settings (Amato-Zech, Hoff, & Doepke, 2006; Bear, 2005; Mitchem & Young, 2001). Using strategies such as self-monitoring, self-evaluation, and self-reinforcement, students can be taught to increase their behavioral self-control and decrease inappropriate behavior (Cole & Bambara, 2000).

The establishment of clarifying schoolwide rules that prohibit bullying and discourage onlooking is the single most important contribution to student self-control of bullying (Limber, Nation, Tracy, Melton, & Flerx, 2004). Three recommended rules include: we will not bully other students; we will try to help students who are bullied; and we will make it a point to include all students who are easily left out (Olweus, 1993). The rules are even more effective in supporting self-control if they have been developed collaboratively with the classroom's students and are responsive to student-generated examples of bullying. We have used scenes from commercial videos or children's literature to prompt rich discussions of these rules. For example, one scene from the film *Little Man Tate* shows Fred Tate carefully handing out birthday party invitations to all of the children in his elementary school class, only to have the children throw the invitations on the ground before running in from recess. After viewing the scene, we have asked classes to consider, "Whose job is it to fix Fred Tate's problem? What should Fred do differently? What should the other children do differently? Do you know any Fred Tates that might need your help?" Such classroom conversations can foster student empathy through the exploration of the thoughts and feelings of victims.

A particular challenge in the face of bullying is to reinforce anti-bullying rules without setting the victims up for revenge by the bully. When adults use strict and punitive contingencies, they raise the risk of infuriating bullies who may, in turn, retaliate by further punishing the victim (Rigby, Smith, & Pepler, 2004). To prevent retaliation, Maines and Robinson's (1998) "No Blame Approach to Bully Prevention" works to induce empathy for the victim on the part of the onlookers and the bully. Once a bullying interaction has been identified in a classroom, teachers meet first with the victim to fully describe the bullying problem, who is involved, and the impact that the bullying has had on the victim's daily life. Next, they assist the victim in communicating their experience of bullying through a written note, picture or film. Then, and without the victim being present, teachers convene a small group including the identified bullies and onlookers to discuss the bullying. They read the victim's note, talk about the tragic impact of the bullying on the victim's life, and ask the group to identify what they will do to stop the bullying. In Maines and Robinson's research, one or two "no blame" meetings were sufficient to stop the bullying in 60% of all cases, by sensitizing the surrounding peer group to the serious harm that they are doing. A related strategy, the method of Shared Concern, has been used with similar success by Rigby (2004) and Pikas (2002) with two procedural differences: teachers or another adult meet individually with the bullying student and the onlookers to secure their commitment to take some action to stop the bullying. Then, the situation is followed over time until there is evidence that the bullying has ended. It is up to the students to devise a plan for resolving the conflict; however, the teacher must closely monitor the course of action that the students choose (Rigby et al., 2004).

Self-determination

Self-determination refers to students' ability to be autonomous and self-directed in making daily life decisions. Self-determined students have goals for their behavior and their achievement. They make choices about daily actions that will advance themselves toward those goals, and routinely evaluate whether or not their progress toward goals is adequate. They are deliberate in revising and refining their actions to maintain consistency with these larger goals. Further, they are self-sufficient in their ability to set goals, make choices and evaluate progress. Although they may weigh the opinions and expectations of others, they are able to act as their own primary causal agent free from undue external influence or interference (Usher & Pajares, 2008).

Self-determination emerges within classroom settings that give students frequent and varied practice, feedback, and direct instruction in goal setting, decision-making, problem-solving, and self-evaluation of their skills and behavior (Zimmerman, Bonner, & Kovach, 1996). A primary strategy for integrating self-determination into the daily activities of classrooms is the provision of frequent and varied opportunities to use self-determination skills with adult guidance that supports but does not supplant the students' choices. These opportunities convey trust and support for students' abilities to independently accomplish age-appropriate tasks (Doll & Sands, 1998; Joussemet, Landry, & Koestner, 2008). Alternatively, adult beliefs that students cannot make good decisions and adult constraints on student opportunities to be self-determined are the most common impediments to students' developing autonomy.

As one example, students can be taught to use problem-solving strategies to avoid peer conflicts and to successfully resolve conflicts that cannot be avoided (Peterson & Skiba, 2000; Roberts & Coursol, 1996; Whitted & Dupper, 2005). Problem-solving instruction can prepare students to identify the conflict, describe both sides, brainstorm alternative solutions, and commit to a shared solution (Soutter & McKenzie, 2000). It will be even more effective if the children are provided with "linguistic cues" that adults can use in natural situations to remind the children of the steps. For many children, the most difficult part of problem solving is generating multiple options. When classroom meetings engage all students in brainstorming multiple options for common peer conflicts, the number and frequency of a classroom's conflicts can be reduced (Murphy, 2002).

Students who practice self-determination gain a confidence in their ability to be self-sufficient, and so become more efficacious. Consequently, self-determination can inoculate students against victimization by countering passivity and inaction in the face of aggression. Instead, students who are victimized can learn to think about their actions as sources of control. For example, in our work with a small group of 2nd graders who said they were frequent victims of bullying, we used problem-solving strategies to help the students identify what they could do to protect themselves from bullying.

TRANSLATING RESEARCH INTO PRACTICE: IMPLICATIONS FOR BULLYING PREVENTION AND INTERVENTION PROGRAMS

Within the ecological perspective of this chapter, we are suggesting that shifts in classroom routines and practices can serve as a first line of defense against peer bullying. Students who bully or students who are victims are presumed to have the potential to interact more effectively with peers, given the proper social context. Creating classroom contexts that discourage aggression can reduce the frequency and the severity of bullying interactions that occur there. In particular, the children's reports emphasized the importance of peer friendships as a defense against peer aggression. Decreased levels of social isolation in a classroom make it more likely that all students will have a supportive circle of friends, and friends provide an ever-present defense against bullying. A second important predictor of aggressive peer interactions in the classroom was students' rule-following behavior. Thus, bullying may also be reduced when teacher routines are altered to include more effective monitoring and more prompt and decisive responses to interactions that look like bullying. For girls, intimidation and victimization were reduced in classrooms where teachers modeled caring and trust, and victims were assured that adults would come to their defense if needed. Peers can also discourage victimization if they are explicitly instructed in their roles as "defenders" and given concrete suggestions for ways to protect potential victims when bullying occurs. Finally, both girls and boys are more resilient in the face of peer aggression when they are more self-determined in their social behaviors. Each of these contextual interventions recognizes bullying as part of a continuum of peer aggression that occurs naturally within classrooms. Failure to attend to the classroom contexts of bullying will be a missed opportunity to understand and prevent bullying in schools.

REFERENCES

Amato-Zech, N.A., Hoff, K.E., & Doepke, K.J. (2006). Increasing on-task behavior in the classroom: Extension of self-monitoring strategies. *Psychology in the Schools, 43*, 211–221.

Asher, S.R., & Coie, J.D. (1990). *Peer rejection in childhood*. New York, NY: Cambridge University Press.

Baker, J.A., Grant, S., & Morlock, L. (2008). The teacher-student relationship as a developmental context for children with internalizing or externalizing behavior problems. *School Psychology Quarterly, 23*, 3–15.

Bauman, S., & Del Rio, A. (2005). Knowledge and beliefs about bullying in schools: Comparing pre-service teachers in the United States and the United Kingdom. *School Psychology International, 24*, 428–442.

Bear, G. (2005). *Developing self-discipline and preventing and correcting misbehavior*. Boston: Allyn & Bacon.

Bollmer, J.M., Milich, R., Harris, M.J., & Maras, M.A. (2005). A friend in need: The role of friendship quality as a protective factor in peer victimization and bullying. *Journal of Interpersonal Violence, 20*, 701–712.

Boulton, M.J. (1997). Teachers' views on bullying: Definitions, attitudes, and ability to cope. *British Journal of Educational Psychology, 67*, 223–233.

Boulton, M.J., & Underwood, K. (1992). Bully/victim problems among middle school children. *British Journal of Educational Psychology, 62*, 73–87.

Bradshaw, C.P., Sawyer, A.L., & O'Brennan, L.M. (2007). Bullying and peer victimization at school: Perceptual differences between students and school staff. *School Psychology Review, 36*, 361–382.

Bru, E., Stephens, P., & Torsheim, T. (2002). Students' perceptions of class management and reports of their own misbehavior. *Journal of School Psychology, 40*, 287–307.

Card, N.A., & Hodges, E. (2008). Peer victimization among schoolchildren: Correlations, causes, consequences, and considerations in assessment and intervention. *School Psychology Quarterly, 23*, 451–461.

Cole, C.L., & Bambara, L.M. (2000). Self-monitoring: Theory and practice. In E. Shapiro & T.R. Kratochwill (Eds.), *Behavioral assessment in schools: Theory, research, and clinical foundations* (2nd ed.) (pp. 202–232). New York, NY: Guilford Press.

Cowie, H. (2004). Peer influences. In C.E. Sanders, & G.D. Phye (Eds.), *Bullying: Implications for the classroom* (pp. 137–157). San Diego, CA: Elsevier Academic Press.

Craig, W.M., Henderson, K., & Murphy, J.G. (2000). Prospective teachers' attitudes toward bullying and victimization. *School Psychology International, 21*, 5–21.

Craig, W., & Pepler, D.J. (1997). Observations of bullying and victimization on the schoolyard. *Canadian Journal of School Psychology, 2*, 41–60.

Doll, B. (1996). Children without friends: Implications for practice and policy. *School Psychology Review, 25*, 165–183.

Doll, B., & Brehm, K. (2010). *Resilient playgrounds.* New York, NY: Routledge.

Doll, B., & Sands, D. (1998). Student involvement in goal setting and educational decision making: Foundations for effective instruction. In M. Wehmeyer & D.J. Sands (Eds.), *Making it happen: Student involvement in educational planning, decision making and instruction* (pp. 45–74). Baltimore: Paul H. Brookes.

Doll, B., & Spies, R.A. (2007, March). The ClassMaps Survey. A paper presented at the Annual Convention of the National Association of School Psychologists, New York, NY.

Doll, B., LeClair, C., & Kurien, S. (2009). Effective classrooms: Classroom learning environments that foster school success. In T. Gutkin & C. Reynolds (Eds.), *The handbook of school psychology* (pp. 791–807). Hoboken, NJ: John Wiley & Sons, Inc.

Doll, B., Murphy, P., & Song, S. (2003). The relationship between children's self-reported recess problems, and peer acceptance and friendships. *Journal of School Psychology, 41*, 113–130.

Doll, B., Zucker, S., & Brehm, K. (2004.) *Resilient classrooms: Creating healthy environments for learning.* New York, NY: Guilford Publications.

Espelage, D. L., & Swearer, S. M. (2003). Research on school bullying and victimization: What have we learned and where do we go from here? *School Psychology Review, 32*, 365–383.

Farmer, T.W., Estell, D.B., Bishop, J.L., O'Neal, K.K., & Cairns, B.D. (2003). Rejected bullies or popular leaders? The social relations of aggressive subtypes of rural African American early adolescents. *Developmental Psychology, 39*, 992–1004.

Fekkes, M., Pijpers, F.I.M., & Verloove-Vanhorick, S.P. (2005). Bullying: who does what, when and where? Involvement of children, teachers and parents in bullying behavior. *Health Education Research, 20*, 81–91.

Fox, C.L., & Boulton, M.J. (2006). Friendship as a moderator of the relationship between social skills problems and peer victimization. *Aggressive Behavior, 32*, 110–121.

Gini, G. (2006). Bullying as a social process: The role of group membership in students' perception of intergroup aggression at school. *Journal of School Psychology, 44*, 51–65.

Grotpeter, J.K., & Crick, N.R. (1996). Relational aggression, overt aggression, and friendship. *Child Development, 67*, 2328–2338.

Harris, A., Hopkins, D., & Wordsworth, J. (2001). The implementation and impact of success for all in English schools. In R.E. Slavin & N.A. Madden (Eds.), *Research and reform in elementary education; success for all* (pp. 81–92). Mahwah, NJ: Lawrence Erlbaum Associates Publishers.

Hazler, R.J., Miller, D.L., Carney, J.V., & Green, S. (2001). Adult recognition of school bullying situations. *Educational Research, 43*, 133–146.

Hertz-Lazarowitz, R. (2001). Success for all: A community model for advancing Arabs and Jews in Israel. In R.E. Slavin & N.A. Madden (Eds.), *Research and reform in elementary education; success for all* (pp. 81–92). Mahwah, NJ: Lawrence Erlbaum.

Hodges, E.V.E., Boivin, M., Vitaro, F., & Bukowski, W.M. (1999). The power of friendship: Protection against an escalating cycle of peer victimization. *Developmental Psychology, 35*, 94–101.

Holt, M.K., & Keyes, M.A. (2004). Teachers' attitudes toward bullying. In D.L. Espelage & S.M. Swearer (Eds.) *Bullying in American schools: A social-ecological perspective on prevention and intervention* (pp. 121–139). Mahwah, NJ: Lawrence Erlbaum.

Hoover, J., Oliver, R., & Hazler, R.J. (1992). Bullying: Perceptions of adolescent victims in the Midwestern USA. *School Psychology International, 13*, 5–16.

Houndoumadi, A., & Pataeraki, L. (2001). Bullying and bullies in Greek elementary schools: Pupils' attitudes and teachers'/parents' awareness, *Educational Review, 53*, 19–27.

Joussemet, M., Landry, R., & Koestner, R. (2008). A self-determination theory perspective on parenting. *Canadian Psychology, 49*, 194–200.

Kochenderfer-Ladd, B., & Pelletier, M.E. (2008). Teachers' views and beliefs about bullying: Influences on classroom management strategies and students' coping with peer victimization. *Journal of School Psychology, 46*, 431–453.

Ladd, G.W. (2005). *Children's peer relations and social competence: A century of progress.* New Haven, CT: Yale University Press.

Leff, S.S., Power, T.J., Costigan, T.E., & Manz, P.H. (2003). Assessing the climate of the playground and lunchroom: Implications for bullying prevention programming. *School Psychology Review, 32*, 418–430.

Lewis, T.J., Sugai, G., & Colvin, G. (1998). Reducing problem behavior through a school-wide system of effective behavioral support: Investigation of a school-wide social skills training program and contextual interventions. *School Psychology Review, 27*, 446–459.

Limber, S.P., Nation, M., Tracy, A.J., Melton, G.B., & Flerx, V. (2004). Implementation of the Olweus bullying prevention programme in the Southeastern United States. In P.K. Smith, D. Pepler, & K. Rigby (Eds.), *Bullying in schools: How successful can interventions be?* (pp. 55–79). Cambridge, UK: Cambridge University Press.

Maines, B., & Robinson, G. (1998). The no blame approach to bullying. In D. Shorrocks-Taylor (Ed.), *Directions in educational psychology* (pp. 281–295). London: Whurr.

Meese, R.L. (1997). Student fights: Proactive strategies for preventing and managing student conflicts. *Intervention in School and Clinic, 33*, 26–33.

Mitchem, K.J., & Young, K.R. (2001). Adapting self-management programs for classwide use: Acceptability, feasibility, and effectiveness. *Remedial and Special Education, 22*, 75–88.

Murphy, P. (2002). The effect of classroom meetings on the reduction of recess problems: A single case design. Unpublished doctoral dissertation, University of Denver, Denver, CO.

National Research Council and the Institute of Medicine. (2004). *Engaging schools: Fostering high school students' motivation to learn*. Washington, DC: The National Academies Press.

Newman, S.R., Murray, B., & Lussier, C. (2001). Confrontation with aggressive peers at school: Student's reluctance to seek help from the teacher. *Journal of Educational Psychology, 93*, 398–410.

Olweus, D. (1993). *Bullying at school: What we know and what we can do*. Cambridge, MA: Blackwell.

Olweus, D., & Limber, S. (1999). The bullying prevention program. In D.S. Elliott (Ed.), *Blueprints for violence prevention*. Boulder, CO: Regents of the University of Colorado.

Orpinas, P., & Horne, A.M. (2006). *Bullying prevention: Creating a positive school climate and developing social competence*. Washington, DC: American Psychological Corporation.

Pellegrini, A.D. (1995). *School recess and playground behavior: Educational and developmental roles*. Albany, NY: State University of New York Press.

Pellegrini, A.D. (2002). Affiliative and aggressive dimensions of dominance and possible functions during early adolescence. *Aggression and Violent Behavior, 7*, 21–31.

Pellegrini, A.D. (2007). Is aggression adaptive? Yes: Some kinds are and in some ways. In P.H. Hawley, T.D. Little, & P.C. Rodkin, (Eds.), *Aggression and adaptation: The bright side to bad behavior* (pp. 85–105). Mahwah, NJ: Lawrence Erlbaum.

Pellegrini, A.D. (2008). The role of aggressive and affiliative behaviors in resource control: A behavioral ecological perspective. *Developmental Review, 28*, 461–487.

Pellegrini, A.D., & Bartini, M. (2001). Dominance in early adolescent boys: Affiliative and aggressive dimensions and possible functions. *Merrill-Palmer Quarterly, 47*, 142–163.

Pellegrini, A.D., & Long, J.D. (2004). Part of the solution and part of the problem: The role of peers in bullying, dominance, and victimization during the transition from primary school through secondary school. In D. L. Espelage & S.M. Swearer (Eds.) *Bullying in American schools: A social-ecological perspective on prevention and intervention* (pp. 107–117). Mahwah, NJ: Lawrence Erlbaum.

Pellegrini, A.D., Bartini, M., & Brooks, F. (1999). School bullies, victims and aggressive victims: Factors relations to group affiliation and victimization in early adolescence. *Journal of Educational Psychology, 91*, 216–224.

Pepler, D.J., Craig, W.M., Ziegler, S., & Charach, A. (1994). An evaluation of an anti-bullying intervention in Toronto Schools. *Canadian Journal of Community Mental Health, 13*, 95–110.

Peterson, R., & Skiba, R. (2000). Creating climates that prevent school violence. *Preventing School Failure, 44*, 122–130.

Pianta, R. (1999). *Enhancing relationships between children and teachers*. Washington, DC: American Psychological Association.

Pikas, A. (2002). New developments of the shared concern method. *School Psychology International, 23*, 307–326.

Rigby, K. (2004). Addressing bullying in schools. *School Psychology International, 25*, 287–300.

Rigby, K., Smith, P.K., & Pepler, D. (2004). Working to prevent school bullying: Key issues. In P.K. Smith, D. Pepler, & K. Rigby (Eds.), *Bullying in schools: How successful can interventions be?* (pp. 1–12). Cambridge, UK: Cambridge University Press.

Rizzo, T.A. (1989). *Friendship development among children in school*. Norwood, NJ: Ablex.

Roberts, W.B., Jr., & Coursol, D.H. (1996). Strategies for intervention with childhood and adolescent victims of bullying, teasing and intimidation in school settings. *Elementary School Guidance and Counseling, 30*, 204–213.

Rodkin, P.C., & Hodges, E.V. (2003). Bullies and victims in the peer ecology: Four questions for psychologists and school professionals. *The School Psychology Review, 32*, 384–400.

Salmivalli, C. (2001). Peer-led intervention campaign against school bullying: Who considered it useful, who benefited? *Educational Research, 43,* 263–278.

Salmivalli, C., Lagerspetz, K., Bjorkqvist, K., Osterman, K., & Kaukiainen, A. (1996). Bullying as a group process: Participant roles and their relations to social status within the group. *Aggressive Behavior, 22,* 1–15.

Schmidt, M.E., & Bagwell, C.L. (2007). The protective role of friendships in overtly and relationally victimized boys and girls. *Merrill-Palmer Quarterly, 53,* 439–460.

Song, S.Y., & Sogo, W. (2010). A hybrid framework for intervention development: Social justice for bullying in low resource schools. In B. Doll, W. Pfohl, & J. Yoon (Eds.), *Handbook of youth prevention science.* New York, NY: Routledge.

Song, S.Y., & Stoiber, K. (2008). Children exposed to violence at school: Understanding bullying and evidence-based interventions. *Journal of Emotional Abuse, 8,* 235–253.

Song, S.Y., Siegel, N.M., Sogo, W., & Doll, B. (2009, February). The protective peer ecology: Informing effective school bullying interventions. A symposium presented at the 2009 Convention of the National Association of School Psychologists, Boston, MA.

Soutter, A., & McKenzie, A. (2000). The use and effects of anti-bullying and anti-harassment policies in Australian schools. *School Psychology International, 21,* 96–105.

Spies, R., Champion, A., Osborn, A., Kurien, S., LeClair, C., & Doll, B. (2007, October). Worries and relationships in the elementary classroom: Results of the ClassMaps Survey from 2006–2007. A paper presented at the 25th Annual Northern Rocky Mountain Educational Research Association Conference, Jackson, WY.

Stephenson, P., & Smith, D. (1989). Bullying in the junior school. In D.P. Tattum & D.A. Lane (Eds.), *Bullying in schools* (pp.45–58). Stoke on Trent, UK: Trentham.

Swearer, S.M., Song, S.Y., & Cary, P.T. (2001). Psychosocial correlates in bullying and victimization: The relationship between depression, anxiety, and bully/victim status. In R.A. Geffner & M. Loring (Eds.), *Bullying behavior: Current issues, research, and interventions* (pp. 95–121). Binghampton, NY: The Haworth Press, Inc.

Usher, E.L., & Pajares, F. (2008). Self-efficacy for self-regulated learning: A validation study. *Educational and Psychological Measurement, 68,* 443–463.

Werner, E.E., & Smith, R.S. (1992). *Overcoming the odds: High risk children from birth to adulthood.* Ithaca, NY: Cornell University Press.

Whitted, K.S., & Dupper, D.R. (2005). Best practices for preventing or reducing bullying in schools. *Children and Schools, 27,* 167–174.

Zimmerman, B.J., Bonner, S., & Kovach, R. (1996). *Developing self-regulated learners: Beyond achievement to self-efficacy.* Washington, DC: American Psychological Association.

Part IV
Beyond the Classroom
Considering School Climate, Family Relationships, Social Support, and Innovative School Partnerships

13

SCHOOL CLIMATE AND CHANGE IN PERSONALITY DISORDER SYMPTOM TRAJECTORIES RELATED TO BULLYING

A Prospective Study

STEPHANIE KASEN, JEFFREY G. JOHNSON, HENIAN CHEN, THOMAS N. CRAWFORD, AND PATRICIA COHEN

School exerts considerable impact on the cognitive, emotional, and social development of children (Ringeisen, Henderson, & Hoagwood, 2003), and is the primary social context for the peer culture in which bullying involvement occurs (Olweus, 1978, 1993). In particular, a school's social and emotional climate is reported to determine in large part its effectiveness as both a learning environment (Brand, Felner, Shim, Seitsinger, & Dumas, 2003), and a socializing agent to promote healthy development and reduce maladaptive behavior in youths (e.g., Battistich & Horn, 1997; DeWitt et al., 2000; Goldstein, Young, & Boyd, 2008; Gottfredson, Gottfredson, Payne, & Gottfredson, 2005; Kuperminc, Leadbeater, & Blatt, 2001; McEvoy & Welker, 2000; Noam & Hermann, 2002). Nonetheless, few studies have examined associations between school climate and negative student characteristics that denote more serious psychiatric disturbance, and whether those associations continue into adulthood.

In this chapter we extend our work on the predictive effects of perceived school climate on psychiatric disturbance in youths to examine whether school experiences influence the continuity of adolescent personality disorders into adulthood. The study is based on prospective data drawn from the Children in the Community (CIC), an ongoing longitudinal study of social risk indicators of early psychopathology in a randomly selected community-based population of youths. Albeit information specific to identifying youths as bullies or victims is limited, psychiatric disorders (both clinical and personality disorders) were assessed multiple times according to standard diagnostic criteria since the sample was, on average, 13.7 years old.

There is indication that such psychiatric conditions are elevated in youths who bully or are being bullied (e.g., Coolidge, DenBoer, & Segal, 2004; Kumpulainen et al., 1998; Kumpulainen, Räsänen, & Puura, 2001); moreover, albeit limited, there also is evidence that those conditions may continue or worsen (e.g., Kim, Leventhal, Koh, Hubbard, & Boyce, 2006; Kumpulainen, Räsänen, & Henttonen, 1999). However, few studies have examined whether salient aspects of the school climate are implicated in the continuity or development of early psychopathology that likely may co-exist in both bullies and victims.

WHAT MALADAPTIVE CHARACTERISTICS CO-EXIST IN BULLIES AND VICTIMS?

A number of studies have linked involvement in bullying to maladaptive attitudes, behaviors, and self-concepts: Compared to youths not identified, youths identified as bullies, victims, and bully-victims (i.e., those who both bully and are bullied) are reported to have more internalizing (e.g., sad, fearful, apathetic, worried, poor self-esteem) or externalizing (e.g., fighting, disobedient, hyperactive, lying, stealing) problems or both, and are more likely to be referred for mental health services (e.g., Kaltiala-Heino, Rimpelä, Rantanen, & Rimpelä, 2000; Kumpulainen et al., 2001; Marsh, Parada, Yeung, & Healey, 2001; Nansel et al., 2001; Slee & Rigby, 1993). In addition, psychological disturbance among youths involved in bullying may continue (Kumpulainen & Räsänen, 2000; Kumpulainen et al., 1999).

Recently, Kim and colleagues reported that bullying involvement may be causally implicated in future pathologic features: Ten months following identification of bullying status, victims had more social problems, perpetrators were more aggressive, and victim-perpetrators were more aggressive and had a higher level of other externalizing problems (Kim et al., 2006). Based on data from males in the Finnish Epidemiologic Child Psychiatric Study, Sourander and colleagues (2007) found that involvement in bullying at eight years old significantly increased the odds of psychiatric disorder when screened for the military 10 to 15 years later: After adjusting for earlier maladaptive behavior and other salient controls, bully status predicted antisocial personality disorder, victim status predicted anxiety disorder, and bully-victim status predicted both. Other recent findings indicate that among 14 to 16-year-old students, those involved in bullying were more predisposed to psychotic experiences, including auditory hallucinations, paranoia, and dissociation (Campbell & Morrison, 2007). We are aware of only one study that examined personality disorder in conjunction with bullying: Compared to matched controls, youths involved in bullying had higher rates of co-existing attention-deficit/hyperactivity, conduct, depressive, and oppositional defiant disorder, and more likely to be diagnosed with dependent, histrionic, paranoid, and passive-aggressive personality disorders and to show neuropsychological and executive function deficits (Coolidge et al., 2004).

WHICH SCHOOL CLIMATE FEATURES INFLUENCE STUDENT CHARACTERISTICS?

School climate refers to the attitudes, values, and norms that underlie instructional and management practices, and is based on perceptions of individuals who experience and respond to those forces (Emmons, Comer, & Haynes, 1996; Sarason & Klaber, 1985); thus, it reflects the overall social and emotional ethos of the school. Features assessed typically include organization of the school into an effective learning environment; school spirit and motivation; opportunities for student decision-making; and quality of student–student and student–teacher relationships. Such features are a product of the interaction dynamics among and between students and teachers, and establish the parameters for acceptable behavior and school norms (Emmons et al., 1996; Kuperminc, Leadbeater, Emmons, & Blatt, 1997). Positive aspects of school climate, including support and cooperation, have been related to improved psychosocial skills and self-esteem in students (Ames, 1992; Goodenow, 1993; Glisson & Hemmelgarn, 1998), while negative aspects, including ineffective disciplinary practices and low levels of school spirit, teacher or peer support, and student autonomy have been related to elevated externalizing problems (De Wit et al., 2000; Noam & Hermann, 2002). Negative perceptions of school climate also have been found among school-age bullies (Nansel et al., 2001) and victims (Swearer, Turner, Gibbons, & Pollack, 2008).

Perceived school climate also is reported to influence subsequent emotional and behavioral symptoms in students (Kuperminc et al., 2001; Roeser & Eccles, 1998). We found that adolescent perceptions of a low level of learning focus and a high level of student–student and student–teacher conflict were related to increased conduct and other externalizing problems 2.5 years later, whereas perceptions of a high level of personal ties (interpersonal informality/familiarity) were associated with elevated anxiety and depression (Kasen, Berenson, Cohen, & Johnson, 2004; Kasen, Johnson, & Cohen, 1990). Negative perceptions of school climate also had young adult consequences that included increased involvement in criminal and other antisocial activities (Kasen, Cohen, & Brook, 1998). Moreover, perceived school climate predicted continuity into young adulthood of adolescent personality disorder symptoms aggregated at the cluster level (Kasen, Cohen, Chen, Johnson, & Crawford, 2009), with associations between high learning focus and decreased cluster B (antisocial, borderline, histrionic, and narcissistic) symptoms, high autonomy and decreased cluster A (paranoid, schizoid, and schizotypal) symptoms, and high conflict and high personal ties and increased cluster A and cluster C (avoidant and dependent) symptoms.

In this chapter we will examine whether those school climate features (Learning Focus, Autonomy, Personal Ties, and Conflict) are related to change in symptom trajectories of specific personality disorders from adolescence into adulthood by utilizing repeated measures of personality disorder (over a 17-year period) in growth curve analyses.

ARE ADOLESCENT PERSONALITY DISORDERS A MEANINGFUL CONSTRUCT?

Personality disorders are a class of psychiatric disorders characterized by maladaptive patterns of thoughts and actions that are stable, rigid, and pervasive across situations; deviate widely from cultural expectations; and cause significant distress or impaired function (American Psychiatric Association (APA), 1994). Despite an underlying presumption that personality disorders are resistant to change, the evidence indicates that personality may be altered by life experience (Roberts & DelVecchio, 2000). The ten personality disorders defined on Axis II of the *Diagnostic Statistical Manual for Mental Disorders, 4th edition* (DSM-IV: APA, 1994) include antisocial, avoidant, borderline, dependent, histrionic, narcissistic, obsessive-compulsive, paranoid, schizoid, and schizotypal personality disorder; two additional personality disorders, depressive and passive aggressive, are listed in the appendix. Although typically not assessed before late adolescence, there is increasing recognition that personality disorders have their origins in childhood (Cohen, Crawford, Johnson, & Kasen, 2005; De Clercq, De Fruyt, Van Leeuwen, & Mervielde, 2006; Shiner, Masten, & Roberts, 2003). We found that early adolescent personality disturbance elevates risk for personality disorder in mid-adolescence (Bernstein et al., 1993; Bernstein, Cohen, Skodol, Bezirganian, & Brook, 1996), young adulthood (Kasen, Cohen, Skodol, Johnson, & Brook, 1999), and into the fourth decade of life (Cohen et al., 2005; Crawford et al., 2005). Moreover, adolescent personality disorder also increased risk for impaired adult role function (Chen et al., 2004; Johnson, Cohen, Kasen, & Brook, 2008; Skodol, Cohen, Sneed, Johnson, & Crawford, 2007) and psychotropic medication use (Kasen et al., 2007).

Additional support for the existence of serious personality disturbance prior to adulthood may be found in the bullying literature. Olweus (1994) identified adolescent bullies as having an antisocial personality pattern combined with physical strength, whereas victims were found to have an anxious personality pattern combined with physical weakness. Maladaptive personality traits noted in child and adolescent victims include being overly sensitive to critical evaluation, introverted, passive and submissive, and having low self-worth and a tendency toward self-blame in negative situations not of their making; in contrast, child and adolescent bullies are described as aggressive, needing power or dominance, lacking empathy, and violating others' rights (Lagerspetz, Björkqvist, Berts, & King, 1982; Boulton & Smith, 1994; Olweus, 1994; Mynard & Joseph, 1997). Both bullies and victims have been found to demonstrate high levels of emotional instability and low levels of social extroversion (Tani, Greenman, Schneider, & Fregosa, 2003). However, bully-victims may be the most disturbed group, and, relative to youths identified as either bullies or victims, are reported to be more neurotic, have more psychotic experiences (Mynard & Joseph, 1997), be more provocative in eliciting negative attention from peers (Olweus, 1994), and have lower self-esteem (Slee & Rigby, 1993). Those findings support the likelihood that personality disturbance may co-exist with bullying involvement and worsen with time; thus, it is important to examine potentially meaningful risk (and protective) factors for early personality disorder that are amenable to transformation.

THE CURRENT STUDY

We draw on longitudinal data from a community sample of over 700 youths to examine associations between perceived school climate assessed at mean age 13.7 and subsequent symptom trajectories for nine personality disorders. Four school climate factors are examined: learning focus, autonomy, personal ties, and conflict. Covariates include adolescent academic achievement and personality disorder symptoms assessed at mean age 13.7 and demographic characteristics (age at time of school climate assessment, sex, and family socioeconomic status (SES)).

Method

Sample. This study is based on data drawn from the CIC Study, an ongoing longitudinal investigation of early risk for psychopathology. A cohort of 776 children (51% female) whose families were selected randomly from two upstate New York counties for study participation first were assessed for school experiences and personality disorder in

1983 (T1) at mean age 13.7 (SD 2.6, range 9–18). Racial distribution (91% Caucasian, 8% African American, 1% other), family SES (20% at or below poverty line according to Federal Guidelines for families of similar size, 25% with upper-middle-class education and incomes), and residence (50% urban, 25% suburban, 25% rural or small town) represented the sampled region according to 1980 census data (Cohen & Cohen, 1996). Youths were re-interviewed in 1985–1986 (T2), 1991–1994 (T3), and 2001–2004 (T4) at mean ages 16.4 (SD 2.8, range 11–20), 22.4 (SD 2.8, range 17–27), and 33.2 (SD 2.9, range 27–39). Mothers were interviewed about study youths in T1, T2, and T3.

Attrition rate was low at T2 and T3 (< 5%). At T4, 680 persons were re-interviewed, a retention rate of 87.6% over 20 years. Those interviewed at T1 but not at T4 were more likely to be male than those interviewed both times (70.4% vs. 47.2%) ($\chi^2 = 24.55$, df, = 1, $p < 0.001$). Groups did not differ significantly with regard to other study variables.

Procedure. Written consent was obtained from all participants at each study wave. Trained interviewers collected data from participants at home in T1–T4; youths and their mothers were interviewed simultaneously but separately in T1–T3. This study was approved by the Institutional Review Board of the New York State Psychiatric Institute and Columbia University. Study data are protected by a Certificate of Confidentiality issued by the National Institute of Mental Health.

Assessment of Personality Disorder Symptoms

Most interview items used to assess personality disorder symptoms were selected at T1, when youths were mean age 13.7. Because no age-appropriate measure of personality disorder was available then, items corresponding to criteria outlined in the *Diagnostic and Statistical Manual of Mental Disorders 3rd edition* (DSM-III: American Psychiatric Association [APA], 1980) were drawn from existing adult measures, primarily the Personality Diagnostic Questionnaire (Hyler, Rieder, Spitzer, & Williams, 1982), and revised for age as needed. To maximize correspondence with updated criteria in the revised edition of the DSM-III (DSM-III-R: APA, 1987), new items adapted from an early version of the Structured Clinical Interview for DSM-III-R Personality Disorders (SCID-II: Spitzer & Williams, 1986) were added to the study protocol in subsequent assessments.

Personality disorder symptoms were assessed by parent- and child-report in adolescence and by self-report in adulthood. Repeated measurement of the same dependent variables over time is required for the trajectory analyses done here; thus repeated measures of antisocial, avoidant, borderline, dependent, histrionic, narcissistic, paranoid, schizoid, and schizotypal personality disorder symptoms assessed by self-report at mean ages 16.4, 22.4, and 33.2 are used. Personality disorder algorithms were revised so that self-report measures corresponded to DSM-IV criteria (APA, 1994); these measures are highly correlated with our combined parent–child measures, for which considerable evidence of validity exists (Cohen et al., 2005; Crawford et al., 2005). Internal consistencies (median $\alpha = .76$, range = .44 to .82) are comparable to other personality disorder symptom scales based on self-report (grand median $\alpha = .76$, range = .36 to .96) (Clark & Harrison, 2001). Abbreviated versions of these scales at T1 serve as covariates to adjust for adolescent personality disorder symptoms in the analyses (median $\alpha = .59$). Detailed information on scale construction and psychometric characteristics may be found elsewhere (Crawford et al., 2005).

Obsessive–compulsive personality disorder was not examined because, as measured

Table 13.1 Central Characteristics of Nine Personality Disorders Grouped by Traditional DSM-IV Axis II Clusters A, B, and C

Cluster A Personality Disorders: The Odd Eccentric Personality Disorders

Paranoid	Difficult interpersonal relations, excessive suspiciousness and hostility, hyper-vigilant
Schizoid	Detachment from social relationships, restricted range of expressed emotions
Schizotypal	Social/interpersonal deficits, acute social discomfort, cognitive/perceptual distortions and behavioral eccentricities

Cluster B Personality Disorders: The Dramatic Erratic Personality Disorders

Antisocial	Disregard for basic rights of others and serious violation of societal norms/rules
Borderline	Marked impulsivity and instability of interpersonal relations, self-image, and emotions
Histrionic	Excessive emotionality, attention-seeking, suggestible
Narcissistic	Grandiosity, need for admiration, lack of empathy

Cluster C Personality Disorders: The Anxious Fearful Personality Disorders

Avoidant	Social inhibition, feelings of inadequacy, hypersensitivity to negative evaluation
Dependent	Need to be taken care of leading to submissive clinging behavior and separation fears

in this study (and unlike the other personality disorders), this disorder did not predict negative adult consequences (Cohen et al., 2005). However, albeit not usually diagnosed prior to age 18, we do examine antisocial personality disorder, which is estimated at mean ages 13.7 and 16.4. Central features of each personality disorder are shown in Table 13.1. Personality disorders are grouped by DSM-IV clusters owing to their overlapping features within clusters A (paranoid, schizoid, schizotypal), B (antisocial, borderline, histrionic, narcissistic), and C (avoidant, dependent).

Table 13.2 shows raw score means (standard deviation (SD)) for the personality disorder symptom scales at T1, T2, T3, and T4.

Table 13.2 Personality Disorder (PD) Symptom Scales: Raw Means and Standard Deviations (SD)

Scales	T1 (1983)		T2 (1985–1986)		T3 (1991–1994)		T4 (2001–2004)	
	Mean	(SD)	Mean	(SD)	Mean	(SD)	Mean	(SD)
Cluster A PDs								
Paranoid	37.0	(15.0)	37.4	(13.4)	34.8	(14.1)	30.2	(14.5)
Schizoid	25.7	(10.8)	31.7	(9.3)	29.2	(9.5)	27.7	(9.0)
Schizotypal	19.6	(9.2)	23.3	(9.4)	22.4	(9.1)	21.5	(9.0)
Cluster B PDs								
Antisocial	17.7	(12.0)	18.7	(12.7)	19.9	(13.2)	16.3	(13.2)
Borderline	26.0	(11.9)	24.9	(10.4)	24.0	(10.7)	19.7	(11.0)
Histrionic	38.7	(16.3)	35.1	(13.1)	31.7	(13.5)	26.0	(12.9)
Narcissistic	41.8	(15.7)	37.6	(13.9)	36.8	(12.3)	30.3	(13.6)
Cluster C PDs								
Avoidant	34.7	(12.2)	32.7	(10.9)	30.5	(11.6)	30.0	(12.6)
Dependent	34.8	(11.2)	34.1	(10.3)	31.2	(10.9)	26.9	(11.1)

Assessment of School Climate

The 756 youths attending grades 5 to 12 in about 450 schools at T1 responded to 45 items assessing school features based on Moos's school climate dimensions (Moos, 1987; Moos & Trickett, 1979) and Rutter and colleagues' school process dimensions (Rutter, Maughan, Mortimore, Ouston, & Smith, 1979). Principal factor analysis, described elsewhere (Kasen et al., 1990), yielded four factors: The 12-item Learning Focus Scale (formerly Academic Focus) ($\alpha = .68$) assesses student and teacher attitudes and behaviors indicative of learning goals and adequate structure and organization (e.g., "Teachers usually return marked homework to students," "Teachers really work hard to make the work interesting"). The 6-item Autonomy Scale ($\alpha = .60$) assesses the degree to which students are involved in decision-making regarding coursework and other school activities (e.g., "Students have a lot of opportunities to work on what interests them," "Students are strongly encouraged to say what they think"). The 7-item Personal Ties Scale (formerly Social Facilitation) ($\alpha = .44$) assesses the degree that student–student and student–teacher interactions may be characterized as informal and familiar (e.g., "Students can call teachers by their first names," "Teachers lead discussions of personal or family problems students may have"). The 15-item Conflict Scale ($\alpha = .82$) assesses the degree to which interactions among and between students and teachers are characterized by disrespect, arguing, and fighting (e.g., "Teachers often shout at students," "There is a lot of fighting between students in and around the school"). A 3-point response option scale was used for each item (1 = not true of my school, 2 = somewhat true, 3 = definitely true).

Raw mean scores (SD) were 29.5 (3.3), 12.9 (2.4), 12.1 (2.0), and 27.8 (5.4) for the Learning Focus, Autonomy, Personal Ties, and Conflict Scales, respectively. Predictive validity of the school climate scales have been supported by associations with change in adolescent internalizing and externalizing problems (Kasen et al., 1990, 2004) and increased risk for criminal and other deviant activities in young adulthood (Kasen et al., 1998).

Assessment of Academic Achievement

The 5-item Academic Achievement Scale (α .61) (Brook, Lukoff, & Whiteman, 1977) is based on T1 mother and child reports of reading and math ability (1 = very poor, 5 = well above average) and frequency of homework completion (1 = never, 5 = most or all the time), and teacher grades (1 = very poor (mostly F), 5 = excellent (mostly A)). Raw score mean (SD) was 17.5 (4.1). The predictive validity of this scale has been supported by prospective relations with deviant behaviors and role dysfunction in young adulthood (Kasen et al., 1998).

Data Analytic Models

We used the PROC MIXED procedure from the SAS statistical package (Littell, Miliken, Stroup, & Wolfinger, 1996) to estimate effects of adolescent-reported school climate (i.e., at mean age 13.7) on the symptom trajectory of each personality disorder assessed at mean ages 16.4, 22.4, and 33.2. Growth curve models accommodate time-varying repeated measures of personality disorder symptoms, thus fully exploiting our longitudinal data (Chen & Cohen, 2006). This method also estimates both linear and non-linear change in dependent variables over time, tolerates unequal intervals between assessments, combines data from persons assessed at different ages, and permits inclusion of persons not assessed at all time points.

Basic models examine effects of linear (age) and quadratic (age^2) change in personality disorder symptom trajectories. Main models examine additional effects of the school climate scales, adolescent levels of corresponding personality disorder symptoms, and academic achievement. Interactions between school climate scales and age and age^2 also were examined in main models to determine whether associations between school climate features and symptom trajectories attenuate with age. The impact of a negative school climate may be greater for antisocial students (McEvoy & Welker, 2000); thus, to determine if predictive associations between perceived school climate and trajectory of antisocial personality disorder symptoms are greater for such "high risk" youths, interactions between the school climate scales and adolescent antisocial symptom level were examined. Main models are controlled for T1 age, sex, and family socioeconomic status (SES), the latter measured by a standardized index of parents' education and occupation and family income (these effects are not reported). For each personality disorder dependent variable, symptoms for each personality disorder were aggregated over the T2, T3, and T4 assessments and resulting scores standardized; that strategy preserved the age differences in repeated measures of personality disorder symptoms and produced effect estimates that may be interpreted as standardized mean differences or partial correlations. Because ranges and internal reliabilities of predictor scales varied, they also were standardized so that comparisons of effect magnitudes for regression coefficients would be more meaningful. All covariates and demographic controls were centered at their respective means. Linear age was centered at age 22, an age that typically signals the end of adolescence and entry into young adulthood; intercepts for personality disorder symptom trajectories reflect reference group means at that age (shown in Table 13.4). Cutoffs of ± 1 SD, representing high and low school climate scale values, were used to plot significant interactions with age, age^2 or adolescent antisocial symptoms.

Results

Correlations between adolescent personality disorder symptoms and school-related covariates. Correlations coefficients over .08 are significant at the p < .05 level (Table 13.3). Strength of associations between adolescent personality disorders and academic achievement ranged from -.131 (for schizoid symptoms) to -.314 (for antisocial symptoms). Associations with Learning Focus ranged from -.006 (for avoidant symptoms) to -.280 (for antisocial symptoms). Associations with Autonomy ranged from -.018 (for narcissistic symptoms) to -.262 (for dependent symptoms). Associations with Personal Ties ranged from .000 (for dependent symptoms) to .126 (for narcissistic symptoms). Associations with Conflict ranged from .146 (for schizoid symptoms) to .367 (for borderline symptoms).

Basic models. Basic models examined linear (age) and quadratic (age^2) changes in personality disorder symptom trajectories between mean ages 16.4 and 33.2 (data not tabulated). During that 17-year period, there was a significant linear decrease in symptoms at an average yearly rate of 031, .032, and .014 SD for paranoid, schizoid, and schizotypal symptoms, respectively; .027, .035, and .020 SD for borderline, histrionic, and narcissistic symptoms; and .019 SD for avoidant symptoms and .043 SD for dependent symptoms. Thus, the greatest decline was for dependent symptoms, at about 0.75

Table 13.3   Correlations between Personality Disorder (PD) Symptoms and School Covariates Assessed During Adolescence (T1)

	Academic achievement	Learning focus	Autonomy	Personal ties	Conflict
Cluster A PDs					
Paranoid	−.224**	.034	−.101**	.067	.280**
Schizoid	−.131**	−.047	−.259**	−.057	.146**
Schizotypal	−.168**	.011	−.255**	.029	.275**
Cluster B PDs					
Antisocial	−.314**	−.280**	.044	−.031	.324**
Borderline	−.229**	−.027	−.138**	.063	.367**
Histrionic	−.180**	-.081*	−.088*	.109**	.361**
Narcissistic	−.193**	−.084*	−.018	.126**	.331**
Cluster C PDs					
Avoidant	−.176**	−.006	−.115**	.046	.260**
Dependent	−.168**	.011	−.262**	.000	.225**
Academic achievement		.085*	.082*	.030	−.236**
Learning focus			.130**	.228**	−.305**
Autonomy				.233**	−.082*
Personal ties					.036

Note: * p < .05; ** p < .01

of a standard deviation over the assessed period (.043 decline annually over 17 years = .731 SD), while the least decline was for schizotypal symptoms at nearly 0.25 of a standard deviation ($17 \times .014$ SD = .238 SD). Albeit there was no significant linear decline in antisocial symptoms, quadratic effects showed significantly greater declines later in the assessed period for antisocial, histrionic, and narcissistic symptoms (by an additional .002, .0007, and .002 SD per year).

Main models. Main models were adjusted for effects of all demographic controls and covariates as noted in Table 13.4. Significant effects of the school climate scales on subsequent personality disorder symptom trajectories are illustrated in Figures 13.1 (for Learning Focus), 13.2 (for Autonomy), 13.3 (for Personal Ties), and 13.4 (for Conflict). School climate interactions (as described above) examined in main models are not tabulated; however, significant interactions are noted in the text and plotted in the appropriate figure (i.e., corresponding to the school climate scale involved). Effect magnitudes noted below for symptom trajectories pertain to a 1 SD increase in the scaled predictor covariate.

A 1 SD elevation in adolescent personality disorder symptoms was related to a significantly higher level of corresponding symptoms at age 22 across all personality disorders (Table 13.4), increasing by 311, .254, and .260 SD for paranoid, schizoid, and schizotypal symptoms, respectively; by .493, .355, .396, and .366 SD for antisocial, borderline, histrionic, and narcissistic symptoms; and by .330 SD for avoidant symptoms and .278 SD for dependent symptoms.

A 1 SD elevation in academic achievement in adolescence was related to a significantly lower level of borderline, avoidant, and dependent personality disorder symptoms at age

Table 13.4 Adolescent Predictors of Subsequent Personality Disorder (PD) Symptom Trajectories (Intercept Set at Age 22)

	Cluster A PDs			Cluster B PDs			Cluster C PDs		
	1	2	3	4	5	6	7	8	9
Intercept									
β	.037	−.004	.022	.134****	.080**	.103***	.148****	−.042	.017
(SE)	(.028)	(.030)	(.030)	(.029)	(.028)	(.029)	(.029)	(.030)	(.029)
Annual linear change									
β	−.030****	−.030****	−.012****	−.024	−.026****	−.038****	−.021****	−.015****	.043****
(SE)	(.003)	(.003)	(.003)	(.003)	(.003)	(.003)	(.003)	(.003)	(.003)
Quadratic change									
β	.0003	.001*	.0003	−.002****	−.0005	−.0007†	−.002****	.001**	.001**
(SE)	(.0003)	(.0004)	(.0003)	(.0003)	(.0003)	(.0004)	(.0003)	(.0003)	(.0003)
Corresponding adolescent PD									
β	.311****	.254****	.260****	.493****	.355****	.396****	.366****	.330****	.278****
(SE)	(.027)	(.027)	(.030)	(.030)	(.028)	(.027)	(.028)	(.028)	(.028)
Academic achievement									
β	−.032	−.035	−.033	.006	−.061*	.002	.067*	−.085**	−.054*
(SE)	(.026)	(.027)	(.026)	(.026)	(.026)	(.025)	(.026)	(.027)	(.026)
Learning focus									
β	.033	−.021	−.005	−.020	−.029	.002	−.036	−.035	−.011
(SE)	(.029)	(.029)	(.031)	(.032)	(.029)	(.032)	(.030)	(.034)	(.030)
Autonomy									
β	−.092**	−.031	−.050	−.071*	−.069*	−.047	−.053	−.008	−.026
(SE)	(.029)	(.030)	(.031)	(.032)	(.029)	(.033)	(.033)	(.034)	(.030)
Personal ties									
β	.050*	.101**	.022	.011	.053*	.008	.050†	.039	.050†
(SE)	(.025)	(.031)	(.027)	(.025)	(.025)	(.025)	(.026)	(.037)	(.026)
Conflict									
β	.082**	.054*	.062*	.012	.041	.022	.021	.056*	.088**
(SE)	(.027)	(.027)	(.029)	(.026)	(.028)	(.027)	(.028)	(.028)	(.028)

Note: Symptom trajectories: 1 = paranoid, 2 = schizoid, 3 = schizotypal, 4 = antisocial, 5 = borderline, 6 = histrionic, 7 = narcissistic, 8 = avoidant and 9 = dependent. Parameter entries are maximum–likelihood estimates using SAS PROC MIXED. SE = standard error. Model adjusted for age at T1, sex, family SES, school climate interactions, and all tabulated effects. All scaled variables were standardized.

† p < .10; * p < .05; ** p < .01; *** p < .001; **** p < .0001

22 (.061, .085, and .054 SD lower, respectively), but also to a significantly *higher* level of narcissistic personality disorder symptoms (.067 SD higher) (Table 13.3).

Learning Focus was not significantly associated with personality disorder symptom levels at age 22 independently of other covariates (Table 13.4), but did significantly moderate rate of change in symptom trajectories (Figure 13.1). An interaction between Learning Focus and age indicated that the early gap in antisocial symptom trajectories between youths who had perceived school as high in Learning Focus (high LF group) and youths who had perceived school as low in Learning Focus (low LF group), narrowed by age 20 owing to an increasing symptom trajectory in the high LF group (β = .006, SE = .003, p < .05). However, an interaction with age^2 also showed that the decline in antisocial symptoms in the mid-20s apparent in both groups was more rapid in the

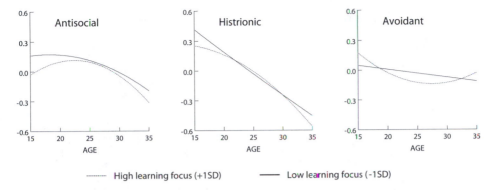

Figure 13.1 Adjusted effects of adolescent perceived school Learning Focus on personality disorder symptom trajectories over 17 years.

high LF group (β = -.046, SE = .023, p < .05). In a similar interaction with age^2 histrionic symptoms also declined more rapidly with increasing age in the high LF group relative to the low LF group (β = -.0008, SE = .0003, p < .05). In addition, an interaction between Learning Focus and age indicated a more rapid decline in avoidant symptoms in the high LF group ((-.015) + (-.007) = -.022 per year) compared to the low LF group ((-.015) + (+.007) = -.008 per year) (β = -.007, SE = .003, p < .05).

Perceptions of greater Autonomy were associated with significantly lower levels of paranoid, antisocial, and borderline symptoms (.092, .071, and .069 SD, respectively) at age 22 independently of other covariates (Table 13.4, Figure 13.2), and significantly moderated rate of change in symptom trajectories (Figure 13.2). An interaction between Autonomy and age indicated that the early gap in schizoid trajectories between youths who had perceived school as high in Autonomy (high AUTO group) and youths who had perceived school as low in Autonomy (low AUTO group) narrowed by the mid-20s owing to a sharper symptom decline in the low AUTO group (β = .006, SE = .003, p < .05). Interactions between Autonomy and age^2 indicated that earlier gaps in symptom trajectories (lower levels in the high AUTO group) narrowed owing to a sharper decline with increasing age in antisocial (β = .0006, SE = .0003, p < .05), histrionic (β = .0009, SE = .0003, p < .01) and narcissistic (β = .0007, SE = .0003, p < .05) symptoms in the low AUTO group. In an additional interaction between Autonomy and age,^{2} there was an upswing in avoidant symptom trajectory after a decline (from above mean level) in the low AUTO group, whereas in the high AUTO group, avoidant symptoms showed a gradual but steady decline from mean level.(β = -.0008, SE = .0003, p < .01).

Perceptions of greater Personal Ties predicted significantly higher levels of para-noid, schizoid, and borderline symptoms (.050, .101, and .053 SD, respectively) at age 22 independently of other covariates (Table 13.4, Figure 13.3). An interaction between Personal Ties and age^2 indicated that schizoid symptoms declined more sharply to below mean level (and at an earlier age) before decline tapered off in youths who had perceived school as low in Personal Ties compared to youths who had perceived school as high in Personal Ties (β = -.0008, SE = .0003, p < .01) (Figure 13.3). Additionally, an interaction between Personal Ties and adolescent antisocial symptoms indicated that in individuals with low adolescent antisocial symptoms, perceptions of high Personal Ties predicted *more* subsequent antisocial symptoms, whereas in individuals with high adolescent antisocial symptoms, perceptions of high Personal Ties predicted *less* subsequent anti-social symptoms (β = -.057, SE = .023, p < .05) (Figure 13.3).

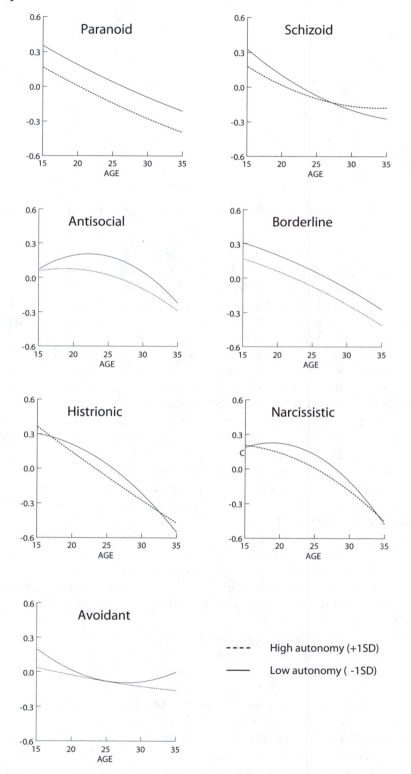

Figure 13.2 Adjusted effects of adolescent perceived school Autonomy on personality disorder symptom trajectories over 17 years.

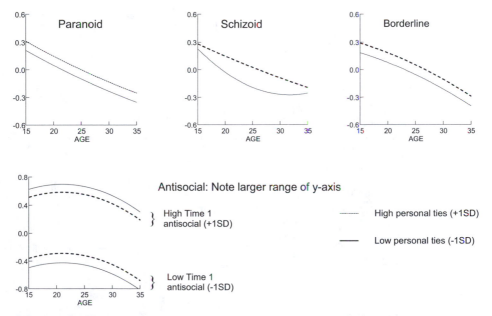

Figure 13.3 Adjusted effects of adolescent perceived school Personal Ties on personality disorder symptom trajectories over 17 years.

Perceptions of greater Conflict predicted significantly higher levels of paranoid, schizoid, schizotypal, avoidant, and dependent symptoms (.082, .054, .062, .056, and .088 SD, respectively) at age 22 independently of other covariates (Table 13.4, Figure 13.4). An interaction between Conflict and adolescent antisocial symptoms indicated that among individuals with low adolescent antisocial symptoms, perceptions of a high level of Conflict predicted *more* subsequent antisocial symptoms, whereas among individuals with high adolescent antisocial symptoms, perceptions of a high level of Conflict predicted *less* subsequent antisocial symptoms (β = -.046, SE = .023, p < .05) (Figure 13.4).

Discussion

Key findings. The finding that earlier perceived school climate is related to subsequent personality disorder symptom trajectories independently of demographic characteristics, adolescent symptoms, and academic achievement extends previous work on the impact of school climate on the psychosocial and behavioral development and mental health of students. Additionally, results suggest that school experiences may either exacerbate or attenuate symptom trajectories of personality pathology. Those findings have implications for implementing system-based school programs designed to improve psychosocial function and reduce existing maladaptive personality tendencies that include pathologic features related to bullying. Moreover, these findings also support the hypothesis that pertinent features of the broader social context are implicated in the origins or continuity of early disturbances in personality development (Sameroff, Seifer, & Bartko, 1997). It is important to note that this study was based on prospective data; examined repeated symptom measures of nine of the ten DSM-IV personality disorders listed on Axis II, many of which have received only limited attention in the literature, especially in community individuals; and was among the few to identify perceived school climate factors that covary with symptoms of specific personality disorders.

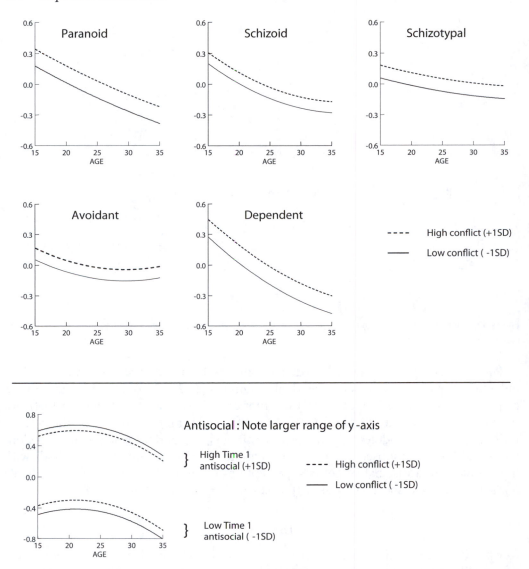

Figure 13.4 Adjusted effects of adolescent perceived school Conflict on personality disorder symptom trajectories over 17 years.

Normative age-related changes in personality disorder symptom trajectories. The significant age-related decline in eight of the nine personality disorder symptom trajectories examined corroborates earlier work on this (Johnson et al., 2000) and other (e.g., Lenzenweger, 1997) cohorts, and likely reflects increased exposure to social learning experiences and maturational growth. There was no significant linear decline in antisocial symptoms; however, there was a sharp drop in symptoms by the mid-20s following a rise, which is compatible with reports of a peak in antisocial deviant behaviors in the early twenties in other community samples (Bachman, Johnston, O'Malley, & Schulenberg, 1996; Jessor, Donovan, & Costa, 1991; Schulenberg, Bryant, & O'Malley, 2004).

Continuity of adolescent personality disorder symptoms. For all personality disorders, elevated adolescent symptoms (at average age 13.7) predicted a significant increase in corresponding symptoms at age 22: Magnitude of effects ranged from 0.5 standard deviation increase for antisocial symptoms to 0.25 standard deviation increase for schizoid symptoms with each 1 standard deviation elevation in corresponding adolescent symptoms. That finding is consistent with our earlier findings at the diagnostic level regarding the increased odds of continuity of adolescent personality disorders in young adulthood (Kasen et al., 1999), and bolsters the argument that the origins of adult personality disorder may be traced back to earlier manifestations of disturbance during childhood (e.g., DeClerq et al., 2006; Shiner et al., 2003). Also in line with our findings are reports that, among youths identified as bullies and victims, pathologic personality traits—for example, emotional dysregulation, a central feature of the Cluster B personality disorders—were stable over a two-year period (Marsh et al., 2001) and predicted adult role impairment and disorder (e.g., Sourander et al., 2007).

Predictive effects of academic achievement. High academic achievement during adolescence predicted lower levels of borderline, avoidant, and dependent symptoms by age 22, providing prospective evidence that academic competence may reduce early personality pathology. High academic achievement also predicted a *higher* mean level of narcissistic symptoms at age 22; such competence may fuel feelings of omnipotence typically expressed by narcissistic individuals. High academic achievement, although related significantly to a lower level of adolescent antisocial symptoms (r = -.314, Table 13.3), was not predictive of subsequent symptom levels or change in symptom trajectory independent of other covariates. The low valence likely attached to academic proficiency among antisocial youths may diminish its utility as a predictor of subsequent antisocial symptom trajectory.

Predictive effects of school climate. Learning focus was not related significantly to personality disorder symptom level at age 22, but variations in learning focus did predict disparities in symptom trajectories. Individuals who had perceived high learning focused schools showed a more rapid decline in avoidant symptoms and a lower level of antisocial symptoms early in the trajectory compared to individuals who had perceived low learning focused schools. Although the latter effect appeared to fade somewhat with age, a sharp decline in antisocial (and histrionic) symptoms by the mid-20s among individuals who had perceived schools as high in learning focus suggest that effects of learning focus may have long-term benefits. Academic skills gained in such an environment may increase sense of accomplishment and personal worth, self-concepts incompatible with avoidant personality disorder, and may provide more positive options for future role endeavors incongruent with antisocial or histrionic personality disorder.

Greater student autonomy predicted lower mean levels of paranoid, antisocial, and borderline symptoms at age 22; a more rapid decline with increasing age in antisocial, histrionic, and narcissistic symptoms; an earlier decline in schizoid symptoms to the sample mean; and a continuous decline in avoidant symptoms that stayed below the mean. Autonomous behavior is the ability to consider and act on one's wishes within a framework of contextual demands imposed by rules that protect others' rights, and to synthesize these competing forces (Ryan & Deci, 2000); thus, behaviors are both self-endorsed and self-regulated. Schools that support student autonomy promote a sense of personal accomplishment, self-confidence, and self-regulation (Siegel & Scovill, 2000). Support of autonomy also engenders acceptance and trust, while efforts to control may cause rebellion and rejection of authority, especially in adolescents (Deci & Ryan, 1987; Ryan & Lynch, 1989). Hence, fostering student autonomy may (1) raise regard for school authority figures and commitment to social institutions, quelling antisocial behavior and increasing social trust and attachment among individuals with a tendency to distrust others; (2) increase opportunities for student success, alleviating perceived inadequacies and fear of criticism; and (3) strengthen self-regulatory skills, improving impulse control, stabilizing affect, and lead to more mature interpersonal relatedness.

A high level of student–student and student–teacher personal ties (i.e., greater interpersonal informality/familiarity) predicted higher levels of paranoid, schizoid, and borderline symptoms at age 22, a trend for higher levels of narcissistic and dependent symptoms, and a slower decline in schizoid symptoms over time. In prior work, we found that a high level of personal ties fostered arguing with and talking back to teachers and other school problems (Kasen et al., 2004), and increased the risk of student depression and anxiety (Kasen et al., 1990). Too much socializing among students and teachers is reported to weaken school standards (Noguera, 1995), which may create a climate that reinforces unstable interpersonal relationships and emotional dysregulation (borderline symptoms). Moreover, disclosure of personal vulnerabilities and problems in the class-room, the basis of many therapeutic interventions, is a risk factor for psychopathology (Hansell & Mechanic, 1985), and may be especially threatening to students with per-sonality disturbance indicative of social distrust or discomfort (paranoid and schizoid symptoms) or extreme anxiety (dependent symptoms). The need for meaningful rela-tionships with caring adults may better be served by school-based mentoring programs than by teachers, whose attempts at close relationships with students may impede their roles as authority figures (McEvoy & Welker, 2000; Noam & Hermann, 2002). Personal ties also interacted with adolescent antisocial symptom levels so that among adolescents with low antisocial symptoms, high personal ties predicted more subsequent antisocial symptoms, whereas among adolescents with high antisocial symptoms, high personal ties predicted less subsequent antisocial symptoms. Nonetheless, the disparity in sub-sequent antisocial symptoms attributable to high or low levels of adolescent antisocial symptoms far outweighed differences based on perceptions of high or low personal ties. High personal ties may provide a context in which antisocial tendencies are maximized, providing models for students with low antisocial tendencies to increase that behavior. There may also be a dampening effect on symptoms for students with high antisocial tendencies as they move on to social contexts less conducive to such deviant behaviors.

A high level of student–student and student–teacher conflict predicted higher levels of paranoid, schizoid, schizotypal, avoidant, and dependent symptoms at age 22. That finding is compatible with reports that a school conflict contributes to increased student fears regarding their safety (Goldstein et al., 2008), relational student aggression (Got-tfredson et al., 2005), and overall maladaptive adjustment in youths in (Kuperminc et al., 2001) and out-of-school settings (De Wit et al., 2000; Kasen et al., 1990, 1998, 2004, 2009). As with personal ties, conflict interacted with adolescent antisocial symptom level so that among individuals with low adolescent antisocial symptoms, high conflict predicted more subsequent antisocial symptoms, whereas among adolescents with high antisocial symptoms, high conflict predicted less subsequent antisocial symptoms. A high conflict school context also may maximize antisocial tendencies and thus provide models for low risk students to increase antisocial behavior. Such behavior necessitates control efforts by teachers that may detract from or preclude academic activities and goals. Additionally, authority figures that model punitive measures as acceptable means by which to gain control of a situation cultivate a school climate that condones coer-cive or aggressive acts, thus elevating anxiety and inviting like behavior in students (Sharp, 1995). Antisocial adolescents may exploit such contexts by becoming even more antisocial (note that school conflict and concurrent adolescent antisocial symptoms are highly correlated in Table 13.3), but then may hold back that proclivity as they likely move on to less compatible social contexts.

Limitations

Study limitations should be taken into consideration when interpreting these findings. The adolescent-reported perceptions of school climate used here to assess school experiences may be biased by the very individual characteristics that are under investigation. School features assessed by a more objective rating system are necessarily limited, however, and do not represent the social and emotional features of the school climate as experienced by students. Additionally, in contrast to studies that are school based, most of which assess school factors in a limited number of schools, community-based epidemiological studies cover large geographic areas; thus, as was the case in our sample, few if any participants attend the same school, making it impractical to use outside raters. Furthermore, other findings based on student-reported school climate indicate good predictive validity for the consequences of such ratings (Kasen et al., 1990, 1998, 2004, 2009; Kuperminc et al., 2001). Accordingly, it is useful to complement school studies using objective raters with student-perceived ratings, particularly when, as in this study, student consequences are assessed at a later point in time. The Personal Ties Scale had relatively low internal consistency. This measure taps a school feature rarely examined that may have negative consequences for high-risk youths. Our finding that high personal ties is related to later elevated personality pathology characterized by social inhibition, anxiety, and fearfulness (vs. more dramatic pathologic features, for example, emotional dysregulation and impulsivity) is compatible with prior reported links between personal ties and social avoidance, anxiety, and depression (Kasen et al., 1990, 2009), thus indicating a repeated pattern. These findings should be considered with that caveat in mind, however. Participants in this study are primarily Caucasian; thus, findings cannot be generalized to other racial groups. Nonetheless, as participants in this sample are demographically representative of other individuals in the Northeastern region of the United States at time of sampling, the current findings apply to a substantial proportion of the population.

TRANSLATING RESEARCH INTO PRACTICE: IMPLICATIONS FOR BULLYING PREVENTION AND INTERVENTION PROGRAMS

Schools play a key role in identifying and treating childhood psychological disturbance, providing 70% to 80% of all child mental health services (Burns et al., 1995). Moreover, school attendance is compulsory for most children between, on average, ages 7 to 16; thus, schools also serve as a vanguard for the healthy development and well-being of nearly all children. Nonetheless, efforts at school reform that target academic or social skill development, especially in vulnerable populations, often have unsatisfactory results, as programs implemented do not consider the school contexts in which children learn and interact with others (McEvoy & Welker, 2000; Ringeisen et al., 2003). School-based mental health intervention and prevention programs also focus on specific student behaviors for modification; however, the findings here suggest that it is also important to consider a more system-based approach that will benefit all students.

Targeting characteristics of the child such as poor impulse control (as with borderline personality disorder) or rule-breaking/violation of others' rights (as with antisocial personality disorder) does little to modify contextual features that may sustain them. Moreover, others have found that undesirable school climate features can have a negative influence on the effectiveness of school-based intervention efforts (Gottfredson, Jones, & Gore, 2002). Thus, the emphasis on individual traits needs to be complemented by an equal emphasis on features of the school climate that may change maladaptive predispositions and behavioral patterns over time.

These results also support a dual emphasis that takes into account school climate features that bolster desirable developmental pathways and those that may reinforce undesirable ones. Our findings suggest that schools that provide ample opportunity for students to act autonomously and exercise decision-making skills create a climate that fosters regard for others, self-regulation of behavior and affect, and self-reliance. On the other hand, they also indicate that schools that tolerate student aggression or unruly behavior, support the use of coercive teacher practices to maintain order, or fail to draw boundaries regarding student–student and student–teacher social relations create a climate that may provide a model for relational aggression and increase social anxiety and fearfulness. Ongoing associations with learning-focused schools also warrant further attention. The findings here also have heuristic value, particularly with regard to research on school climate effects on the continuity of co-existing personality disturbance in children involved in bullying into adulthood.

REFERENCES

American Psychiatric Association (APA). (1980). *Diagnostic and statistical manual of mental disorders* (3rd ed.), Washington, DC: Author.

American Psychiatric Association. (1987). *Diagnostic and statistical manual of mental disorders* (3rd ed. revised), Washington, DC: Author.

American Psychiatric Association. (1994). *Diagnostic and statistical manual of mental disorders* (4th ed.), Washington, DC: Author.

Ames, C. (1992). Classrooms: Goals, structure, and student motivation. *Journal of Educational Psychology, 84,* 261–271.

Bachman, J.G., Johnston, L.D., O'Malley, P., & Schulenberg, J. (1996). Transitions in drug use during late adolescence and young adulthood. In J.A. Graber, J. Brooks-Gunn, & A.C. Petersen (Eds.), *Transitions through adolescence: Interpersonal domains and context* (pp. 111–140). Mahwah, NJ: Lawrence Erlbaum.

Battistich, V., & Hom, A. (1997). The relationship between students' sense of their school as a community and their involvement in problem behaviors. *American Journal of Public Health, 87,* 1997–2001.

Bernstein, D.P., Cohen, P., Skodol, A., Bezirganian, S., & Brook, J.S. (1996). Childhood antecedents of adolescent personality disorders. *American Journal of Psychiatry, 153,* 907–913.

Bernstein, D.P., Cohen, P., Velez, C.N., Schwab-Stone, M., Siever, L.J., & Shinsato, L. (1993). Prevalence and stability of the DSM-III-R personality disorders in a community-based survey of adolescents. *American Journal of Psychiatry, 150,* 1237–1243.

Boulton, M.J., & Smith, P.K. (1994). Bully/victim problems in middle-school children: Stability, self-perceived competence, peer perceptions and peer acceptance. *British Journal of Developmental Psychology, 12,* 315–329.

Brand, S., Felner, R., Shim, M., Seitsinger, A., & Dumas, T. (2003). Middle school improvement and reform: Development and validation of a school-level assessment of climate, cultural pluralism, and school safety. *Journal of Educational Psychology, 95,* 570–588.

Brook, J.S., Lukoff, I.F., & Whiteman, M. (1977). Correlates of adolescent marijuana use as related to age, sex, and ethnicity. *Yale Journal of Biology and Medicine, 50,* 383–390.

Burns, B.J., Costello, E.J., Angold, A., Tweed, D., Stangl, D., Farmer, E.M., & Erkanli, A. (1995). Children's mental health service use across service sectors. *Health Affairs, 14,* 147–159.

Campbell, M.L.C., & Morrison, A.P. (2007). The relationship between bullying, psychotic-like experiences, and appraisals in 14–16-year-olds. *Behaviour Research and Therapy, 45,* 1579–1591.

Chen, H., & Cohen, P. (2006). Using individual growth model to analyze the change in quality of life from adolescence to adulthood. *Health and Quality of Life Outcomes, 4,* 10, doi: 10.1186/1477-7525-4-10. This article is available from www.hqlo.com/content/4/1/10.

Chen, H., Cohen, P., Johnson, J.G., Kasen, S., Sneed, J.R., & Crawford, T.N. (2004). Adolescent personality disorders and conflict with romantic partners during the transition to adulthood. *Journal of Personality Disorders, 18,* 507–525.

Clark, A.L., & Harrison, J.A. (2001). Assessment instruments. In W.J. Livesley (Ed.), *Handbook of personality disorders* (pp. 277–306). New York, NY: Guilford Press.

Cohen, P., & Cohen, J. (1996). *Life values and adolescent mental health.* Hillsdale, NJ: Lawrence Erlbaum.

Cohen, P., Crawford, T.N., Johnson, J.G., & Kasen, S. (2005). The Children in the Community Study of developmental course of personality disorder. *Journal of Personality Disorders, 19,* 466–486.

Coolidge, F.L., DenBoer, J.W., & Segal, D.L. (2004). Personality and neuropsychological correlates of bullying behavior. *Personality and Individual Differences, 36,* 1559–1569.

Crawford, T.N., Cohen, P., Johnson, J.G., Kasen, S., First, M.B., Gordon, K., & Brook, J.S. (2005). Self-reported personality disorder in the Children in the Community sample: Convergent validity and prospective validity in late adolescence and adulthood. *Journal of Personality Disorders, 19,* 30–52.

Deci, E.L., & Ryan, R.M. (1987). The support of autonomy and the control of behavior. *Journal of Personality and Social Psychology, 53,* 1024–1037.

De Clercq, B., De Fruyt, F., Van Leeuwen, K., & Mervielde, I. (2006). The structure of maladaptive personality traits in childhood: A step toward an integrative developmental perspective for DSM-V. *Journal of Abnormal Psychology, 115,* 639–657.

DeWit, D.J., Offord, D.R., Sanford, M., Rye, B.J., Shain, M., & Wright, R. (2000). The effect of school culture on adolescent behavioural problems: Self-esteem, attachment to learning, and peer approval of deviance as mediating mechanisms. *Canadian Journal of School Psychology, 16,* 15–38.

Emmons, C.L., Comer, J.P., & Haynes, N.M. (1996). Translating theory into practice: Comer's theory of school reform. In J.P. Comer, N.M. Haynes, & M. Ben-Avie (Eds.), *Rallying the whole village* (pp. 27–41). New York, NY: Teachers College Press.

Glisson, C., & Hemmelgarn, A. (1998). The effects of organizational climate and interorganizational coordination on the quality and outcomes of children's service systems. *Child Abuse & Neglect, 22,* 401–421.

Goldstein, S.E., Young, A., & Boyd, C. (2008). Relational aggression at school: Associations with school safety and social climate. *Journal of Youth & Adolescence, 37,* 641–654.

Goodenow, C. (1993). Classroom belonging among early adolescent students: Relationships to motivation and achievement. *Journal of Early Adolescence, 13,* 21–43.

Gottfredson, G.D., Jones, E.M., & Gore, T.W. (2002). Implementation and evaluation of a cognitive-behavioral intervention to prevent problem behavior in a disorganized school. *Prevention Science, 3,* 43–56.

Gottfredson, G.D., Gottfredson, D.C., Payne, A.A., & Gottfredson, N.C. (2005). School climate predictors of school disorder: Results from a national study of delinquency prevention in schools. *Journal of Research in Crime and Delinquency, 42,* 412–444.

Hansell, S., & Mechanic, D. (1985). Introspectiveness and adolescent symptom reporting. *Journal of Human Stress, 11,* 165–176.

Hyler, S.E., Reider, R., Spitzer, R.L., & Williams, J.B.W. (1982). *The Personality Diagnostic Questionnaire (PDQ).* New York, NY: New York State Psychiatric Institute.

Jessor, R., Donovan, J.E., & Costa, F.M. (1991). *Beyond adolescence: Problem behavior and young adult development.* New York, NY: Cambridge University Press.

Johnson, J.G., Cohen, P., Kasen, S., & Brook, J.S. (2008). Psychiatric disorders in adolescence and early adulthood and risk for child-rearing difficulties during middle adulthood. *Journal of Family Issues, 29,* 210–233.

Johnson, J.G., Cohen, P., Kasen, S., Skodol, A.E., & Brook, J.S. (2000). Change in personality disorder symptom levels between childhood and adulthood: A community-based longitudinal investigation. *Acta Psychiatrica Scandinavica, 102,* 265–275.

Kaltiala-Heino, R., Rimpelä, M., Rantanen, P., & Rimpelä, A. (2000). Bullying at school—an indicator of adolescents at risk for mental disorders. *Journal of Adolescence, 23,* 661–674.

Kasen, S., Cohen, P., & Brook, J.S. (1998). Adolescent school experiences and dropout, adolescent pregnancy, and young adult deviant behavior. *Journal of Adolescent Research, 13,* 49–72.

Kasen, S., Johnson, J., & Cohen, P. (1990). The impact of school emotional climate on student psychopathology. *Journal of Abnormal Child Psychology, 18,* 165–177.

Kasen, S., Berenson, K., Cohen, P., & Johnson, J.G. (2004). Effects of school climate on changes in aggressive and other behaviors related to bullying. In D.L. Espelage & S.M. Swearer (Eds.), *Bullying in American schools* (pp. 187–210). Mahwah, NJ: Lawrence Erlbaum.

Kasen, S., Cohen, P., Chen, H., Johnson, J.G., & Crawford, T.N. (2009). School climate and continuity of adolescent personality disorder symptoms. *Journal of Child Psychology and Psychiatry, 50,* 1504–1512.

Kasen, S., Cohen, P., Skodol, A.E., Johnson, J.G., & Brook, J.S. (1999). Influence of child and adolescent psychiatric disorders on young adult personality disorder. *American Journal of Psychiatry, 156,* 1529–1535.

Kasen, S., Cohen, P., Skodol, A. E., First, M. B., Johnson, J. G., Brook, J. S., & Oldham, J. M. (2007). Comorbid personality disorder and treatment use in a community sample of youths: A 20-year follow-up. *Acta Psychiatrica Scandinavica, 115,* 56–65.

Kim, Y.S., Leventhal, B.L., Koh, Y-J., Hubbard, A., & Boyce, W.T. (2006). School bullying and youth violence: Causes or consequences of psychopathologic behavior. *Archives of General Psychiatry, 63,* 1035–1041.

Kumpulainen, K., & Räsänen, E. (2000). Children involved in bullying at elementary school age: Their psychiatric symptoms and deviance in adolescence. *Child Abuse & Neglect, 24,* 1567–1577.

Kumpulainen, K., Räsänen, E., & Henttonen, I. (1999). Children involved in bullying: Psychological disturbance and the persistence of involvement. *Child Abuse & Neglect, 23,* 1253–1261.

Kumpulainen, K., Räsänen, E., & Puura, K. (2001). Psychiatric disorders and the use of mental health services among children involved in bullying. *Aggressive Behavior, 27,* 102–110.

Kumpulainen, K., Räsänen, E., Henttonen, I., Almqvist, F., Kresanov, K., Linna, S.L., Piha, J., Puura, K., & Tamminen, Y. (1998). Bullying and psychiatric symptoms among elementary school-age children. *Child Abuse & Neglect, 22,* 705–717.

Kuperminc, G.P., Leadbeater, B.J., & Blatt, S.J. (2001). School social climate and individual differences in vulnerability to psychopathology among middle school students. *Journal of School Psychology, 39,* 141–159.

Kuperminc, G.P., Leadbetter, B.J. Emmons, C.L., & Blatt, S.J. (1997). Perceived school climate and difficulties in the social adjustment of middle school students. *Applied Developmental Science, 1,* 76–88.

Lagerspetz, K., Björkqvist, K., Berts, M., & King, E. (1982). Group aggression among school children in three schools. *Scandinavian Journal of Psychology, 23,* 45–52.

Lenzenweger, M.F. (1997). Stability and change in personality disorder features: The longitudinal study of personality disorders. *Archives of General Psychiatry, 56,* 1009–1015.

Littell, R.C., Miliken, G.A., Stroup, W.W., & Wolfinger, R.D. (1996). *SAS system for fixed models.* Cary, NC: SAS Institute.

Marsh, H.W., Parada, R.H., Yeung, A.S., & Healey, J. (2001). Aggressive school troublemakers and victims: A longitudinal model examining the pivotal role of self-concept. *Journal of Educational Psychology, 93,* 411–419.

McEvoy, A., & Welker, R. (2000). Antisocial behavior, academic failure, and school climate: A critical review. *Journal of Emotional and Behavioral Disorders, 8,* 130–140.

Moos, R.H. (1987). *Evaluating educational environments: Procedures, measures, findings and policy implications.* San Francisco: Jossey-Bass.

Moos, R.H., & Trickett, E.J. (1979). *Classroom Environment Scale Manual* (2nd ed.). Palo Alto, CA: Consulting Psychologists Press.

Mynard, H., & Joseph, S. (1997). Bully/victim problems and their association with Eysenck's personality dimensions in 8 to 13 year-olds. *British Journal of Educational Psychology, 67,* 51–54.

Nansel, T.R., Overpeck, M., Pilla, R.S., Ruan, W.J., Simons-Morton, B., & Scheidt, P. (2001). Bullying behaviors among U.S. youth. *JAMA, 285,* 2094–2100.

Noam, G.G., & Hermann, C.A. (2002). Where education and mental health meet: Developmental prevention and early intervention in schools. *Development and Psychopathology, 14,* 861–875.

Noguera, P. (1995). Preventing and reducing violence: A critical analysis of responses to school violence. *Harvard Educational Review, 69,* 189–212.

Olweus, D. (1978). *Aggression in the schools: Bullies and whipping boys.* Washington, DC: Hemisphere Press (Wiley).

Olweus, D. (1993). *Bullying at school.* Oxford, UK: Blackwell Publishers.

Olweus, D. (1994). Annotation: Bullying at school: Basic facts and effects of a school based intervention program. *Journal of Child Psychology and Psychiatry and Allied Disciplines, 35,* 1171–1190.

Ringeisen, H., Henderson, K., & Hoagwood, K. (2003). Context matters: Schools and the research to practice gap in children's mental health. *School Psychology Review, 32,* 153–168.

Roberts, B.W., & DelVecchio, W.F. (2000). The rank-order consistency of personality traits from childhood to old age: A quantitative review of longitudinal studies. *Psychological Bulletin, 126,* 3–25.

Roeser, R.W., & Eccles, J.S. (1998). Adolescents' perceptions of middle school: Relation to longitudinal changes in academic and psychological adjustment. *Journal of Research on Adolescence, 8,* 123–158.

Rutter, M., Maughan, B., Mortimore, P., Ouston, J., & Smith, A. (1979). *Fifteen thousand hours: Secondary schools and their effects on children.* Cambridge, MA: Harvard University Press.

Ryan, R.M., & Deci, E.L. (2000). Self-determination theory and the facilitation of intrinsic motivation, social development, and well-being. *American Psychologist, 55,* 68–78.

Ryan, R.M., & Lynch, J.H. (1989). Emotional autonomy versus detachment: Revisiting the vicissitudes of adolescence and young adulthood. *Child Development, 60,* 340–356.

Sameroff, A.J., Seifer, R., & Bartko, W.T. (1997). Environmental perspectives on adaptation during childhood and adolescence. In S.S. Luthar, J.A. Burack, D. Cicchetti, & J.R. Weisz (Eds.), *Developmental psychopathology: Perspectives on adjustment, risk, and disorder* (pp. 507–526). New York, NY: Cambridge University Press.

Sarason, S.B., & Klaber, M. (1985). The school as a social situation. *Annual Review of Psychology, 36,* 115–140.

Schulenberg, J.E., Bryant, A.L., & O'Malley, P. (2004). Taking hold of some kind of life: How developmental tasks relate to trajectories of well-being during the transition to adulthood. *Development and Psychopathology, 16,* 1119–1140.

Sharp, S. (1995). How much does bullying hurt? The effects of bullying on the personal well-being and educational progress of secondary aged students. *Educational and Child Psychology, 12,* 81–88.

Shiner, R.L., Masten, A.S., & Roberts, J.M. (2003). Childhood personality foreshadows adult personality and life outcomes two decades later. *Journal of Personality, 71,* 1145–1170.

Siegel, A.W., & Scovill, L.C. (2000). Problem behavior: The double symptom of adolescence. *Development and Psychopathology, 12,* 763–793.

Skodol, A.E., Johnson, J.G., Cohen, P., Sneed, J.R., & Crawford, T.N. (2007). Personality disorder and impaired functioning from adolescence to adulthood. *British Journal of Psychiatry, 190,* 415–420.

Slee, P.T., & Rigby, K. (1993). The relationship of Eysenck's personality factors and self-esteem to bully-victim behaviour in Australian schoolboys. *Personality and Individual Differences, 14,* 371–373.

Sourander, A., Jensen, P., Rönning, J.A., Niemelä, S., Helenius, H., Sillanmäki, L., Kumpulainen, K., Piha, J., Tamminen, T., Moilanen, I., & Almqvist, F. (2007). What is the early adult outcome of boys who bully or are bullied in childhood? The Finnish "From a Boy to a Man" Study. *Pediatrics, 1220,* 397–404.

Spitzer, R.L, & Williams, J.B.W. (1986). *Structured Clinical Interview for DSM III-R Disorders (SCID-II).* New York, NY: New York State Psychiatric Institute.

Swearer, S.M., Turner, R.K., Givens, J.E., & Pollack, W.S. (2008). "You're so gay!": Do different forms of bullying matter for adolescent males? *School Psychology Review, 37,* 160–173.

Tani, F., Greenman, P.S., Schneider, B.H., & Fregosa, M. (2003). Bullying and the Big Five: A study of childhood personality and participant roles in bullying incidents. *School Psychology International, 24,* 131–146.

14

THE ROLE OF SOCIAL SUPPORT IN THE LIVES OF STUDENTS INVOLVED IN BULLYING

MICHELLE K. DEMARAY AND CHRISTINE K. MALECKI

The study of social support as a contributing variable in bullying situations is especially important to investigate from an ecological perspective of bullying (Swearer & Doll, 2001). The level of support that students perceive from significant individuals (e.g., peers, teachers, and parents) in their environments may be related to their involvement in bullying or the potential to intervene or defend students who are victims of bullying. Because social support is related to many positive outcomes for students that possess it and negative outcomes for students who lack it, understanding how this aspect of the environment is related to bully and victim problems is important. This chapter will provide a review of social support and the theoretical models of this construct that may lend support for past, present, and future empirical research on bullying and social support. A brief discussion of the measurement of social support will also be presented. An overview of the research on the perceptions of support for students who are victims of bullying and students who bully will be presented followed by the research on how social support relates to outcomes for students involved in bullying. Finally, conclusions, implications, and future directions will be discussed.

SOCIAL SUPPORT

Social support has been defined in a number of ways, including Cobb's (1976) classic description of the three components of social support: feeling loved, feeling valued or esteemed, and belonging to a social network. Tardy (1985) defined five dimensions in the conceptualization of social support: direction, disposition, description or evaluation, content, and network. In this model, *direction* refers to whether social support is being *given* or *received*. *Disposition* refers to social support being *available* (accessible) or *enacted* (actually utilized). Tardy distinguishes that in research social support may be *evaluated* or simply *described*. *Content* refers to four types of social support based on House's (1981) categories including *emotional*, *instrumental*, *informational*, and/or *appraisal* support. Emotional support consists of support in the form of trust, love, and empathy. Instrumental support includes resources such as money, tangible resources, and time. Informational support is advice or information provided to someone. Appraisal support consists of evaluative feedback given to individuals. Finally, Tardy's *network* refers to the source(s) or the member(s) of an individual's support network. For children and adolescents this may include a variety of sources, such as parents, teachers, classmates, friends, club members, or school staff. For students who are involved in bullying, the content and networks of their social support may differ from other students. Students who are victims of bullying may not receive the emotional support from peers or classmates that they would like. They may, however, seek out emotional support from others (e.g., parents, teachers, close friends) to help them cope with the bullying. Students who bully may lack emotional support from important sources. They may, for example, receive less emotional support from adults (e.g., parents and teachers) due to their negative behaviors.

Broad Theoretical Orientation: Stress-Buffering and Main Effect Theories

Throughout the literature, the relationship between perceived social support and children and adolescents' functioning can be explained by two primary theoretical orientations: the *stress-buffering model* and the *main effect model* (Cohen, Gottlieb, & Underwood, 2000). The stress-buffering model advocates that the positive benefits of social support primarily aid children who are at-risk or under stress (Barrera, 1986; Cohen et al., 2000; Cohen & Wills, 1985). For example, using the stress-buffering hypothesis, a researcher might examine the potential protective effects of social support for students who are victims of bullying. Stress-buffering theory would posit that if students who are victims of bullying receive social support, that social support may buffer them from negative outcomes, such as anxiety, depression, and drug use.

The main-effect model advocates that social support has a positive benefit for *all* children and adolescents (Cohen et al., 2000; Cohen & Wills, 1985), regardless of stress levels or circumstances. The main-effect model presumes that access to social support improves one's overall psychological state (e.g., sense of worth and belonging, security, stability) and may provide the individual with support, which in turn reduces psychological problems (Cohen et al., 2000).

Both the stress-buffering and the main-effect models may be used as tools in explaining the role of social support in the lives of students involved in bullying. For example, according to the stress-buffering model, students who are victims of bullying may be under greater stress and the presence of social support from significant people in their lives may buffer them from developing negative social or psychological outcomes (e.g., depression, anxiety) as a result of being bullied. On the other hand, according to the main effect model, social support may help all students, not just those under stress. Therefore, both students who are victims of bullying and those who bully may benefit from social support as an overall positive influence, regardless of the stress they may be under as a result of bullying behaviors.

Measuring Social Support

Key to being able to examine the relations between social support and bullying behavior is having an appropriate measure of social support. Rating scales are one methodology available to assess students' perceptions of social support. Several of these will be briefly described.

Survey of Children's Social Support—Appraisals Scale (SOCSS-APP; Dubow & Ullman, 1989). The APP is a 31-item rating scale that measures perceived social support from children and adolescents' family, peers, and teachers. Students answer questions such as "Some kids have friends who like to hear their ideas, but other kids do not. Do your friends like to hear your ideas?" on a 5-point rating scale (1 = Never to 5 = Always). Items primarily reflect supportive behaviors in the form of caring, love, and feeling valued. Dubow and Ullman (1989) reported internal consistency evidence with a coefficient alpha of .88 on the total score. In addition, they reported a three to four-week test–retest reliability coefficient of .75. Validity evidence for the APP has been demonstrated via a three-factor structure (family, teacher, and peer support) and via significant correlations (rs = .42 to .66) with the corresponding subscales on the *Social Support Scale for Children* (SSSC; Harter, 1985a). No information has been found on administration time, but from the present authors' experience, the APP requires approximately 10 to 15 minutes of children's time. The APP is one part of the *Survey of Children's Social Support* (Dubow & Ullman, 1989) which includes the *Scale of Available Behaviors* (SAB), the APP, and a measure of children's social network size (NET), all self-report measures. See Dubow and Ullman (1989) for more information.

Social Support Scale for Children (SSSC; Harter, 1985a). The SSSC is a 24-item rating scale that assesses 8 to 12-year-old children's perceptions of social support from four sources (parents, teachers, classmates, and friends). Children read two statements and decide which one is more like them. For example, "Some kids have parents who don't really understand them BUT Other kids have parents who really do understand them." Students decide if the appropriate statement is sort of true or really true of them. The SSSC takes approximately 15 to 20 minutes to complete. The SSSC measures primarily social support in the form of positive regard from others. There is only one form (student self-rating) of the SSSC. Harter (1985a) has reported evidence for internal consistency with alpha coefficients of .72 to .82 on the four subscales in two elementary school samples and coefficients of .74 to .88 on the four subscales in two middle school samples. Furthermore, Harter has provided evidence of validity with correlations from .35 to .49 between the SSSC subscales and the Self-Perception Profile for Children (Harter, 1985b) total score. See Harter (1985a) for further details.

The Child and Adolescent Social Support Scale (CASSS; Malecki, Demaray, & Elliott, 2000). The CASSS measures the frequency and importance of perceived support from five sources: parents, teachers, classmates, close friends, and the school. "My parents understand me" is an example item. Frequency ratings consist of a 6-point Likert Scale (1 = Never to 6 = Always). Importance ratings consist of a 3-point Likert Scale (1 = Not Important to 3 = Very Important). The CASSS also contains items that tap each of the four types of support including emotional, informational, instrumental, and appraisal. This self-report measure is designed for students in grades 3 through 12 and takes students approximately 15 minutes to complete.

Evidence for the reliability of scores on the CASSS have been demonstrated via alpha coefficients for the Total Frequency and Total Importance scores both being .97 (Malecki & Demaray, 2003). Subscale scores have produced alpha coefficients ranging from .92 to .96 and .89 to .95 for the Frequency and Importance subscales, respectively. Test–retest reliability evidence has been demonstrated for the frequency scores with eight to ten-week coefficient of .85 on the Total Frequency score (Malecki & Demaray, 2003). Validity evidence in the form of correlations with similar measures of social support has been demonstrated. For example, the Total Frequency score on the CASSS has been related to total scores on the *Social Support Scale for Children* (Harter, 1985a), $r = .58$, and the *Social Support Appraisals Scale* (Dubow & Ullman, 1989), $r = .61$ (Malecki & Demaray, 2003).

Using a measure such as the CASSS or other multidimensional measures in the research of social support and bullying behavior can help advance our understanding of social support as it relates to bullying. For example, it may help understand how social support forms specific sources that may buffer victims of bullying from negative outcomes.

SOCIAL SUPPORT AND BULLYING BEHAVIOR

In recent years, more research on the role of social support in bullying situations has been conducted. Specifically, research on the role of social support in the lives of students who are victims of bullying has increased. Much of this work is focused on the possible protective factor of social support for students who are victims of bullying (Cheng, Cheung, & Cheung, 2008; Davidson & Demaray, 2007; Holt & Espelage, 2007). It may be that researchers are focusing on broader aspects of the environment, as advocated by the social–ecological model (e.g., parent support, peer support), that may buffer students who are victims of the negative effects of bullying. Although there is relatively more research on this topic since the last edition of this book, more work is needed to thoroughly understand the role of social support in the lives of those involved in bullying. The majority of the research that has been conducted on bully-victim problems and social support is focused on two main areas, which include (1) describing the perceptions of social support for students who are classified in various bully roles (i.e., bullies, victims, bully-victims), and (2) investigating the relationship of social support to relevant outcomes for students involved in bullying. The research in these areas is described below. Although bullying overlaps with peer-victimization and the aggression literature (Hunter, Boyle, & Warden, 2007), the focus of current review will be on studies that include social support and bullying, not general peer victimization or aggression.

Perceptions of Social Support for Students who are Involved in Bullying

Some research has focused on understanding levels of perceived social support among the groups of participants involved in the bullying situation. Although the majority of this research has focused on the students who are involved in bullying as the bully, the victim, or the bully-victim, some research has begun to investigate perceptions of social support for students who are bystanders of the bullying situation (Summers & Demaray, 2009a). Below, the research on levels of support for various roles in the bullying dynamic is described.

In a seminal study to investigate the perceptions of social support by students experiencing victim and bullying behaviors, Demaray and Malecki (2003) investigated perceptions of support for victims, bullies, bully-victims, and a comparison group. This study included 499 students in grades 6 through 8 in a predominately Hispanic and lower socioeconomic status sample. Demaray and Malecki (2003) investigated perceptions of both the frequency and the importance of social support, assessed via the CASSS. It was found that the comparison group perceived more overall total support than all other groups (Bullies, Victims, and Bully-Victims). When comparing specific *sources* of support, again, significant differences were found among the groups. For parent support, comparison students reported perceiving more support from parents than bullies or bully-victims. With regard to teacher support, the comparison group perceived significantly more support from teachers than did bullies. Interestingly, *both* the comparison and the bully groups perceived more support from classmates than victims and bully-victims. This makes sense given that the victims and bully-victims are on the receiving end of bullying behavior from peers in the school. Analyses indicated that there was not a significant difference on perceptions of close friend support by bully-victim status. Lastly, for school support, the comparison group reported significantly more support than the bully-victim group.

A very different pattern of results was found when investigating the differences in perceptions of the *importance* of social support by bully-victim status compared to the frequency results. The victim and bully-victim groups rated total social support as more important than the bully and comparison groups. Significant differences on importance ratings were also found with regards to the various sources of support. Victims and bully-victims rated the importance of parent and teacher support as more important than the comparison group. The importance of classmate and close friend support was rated higher by the victim group than the bully group and the bully-victim group reported higher ratings of importance than the bully and comparison groups. One of the major themes found in the comparisons of the groups' ratings of both frequency and importance of social support is that in general, victims and bully-victims reported less frequency of perceived social support; however, they placed greater importance on social support than the other groups.

Recently, Holt and Espelage (2007) conducted a study of 784 middle and high school students in which they investigated perceptions of social support among bullying groups (Bully, Victim, Bully-victim, and Uninvolved) and the role of social support as a moderator in the relationship between bullying behaviors, anxiety and depression. With regards to perceptions of social support, Holt and Espelage utilized the Support/ Cohesion Microsystem Scale (Seidman et al., 1995) and asked participants to rate support from their mothers and close friends. They found that uninvolved youth reported significantly more peer social support than victims or bully-victims and significantly more maternal social support than victims.

A recent study by Summers and Demaray (2009a) added to the prior work by investigating social support, school climate, and bullying participant roles. As part of this study, they investigated perceptions of social support among not only the bully and victim, but also other bystander participants in the bullying situation. Summers and Demaray (2009a) utilized the Bully Participant Role Survey (BPRS; Summers & Demaray, 2009b) to categorize children into the following groups: Comparison, Bully, Victim, Bully-Victim, Defender, Victim-Defender, and Outsider. They measured social support via the CASSS (Malecki et al., 2000). Group differences (Comparison, Bully, Victim, Bully-Victim, Defender, Victim-Defender, and Outsider) were investigated by conducting a multivariate analysis of variance (MANOVA) on the sources of support (Parent, Teacher, Classmate, Close Friend, and School). The overall MANOVA was significant, $p < .001$. Follow-up analyses of variance (ANOVAs) for each of the sources of support were also significant at the $p < .001$ level with the exception of close friend support which was significant at $p < .01$. Post hoc Scheffé analyses were conducted to determine significant differences among the groups. With regard to parent support, the Comparison, Bully, Defender, and Outsider groups all perceived more social support than the Bully-Victim group. For teacher support, the Comparison, Defender and Outsider groups all perceived more social support than the Bully-Victim group and the Defender group perceived more social support than the Bully group. With respect to classmate support, the Comparison, Bully, and Defender groups all perceived more social support than the Victim group. In addition, the Defender group perceived more social support than the Victim-Defender and Outsider group. The only significant difference in perceptions of close friend support was that the Defender group perceived more support than the Victim group. For school support, the Comparison and Defender groups perceived more support than Bully-Victims; in addition, the Defender Group perceived more support than Victims and Outsiders. In sum, victims and bully-victims often perceived lower levels of social support while the Comparison and Defender groups often perceived higher levels of support. This has important implications for understanding why some youth defend victims, suggesting that perhaps higher perceptions of social support allow them to stand up to bullies in bullying situations.

Thus, although not a lot of work has been done investigating perceptions of support for students involved in bullying situations, these studies demonstrate that there are differences in perceptions of social support from varying sources for students who are involved in bully situations at school. Since in general higher perceptions of social support are linked to many positive outcomes for students (Bender & Losel, 1997; Compas, Slavin, Wagner, & Vannatta, 1986; Levitt, Guacci-Franco, & Levitt, 1994), it seems important for researchers to also investigate outcomes for bullies or victims in relation to their perceptions of support.

Social Support and Outcomes for Students Involved in Bullying

The research focused on social support and outcomes for students involved in bullying situations has consisted of researching both the moderating and the mediating role of social support. The goal of much of this research is to investigate the potential role of social support to buffer victims from the negative outcomes commonly associated with victimization due to bullying. This area of research has seen some growth since the last edition of this book (e.g., Cheng et al., 2008; Davidson & Demaray, 2007; Holt & Espelage, 2007).

In a seminal study on social support and victimization, Rigby (2000) investigated the effects of victimization and perceived support on the overall well-being of 845 school-age (12 to 16 years old) children in Australia. Social support was assessed by asking children how much help they would get from their teacher, best friend, classmates, mother, and father if they were having a serious problem at school. The researchers found that both peer victimization and low levels of perceived social support contributed significantly to lower overall well-being. The researchers also investigated the possible buffering effect of social support for students who had positive general well-being scores despite having high victimization scores; however, no buffering effect was supported via analyses.

Rigby and Slee (1999) conducted similar research investigating the relationship among social support, bully-victim problems and suicidal ideation. They investigated this topic with two brief studies on 1103 children (ages 12 to 18) and 845 children (ages 12 to 16). Social support was assessed in the same method as previously described. They found that bully and victim problems as well as social support made independent and significant contributions to suicidal ideation. However, interactions with bullying, social support, and victim problems and social support were not significant in contributing to suicidal ideation. Thus, a mediating role of social support was not found.

Focused specifically on students who bully, Natvig, Albrektsen, & Qvarnstrom (2001) investigated the relationship among bullying behavior, school stress, self-efficacy, decision control and social support from teachers and peers in a sample of 885 students in Norway. They assessed social support via three self-report questions focused on emotional support from teachers and classmates. Students with higher perceived social support had a decreased risk of demonstrating bullying behaviors. Thus, social support not only protects victims of negative outcomes but may also prevent students from exhibiting bullying behaviors in the first place.

Malecki, Demaray, and Davidson (2008) investigated the role of social support in relationship to students' outcomes for victims in a sample of 142 students in 6th to 8th grade at an urban middle school in Illinois. The majority of the students were Hispanic and received free or reduced lunch prices. Social support was assessed via the CASSS. They found that students' perceptions of total social support were partial mediators of the relationship between levels of victimization and several outcomes including students' personal adjustment, clinical maladjustment, and emotional symptoms. Students' levels of being victimized were related to personal adjustment, clinical maladjustment, and emotional symptoms, but after social support was taken into account, the predictive power of being victimized was reduced. Furthermore, evidence for pure mediation between victimization and school maladjustment was found. Specifically, the predictive power of being victimized was eliminated after total social support was taken into account. These results provide evidence that social support may mediate the relationship between students' victimization in schools and their adjustment.

In the study described earlier, Holt and Espelage (2007) not only investigated perceptions of social support, but also the potential protective role social support may play in the relationship between victimization and anxiety and depression. Their study included 784 middle and high school students. Social support was assessed via the Support/Cohesion Microsystem Scale (Seidman et al., 1995) and focused on maternal and peer support. After dividing their sample into groups (uninvolved, bullies, victims, and bully-victims), they tested the moderating role of social support in relation to anxiety and depression. They found that bullies, victims, and bully-victims with moderate levels of peer support had the lowest levels of anxiety and depression. Ironically, those with the lowest and highest levels of peer support had higher (than the moderate social support group) levels of anxiety and depression. However, moderate levels of support were found to buffer bullies, victims, and bully-victims from higher levels of anxiety and depression.

Another recent study investigating the role of social support in the relationship between victimization due to bullying and internalizing–externalizing distress from bullying also found a moderating effect. Davidson and Demaray (2007) conducted a study of 355 middle school students and assessed social support via the CASSS. The outcome of interest in this study was internalizing and externalizing distress due to bullying as assessed by the Bully-Victimization Distress Scale (BVDS; Reynolds, 2003). This measure assesses internalizing and externalizing distress specifically due to victimization. They found that teacher, classmate, and school support for males moderated the relationship between victimization and internalizing distress due to bullying. Thus, boys with high victimization and high support (teacher, classmate, or school) had lower internalizing scores than boys with high victimization and low support. The same moderating role was found for parent support with girls. Thus, social support was found to buffer negative effects of internalizing distress due to bullying.

Translating Research into Practice: Implications for Bullying Prevention and Intervention Programs

Since the last edition of this book, additional research has investigated the role of social support in the lives of students involved in bullying situations. This research has focused on perception of social support among students involved in bullying and on the relationship of those perceptions of support to various outcomes for students. Regarding perceptions of support, as one might expect, students who are victims of bullying or students who are involved in both victimization and bullying perceive lower levels of support from classmates and peers (Demaray & Malecki, 2003; Holt & Espelage, 2007; Summers & Demaray, 2009a). Regarding parent support, Demaray and Malecki (2003) found that students who are involved in bullying and those who are involved in bullying and are victimized perceived less parent support; additionally Holt and Espelage (2007) found that students who were victimized perceived less maternal support. Students who bully have also been found to report less support from teachers (Demaray & Malecki, 2003). These perceptions of social support may be one place that could be targeted for interventions aimed at bullying. Making sure that adult (parent and teacher) support is provided for students who are involved in bullying situations and are not obtaining peer support may be an important part of intervention. Likewise, additional work investigating the role of social support for bystanders in bullying situations may also assist in indentifying variables that help students defend victims from bullying. For example, Summers and Demaray (2009a) found that students who defended victims from bullying perceived more social support than students who were victimized. Much more research is needed to understand this relationship.

Additionally, research has focused on the role of social support as a mediator or moderator in the relation between victimization and various outcomes. Again, these studies provide important implications for future research and intervention ideas to understand how social support may buffer students who are victimized from negative outcomes. A growing body of literature is supporting the notion that students who are victims of bullying are protected from negative outcomes via social support (Davidson & Demaray, 2007; Holt & Espelage, 2007; Malecki et al., 2008; Rigby, 2000; Rigby & Slee, 1999).

The contextual factor of social support appears to be important for both students who perpetuate bullying and victims of bullying. Future research on this important element of bullying should take several directions. First, the nature of the relationship between bullying behavior and social support (for both bullies and victims) should be further investigated. Second, using the theoretical approaches described in this chapter, researchers should examine other outcomes important to students and determine whether there is a stress-buffering mechanism in place for students who are victims. Finally, intervention planning and development should be based on an ecological framework and include social support as one of many contextual factors.

REFERENCES

Barrera, M. (1986). Distinctions between social support concepts, measures, and models. *American Journal of Community Psychology, 14*, 413–445.

Bender, D., & Losel, F. (1997). Protective and risk effects of peer relations and social support on antisocial behavior in adolescents from multi-problem milieus. *Journal of Adolescence, 20*, 661–678.

Cheng, S.T., Cheung, K.C.C., & Cheung, C. (2008). Peer victimization and depression among Hong Kong adolescents. *Journal of Clinical Psychology, 64*, 766–776.

Cobb, S. (1976). Social support as a moderator of life stress. *Psychosomatic Medicine, 38*, 300–314.

Cohen, S., & Wills, T. (1985). Stress, social support, and the buffering hypothesis. *Psychological Bulletin, 98*, 310–357.

Cohen, S., Gottlieb, B.H., & Underwood, L.G. (2000). Social relationships and health. In S. Cohen, L.G. Underwood, & B.H. Gottlieb (Eds.), *Social support measurement and intervention: A guide for health and social scientists* (pp. 3–25). New York, NY: Oxford University Press.

Compas, B.E., Slavin, L.A., Wagner, B.A., & Vannatta, K. (1986). Relationship of life events and social support with psychological dysfunction among adolescents. *Journal of Youth and Adolescence, 15*, 205–221.

Davidson, L.M., & Demaray, M.K. (2007). Social support as a moderator between victimization and internalizing-externalizing distress from bullying. *School Psychology Review, 36*, 383–405.

Demaray, M.K., & Malecki, C.K. (2003). Perceptions of the frequency and importance of social support by students classified as victims, bullies, and bully/victims in an urban middle school. *School Psychology Review, 32*, 471–489.

Dubow, E.F., & Ullman, D.G. (1989). Assessing social support in elementary school children: The survey of children's social support. *Journal of Clinical Child Psychology, 18*, 52–64.

Harter, S. (1985a). *Manual for the social support scale for children.* Denver: University of Denver.

Harter, S. (1985b). *Manual for the self-perception profile for children.* Denver: University of Denver.

Holt, M.K., & Espelage, D.L. (2007). Perceived social support among bullies, victims, and bully-victims. *Journal of Youth and Adolescence, 36*, 984–994.

House, J. (1981). *Work stress and social support.* Reading, MA: Addison-Wesley.

Hunter, S.C., Boyle, J.M.E., & Warden, D. (2007). Perceptions and correlates of peer-victimization and bullying. *British Journal of Educational Psychology, 77*, 797–810.

Levitt, M.J., Guacci-Franco, N., & Levitt, J.L. (1994). Social support achievement in childhood and early adolescence: A multicultural study. *Journal of Applied Developmental Psychology, 15*, 207–222.

Malecki, C.K., & Demaray, M.K. (2003). What type of support do they need? Investigating student adjustment as related to emotional, informational, appraisal, and instrumental support. *School Psychology Quarterly, 18*, 231–52.

Malecki, C.K., Demaray, M.K., & Davidson, L.M. (2008). The relationship among social support, victimization, and student adjustment in a predominantly Latino sample. *Journal of School Violence, 7*, 48–71.

Malecki, C.K., Demaray, M.K., & Elliott, S.N. (2000). *The child and adolescent social support scale.* DeKalb, IL: Northern Illinois University.

Natvig, G.K., Albrektsen, G., & Qvarnstrom, U. (2001). School-related stress experiences as a risk factor for bullying behavior. *Journal of Youth and Adolescence, 30*, 561–575.

Reynolds, W.M. (2003). *Reynolds bully-victimization scales for schools.* San Antonio, TX: The Psychological Corporation.

Rigby, K. (2000). Effects of peer victimization in schools and perceived social support on adolescent well-being. *Journal of Adolescence, 23*, 57–68.

Rigby, K., & Slee, P.T. (1999). Suicidal ideation among adolescent school children, involvement in bully-victim problems, and perceived social support. *Suicide and Life-Threatening Behavior, 29*, 119–130.

Seidman, E., Allen, L., Aber, J.L., Mitchell, C., Feinman, J., Yoshikawa, H., et al. (1995). Development and validation of adolescent-perceived microsystem scales: Social support, daily hassles, and involvement. *American Journal of Community Psychology, 23*, 355–388.

Summers, K.H., & Demaray, M.K. (2009a). Defending victims of bullying: The role of social support and school climate. Manuscript submitted for publication.

Summers, K.H., & Demaray, M.K. (2009b). *The bully participant role survey (BPRS).* DeKalb, IL: Northern Illinois University.

Swearer, S.M., & Doll, B. (2001). Bullying in schools: An ecological framework. *Journal of Emotional Abuse, 2*, 7–23.

Tardy, C.H. (1985). Social support measurement. *American Journal of Community Psychology, 13*, 187–202.

15

FAMILY RELATIONSHIPS OF BULLIES AND VICTIMS

RENAE D. DUNCAN

This chapter examines characteristics of parents, siblings, and families of children involved in bullying and offers suggestions on how this information might be used to help reduce school bullying. Because the family is where the child first sees and experiences relationships, it is through the family that the child will learn what to expect in relationships, how to behave in relationships, and the interpersonal skills to be used in relationships. Therefore, it is likely that at least some of the characteristics that predispose children to becoming victims or bullies develop before the child enters school and that some of these characteristics are developed through experiences within the family.

PARENTS AND FAMILIES OF VICTIMS

Family Systems Theory proposes that the family is a single unit made up of a variety of interconnected relationships. Due to this interconnectedness, when a child (or adult) experiences emotional or behavioral difficulties, these problems are viewed as a reflection of dysfunction within the family unit rather than being evidence of something that is "wrong" with the child. Therefore, Family Systems Theory would propose that those behaviors which predispose a child to becoming a victim of peer aggression at school are a reflection of problems within the family system. Difficulties within the families of victims are reflected in one study which found that parents of victims described their family members as being highly critical of each other (Holt, Kaufman Kantor & Finkelhor, 2009). However, most other studies have found that families of victims are excessively close and that parents are overly involved in their children's lives. For example, families of victims have been found to be cohesive yet enmeshed (Berdondini & Smith, 1996) and the parents of victims are described as being overly intense with their children (Bowers, Smith & Binney, 1994). Similarly, the mother–child relationship has been described as more emotionally close than typically seen (Ladd & Ladd, 1998), with mothers who are highly responsive, overprotective (Georgiou, 2008a) and overly controlling of their children (Ladd & Ladd, 1998; Olweus, 1993b; Rigby, 2002).

It is possible that this overly controlling parenting style leads to an inhibition of the child's sense of autonomy. Putallaz (1987) found that children whose autonomy was restricted by their mothers were less assertive with peers than were those whose mothers allowed more autonomy. In addition, Perry, Hodges and Egan (2001) suggested that because of the mother's overprotective parenting style, the child has difficulty exploring and experiencing new situations alone or with peers. Because the child is sheltered from potentially negative experiences, those skills necessary to handle conflict and discomfort are not developed. Perry and colleagues also suggested that the controlling style seen in parents of victims leads the child to believe that his or her feelings and thoughts are wrong, which in turn can lead to a variety of internalizing symptoms and behaviors such as those commonly seen in victims of bullying. Indeed, several studies have found that children display significant levels of anxiety and even panic when they are raised by parents who use excessively high levels of care and control with their children (e.g., Silove, Parker, Hadzi-Pavlovic, Manicavasagar, & Blaszczynski, 1991) or who are simply perceived as being overly controlling of the child (e.g., Parker, 1979). These internalizing symptoms and weak assertiveness skills may then place the child at risk for victimization at the hands of their peers. It is important to note, however, that these mothers may become overprotective because they believe their children are weak and fragile rather than making their children weak and fragile due to their overprotectiveness (Georgiou, 2008a). Georgiou (2008b) goes on to say that children whose mothers are anxious and overprotective tend to become passive and submissive, which then increases the likelihood that they will become victims of bullying.

In addition to being overly controlling, some researchers have found that parents of victims are overly involved in their children's lives (e.g., Bowers et al., 1994). This is evident in a survey of 15,686 U.S. school children in which Nansel and colleagues (2001) found that parents of victims were highly likely to be involved in their children's schools. The authors propose that this parental involvement may reflect concern that the parents have about the difficulties their children are experiencing with their peers. However, they also suggest that the parental involvement may reflect the notion that victims are less independent than their peers, potentially leaving them more vulnerable to attacks. The opposite relationship between parental involvement in school and victimization was noted by Jeynes (2008) who found that children whose parents were highly involved in their schooling were less likely than other children to become victims of bullying.

The studies discussed above most often examined male and female victims together, which may lead to inaccurate depictions of the relationship between victims and their parents. Indeed, in most studies in which male and female victims were examined separately, differences were found in the parent–child relationships depending on the sex of the child. For example, research examining males found that victims had mothers who were overprotective (Olweus, 1993a), coddling, controlling, and restrictive of their sons (Olweus, 1993b). Olweus (1994) also found that although male victims reported a close and positive relationship with their mothers, the boys' teachers believed the mothers were overprotective. Ikemoto (2009) found similar results in which 71% of male victims described their mothers as using affectionate constraint (high levels of care and control) with their sons. Finnegan, Hodges, and Perry (1998) found that those boys who had both a fearful coping style and overprotective mothers were the most likely to be victimized by peers. Interestingly, male victims were more likely than other boys to report that their mothers allowed the boys to express themselves during family arguments. Finnegan and colleagues suggest that the "animated, positively toned discussions, even lively debates" (p. 1082) between mother and son are evidence of the enmeshed relationships found in other studies.

Although the mothers of victimized males appear to be overly protective, perhaps even overcontrolling, researchers have found fathers of victims to be distant and critical (Olweus, 1993a), uninvolved (Flouri & Buchanan, 2002) or absent (Fosse & Holen, 2002). Ikemoto (2009) found that male victims were more likely than those not involved in bullying to have fathers who were neglectful, showed little care, and maintained a high level of control over the child. Flouri and Buchanan (2002) found that of all students, victims of bullying were the most likely to have uninvolved fathers. Further, they found that the worse the victimization, the less the father was involved in the child's life. Similarly, Jeynes (2008) found that children who lived with both parents were least likely to become victims of bullying. Fosse and Holen (2002) theorize that because fathers play a critical role in teaching their sons how to interact with other males, having a father who is involved in the life of his son would help the boy develop skills that would keep him safe from bullies. Further, early research found that boys' popularity with peers was related to physically playful and affectionate interactions with the father (MacDonald & Parke, 1984). Thus, fatherless boys or boys with uninvolved or neglectful fathers do not develop these skills to the same degree as do boys who spend a good deal of time with their fathers. Therefore, it is likely that father involvement acts as a protective factor in bully victimization (Flouri & Buchanan, 2002).

A different pattern has been noted in the parent–child relationships of female victims. Whereas mothers of victimized boys tend to be overly protective of their sons, victimized girls tend to have a negative attitude toward their mothers (Rigby, 1993). In addition, female victims are more likely to experience poor family functioning, inadequate family communication and lower family affect than non-victims of bullying (Rigby, 1994). Similarly, Ikemoto (2009) found that female victims were more likely than females not involved in bullying to have mothers and fathers who were overly controlling and who displayed little care toward their daughters, though the relationship between victimization and mother's parenting was much stronger than that for fathers. Ikemoto also found that female victims were more likely than those not involved in bullying to have mothers and fathers categorized as using affectionless control with their daughters and were less likely than their peers to have mothers and fathers who displayed optimal parenting.

Further evidence of the unhealthy female victim–parent relationship is reflected in an examination of persons seeking outpatient mental health treatment. It was found that female outpatients with histories of bully victimization were more likely than non-bullied female outpatients to have been abused or neglected by their parents (Fosse & Holen, 2002). Similarly, Finnegan et al. (1998) found that female victims described their mothers as hostile and rejecting and described mothers who would withdraw their love and threaten to reject and abandon the girls when they misbehaved. They further stated that the parenting behaviors used by the mothers were "likely to threaten girls' need for communion and their development of the social skills needed to relate closely and effectively with others" (p. 1082).

Finnegan and colleagues (1998) hypothesized that the behaviors of mothers have a differential impact on children depending on the gender of the child. For example, the overprotected male child is unable to develop the autonomy necessary to obtain and maintain status in the peer group. Thus, the overprotected boy (who may already be rejected by other boys) feels helpless and anxious when he encounters a difficult situation involving peers because he has not learned the skills necessary to handle these situations effectively. In contrast, the mothers of female victims are described as emotionally abusive, hostile, and rejecting of their daughters. Finnegan et al. (1998) propose that this hostile and rejecting parenting style leads to the development of depression, anxiety or other internalizing symptoms in the daughter. Indeed, numerous studies have found a link between depression and affectionless or overly controlling parenting (e.g., Parker, 1986). Additionally, Finnegan and colleagues propose that because the mother fails to model healthy interpersonal skills, the daughter has difficulty learning those skills necessary for developing relationships with other girls. Finnegan and colleagues suggest that these girls become victims of bullying because they have difficulty regulating their emotions, feeling or expressing empathy, and communicating effectively, all of which may make them easy targets for victimization by peers.

FAMILIES AND PARENTS OF BULLIES AND BULLY-VICTIMS

Families of bullies have been characterized as having low cohesion (Berdondini & Smith, 1996; Bowers et al., 1994; Stevens, De Bourdeaudhuij, & Van Oost, 2002), little warmth, and high needs for power (Bowers et al., 1994). Ahmed and Braithwaite (2004) found that bullying was related to family disharmony, which includes being ignored by parents, difficulties, arguments, and disagreements between family members. Similarly, Stevens and colleagues (2002) found that bullies perceive high conflict and low levels of expressiveness, organization, control, and social orientation within their families. Additionally, bullies described their families as using destructive problem-solving strategies and reported high levels of negative affect within their families. Similar difficulties within the families of bullies were reported by Connolly and O'Moore (2003) who found that bullies have ambivalent relationships with their siblings, mothers, and fathers. Bullies were also found to believe that they receive few positive emotions from their families and said that they give few positive and many negative emotions in return. The ambivalent relationships between bully, sibling, and parents could be a result of communication problems, given that difficulty communicating with parents was one of the few characteristics found in an examination of 11,033 school children to be related to bullying in all racial and ethnic groups (Spriggs, Iannotti, Nansel, & Haynie, 2007).

Family relationship problems were also noted by Rigby (1993) who found that bullies reported having poor relationships with their parents and unhealthy family functioning. The importance of parent and family characteristics was also reflected in the results of a seven-year longitudinal investigation of bullying in which it was found that children who had relationship problems with their parents when in elementary school were two to four times more likely than their peers to perpetrate high levels of bullying throughout their school years (Pepler, Jiang, Craig & Connolly, 2008). Pepler and colleagues also found that bullies report high conflict and low trust with their parents and report that their parents do not monitor their behavior. Indeed, Olweus (1994) notes that parents of bullies fail to place limits on their children's aggressive behaviors and are "generally permissive and tolerant" of aggression toward others (p. 1182). This acceptance of aggression may be reflected in the fact that fathers who were bullies in childhood and those who had been convicted of violent crimes were more likely than other fathers to have children who bullied their peers (Farrington, 1993).

Espelage, Bosworth and Simon (2000) suggested that the messages parents give their children about violence, aggression, and fighting, as well as the time they spend with their children, have a strong impact on whether their children will become bullies. In addition to providing positive messages about aggression, Rigby (1994) found that bullies rated their families as having high negative affect while providing little emotional support and Georgiou (2008a) found that bullies have mothers who are unresponsive to their children. This negative, unsupportive, and unresponsive family environment could be a result of parental depression. Indeed, Georgiou (2008b) found that male (but not female) bullies are likely to have depressed mothers. Georgiou suggests that maternal depression impacts boys differently from girls (in regard to bullying) because boys may need more monitoring—a need that goes unmet when the mother is depressed. Georgiou also suggests that because boys tend to be more active than girls, their behavior might elicit harsh and punitive responses from their depressed mothers. However, Georgiou acknowledges that the mother may become depressed as a result of her child's misbehavior if he is aggressive and argumentative at home.

Various researchers have found that parents of bullies display characteristics of both the authoritarian and the indifferent–uninvolved parenting styles. For example, Baldry and Farrington (2000) found that bullies had parents who were authoritarian, punitive, and unsupportive, and who disagreed with each other. Olweus (1994) and Strassberg, Dodge, Pettit and Bates (1994) found that parents of bullies were both physically and emotionally aggressive with their children. Similarly, in their examination of children enrolled in Head Start, Curtner-Smith and colleagues (2006) found that mothers who exerted power over their children had children who engaged in more relational bullying than did children whose mothers fostered independence in their children. Curtner-Smith and colleagues also found that the children of mothers who had low empathy for their children displayed higher levels of relational and overt bullying. Interestingly, Curtner-Smith and colleagues also found that mothers who had inappropriate developmental expectations for their children produced children who engaged in higher levels of relational bullying than their peers.

Evidence of indifferent–uninvolved parenting comes from several studies in which parents of bullies were found to be overly indulgent of their children (Olweus, 1994) while at the same time failing to supervise or monitor them (Espelage et al., 2000; Holt et al., 2009). Flouri and Buchanan (2003) found that when fathers and mothers were uninvolved with their children, the children were likely to become bullies in school. The researchers also found that father involvement was an important protective factor when mother involvement was low and that the impact of parental involvement was the same whether the family was divorced or intact. The impact of parental involvement in their children's lives is also reflected in the finding that bullies are less likely than other children to have a father in the home (Berdondini & Smith, 1996; Bowers et al., 1994; Holt et al., 2009). In fact, in one of the few longitudinal studies of bullying, Pepler and colleagues (2008) found that children involved in high levels of bullying throughout childhood were the least likely of all children to live with both natural parents. However, Spriggs and colleagues (2007) found that the link between parent absence and involvement in bullying was true only among White, but not Black or Hispanic children.

Perhaps the best evidence supporting the role of parents in increasing or decreasing the likelihood that their children will become involved in bullying comes from an examination of 558 middle school children by Espelage and colleagues (2000). In this study, the researchers found that physical discipline was related to bullying and that less bullying occurred when children were exposed to adults who used non-violent strategies to handle conflict. In fact, Espelage and colleagues found the strongest predictor of the absence of bullying was being exposed to positive adult role models. Thus, children who bully their peers are likely to have modeled the aggressive behavior of their parents, whereas those who were not involved in bullying modeled the non-violent problem-solving behaviors of the adults around them. In fact, Espelage and colleagues found that the adult influence on bullying remained even when peer influences were controlled.

There have been few studies that specifically examine characteristics of the parents of bully-victims (those who both bully and are victimized by their peers). However, Bowers and colleagues (1994) found that bully-victims report troubled relationships with their parents, poor parental warmth, abusive and inconsistent discipline and monitoring, and neglect. Bully-victims also viewed their mothers as relatively powerless, perhaps as a result of domestic violence that occurs more often in these families than in the families of other children. Similarly, indirect (but not direct) bully-victims were more likely than any other children to report feeling alienated from their mothers (Marini, Dane, Bosacki, & YLC-CURA, 2006). Specifically, bully-victims report that they are both neglected by and inconsistently monitored by their parents (Bowers et al., 1994). However, bully-victims have also described their parents as authoritarian, punitive, and unsupportive (Baldry & Farrington, 1998).

SIBLING CHARACTERISTICS

Numerous studies have shown that the most prevalent form of violence within the family occurs between siblings (e.g., Gelles & Straus, 1988). Patterson (1984) argues that it is through the modeling and reinforcement of sibling behavior that the child learns to behave appropriately or inappropriately with peers. Therefore, if there is a large amount of aggression between siblings, there is also likely to be a great deal of aggression against peers. Patterson's assertion is supported by Duncan (1999b) who found that children involved in bullying at school were the most likely of any of the 375 middle school students surveyed to be involved in bullying at home with their siblings. Duncan also noted that the majority of school bullies and bully-victims bullied their siblings and the majority of school bully-victims reported that they were frequently victimized by their siblings.

This relationship between sibling aggression and school bullying was supported by Wolke and Samara (2004) who found that children who were bullied by siblings were significantly more likely than other children to be involved in bullying at school. Additionally, Holt, Finkelhor and Kaufman Kantor (2007) found that bully-victims and victims reported more victimization at the hands of their siblings than did bullies or those who were not involved in school bullying. Interestingly, Ma (2001) found that children who had many siblings were more likely to bully their peers than were children from small families. Ma proposed that large families increase the likelihood of sibling bullying and that the long-term bullying experienced at home might become internalized. This internalization of bullying causes a "carry over effect" in that the child who has experienced years of sibling bullying comes to believe that bullying is an appropriate style of interaction. Indeed, using peer nominations of bullies and victims, Chan (2006) found numerous cases in which children in one grade would describe as a bully the sibling of another child who was listed as being a bully by children in a different grade. This indicates that multiple children within one household were identified as bullies by their peers at school.

The relationship between sibling violence and school aggression is supported by the research of Berndt and Bulleit (1985) who found that preschoolers who were aggressive with their siblings were more likely than other preschoolers to be aggressive with peers. Also, Stormshak, Bellanti, and Bierman (1996) found that children who experience high sibling conflict were rated by teachers as displaying high aggression and low social competence at school. Similarly, bullies have been found to have ambivalent and somewhat negative relationships with their siblings and to view their siblings as being more powerful than themselves (Bowers et al., 1994).

The link between sibling and peer aggression suggests that the maladaptive social interactions of bullies and victims may be related to problems within the sibling relationship. Bank, Patterson, and Reid (1996) found that children whose older siblings displayed aggressive behavior were unlikely to have positive experiences in their relationships with peers and Lockwood, Kitzmann and Cohen (2001) found that children whose relationships with siblings were characterized by high levels of warmth had the most positive relationships with peers. In addition, children with high levels of sibling warmth were less likely than other children to be viewed as victims or as rejected by peers. Lockwood and colleagues propose that children in warm sibling relationships are able to learn and practice healthy interpersonal skills through interactions with the sibling and that children who have positive relationships with peers may take these positive interactions back into the sibling relationship, which then encourages even more sibling warmth. However, Lockwood and colleagues found that sibling warmth did not mediate the likelihood of peer aggression when the siblings also engaged in high levels of conflict. In fact, the authors noted that sibling conflict has both risks and benefits for children. Children who experience low levels of sibling conflict had a lower social status among peers and were more likely to be victimized than other children as supported by the findings of Bowers and colleagues (1994) who noted that victims report extremely close, if not enmeshed, relationships with their siblings. Lockwood and colleagues also found that children from homes with high levels of sibling conflict were more likely than the other children to be rejected by their peers and were somewhat more aggressive than the low sibling conflict children. The authors propose that children who experience little sibling conflict fail to develop the social skills necessary to successfully interact with peers in the school setting. Additionally, Lockwood and colleagues suggest that children who experience high levels of sibling conflict develop a negative attributional bias, which predisposes the child to handling uncomfortable peer interactions with aggression.

DOMESTIC VIOLENCE, CHILD ABUSE, AND INVOLVEMENT IN BULLYING

MacKinnon-Lewis, Starnes, Volling and Johnson (1997) suggest that the relationship with family members acts as a "training ground" for the child in that children who are aggressive with peers are "trained" to behave in such a manner through their interpersonal interactions at home. When children witness aggressive behavior on the part of their parents, Social Learning Theory would propose that some children model the behavior of the aggressive parent by becoming bullies whereas others model the behavior of the parent who was aggressed against by becoming victims of bullying. This hypothesis is supported by a variety of studies which found that domestic violence is more likely to occur in families of bullies (Baldry, 2003; Holt et al., 2009), victims of bullying (Baldry & Winkel, 2004), and bully-victims (Schwartz, Dodge, Pettit, & Bates,

1997) than in families of those not involved in bullying. In fact, Baldry (2003) found that domestic violence, especially when the violence was perpetrated by the mother against the father, better predicted both bullying and victimization than did age, gender, or being a victim of child abuse. Baldry also proposed that children who witness domestic violence become depressed and fearful and develop low self-esteem, all of which makes them less likely than their peers to become assertive when faced with aggression by peers. Baldry states that in these cases, "the vicious cycle of victimization starts at home and continues at school" (p. 728).

In addition to finding that male 3rd and 4th grade bully-victims were likely to have witnessed domestic violence when they were in preschool, Schwartz and colleagues (1997) found that these boys were likely to have been physically abused and to have had a hostile mother who used restrictive discipline with the child. This suggests that modeling of aggressive behavior might also take place when children are abused by their parents. If this hypothesis is correct, we would expect to see a higher prevalence of child abuse among children involved in bullying than in those who are not involved. This hypothesis is supported by a variety of studies, such as those conducted by Olweus (1994) and Strassberg and colleagues (1994) which found that parents of bullies are often physically and emotionally aggressive in their interactions with their children. Additionally, several studies found that 5th grade children who were bullies, victims, or bully-victims were more likely to have been abused by their parents than children who were not involved in bullying, with bully-victims experiencing the highest rates of abuse (Holt et al., 2007, 2009). This abusive parenting style was also found in a study in which college students who were victims of childhood bullying reported a significantly higher level of physical and emotional abuse by parents than did non-victims of bullying (Duncan, 1999a). Similarly, Baldry and Winkel (2004) found a positive correlation between abuse by mothers, abuse by fathers and bully victimization. Baldry (2003) also found that boys who were abused by their fathers had a higher risk of involvement in bullying as either bullies or victims than did their non-abused peers. In a cross-cultural examination of bullying in which Dussich and Maekoya (2007) found that 72% of children who were physically harmed by their parents were involved in bullying as victims, bullies, or bully-victims, and Shields and Cicchetti (2001) found that maltreated boys and girls—especially those who were physically or sexually abused—were more likely than those who were not abused to become bullies or victims of bullying while at a summer day camp.

Finkelhor and Browne (1985) proposed that when children are abused, they learn that they are powerless, they become less self-confident and they are less able to assert their needs. Additionally, they suggest that abused children lose the ability to determine whether others are trustworthy. Cicchetti and Lynch (1995) propose that because of problematic relationships with their parents, abused children come to expect that all relationships are filled with violence and exploitation, which then leads to the anxiety and hyperarousal seen in abused children who become victims of bullying (Shields & Cicchetti, 2001). Although being on-guard and ready for harm might be adaptive for living in a violent home, Shields and Cicchetti suggest that this behavior puts the child at risk of bullying in social situations with peers, especially when the situation is novel. They propose that abused children come to expect to be harmed, fail to recognize danger, and are thus less able to protect themselves when they encounter others who might be harmful to them. Then, seeing a vulnerable child who will not retaliate when attacked, the bully targets the child abuse victim. Research indicates that children with low self-esteem (Sharp, 1996), passive response styles (Bernstein & Watson, 1997; Sharp, 1996), and submissive and unassertive tendencies with peers (Schwartz, Dodge, & Coie, 1993)—all of which are characteristics common in child abuse survivors—are bullied more than others. Indeed, Perry, Williard, and Perry (1990) found that children easily detect which of their peers are most submissive and who fail to assert their needs. Children expect that these submissive peers will not retaliate and will show more suffering when picked on by bullies, which, in turn, rewards the bully's behavior.

Further, Holt and colleagues (2007) propose that being a victim of child abuse might increase the likelihood that a child will become a bully because child abuse so often causes aggression in peer relationships. For example, early research examining peer relationships of children who had been abused by parents found that toddlers who were physically abused by parents were aggressive toward peers and caregivers (George & Main, 1979) and that abused children responded to aggression with aggression, which caused the inappropriate behavior to escalate (Howes & Eldredge, 1985). Perhaps of more importance in understanding bullying behavior, Howes, Eldredge, Main, and George (1985) found that when faced with a peer in distress, abused children responded to that peer's distress with aggression. Interestingly, Perry and colleagues (1990) found that bullies target children who openly display distress as a response to being humiliated or physically harmed by the bully and that bullies are rewarded by the victim's suffering.

Child abuse is also likely to lead to bullying because physical abuse teaches the child to use aggression to get what he or she wants from others (Schwartz et al., 1997). Thus, if bullies want to gain status, get attention from peers, or simply gain pleasure from tormenting other children, they can do so by being aggressive against those who are weaker than themselves because that is what was modeled by their parents. Additionally, because some abused children survive the abuse by constricting their emotions, they may become less empathetic and less emotionally responsive to peers. This, in turn, might make them more prone to bullying those they consider weak or vulnerable (Shields & Cicchetti, 2001).

SUMMARY OF THE RESEARCH EXAMINING PARENT AND FAMILY CHARACTERISTICS

Reviewing existing research which examines families of children involved in bullying reveals several interesting patterns (see Table 15.1). Specifically, male victims appear to be overly close with their siblings and with their coddling, overprotective mothers. In contrast, male victims are likely to have fathers who are neglectful or who show little care and a high level of control over their sons. The overly close sibling relationship and mother's over involvement appear to stifle the male victim's autonomy, while the same time victimized boys fail to learn from their fathers the skills needed to reduce the likelihood they will be victimized by their peers.

Female victims appear to come from families very different from those of male victims. Whereas the boys' families are close to the point of enmeshment, families of female victims are characterized as emotionally abusive and unhealthy. Female victims view their fathers as uncaring, yet overcontrolling and report that their mothers withdraw love and threaten abandonment when the girls do not follow their mothers' directives. Because the girls are unable to model appropriate interpersonal behaviors from their mothers, they are left without the skills needed to become involved in healthy friendships with

Table 15.1 Family Characteristics of Bullies and Bully-Victims

Bullies	Bully-victims
Absent Father	Physical Abuse
Low Cohesion	Domestic Violence
Little Warmth	Hostile Mother
High Power Needs	Powerless Mother
Permit/Encourage Aggression	Indifferent/Uninvolved Parents
Physical Abuse	Neglect
Poor Family Functioning	Low Warmth
Negative Affect	Inconsistent Discipline
Authoritarian Parenting	Negative Environment
Harsh Physical Punishment	

other girls. Additionally, the emotionally abusive behaviors directed toward the daughter may lead the girl to develop depression and anxiety which, when paired with poor interpersonal skills, leaves the child at risk for rejection and victimization.

Families of bullies are often characterized by a lack of warmth, a lack of closeness and, as focused on, power (see Table 15.2). Bullies are likely to grow up in homes without a father figure and are also likely to have been physically and emotionally maltreated while growing up. Bullies also acknowledge that they frequently mistreat their siblings, which parallels the aggression they perpetrate on their peers. Similarly, the families of bully-victims often exhibit high levels of aggression and violence and low levels of warmth. The parents are likely to provide inconsistent discipline and are unlikely to monitor the behavior of their children. In fact, mothers tend to be described as neglecting their children and are often viewed as relatively powerless. A high level of sibling violence is often found in the homes of bully-victims, with the majority of bully-victims admitting that they both bully and are victimized by their siblings.

A finding of great concern is the relatively high prevalence of child abuse among children involved in bullying. Research indicates that bullies, victims, and bully-victims are each more likely to be victims of child abuse than children who are not involved in bullying. The highest prevalence of physical and sexual abuse and neglect occurs among bully-victims, which likely contributes to the variety of behavioral and emotional problems these children experience. Overall, it is clear that when children are victims of

Table 15.2 Parent Characteristics of Male and Female Victims

Male Victims		Female Victims	
Mothers	**Fathers**	**Mothers**	**Fathers**
Overprotective	Distant	Hostile	Uncaring
Controlling	Critical	Rejecting	Affectionless Control
Restrictive	Absent	Withdraw Love	
Coddling	Uncaring	Threatening	
Overinvolved	Neglectful	Controlling	
Warm	Affectionless Control		

abuse at the hands of their parents, they are at increased risk of becoming involved in bullying at school.

TRANSLATING RESEARCH INTO PRACTICE: IMPLICATIONS FOR BULLYING PREVENTION AND INTERVENTION PROGRAMS

Research examining parents and families of bullies, victims, and bully-victims finds behaviors within the families which may predispose children to involvement in bullying. Therefore, it is likely that the most successful intervention and treatment programs would involve not only the child, but also the parents and siblings. Thus, future research examining the inclusion of family members in bully prevention programs would be invaluable.

Additionally, it may benefit educators to be mindful of the family environment when attempting to modify the problematic behavior of their students. Thus, school counselors might find that helping the bully *and* his or her parents find more appropriate outlets for their power needs will decrease the child's level of aggression toward peers and siblings. Also, teaching the parents to use alternative (non-violent) forms of punishment and to model non-violent problem solving techniques will in turn teach the bully and his or her siblings to handle discomfort without aggression. Similarly, helping the parents recognize the inappropriateness of their children's aggressive behaviors may enable them to actively discourage bullying by their children both at school and at home. Overall, it is expected that changing the aggressive and power-focused climate of the family will result in changes in the bully's interactions with siblings and peers.

Similarly, a change in the family environment of male victims may help the victim stand up for himself when faced with conflict. School counselors and teachers might find it beneficial to encourage mothers of male victims to allow more risk-taking and autonomous behaviors in their sons. At the same time, helping the father to develop a closer and less critical relationship with the son will better enable the male victim to learn healthier ways to handle conflict with peers and may encourage the child to become more independent. Counselors will also need to ensure that siblings are not enabling the male victim to remain isolated by serving as their only friend. While sibling warmth is important, counselors should be careful to ensure that siblings allow and even encourage the victim to take chances with developing new friendships. In addition to involving the parents and siblings in the male victim's treatment, it would be beneficial for teachers and counselors to help the male victim learn to respond to bullying in a more controlled and less emotional manner. Responding to teasing and harassment in a calm, unemotional manner will remove some of the fodder that fuels the bully's behavior.

Similar interventions might be used with bully-victims and female victims. In both groups of children we may see emotional abuse as well as little warmth and open hostility expressed by the parents toward the children. Counselors might find it beneficial to help the parents become more nurturing and accepting of their children while also teaching them to handle their children's misbehavior with more consistent and appropriate consequences. Also, assessing and treating symptoms of psychological distress in the victim and bully-victim will be vital. As with the male victim, helping the female victim and bully-victim face harassment without becoming overly emotional will remove at least some of the reinforcement the bully receives from victimizing his or her peers.

Finally, counselors and teachers should be aware that children involved in bullying, regardless of gender or whether they are bullies, victims, or bully-victims, are more likely than their peers to be victims of child abuse. If it is suspected that abuse is occurring, local social services agencies will need to be involved. Additionally, intervention by mental health professionals trained specifically in the treatment of child abuse will be important.

REFERENCES

Ahmed, E., & Braithwaite, V. (2004). "What me ashamed?" Shame management and school bullying. *Journal of Research in Crime and Delinquency, 41*, 269–294.

Baldry, A.C. (2003). Bullying in schools and exposure to domestic violence. *Child Abuse and Neglect, 27*, 713–732.

Baldry, A. C., & Farrington, D.P. (1998). Parenting influences on bullying and victimisation. *Criminal and Legal Psychology, 3*, 237–254.

Baldry, A.C., & Farrington, D.P. (2000). Bullies and delinquents: Personal characteristics and parental styles. *Journal of Community and Applied Social Psychology, 10*, 17–31.

Baldry, A.C., & Winkel, F.W. (2004). Mental and physical health of Italian youngsters directly and indirectly victimized at school and at home. *International Journal of Forensic Mental Health, 3*, 77–91.

Bank, L., Patterson, G.R., & Reid, J.B. (1996). Negative sibling interaction patterns as predictors of later adjustment problems in adolescent and young adult males. In G.H. Brody (Ed.), *Sibling relationships: Their causes and consequences* (pp. 197–229). Norwood, NJ: Ablex.

Berdondini, L., & Smith, P.K. (1996). Cohesion and power in the families of children involved in bully/victim problems at school: An Italian replication. *Journal of Family Therapy, 18*, 99–102.

Berndt, D.J., & Bulleit, T.N. (1985). Effects of sibling relationships on preschoolers' behavior at home and at school. *Developmental Psychology, 21*, 761–767.

Bernstein, J.Y., & Watson, M.W. (1997). Children who are targets of bullying: A victim pattern. *Journal of Interpersonal Violence, 12*, 483–498.

Bowers, L., Smith, P.K., & Binney, V. (1994). Perceived family relationships of bullies, victims and bully/victims in middle childhood. *Journal of Social and Personal Relationships, 11*, 215–232.

Chan, J.H.F. (2006). Systematic patterns in bullying and victimization. *School Psychology International, 27*, 352–369.

Cicchetti, D., & Lynch, M. (1995). Failures in the expectable environment and their impact on individual development: The case of child maltreatment. In D. Cicchetti & D.J. Cohen (Eds.), *Developmental psychopathology: Vol. 2. Risk, disorder and adaptation* (pp. 32–71). New York, NY: Wiley.

Connolly, I., & O'Moore, M. (2003). Personality and family relations of children who bully. *Personality and Individual Differences, 35*, 559–567.

Curtner-Smith, M.E., Culp, A.M., Culp, R., Scheib, C., Owen, K., Tilley, A., Murphy, M., Parkman, L., & Coleman, P.W. (2006). Mothers' parenting and young economically disadvantaged children's relational and overt bullying. *Journal of Child and Family Studies, 15*, 181–193.

Duncan, R.D. (1999a). Maltreatment by parents and peers: The relationship between child abuse, bully victimization and psychological distress. *Child Maltreatment, 4*, 45–55.

Duncan, R.D. (1999b). Peer and sibling aggression: An investigation of intra- and extra-familial bullying. *Journal of Interpersonal Violence, 14*, 871–886.

Dussich, J.P.J., & Maekoya, C. (2007). Physical child harm and bullying-related behaviors: A comparative study in Japan, South Africa, and the United States. *International Journal of Offender Therapy and Comparative Criminology, 51*, 495–509.

Espelage, D.L., Bosworth, K., & Simon, T.R. (2000). Examining the social context of bullying behaviors in early adolescence. *Journal of Counseling and Development, 78*, 326–333.

Farrington, D.P. (1993). Understanding and preventing bullying. In M. Tonry, & N. Morris (Eds.), *Crime and justice: An annual review of research* (Vol. 17). Chicago: University of Chicago Press.

Finkelhor, D., & Browne, A. (1985). The traumatic impact of child sexual abuse: A conceptualization. *American Journal of Orthopsychiatry, 55*, 530–541.

Finnegan, R.A., Hodges, E.V.E., & Perry, D.G. (1998). Victimization by peers: Associations with children's reports of mother-child interaction. *Journal of Personality and Social Psychology, 75*, 1076–1086.

Flouri, E. & Buchanan, A. (2002). Life satisfaction in teenage boys: The moderating role of father involvement and bullying. *Aggressive Behavior, 28*, 126–133.

Flouri, E., & Buchanan, A. (2003). The role of mother involvement and father involvement in adolescent bullying behavior. *Journal of Interpersonal Violence, 18,* 634–644.

Fosse, G.K., & Holen, A. (2002). Childhood environment of adult psychiatric outpatients in Norway having been bullied in school. *Child Abuse & Neglect, 26,* 129–137.

Gelles, R.J., & Straus, M.A. (1988). *Intimate violence.* New York, NY: Simon and Schuster.

George, C., & Main, M. (1979). Social interactions of young abused children: Approach, avoidance, and aggression. *Child Development, 50,* 306–318.

Georgiou, S. (2008a). Parental Style and child bullying and victimization experiences at school. *Social Psychology of Education, 11,* 213–227.

Georgiou, S.N. (2008b). Bullying and victimization at school: The role of mothers. *British Journal of Educational Psychology, 78,* 109–125.

Holt, M.K., Finkelhor, D., & Kaufman Kantor, G. (2007). Multiple victimization experiences of urban elementary school students: Associations with psychosocial functioning and academic performance. *Child Abuse and Neglect, 31,* 503–515.

Holt, M.K., Kaufman Kantor, G., & Finkelhor, D. (2009). Parent/child concordance about bullying involvement and family characteristics related to bullying and peer victimization. *Journal of School Violence, 8,* 42–63.

Howes, C., & Eldredge, R. (1985). Responses of abused, neglected, and non-maltreated children to the behaviors of their peers. *Journal of Applied Developmental Psychology, 6,* 261–270.

Ikemoto, R. (2009). Family characteristics of bully victims: A cross-cultural examination of Americans and Japanese. Unpublished master's thesis. Murray State University, Murray, KY.

Jeynes, W.H. (2008). Effects of parental involvement on experiences of discrimination and bullying. *Marriage and Family Review, 43,* 255–268.

Ladd, G.W., & Ladd, B.K. (1998). Parenting behaviors and parent-child relationships: Correlates of peer victimization in kindergarten. *Developmental Psychology, 34,* 1450–1458.

Lockwood, R.L., Kitzmann, K.M., & Cohen, R. (2001). The impact of sibling warmth and conflict on children's social competence with peers. *Child Study Journal, 31,* 47–69.

Ma, X. (2001). Bullying and being bullied: To what extent are bullies also victims? *American Educational Research Journal, 38,* 351–370.

MacDonald, K., & Parke, R.D. (1984). Bridging the gap: Parent-child play interaction and peer interactive competence, *Child Development, 55,* 1265–1277.

MacKinnon-Lewis, C., Starnes, R., Volling, B., & Johnson, S. (1997). Perceptions of parenting as predictors of boy's sibling and peer relations. *Developmental Psychology, 33,* 1024–1031.

Main, M., & George, C. (1985). Responses of abused and disadvantaged toddlers to distress in agemates: A study in the day care setting. *Developmental Psychology, 21,* 407–412.

Marini, Z.A., Dane, A.V., Bosacki, S.L., & YLC-CURA (2006). Direct and indirect bully-victims: Differential psychosocial risk factors associated with adolescents involved in bullying and victimization. *Aggressive Behavior, 32,* 551–569.

Nansel, T.R., Overpeck, M., Pilla, R.S., Ruan, W.J., Simons-Morton, B., & Scheidt, P. (2001). Bullying behaviors among U.S. youth: Prevalence and association with psychosocial adjustment. *Journal of the American Medical Association, 285,* 2094–2100.

Olweus, D. (1993a). *Bullying at school.* Cambridge, MA: Blackwell Publishers.

Olweus, D. (1993b). Victimization by peers: Antecedents and long-term consequences. In K.H. Rubin & J.B. Asendorph (Eds.), *Social withdrawal, inhibition, and shyness in childhood* (pp. 315–341). Hillsdale, NJ: Lawrence Erlbaum.

Olweus, D. (1994). Annotation: Bullying at school: Basic facts and effects of a school based intervention program. *Journal of Child Psychology and Psychiatry, 35,* 1171–1190.

Parker, G. (1979). Reported parental characteristics in relation to trait depression and anxiety in a non-clinical group. *Australian and New Zealand Journal of Psychiatry, 13,* 260–264.

Parker, G. (1986). Validating an experimental measure of parental style: The use of a twin sample. *Acta Psychiatrica Scandinavica, 73,* 22–27.

Patterson, G.R. (1984). Siblings: Fellow travelers in coercive family processes. In R. J. Blanchard (Ed.), *Advances in the study of aggression* (pp. 174–213). New York, NY: Academic Press.

Pepler, D., Jiang, D., Craig, W., & Connolly, J. (2008). Developmental trajectories of bullying and associated factors. *Child Development, 79,* 325–338.

Perry, D.G., Hodges, E.V.E., & Egan, S.K. (2001). Determinants of chronic victimization by peers. In J. Juvonen & S. Graham (Eds.) *Peer harassment in schools: The plight of the vulnerable and victimized* (pp. 73–104). New York, NY, Guilford Press.

Perry, D.G., Williard, J.C., & Perry, L.C. (1990). Peers' perceptions of the consequences that victimized children provide aggressors. *Child Development, 61,* 1310–1325.

Putallaz, M. (1987). Maternal behavior and children's sociometric status. *Child Development, 58,* 324–340.

Rigby, K. (1993). School children's perceptions of their families and parents as a function of peer relations. *The Journal of Genetic Psychology, 154,* 501–513.

Rigby, K. (1994). Psychosocial functioning in families of Australian adolescent schoolchildren involved in bully/victim problems. *Journal of Family Therapy, 16,* 173–187.

Rigby, K. (2002). *New Perspectives on Bullying.* Philadelphia, PA: Jessica Kingsley Publishers.

Schwartz, D., Dodge, K.A., & Coie, J.D. (1993). The emergence of chronic peer victimization in boys' play groups. *Child Development, 64,* 1755–1772.

Schwartz, D., Dodge, K.A., Pettit, G.S., & Bates, J.E. (1997). The early socialization of aggressive victims of bullying. *Child Development, 68,* 665–675.

Sharp, S. (1996). Self-esteem, response style and victimization: Possible ways of preventing victimization through parenting and school based training programmes. *School Psychology International, 17,* 347–357.

Shields, A. & Cicchetti, D. (2001). Parental maltreatment and emotion dysregulation as risk factors for bullying and victimization in middle childhood. *Journal of Clinical Child Psychology, 30,* 349–363.

Silove, D., Parker, G., Hadzi-Pavlovic, D., Manicavasagar, V., & Blaszczynski, A. (1991). Parental representations of patients with panic disorder and generalised anxiety disorder. *British Journal of Psychiatry, 159,* 835–841.

Spriggs, A.L., Iannotti, R.J., Nansel, T.R., & Haynie, D.L. (2007) Adolescent bullying involvement and perceived family, peer and school relations: Commonalities and differences across race/ethnicity. *Journal of Adolescent Health, 41,* 283–293.

Stevens, V., De Bourdeaudhuij, I., & Van Oost, P. (2002). Relationship of the family environment to children's involvement in bully/victim problems at school. *Journal of Youth and Adolescence, 31,* 419–428.

Stormshak, E.A., Bellanti, C.J., & Bierman, K.L. (1996). The quality of sibling relationships and the development of social competence and behavioral control in aggressive children. *Developmental Psychology, 32,* 79–89.

Strassberg, Z., Dodge, K.A., Pettit, G.S., & Bates, J.E. (1994). Spanking in the home and children's subsequent aggression toward kindergarten peers. *Development and Psychopathology, 6,* 445–461.

Wolke, D., & Samara, M.M. (2004). Bullied by siblings: Association with peer victimisation and behaviour problems in Israeli lower secondary school children. *Journal of Child Psychology and Psychiatry, 45,* 1015–1029.

16

CONSIDERATIONS WHEN MEASURING OUTCOMES TO ASSESS FOR THE EFFECTIVENESS OF BULLYING- AND AGGRESSION-PREVENTION PROGRAMS IN THE SCHOOLS

STEPHEN S. LEFF, MELANIE A. FREEDMAN, JULIE
P. MACEVOY, AND THOMAS J. POWER

Over the past ten years there has been an increasing emphasis on taking preventative approaches to reduce bullying and victimization in schools (Berger, 2007). In the wake of the horrific school shootings in Columbine and other areas in the United States, it is not surprising that schools have been focusing upon bullying prevention and social skills promotion in order to try to prevent future acts of violence and to create safer and more productive environments for youth (Modzeleski, 2007). A number of bullying prevention programs have been designed to promote children's social skills, empathy and perspective taking skills, and problem-solving skills and have demonstrated some positive effects (Frey, Nolan, Van Schoiack-Edstrom, & Hirschstein, 2005; Leff et al., 2009; Lochman & Wells, 2004). At the same time, many bullying prevention programs that are being implemented across the country still lack empirical support and/or are not currently implemented or evaluated systematically (Leff, Power, Manz, Costigan, & Nabors, 2001; Perepletchikova, Treat, and Kazdin, 2007). Most notably, there is an increasing need to develop, validate, and utilize community responsive outcome measures in order to more successfully monitor how interventions are carried out and received within the schools (Leff, Power, Costigan, & Manz, 2003). This chapter will provide a summary of the most common classes of outcome measures being used to evaluate school-based bullying and aggression prevention programs, and a detailed description of their strengths, limitations, and recommended uses. In addition, the chapter will also discuss the importance of integrity monitoring assessment in bullying prevention programming (Leff, Hoffman, & Gullan, 2009). Finally, the chapter will conclude with a review of several important considerations in assessing outcomes of school-based aggression and/or bullying prevention programming.

DEFINING SCHOOL BULLYING

Prior research on bullying has allowed for a relatively standard definition of this construct (e.g., Nansel & Overpeck, 2003; Rigby, 2002). For instance, bullying is typically defined as a systematic abuse of power, such that there is a power differential utilized (Smith & Sharp, 1994). Peer bullying occurs within the context of a social relationship and when three key criteria are met. First, the bully exhibits behavior directed toward the victim that is designed to hurt or harm the victim physically, socially, or emotionally. Second, this behavior occurs only in situations where the bully has more power than the victim, either physically (i.e., being physically stronger or larger than the victim) or psychologically (i.e., being able to damage the victim's social status). Third, the bullying behavior happens repeatedly over time. This definition of bullying is broad enough to incorporate both physical and relational means of bullying others. In simple terms, bullying can be distinguished from aggression by its repetition and also by its occurrence within a relationship characterized by an imbalance in power.

Much of what we know about school bullying has been drawn from the literature related to physical bullying (i.e., hitting, fighting, kicking). As such, many studies have focused upon better understanding and describing the characteristics and comorbidities associated with the physical manifestations of bullying. However, over the past 15 years, research has more clearly demonstrated that children express their anger toward others in both physical and non-physical ways (see Card, Stucky, Sawalani, & Little, 2008). For example, research has found that while girls only occasionally display physical aggression, they are more likely to use relational aggression, defined as harming others by manipulating or damaging their social standing through gossip or social exclusion (Crick & Grotpeter, 1995).

OVERVIEW OF OUTCOME MEASURES

Much research from the developmental psychology literature has demonstrated that the perpetrators and victims of aggression are at great risk of developing behavioral and emotional adjustment problems and academic deficits (e.g., Berger, 2007). Therefore, it has become much clearer that equipping schools with best practice knowledge on school bullying prevention programs and related outcome assessment measures is crucial. As such, the purpose of this chapter is to review the classes of outcome measures that are most appropriate to use to evaluate the effectiveness of bullying prevention programs. Classes of outcome measures reviewed include student self-report, teacher report, peer sociometric, behavioral observations, and playground and lunchroom supervisor report measures. In addition, integrity monitoring indices were also reviewed given recent research suggesting that prevention programs are generally more successful when they are implemented in a systematic and culturally sensitive manner (Power et al., 2005). Parent report measures of bullying were not reviewed because there are few measures of this type available and because parents are not typically present at school to witness bullying episodes. In addition, we chose not to review nursing logs of injuries or discipline referrals due to their limited utility and lack of standardization (Nelson, Benner, Reid, Epstein, & Currin, 2002). A brief overview of strengths, limitations, and recommended use for each class of measures is provided in Table 16.1.

Table 16.1 Summary of Outcome Measures

Measure	Strengths	Limitations	Recommended Uses
Self-Report Measures	✓ Widely accepted by researchers, educators, and students ✓ Established psychometric properties for some measures ✓ Some measures appear to be sensitive to relational and physical bullying and victimization ✓ Provides unique information about bullying or victimization experience	• Biases in reporting may underestimate rates of bullying and victimization • Administration/data collection may interfere with class time • Using anonymous self-reports makes analyzing change over time difficult • Accuracy and sophistication of use may depend, in part, on child's age and cognitive maturity	➢ To better understand subjective experiences of bully and/or victim ➢ As an outcome measure for universal or indicated interventions (provided that the same children participate at pre- and post-testing)
Teacher Report Measures	✓ Easy to administer, score, interpret ✓ Established psychometrics for many measures ✓ May eliminate parent concerns about children participating in peer report methods	• May be too time consuming to complete on multiple students • May not be sensitive to playground context • May not be sensitive to relational bullying	➢ Can be used to screen out children who are not involved in bullying problems ➢ In conjunction with peer reports to identify aggressive children ➢ As an outcome measure for indicated intervention for physical aggression/bullying
Peer Sociometric Measures (Peer Nominations and Peer Rating Scales)	✓ Widely accepted by researchers ✓ Strong psychometric properties ✓ Sensitive to relational and physical aggression and victimization ✓ Sensitive to all school contexts	• Labor- and time-intensive • Parents, teachers, and institutional review boards may not fully understand or appreciate the reasons for using • Low participation rates may compromise generalizability	➢ Arguably, the best method to identify bullies, aggressors, and victims (physical and relational) ➢ Peer-rating scales can be used as outcome measures for indicated or universal intervention
Behavioral Observations	✓ Can be used in playground or classroom settings ✓ Has been used to document impact of bullying programs ✓ Adequate psychometrics have been established for some systems	• More complicated systems are time- and labor-intensive • May require extensive training of coders • Reactivity issues • Has not been used for relational aggression for elementary or middle school-age children • Requires validation in each new school used in	➢ Can be used as an outcome measure for universal or indicated intervention ➢ Strong method for examining children's play behaviors and/or physical aggression on playground, especially for preschoolers
Playground Supervisor Methods	✓ Feasibility and ease of use ✓ No disruption of classroom learning ✓ Created in partnership with school staff and community members ✓ Sensitive to playground/lunchroom context ✓ Provides school-level data ✓ Focuses upon important school climate variables	• Does not provide data on individual children • More research needed related to relational aggression • Has not been used in many prior studies	➢ Guide decision making when choosing a bullying prevention program ➢ As a supplement to other measures in determining outcome of universal bullying prevention programs

SELF-REPORT MEASURES

Brief Description

Self-report may be the most commonly used method for examining the prevalence of bullying and victimization (Rigby, 2002). Typically, children are provided definitions for bullying or victimization and then asked to rate how often these behaviors occur at school. The most widely known and used self-report measure of bullying is the Bully-Victim Questionnaire (e.g., Olweus, 1993). This questionnaire assesses the frequency of bullying perpetration and victimization across varied school contexts, and what others may do to help with these issues. The original questionnaire has been translated, disseminated, and adapted for use in many countries across the world, including the United States, The Netherlands, Norway, England, and Japan (Smith, Cowie, Olafsson, & Liefooghe, 2002).

Psychometric Properties

Although the Bully-Victim Questionnaire has been used by numerous researchers, nationally and internationally, the psychometric properties of this and related measures are difficult to determine. This is primarily due to the fact that, when the measure is translated into a new language, its psychometric properties need to be re-established in that language and with the new population to which the measure is administered. Oftentimes, information about the psychometric properties of the measures within specific populations is lacking.

Results of psychometric analyses have been reported on several other self-report measures. For example, Ladd and Kochenderfer-Ladd (2002) provided data suggesting that a brief, four-item, self-report measure of victimization had moderate internal consistency (i.e., the items appear to measure the same dimension), was relatively stable across grade, and correlated in the expected directions with indices of psychosocial adjustment (i.e., loneliness and peer rejection). In addition, factor analyses, internal consistency analyses, and correlations with related measures have been reported for a self-report measure of physical and relational aggression (Children's Peer Relations Scale; Crick & Grotpeter, 1995) and for a self-report measure of physical and relational victimization (Social Experience Questionnaire; Crick & Grotpeter, 1996). These latter two measures provide information related to both physical and relational forms of bullying and victimization making them a popular choice by researchers.

Strengths

Much of what we know about bullying and victimization has come from self-report measures, and they are widely accepted by researchers, teachers, and students. Some of these measures appear to be sensitive to relational and physical forms of aggression and victimization (e.g., Crick & Grotpeter, 1995, 1996) and are particularly helpful for a better understanding of the child's own understanding of victimization, especially related to internalizing symptoms such as loneliness and depression (Ladd & Kochenderfer-Ladd, 2002). In addition, self-reports of victimization can provide unique information that may not overlap with other informants' assessments of victimization.

Limitations

There are several broad limitations to using self-report measures. First, although the psychometric properties have been established for some of the measures, they are still questionable and limit the way in which the data may be used. Although the Bully-Victim Questionnaire has been widely disseminated, the fact that different countries and societies apply somewhat different terminology when describing bullying makes cross-national comparisons difficult (Smith et al., 2002). In addition, in many of the larger scale bullying intervention programs (e.g., Olweus, 1993), the self-report measures used as primary outcome measures are completed anonymously. This method protects the confidentiality of the respondent, but it makes it difficult, if not impossible, to compare an individual student's responses before and after an intervention. As a result, self-report measures completed anonymously may not be helpful if one is interested in the effects of a targeted intervention on a given student's behavior. They may, however, have value in determining the effectiveness of a universal intervention, assuming the same group of children completes the measure at pre- and post-testing.

Relying on children to be primary informants introduces another limitation. For example, the accuracy and sophistication of children's responses on these measures are, in part, related to children's age and cognitive maturity. Research suggests that younger children may define bullying more broadly than older children (Monks & Smith, 2006). As a result, younger children completing self-report measures may be less discriminating as to what constitutes bullying behavior than older children. It is also possible that children may confuse "bullying" with "aggression" when responding to questionnaires (Rigby, 2002). Both of these issues may independently influence the construct validity of the measure; the respondents (children) may apply a definition of bullying that is different from the one intended by the researchers. In addition, bullies may minimize their involvement in bullying episodes (e.g., Craig & Pepler, 1997; Smith & Sharp, 1994), and victims may not wish to recall an incident of victimization if it was embarrassing or upsetting for them (Ladd & Kochenderfer-Ladd, 2002). Further, there may be social pressures against children reporting instances of victimization, as victims may fear retribution if they report the bullying (Newman & Murray, 2005).

Future Directions

Although self-report measures are arguably the most commonly used outcome measures, there are still many ways in which this methodology can be strengthened and improved. First, it is recommended that researchers partner with students to design, adapt, and modify existing self-report measures (e.g., Leff et al., 2006), so that these measures reflect the concerns of children and are worded in a manner that is developmentally appropriate. Second, it is suggested that practitioners train children on how to complete self-report surveys, helping to ensure that the measures employed are well understood and completed in an appropriate manner by children.

Some researchers have developed innovative ways in which to address limitations of self-report measures. One example is the use of field diaries as a way of gathering students' perspectives on bullying and victimization episodes immediately after a recess period, or in places where direct observations are not feasible, such as in bathrooms and locker rooms (see Pellegrini, 2001). This method may provide more objective reporting that is not impaired by selective memory, and may help researchers to better understand contextual factors related to bullying and victimization.

TEACHER REPORT MEASURES

Brief Description

Teacher report measures of behavior problems are often used in both school- and clinic-based settings to help with educational planning and intervention monitoring. Such measures vary considerably in their length and comprehensiveness. For instance, several studies have utilized measures such as the Child Behavior Checklist–Teacher Report Form (TRF; Achenbach, 1991) and the Behavior Assessment System for Children (BASC; Reynolds & Kamphaus, 1991) to assess children's overall externalizing and internalizing behavioral functioning across multiple domains (e.g., Kamphaus, Huberty, DiStefano, & Petoskey, 1997; McConaughy & Achenbach, 1996). In addition, several researchers have designed teacher measures focused specifically on aggression or bullying (e.g., Crick, 1996; Huesmann, Eron, Guerra, & Crawshaw, 1994). An example of the latter is the Children's Social Behavior Questionnaire (CSB; Crick, 1996), which requests teachers to rate a given student's levels of overt aggression, relational aggression, and prosocial behaviors. Several teacher report measures have also been utilized to assess the classroom social climate that impacts student behavior and classroom learning (e.g., Thomas & Bierman, 2006). For instance, the Teacher Observation of Classroom Adaptation-Revised (TOCA-R) asks teachers to rate each student on the frequency with which they exhibit a variety of behaviors indicative of aggression, poor peer relations, and poor academic focus, which can then be averaged across students to estimate an overall classroom climate score (Barth, Dunlap, Dane, Lochman, & Wells, 2004).

Psychometric Properties

Some of the most commonly used and broadest teacher report measures (e.g., BASC and TRF) have demonstrated strong psychometric properties (i.e., reliability and validity) across many studies (e.g., Kamphaus et al., 1997; McConaughy & Achenbach, 1996). In addition, brief teacher report measures examining specifically aggression, such as the CSB, have demonstrated adequate psychometric properties across several studies (i.e., factor analyses and internal consistency analyses; Crick, 1996; Rys & Bear, 1997). Teacher report measures have been found to correlate moderately with peer nominations and behavioral observation systems (e.g., Achenbach, McConaughy, & Howell, 1987; Rys & Bear, 1997).

Strengths

Teacher report measures are generally easy to administer, score, and interpret. Using teacher report measures of aggression and bullying is consistent with school practice as teachers regularly rate children's academic performance and competence. Teacher report measures may also eliminate parents' concerns about children participating in peer sociometric procedures (Leff, Kupersmidt, Patterson, & Power, 1999). Recent research by Cullerton-Sen and Crick (2005) suggest that teacher reports may significantly predict students' level of social and emotional adjustment beyond information obtained solely from peer and self-reports.

Brief teacher report measures may have their greatest use as an initial step in a multiple gating procedure to screen out children who are not the perpetrator or victim of bullying (Leff et al., 1999). The more in-depth measures (i.e., peer sociometric measures, behavioral observations, or more comprehensive teacher report measures) can then be used with the remaining children to identify those at highest risk for being a bully or victim.

Limitations

Teacher report measures have some limitations that may make their use somewhat problematic as a sole outcome measure for a bullying or aggression prevention program. Generally, they are not particularly sensitive to behaviors in the playground setting or to more subtle forms of aggression, which limits both their contexts of use and the type of information they provide. In general, it is unclear how well teachers understand and are concerned by the more subtle forms of aggression and bullying. In addition, the most commonly used teacher report measures are quite lengthy, making it difficult for busy teachers to find time to rate multiple students' behaviors. Even brief teacher report measures (e.g., 17-item CSB) may be too time-consuming for teachers to complete on multiple students. Finally, some research has also demonstrated that teacher and self-report measures may vary considerably depending upon multiple factors (e.g., settings in which the behavior occurs, the age and cognitive maturity of the student, how covert the behavior being examined is; whether the teacher is privy to this information; see Smith, 2004). Thus, it is important to keep in mind that teacher report measures may sometimes provide different though complementary information to self-report measures.

Future Directions

Several innovative techniques can be used to improve the accuracy of teacher reports in identifying bullies and victims. Huesmann and colleagues (1994) developed a procedure whereby they ask teachers to estimate peer ratings of aggression (as opposed to asking teachers for their own opinions). Having teachers take the perspective of peers may be a feasible alternative to using the more labor- and time-intensive peer sociometric procedures in some situations for identifying peer aggressors and victims. Second, Leff and colleagues have found that including reports from multiple teachers (e.g., homeroom teacher plus related arts teachers) greatly increases the correspondence between peer and teacher reports (Leff et al., 1999). Third, it is important to focus additional research on gaining a better understanding of teachers' perceptions of relational bullying. Knowing how teachers view relational bullying will help researchers and professionals to determine the utility of teacher reports for assessing relational aggression. Finally, more research on the development of teacher report measures regarding the social climate of their classrooms would be helpful and may have implications for intervention.

PEER SOCIOMETRIC MEASURES

Brief Description

Systematic research using sociometric techniques to examine the relationship between children's peer acceptance and their social behavior dates back to the 1930s. In general, there are two sociometric techniques that are used to assess peer acceptance. One technique, the nomination method, typically involves asking children to nominate the three peers in their class whom they like most and the three peers whom they like least (Coie, Dodge, & Coppotelli, 1982). Based on the average number of each type of vote that a child receives, he or she is then classified into one of five status groups: popular, average, rejected, neglected, and controversial. The other technique, the rating-scale method, involves asking children to rate each of their classmates on a Likert scale in response to a question such as, "How much do you like to play with this child?" (e.g., Singleton & Asher, 1977). The average rating each child receives from all classmates is calculated and children are then classified as high-accepted, average-accepted, or low-accepted. These same techniques have also been used in many studies to identify children who exhibit high levels of behavioral difficulties (e.g., relational and physical aggression; see Crick & Grotpeter, 1995).

Psychometric Properties

The psychometric strength of peer sociometric measures has been clearly documented across a large number of studies. These measures have high test–retest reliability (e.g., Pekarik, Prinz, Liebert, Weintraub, & Neale, 1976), and have shown the sociometric categories of popular- and rejected-status to be particularly stable over time (e.g., Zettergren, 2007) and across context (Coie & Kupersmidt, 1983). In addition, Terry (2000) has found that brief peer nomination procedures have extremely high inter-rater consensus reliability—an index of agreement between all peer raters in their rating of each particular classmate.

Importantly, sociometric measures have also shown strong concurrent and predictive validity (Terry & Coie, 1991). For example, children who are well-liked according to sociometric indices are usually friendly and do well academically and athletically (see Cillessen & Mayeux, 2004). In contrast, children who are sociometrically rejected by their peers tend to exhibit elevated levels of aggressive or withdrawn behavior. Furthermore, sociometric ratings of peer acceptance during childhood predict school dropout, delinquency, job performance, and mental health difficulties later in life (Parker & Asher, 1987).

Strengths

Perhaps the greatest strength of peer sociometric measures lies in their ability to identify youth at risk for concurrent and future adjustment problems. Additionally, these measures can be particularly helpful in identifying subtle social behaviors that may not be easily seen by parents and teachers, such as relational aggression. Peer sociometric measures have also often been used in conjunction with teacher report measures for identifying at-risk children for research and intervention efforts (e.g., Conduct Problems Prevention Research Group, 1999). Finally, a particular strength of continuous measures of peer acceptance and behavioral difficulties (but not of the categorical, nomination measures) is that they can be used in multilevel statistical modeling (Jiang & Cillessen, 2005).

Limitations

Despite the considerable strengths inherent in the use of peer sociometric techniques, these measures present a few limitations. First, a weakness that is particular to the categorical approach to sociometric assessment is that children who do not fall into one of the pre-determined status groups are typically dropped from analyses (see DeRosier &

Thomas, 2005). A continuous approach, however, alleviates this problem. In addition, as peer nomination methods are relative rating measures, they always categorize some children as exhibiting problematic behaviors. This fact may limit the use of peer nomination methods for determining the effectiveness of school-level bullying or aggression prevention programs. For example, a child's social behavior may improve dramatically following an intervention. However, if the child is still viewed as having more of a problem than their peers, the child's sociometric standing on this relative rating measure may not change. In addition, because peer sociometric measures are relatively stable over time, they may not be sensitive to intervention effects.

Another limitation of peer sociometric measures is that although many researchers have used this methodology for identifying high-risk children in the schools, it can be extremely labor-intensive and time-consuming. This method necessitates involving all children in a class (and/or grade), which typically requires that time be set aside by the classroom teacher for the peer sociometric procedure to be group-administered to all participating students. Finally, the data entry and analyses associated with peer sociometric measures are more complex and time-consuming than evaluating teacher or self-report questionnaires.

Although research has shown no deleterious effects upon children when completing sociometric measures (e.g., Mayeux, Underwood, & Risser, 2007), it should also be noted that some parents and school staff may be uncomfortable with the idea of having children say which of their peers they like least or having them identify peers who exhibit high levels of negative behavior. Some parents and school staff may find the continuous, rating-scale approach more palatable because they do not require children to single out peers (Asher & Dodge, 1986). Regardless of whether a categorical or continuous approach is employed, to successfully implement a peer sociometric method in a school, the researcher is encouraged to explain, thoroughly and clearly, the procedure to children, parents, teachers, and institutional review boards. Concerns about the use of peer sociometric measures may also translate into relatively low participation rates (i.e., 50% to 60%), which may affect the generalizability of the procedure (Hamilton, Fuchs, Fuchs, & Roberts, 2000). Recent research indicates that when participation rates are lower than 75%, standard peer nomination procedures may not be able to provide accurate estimates of children's social standing within the classroom or grade (Hamilton et al., 2000). One approach to address this issue is the use of unlimited peer nominations, in which children are not restricted to selecting only a certain number of their peers for each item. Unlimited peer nominations demonstrate strong psychometric properties and appear to be more robust for low participation rates than the standard limited peer nomination (Terry, 2000).

Future Directions

As described above, sociometric measures have significant clinical utility for identifying children at risk for future adjustment problems. However, some school districts and Institutional Review Boards are concerned by the use of sociometric measures because they perceive potential negative repercussions from using these methods, despite research to show that there are no such deleterious effects. It will therefore be important for researchers to develop measures that are not only strong predictors of social functioning and adjustment, but also viewed as acceptable for use with children.

BEHAVIORAL OBSERVATIONS

Brief Description

Observational systems allow for the coding of social behaviors in a relatively objective way that is not impacted by prior relationships or pre-existing reputations. Behavioral observation systems range considerably in breadth and complexity. For example, some systems are relatively straightforward and provide basic information on the frequency with which different behaviors occur. In contrast, other observation systems are designed to better understand the ways in which children engage in social interactions, and the antecedents and consequences of different peer-directed behaviors.

Psychometric Properties

Some observation systems have demonstrated adequate reliability and precision in examining children's play behaviors (see Leff & Lakin, 2005 for a review of these systems), and others in understanding classroom climate and/or process variables underlying classroom climate (Fish & Dane, 2000; La Paro, Pianta, & Stuhlman, 2004). However, each specific observational system must be examined for reliability and cultural-relevance within a specific population of interest (i.e., are the behavioral codes meaningful and can coders use the system to categorize behaviors consistently within each context?). With appropriate and systematic training, observers are able to use observation rating systems to make important distinctions between behaviors, such as rough, vigorous play versus aggressive behaviors (e.g., Smith & Hunter, 1992) or bullying versus non-bullying aggression (Frey, Hirschstein, Edstrom, & Snell, 2009). Further, this methodology can be used to examine children's play and aggressive behaviors in various contexts. For example, it can be used in contrived laboratory situations in which researchers retain much experimental control, in naturalistic settings that can be recorded live, and in settings using sophisticated audio- and video-recording systems (see Leff & Lakin, 2005 for a review). Increasingly, there are also several broader-based behavioral observation systems that allow a better understanding of the classroom social climate that may impact on both academic learning and students' social behaviors (Fish & Dane, 2000; LaParo et al., 2004) and/or various unstructured school settings (hallways, cafeterias, play areas; Cushing, Horner, & Barrier, 2003; Frey et al., 2009).

Strengths

A number of researchers have used behavioral observation systems as a means to identify and/or better understand children who engage in aggression, bullying, and victimization (see Leff & Lakin, 2005). In particular, several researchers have focused their observational research on developing systems to examine these behaviors on the school playground (e.g., Frey et al., 2009; Leff, Costigan, & Power, 2004; McNeilly-Choque, Hart, Robinson, Nelson, & Olsen, 1996; Pepler & Craig, 1995). Further, research has successfully employed behavioral observation methodologies to determine whether children's behavior and/or school climate improves following an intervention (e.g., Conduct Problems Prevention Research Group, 1999; Frey et al., 2009; Leff et al., 2004).

Limitations

Although behavioral systems designed to record discrete child behaviors are relatively easy to use and evaluate, the more complicated observation systems investigating interactional patterns are usually time- and labor-intensive to design, adapt, and implement. In addition, these more complicated systems typically require extensive training of coders in order to ensure adequate inter-rater reliability (see Leff & Lakin, 2005). Further, observational systems often require a considerable baseline period during which data is not analyzed, as children become comfortable with the system and reactivity is minimized. Finally, time needs to be spent to ensure that the behaviors targeted are viewed as meaningful by school staff, community members, and/or students (Leff et al., 2004).

It is unclear how well any of the methodologies can be used to identify the more subtle forms of aggression, such as relational aggression. For example, to accurately code relationally aggressive behaviors, it is necessary to see each child's facial and body expressions, hear their ongoing conversation, and understand the particular social context in which the behavior occurs. While several researchers have developed observational systems to examine preschoolers' relationally aggressive actions (McNeilly-Choque et al., 1996; Ostrov & Keating, 2004), similar systems have not yet been fully developed and validated for children of elementary and middle school age.

The challenge of accurately coding low-base rate behaviors (e.g., relational aggression) can also make an observational system difficult to utilize and ultimately to validate. For instance, it is necessary to conduct a number of observations in order to see a child exhibit a full range of behaviors, especially those of low frequency (Leff & Lakin, 2005).

Future Directions

Future research is needed in establishing systems that can reliably code children's naturally occurring relationally aggressive behaviors across contexts. This will be especially important in better understanding girls' bullying and victimization episodes. Perhaps techniques such as the use of microphones and video-recording systems from remote locations of the playground during recess may help advance our knowledge in this important area (Pepler & Craig, 1995). In addition, more research is needed to develop classroom-based observation systems to better understand classroom climate and teacher–student relationships that can greatly impact students' social and behavioral competence.

PLAYGROUND AND LUNCHROOM SUPERVISOR MEASURES

Brief Description

In many schools, teachers do not supervise children in the unstructured school settings (i.e., during lunch and recess periods). Rather, lunchtime supervisors, who are often paraprofessionals, parents, and/or community members, oversee children's lunchroom and playground behavior (Leff et al., 2004; McCurdy, Lannie, & Barnabas, 2009). Surprisingly, few, if any, measures have been designed to assess these individuals' perspective, despite the important roles they serve related to children's peer relationships. Leff and colleagues have partnered with lunchtime supervisors to combine theory and prior empirical research with extensive feedback from key stakeholders to design the Playground and Lunchroom Climate Questionnaire (PLCQ; Leff et al., 2003). The PLCQ is a 23-item questionnaire that assesses playground and lunchroom supervisors' perceived communication skills, the availability and appropriateness of play activities during recess, the use of clear and consistent rules in the lunchroom and on the playground, and the frequency and appropriateness of adult supervision across these settings.

Psychometric Properties

Playground and lunchroom personnel from seven urban elementary schools and two community members worked with the research team to ensure that each item on the questionnaire measured important aspects of playground and lunchroom climate, and that items and response scales were worded in a developmentally appropriate and culturally sensitive manner (Leff et al., 2003). Then, 122 school staff who worked in the lunchroom and playground setting from 17 urban schools (12 elementary schools, 3 kindergarten to 8th grade schools, and 2 middle schools) completed the finalized versions of the PLCQ as part of a series of bullying prevention workshops. Results of factor analyses of the PLCQ revealed that there are two main dimensions measured by the questionnaire: (1) Structure for Activities and Monitoring (ten items including "There are many games for children to play on the playground," "There are enough staff to monitor children on the playground") and (2) Staff Collaboration (nine items including "Staff members work well together and as a team"). These dimensions were internally consistent and stable over a three-week interval (see Leff et al., 2003 for details). Finally, initial results suggest that these two dimensions are sensitive to playground intervention effects (Nabors, Leff, & Power, 2004).

Strengths

A strength of the PLCQ measure is that it is sensitive to the dynamics that occur within the playground and lunchroom settings. In addition, this measure was designed through partnerships with diverse school staff and community members. These collaborations helped to ensure that the measure was able to provide valuable information about often neglected school climate and contextual variables that may contribute to bullying behaviors. Another strength of this measure is that it is brief, can be administered to a group within about ten minutes, and does not disrupt class time. Measures such as the PLCQ have the potential for helping schools to conduct a thorough needs assessment that can be used to guide intervention planning. In addition, this type of measure can be used to provide school-level data at multiple time periods during the implementation of bullying programs.

Limitations

A measure such as the PLCQ is not designed to provide information about specific at-risk children. Thus, this measure would not be recommended to track student outcomes for a selective/indicated intervention program (e.g., with high-risk youth). Similar to teacher report indices, more research is also needed to determine playground/lunchroom supervisors' perceptions of relational aggression.

Future Directions

In general, the development of playground and lunchroom supervisor measures that are constructed through active partnership with school and community members is a fruitful area for research (Leff et al., 2004; McCurdy et al., 2009). Given the increasing focus upon the playground and/or lunchroom setting as a key intervention setting within the schools (Leff et al., 2004; McCurdy et al., 2009), it will be extremely important to better capitalize on the perspective of playground and lunchroom supervisors. More specifically, how these individuals view different types of bullying behaviors (i.e., physical versus relational), which strategies they believe are most successful across the unstructured school contexts, and how their ideas can be better incorporated into bullying prevention efforts will be fruitful future directions to explore.

TRANSLATING RESEARCH INTO PRACTICE: IMPLICATIONS FOR BULLYING PREVENTION AND INTERVENTION PROGRAMMING

Using Community Partnership-Based Methods

Developing and validating measures for use in schools typically is a process directed primarily by experts from the research community (Power et al., 2005). The advantage of an expert-driven approach to measure development is that dimensions of the scale and items pertaining to each dimension are likely to relate closely with theoretically based and empirically supported psychological constructs. A notable limitation to this approach is that the structure and content of measures may be lacking in relevance to participants in the community (i.e., lacking in ecological validity). Low levels of ecological validity can have an effect on the construct validity of a measure in that items may convey a different meaning to participants than that which was intended by researchers. Further, low levels of ecological validity may lead to poor participant response rates to measures, which can have an effect on the generalizability of findings.

Establishing partnerships among researchers and participants in the research process (e.g., educators, students, parents, community members) can be an effective way of improving the validity, feasibility, and acceptability of measures used to evaluate program effectiveness. A partnership-based approach to measurement development is based upon principles of participatory action research (PAR; Nastasi et al., 2000), and is distinguished from other scientific models by several key features. First, a strong emphasis is placed upon how the researcher can form a working alliance with key stakeholders to foster collective ownership of the process (Nastasi et al., 2000). Second, the partnership process involves the integration of theory and empirical research with ideas generated by key stakeholders to delineate dimensions of the measure, identify items pertaining to each dimension, and refine item content (e.g., Leff et al., 2006; Power, Dombrowski, Watkins, Mautone, & Eagle, 2007). Third, measurement development within the framework of a partnership-based approach is a recursive process consisting of multiple iterations that involves input from participants and researchers in developing and refining the measures. The methodology employed in a partnership-based approach is not only rigorous, but is also responsive to the needs of the school and community. As a result, a partnership-based model is more likely to result in higher levels of sustainability and institutionalization than an approach relying more on expert-driven methods (Nastasi et al., 2000). An example of this approach is described by Leff and colleagues (2006);

this research team entered into a partnership with educators and students from schools situated in a low-income, urban district to develop and refine a cartoon-based measure of hostile attribution bias adapted from a measure originally developed by Crick (1995). Through the iterative process of measure development, Leff and colleagues developed a cartoon measure that was engaging for student participants, depicted characters in cartoons in a manner that was developmentally appropriate and acceptable to the children, ensured that the cartoons corresponded closely to the written items developed by Crick (1995), and demonstrated that respondents were responding reliably to the items. By so doing, these researchers were able to develop a measure that had strong construct and ecological validity, thereby meeting both the rigorous standards of the research community and the expectations of the school community.

Using Multimethod, Multi-Informant Outcome Measures

Although each set of measures reviewed has potential strengths and limitations, no single method is sufficient for assessing the process and outcomes of bullying prevention programs. A combination of measurement methods is needed to assess program effectiveness and identify strategies for improving outcomes. Researchers and interventionists are encouraged to partner with school administrators to determine which combination of methods will provide the most comprehensive, valid, and feasible approach to assessment. In addition, it is important for researchers and practitioners to ensure assessment strategies are relevant and appropriate for cultural groups served by the school (Leff et al., 2001).

Including Integrity Monitoring Procedures

Treatment integrity is traditionally defined as the provision of an intervention as intended (see Leff et al., 2009). In other words, integrity refers to the degree to which a therapist or other treatment provider adheres to the protocol and delivers core or critical content of an intervention. This type of *procedural* or *content* integrity has long been considered the hallmark feature of treatment integrity (Schlosser, 2002). However, the available literature has recently expanded the integrity construct to include other important aspects that capture the *process* of treatment. For example, the skill and competence of a therapist, including the therapist's ability to effectively deliver treatment components, respond appropriately to questions, engage participants in session activities, and address significant behavioral challenges exhibited by participants are important areas to consider when delivering bullying prevention programs (see Gullan, Feinberg, Freedman, Jawad, & Leff, 2009; Power et al., 2005). In school-based intervention work, including all of these components in the definition of treatment integrity captures not only what is covered by the intervention (e.g. key content) but also how well it is covered and received (e.g., process-oriented variables).

Researchers have emphasized the importance of examining the relationship between treatment integrity and therapeutic outcomes, suggesting that evaluating integrity is clearly required before inferences pertaining to treatment effectiveness and mechanisms of change can be drawn (Leff et al., 2009; Schlosser, 2002). Despite its value, it is surprising that few therapeutic outcome studies have documented indices of treatment integrity. For example, Perepletchikova and colleagues (2007) reported that fewer than 4% of the reviewed psychotherapy outcome studies applied treatment integrity procedures.

Nonetheless, the systematic monitoring of treatment integrity is important in school-based outcome research for several reasons. First, integrity monitoring informs researchers about how well critical intervention components are covered. If researchers assess that key session components were excluded or poorly implemented, they can offer alternative explanations for a lack of desired outcome. Consistently evaluating integrity prevents the erroneous attribution that non-significant findings are due to overall study design or conceptualization problems (Dane & Schneider, 1998). Second, the inclusion of monitoring procedures permits the comparison of therapists who provide the intervention at different sites or time periods. This addresses the possibility that differences in treatment outcomes depend upon site or seasonal effects. Third, monitoring both *procedural-* and *process-*oriented integrity bolsters the identification of potential obstacles to successful implementation. For these reasons we suggest that researchers consider how they can determine whether crucial program components are implemented (procedural integrity) and how they are received by participants (process integrity) when determining outcome assessment measures for use with aggression and/or bullying prevention programs (see Gullan et al., 2009).

Selecting Measures and Partnering with School Staff

In order to determine which sets of measures might be most appropriate for use within a particular school, it is suggested that researchers and practitioners consider the following questions:

1. What particular behaviors are being targeted by the bullying intervention (e.g., rough, physical play on the playground, relational bullying in the lunchroom, etc.)?
2. What intervention processes should be assessed to evaluate the integrity of treatment implementation?
3. What measurement methods have been developed and are available to assess each intervention process and target behavior?
4. To what extent are the available methods developmentally appropriate and culturally responsive?
5. Which measurement methods need to be adapted to make them more feasible, acceptable, and culturally relevant?
6. Which school and community stakeholders ought to be engaged in the process of adapting measures to make them relevant for the project?
7. What procedures are needed to insure a high rate of response at each of the measurement points (e.g., baseline, mid-treatment, post-treatment, follow up) to evaluate outcomes?

Challenges for the Future

While there have been a number of recent advances in the field of bullying prevention programming and in the development of related outcome measures over the past few years, there also remain a number of challenges. First, given the high need for quality programming in the area of aggression and bullying prevention and social skills promotion within the schools, it is necessary for researchers to better recognize the importance of providing needed services quickly and efficiently, which do not always align themselves with research goals (e.g., to set up a controlled and systematic study of an intervention and/or outcome assessment measure). While every effort should be taken to match interventions and outcome batteries with the specific needs of particular schools and school districts, the balance between providing a needed service and conducting meaningful research can at times be challenging to negotiate. This is why the authors of the current chapter recommend the use of a partnership-based approach, which often results in a shared vision and goal between researchers, schools, and participants (Leff et al., 2004). Second, researchers interested in using behavioral observational approaches on the playground during school recess to assess for students' behaviors must first ensure that the school has a plan for providing support to students who are repeatedly subjected to aggressive or harmful behaviors that may be observed by coders. It is recommended that researchers talk openly with school officials before conducting playground observations and develop contingency plans, whereby they can be assured of the safety of the students they are observing. For instance, researchers need to be open to abandoning their coding systems in the event that a conflict is not addressed by school support staff. Despite these challenges, observational approaches have the potential to contribute greatly to our knowledge of the impact of bullying prevention programs within the schools.

CONCLUSION

The research base regarding bullying has grown exponentially since Dan Olweus's pioneering intervention research in the late 1970s and early 1980s. However, the field is still developing as researchers are developing and utilizing more sophisticated outcome assessment batteries. Several types of measures have been developed to assist school professionals in monitoring the progress of bullying interventions. It is recommended that practitioners and educators work together to identify a set of measures for determining the effectiveness of school-based bully prevention programs. It is also important that the field moves beyond trying to select the "best method" for assessing intervention outcomes. Instead, the development and validation of integrated multimethod protocols that assess social behavior across multiple contexts and are responsive to the needs of children, families, and schools are critical goals for future research.

REFERENCES

Achenbach, T.M. (1991). *Manual for the teacher's report form & 1991 profile*. Burlington, VT: University of Vermont, Depatment of Psychiatry.

Achenbach, T.M., McConaughy, S.H., & Howell, C.T. (1987). Child/Adolescent behavioral and emotional problems. Implications of crossinformant correlations for situational specificity. *Psychological Bulletin, 101,* 213–232.

Asher, S.R., & Dodge, K.A. (1986). Identifying children who are rejected by their peers. *Developmental Psychology, 22,* 444–449.

Barth, J.M., Dunlap, S.T., Dane, H., Lochman, J.E., & Wells, K.C. (2004). Classroom environment influences on aggression, peer relations, and academic focus. *Journal of School Psychology, 42,* 115–133.

Berger, K.S. (2007). Update on bullying at school: Science forgotten? *Developmental Review, 27,* 90–126.

Card, N.A., Stucky, B.D., Sawalani, G.M., & Little, T.D. (2008). Direct and indirect aggression during childhood and adolescence: A meta-analytic review of gender differences, intercorrelations, and relations to maladjustment. *Child Development, 79,* 1185–1229.

Cillessen, A.H.N., & Mayeux, L. (2004). Sociometric status and peer group behavior: Previous findings and current directions. In K.A. Dodge & J.B. Kupersmidt (Eds.), *Children's peer relations: From development to intervention* (pp. 3–20). Washington, DC: American Psychological Association.

Coie, J.D., & Kupersmidt, J.B. (1983). A behavioral analysis of emerging social status in boys' groups. *Child Development, 54*, 1400–1416.

Coie, J.D., & Dodge, K.A., & Coppotelli, H. (1982). Dimensions and types of social status: A cross-age perspective. *Developmental Psychology, 18*, 557–570.

Conduct Problems Prevention Research Group (1999). Initial impact of the Fast Track Prevention Trial of Conduct Problems: I. The High Risk Sample. *Journal of Consulting and Clinical Psychology, 67*, 631–647.

Craig, W.M., & Pepler, D.J. (1997). Observations of bullying and victimization in the school yard. *Canadian Journal of School Psychology, 13*, 41–59.

Crick, N.R. (1995). Relational aggression: The role of intent attributions, feelings of distress, and provocation type. *Development and Psychopathology, 7*, 313–322.

Crick, N.R. (1996). The role of overt aggression, relational aggression, and prosocial behavior in the prediction of children's future social adjustment. *Child Development, 67*, 2317–2327.

Crick, N.R., & Grotpeter, J.K. (1995). Relational aggression, gender, and social-psychological adjustment. *Child Development, 66*, 710–722.

Crick, N.R., & Grotpeter, J.K. (1996). Children's treatment by peers: Victims of relational and overt aggression. *Development and Psychopathology, 8*, 367–380.

Cullerton-Sen, C., & Crick, N.R. (2005). Understanding the effects of physical and relational victimization: The utility of multiple perspectives in predicting social-emotional adjustment. *School Psychology Review, 34*, 147–160.

Cushing, L.S., Horner, R.H., & Barrier, H. (2003). Validation and congruent validity of a direct observation tool to assess student social climate. *Journal of Positive Behavior Interventions, 5*, 225–237.

Dane, A., & Schneider, B. (1998). Program integrity in primary and early secondary prevention: Are implementation effects out of control? *Clinical Psychology Review, 18*, 23–45.

DeRosier, M.E., & Thomas, J.M. (2005). Strengthening sociometric prediction: Scientific advances in the assessment of children's peer relations. *Child Development, 74*, 1379–1392.

Fish, M.C., & Dane, E. (2000). The Classroom Systems Observation Scale: Development of an instrument to assess classrooms using a systems perspective. *Learning Environments Research, 3*, 67–92.

Frey, K.S., Hirschstein, M.K., Edstrom, L.V., & Snell, J.L. (2009). Observed reductions in school bullying, non-bullying aggression, and destructive bystander behavior: A longitudinal evaluation. *Journal of Educational Psychology, 101*, 466–481.

Frey, K.S., Nolen, S.B., Van Schoiack-Edstrom, L., & Hirschstein, M.K. (2005). Evaluating a school-based social competence program: Linking behavior, goals and beliefs. *Journal of Applied Developmental Psychology, 26*, 171–200.

Gullan, R.L., Feinberg, B.E., Freedman, M.A., Jawad, A., & Leff, S.S. (2009). Using participatory action research to design an intervention integrity system in the urban schools. *School Mental Health, 1*, 118–30.

Hamilton, C., Fuchs, D., Fuchs, L.S., & Roberts, H. (2000). Rates of classroom participation and the validity of sociometry. *School Psychology Review, 29*, 251–266.

Huesmann, L.R., Eron, L.D., Guerra, N.G., & Crawshaw, V.B. (1994). Measuring children's aggression with teachers' predictions of peer nominations. *Psych. Assessment, 6*, 329–336.

Jiang, X.L., & Cillessen, A.H.N. (2005). Stability of continuous measures of sociometric status: A meta-analysis. *Developmental Review, 25*, 1–25.

Kamphaus, R.W., Huberty, C.J., DiStefano, C., & Petoskey, M.D. (1997). A typology of teacher-rated child behavior for a national U.S. sample. *Journal of Abnormal Child Psychology, 25*, 453–463.

Ladd, G.W., & Kochenderfer-Ladd, B. (2002). Identifying victims of peer aggression from early to middle childhood: Analysis of cross-informant data for concordance, estimation of relational adjustment, prevalence of victimization, and characteristics of identified victims. *Psychological Assessment, 14*, 74–96.

La Paro, K., Pianta, R.C., & Stuhlman, M. (2004). The Classroom Assessment Scoring System: Findings from the prekindergarten year. *The Elementary School Journal, 104*, 409–426.

Leff, S.S., & Lakin, R. (2005). Playground-based observation systems: A review and implications for practitioners and researchers. *School Psychology Review, 34*, 475–489.

Leff, S.S., Costigan, T.E., & Power, T.J. (2004). Using participatory-action research to develop a playground-based prevention program. *Journal of School Psychology, 42*, 3–21.

Leff, S.S., Hoffman, J.A., & Gullan, R.L. (2009). Intervention integrity: New paradigms and applications. *School Mental Health, 1*, 103–106.

Leff, S.S., Kupersmidt, J.B., Patterson, C., & Power, T.J. (1999). Factors influencing teacher predictions of peer bullying and victimization. *School Psychology Review, 28*, 505–517.

Leff, S.S., Power, T.J., Costigan, T., & Manz, P.H. (2003). Assessing the climate of the playground and lunchroom: Implications for bullying prevention programming. *School Psychology Review, 32,* 418–430.

Leff, S.S., Power, T.J., Manz, P.H., Costigan, T.E., & Nabors, L.A. (2001). School-based aggression prevention programs for young children: Current status and implications for violence prevention. *School Psychology Review, 30,* 343–360.

Leff, S.S., Crick, N.R., Angelucci, J., Haye, K., Jawad, A.F., Grossman, M., & Power, T.J. (2006). Social cognition in context: Validating a cartoon-based attributional measure for urban girls. *Child Development, 77,* 1351–1358.

Leff, S.S., Gullan, R.L., Paskewich, B.S., Abdul-Kabir S., Jawad, A.F., Grossman, M., Munro, M.A., & Power, T.J. (2009). An initial evaluation of a culturally-adapted social problem solving and relational aggression prevention program for urban African American relationally aggressive girls. *Journal of Prevention and Intervention in the Community, 37,* 260–274.

Lochman, J.E., & Wells, K.C. (2004). The Coping Power program for preadolescent aggressive boys and their parents: Outcome effects at the 1-year follow-up. *Journal of Consulting and Clinical Psychology, 72,* 571–578.

Mayeux, L., Underwood, M.K., & Risser, S.D. (2007). Perspectives on the ethics of sociometric research with children. *Merrill-Palmer Quarterly, 53,* 53–78.

McConaughy, S.H., & Achenbach, T.M. (1996). Contributions of a child interview to multimethod assessment with EBD and LD. *School Psychology Review, 25,* 24–39.

McCurdy, B.L., Lannie, A.L., & Barnabas, E. (2009). Reducing disruptive behavior in an urban school cafeteria: An extension of the Good Behavior Game. *Journal of School Psychology, 47,* 39–54.

McNeilly-Choque, M.K., Hart, C.H., Robinson, C.C., Nelson, L.J., & Olsen, S.F. (1996). Overt and relational aggression on the playground: Correspondence among different informants. *Journal of Research in Childhood Education, 11,* 47–67.

Modzeleski, W. (2007). School-based violence prevention programs: Offering hope for school districts. *American Journal of Preventive Medicine, 33,* S107-S108.

Monks, C., & Smith, P.K. (2006). Definitions of bullying: Age differences in understanding of the term, and role of experience. *British Journal of Developmental Psychology, 24,* 801–821.

Nabors, L.A., Leff, S.S., & Power, T.J. (2004). Quality improvement activities and expanded school mental health services. *Behavior Modification, 28,* 596–618.

Nansel, T.R., & Overpeck, M. (2003). Operationally defining "bullying" (Reply). *Archives of Pediatrics and Adolescent Medicine, 157,* 1135–1136.

Nastasi, B.K., Varjas, K., Schensul, S.L., Silva, K.T., Schensul, J.J., & Ratnayake, P. (2000). The participatory intervention model: A framework for conceptualizing and promoting intervention acceptability. *School Psychology Quarterly, 15,* 207–232.

Nelson, J.R., Benner, G.J., Reid, R.C., Epstein, M.H., & Currin, D. (2002). The convergent validity of office discipline referrals with the CBCL-TRF. *Journal of Emotional and Behavioral Disorder, 10,* 181–188.

Newman, R.S., & Murray, B.J. (2005). How students and teachers view the seriousness of peer harassment: When is it appropriate to seek help. *Journal of Educational Psychology, 97,* 347–365.

Olweus, D. (1993). *Bullying at school.* Cambridge, MA: Blackwell.

Ostrov, J.M., & Keating, C.F. (2004). Gender differences in preschool aggression during free play and structured interactions: An observational study. *Social Development, 13,* 255–277.

Parker, J.G., & Asher, S.R. (1987). Peer relations and later personal adjustment: Are low-accepted children at risk? *Psychological Bulletin, 102,* 357–389.

Pekarik, E.G., Prinz, R.J., Liebert, D.E., Weintraub, S., & Neale, J.M. (1976). The pupil evaluation inventory: A sociometric technique for assessing children's social behavior. *Journal of Abnormal Child Psychology, 4,* 83–97.

Pellegrini, A.D. (2001). Sampling instances of victimization in middle school. In J. Juvonen & S. Graham (Eds.), *Peer harassment in school: The plight of the vulnerable and victimized* (pp. 125–144). New York, NY: Guilford Press.

Pepler, D.J., & Craig, W.M. (1995). A peek behind the fence: Naturalistic observations of aggressive children with remote audiovisual recording. *Developmental Psychology, 31,* 548–553.

Perepletchikova, F., Treat, T., & Kazdin, A. (2007). Treatment integrity in psychotherapy research: Analysis of the studies and examination of the associated factors. *Journal of Consulting and Clinical Psychology, 75,* 829–841.

Power, T.J., Blom-Hoffman, J., Clarke, A.T., Riley-Tillman, T.C., Kelleher, C., & Manz, P.H. (2005). Reconceptualizing intervention integrity: A partnership-based framework for liking research with practice. *Psychology in the Schools, 42,* 495–507.

Power, T.J., Dombrowski, S.C., Watkins, M.W., Mautone, J.A., & Eagle, J.W. (2007). Assessing children's homework performance: Development of multi-dimensional, multi-informant rating scales. *Journal of School Psychology, 45*, 333–348.

Reynolds, C.R., & Kamphaus, R.W. (1991). *Behavior Assessment System for Children (BASC)*. Circle Pines, MN: American Guidance Service, Inc.

Rigby, K. (2002). *Bullying in childhood*. In P. Smith & C. Hart (Eds.), *Childhood Social Development*. Malden, MA: Blackwell Publishing.

Rys, G.S., & Bear, G.G. (1997). Relational aggression and peer relations: Gender and developmental issues. *Merrill Palmer Quarterly, 43*, 87–106.

Schlosser, R.W. (2002). On the importance of being earnest about treatment integrity. *Augmentative and Alternative Communication, 18*, 36–44.

Singleton, L., & Asher, S.R. (1977). Peer preferences and social interaction among third-grade children in an integrated school district. *Journal of Educational Psychology, 69*, 330–336.

Smith, P.K. (2004). Bullying: Recent developments. *Child and Adolescent Mental Health, 9*, 98–103.

Smith, P.K., & Hunter, T. (1992). Children's perceptions of playfighting, playchasing and real fighting: a cross-national interview study. *Social Development, 1*, 211–229.

Smith, P.K., & Sharp, S. (1994). *School bullying: Insights and perspectives* (1–19). London: Routledge.

Smith, P.K., Cowie, H., Olafsson, R.F., & Liefooghe, A.P.D. (2002). Definitions of bullying: A comparison of terms used, and age and gender differences, in a fourteen-country international comparison. *Child Development, 73*, 1119–1133.

Terry, R. (2000). Recent advances in measurement theory and the use of sociometric techniques. In A. Cillessen and W. Bukowski (Eds.), *Recent advances in the measurement of acceptance and rejection in the peer system: New directions in child and adolescent development* (pp. 27–53). San Francisco: Jossey-Bass.

Terry, R., & Coie, J.D. (1991). A comparison of methods for defining sociometric status among children. *Developmental Psychology, 27*, 867–880.

Thomas, D.E., & Bierman, K.L. (2006). The impact of classroom aggression on the development of aggressive behavior problems in children. *Development and Psychopathology, 18*, 471–487.

Zettergren, P. (2007). Cluster analysis in sociometric research: A pattern-oriented approach to identifying temporally stable peer status groups of girls. *Journal of Early Adolescence, 27*, 90–114.

Part V

Effective Prevention and Intervention Programs

17

BULLY BUSTERS

A Resource for Schools and Parents to Prevent and Respond to Bullying

ARTHUR M. HORNE, CHRISTOPHER D. BELL,
KATHERINE A. RACZYNSKI, AND JENNIFER L. WHITFORD

IS BULLYING REALLY A PROBLEM IN SCHOOLS?

As illustrated in the following fable, violence, aggression, and conflict between those of differing abilities, strengths, and status appear to be ubiquitous:

> The beasts of the field and forest had a Lion as their king. He was neither wrathful, cruel, nor tyrannical, but just and gentle as a king could be. During his reign he made a royal proclamation for a general assembly of all the birds and beasts, and drew up conditions for a universal league, in which the Wolf and the Lamb, the Panther and the Kid, the Tiger and the Stag, the Dog and the Hare, should live together in perfect peace and amity. The Hare said, "Oh, how I have longed to see this day, in which the weak shall take their place with impunity by the side of the strong." And after the Hare said this, he ran for his life.
>
> (Aesop, 1880)

It appears that what was true for Aesop's era is still true today—examples are evident worldwide. Even though violence, aggression, and conflict seem to be "hard-wired" into the experience of life (human or otherwise), there is still every reason to work to make our nations, corporations, communities, and schools less conflict-oriented: safer.

Unfortunately, as the Hare instinctively knows, this can be a dangerous undertaking. Even in our schools, where ideas such as social justice should be held as sacred, children and adolescents are indoctrinated into the world of aggression on a daily basis. As schools in the United States have been described as microcosms of the general culture (Newman, 1999), it should not be surprising that the violence and aggression expressed in the general culture are also reflected in our classrooms (Horne, Glaser, & Sayger, 1994).

Despite statistics indicating that school violence is diminishing (Glasser, 2000), adults should be concerned about any risk of students being harmed at school. The school shootings at Columbine in 1999, and the tragedy at Virginia Tech in 2007 provides sobering support of this assertion. Recent reports on the Youth Risk Behavior Survey (Eaton et al., 2006) indicate that as many as 6% of high school students admit to carrying a weapon—a gun, knife, or club—to school. Further, even when the violence is not as starkly expressed as in the above examples, children still face violence and aggression regularly. For example, the Youth Risk Behavior Survey indicates that 43% of boys and 28% of girls have been in fights and that 30% of students in grades 6 to 10 have been involved in a bully-victim dyad (Whitted & Dupper, 2005). Such high percentages strongly suggest that social interactions are a major source of our nation's violence-indoctrination (Espelage & Holt, 2001; Hoover, Oliver, & Hazler, 1992; Newman-Carlson & Horne, 2004).

With regard to grade-based prevalence, Grunbaum and colleagues (2004) reported that 13% of 6th graders and 5% of 10th graders acknowledged engaging in bullying behaviors. In another survey of almost 5,000 elementary school students, over 14% of students had engaged in name-calling, teasing, and low-level physical aggression (e.g., pushing and kicking) within the past month (Silvernail, Thompson, Yand, & Kopp, 2000). Bullying researchers initially believed that as students become older they experience less bullying (Olweus, 1991), but recent reports indicate that as many as 30% of students in middle and high school report experiencing bullying, either as perpetrators or victims (Klomek, Marrocco, & Kleinman, 2007).

SO, THEN, WHAT IS BULLYING?

It is important that teachers, students, and parents understand how bullying is different from play and recognize it for what it is—an abuse of power. While definitions of bullying vary among scholars, researchers, and practitioners, three components appear to be common to all definitions: bullying behavior is purposeful, unbalanced in power, and repeated. One highly accessible definition that can be used with even young students is the PIC acronym: *PIC*: *P*urposeful, *I*mbalanced, and *C*ontinual. The PIC definition means that bullying behavior is *purposeful* in that it is done on purpose. Second, bullying behavior is *imbalanced*, because the bully has more power or influence than the victim. Third, bullying is *continual*, meaning that it occurs more than once.

BASIC ASSUMPTIONS OF THE BULLY BUSTERS PROGRAM

The elementary and middle school educational experience for children involves learning academic subjects and educational material, but it should also entail learning appropriate social skills and behaviors. The ability to resolve conflict, to play fairly, to treat each other with kindness, and to share are not innate characteristics of most children; learning these skills should be a part of good educational programs. A key facet of the most effective school antiviolence programs is building social skills to improve interpersonal interactions (Gregg, 1998). As bullying prevention researchers, our hope is that children will incorporate these skills, value the safety of a bully-free school environment, and perpetuate a non-violent approach to social interactions throughout their school years.

The overall goal of the Bully Busters Program is to effect change in the social system so that bullying does not occur. Bully Busters has primarily focused on enhancing the social environment in schools (middle school: Newman, Horne, & Bartolomucci, 2000; elementary school: Horne, Bartolomucci, & Newman-Carlson, 2003). This involves enhancing awareness of bullying among school staff, changing teachers' responses to aggression, and developing student norms that reject bullying. In short, our goal is for all people within the school system to support a peaceful environment, to be informed of the nature of the problem, and to be prepared to prevent and respond to bullying.

A companion parenting guide is available for use in conjunction with a school-wide implementation of the Bully Busters Program, or it can be used alone (Horne, Stoddard, & Bell, 2007). Parents and families of students play an integral role in responding to and preventing bullying. The parenting guide mirrors the materials presented in the school-focused books, along with additional information about how families can support children who have been impacted by bullying. The principles that guide the parenting program are the same as the school-based Bully Busters curriculum.

SETTING UP FOR SUCCESS WITHIN A SCHOOL

In establishing the Bully Busters Program in a school setting, teachers need to learn basic skills of setting up their classrooms for success. These are briefly summarized in the sections below.

Establish a Bully Busters Teacher Support Team

Teachers have enormous resources available to share with one another, but this often does not happen unless a formalized structure is established. Bully Busters Teacher Support Teams are composed of a small group of teachers (by grade level, subject level, team level, etc.) who meet every two to three weeks to review new interventions, problem-solve current conflicts with students, and share ideas on effective classroom management. Teachers benefit greatly by having co-workers available to facilitate problem-solving and to provide support and encouragement during difficult times. The teams fulfill several roles:

1. They remind teachers to continue addressing the problem of bullying.
2. They allow the opportunity to discuss problems in the classroom or with specific students that continue to be problematic.
3. They offer the chance to review what works, and what does not work.
4. They are an opportunity for creativity and fun.
5. The group provides a supportive and understanding experience.

Understand the ABCs

Teachers who understand basic behavioral principles can better interpret the actions and reactions of students with regard to bullying. The ABCs of behavior—understanding the Antecedents, Behaviors, and Consequences of bullying behavior—allow teachers to predict and prevent problems before they happen. When bullying occurs and one child is hurt, embarrassed, or loses something such as lunch money, the consequence needs to be changed. This can be facilitated by changing the antecedent (i.e., what led up to the bullying) or the behavior. Understanding how the antecedent influences the outcome helps teachers *prevent* problems from occurring in the first place.

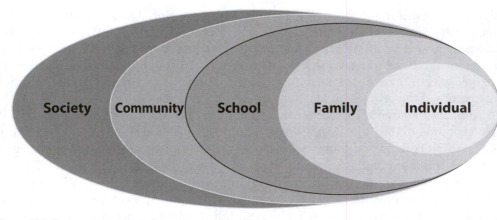

Figure 17.1 Ecological–systemic influences on a child's behavior

Understand the sphere of influence

Most teachers intuitively understand that bullying behavior has a number of contributing factors. These factors are often represented by the concentric circles presented in Figure 17.1. This figure represents the ecological–systemic perspective on bullying.

The first circle represents the characteristics of the child, including temperament, gender, intellectual ability, and other individual factors that influence behavior. The second circle indicates that family influence is very powerful and that the circumstances of the family, such as family structure, parenting approaches, size, socioeconomic status, and other related factors strongly influence the child. The third circle denotes school influences and includes such factors as the adequacy of the school facilities, the teaching staff, the size of the classrooms, the makeup of the student body, and related factors. The fourth circle represents the community and is indicative of how the community can influence the development of a child, including the economics of the community, the focus on safety and health in the area, and whether it is urban, suburban, or rural. The fifth circle is indicative of cultural influences on children's development and includes ethnicity, popular entertainment such as television, films and music, and the political nature of the cultural group.

Teachers' influence, for the most part, is limited to the classroom and school environment. Thus, teachers are encouraged to focus their energy and resources on changing the areas within their sphere of influence—the classroom and school.

Establish Clear Classroom Guidelines and Be Consistent

Teachers should aim to clearly communicate their classroom rules and apply them consistently. The Bully Busters Teacher Support Team can serve as consultants to one another regarding the establishment of effective classroom rules and overcoming barriers to consistently applying the rules.

Value All Students

The foundation of the Bully Busters Program is *respect*. When adults ask students to demonstrate respect for one another, students will expect those adults to model respect in their own language and behavior. Three primary values underpin the Bully Busters program:

1. All children can learn.
2. All people in school deserve to be treated with respect and dignity.
3. There is no place for violence, aggression, or bullying in our schools.

Bully Busters Teacher Support Team can review effective and less effective means of talking with students about aggression and bullying. The most appropriate language is polite, respectful, clear, and specific—not sarcastic, critical, or punitive.

Teach New Skills

Some students may lack the skills necessary to engage in positive peer relationships. If students do not have these important social skills, then it becomes the responsibility of teachers to incorporate the appropriate skill development into their work. As teachers and researchers, we truly believe that students need to develop the skills necessary to lead an effective life—being able to live and work with one another harmoniously. Effective people skills, problem-solving skills, and personal responsibility are equally as important as the content of the subject matter we teach our students. To assist students in developing their social and problem-solving skills, teachers need to know how to evaluate the level of skills students already have, what their current ability level is for the particular skill, and what additional skills need to be learned. Then, teachers need to provide opportunities for students to learn such skills.

Use a Solution-Focused Approach to Problems

Discussions that focus on problems often end without developing effective strategies that lead to solutions. Problem-focused approaches to dealing with children's behavior problems focus on the root causes of the problem, the background that has led to the current situation, and the reason for the behavior. While it is helpful for teachers to understand why a problem exists, this understanding does not always lead to answers about what to do about solving the problem. This emphasis can lead to frustration, exasperation, and hopelessness. Students may be left with teachers who want to give up. In contrast, being solution-focused leads teachers to become more proactive rather than reactive and to search out and identify solutions to the problems. As teachers learn to focus on solutions, their beliefs and expectations of their students will likely become more positive.

Use the Big Questions

The Big Questions provide a solution-focused technique that can help teachers become more efficient and effective problem-solvers, and thus more impactful with bullying problems. The Big Questions are:

1. What is my goal?
2. What am I doing?
3. Is what I am doing helping me achieve my goal?

4.   If not, what can I do differently that will help me achieve my goal?

An example of the Big Questions might be:

Question 1:   What is my goal? (Identify what you hope to achieve)
My goal is to help teach my students this history lesson. If we get behind in the schedule, they are not going to be ready for end of the year testing.
Question 2:   What am I doing? (Identify the problem)
I am trying to teach, but I don't have the attention of the students. Kevin is whispering to Peter, and Renee is spacing out. I am feeling upset, tired, and frustrated.
Question 3:   Is what I am doing helping me to achieve my goal? (Evaluate the effectiveness of the solutions)
No, if I keep going, I will make it through the lesson, but the students will not have learned the material, and they won't be prepared.
Question 4:   What can I do differently that will help me achieve my goal? (Generate alternative/new solutions)
I am going to take a minute and think about what is happening in my classroom. What usually gets the students' attention and allows them to have a good time while learning something new? Sometimes, it is better if we sit on the floor together in a circle or if I ask for several volunteers to help teach. Let's try that.

Teachers may also use the Big Questions with students to help them learn more effective means of managing conflict.

Teacher: Shana, I asked you to stay after class because you made a mean comment when Cory gave a wrong answer. What was your goal in doing that?
Shana: I don't know, I just said it.
Teacher: Was your goal for the class to think you are a mean person?
Shana: No, I was just trying to be funny.
Teacher: You were trying to be funny, so what did you do?
Shana: I made the comment about Cory. But I wasn't trying to be mean.
Teacher: Did making the comment help you accomplish that goal?
Shana: I don't know.
Teacher: It didn't, because you ended up in conflict with Cory and then in a time out period. Plus, even if some of the class thought the comment was funny, a lot of people are now afraid you might say something mean about them. So, what could you do next time?
Shana: Not make the comment.
Teacher: Right. You *do* have a good sense of humor, Shana. And people will like you even more if you use it in a way that doesn't cut other people down.
Shana: Okay, thanks.

Teachers can use the Big Questions to examine their own methods of working with disruptive students and to help students develop healthy ways of resolving conflicts. The process facilitates using the ABCs (Antecedents, Behaviors, and Consequences) and the core components of Setting Up For Success. Using the Big Questions takes practice and support to use, but when teachers incorporate the process into their thinking and practice, it is very powerful for impacting change and reducing bullying behaviors.

IMPLEMENTATION OF THE BULLY BUSTERS PROGRAM

In the school setting, the Bully Busters Program is implemented through teacher training groups, with training being offered to as many teachers as are interested. The training with teachers needs to be long enough to cover the overview and basic theoretical material (presented above), and to provide training in the classroom material that follows. While the overview material can be didactic, the activities for teachers to cover with students in the classroom need to be demonstrated and practiced. The training should provide the opportunity for small group experiences with some supervision of the role plays and skill development by the trainer. Generally, the training may be accomplished in one full day but can be provided during two days of training, as well. After the initial training, Bully Busters Teacher Support Teams meet regularly throughout the year.

After several years of facilitating Bully Busters trainings for teachers, school personnel asked for a similar training program for parents. In response to this request, we piloted weekly parenting groups that lasted about an hour after school for four weeks. The materials we developed eventually became the Bully Busters for Parents book (Horne, Stoddard, & Bell, 2007). The parenting groups fulfilled several purposes. First, staff in the schools believed that parents could benefit from the type of information provided in the Bully Busters curriculum. The behavioral principles presented in the books for interacting with children are effective for strengthening parent–child relationships as well as teacher–student relationships. The schools also viewed the Bully Busters Program as a way to strengthen the bond between schools and home. Parents attending the parenting program learn about the steps the school is taking to minimize bullying at the school and what their child will be learning about in the Bully Busters activities. The group also provides an opportunity for parents to interact with school counselors or other personnel leading or assisting with the program and to provide feedback about the way bullying is handled at the school.

THE BULLY BUSTERS SERIES

At present, there are three books in the Bully Busters series: an elementary school book, a middle school book, and a parenting guide. The school-focused books divide content into modules. Each module addresses a particular element of the bully–victim problem and provides background information for teachers along with numerous classroom activities related to the topic. The parenting book is divided into chapters with content similar to the modules and includes activities for parents and families to do together. Throughout the three Bully Busters books, common topics are covered. In the following sections we provide an overview of the concepts covered in the Bully Busters series.

Module 1: Increasing Awareness of Bullying

Module 1 is focused upon increasing awareness of the definition of bullying, types of bullying, and the extent of the problem. Efforts to prevent and reduce bullying will not be successful until adults are aware of the extent of the problem and can identify bullying when it occurs. A first step in this process is evaluating the level of bullying that is taking place in school from the perspective of adults and students. This includes having teachers and students rate the extent of the problem of bullying, teasing, name-calling, fighting, rumor spreading, social exclusion, weapon-carrying, unsafe areas of school, teacher help with bullying and other related problems. Most frequently students report a much higher level of bullying than teachers. Students also tend to report a much lower level of teacher help and assistance with bullying problems than teachers believe they give to their students. This information usually comes as a surprise to teachers, and many discount the accuracy of the feedback. But it is important to address students' perceptions, even if teachers do not share the same views on the school environment as the students.

Parents who participate in the Bully Busters for Parents groups are generally more aware that bullying is occurring. Often parents are participating in the group because their child has experienced or witnessed bullying. While these parents have a particular interest in understanding bullying, they often require clarification about the definition and different types of bullying.

Module 1 also provides definitions of bullying that are acceptable and usable by teachers, parents and students, such as the PIC definition discussed earlier. This module differentiates rough and tumble play (normal), bullying (requiring action from parents, teachers and peers), and conduct disorders or delinquency (legal or police action, or perhaps requiring consultation from counselors or school psychologists and special education staff).

Adults also need to be able to identify different types of bullying. The following types of bullying are discussed in Module 1:

- *Physical bullying:* Bullies physically harm a victim. This type of bullying is "action-oriented" and includes any type of behavior that intentionally inflicts bodily harm such as hitting, pushing, punching, and kicking.
- *Emotional bullying:* Bullies emotionally harm a victim. This type of bullying is "word or verbally oriented" and includes using words to humiliate or hurt the victim such as name-calling, teasing, racial slurs, and insults.
- *Relational bullying:* Bullies attempt to harm the relationships of the victims. This type of bullying is "peer-oriented" and includes peer exclusion and peer rejection through rumors, lies, embarrassment, and manipulations. This type of bullying is closely associated with verbal bullying.
- *Bystander victimization:* Bullies indirectly harm innocent bystanders. This type of bullying is "bystander-oriented." These students watch bullying occur and do not feel they have the power to address the bully or fear they may be the bullies' next direct target.

Module 1 also provides teachers and parents with information on common locations where bullying occurs, such as the lunchroom, and myths or misconceptions that many adults hold about bullying. Our experience is that many adults hold erroneous beliefs about bullying, and until these beliefs change, adult behavior will not change either.

Module 2: School-level Prevention

The primary focus of Module 2 is on prevention efforts, including the Setting Up For Success information presented earlier. The module includes information about how to foster administrative support for the program—a crucial element. Steps include:

1. Sharing with administrators the importance of preventing the problem.
2. Sharing data collected about student and teacher perceptions of the problem.
3. Identifying the cost to respond to bullying problems after they have developed versus the cost of prevention.

The parenting book provides information for parents about how they can work together with schools to foster a positive school climate and respond to bullying incidents. Parents often feel unsure about how to interact with the school when their child is involved in a bullying situation, either as the target or instigator of the bullying. The book provides guidelines for parents to facilitate communication with teachers and school personnel to help resolve the situation, specifically by using the Big Questions to establish a plan that will help their child.

The parenting guide also provides information about prevention at the family level. This chapter is called "Tools for Strong Families" and includes guidelines for maintaining positive relationships within the family, such as modeling desirable behavior and being respectful, encouraging, honest, firm, and fair. The Family Council meeting is discussed, and parents are given advice for using the Big Questions to solve family conflicts. The chapter highlights the importance of emotional intelligence and provides four steps for parents to help foster emotional intelligence in their children:

1. Becoming aware of your own emotions and your child's emotions.
2. Recognizing your child's emotion as an opportunity for intimacy and teaching.
3. Listening empathically and validating your child's feelings.
4. Helping your child find words to label the emotions he or she is feeling.

Module 3: Building Personal Power

One important component in bullying prevention is supporting the development of personal power for all students. Personal power can be thought of as a combination of the personal strengths, self-reliance, and resiliency that empower students to interact with others with dignity and respect. Bullies victimize those whom they perceive as lacking in power. One way to help children develop a sense of power is by helping them develop a narrative—a story to themselves—about their strengths and abilities. The activities include helping students learn how to request help and support from peers and teachers, and how to take risks to address problems they are experiencing. They are also taught the use of humor and laughter, how to deflect criticism, and how to avoid confrontations.

Module 4: Understanding Children Who Bully

This module places considerable emphasis on helping teachers and parents recognize the risk and developmental factors that contribute to the development of bullying and aggressive behaviors in children. It helps teachers identify risk factors that may be operating in the classroom and school environment, as well as family and external factors that influence bullying behaviors. Several distinct types of bullying have been identified by researchers, including aggressive bullying, passive bullying, and relational bullying. Boys and girls display somewhat different patterns of behavior in terms of bullying. Male students often exhibit direct, aggressive forms of bullying, while girls frequently use less visible and more indirect means of bullying.

Module 5: Understanding Targets of Bullying

Students who are the victim of name-calling, exclusion, or physical forms of bullying endure pain and humiliation and may suffer from lifelong psychological struggles. This trauma has been linked to depression, feelings of helplessness, and risk of suicide. Children who are victimized often go unnoticed, forgotten, or ignored, which perpetuates the problem. Most frequently it is the child who bullies who receives the attention, while the victims go unnoticed or are blamed for being the victim. The purpose of this module is to assist in understanding the victim and the victim's role in the bully–victim interaction. There are several types of victims, including passive, provocative, and bystander victims. This module prepares teachers to conduct skills training activities to help all students learn more effective methods for managing the bully problem.

Module 6: Helping Children who Bully

The sixth module provides specific suggestions for helping children who bully. Adults are better able to prevent bullying when they establish a working relationship with students who bully. This involves balancing support and firmness. We advocate an invitational approach to interacting with students, allowing the student to talk and share while affirming that the student is worthy of care and support. Students who bully need to know that adults believe they are capable of learning new skills and changing their behaviors. The key to successful bully prevention is to use what we call the Four Rs of Bully Control:

1. Recognize that a problem exists and remember to stay calm.
2. Remove yourself or step back from the situation if you do not feel you can effectively intervene.
3. Review the situation to figure out whether what you are doing is working to solve the problem.
4. Respond to the situation. If you feel competent to intervene, then do so. If you are uncertain how to intervene, assist students in finding help elsewhere.

Module 7: Helping Targets of Bullying

Module 7 focuses on interventions that assist the targets of bullying. Adults can help victims in many ways. Teachers and parents often think that helping the victim will only make matters worse for them. This is a mistaken belief. Victims are desperately in need of the help of a caring adult. Direct assistance to the victim openly communicates that they are believed and that they are worth the teachers' time and energy. Many children who are not victimized have learned skills or have characteristics that buffer them from victimization. Children need training, skills, and support to stop bullying.

Adults can support victims through social skills building, treating every child with respect, assisting children in mediating conflict and managing problem-solving, and developing a culture of support that includes other adults and children in the environment. Adults also need to teach victims skills to protect themselves from the bullying interaction. These skills can help victims feel empowered. Rather than feeling like a helpless recipient of undue attention from the bully, victims will learn how to take an active role in changing the bully–victim interaction.

Module 8: Relaxation and Coping Skills

Module 8 addresses ways that adults and children can cope with stress. How teachers and parents deal with stress has a profound effect on their ability to positively interact with children. Children also face a considerable amount of stress in their daily lives. It can be challenging for youth to cope with stress, especially when they may lack the skills to do so effectively. The activities in module 8 provide a way for both adults and children to take a moment to relax and counteract stress. Effective strategies include using meditation, humor, exercise, and a social support network.

TRANSLATING RESEARCH INTO PRACTICE: IMPLICATIONS FOR BULLYING PREVENTION AND INTERVENTION PROGRAMS

When bullying prevention programs are implemented in a school, administrators and teachers justifiably want to know that their efforts are producing positive results. The Bully Busters Program has been evaluated in a number of different settings, with both qualitative and quantitative methodologies. These evaluations have yielded positive results in terms of teacher and student outcomes, and more research is needed.

In an evaluation of the Bully Busters middle school curriculum (Newman-Carlson & Horne, 2004), teachers who participated in the program reported a number of statistically significant positive outcomes compared to the control group. These teachers reported significant increases in knowledge and use of bullying intervention skills. Teachers in the treatment group also reported significant increases in personal self-efficacy, and self-efficacy related to working with specific types of children. Further, these teachers demonstrated a significant reduction in bullying as measured by the number of disciplinary referrals. These results provide evidence that the middle school Bully Busters curriculum effectively increases teachers' knowledge and effective use of bullying intervention techniques. An earlier study (Howard, Horne, & Jolliff, 2002) produced similar findings. After one year of treatment, middle school teachers reported significant increases in knowledge and use of bullying intervention skills, higher self-efficacy, and reductions in discipline referrals. Further, an evaluation of an abbreviated version of the middle school program found significant increases in teacher self-efficacy for intervening with victims of bullying, and in teachers' positive expectations for bullies and victims (Bell, 2008). A limitation is that the study designs were quasi-experimental.

Several studies have evaluated Bully Busters at the elementary school level. Browning, Cooker, and Sullivan (2005) evaluated outcomes of the elementary school curriculum on teacher knowledge and skills for responding to bullying. A randomly assigned group of teachers and school staff participated in a three-day teacher training which covered the elementary school Bully Busters curriculum. At the conclusion of the training, participants in the treatment group demonstrated significantly better results than the control group on seven outcomes:

1. Awareness of bullying.
2. Knowledge of prevention strategies that can be used in the classroom.
3. Identification of behavior characteristics of bullies and victims.
4. Interventions for reducing bullying behavior.
5. Ways to help victims of bullying.

6. Techniques for relaxation and stress management for students.
7. Personal stress reduction.

Further, these teachers retained much of this knowledge six weeks after the training. A limitation of this study is the somewhat narrow scope of outcomes measured. Additional outcomes focused on teacher and student behaviors would have bolstered the findings of this study.

Orpinas, Horne, and Staniszewski (2003) evaluated a school-wide bullying prevention program that included components of the elementary school Bully Busters curriculum. This study provides evidence that the Bully Busters Program reduced student-reported bullying and victimization at the elementary school level. After one year of intervention, students in kindergarten through 2nd grade reported a statistically significant reduction in self-reported aggressive behaviors. This result was particularly pronounced among students who reported high levels of aggression at pre-test. Further, a statistically significant decline in self-reported victimization was observed at post-test for all students in the school (grades K–5). The findings of this study were positive; however, the results should be interpreted with a measure of caution because the study design was quasi-experimental, and the Bully Busters curriculum was implemented in conjunction with other bullying-reduction efforts.

Evaluations of the Bully Busters Program in a number of settings have yielded positive results, and further research is needed to conclusively demonstrate that implementing Bully Busters is an effective way to reduce bullying in schools. Studies with a rigorous experimental design are particularly needed, although they are difficult to conduct given the constraints of working within schools. Random assignments to treatment and control groups can be particularly problematic. In a review of 14 published studies of whole school bullying prevention programs, only eight studies had control groups, and four had random assignment to treatment or control condition (Smith, Schneider, Smith, & Ananiadou, 2004).

Evaluations of the Bully Busters curriculum suggest several important implications for the field of bullying prevention. These implications are discussed below.

Bullying prevention efforts are necessary and desired

The implementation of Bully Busters Programs in elementary and middle schools provides evidence that bullying is widespread. Baseline rates of reported bullying and victimization were quite high. For example, in one elementary school, over 85% of students reported being victimized in the week prior to the baseline survey (Orpinas, Horne, & Staniszewski, 2003). A qualitative study of student perceptions of the Bully Busters Program in a middle school concluded that students view bullying as a significant problem, and that they want adults to address it (Hunter, 2007). Students indicated that they wanted teachers to be aware of bullying and to act to make the school a safer place. Students were supportive of the Bully Busters Program and reported that they had observed a decrease in bullying during the year of implementation (Hunter, 2007).

Programs that target teachers are promising

The Bully Busters Program has repeatedly demonstrated increases in teacher knowledge, skills and self-efficacy with regard to intervening in bullying situations. Students look to adults to set the tone of the school. In interviews, students expressed frustration with teachers who ignored evidence of bullying and refused to intervene (Hunter, 2007). These results indicate that teachers should act to send a clear, consistent message that bullying is wrong and not acceptable in school.

Because teachers remain in the school much longer than individual students, programs that target teachers provide an opportunity for program effects to be sustained over many years. Additional research should focus on the best ways to maintain the knowledge and skills learned to address bullying, especially given variable rates of teacher attrition across schools.

Program effectiveness may be impacted by teacher buy-in

The impact of a school-wide program may hinge on the willingness of teachers to participate in and implement the program as intended. In interviews, students linked the investment of their teacher to the effectiveness of the program (Hunter, 2007). Students who were satisfied with the Bully Busters Program reported that their teacher conducted all of the components of the program (e.g., activities and frequent class discussions) and valued the opportunity to discuss bullying with students. Other students reported that their teachers were resistant to the program. These teachers were viewed as disinterested, or, in some cases, hostile toward the program. Students reported feeling frustrated with these teachers because the students saw bullying as a legitimate problem that warranted teachers' attention (Hunter, 2007). An important line of future research will be identifying characteristics of engaged versus unengaged teachers and pinpointing ways to increase program buy-in.

SUMMARY

This chapter has provided an overview of the Bully Busters Program and a series of resources for working with students, teachers, and parents to prevent and respond to bullying. This program has been developed from decades of research on bullying prevention by the Bully Busters team and has been implemented successfully in elementary and middle schools around the Unites States. The Bully Busters Program takes a psychoeducational approach to bullying prevention, including focus on the individual and context-based factors that influence the development of bullying behaviors. An important aspect of the Bully Busters series is translating research-based knowledge into a format that is easily accessed and implemented by teachers and parents. The text of the modules provides bullying prevention information written for adult readers, and the activities provide an engaging method for teaching students the skills and knowledge they need to counteract bullying.

REFERENCES

Aesop (1880). The kingdom of the lion. In G. Townsend (Ed.), *Fables*. (10th ed.) Retrieved from http://etext. virginia.edu/toc/modeng/public/AesFabl.html.

Bell, C.D. (2008). Evaluation of an abbreviated bully prevention program for reducing aggression in a middle school. Unpublished doctoral dissertation. University of Georgia, Athens.

Browning, C.M., Cooker, P.G., & Sullivan, K. (2005). Help for the bully/peer abuse problem: Is Bully Busters in-service training effective? In G. Walz & R. Yep (Eds.), *Vistas compelling perspectives on counseling* (pp. 231–234). Alexandria, VA: American Counseling Association.

Eaton, D.K., Kann, L., Kinchen, S., Ross, J., Hawkins, J., Harris, W.A., & Wechsler, H. (2006). Youth risk behavior surveillance–United States, 2005. *Journal of School Health, 76,* 353–372.

Espelage, D., & Holt, M.K. (2001). Bullying and victimization during early adolescence: Peer influences and psychosocial correlates. *Journal of Emotional Abuse, 2,* 123–142.

Glasser, W. (2000). School violence from the perspective of William Glasser. *Professional School Counseling, 4,* 77–80.

Gregg, S. (1998). *School-based programs to promote safety and civility* (Policy Brief). Charleston, WV: Appalachia Educational Laboratory.

Grunbaum, J.A., Kann, L., Kinchen, S., Ross, J., Hawkins, J., Lowry, R., & Collins, J. (2004). Youth risk behavior surveillance–United States, 2003. *Morbidity and Mortality Weekly Report, 53(SS-2),* 1–96.

Hoover, J.H., Oliver R. & Hazler R.J. (1992). Bullying: Perceptions of adolescent victims in the Midwestern USA. *School Psychology International, 13,* 5–16. doi:10.1177/0143034392131001.

Horne, A.M., Bartolomucci, C.L., & Newman-Carlson, D. (2003). *Bully Busters: A teachers' manual for helping bullies, victims, and bystanders (grades K–5).* Champaign, IL: Research Press.

Horne, A.M., Glaser, B., & Sayger, T. (1994). Bullies. *Counseling and Human Development, 27,* 1–12.

Horne, A.M., Stoddard, J.L., & Bell, C.D. (2007). *A parent's guide to understanding and responding to bullying: The Bully Busters approach.* Champagne, IL: Research Press.

Howard, N., Horne, A., & Jolliff, D. (2002). Self-efficacy in a new training model for the prevention of bullying in schools. In R. Geffner, M. Loring, & C. Young (Eds.), *Bully behavior: Current issues, research, and interventions* (pp. 181–192). New York, NY: Haworth Press.

Hunter, G.H. (2007). *Students' perception of effectiveness of a universal bullying intervention.* Unpublished manuscript, University of Georgia, Athens.

Klomek, A.B., Marrocco, F., Kleinman, M. (2007). Bullying, depression, and suicidality in adolescents. *Journal of the American Academy of Child & Adolescent Psychiatry, 46,* 40–49. doi: 10.1097/01.chi.0000242237.84925.18.

Newman, D.A. (1999). *The effectiveness of a psychological intervention for classroom teachers aimed at reducing bullying behavior in middle school students.* Unpublished doctoral dissertation. University of Georgia, Athens.

Newman, D.A., Horne, A.M., & Bartolomucci, C.L. (2000). *Bully Busters: A teacher's manual for helping bullies, victims, and bystanders.* Champaign, IL: Research Press.

Newman-Carlson, D.A., & Horne, A.M. (2004). Bully Busters: A psychoeducational intervention for reducing bullying behavior in middle school students. *Journal of Counseling and Development, 82,* 259–268.

Olweus, D. (1991). Bully-victim problems among school children: Basic facts and effects of a school based intervention program. In K. Rubin & D. Pepler (Eds.), *The development and treatment of childhood aggression* (pp. 411–448). Hillsdale, NJ: Erlbaum.

Orpinas, P., Horne, A.M., & Staniszewski, D. (2003). School bullying: Changing the problem by changing the school. *School Psychology Review, 3,* 431–444.

Silvernail, D.L., Thompson, A.M., Yang, Z., & Kopp, H.J.P. (2000). *A survey of bullying behavior among Maine third graders* (Technical Report). Retrieved from University of Southern Maine, Center for Educational Policy, Applied Research, and Evaluation website: http://lincoln.midcoast.com/~wps/against/bullying.html.

Smith, J.D., Schneider, B.H., Smith, P.K., & Ananiadou, K. (2004). The effectiveness of whole-school antibullying programs: A synthesis of evaluation research. *School Psychology Review, 4,* 547–560.

Whitted, K.S., and Dupper, D.R. (2005). Best practices for preventing or reducing bullying in schools. *Children and Schools, 27,* 167–174.

18

INTEGRATING STRATEGIES FOR BULLYING, SEXUAL HARASSMENT, AND DATING VIOLENCE PREVENTION

The Expect Respect Elementary School Project

BARRI ROSENBLUTH, DANIEL J. WHITAKER,
LINDA ANNE VALLE, AND BARBARA BALL

The Expect Respect Program at SafePlace in Austin, Texas has partnered with local schools to prevent dating violence, sexual harassment, and bullying for more than 20 years. The prevalence of these behaviors and their negative impact on students' health and safety is widely reported (e.g., AAUW, 2001; Lenhart, 1996; Foshee et al., 1996; Ackard & Neumark-Sztainer, 2002; Coker et al., 2000; Olweus, 1993; Silverman, Raj, Mucci, & Hathaway, 2001; Thompson, Wonderlich, Crosby & Mitchell, 2001). It has also been suggested that bullying, sexual harassment, and dating violence represent a continuum of interpersonal violence in students' relationships (Stein, 1995) and studies have linked perpetration of bullying with perpetration of sexual harassment (Pellegrini, 2001) and aggression in dating relationships (Connolly, Pepler, Craig & Taradash, 2000). Molidor, Tolman, and Kober (2000) concluded that dating violence, like other forms of school violence, should be addressed in order to maintain a safe and equitable learning environment for all students.

This chapter describes the Expect Respect Elementary School Project (1997–2000), an intervention developed by SafePlace to prevent dating violence by reducing bullying and sexual harassment in elementary schools. The results of this project and subsequent efforts by SafePlace to address these related behaviors will be discussed.

THE EXPECT RESPECT ELEMENTARY SCHOOL PROJECT 1997–2000

Recognizing an opportunity to prevent dating violence before it starts, SafePlace initiated the Expect Respect Elementary School Project in 1997 with funding and technical assistance from the Centers for Disease Control and Prevention (CDC; see Rosenbluth, Whitaker, Sanchez, & Valle, 2004, for a full description). This project used a multilevel approach to prevent bullying and sexual harassment—problems identified by local elementary school personnel as prevalent and harmful to individuals and school climate.

The goal of the project was to prevent violence and abuse in future dating relationships by increasing effective responses to bullying and sexual harassment among students and adults who witness these behaviors. The program evaluation design involved six pairs of schools that were matched on selected demographic and academic characteristics. Schools in each pair were randomly assigned to the intervention or comparison condition. Intervention schools participated in program activities over a two-year period. Comparison schools participated in the evaluation but did not receive any program services.

The theoretical foundation of the Expect Respect Project was based on the multi-level, multicomponent, school-based prevention program developed by Dan Olweus and colleagues. The Olweus Bullying Prevention Program demonstrated reductions in bullying, general antisocial behavior and improved school climate (Olweus, Limber, & Mihalic, 1999; Olweus, 1993). Like the Olweus program, the Expect Respect Project engaged all members of the school community in learning how to recognize and respond effectively to these behaviors. The Expect Respect Project utilized five program components: a 12-week classroom curriculum entitled *Bullyproof* for 5th grade students (Stein & Sjostrom, 1996), trainings for staff, education for parents, guidance to administrators for policy development, and support services for students who had been affected by bullying, sexual harassment, or sexual or domestic violence. At the beginning of the intervention, there were 929 and 834 students in the intervention and control schools, respectively. The sample was evenly split between boys (50.3%) and girls (48.3%). There were 55% who self-identified as White, 27.6% as Hispanic, and 15.4% as African American. Ethnic distribution was similar across the intervention (54.9% White, 27.1% Hispanic, 15.9% African American) and comparison schools (55.1% White, 28.0% Hispanic, 15.0% African American).

Questionnaires were used to assess the impact of the Expect Respect Project at three time points. This chapter reports data regarding students' self-reports of actual bullying behaviors, students' reactions to verbal and physical bullying, students' perceptions of staff reactions to verbal and physical bullying, and students' identification of bullying and sexual harassment. For analyses of other outcomes, please see the first edition of this book (Whitaker, Rosenbluth, Valle, & Sanchez, 2004).

Bullying Behaviors

Students were asked at baseline if they had ever bullied another student and if they had ever been bullied. At post-intervention, students were asked if they had bullied another student in the past three months and been bullied in the past three months. Students were asked what the bully did (i.e., name-calling, threatening, hitting, kicking, or shoving) and how they responded. Responses to physical bullying (i.e., hitting, kicking, or shoving) and verbal bullying (i.e., name-calling, threats) were examined separately. Students' self-reported responses to being bullied were factor analyzed, with three factors emerging: told an adult (two items: told a parent, told an adult at school), made a verbal response (three items: told the bully to stop, asked friends for help, said something to make the bully stop), or ignored or did not respond to the bullying (two items: ignored the behavior or a lack of physical response such as hit, kicked, or shoved the bully). In addition, students reported how often they had witnessed bullying in the past week (never, once or twice, almost every day). This measure was dichotomized into either witnessed or did not witness bullying.

Reactions to Witnessing Bullying Behaviors

Students were asked about the probable responses made by themselves and by other students upon witnessing physical bullying (i.e., a student beating up on another student) and verbal bullying (i.e., a student calling another student names). For each question, a number of responses were provided and the respondent was asked to check all that apply.

For students' responses about their own intended actions upon witnessing another student being bullied, two factors each were derived for witnessing physical bullying and witnessing verbal bullying: telling someone (two items: telling a parent, telling an adult at school) and directly intervening (two items: telling the bully to stop, helping the student get away). For students' perceptions about school adults' actions upon witnessing physical bullying, two factors were derived: adult intervention (five items: calling the parent, sending the bully to the office, punishing the bully, telling the bully to stop, sending the bully to an alternative school) and no adult intervention (three items: tell the student to ignore the bullying, do nothing, don't know). For students' perception of adults' responses to verbal bullying, three factors emerged through factor analyses: strong intervention (three items: calling the parents, sending the bully to the office, sending the bully to an alternative school), mild intervention (three items: telling the bully to stop, punishing the bully, telling the victim to ignore the bully), and no intervention (two items: do nothing, don't know).

Identification of Bullying and Sexual Harassment

As a measure of bullying identification, students were asked to indicate on the survey instrument whether or not 14 behaviors were examples of bullying. Nine items consisted of bullying behaviors (e.g., pushing, taking things, threatening), and five items did not (e.g., telling someone to leave you alone, not sharing). The measure of bullying identification was the number of behaviors correctly identified as a bullying or non-bullying item (range 0–14). Similarly, students indicated if they believed each of nine behaviors constituted sexual harassment. Six items consisted of sexual harassment behaviors (e.g., making fun of someone's private body parts), and three did not (e.g., telling someone you like him or her). The measure of sexual harassment identification was the number of behaviors students correctly identified (range 0–9).

Statistical Analyses

All dependent measures were analyzed with hierarchical modeling using the SAS Proc Mixed for normally distributed dependent variables and the SAS macro GLIMMIX for non-normally distributed dependent variables. School was used as a clustering variable to account for the relations among responses within a school. For analysis of each dependent measure (perpetration, victimization, and witnessing of bullying behaviors; students' responses to being bullied; students' intended actions upon witnessing bullying; students' perceptions of others' reactions upon witnessing bullying; and student identification of bullying and sexual harassment behaviors), the statistical model crossed Group (intervention vs. comparison) and Time (baseline vs. post or baseline vs. follow-up) to examine changes by intervention group from baseline to post-intervention (reflected by the Group x Time interaction). Year (1 vs. 2) was included as a control variable in all analyses (differences in group effects over time were examined by Year but were negligible.) For analyses of student data, gender was also included in the model and fully crossed with the other variables of interest to examine differential effects of the program on boys versus girls. Semester of intervention (fall vs. spring) was also included because students at different schools received the intervention in different semesters.

Results

Tables 18.1–18.4 show the means and standard deviations (in parentheses) or percentages and significant effects for all dependent measures. Means or percentages for each dependent variable are shown by Group (intervention vs. comparison) and Time (baseline vs. post), with the final column indicating significant effects for Group (G), Time (T), and for the student variable Gender (S). For analyses of student data, where Gender moderated the Group x Time interaction, follow-up analyses were conducted separately for boys and girls, and results are shown by Gender. In describing the results, the focus is on those variables for which there were Group x Time interactions, which indicated significant differences in how the intervention and comparison schools changed from baseline to post-intervention.

Bullying behaviors and reactions to being bullied. Table 18.1 shows the means, standard deviations (in parentheses), or percentages for bully perpetration, victimization, and witnessing, and students' self-reported reactions to being bullied. For bullying perpetration, the Group x Time interaction was not significant. For having been bullied, the Group x Time interaction was significant. Students in the intervention group reported equal amounts of being bullied at baseline and post-intervention ($p = .10$), whereas students in the comparison schools reported having been bullied less at post-intervention than baseline ($p < .001$). There was no significant Group x Time interaction for students' reports of having been physically bullied, but the interaction was significant for verbal bullying. The pattern was identical to the findings for overall bullying; students in the intervention schools reported no change ($p = .60$), whereas students in the comparison schools reported a decrease in verbal bullying ($p < .001$). Thus, the decrease in overall bullying in the comparison schools appears to be due to the decrease in verbal bullying from baseline to post-intervention. Finally, for witnessing bullying there was a Group x Time interaction for student reports. Students in the intervention schools reported an increase from baseline to post-intervention in witnessing bullying ($p < .001$), whereas students in the comparison schools did not ($p = .06$).

Because students' reactions to physical and verbal bullying are likely to differ, students' self-reports of what they did when they were physically or verbally bullied were analyzed separately (displayed in the lower half of Table 18.1). For physical bullying, the Group x Time interaction for the response of telling an adult was significant ($p < .001$). Students in the intervention group did not change from baseline to post-intervention in their self-reports of telling an adult ($p = .49$), whereas students in the comparison schools were less likely to tell an adult ($p < .01$). There was a significant Gender x Group x Time interaction for making a verbal response after being physically bullied. Separate analyses for boys and girls indicated the effect was limited to boys. In the intervention schools, boys' verbal responses to being physically bullied did not change from baseline to post-intervention ($p = .11$), whereas boys in the comparison schools reported a decrease in verbal responses ($p < .01$). There was also a Gender x Group x Time interaction ($p < .05$) for the response of ignoring physical bullying, and here the Group x Time

Table 18.1   Perpetration, Victimization, and Witnessing of Bullying Behaviors, and Students' Self-reported Responses to being Bullied

Variable	Intervention		Comparison		Significant Effects
	Baseline	Post	Baseline	Post	
Bullying behaviors					
Student: Bullied another student	10.6%	17.0%	11.2%	17.8%	T, G
Student: Been bullied	40.8%	36.7%	47.5%	34.7%	T, G x T
Student: Been physically bullied	15.2%	11.1%	19.5%	13.4%	G, T
Student: Been verbally bullied	31.2%	29.8%	36.8%	26.8%	T, G x T
Student: Witnessed bullying	38.4%	60.6%	47.3%	53.0%	T, G x T
Student responses to being physically bullied					
Told an adult	0.77	0.87	0.83	0.55	G x T
	(.82)	(.71)	(.80)	(.79)	
Verbal response	0.84	1.04	0.90	0.77	S x G x T
	(.87)	(.80)	(.83)	(.79)	
Boys	0.87	1.04	0.90	0.54	G x T
	(.93)	(.86)	(.84)	(.65)	
Girls	0.81	1.03	0.90	1.08	None
	(.81)	(.72)	(.82)	(.87)	
Ignored/did not respond	1.06	1.14	0.93	1.00	S x G x T
	(.61)	(.60)	(.65)	(.74)	
Boys	1.01	1.06	0.83	1.10	T
	(.59)	(.62)	(.67)	(.79)	
Girls	1.11	1.26	1.07	0.86	G x T
	(.63)	(.57)	(.60)	(.64)	
Student responses to being verbally bullied					
Told an adult	0.59	0.44	0.64	0.48	S, T
	(.69)	(.66)	(.75)	(.72)	
Made verbal response	0.59	0.60	0.70	0.58	S
	(.76)	(.68)	(.75)	(.72)	
Ignored/did not respond	1.34	1.33	1.34	1.39	None
	(.60)	(.59)	(.59)	(.64)	

effect was limited to girls. In the intervention schools, girls' reports of ignoring physical bullying did not change from baseline to post-intervention ($p = .42$), whereas girls in the comparison schools reported a decrease in ignoring bullying ($p < .05$). For all students' responses to verbal bullying, the Group x Time interactions were not significant.

Student intended actions upon witnessing bullying. Table 18.2 shows the means, standard deviations (in parentheses), and significant effects from the analyses of students' responses to what they would do if they witnessed physical bullying (i.e., a student beating up on another student) and what they would do if they witnessed verbal bullying (i.e., name-calling). Students' intentions to tell an adult if they witnessed physical bullying resulted in only Gender and Time main effects, but students' intentions to directly intervene if they witnessed physical bullying revealed a Group x Time interaction. Students in both the intervention ($p < .001$) and comparison schools ($p < .01$) reported an

Table 18.2   Intended Actions by Students upon Witnessing Physical or Verbal Bullying

Variable	Intervention		Control		Significant Effects
	Baseline	Post	Baseline	Post	
Students' intended actions upon witnessing physical bullying					
Tell an adult	1.06	1.21	1.02	1.14	T, S
	(.75)	(.78)	(.75)	(.80)	
Directly intervene	0.90	1.26	0.94	1.06	T, G x T
	(.81)	(.81)	(.81)	(.83)	
Students' intended actions upon witnessing verbal bullying					
Tell an adult	0.85	0.88	0.80	0.88	T, S x T x G
	(.78)	(.86)	(.78)	(.83)	
Boys	0.70	0.67	0.67	0.79	G x T
	(.76)	(.83)	(.76)	(.82)	
Girls	1.00	1.09	0.93	0.96	T
	(.76)	(.84)	(.78)	(.83)	
Directly intervene	0.86	1.08	0.93	0.92	T, G x T
	(.75)	(.76)	(.76)	(.80)	

increase in intentions to directly intervene from baseline to post-intervention, but the pre- to post-intervention mean difference was larger for students in the intervention schools. Analyses of students' intentions to tell an adult upon witnessing verbal bullying resulted in a Gender x Group x Time interaction. The Group x Time interaction was limited to boys. Those in the intervention schools reporting no change over time (p = .71), whereas boys in the comparison schools reported an increase from baseline to post-intervention in their intent to tell someone upon witnessing verbal bullying ($p < .01$). Students' intentions to intervene directly upon witnessing name-calling also revealed a Group x Time interaction, with significant increases in intentions to tell an adult from baseline to post-intervention found for students in the intervention group ($p < .001$), but not in the comparison group ($p = .60$).

Perceptions of others' reactions upon witnessing bullying. Of the five dependent variables analyzed to examine students' perceptions of staff's reactions to physical and verbal bullying (Table 18.3), the only Group x Time interaction found was for adults' mild intervention upon witnessing verbal bullying. Although the intervention and comparison groups were each more likely to believe adults would respond with a mild intervention at post-intervention than baseline ($ps < .001$), the baseline to post-intervention mean difference was greater for students in the intervention schools than the comparison schools.

Identification of bullying and sexual harassment. Table 18.4 shows the means, standard deviations (in parentheses), and percentages for students' identification of bullying and sexual harassment behaviors. The Group x Time interaction for bullying identification was not significant for students. There was a significant Group x Time interaction for students' identification of sexual harassment behaviors. Sexual harassment identification increased from baseline to post-intervention for students in both the intervention and the comparison schools ($ps < .001$), but the baseline to post-intervention mean difference was greater for students in the intervention schools.

Table 18.3   Students' Perceptions of Others' Reactions upon Witnessing Bullying

Variable	Intervention		Control		Significant Effects
	Baseline	Post	Baseline	Post	
Students' perceptions of staff's actions upon witnessing physical bullying					
Intervention	2.50	2.91	2.59	2.88	T
	(1.46)	(1.51)	(1.49)	(1.53)	
No intervention	0.19	0.26	0.17	0.20	G, T
	(.44)	(.49)	(.41)	(.44)	
Students' perception of staff's actions upon witnessing verbal bullying					
Strong intervention	0.94	0.85	0.97	0.97	None
	(1.00)	(1.04)	(1.02)	(1.06)	
Mild intervention	0.95	1.20	1.04	1.17	T, G x T
	(.74)	(.75)	(.78)	(.78)	
No intervention	0.11	0.14	0.07	0.13	G, T
	(.34)	(.37)	(.27)	(.35)	

Summary of Results

The Expect Respect Elementary School Project aimed to increase awareness of bullying and sexual harassment and increase students' ability and willingness to intervene on behalf of targeted students. With respect to awareness of bullying and sexual harassment, the only statistically significant change among the students occurred in students' identification of behaviors constituting sexual harassment. Although students in the intervention and comparison schools each demonstrated greater accuracy over time in identifying behaviors that constitute sexual harassment, the increase in accuracy was greater for students in the intervention schools. No significant differences in students' bullying identification were observed. The absence of significant results in bullying identification may be associated, in part, with a mismatch between the design of the student questionnaire and the curriculum. The questionnaire asked students to identify behaviors that constituted bullying and sexual harassment from a simple listing of behaviors, whereas the curriculum focused on discriminating bullying and sexual harassment behaviors within specific contexts that were absent in the survey.

With respect to responses to actual situations of having been bullied, the intervention appeared to be related to student group differences. For actual responses to being physically bullied, students in the comparison schools were less likely from baseline to

Table 18.4   Student Identification of Bullying and Sexual Harassment Behaviors

Variable	Intervention		Control		Significant Effects
	Baseline	Post	Baseline	Post	
Student Awareness					
Bullying behavior identification	11.16	11.66	11.19	11.46	T, S
	(2.77)	(2.27)	(2.74)	(2.45)	
Sexual harassment behavior identification	7.11	8.09	7.13	7.85	T, G x T
	(1.53)	(1.18)	(1.52)	(1.30)	

post-intervention to tell an adult, verbally respond to the bully (boys only) or ignore the bullying (girls only). Intervention students did not demonstrate decreases in these types of responses over time. It may be that as students get older, there is a greater stigma associated with behaviors such as telling the teacher or ignoring the bully when physically bullied. The intervention curriculum may have buffered students from that stigma by making these responses more socially appropriate. However, a similar pattern was not observed in students' responses to having been verbally bullied.

With respect to students' intent to respond to witnessing hypothetical bullying scenarios, the intervention was associated with increases in students' intentions to directly intervene upon witnessing physical and verbal bullying. The intervention appeared to have minimal impact on students' intentions to tell an adult, whereas boys in the comparison schools indicated they were more likely to tell an adult about verbal bullying at post-intervention than baseline. The *Bullyproof* curriculum encouraged students to intervene directly or get help from an adult when they witnessed bullying or sexual harassment. Increases in intervention students' expressed intent to directly intervene for a victim may indicate that these students believed they were capable of intervening on their own without help from adults. Students in the intervention schools, relative to those in comparison schools, showed an increase in their belief that school staff would be more likely to mildly intervene (i.e., tell the bully to stop, punish the bully, tell the victim to ignore the bullying) in a situation involving verbal bullying.

The results of self-reported bullying behavior are difficult to interpret. Although both groups of students were more likely to report having bullied another student at post-intervention, students in the intervention schools reported no significant change from baseline to post-intervention in being bullied, whereas students in the comparison schools reported a decrease. Students in the intervention schools reported an increase from baseline to post-intervention in witnessing bullying, whereas in the comparison schools did not. It is unclear whether the observed changes reflect an actual increase in bullying in the intervention schools relative to the comparison schools or whether the changes reflect an increase in intervention students' awareness of, attendance to, and willingness to report bullying behaviors.

Limitations

There are several limitations to the findings reported in this chapter. First, because many analyses were conducted with relatively few significant effects and there was no correction for multiple analyses, some of the observed group differences may have been due to chance. Moreover, the mean differences, standard deviations, and percentages suggest that the effect sizes of the statistically significant findings were relatively small. Thus, the practical significance of the observed changes appears to be limited. Second, there were strong effects associated with the passage of time for many of the variables. It is unclear whether these time effects were due to repeated administrations of the survey, experimental demand, or some naturally occurring event external to the intervention. For example, the April 1999 shootings at Columbine High School would have been likely to have similar effects in increasing awareness of bullying and aggression in the intervention and comparison schools.

The lack of clarity in the findings may result from assessment and implementation issues. The measurement of outcomes for this study relied solely on self-report questionnaires completed by students. Most of the items used in the questionnaires were constructed for the purpose of this project, and evidence for the validity and reliability of the questionnaires is lacking. For example, the degree to which the items actually assessed perceptions of school climate and tolerance for bullying behaviors is not known. In addition, there were no independent behavioral measures of bullying. As a result, students' reports of the increased level of bullying in the intervention schools relative to comparison schools are impossible to interpret.

PROGRAM DEVELOPMENT FOLLOWING THE EXPECT RESPECT ELEMENTARY SCHOOL PROJECT

Despite ambiguous quantitative results, the Expect Respect Elementary School Project was viewed positively by school personnel because of its effectiveness at building awareness about bullying and sexual harassment and its emphasis on responding to and preventing such behaviors. Following completion of the Project, SafePlace was contracted by Austin Independent School District (AISD) to provide similar bullying prevention activities in 14 additional elementary schools. A separate initiative expanded this effort to 20 additional schools over a five-year period. *Bullyproof*, and its companions *Quit It! A Teacher's Guide on Teasing and Bullying for Use with Students in Grades K–3* (Froschl, Sprung, & Mullin-Rindler, 1998) and *Flirting or Hurting? A Teacher's Guide on Student-to-Student Sexual Harassment in Schools (Grade 6–12)* (Stein & Sjostrom, 1994) were provided by AISD to all school counselors serving students in corresponding grades.

District administrators expanded efforts to develop school policy that had begun with schools in the project. In 2004 a district-wide policy concerning bullying, sexual harassment, and dating violence was established with assistance from SafePlace. This policy, which includes a complaint process for students and protocol for administrators, also informed legislation in 2007 requiring all Texas school districts to address dating violence.

Building upon previous efforts to promote active bystander behavior in participating elementary schools, SafePlace developed a new program component to promote youth leadership in preventing dating violence, sexual harassment, and bullying. In secondary schools, youth participate in *SafeTeens*, an eight-session curriculum and school-based service project. In elementary schools, a similar curriculum entitled *Heroes* provides four sessions and a service project. Older students address issues including dating abuse and sexual harassment, while younger students address issues of concern in their relationships including teasing, bullying, rumors, and gossip. Following the curriculum sessions, participants identify a problem on their campus concerning students' relationships and develop a youth-led project to address it. Examples of youth-led projects include public service announcements, interviews or articles for local and school newspapers, classroom presentations and school assemblies, and the creation of T-shirts, bookmarks, poetry, skits, and posters featuring prevention themes and messages. As experts on their peers, teens are in a unique position to identify approaches, messages, designs, colors, and language that are relevant and attractive to other teens. Youth in *SafeTeens* and *Heroes* become active bystanders and role models for healthy relationships on their campus. Engaging youth as leaders has been identified as essential for developing effective violence prevention strategies (NCVC & NCPC, 2005; Nation et al., 2003; Forum for Youth Investment, n.d.).

The Expect Respect Program (2009) serves over 45, K–12 schools in the Austin area with a menu of services designed to engage all members of the school community in promoting healthy relationships and preventing dating violence, sexual harassment, and bullying. A program manual for secondary schools was published in 2008 with assistance from the CDC (Ball, Rosenbluth, Aoki, & Randolph, 2008). The Expect Respect Program has three primary program components:

1. School-based support groups and counseling for youth in abusive relationships and those at risk due to family violence or sexual abuse (Ball, Kerig, & Rosenbluth, 2009).
2. Youth leadership programs including *SafeTeens* (grades 6–12), *Heroes* (grades 4–5) and the Changing Lives Youth Theatre Ensemble.
3. School-wide prevention strategies including policy, staff and parent training, and school-wide prevention education. These components are designed to work together to create safe and respectful learning environments, positive social norms and skills for healthy relationships.

TRANSLATING RESEARCH INTO PRACTICE: IMPLICATIONS FOR BULLYING PREVENTION AND INTERVENTION PROGRAMS

SafePlace has a history of developing innovative programs responsive to school and community needs. One of these was the Expect Respect Elementary School Project 1997–2000. This project positively impacted children's awareness of sexual harassment and intentions to intercede upon witnessing bullying. However, it should be noted that the observed changes were small. The impact of the project on other outcomes, such as school climate, staff responses to bullying and sexual harassment, and actual incidence rates of bullying (rather than students' self-reports) and sexual harassment could not be determined with the existing data. The project's implementation, however, contributed to increased awareness and support for comprehensive programs to prevent dating violence, sexual harassment and bullying in Austin schools. A school district policy and state law now provide increased protections for victimized students and counseling for youth affected by dating, sexual, or domestic violence and is available in many of Austin's schools.

CONCLUSIONS

The Expect Respect Elementary School Project engaged youth and adults in recognizing and responding to bullying and sexual harassment among students as a way to prevent future dating violence. The strategies employed included a classroom-based curriculum for students, staff training and parent education sessions, parent newsletters, policy development and counseling for affected students. In subsequent years, SafePlace developed a youth leadership program to further engage youth as leaders in promoting positive peer relationships. If indeed bullying, sexual harassment, and dating violence represent a continuum of interpersonal violence in students' relationships, then these behaviors may most effectively be prevented through integrated, multilevel, and youth-led approaches. Valid assessment tools and methods are needed more than ever to evaluate the full range of activities that may be important agents of change.

REFERENCES

Ackard, D.M., & Neumark-Sztainer, D. (2002). Date violence and date rape among adolescents: Associations with disordered eating behaviors and psychological health. *Child Abuse & Neglect, 26*, 455–473.

American Association of University Women (AAUW) (2001). *Hostile hallways: Bullying, teasing, and sexual harassment in school.* Washington, DC.

Ball, B., Kerig, P., & Rosenbluth, B. (2009). Like a family but better because you can actually trust each other. The Expect Respect Dating Violence Prevention Program For At-Risk Youth. *Health Promotion Practice, Supplement to volume 10, Issue 1, January 2009,* 45S–58S.

Ball, B., Rosenbluth, B., Aoki, A., & Randolph, R. (2008). *Expect Respect: A school-based program for preventing teen dating violence and promoting safe and healthy relationships.* SafePlace, Austin, Texas.

Coker, A.L., McKeown, R.E., Sanderson, M., Davis, K.E., Valois, R.F., & Huebner, E.S. (2000). Severe dating violence and quality of life among South Carolina high school students. *American Journal of Preventive Medicine, 19*, 220–227.

Connolly, J., Pepler, D., Craig, W., & Taradash, A. (2000). Dating experiences of bullies in early adolescence. *Child Maltreatment, 5*, 299–310.

Forum for Youth Investment (n.d.). *Youth Development Approach.* Retrieved May 10, 2007, from www.forumfyi.org.

Foshee, V.A., Linder, G.F., Bauman, K.E., Langwick, S.A., Arriaga, X.B., Heath, J.L., McMahon, P.M., & Bangdiwala, S. (1996). The Safe Dates Project: Theoretical basis, evaluation design, and selected baseline findings. *American Journal of Preventive Medicine, 12 (Suppl. 5),* 39–47.

Froschl, M., Sprung, B., & Mullin-Rindler, N. (1998). *Quit It! A Teacher's Guide on Teasing and Bullying for Use with Students in Grades K–3.* Wellesley MA: Wellesley College Center for Research on Women and the NEA Professional Library.

Lenhart, S. (1996). Physical and mental health aspects of sexual harassment. In D. K. Shrier (Ed.), *Sexual harassment in the workplace and academia: Psychiatric issues. Clinical practice series, No. 38.* (pp. 21–38). Washington, DC: American Psychiatric Press.

Molidor, C., Tolman, R., & Kober, J. (2000). Gender and contextual factors in adolescent dating violence. *The Prevention Researcher, 7*, 1–4.

Nation, M., Crusto, C., Wandersman, A., Kumpfer, K., Seybolt, & Morissey-Kane, E., et al. (2003). What works in prevention: Principles of effective prevention programs. *American Psychologist, 58*, 449–456.

National Center for Victims of Crime (NCVC) and the National Crime Prevention Council (NCPC). (2005). *Reaching and serving teen victims: A practical handbook.* Retrieved January 10, 2007, from www.ncvc.org.

Olweus, D. (1993). *Bullying at school: What we know and what we can do.* Willinslon, VT: Blackwell.

Olweus, D., Limber, S., & Mihalic, S.F. (1999). *Blueprints for violence prevention: Book nine, bullying prevention program.* Boulder, CO: Center for the Study and Prevention of Violence.

Pellegrini, A.D. (2001). A longitudinal study of heterosexual relationships, aggression, and sexual harassment during the transition from primary school through middle school. *Applied Developmental Psychology, 22*, 119–133.

Rosenbluth, B., Whitaker, D., Sanchez, E., & Valle, L.A. (2004). The Expect Respect Project: Preventing bullying and sexual harassment in U.S. elementary schools. In P.K. Smith, D. Pepler, & K. Rigby (Eds.), *Bullying in schools: How successful can interventions be?* (pp. 211–233). Cambridge, UK: Cambridge University Press.

Silverman, J.G., Raj, A., Mucci, L.A., & Hathaway, J.E. (2001). Dating violence against adolescent girls and associated substance use, unhealthy weight control, sexual risk behavior, pregnancy, and suicidality. *Journal of the American Medical Association, 286*, 572–579.

Stein, N. (1995). Sexual harassment in school: The public performance of gendered violence. *Harvard Educational Review, 65*, 145–162.

Stein, N. & Sjostrom, L. (1994). *Flirting or hurting? A teacher's guide on student-to-student sexual harassment in schools (grade 6–12).* Wellesley, MA: Wellesley College Center for Research on Women and the NEA Professional Library.

Stein, N., & Sjostrom, L. (1996). *Bullyproof: A teacher's guide on teasing and bullying for use with fourth and fifth grade students.* Wellesley, MA: Wellesley College Center for Research on Women and the NEA Professional Library.

Thompson, K.M., Wonderlich, S.A., Crosby, R.D., & Mitchell, J.E. (2001). Sexual violence and weight control techniques among adolescent girls. *International Journal of Eating Disorders, 29*, 166–176.

Whitaker, D.J., Rosenbluth, B., Valle, L.A., & Sanchez, E., (2004). Expect Respect: A school-based intervention to promote awareness and effective responses to bullying and sexual harassment. In D.L. Espelage & S.M. Swearer (Eds.), *Bullying in American schools* (pp. 327–350). Hillsdale, NJ: Lawrence Erlbaum Associates.

19

BULLY-PROOFING YOUR SCHOOL

Overview of the Program, Outcome Research, and Questions that Remain about how Best to Implement Effective Bullying Prevention in Schools

AMY PLOG, CARLA GARRITY, KATHRYN JENS, AND WILLIAM PORTER

OVERVIEW OF BULLY-PROOFING YOUR SCHOOL

Bully-Proofing Your School (BPYS) was developed in the early 1990s as a comprehensive prevention program designed to reduce bullying and improve overall climate in elementary schools. The authors of the program, most of whom were school-based practitioners, recognized that pull-out groups for bullies and victims were not effective and began to research what was known about effective intervention with bullying in schools. Building on the pioneering ideas of Olweus (1991) in Norway and Sharp and Smith (1991) in England, a school-wide, systemic bullying intervention with teacher training and a student curriculum was created. BPYS, the first bullying prevention program developed in the United States, was originally published in 1994 and has been updated in two revisions (in 2000 and 2004; Garrity, Jens, Porter, Sager, & Short-Camilli. 1994, 2004). Consistent across these revisions, the focus of BPYS has continued to be on developing a safe, caring school climate that does not condone aggression and bullying behavior but rather promotes kindness and caring. This desired environment must be created, nurtured and sustained by students, parents, teachers, and staff.

Although originally developed for elementary schools, Bully-Proofing Your School has been adapted across all age ranges from early childhood through high school. Key components of the BPYS program are present in each of the various developmental level curricula. Specifically, the program aims to train all staff who then instruct all students and teach the parents and school community about the program concepts and language. Schools are advised to follow a three-phase implementation process: pre-implementation, implementation, and sustained implementation. During the pre-implementation phase, administration and staff acknowledge bullying as a problem, assess the types and frequency of bullying using the Colorado School Climate Survey, and put behavioral expectations and discipline plans in place. As with any school-based prevention program, initial and ongoing support from the administration and school staff are crucial for program success (Lohrmann, Forman, Martin, & Palmieri, 2008). A staff committee (or cadre) guides the five components of the intervention described below.

Staff Training

This is typically comprised six lessons that can be covered in a one-day workshop. Lessons include the following essential information:

- The definition of bullying and how it differs from normal peer conflict.
- Bully, victim, and bystander roles and characteristics.
- Education on the dynamics of bullying, including the ongoing impact on learning as well as longer-term consequences for victims (e.g., depression and suicidality; Espelage & Swearer, 2003; Juvonen, Graham, & Schuster, 2003; Nansel et al., 2001) and bullies (e.g., criminal behavior and domestic violence; Olweus, 1993; Smith, Bowers, Binney, & Cowie, 1993).
- The serious nature of bullying and the need for adults to help children with bullying.
- Adult conflict management styles that are most effective with bullies, victims, and bystanders (no-nonsense style for bullies and supportive style for victims).
- The important role that peers or bystanders have in maintaining or changing bullying patterns (Espelage & Swearer, 2003).
- Review of the student curriculum and practice in teaching it.

Student Instruction

Six lessons for the primary grades and six lessons for the intermediate grades cover the following essential concepts:

- The definitions of bullying and bully, victim, and bystander roles.
- The difference between bullying and normal peer conflict.
- The three bully-proofing rules: (1) We will not bully other students; (2) We will help others who are being bullied by speaking out and by getting adult help; and (3) We will use extra effort to include all students in activities at out school.
- HA HA SO (Help, Assert, Humor, Avoid, Self-talk, Own it), the six techniques students can use to protect themselves from bullying.
- CARES (Creative problem-solving, Adult help, Relate and join, Empathy, Stand up and Speak out), the five techniques a student can use to help another student who is being bullied.
- Practice of the HA HA SO and CARES techniques using role plays.
- The difference between tattling and telling.
- Recognition and rewards for caring behaviors that help develop a Caring Community.
- For primary students, instruction that emphasizes friendship skills.

Individualized Interventions for Victims

Six lessons to be used with one student or a small group of students are available that cover:

- Instruction in friendship-making skills due to the strong relationship between social isolation, poor social skills, and victimization (e.g., Juvonen et al., 2003).
- Instruction about self-esteem and communication skills.
- Identification of trusted and effective adults within the school who students believe will effectively intervene in bullying situations.

Individualized Interventions for Bullies

Six lessons to be used with one student or a small group of students are available that cover:

- Instruction about the thinking errors that contribute to antisocial behavior (Samenow, 1989), along with strategies to alter these thinking errors.
- Instruction in anger management, social problem-solving, and empathy development.

Parent and Community Involvement

Such involvement can occur in a variety of ways (e.g., communication from the school via newsletters or local newspaper articles, caring awards sponsored by local businesses, or family nights) and includes:

- Education about the language and concepts of the program so that BPYS is supported not only at school, but also on the way to and from school; waiting at the bus stop and outside of school; and at youth sports, scouting, and other community activities.
- Emphasis on the philosophy that bullying is not tolerated and that kindness is rewarded.

In addition to these five intervention components, ongoing evaluation is also an important aspect of effective implementation of the BPYS program. Evaluation guides initial program implementation and is carried over into the final phase of BPYS—the sustained implementation phase. This phase occurs once BPYS is being used at a school. In addition to ongoing evaluation, sustained implementation stresses the need for regular cadre meetings, accommodation of staff changes, efforts to keep the program visible and fresh, integration of BPYS with other programs and the stated goals of the school, empowerment of students, and continued technical assistance and financial resources. In order to ensure success during this final phase, it is important to have a long-term focus (i.e., three to five years) from the outset of the program and to pay attention to implementation fidelity (Elliott, 2006).

Over time, the authors have observed some schools struggle with sustaining intervention efforts and have learned the importance of providing schools with additional tools, such as ongoing classroom meetings to promote open and constructive communication. A section on Caring Community Development has been added to the teacher training and student instruction and includes four guiding principles:

1. Identifying the behaviors and characteristics of a caring community.
2. Recognizing and reinforcing these caring behaviors.

3. Developing classroom and school-wide caring community groups.
4. Using teachable moments and ongoing classroom discussions.

Many concepts in BPYS are similar to Olweus's Bullying Prevention Program (Olweus, 1991). Specifically, the use of explicit rules, involvement of the entire community, and increased adult supervision are components that are not unique to BPYS. Concepts that are *unique* to BPYS include:

*   emphasis on climate change and turning bystanders into a "caring majority";
*   staff use of a no-nonsense interaction style with bullies and a supportive style with victims;
*   specific sets of strategies for students to use when experiencing (HA HA SO) or witnessing (CARES) bullying;
*   charts for bullying versus normal peer conflict and for tattling versus telling;
*   use of Samenow's (1989) antisocial thinking errors in teaching about bullies;
*   use of prosocial consequences and avoidance of power struggles with bullies;
*   caring community development strategies, including teachable moments.

The BPYS teacher training and student instruction curricula were developed based on bullying prevention research and programs that began in Europe (e.g., Olweus, 1991; Sharp & Smith, 1991). Emphasizing comprehensiveness and climate change, the program seeks to work with teachers, bystanders, victims, bullies, parents, and community members. By teaching all members of the school community their role in preventing bullying and the importance of becoming a caring community member, the program aims to improve school climate and change the behavior and well-being of these varied participants. Research has begun to support the positive impact of BPYS in schools.

REVIEW OF RESEARCH ON BULLY-PROOFING YOUR SCHOOL

Schools today are increasingly called upon to implement interventions that are research- and/or evidence-based. This is a prudent expectation given that programs with a solid foundation in research and evidence of previous positive impact are more likely to be effective than programs without such a foundation (Elliott, 2006; Nation et al., 2003). Several recent reviews of research on the outcome of bullying interventions have been conducted that address the general effectiveness of bullying interventions. Unfortunately, some of these reviews conclude that such interventions in schools have no practical effect in reducing bullying or other violent behaviors (Ferguson, San Miguel, Kilburn, & Sanchez, 2007), while others point to a limited or variable impact (Merrell, Gueldner, Ross, & Isava, 2008; Smith, Schneider, Smith, & Ananiadou, 2004; Vreeman & Carroll, 2007). This is not surprising given that, despite some general commonalities across programs, variability exists in what is included in bullying interventions (Rigby, Smith, & Pepler, 2004), as well as populations studied, which outcome variables are assessed, and how they are assessed.

Despite this inconsistency, the current research-base can be used to support the importance of the key components of Bully-Proofing Your School. The first factors that are discussed as important components of bullying intervention are assessment of bullying in the school paired with increased awareness of the dynamics of bullying (Olweus, 1997; Orpinas, Horne, & Staniszewski, 2003; Rigby et al., 2004). The Colorado School Climate Survey was developed for BPYS in order to assess bullying behaviors, perceptions of safety, and overall school climate; BPYS trainings for students, staff, and parents include information on bullying dynamics. The school-wide, systemic approach as found in BPYS has also been identified as an important component of successful bullying interventions (Olweus, 1997; Orpinas et al., 2003; Pepler, Smith, & Rigby, 2004). Because bullying is thought of as a systemic group process involving not only victims and bullies, but also peers, adults at school, parents, and the community as a whole (Swearer & Espelage, 2004), it is not surprising that interventions that address only one level (i.e., skills-based classroom curriculum interventions) have not been found to impact bullying behaviors in schools (Vreeman & Carrol, 2007).

The establishment of rules and/or a policy regarding bullying (Olweus, 1997; Orpinas et al., 2003; Rigby et al., 2004) is mentioned as a necessary, though not sufficient, component of effective bullying interventions and is addressed in BPYS through classroom rules and the adoption of a school-wide discipline plan that addresses bullying behaviors. Research has discussed the importance of interventions for both bullies and victims (Eslea & Smith, 1998; Stevens, Van Oost, & DeBourdeaudhuij, 2000); although it is thought to be critical to provide support and protection for victims, the approaches with bullies have been more variable across bullying interventions (Pepler et al., 2004). BPYS includes the HA HA SO strategies to provide students with tools to become less attractive as victims, places emphasis on no-nonsense staff responses to bullies and the importance of support for victims, and contains supplemental interventions for victims and bullies.

A final component identified by research as critical for effective bullying intervention is the involvement of peers in the intervention (Cowie, 2000; Orpinas et al., 2003; Stevens et al., 2000). Peers are an important part of the dynamics of bullying for several reasons. Bullying is a problem that includes the bully and the victim, but is also impacted by the social environment in which bullying occurs (Espelage & Swearer, 2003). Within this environment, other students and not adults are often the ones who are aware of the bullying (Pepler, Craig, Ziegler, & Charach, 1994). Further, though students typically report they do not condone bullying behavior, they often behave in ways that exacerbate rather than diminish bullying (Salmivalli, 1999). BPYS includes lessons that teach strategies to students who are bystanders to the bullying. Further, the core of Bully-Proofing Your School is its emphasis on Caring Community development, which relies on the involvement of the entire peer community.

In addition to its foundation in research on effective bullying intervention, research has been conducted that more directly assesses the impact of Bully-Proofing Your School. Berkey, Keyes, and Longhurst (2001) interviewed over 200 students and school staff in schools where BPYS had been implemented. They found that BPYS had a positive impact on discipline and behavior at the elementary but not secondary level. A four-year longitudinal study by Epstein, Plog, and Porter (2002) reported on the impact of BPYS in a suburban elementary school. Significant decreases in bullying behaviors (physical, verbal, and exclusionary) and improved perceptions of safety across four school locations were found using time-lagged contrasts between equivalent groups. A study by Beran and Tutty (2002) improved upon this methodology and included both an intervention (an adaptation of BPYS) and a comparison school. They found significantly decreased reports of witnessed bullying in an intervention school, but not in a comparison school.

They also found decreased positive attitudes toward victims in a comparison school, but not in an intervention school.

This preliminary research provides initial support for the positive impact of the BPYS program at the elementary level. More solid support comes from a methodologically rigorous study of BPYS conducted by the Center for the Study and Prevention of Violence. This study was conducted in five treatment and four comparison schools in rural and suburban Colorado over the course of five years (Menard, Grotpeter, Gianola, & O'Neal, 2007). Approximately 700 elementary and 300 middle school students were surveyed prior to the implementation of BPYS—each of the three years during which it was implemented in the treatment schools, and one year following the intervention. Students provided information on the degree to which bullying was discouraged at their school, their attitudes toward bullying and perceptions of safety at school, as well as on the prevalence of bullying and other aggressive behavior. Although schools were not randomly assigned to treatment and control conditions, attempts were made to match treatment and control schools using sociodemographic variables. Despite these attempts, significant differences that favored the treatment schools emerged on some of the outcome variables at the baseline measurement at the middle school level. Although these differences were inconsistent, they led the authors to conclude that the generally positive results that were found (increased perception that bullying is discouraged at their school, a positive impact on attitudes toward physical and relational aggression, and mild support for improved perceptions of safety at school and reductions in bullying behavior) could not be attributed to the BPYS intervention. Therefore, the following discussion will focus only on the elementary-level findings.

Analyses were conducted to assess treatment and comparison differences at the survey-item level, based on composite scale scores and ratings of the quality of the implementation of the intervention, and using multivariate analysis to consider other variables which may have influenced the results. Across these different methodologies, BPYS was found to lead to improved recognition that bullying was discouraged in their school, reductions in bullying and related behaviors, improved perceptions of safety (though only at school, not on the bus or going to and from school), and more negative attitudes toward physical and relational aggression. The quality of implementation in the schools impacted the results; results were quicker to materialize and more persistent over time in schools with good implementation fidelity. Finally, the authors found that the impact of BPYS on bullying behaviors appeared to be mediated through its impact on attitudes toward aggression and violence; those students with a more favorable view of aggression and violence were more likely to perpetrate and witness physical and relational aggression and bullying. The authors conclude that "there is clear evidence of success in meeting the objectives of the three major components [defined by the authors as: heightened awareness of the problem of bullying, teaching protective skills for dealing with bullying, and creation of a positive school climate] of BPYS" (Menard et al., 2007, p. 95).

Thus, research on the impact of Bully-Proofing Your School has generally shown that BPYS has a positive impact on student attitudes toward bullying and perceptions of safety at school as well as reductions in bullying behavior, in particular at the elementary level. As rigorous evaluation of BPYS at the middle school level failed to yield conclusive results (Menard et al., 2007), more research will be needed to determine whether these promising initial results are attributable to BPYS at the middle school level. In addition, more research is needed to determine whether the above results can be replicated at the elementary level.

REMAINING QUESTIONS ABOUT EFFECTIVE BULLYING INTERVENTION

Although preliminary evidence of effectiveness of the bully-proofing has been found, as is true with other bullying interventions, questions still remain. As stated by Smith and colleagues (2004), research generally concludes that bullying interventions "can succeed, but not enough is known to indicate exactly how and when" (p. 558). The following discussion focuses on factors that, based on the authors' experience working to implement BPYS in schools, appear to play a role in the "how and when" of effective bullying intervention.

Climate Change

Brand, Felner, Shim, Seitsinger, and Dumas (2003) defined school climate to include dimensions such as disciplinary practices, positive and negative peer interactions, rules and expectations, and safety. More generally, the "climate" of a school can be said to describe the milieu of a building, how people treat each other, and what is valued there. BPYS aims to reduce bullying in a school by changing the climate from one that allows bullying through attitudes that do not notice or intervene with bullying to a climate that emphasizes "safe and caring", values kindness and inclusion, and works toward a goal of no bullying in the school. This change in climate takes place over time and is thought to be a key component in the reduction of bullying. Shared language and visible goals, system-wide involvement including parents, and long-term focus play an important role in this process.

Shared language and visible values. For BPYS, this language includes phrases such as "caring community," "no bullying allowed," "protect yourself with HAHASO," and "take a stand for what is right." In order to be visible, this language and set of values should appear in signs and posters around the school, school newsletters, the school's mission statement and accountability goals, and potentially even on items such as T-shirts, rulers, and/or bookmarks. Common language is one part of ensuring that school-wide bully-proofing efforts become a part of the practices and belief of the school and community. Such integration of an intervention into normal school operations is thought to be one important component of effective implementation of prevention programs in schools (Elliott, 2006; Gottfredson & Gottfredson, 2002).

System-wide involvement. Everyone who is part of the school should know the reasons why BPYS is being implemented and should be familiar with its concepts and interventions. In addition, all members of a school community, including parents, should know and support the caring community values and understand what to do should bullying occur. The importance of involving the entire school community is supported by several lines of research. First, when skill-building interventions are accompanied by environmental change (multiple interventions or contexts), there is a greater likelihood of success than when skill building occurs without the accompanying environmental change (Elliott, 2006; Gottfredson, 1997; Greenberg et al., 2003; Weissberg, 2004). Also, interventions that include the involvement of parents, school staff, and the community in intervention have been noted to be part of effective prevention programming (Greenberg et al., 2003). Finally, as Roland (2000) noted based on his observation of 15 years of bullying intervention in Norway, schools that implement bullying interventions in a more complete and systematic manner are more likely to obtain positive results.

Long-term focus. Climate change programs can typically take as long as three to five years for the program to become fully integrated into the school culture (Elliott, Kratochwill, & Roach, 2003; Weissberg, 2004). Conceptually it makes sense that creating a more positive school climate through shared language and visible goals, system-wide involvement, and a long-term focus could enhance bullying prevention efforts in schools. In addition, research generally supports a reciprocal and inverse relationship between bullying and school climate (e.g., Buckley, Storino, & Sebastiani, 2003; Limber & Small, 2003; Nansel et al., 2001). Even so, understanding how changes to climate impact changes in bullying warrants additional empirical study.

CONFLICT RESOLUTION AND BULLYING PREVENTION

Some confusion exists in the literature as to the appropriateness of conflict resolution as an intervention to reduce bullying. Some authors have noted that conflict resolution, in particular peer mediation, is not an appropriate bullying intervention because conflict resolution fails to recognize the imbalance of power involved in bullying and therefore sends an inappropriate message that both parties are equally responsible (Jacobs, 2007; Limber, 2004; Sampson, 2002). Further, it is argued that these approaches can traumatize the victim even more and have not been shown to be effective in reducing bullying (Jacobs, 2007; U.S. Department of Health and Human Services, n.d.). The general effectiveness of peer mediation also has been questioned (U.S. Department of Health and Human Services, 2001), though Jones's (2004) review of research on conflict resolution education, including peer mediation, concludes that this form of intervention is effective in increasing students' conflict knowledge, improving school climate, and reducing negative behavior. Other authors have also reported a positive impact of peer mediation and conflict resolution interventions (Peterson & Skiba, 2001).

Part of the confusion over the appropriateness of conflict resolution interventions may stem from the different forms of conflict resolution; some approaches rely on a whole-school skill building approach, while peer mediation provides a select group of students with skills to mediate disputes between other students (Powell, Muir-McClain, & Halasyamani, 1995). Many of the concerns about conflict resolution apply more clearly to peer mediation approaches. Despite some evidence of general positive impact, peer mediation bears little resemblance to the characteristics of effective bullying interventions described above. Therefore, peer mediation should be included only as one component of a comprehensive approach (if used at all) and should only be considered at the victim's request and with adequate preparation and supervision (Limber, 2004).

Although peer mediation may have at best a very limited role in bullying intervention, questions remain about the appropriateness of skills-based conflict resolution approaches in bullying prevention. The use of a curriculum to teach such skills alone is inadvisable simply because of the systemic nature of bullying; in fact, such curricular types of conflict resolution programs have been noted to be ineffective in preventing bullying (Vreeman & Carrol, 2007). Not all conflict resolution approaches are based on the delivery of an isolated curriculum, however. In fact, whole-school approaches to conflict resolution, such as Responding to Conflict Creatively and Peacebuilders, have been shown to have a positive impact on variables such as social competence and aggressive behaviors (Brown, Roderick, Lantieri, & Aber, 2004; Flannery, et al., 2003; Jones, 2004). On a theoretical level, although normal conflict and bullying are not the same, a potential way to integrate the two can come from viewing a continuum of conflictual, aggressive behavior.

This model, presented by Doll, Song, and Siemers (2004), proposes that viewed on a continuum, bullying as an aggressive behavior is a more extreme form of normal conflict in terms of its malicious intent and inequality of power. They argue that the normal conflicts that can and do arise in a classroom can be resolved more effectively when students have the skills needed to successfully negotiate conflict and when the adults in the children's lives model successful execution of these skills. The successful resolution of conflicts before they escalate to bullying might also diminish the frequency of bully behaviors. Given this view, it is not surprising that some authors have recommended integrating conflict resolution education as one part of bullying interventions (Cornell, 2006; National Association of School Psychologists Bullying Workgroup, 2007).

On a practical level, integration of bullying prevention and conflict resolution is appealing. Conflicts between children more commonly do not involve an imbalance of power (Doll et al., 2004); it has been the authors' experience in schools that normal conflict between peers coexists with bullying. Therefore, schools may need an intervention or interventions that address both areas of concern. How to integrate the two is somewhat less clear. Of concern is the tendency to blur the distinction between bullying and normal conflict. Some of the reviews of the effectiveness of bullying prevention have included studies of the impact of more traditional conflict-resolution programs (Ferguson et al., 2007), even though these programs were not specifically designed to address bullying. Within the conflict-resolution field, bullying has been discussed as a specific content area of the curricula (Jones, 2004). This view does not necessarily incorporate all the components (e.g., systemic approach, policy on bullying, involvement of the peer community) that are thought to be necessary for effective bullying prevention. A second concern comes from the logistics involved should a school select a whole-school bullying intervention and a whole-school conflict resolution intervention (not to mention the possible need to address other areas of social emotional learning); integration of the two approaches could prove a time-consuming task and failure to integrate the two would likely stretch already limited resources. Although one study of a program designed to impact both bullying and conflict resolution has found a positive impact on conflict resolution skills, perceptions of safety, and bullying behaviors (Heydenberk, Heydenberk, & Tzenova, 2006), clearly more work is needed to determine how to best integrate bullying prevention and conflict resolution education.

EARLY CHILDHOOD INTERVENTION

When bully prevention programs were first developed over 20 years ago, it was commonly assumed that bullying behavior could not be specifically identified until approximately 2nd grade (Perry, Kusel, & Perry, 1988) despite anecdotal reports from preschool and early elementary parents, staff, and students to the contrary. Because of this, bullying interventions typically have been designed for children of later elementary and middle school age. Recent research has begun to demonstrate the salience of bullying in the early childhood years. Initial research conducted abroad on early childhood students suggests that relational and physical aggression do occur in the preschool years (Russell, Hart, Robinson, & Olsen, 2003). Observational studies in the United States lend further support to these findings. For example, Ostrov, Woods, Jansen, Casas, and

Crick (2004) observed that under conditions of limited resources, a majority of boys engaged in physical aggression and girls employed social aggression, such as spreading rumors, telling secrets, and gossiping.

Other studies of preschool-aged children not only find bullying is present in this age group, but also begin to point to the importance of early intervention tailored specifically to the needs of these students. One such study (Monks, Ortega Ruiz, & Torrado Val, 2002) on the stability of victim and bully behavior reported that children victimized during the preschool years display different characteristics from children who are not victimized until they are older. Rather than being timid, physically weak or socially isolated as is often found of older victims, the early childhood victims were aggressive. These physically aggressive behaviors have been found to increase a child's risk for future victimization (Barker et al., 2008). Chronically victimized children have been found to exhibit "a multitude of psychiatric and physical health problems" (Barker et al., 2008, p. 1185) such as loneliness, depression, self-harm and suicidal ideation; low self-esteem and social withdrawal; alcohol and/or drug use; and school avoidance and decreased school performance.

Researchers have also found a relatively stable group of preschoolers who used physical aggression to victimize their peers. Ostrov and Keating (2004) not only documented aggression toward peers as early as age two and a half but also found the behavior to be relatively stable and to grow more serious as children moved into the elementary years. Because early research suggests that perpetrators and victims of bullying can be identified in the early preschool years and that without intervention these students may continue on in perpetrator and victim roles into their elementary years, it follows that intervention programs targeting this age group could be of great benefit in reducing bullying, not only in the preschool, but also the elementary years.

Bully-Proofing in Early Childhood: Building a Caring Community (McCarnes, Nelson, & Sager, 2005) was developed in an effort to address the need for bullying intervention with preschool-aged children. Although empirical evidence of the efficacy of BPYS with this age group has yet to be demonstrated, the curriculum extends the principles that have been found to have a positive impact on bullying during the elementary school years. Clearly, additional research is needed to determine the potential of early childhood bullying prevention programs to positively impact current and future levels of bullying behaviors in schools.

TRANSLATING RESEARCH INTO PRACTICE: IMPLICATIONS FOR BULLY PREVENTION AND INTERVENTION PROGRAMS

Bully-Proofing Your School (BPYS) is a developmentally based comprehensive prevention program designed not only to reduce bullying but also to shift the school climate in a systemic way that can be sustained over time. It includes specific, hands-on materials relevant and developmentally appropriate to students from early childhood through high school. Staff training, student instruction, individualized interventions for victims, individualized interventions for bullies, and parent and community involvement are thought to be essential in order to achieve positive outcomes. The desired outcomes for these five program components and their impact on the school climate are shown in Figure 19.1 (Garrity et al., 2004).

Preliminary research has begun to provide support for the positive impact of BPYS

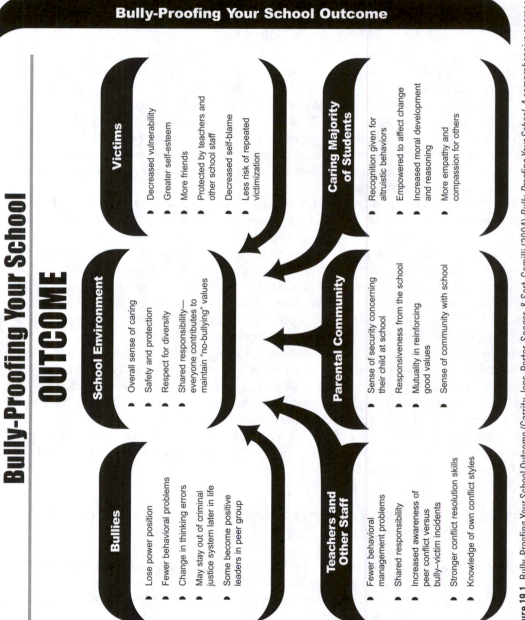

Figure 19.1 Bully-Proofing Your School Outcome (Garrity, Jens, Porter, Saager, & Sort-Camilli (2004) *Bully-Proofing Your School: A comprehensive approach for elementary schools*. 2nd ed. Longmont, CO: Sopris West. Reproduced with permission.)

on bullying behavior, perceptions of safety, and attitudes toward bullying in schools. Despite this initial evidence of positive impact, more research is needed to definitively support the effectiveness of BPYS. Additional research is also needed to clarify the hypothesized central role of climate change in bullying prevention, the overlapping roles of conflict resolution and bullying prevention in schools, and the potential impact of bullying prevention with preschool-aged children. Based on both available research and experience implementing BPYS in schools, it is thought that interventions should address bullying not just as a problem behavior, but rather should also focus on the overall climate of the school. Such a focus helps address a broader goal of proactively building comprehensive programs that help children develop socially and emotionally (Shriver & Weissberg, 1996). Through such a lens, schools should be better prepared to integrate interventions aimed at both normal conflict and bullying. As it is critical that school staff be taught the difference between normal conflict and bullying to ensure appropriate interventions (Limber, 2004), it is also critical that interventions for each are implemented in an integrated fashion when both are needed. A final recommendation is that because chronic, destructive bullying patterns can begin in preschool and younger (Barker et al., 2008), schools should not overlook this age group in their bullying assessments and should also consider intervention with their youngest students.

REFERENCES

Barker, E., Boivin, M., Brendgen, M., Fontaine, N., Arsenault, L., Vitaro, F., Bissonnette, C., & Tremblay, R.E. (2008). The predictive validity and early predictors of peer victimization trajectories in preschool. *Archives of General Psychiatry, 65,* 1185–1192.

Beran, T.N., & Tutty, L. (2002). An Evaluation of the Dare to Care Bully-Proofing Your School Program. Unpublished, Calgary, Alberta. RESOLVE Alberta.

Berkey, L.G., Keyes, B.J., & Longhurst, I.E. (2001). Bully-Proofing: What one district learned about improving school climate. *Reclaiming Children and Youth, 9,* 224–228.

Brand, S., Felner, R., Shim, M., Seitsinger, A., & Dumas, T. (2003). Middle school improvement and reform: Development and validation of a school-level assessment of climate, cultural pluralism, and school safety. *Journal of Educational Psychology, 95,* 570–588.

Brown, J.L., Roderick, T., Lantieri, L., & Aber, J.L. (2004). The Resolving Conflict Creatively Program: A school-based social and emotional learning program. In J.E. Zins, R.P. Weissberg, M.C. Wang, & H.J. Walberg (Eds.), *Building academic success on social and emotional learning: What does the research say?* (pp. 151–169). New York, NY: Teachers College, Columbia University.

Buckley, M.A., Storino, M., & Sebastiani, A.M. (2003). The impact of school climate: Variation by ethnicity and gender. Poster presented at the annual meeting of the American Psychological Association, Toronto.

Cornell, D. (2006). *School violence: Fears versus facts.* Mahwah, NJ: Lawrence Erlbaum.

Cowie, H. (2000). Bystanding or standing by: Gender issues in coping with bullying in English schools. *Aggressive Behavior, 26,* 85–97.

Doll, B., Song, S., & Siemers, E. (2004). Classroom ecologies that support or discourage bullying. In D.L Espelage & S.M. Swearer (Eds.), *Bullying in American schools: A social-ecological perspective on prevention and intervention* (pp. 161–183). Mahwah, New Jersey: Lawrence Erlbaum.

Elliott, D.S. (2006, March). Improving the effectiveness of delinquency, drug and violence prevention efforts: Promise and practice. Presentation at the Blueprints Conference, Denver, Colorado.

Elliott, S.N., Kratochwill, T.R., & Roach, A.T. (2003). Commentary: Implementing social-emotional and academic innovations: Reflections, reactions, and research. *School Psychology Review, 32,* 320–326.

Epstein, L., Plog, A.E., & Porter, W. (2002). Bully-Proofing Your School: Results of a four-year intervention. *The Report on Emotional and Behavioral Disorders in Youth. 2,* 55–56, 73–77.

Eslea, M. & Smith, P.K. (1998). The long-term effectiveness of anti-bullying work in primary schools. *Education Research, 40,* 203–218.

Espelage, D.L., & Swearer, S. (2003). Research on school bullying and victimization: What have we learned and where do we go from here? *School Psychology Review, 23,* 365–383.

Ferguson, C.J., San Miguel, C., Kilburn, J.C., & Sanchez, P. (2007). The effectiveness of school-based anti-bullying programs. *Criminal Justice Review, 32*, 401–414.

Flannery, D.J., Vazsonyi, A.T., Liau, A.K., Guo, S., Powell, K.E., Atha, H., Vesterdal, W., & Embry, D. (2003). Initial behavior outcomes for the PeaceBuilders universal school-based violence prevention program. *Developmental Psychology, 39*, 292–308.

Garrity, C., Jens, K., Porter, W., Sager, N., & Short-Camilli. C. (1994). *Bully-Proofing Your School: A comprehensive approach for elementary schools.* Longmont, CO: Sopris West.

Garrity, C., Jens, K., Porter, W., Sager, N., & Short-Camilli. C. (2004). *Bully-Proofing Your School: Administrators guide to staff development in elementary schools* (3rd ed.). Longmont, CO: Sopris West.

Gottfredson, D. (1997). School-based crime prevention. In L. Sherman, D. Gottfredson, D. Mackenzie, J. Ect, P. Reuter, & S. Bushway (Eds.), *Preventing crime: what works, what doesn't, and what's promising.* Retrieved March 2006, from www.ncjrs.gov/works/chapter5.htm.

Gottfredson, D.C., & Gottfredson, G.D. (2002). Quality of school-based prevention programs: Results from a national survey. *Journal of Research in Crime & Delinquency, 39*, 3–35.

Greenberg, M.T., Weissberg, R.P., O'Brien, M.U., Zins, J.E., Fredricks, L., Resnick, H., & Elias, M. (2003). Enhancing school-based prevention and youth development through coordinated social, emotional, and academic learning. *American Psychologist, 58*, 466–474.

Heydenberk, R.A., Heydenberk, W.R., & Tzenova, V. (2006). Conflict resolution and bully prevention: Schools for success. *Conflict Resolution Quarterly, 24*, 55–69.

Jacobs, A.K. (2007). Components of evidence-based interventions for bullying and peer victimization. In R.G. Steele, T.D. Elkin, & M.C. Roberts (Eds.), *Evidence-based therapies for children and adolescents: Bridging science and practice* (pp. 261–279). New York, NY: Springer.

Jones, T.S. (2004). Conflict resolution education: The field, the findings, and the future. *Conflict Resolution Quarterly, 22*, 233–267.

Juvonen, J., Graham, S., & Schuster, M.A. (2003). Bullying among young adolescents: The strong, the weak, and the troubled. *Pediatrics, 112*, 1231–1237.

Limber, S. (2004). Implementation of the Olweus Bullying Prevention Program in American schools: Lessons learned from the field. In D.L Espelage & S.M. Swearer (Eds.), *Bullying in American schools: A social-ecological perspective on prevention and intervention* (pp. 351–362). Mahwah, NJ: Lawrence Erlbaum.

Limber, S., & Small, M.A. (2003). State laws and policies to address bullying in schools. *School Psychology Review, 23*, 445–455.

Lohrmann, S., Forman, S., Martin, S., & Palmieri, M. (2008). Understanding school personnel's resistance to adopting a schoolwide positive behavior support at a universal level of intervention. *Journal of Positive Behavior Intervention, 10*, 256–269.

McCarnes, K., Nelson, K., & Sager, N. (2005) *Bully-proofing in early childhood: Building a caring community.* Longmont, CO: Sopris West.

Menard, S., Grotpeter, J., Gianola, D., & O'Neal, M. (2007). *Evaluation of Bullyproofing Your School: Final Report.* Retrieved June 2008, from www.ncjrs.gov/App/Publications/abstract.aspx?ID=242926.

Merrell, K.W., Gueldner, B.A., Ross, S.W., & Isava, D.M. (2008). How effective are school bullying intervention programs? A meta-analysis of intervention research. *School Psychology Quarterly, 23*, 26–42.

Monks, C., Ortega Ruiz, R., & Torrado Val, E. (2002). Unjustified aggression in preschool. *Aggressive Behavior, 28*, 458–476.

Nansel, T.R., Overpeck, M., Pilla, R.S., Ruan, W.J., Simons-Morton, B., & Scheidt, P. (2001). Bullying behaviors among U.S. youth: Prevalence and association with psychosocial adjustment. *Journal of the American Medical Association, 285*, 2094–2100.

Nation, M., Crusto, C., Wandersman, A., Kumpfer, K.L., Seybolt, Morrisey-Kane, E., & Davino, K. (2003). What works in prevention: Principles of effective programs. *American Psychologist, 58*, 449–456.

National Association of School Psychologists Bullying Workgroup (2007). *School bullying prevention and intervention: Tips for the school psychologist.* Retrieved January 16, 2009, from http://nasponline.org/prepare/cpipresentations/bullying.ppt.

Olweus, D. (1991). Bully/victim problems among schoolchildren: Basic facts and effects of a school based intervention program. In K. Rubin & D. Pepler (Eds.), *The development and treatment of childhood aggression* (pp. 411–448). Hillsdale, NJ: Erlbaum.

Olweus, D. (1993). Bully/victim problems among schoolchildren: Long-term consequences and an effective intervention program. In S. Hodgins (Ed.), *Mental Disorder and Crime* (pp. 317–349). Newbury Park, CA: Sage.

Olweus, D. (1997). Bully/victim problems in school: Facts and intervention. *European Journal of Psychology of Education, 12*, 495–110.

Orpinas, P., Horne, A.M., & Staniszewski, D. (2003). School bullying: Changing the problem by changing the school. *School Psychology Review, 23*, 431–444.

Ostrov, J. & Keating, C. (2004). Gender differences in preschool aggression during free play and structured interactions: An observational study. *Social Development*, 13, 255–277.

Ostrov, J., Woods, K., Jansen, E. Casas, J. & Crick, N. (2004). An observational study of delivered and received aggression, gender and social-psychological adjustment in preschool: "This White Crayon Doesn't Work…". *Early Childhood Research Quarterly, 19*, 355–371.

Pepler, D., Smith, P.K., & Rigby, K. (2004). Looking back and looking forward: Implications for making interventions work effectively. In P.K. Smith, D. Pepler, & K. Rigby (Eds.), *Bullying in schools: How successful can interventions be?* (pp. 307–322). Cambridge, UK: Cambridge University Press.

Pepler, D.J., Craig, W.M., Ziegler, S., & Charach, A. (1994). An evaluation of an anti-bullying intervention in Toronto schools. *Canadian Journal of Community Mental Health, 13*, 95–110.

Perry, D., Kusel, S., & Perry, L. (1988). Victims of Peer Aggression. *Developmental Psychology, 24*, 807–814.

Peterson, R.L., & Skiba, R. (2001). Creating school climates that prevent school violence. *The Clearing House, 74*, 155–163.

Powell, K.E., Muir-McClain, L., & Halasyamani, L. (1995). A review of selected school-based conflict resolution and peer mediation projects. *Journal of School Health, 65*, 426–431.

Rigby, K., Smith, P.K., & Pepler, D. (2004). Working to prevent school bullying: key issues. In P.K. Smith, D. Pepler, & K. Rigby (Eds.), *Bullying in schools: How successful can interventions be?* (pp. 1–12). Cambridge, UK: Cambridge University Press.

Roland, E. (2000). Bullying in school: Three national innovations in Norwegian schools in 15 years. *Aggressive Behavior, 26*, 135–143.

Russell, A., Hart, C. Robinson, S., & Olsen, S. (2003). Children's sociable and aggressive behavior with peers: A comparison of the U.S. and Australia and contributions of temperament and parenting styles. *International Journal of Behavioral Development, 27*, 74–86.

Salmivalli, C. (1999). Participant role approach to school bullying: Implications for interventions. *Journal of Adolescence, 22*, 453–459.

Samenow, S. (1989). *Before it's too late: Why some kids get into trouble and what parents can do about it.* New York, NY: Times Books.

Sampson, R. (2002). Bullying in schools. Problem-oriented guides for police. Problem-Specific Guides Series No. 12 U.S. Department of Justice, Office of Community Oriented Policing Services. Retrieved January 16, 2009, from www.cops.usdoj.gov/files/ric/CDROMs/Tribal/law/BullyingInSchools.pdf.

Sharp, S., & Smith, P. K. (1991). Bullying in UK schools: The DES Sheffield Bullying Project. *Early Child Development and Care, 77*, 47–55.

Shriver, T.P., & Weissberg, R.P. (1996). No new wars! *Education Week, 15*, 33, 37.

Smith, J.D., Schneider, B.H., Smith, P.K., & Ananiadou, K. (2004). The effectiveness of whole-school antibullying programs: A synthesis of evaluation research. *School Psychology Review, 33*, 547–560.

Smith, P.K., Bowers, L., Binney, V., & Cowie, H. (1993). Relationships of children involved in bully/victim problems at school. In S. Duck (Ed.), *Learning about relationships*. Understanding Relationship Processes Series, V.2 (pp. 184–204). Newbury Park, CA: Sage

Stevens, V., Van Oost, P., & De Bourdeaudhuij, I. (2000). The effects of an anti-bullying intervention programme on peers' attitudes and behaviour. *Journal of Adolescence, 23*, 21–34.

Swearer, S.M., & Espelage, D.L. (2004). Introduction: A social ecological framework of bullying among youth. In D.L Espelage, & S.M. Swearer (Eds.), *Bullying in American schools: A social-ecological perspective on prevention and intervention* (pp. 1–11). Mahwah, NJ: Lawrence Erlbaum.

U.S. Department of Health and Human Services. (2001). Surgeon General's Report on Youth Violence. Retrieved December 2008, from http://mentalhealth.samhsa.gov/youthviolence/surgeongeneral/SG_Site/home.asp.

U.S. Department of Health and Human Services, Health Resources and Services Administration (n.d.). Misdirections in bullying prevention and intervention. Retrieved January 16, 2009 from http://stopbullyingnow.hrsa.gov/HHS_PSA/pdfs/SBN_Tip_5.pdf.

Vreeman, R.C., & Carroll, A.E. (2007) A systematic review of school-based interventions to prevent bullying. *Archives of Pediatric and Adolescent Medicine, 161*, 78–88.

Weissberg, R.P. (2004). Statement before the subcomittee on substance abuse and mental health services, U.S. Senate committee on health, education, labor and pensions. Retrieved March 2006, from www.k12coordinator.org/testimony.pdf.

20

TEACHER SUPPORT OF BULLYING PREVENTION
The Good, the Bad, and the Promising

KARIN S. FREY, DIANE CARLSON JONES,
MIRIAM K. HIRSCHSTEIN, AND LEIHUA V. EDSTROM

Bullying and victimization are persistent school problems that impede learning and threaten the psychological well-being of students. The effects of repeated hurtful, intimidating, and exclusionary actions are not limited to the individuals directly involved in bullying episodes. Student bystanders may feel afraid or envious of the aggressor. They may also feel confused or guilty if they enjoy watching the event (Bradshaw, Sawyer, & O'Brennan, 2007; O'Connell, Pepler, & Craig, 1999). On days in which middle school students witness others being victimized, they may feel increased anxiety or dislike of schools (Nishina & Juvonen, 2005). Some schools and classrooms develop "cultures of bullying" (Unnever & Cornell, 2003) in which abusive treatment is expected and tolerated.

Teachers are central figures in schools' efforts to intervene effectively and limit the negative effects of school bullying among students (Doll, 2004; Kallestad & Olweus, 2003). Teachers are generally expected to monitor student behavior and to respond to instances of victimization both in the classroom (Atlas & Pepler, 1998) and in the larger school context (Parault, Davis, & Pelligrini, 2007). Teachers are also frequently relied upon to implement anti-bullying curricula at the classroom level (e.g., Committee for Children, 2001; Horne, Orpinas, Newman-Carlson, & Bartolomucci, 2004; Stein & Sjostrom, 1996).

The importance of teachers is confirmed in research on the effectiveness of intervention programs. In the context of a successful school-wide anti-bullying program, even occasional interventions by teachers predicted higher-than-average declines in observed victimization, non-bullying aggression (including responses to bullying), and bystander encouragement of bullying (Hirschstein, Edstrom, Frey, Snell, & MacKenzie, 2007).

In this chapter, we examine the role of teachers in changing the dynamics of bullying and victimization. We are particularly interested in the ways in which teachers help students acquire empathy for each other and skills that enable them to effectively respond to bullying. Teachers can be powerful agents of change—aiding students by providing emotional support (Hunter, Boyle, & Warden, 2004), facilitating student problem-solving (Hirschstein et al., 2007), and fostering prosocial behavior (Frey, Nolen, Van Schoiack Edstrom, & Hirschstein, 2005).

It is particularly important to examine teacher intervention strategies because of the variations in the effectiveness of existing school-wide intervention programs (Smith, Schneider, Smith, & Ananiadou, 2004). Teachers show significant variability in the degree to which they acknowledge, interpret, and intervene to limit victimization (Bradshaw et al., 2007; Mishna, Scarcello, Pepler, & Wiener, 2005). Inconsistent findings across classrooms can be related to the different levels as well as types of strategies that teachers use in response to bullying and victimization. Information is needed about outcomes associated with specific teachers' intervention behaviors as they address bullying and victimization among students. In addition to describing briefly the Steps to Respect program (Committee for Children, 2001) and evidence of its effectiveness, we will examine the role of specific teacher actions as they relate to aspects of schoolyard bullying and non-bullying aggression.

We are guided in our analysis by the social–ecological approach (Swearer & Espelage, 2004), which assumes that bullying is embedded in a larger sociocultural context and reflects the norms, attitudes, and standards for conduct in the school community. Figure 20.1 represents the aspects of the teacher–student relationships that have potential impact on bullying and victimization. These relationships are experienced in the larger context of the classroom and the school community norms. In this chapter, we focus primarily on the ways in which teachers may influence classroom peer dynamics as well

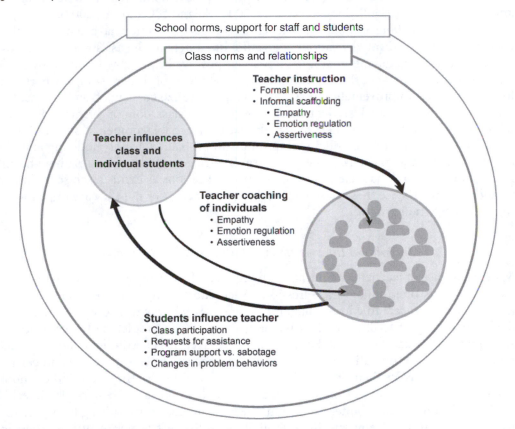

Figure 20.1 Teacher–student influences within the classroom and school context

as individual student behavior. We note, however, that the direction of influence is not unidirectional from teacher to students. Whether students participate, show positive change, or attempt to sabotage the instruction of anti-bullying curricula will influence teachers' motivation and effectiveness in creating a positive classroom culture.

CLASS-WIDE EFFORTS TO INFLUENCE THE QUALITY OF PEER INTERACTION

Formal class rules and instruction

The centrality of the role of teachers reflects, in part, the amount of regular contact they have with students as prominent authority figures in organizing the classroom context. Familiar with their students' characteristics and relationships, teachers must skillfully manage classroom dynamics daily if they are to create a respectful learning environment governed by positive norms and rules. Within the context of school-wide policies and procedures, teachers lead their classes to develop rules that guide peer interactions. They often provide formal instruction of expected behavior, especially in elementary school. Subject matter lessons such as social studies and literature may include themes of empathy or ethical behavior. Finally, there are formal programs such as Steps to Respect that attempt to foster non-exploitive, cooperative peer relationships. Students indicate less bullying when their teachers provide safe, structured classrooms that promote inclusion and prosocial values (Doll, Song, & Siemers, 2004; Roland & Galloway, 2002).

Informal instruction: Scaffolding. Teachers also engage in less formal avenues to influence peer relations through scaffolding. Scaffolding refers to the assistance offered by the teacher to help students acquire and practice positive behavior with peers. By scaffolding behaviors that are slightly beyond the current level of student skill, teachers can foster continued improvement. To reinforce and generalize concepts from lessons, for example, teachers may ask students to resolve common classroom problems (e.g., equitably sharing resources). Teachers may make use of "teachable moments" such as intervening in a work-partner conflict with prompts to problem-solve or modeling audible anger management "self-talk" when they feel frustrated with the class. Although our intervention research has referred to these informal actions as *extra-lesson* scaffolding, teachers frequently use these class-wide techniques whether or not they are implementing an intervention program.

Individual Interventions to Influence Peer Relations

Many examples of teacher scaffolding are directed at the entire class. Efforts with individual students often follow transgressions. Such efforts range from entirely punitive (e.g., "zero tolerance") to educational and supportive. The way transgressions are handled is revealing of teacher–student relationship quality, a predictor of peer relationship quality (Loukas, Suzuki, & Horton, 2006; Wentzel, 1997). Middle school students report less peer victimization when they perceive teachers to be supportive and caring (Marachi, Astor, & Benbenishty, 2007; Barboza et al., 2009). Victimized middle school students rate social support from teachers as especially important (Demaray & Malecki, 2003). Such support may buffer boys from internalizing distress resulting form victimization (Davidson & Demaray, 2007). The Steps to Respect program utilizes specific techniques to coach students involved in bullying as aggressors or targets.

CONTENT OF THE STEPS TO RESPECT PROGRAM

Since our research on scaffolding has been done in the context of an experimental evaluation of the Steps to Respect bullying prevention program, we will briefly describe the program, emphasizing the content of classroom lessons in grades 3 to 6. These lessons use a cognitive-behavioral approach (Kendall, 1993) and are coordinated with a school-wide environmental intervention (Olweus, 1993) and selective coaching for those involved in bullying. Classroom lessons use literature, discussions, and skill rehearsals to (1) guide safety-oriented decisions and procedures, (2) promote empathic attitudes and behavior, and (3) foster self-regulatory skills such as emotion management and assertiveness.

Decision-making

Since bullying may pose immediate risks to students, lessons teach students to assess safety risks, identify responses they can use on their own, and/or seek assistance. These are presented in the context of increased adult supervision, anti-bullying policies, and anti-bullying pledges. Constructive problem-solving is also taught explicitly and may help students build the supportive friendships necessary to protect against bullying (Kochenderfer & Ladd, 1997; Hodges, Malone, & Perry, 1997).

Empathy

Bullying and reinforcement of bullying by bystanders is associated with lack of empathy for victims (Endresen & Olweus, 2001; Rigby, 2005). The lack of emotional connection with victims is frequently accompanied by cognitive mechanisms that individuals use to rationalize cruel or oppressive behavior (Bandura, 2002). Common attitudes about bullying (Oliver, Hoover, & Hazler, 1994; Terasahjo & Salmivalli, 2003) correspond to several of these mechanisms: minimizing consequences ("She's not hurt"), euphemistic labeling ("We're just joking around with her"), and victim blaming ("She's such a weirdo"). Hymel, Rocke-Henderson, and Bonanno (2005) show that this type of *moral disengagement* is closely tied to bullying behavior. Lessons in Steps to Respect expose the lack of ethical justification for bullying and promote empathic understanding of the feelings of others. The lessons aim to reduce perceptions that victims are "outsiders" by emphasizing emotional understanding and support of peers who are excluded or harassed.

Self-regulation of Emotion and Behavior

Harassment and ostracism decreases student self-regulatory capacity (Williams, 2001). Hence, a third foci of Steps to Respect lessons is (1) emotion regulation and (2) assertiveness. Emotionally and behaviorally dysregulated students often become favored targets for bullying. Typified by non-bullying, retaliatory aggression, they are often rejected by peers, creating a vicious cycle of victimization and aggression (Camodeca, Terwogt, & Schuengel, 2002; Olweus, 1993). Self-calming techniques may help students respond more effectively when they are experiencing intense emotions. Assertiveness skills (e.g., being calm, polite, and strong) appear to reduce bullying (Espelage, Bosworth, & Simon, 2001) and deter victimization (Schwartz, Dodge, & Coie, 1993). Improving self-regulatory skills may also enable bystanders to manage emotional distress and channel their concern into socially responsible behavior (Eisenberg et al., 1996).

Individual Coaching Interventions

In addition to utilizing teachable moments in class and providing practice opportunities for students, the Steps to Respect program trains teachers to provide brief individual coaching sessions with each participant in a bullying episode. Teachers talk to participants individually, after allowing for natural "cooling off" periods. The StR coaching protocols (one for perpetrators, one for targets of bullying) provide for emotional support, discussion of school norms, student problem-solving, future behavior plans, practice of skills, and later follow-up to see if problems have been resolved. When intervention teachers provided more coaching, their students showed declines in playground victimization, non-bullying aggression, and bystander reinforcement of aggression (Hirschstein et al., 2007). The simultaneous decrease in victimization and non-bullying aggression suggests that those targeted for bullying may have learned more effective ways of responding other than retaliation.

Student Outcomes Associated with Specific Scaffolding Strategies

Steps to Respect coaching protocols, similar to lessons, are highly scripted. Intervention teachers also engaged in informal, less scripted scaffolding. Analyses within the intervention group showed no links between this less scripted scaffolding and playground behavior (Hirschstein et al., 2007). The analyses, however, did not examine the specific content of teachers' actions. Furthermore, we confirmed that although control-group teachers in the experimental evaluation did not have access to StR coaching protocols, they still attempted to scaffold positive peer interactions using more informal practices. Therefore we used data from both intervention and control-group classrooms in the current analyses to examine *specific* relationships between the use of scaffolding to support empathy, emotion regulation, assertiveness and changes in student behaviors and beliefs. This necessitated the grouping of teacher-reported scaffolding items into content-specific subscales with relatively few items. Although internal reliability remains high due to repeated measurement, these results are exploratory.

Content of scaffolding efforts

Based on the evidence described earlier, we hypothesized:

1. More frequent *empathy scaffolding* would predict later decreases in playground bullying, non-bullying aggression, bystander reinforcement of aggression, and beliefs supporting aggression.
2. More frequent prompting of *emotion regulation* would predict later decreases in playground victimization and non-bullying aggression.
3. More frequent *assertion scaffolding* would predict later increases in assertion self-efficacy and decreases in playground victimization and bystander reinforcement of aggression.

Scaffolding subscales

Our previous research indicated that observations of teacher behavior were moderately to strongly correlated with self-reports of scaffolding efforts (Hirschstein, Van Schoiack-

Edstrom, Frey, & Nolen, 2001). Over the four months between fall and spring observations, teachers estimated how frequently they used 11 specific behaviors with their students. Five of the 11 items (Hirschstein et al., 2007) were intended to foster empathic understanding (e.g., "I intervened in a student conflict by asking students to report how the other party felt") and behavior (e.g., "I encouraged student(s) to be friendly to someone who was being left out"). Five items referred to self-regulatory skills. Three of these specified emotion regulation ("I intervened in a student conflict by prompting students to manage their emotions"). Two items were meant to foster assertiveness skills ("I helped student(s) respond assertively to peer pressure"). A final item was deleted from our analyses because it specified more than one type of student behavior and was the only item that relied on teacher modeling rather than student prompts. Coefficient alphas were .92 for empathy, .90 for emotion regulation, and .83 for assertion. Means were calculated for each scaffolding type by summing across four data points for each item within the three scales.

Student behavior and beliefs

For two-and-a-half months in the fall and spring, coders who were blind to condition made second-by-second observations of playground behavior, including bullying, victimization, non-bullying aggression, and bystander reinforcement of aggression (Frey et al., 2005). We defined bullying as proactive aggression directed toward a victim having lesser power due to age, strength or number of supporters. Retaliatory responses to bullying (e.g., a student becomes highly aroused and screams at a group of mocking peers) were categorized as non-bullying aggression. The inter-rater reliabilities for each of the playground behaviors were adequate to excellent. In addition, coders showed an excellent ability to discriminate between the two types of aggression (*kappa* = .80). Students were surveyed twice a year in class regarding their beliefs supporting aggression and self-efficacy for assertiveness. Playground observations over two years showed substantial decreases in bullying, retaliatory aggression, argumentative behavior, and bystander encouragement of aggression in the intervention, but not the control group. Improvements in beliefs about aggression and self-efficacy were also limited to the intervention group (Frey, Hirschstein, Edstrom, & Snell, 2009).

Analyses

To test our predictions regarding the role of informal scaffolding, we aggregated student data and analyzed student outcomes at the classroom level. Preliminary findings did not reveal significant group by scaffolding type predictors. Analyses proceeded using separate hierarchical regression analyses to predict spring levels of four observed student behaviors (bullying, non-bullying aggression, bystander reinforcement of aggression, and victimization) and two types of self-reported beliefs (aggression and assertiveness). In the first step of the regression analyses, fall pre-test levels of the student behavior or beliefs were entered as control variables. In the second step, we entered the three scaffolding types simultaneously. Although our main interest lay with hypothesized relationships, we analyzed for each scaffolding type, allowing for the possibility of unexpected relationships. Table 20.1 shows the results predicting student outcomes in spring (time 3), from teacher scaffolding in winter (time 2) after controlling for respective baseline values (time 1).

Table 20.1 *Beta* Weights for Time 3 Class-aggregated Behaviors and Beliefs

Time 2 teacher scaffolding	*Beta* weights for Time 3 class-aggregated behaviors and beliefs					
	Bullying	Non-bullying aggression	Bystander reinforcement	Victim-ization	Aggressive beliefs	Assertive self-efficacy
Empathy	−.08	.08	−.46*	.15	−.49**	−.03
Emotion regulation	.32†	.21	.52**	.12	.16	−.06
Assertiveness	−.10	.12	−.20	−.32†	.23	.21
$F_{(4,67)}$	1.40	5.17**	9.19**	1.42	24.15**	8.58**
Step 1 R^2	.03	.18	.20	.03	.53	.32
Step 2 ΔR^2	.05ª	.05	.15	.04	.06	.02
Total R^2	.08	.24	.35	.08	.59	.34

Note: Step 1 entry: relevant behavior or belief; Step 2 entry: three scaffolding types. Betas are presented for the final model.
ª R^2 change values account for entry of all three types of scaffolding.
† $p < .10$, *$p < .05$, **$p < .01$, two-tailed

Empathy

We hypothesized that teacher scaffolding of empathic cognitions and behavior would forecast decreases in spring bullying, non-bullying aggression, bystander reinforcement of aggression, and beliefs supporting aggression. Two hypotheses were confirmed. Bystander reinforcement of aggression and beliefs supporting aggression were negatively related to empathy scaffolding. These results indicated that teachers who more frequently engaged in empathy scaffolding had students who were observed to engage less in bystander reinforcement of bullying and were less likely to report aggressive beliefs.

Predicted links to bullying and non-bullying aggression, however, did not emerge. As expected, neither self-efficacy for assertion nor victimization was related to teacher efforts to scaffold student empathy.

Emotion regulation

Contrary to predictions, scaffolding of emotion regulation forecast later *increases* in bystander reinforcement of aggression. Although not significant, the *Beta* weights for bullying and non-bullying aggression also suggest cause for concern.

Assertiveness

We predicted that scaffolding of assertion would be followed by decreased victimization, bystander reinforcement, and increased assertion self-efficacy. Analyses offered qualified support for victimization *(p < .10)*. *Beta* weights for bystander reinforcement and assertion self-efficacy were supportive, but not significant. Having only two items in this subscale is a clear limitation. A larger, more representative selection of items is needed for future research.

DISCUSSION

This study provides new insights on the effects of teacher efforts for bullying prevention. Our analyses show behavior-specific links between type of teacher scaffolding and later student behaviors and beliefs. The nature of those links varied, however, from those suggestive of best practices to those that may have unintended negative consequences.

Empathy scaffolding appears to be an important classroom strategy for teachers. Bystander reinforcement of aggression and beliefs supporting aggression were strongly and negatively related to teachers' efforts. When teachers intervened with appeals to the emotions and perspectives of others, then students in the spring observations were less likely to be engaged in the bystander role of supporting bullying and were less likely to endorse aggressive beliefs. These results support the importance of empathy in the development of prosocial behavior (Bandura, Caprara, Barbaranelli, Gerbino, & Pastorelli, 2003). These outcomes suggest that the teachers' informal strategies are effective in changing the norms and expectations among students about the appropriateness of bullying. More generally, it illustrates the need for educators to actively teach social–emotional skills and positive values.

At the same time, neither bullying nor non-bullying aggression showed immediate links to teacher scaffolding of empathy. The absence of a direct relationship could be accounted for in several ways. First, the relationship between empathy scaffolding and bullying could be indirect and mediated through beliefs supporting aggression, which have been found to predict later changes in aggressive behavior (Huesmann & Guerra, 1997).

Another possible pathway to aggression reduction is the withdrawal of bystander reinforcement (Frey & Nolen, 2010). This may be particularly relevant for high-status bullies, who are likely to be sensitive to social rewards (Rodkin, Farmer, Pearl, & Van Acker, 2000; Vaillancourt, Hymel, & McDougall, 2003). The impact of withdrawal of bystander reinforcement may require longer periods of study in order to document the effects on bullying (cf. Frey et al., 2009). Finally, other teacher actions that we did not measure, such as monitoring, would also be expected to impact on bullying as part of the program effects. Longitudinal studies are needed to examine possible direct and indirect pathways between specific teacher actions and student behavior.

Despite the restricted range of the assertion subscale, results tentatively suggest that assertion scaffolding may be a useful tool for teachers to use in support of students who are victimized or who reinforce aggression in others. Reductions in victimization following assertion scaffolding appear promising. Self-efficacy for assertion and bystander reinforcement may also be linked to assertion scaffolding, although neither relationship achieved significance. Why might self-efficacy for assertion be related to bystander reinforcement? Not all reinforcement is intentional. Bystanders experience a range of emotions including fear, shame, and confusion. Bystanders who feel confident of their ability to assert themselves when pressured may not feel it necessary to display the typical levels of respect accorded to students who bully (O'Connell et al., 1999), leading to transactional change (Frey & Nolen, 2010).

The predicted improvement in bullying, non-bullying aggression, and victimization did not emerge following teacher prompting of emotion regulation. Instead, aggressive playground behaviors were positively related to this type of teacher activity. Two possible explanations relate to (1) the timing of the cues and (2) teachers' skill at providing regulatory support. One of the three emotion regulation items explicitly denotes cues provided during a conflict, and a second item easily lends itself to similar high-arousal events. By interfering with higher-level cognitions and judgment (see review by Anderson & Bushman, 2002), anger may reduce receptivity to "in the moment" cues. In contrast, our previous research showed declines in non-bullying aggression and victimization following Steps to Respect coaching by intervention teachers (Hirschstein et al., 2007). Coaching, occurring after the event has passed, includes problem-solving, reiterating school norms about bullying, and, possibly, a more supportive context for emotion coaching.

Another aspect to consider is the stress that teachers often feel when dealing with conflicts and disruptive behaviors (Byrne, 1994). Teachers who cue emotion regulation when they are stressed may communicate a demand to hide negative emotions rather than provide an expectation of an equitable resolution. In the Steps to Respect problem-solving framework, the purpose of arousal-moderation is to enable problem-solving and effective responses to bullying. Failure to communicate such intentions may increase student frustration and aggression (Anderson & Dill, 2000). Further, control teachers and students may not have been trained to resolve feelings of anger through constructive solutions. In support of this reasoning, evaluation of a social skills program found that cueing of emotion regulation by control group teachers was positively linked to later aggression (Van Schoiack, 2000). This reiterates the need to be active in fostering social–emotional competence, rather than rely on haphazard "reminders" of skills that may have never been systematically taught.

TRANSLATING RESEARCH INTO PRACTICE: IMPLICATIONS FOR BULLYING PREVENTION AND INTERVENTION PROGRAMS

While awaiting replication with expanded scales, we recommend that educators provide cooling-off periods and the expectation of constructive problem-solving for high-arousal situations. Schools often have procedures that accomplish this by asking students to take another's perspective and write out ideas for problem resolution while waiting for educators to become available. Given our results, educators may wish to exercise caution about prompting emotion regulation without structured lessons or coaching. Structured Steps to Respect coaching sessions predict later decreases in non-bullying aggression and victimization—problems thought to be exacerbated by emotion dysregulation (Hirschstein et al., 2007). Research on single-component programs that use similar emotion regulation strategies has provided specific evidence of their efficacy (e.g., Lochman & Wells, 2002). Future experimental research is needed to examine *which* elements of multicomponent programs lead to aggression reductions.

CONCLUSIONS

Not enough research has examined teaching practices that attempt to foster social–emotional skills and reduce aggression. These initial analyses may provide stimulus for more content-specific examinations of teacher efforts, including experimental studies of their impact. For now, we propose that scaffolding of empathy and assertiveness are helpful strategies. Links to greater assertion on the part of victims and more socially responsible beliefs and bystander behavior may set the stage for subsequent reductions in aggression (Frey & Nolen, 2010). Such a reduction would be in addition to declines in non-bullying aggression and victimization that follow individual coaching of students, a practice in which "cooling off" periods may enhance learning of social skills and receptivity to school norms.

Our examination suggests both specificity in student responses to teacher scaffolding and an indication that bystander behavior is especially responsive to teacher efforts (see also Frey et al., 2009; Hirschstein et al., 2007). Bystander reinforcement of aggression was repeatedly linked to teacher scaffolding, as well as to coaching. It is possible that students who are followers, rather than leaders, of aggression are the most easily influenced by intervention practices. Given the important role played by bystanders in conceptual models of bullying, more attention is needed to chart these dynamics.

REFERENCES

Anderson, C.A., & Bushman, B.J. (2002). Human Aggression. *Annual Review of Psychology, 53*, 27–51.

Anderson, C.A., & Dill, K.E. (2000). Video games and aggressive thoughts, feelings and behavior in the laboratory and in life. *Journal of Personality and Social Psychology, 78*, 772–790.

Atlas, P.A., & Pepler, D.J. (1998). Observations of bullying in the classroom. *Journal of Educational Research, 92*, 86–99.

Bandura, A. (2002). Selective moral disengagement in the exercise of moral agency. *Journal of Moral Education, 31*, 101–119.

Bandura, A., Caprara, G.V., Barbaranelli, C., Gerbino, M., & Pastorelli, C. (2003). Role of affective self-regulatory efficacy in diverse spheres of psychosocial functioning. *Child Development, 74*, 769–782.

Barboza, G.E., Schiamberg, L.B., Oehmke, J., Korzeniewski, S.J., Post, L.A., & Heraux, C.G. (2009). Individual characteristics and the multiple contexts of adolescent bullying: An ecological perspective. *Journal of Youth and Adolescence, 38*, 101–121.

Bradshaw, C.P., Sawyer, A.L., & O'Brennan, L.M. (2007). Bullying and peer victimization at school: Perceptual differences between students and school staff. *School Psychology Review, 36*, 361–382.

Byrne, B.M. (1994). Burnout: Testing for validity, replication, and invariance of causal structure across elementary, intermediate, and secondary teachers. *American Educational Research Journal, 31*, 645–673.

Camodeca, M., Terwogt, M.M., & Schuengel, C. (2002). Bullying and victimization among school-aged children: Stability and links to proactive and reactive aggression. *Social Development, 11*, 332–345.

Committee for Children. (2001). *Steps to respect: A bullying prevention program.* Seattle, WA: Author.

Davidson, L.M., & Demaray, M.K. (2007). Social support as a moderator between victimization and internalizing-externalizing distress from bullying. *School Psychology Review, 36*, 383–405.

Demaray, M.K., & Malecki, C.K. (2003). Perceptions of the frequency and importance of social support by students classified as victims, bullies, and bully/victims in an urban middle school. *School Psychology Review, 32*, 471–489.

Doll, B. (2004). *Resilient Classrooms.* New York, NY: Guilford Press.

Doll, B., Song, S., & Siemers, E. (2004). Classroom ecologies that support or discourage bullying. In D.L. Espelage & S.M. Swearer (Eds.), *Bullying in American schools* (pp. 161–184). Mahwah, NJ: Erlbaum.

Eisenberg, N., Fabes, R.A., Karbon, M., Murphy, B.C., Carlo, G., & Wosinski, M. (1996). Relations of school children's comforting behavior to empathy-related reactions and shyness. *Social Development, 5*, 330–351.

Endresen, I.M., & Olweus, D. (2001). Self-reported empathy in Norwegian adolescents: Sex differences, age trends, and relationship to bullying. In A.C. Bohart, C. Arthur & D.J. Stipek (Eds.), *Constructive and destructive behavior: Implications for family, school, and society* (pp. 147–165). Washington, DC: American Psychological Association.

Espelage, D.L., Bosworth, K., & Simon, T. R. (2001). Short-term stability and prospective correlates of bullying in middle-school students: An examination of potential demographic, psychosocial, and environmental influences. *Violence and Victims, 16*, 411–426.

Frey, K.S., & Nolen, S.B. (2010). Taking "steps" toward positive social relationships: A transactional model of intervention. In J. Meece & J. Eccles (Eds.), *Handbook of research on schools, schooling, and human development.* New York, NY: Routledge.

Frey, K.S., Hirschstein, M.K., Edstrom, L.V., & Snell, J.L. (2009). Observed reductions in school bullying, nonbullying aggression, and destructive bystander behavior: A longitudinal evaluation. *Journal of Educational Psychology, 101*, 466–481.

Frey, K.S., Nolen, S.B., Van Schoiack Edstrom, L., & Hirschstein, M.K. (2005). Effects of a school-based social-emotional competence program: Linking children's goals, attributions and behavior. *Journal of Applied Developmental Psychology, 26*, 171–200.

Frey, K.S., Hirschstein, M.K., Snell, J.L., Van Schoiack Edstrom, L., MacKenzie, E.P., & Broderick, C.J. (2005). Reducing playground bullying and supporting beliefs: An experimental trial of the *Steps to Respect* program. *Developmental Psychology, 41*, 479–491.

Hirschstein, M.K., Van Schoiack-Edstrom, L., Frey, K., & Nolen, S.B. (2001). The Social-Emotional Learning Checklist (SELF-C): Technical report. Unpublished manuscript: Committee for Children, Seattle, WA.

Hirschstein, M.K., Edstrom, L.V., Frey, K.S., Snell, J.L., & MacKenzie, E.P. (2007). Walking the talk in bullying prevention: Teacher implementation variables related to initial impact of the *Steps to Respect* program. *School Psychology Review, 36*, 3–21.

Hodges, E.V.E., Malone, M.J., & Perry, D.G. (1997). Individual risk and social risk as interacting determinants of victimization in the peer group. *Developmental Psychology, 33*, 94–101.

Horne, A.M., Orpinas, P., Newman-Carlson, D., & Bartolomucci, C.L. (2004). Elementary school Bully Busters program: Understanding why children bully and what to do about it. In D.L. Espelage & S.M. Swearer (Eds.), *Bullying in American schools* (pp. 297–326). Mahwah, NJ: Erlbaum.

Huesmann, L.R., & Guerra, N.G. (1997). Children's normative beliefs about aggression and aggressive behavior. *Journal of Personality and Social Psychology, 72*, 408–419.

Hunter, S.C., Boyle, J.M.E., & Warden, D. (2004). Help-seeking amongst child and adolescent victims of peer aggression and bullying: The influence of school-stage, gender, victimization, appraisal, and emotion. *British Journal of Educational Psychology, 74*, 375–390.

Hymel, S., Rocke-Henderson, N., & Bonanno, R.A. (2005). Moral disengagement: A framework for understanding bullying among adolescents. *Journal of Social Sciences* (Special issue) *8*, 1–11.

Kallestad, J.H., & Olweus, D. (2003). Predicting teachers' and schools' implementation of the Olweus Bullying Prevention Program: A multilevel study. *Prevention and Treatment, 6*, Article 21. Retrieved March 4, 2004, from http://journals.apa.org/prevention/volume6/pre0060021a.html.

Kendall, P.C. (1993). Cognitive-behavioral therapies with youth: Guiding theory, current status, and emerging developments. *Journal of Consulting and Clinical Psychology, 61*, 235–247.

Kochenderfer, B.J., & Ladd, G.W. (1997). Victimized children's responses to peers' aggression: Behaviors associated with reduced versus continued victimization. *Development and psychopathology, 9*, 59–73.

Lochman, J.E., & Wells, K.C. (2002). Contextual social-cognitive mediators and child outcome: A test of the theoretical model in the Coping Power program. *Development and Psychopathology, 14*, 945–967.

Loukas, A., Suzuki, R., & Horton, K.D. (2006). Examining school connectedness as a mediator of school climate effects. *Journal of Research on Adolescence, 16*, 491–502.

Marachi, R., Astor, R.A., & Benbenishty, R. (2007). Effects of student participation and teacher support on victimization in Israeli schools: An examination of gender, culture, and school type. *Journal of Youth and Adolescence 36*, 225–240.

Mishna, F., Scarcello, I., Pepler, D., & Wiener, J. (2005). Teachers' understanding of bullying. *Canadian Journal of Education, 28*, 718–738.

Nishina, A., & Juvonen, J. (2005). Daily reports of witnessing and experiencing peer harassment in middle school. *Child Development 76*, 435–450.

O'Connell, P., Pepler, D., & Craig, W. (1999). Peer involvement in bullying: Insights and challenges for intervention. *Journal of Adolescence, 22*, 437–452.

Oliver, R., Hoover, J.H., & Hazler, R. (1994). The perceived roles of bullying in small-town Midwestern schools. *Journal of Counseling and Development, 72*, 416–420.

Olweus, D. (1993). *Bullying at school: What we know and what we can do.* Oxford, UK: Blackwell Publishers.

Parault, S.J., Davis, H.A., & Pelligrini, A.D. (2007). The social contexts of bullying and victimization. *Journal of Early Adolescence, 27*, 145–174.

Rigby, K. (2005). Why do some children bully at school? The contributions of negative attitudes toward victims, and the perceived expectations of friends, parents, and teachers. *School Psychology International, 26*, 147–161.

Rodkin, P.C., Farmer, T.W., Pearl, R., & Van Acker, R. (2000). Heterogeneity of popular boys: Antisocial and prosocial configurations. *Developmental Psychology, 36*, 14–24.

Roland E., & Galloway D. (2002). Classroom influences on bullying. *Educational Research, 44*, 299–312.

Schwartz, D., Dodge, K.A., & Coie, J.D. (1993). The emergence of chronic peer victimization in boys' play groups. *Child Development, 64*, 580–588.

Smith, J.D., Schneider, B.H., Smith, P.K., & Anadiadou, K. (2004). Effectiveness of whole-school antibullying programs: A synthesis of evaluation research. *School Psychology Review, 33*, 547–560.

Stein, N., & Sjostrom, L. (1996). Bullyproof: A teacher's guide on teasing and bullying for use with fourth and fifth grade students. Wellesley, MA: Wellesley College Center for Research on Women.

Swearer, S.M., & Espelage, D.L. (2004). Introduction: A social-ecological framework of bullying among youth. In D.L. Espelage & S.M. Swearer (Eds.), *Bullying in American schools,* (pp. 1–12). Mahwah, NJ: Erlbaum.

Terasahjo, T., & Salmivalli, C. (2003). "She is not actually bullied." The discourse of harassment in student groups. *Aggressive Behavior, 29*, 134–154.

Unnever, J., & Cornell, D. (2003). The culture of bullying in middle schools. *Journal of School Violence, 2*, 166–172.

Vaillancourt, T., Hymel, S., & McDougall, P. (2003). Bullying is power: Implications for school-based intervention strategies. In M.J. Elias & J.E. Zins (Eds.), *Bullying, peer harassment, and victimization in the schools: The next generation of prevention* (pp. 157–177). New York, NY: Haworth Press.

Van Schoiack, L. (2000). Promoting social-emotional competence: Effects of a social-emotional learning program and corresponding teaching practices in the schools (Doctoral dissertation, University of Washington). *Dissertation Abstracts International, 61*, 2689.

Wentzel, K.R. (1997). Student motivation in middle school: The role of perceived pedagogical caring. *Journal of Educational Psychology, 89*, 411–419.

Williams, K.D. (2001). *Ostracism: The power of silence.* New York, NY: Guilford.

21

DESIGN AND ANALYSIS OF A RANDOMIZED CONTROLLED TRIAL OF STEPS TO RESPECT

A School-Based Bullying Prevention Program

SABINA M. LOW, BRIAN H. SMITH, ERIC C. BROWN,
KATE FERNANDEZ, KOREN HANSON, AND KEVIN P. HAGGERTY

Modern efforts to evaluate bullying prevention programs in schools originated with Dan Olweus and his seminal work in Norway in the early 1990s (Olweus, 1991a, b, 1992a, b, 1993a, b, c, d). Despite increasing attention to the problem of bullying behavior in the United States and the widespread use of bullying prevention programs, there is still a shortage of rigorously designed intervention evaluation studies that can be used to guide prevention efforts (see Ryan & Smith, 2009, for a recent review), making it difficult to draw any consensus about the impact of bullying prevention efforts and the key mechanisms of change. The aims of the current chapter are threefold: first, we will provide a description of how we address some of the analytic and design challenges in our school-randomized evaluation of *Steps to Respect: A Bullying Prevention Program©* (StR; Committee for Children, 2001). Second, we will describe baseline data results from the trial, including psychometrics of outcome measures, baseline equivalency between intervention and controls schools, and the characteristics of our student, teacher, and staff samples as they relate to targeted outcomes and mediators. Lastly, we will present findings and implications of differences in perceived school environment, bullying behavior, and likelihood of effective intervention in bullying incidents between students and staff.

In a recent literature review of the past 25 years of research on bullying prevention program effectiveness, Ttofi, Farrington, and Baldry (2008) examined 593 reports and found that published outcomes were available on only six universal school-randomized bullying prevention intervention trials. The size of these studies varied. The largest, a study of the Dutch Anti-Bullying Program, involved 15 intervention schools and over 15 schools in each of two control conditions (Fekkes, Pijpers, & Verloove-Vanhorick, 2006). The evaluation by Cross, Hall, Hamilton, Pintabona, and Erceg (2004) of the Friendly Schools program involved 15 intervention and 14 control schools. Similar in size, Jenson and Dieterich (2007) evaluated Youth Matters across 28 schools, evenly divided between intervention and control conditions. Twelve schools assigned to intervention and control conditions were included in the evaluations of the Expect Respect program (Rosenbluth,

Whitaker, Sanchez, & Valle, 2004; Whitaker, Rosenbluth, Valle, & Sanchez, 2004). Finally, two bullying prevention interventions were evaluated in trials involving six schools, assigned to intervention or control conditions; StR (Frey, Edstrom, & Hirschstein, 2005; Frey et al., 2005; Hirschstein, Edstrom, Frey, Snell, & Mackenzie, 2007), and the Anti-bullying Intervention in Australian Secondary Schools (Hunt, 2007).

Another recent review by Ryan and Smith (2009) examined the scientific rigor and quality of 31 published bullying prevention evaluations. Deficiencies were found across all studies in the specification of intervention components, evaluation design (e.g., statistical power, unit of randomization), statistical analyses (e.g., multilevel vs. single-level), program implementation monitoring, choice and measurement of outcomes (e.g., bullying behaviors, attitudes, and school climate) or selection of informants. Many studies were noted for failing to have an explicit theory of change guiding the evaluation or not matching the theory of change to the analytic strategy.

Taken together, the Ttofi et al. (2008), and Ryan and Smith (2009) reviews highlight several shortcomings limiting the progression of the field of bullying prevention. These concerns are noteworthy given that group-randomized trials, which are the appropriate design strategy for interventions that target the entire school environment, are subject to additional unique analytic and design considerations compared to clinical trials that randomize individuals to condition. For example, studies that fail to address the clustered nature of the data encounter problems with statistical inference, incorrect degrees of freedom, and biased standard errors (Murray, 1998). In addition, two problems that can occur with group randomized trials are misspecification of the analytic model (e.g., inability to model parameter estimates as random effects) and insufficient power to detect intervention effects. The design and analysis plan used in our evaluation of the StR program avoid these problems.

METHODS

The current study assessed the impact of the StR program on bullying attitudes and behaviors among 3rd through 5th graders over a one-year period. The evaluation used a pre-test–post-test control group design with matching of schools within geographic area, incorporating multi-informant data, and measuring fidelity as a key program moderator. All findings in this study are based on preliminary data obtained during the baseline assessment (fall 2008–09 school year).

Program Description

The StR program has school-wide components that are intended to foster norms by creating and reinforcing policies about bullying and respectful behavior. This includes teacher and staff training aimed at enhancing more knowledgeable and ethical monitoring of students, and instruction on how to effectively intervene in bullying situations. Classroom lessons are predicated on the beliefs that all students can benefit from training in social skills (e.g., assertiveness) and that bullying behavior must not be condoned by peers (i.e., shifting norms). Specifically, lessons:

- help students identify the various forms of bullying;
- provide a rationale and guidelines for socially responsible actions;

- train students in assertiveness, empathy and emotion regulation skills;
- allow students to practice friendship skills and conflict resolution (see Frey et al., 2005 for a detailed description of program elements and training).

Sample

Students and Schools. The sample consisted of 2,940 3rd through 5th grade students, in 33 participating schools.[1] Approximately half (51%) of these students were male, 46% were White, 39% were of Hispanic origin, and 6% were African American. Students ranged in age from 7 to 11 years. The sample was divided between intervention schools (51%) and wait-listed control schools (49%). Schools were sampled from four counties in central-northern California. Schools within each county were matched by ordinally ranking them on school size, number of full-time teachers, change in student enrollment from 2006 to 2007, percentage of students eligible for the free or reduced-price lunch program, percentages of students' race and ethnicity, and the percentage of students that were English language learners. Schools were selected randomly within each matched pair to either begin StR in the ensuing school year (i.e., intervention schools) or wait a year before implementing the program (i.e., wait-listed control schools). There were 25% of the schools from rural areas, 10% from small towns, 50% from suburban areas, and 15% located in mid-sized cities. Schools showed substantial variation in the percentage of students who were eligible for free or reduced price lunch ($M = 39.7$, $SD = 29.4$). Schools also varied substantially by size, with a mean of 479 students per school ($SD = 177$, range = 77 to 749 students).

Teachers. Data on students' classroom behavior were obtained from 128 teachers in both intervention and wait-listed control schools. Three or four teachers from either 3rd and 4th grade classrooms or 4th and 5th grade classrooms were selected randomly from each school to complete web-based assessments of students' social and academic competencies, and bullying-related behaviors. Additionally, teachers in intervention schools were asked to complete classroom curricula implementation logs as a measure of program fidelity.

School staff. School staff data were collected from school administrators, teachers, teacher aides, paraprofessionals, support staff, custodial and cafeteria personnel, bus drivers, and any other adult who regularly worked at the school whether or not they were paid by the school. This broad definition is consistent with the theory of change in the StR program, which posits that all members of the school environment are agents of school-bullying prevention. The average completion rate for the fall 2008–09 school year assessment across all 33 study schools was 79%, which resulted in 1,920 individual surveys of school staff. Respondents represented school administrators (2.8%), teachers (58%), paraprofessionals (10%), cafeteria staff (3.3%), school counselors/psychologists (1.4%), custodial staff (1.4%), bus drivers (0.7%), volunteers (0.1%), and other positions (7.6%). Respondents were 90% female, 12% Hispanic, 88% White, and averaged 46 years of age.

INSTRUMENTS AND MEASURES

Student Survey

Data from students was collected using a revised version of the Bullying Prevention Initiative Student Survey (Csuti, 2008a), which was developed originally for the Colorado

Trust's three-year state-wide Bullying Prevention initiative (see Csuti, 2008a). Because the original instrument was designed to be administered to a slightly older population of students (i.e., 5th through 12th graders), we revised some of the language to be developmentally appropriate for 3rd through 5th grade students. These items were verified to be readable for the targeted age group.

The survey contains information related to students' perceptions of bullying-related problems in their school (e.g., *Students picking fights with other students*), bullying perpetration (*I pushed, shoved, tripped, or picked a fight with a student who I knew was weaker than me*), and bullying victimization (*A particular student or group of students spread rumors or told lies about me*). Proximal student outcomes include students' perceptions of other students (e.g., *Students in my school can be trusted, Students in my school generally get along with each other*), their teachers (e.g., *My teachers are fair*), and their school (e.g., *My school is a good place to be*). Additionally, students are asked to report on their own personal attitudes toward positive (e.g., *Students defend others who are being shoved around by strong students*) and negative (e.g., *Students tease weaker students in front of others*) behaviors related to bullying and their perceptions of how much students and staff intervene in observed bullying. Answers to items on the student survey are recorded using four-point Likert-type response options. Survey scales, the number of items per scale, and coefficient alphas for each scale are presented in Table 21.1.

School Environment Survey

Data were collected from school staff members using the School Environment Survey. This instrument also was adapted from the Colorado Trust's Bullying Prevention Initiative (Csuti, 2008b) and was designed to parallel measures collected from students. Similar to the student survey, school staff reported on their perceptions of bullying-related problems in their school, their perceptions of students and other teachers and staff members, their perceptions of how willing students and staff are at intervening in observed bullying behaviors, and their school's anti-bullying policies and strategies. Answers to items on the staff survey are recorded using four-point Likert-type response options. Additional items on the School Environment Survey are included to measure respondents' personal attitudes toward bullying behaviors (e.g., *Do you feel that it is your* _personal_ *responsibility to prevent bullying in your school?*). Demographic information related to staff members' gender, race or ethnicity, age, position in the school, and length of employment at the school is included in the survey. Survey scales, the number of items per scale, and coefficient alphas for each of the six scales of the School Environment Survey are presented in Table 21.1. One scale, Personal Bullying Intervention, had less than optimal internal consistency and was bolstered with two additional items at post-test to improve scale reliability.

Classroom Curricula Implementation Log Checklists

To monitor the implementation and fidelity of the classroom curriculum portion of the StR program during the original efficacy trial, a series of Classroom Curricula Implementation Log Checklists were developed for each of the 11 lessons of the curriculum (Low, Brown, & Smith, 2008). These checklists were developed to monitor activities for each of three different series (or levels) of the program (i.e., sequences covering Grades

Table 21.1   Student and Staff Survey Baseline Measures

Scale	Student Survey		School Environment Survey	
	Number of items	Coefficient alpha	Number of items	Coefficient alpha
School Bonding[a]	15	.83	na	na
Student Perceptions of School Bonding	na	na	4	.80
Teacher/Staff Perceptions of School Bonding	na	na	7	.89
School Anti-Bullying Policies and Strategies	na	na	8	.92
Bullying-related Problems	6	.86	5	.86
Active Bullying Perpetration	4	.80	na	na
Passive Bullying Perpetration	5	.82	na	na
Personal Bullying Intervention	3	.61	na	na
Bullying Victimization	4	.75	na	na
Student Support	6	.72	na	na
Negative Perceptions of Bullying	7	.85	na	na
Positive Perceptions of Bullying	3	.67	na	na
Student Bullying Intervention	4	.77	5	.84
Teacher/Staff Bullying Intervention	4	.85	5	.95

Notes: na = scale not available or not included. a = Student and Teacher/Staff Perceptions of School Bonding were combined into one scale.

3 and 4, Grades 4 and 5, and Grades 5 and 6, respectively). Items on the checklist query teachers on the percentage of students that participated in the lesson, the amount of time teachers spent preparing for the lesson, the length of the actual lesson, the degree to which students were engaged by the lesson, any modifications teachers made to the program, and any activities that teachers employed on their own to reinforce the lesson. Additionally, teachers were asked if they completed each of approximately five to eight specific activities that were prescribed for that lesson and program series.

Statistical Analyses

The one-year pre-test–post-test control group design (Murray, 1998) used a mixed-model analysis of covariance (ANCOVA) to evaluate the efficacy of the program. Mixed-model ANCOVAs were conducted as multilevel models following the specifications described by Raudenbush and Bryk (2002). These models explicitly accounted for the statistical dependencies that can arise when study data have a clustered structure, such as students grouped in the classroom and classrooms grouped within schools. The models used in this study contained random effects for intercept parameters across classrooms and/or schools, and appropriately partitioned variation in outcome variables among the hierarchies. Intraclass correlation coefficients (ICCs) indicated the proportion of total variability in an outcome that can be attributed to a particular level of clustering. Larger school-level ICCs represent greater variability among schools relative to student and classroom variation and, holding other design characteristics constant, result in less statistical power to detect school-level effects.

Consistent with the program's theory of change and the evaluation's design, we modeled intervention status as a randomly varying school-level effect (i.e., the effects of the intervention can vary across schools). The multilevel models used to assess differences in mean levels of outcome variables measured at baseline (results described below) included regression adjustment for student, classroom, and school-level covariates. Final outcome analyses to assess the efficacy of the StR program will use a similar modeling strategy; however, these analyses will use outcome data collected at the end of the school year as the dependent variables and baseline data as additional model covariates for regression adjustment. All analyses presented here were performed using the HLM for Windows software program (Raudenbush, Bryk, & Congdon, 2004).

RESULTS

Multilevel Models of Baseline Outcome Measures

Student Survey. We used three-level models with students nested within classrooms and classrooms nested within schools to assess baseline (pre-test) equivalency in levels of student outcomes. Results of unconditional multilevel models (i.e., no covariates) indicated significant ($ps < .01$) variation in all 11 student measures across classrooms and schools. ICCs from the unconditional models averaged .033 for classroom-level variation (range = .015 for Student Support to .096 for School Climate) and .050 for school-level variation (range = .014 for Student Bullying Intervention to .078 for Passive Bullying Perpetration). Including covariates in conditional models (i.e., student age and gender, classroom size, and dummy variables for school-matched pairs) reduced variation in outcome measures at both classroom and school levels with conditional ICCs averaging .027 and .001, respectively; however, variability across classrooms and schools remained statistically significant for all outcome measures except for school-level variation in Negative Perceptions of Bullying.

Significant ($ps < .05$) covariate effects were found across all student outcomes. Girls reported greater levels of positive school climate, student support, and belief that school staff would intervene in bullying instances compared to boys. Girls also reported greater norms against bullying behaviors and greater norms supporting appropriate reactions to bullying behaviors. Conversely, boys reported higher levels of passive and active bullying perpetration and bullying victimization than girls. Older students reported less school bonding, bullying-related problems in school, student support, norms against bullying, and norms supporting appropriate reactions to bullying behaviors. Older students also reported more passive and active bullying perpetration and victimization; however, older students also reported a greater likelihood that students would intervene in observed bullying.

School Environment Survey (SES). Unconditional models for SES outcomes indicated significant ($ps < .05$) variations among schools for all six measures. The average ICC from the unconditional models was .164 (range = .042 for Teacher-Staff Bullying Intervention to .269 for School Bullying-Related Problems). Including age, gender, categorized job type, and school matched-pair dummy variables as covariates in conditional models resulted in smaller school-level ICCS ($M = .132$, range = .030 for Teacher-Staff Bullying Intervention to .204 for School Bullying-Related Problems); however, school-level variation remained statistically significant for all outcomes.

Teacher Assessment of Student Behavior. Significant ($ps < .05$) variations were present across both classrooms and schools for all four teacher outcomes. Unconditional ICCs for classroom-level variation were .169 for Bullying Perpetration, .183 for Social Competency, .062 for Academic Competency, and .067 for Academic Achievement. Unconditional ICCs for school-level variation were .067, .080, .045, and .107 for the four respective outcomes. ICCs from conditional models controlling for student age and gender, classroom size, and dummy variables for school-matched pairs were only slightly different for classroom-level variation (.180, .206, .076, and .087, respectively). However, conditional ICCs for school-level variation were substantially smaller (i.e., all less than .01), given the significant associations between the school-pair dummy variables and outcomes, which accounted for an average of approximately 8% of the total variation in the teacher outcome measures.

Teachers reported that older students were significantly ($ps < .01$) more likely to exhibit bullying behaviors and display less social competency, academic competency, and academic achievement compared to younger students. Teachers reported that boys were more likely to exhibit bullying behaviors and have less social competency, academic competency, and academic achievement compared to girls. No significant differences were found in any of the four teacher outcome measures between intervention and control schools.

Student and Staff Perceptions of School Environment and Bullying

We first present comparisons of data between students and school staff for items from four constructs that were measured from both Student Surveys and School Environment Surveys: School Bonding, School Bullying-Related Problems, Student Bullying Intervention, and Teacher/Staff Bullying Intervention. Figure 21.1 presents the proportions of students and school staff that responded *Agree* or *Really/Strongly Agree* on a four-item scale to questions measuring School Bonding.[2] For example, whereas approximately 93% of school staff agreed or really/strongly agreed that *Students in my school get along with each other* in their schools, only 59% of students endorsed this item.

Similar discrepancies between student and staff reports are seen in Figure 21.2, which shows the proportions of respondents that identified items on the School Bullying-

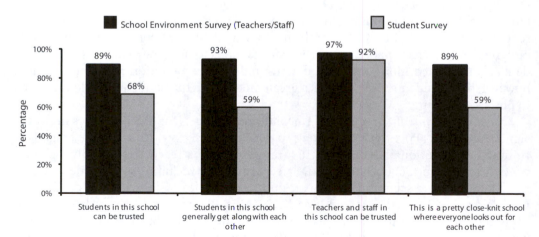

Figure 21.1 Percentages of teachers/staff and students endorsing School Bonding items.

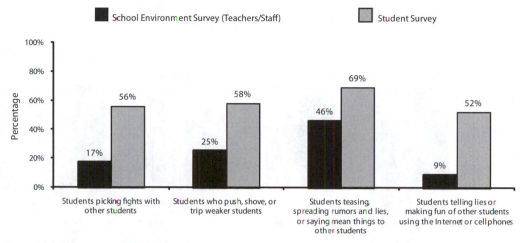

Figure 21.2 Percentages of teachers/staff and students endorsing School Bullying-Related Problems items.

Related Problems scale as a *Huge Problem* or *Pretty Big Problem*. As seen in this figure, over half of students (52%) identified *Telling lies or making fun of other students using the internet or cell phone* as a notable problem in their schools; however, only 9% of school staff identified this as such a problem.

Figures 21.3 and 21.4 show the proportions of students and staff, respectively, that would be expected to intervene in different types of bullying behaviors. Comparing the proportions of staff who responded *Likely* or *Very likely* to proportions of students who responded *Most of the time* or *Always* to different types of bullying behaviors further illustrates the disparity between the two sources of information. For example, 71% of school staff reported that it was likely/very likely students could be counted on to intervene in occasions where *A student or group of students was pushing, shoving, or trying to pick a fight with a weaker student*, whereas only 43% of students responded that students in the school would intervene at least most of the time in these situations. By comparison, 95% of staff reported it was likely/very likely that staff could be counted on to intervene in this scenario; however, only 66% of students thought that staff would help out in those types of bullying incidents at least most of the time.

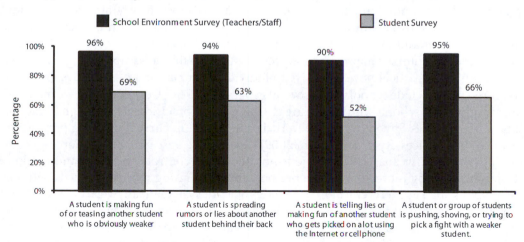

Figure 21.3 Percentages of teachers/staff and students endorsing Staff Bullying Intervention items.

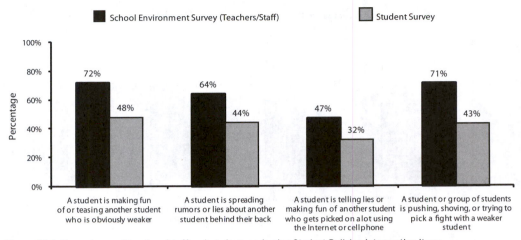

Figure 21.4 Percentages of teachers/staff and students endorsing Student Bullying Intervention items.

SUMMARY

This chapter outlines the study design, sample characteristics, and baseline findings from an evaluation of a bullying prevention intervention carried out with a diverse sample of 3rd through 5th grade students, teachers, and school staff. Goals of the chapter were to detail the steps taken in establishing the school-randomized study design and analytic strategy to test the efficacy of StR, and describe results of multilevel analyses of the trial's baseline data. An additional goal of the chapter was to highlight discrepancies between students and staff on the prevalence of bullying behavior, bullying-related attitudes and school bonding, as knowledge of teacher and school staff attitudes toward bullying and bullying prevention could help inform efforts to effectively reduce bullying through a holistic school approach (Espelage & Swearer, 2003).

A holistic approach to preventing bullying in schools leads to a particular design strategy in their evaluation. As the highest standard in establishing a causal link between intervention and outcomes, this strategy calls for the use of a school-randomized controlled trial. In addition to being consistent with the socio-environmental-oriented theory of change underlying the StR program, randomization of schools to intervention or wait-listed control condition helps avoid problems associated with uneven program implementation and experimental design contamination within schools. A limitation of a school-randomized approach, however, exists in having to sample a larger number of schools for statistical power, relative to individual- or classroom-based designs. This required us to include schools from several geographic areas. Consequently, we matched and randomized schools within each area to improve the precision of the design (Raudenbush, Martinez, & Spybrook, 2007). In their assessment of current bullying prevention evaluation practices, Ryan and Smith (2009) suggest that "researchers use more rigorous designs to identify cause-effect relationships, including control conditions and random assignment, using more appropriate pre-post intervals, using more advanced methods of analyses such as hierarchical linear modeling, and systematically verifying program integrity to obtain dosage data that can be used in the outcome analyses" (p. 248). Our design and evaluation plan to evaluate the efficacy of the StR program are consistent with these recommendations and with the goals of the intervention.

Previous research has found that teachers tend to report lower levels of bullying in their school than students (Pervin & Turner, 1994; Stockdale, Hangaduambo, Duys, Larson, & Sarvela, 2002). This finding was supported in this study. Students were overwhelmingly more likely than staff to report their school had either a *Pretty big* or *Huge* problem across four different types of bullying. The closest they came to agreement was on *Students teasing, spreading rumors and lies, or saying mean things to other students*, but only two-thirds as many staff as students said the behavior was a problem at their school. From twice to over five times as many students as staff identified the other three bullying behaviors as a problem at their school. The largest difference was on what may be an increasingly serious problem—cyberbullying. Whereas fewer than one in ten staff saw bullying over the Internet or cell phones as a problem, over half of students identified this as a *Pretty big* or *Huge* problem.

This study also found notable differences between students and staff on three out of four items related to student bonding to school. Although over 90% of both students and staff felt school staff could be trusted, students were only roughly two-thirds as likely as staff to say that students could be trusted and that they had a *Pretty close-knit school where everyone looks out for each other*. The largest gap between students and staff across the school bonding questions was on the item perhaps most closely linked to bullying—how well students in the school *Generally get along with each other*. Whereas nearly all staff felt this was true (93%), less than two-thirds of students endorsed this item.

Our findings also support previous work suggesting that many students are not confident of the willingness or capability of school staff to help them with bullying and peer conflicts (Rigby & Bagshaw, 2003). Whereas over 90% of staff saw it as likely or very likely that school staff could be counted on to help out when students were being bullied, far fewer students were confident of this, ranging from 52% to 69% across the four items in the survey. In addition, more staff than students also thought that students would be likely to help out in bullying incidents. A high of nearly three-quarters of staff thought students would help out in incidents of teasing or making fun, and just below half thought students would help out in incidents of bullying involving cell phones or the internet. However, student confidence that their peers would help out at least most of the time was below half for all four bullying behaviors, bottoming out at only one-third for cell phone or internet bullying.

TRANSLATING RESEARCH INTO PRACTICE: IMPLICATIONS FOR BULLYING PREVENTION AND INTERVENTION PROGRAMS

There is a strong consensus that bullying prevention in schools should be approached from a social–ecological perspective (Espelage & Swearer, 2003; Swearer, Espelage, & Napolitano, 2009). This ideally involves interventions targeting students, the school as a whole, families and the community (Olweus, Limber, & Mihalic, 1999; Swearer & Doll, 2001). The whole-school approach is a widely advocated and commonly adopted approach to bullying prevention that involves both students and school staff (Espelage & Swearer, 2003; Rigby & Bagshaw, 2003).

The whole-school approach is predicated on the belief that awareness, trust, and reporting of bullying behavior are both integral and essential for a safe school climate. Teachers are often unaware of much of the bullying that occurs in schools, in part because many students do not report bullying (Limber, 2002), and perhaps in part because of the complex and often covert nature of bullying. However, students' willingness to disclose bullying incidents is often hindered by lack of trust in school staff to effectively intervene (Hoover, Oliver, & Hazler, 1992), and students' beliefs that staff do not take bullying seriously (Harris, Petrie, & Willoughby, 2002). Data from the current study round out this literature by showing that students do not see staff as adequately concerned about bullying, do not believe that staff understand student experiences, and think that staff have unrealistic views of the likelihood that either students or staff will intervene in incidents of bullying. Such findings are a concern, and point to the importance of raising awareness and effective responsiveness to bullying incidents, so that trust and cooperation can be engendered between students, staff, and parents. When students see that staff take their concerns seriously and respond appropriately, they also should be more likely to report bullying behavior.

A serious whole-school approach to bullying prevention requires significant commitment on the part of school staff. Staff motivation to make the efforts required to create a safe school environment and respond to student concerns could be harmed by unrealistic appraisals of the conditions for school bonding and the severity of bullying problems experienced by students in their school. The data presented in this chapter suggest that staff in many schools may overestimate how well students get along and support each other, and the extent to which they trust staff and other students. The findings of this study also show that staff underrate the severity of bullying problems experienced by students in their schools.

Staff motivation to actively work to prevent and intervene in incidents of bullying among students could be affected by their perception of student willingness and ability to handle these problems on their own. The findings of this study suggest that staff may be overconfident that bullying will often be effectively addressed by students, which may have the effect of reducing the perceived need for staff to take an active role in bullying prevention. Similarly, if staff overestimate student confidence that they will intervene in bullying, as found here, they may be over confident that they are already adequately addressing the problem and they may overestimate student willingness to enlist staff support and help.

Taken together, the discrepancies between students and staff found in this study reaffirm the importance of educating teachers and other school staff on recognizing the various forms of bullying, and effectively intervening (Espelage & Swearer, 2008). In addition to education about the nature, prevalence, and severity of bullying, it may also be useful to educate school staff about the extent to which students report a more negative school climate, more serious bullying problems and a lower confidence in the likelihood of staff and student intervention in bullying incidents. A misplaced belief by school staff that they understand and have the trust of students could serve to undermine the efforts needed to undertake a whole-school approach to preventing bullying.

The results presented in this chapter should help to confirm and motivate an ecological approach to bullying interventions that target skills, attitudes, norms and behaviors at the level of individual students, peers, and staff. Bullying among students is often difficult for staff to observe, both because students cannot be closely watched at all times and because of the complex social nature of bullying. In addition, as this study makes clear, school staff not only underestimate bullying problems in their school, they also tend to overestimate both student willingness to actively intervene in bullying and student confidence in staff intervention efforts. These findings, coupled with previous work (Harris et al., 2002; Limber, 2002) suggest that it might be risky to rely on staff alone to identify and respond to bullying in schools; student awareness and responsiveness is also critical, especially at the level of the peer social milieu.

NOTES

1. Originally, 34 schools were recruited, though one school withdrew from the study immediately before pretest data collection.
2. Scale responses ranged from 1 to 4 for students and staff, with 1 = *Strongly Disagree* to 4 = *Strongly Agree* for staff, and 1 = *Really Disagree* to 4 = *Really Agree* for students.

REFERENCES

Committee for Children. (2001). *Steps to respect: A bullying prevention program.* Seattle, WA: Author.

Cross, D., Hall, M., Hamilton, G., Pintabona, Y., & Erceg, E. (2004). Australia: The Friendly Schools project. In P.K. Smith, D.J. Pepler, & K. Rigby (Eds.), *Bullying in schools: How successful can interventions be?* (pp. 187–210). Cambridge, UK: Cambridge University Press.

Csuti, N.B. (2008a). The Bullying Prevention Initiative Student Survey. The Colorado Trust: A Grantmaking Foundation. Retrieved from www.coloradotrust.org/attachments/0000/3599/BPI_Student_Survey.pdf.

Csuti, N.B. (2008b). The Bullying Prevention Initiative Staff Survey. The Colorado Trust: A Grantmaking Foundation. Retrieved from www. coloradotrust.org/attachments/0000/3598/BPI_Staff_Survey.pdf.

Espelage, D.L., & Swearer, S.M. (2003). Research on school bullying and victimization: What have we learned and where do we go from here? *School Psychology Review, 32,* 365–383.

Espelage, D.L., & Swearer, S.M. (2008). Current perspectives on linking school bullying research to effective prevention strategies. In T.W. Miller (Ed.), *School violence and primary prevention* (pp. 335–353). New York, NY: Springer Press, Inc.

Fekkes, M., Pijpers, F., & Verloove-Vanhorick, S.P. (2006). Effects of antibullying school program on bullying and health complaints. *Archives of Pediatrics & Adolescent Medicine, 160,* 638–44.

Frey, K.S., Edstrom, L.V.S., & Hirschstein, M.K. (2005). The *Steps to Respect* program uses a multilevel approach to reduce playground bullying and destructive playground behaviors. In D.L. White, M.K. Faber, & B.C. Glenn (Eds.), *Proceedings of persistently safe schools 2005* (pp. 47–55). Washington, DC: Hamilton Fish Institute, George Washington University.

Frey, K.S., Hirschstein, M.K., Snell, J.L., Edstrom, L.V.S., MacKenzie, E.P., & Broderick, C.J. (2005). Reducing playground bullying and supporting beliefs: An experimental trial of the steps to respect program. *Developmental Psychology, 41,* 479–491.

Harris, S., Petrie, G., & Willoughby, W. (2002). Bullying among 9th graders: An exploratory study. *National Association of Secondary School Principals Bulletin, 86,* 630.

Hirschstein, M.K., Edstrom, L.V.S., Frey, K.S., Snell, J.L., & MacKenzie, E.P. (2007). Walking the talk in bullying prevention: Teacher implementation variables related to initial impact of the steps to respect program. *School Psychology Review, 36,* 3–21.

Hoover, J.H., Oliver, R., & Hazler, R.J. (1992). Bullying: Perceptions of adolescent victims in the Midwestern USA. *School Psychology International, 13,* 5–16.

Hunt, C. (2007). The effect of an education program on attitudes and beliefs about bullying and bullying behaviour in junior secondary school students. *Child and Adolescent Mental Health, 12,* 21–26.

Jenson, J.M., & Dieterich, W.A. (2007). Effects of a skills-based prevention program on bullying and bully victimization among elementary school children. *Prevention Science, 8,* 285–296.

Limber, S. (2002). Addressing youth bullying behaviors. In M. Fleming & K. Towey (Eds.), *Educational forum on adolescent health: Youth bullying.* Chicago: American Medical Association.

Low, S.M., Brown, E.C., & Smith, B.H. (2008). Steps to Respect implementation log checklist. Unpublished manuscript.

Murray, D.M. (1998). *Design and analysis of group-randomized trials.* New York, NY: Oxford University Press.

Olweus, D. (1991a). Bully/victim problems among schoolchildren: Basic facts and effects of a school based intervention program. In D.J. Pepler & K.H. Rubin (Eds.), *The development and treatment of childhood aggression* (pp. 411–447). Hillsdale, NJ: Lawrence Erlbaum.

Olweus, D. (1991b). Victimization among school children. In R. Baenninger (Ed.), *Targets of violence and aggression* (pp. 45–102). Oxford, UK: North-Holland.

Olweus, D. (1992a). Bullying among schoolchildren: Intervention and prevention. In R.D. Peters, R.J. McMahon, & V.L. Quinsey (Eds.), *Aggression and violence throughout the life span* (pp. 100–125). Newbury Park, CA: Sage.

Olweus, D. (1992b). Victimization among schoolchildren: Intervention and prevention. In G.W. Albee, L.A. Bond, & T.V.C. Monsey (Eds.), *Improving children's lives: Global perspectives on prevention* (pp. 279–295). Newbury Park, CA: Sage.

Olweus, D. (1993a). Bully/victim problems among schoolchildren: Long-term consequences and an effective intervention program. In S. Hodgins (Ed.), *Mental disorder and crime* (pp. 317–349). Thousand Oaks, CA: Sage.

Olweus, D. (1993b). Bullies on the playground: The role of victimization. In C.H. Hart (Ed.), *Children on playgrounds: Research perspectives and applications* (pp. 85–128). Albany, NY: State University of New York Press.

Olweus, D. (1993c). *Bullying at school: What we know and what we can do.* Malden, MA: Blackwell.

Olweus, D. (1993d). Victimization by peers: Antecedents and long-term outcomes. In K.H. Rubin & J.B. Asendorpf (Eds.), *Social withdrawal, inhibition, and shyness in childhood* (pp. 315–341). Hillsdale, NJ: Lawrence Erlbaum.

Olweus, D., Limber, S.P., & Mihalic, S. (1999). *The bullying prevention program: Blueprints for violence prevention,* Vol. 10. Boulder, CO: Center for the Study and Prevention of Violence.

Pervin, K., & Turner, A. (1994). An investigation into staff and pupils' knowledge, attitudes and beliefs about bullying in an inner city school. *Pastoral Care in Education, 12,* 16–22

Raudenbush, S.W., & Bryk, A.S. (2002). *Hierarchical linear models: Applications and data analysis methods.* Thousand Oaks, CA: Sage.

Raudenbush, S.W., Bryk, A.S., & Congdon, R.T. (2004). HLM 6: Hierarchical linear and non-linear modeling (computer software). Lincolnwood, IL: Scientific Software International, Inc.

Raudenbush, S.W., Martinez, A., & Spybrook, J. (2007). Strategies for improving precision in group-randomized experiments. *Educational Evaluation and Policy Analysis, 29,* 5–29.

Rigby, K., & Bagshaw, D. (2003). Prospects of adolescent students collaborating with teachers in addressing issues of bullying and conflict in schools. *Educational Psychology, 32,* 535–546.

Rosenbluth, B., Whitaker, D.J., Sanchez, E., & Valle, L.A. (2004). The Expect Respect project: Preventing bullying and sexual harassment in U.S. elementary schools. In P.K. Smith, D.J. Pepler, & K. Rigby (Eds.), *Bullying in schools: How successful can interventions be?* (pp. 211–234). Cambridge, UK: Cambridge University Press.

Ryan, W., & Smith, J.W. (2009). Antibullying programs in schools: How effective are evaluation practices? *Prevention Science, 10,* 248–259.

Stockdale, S., Hangaduambo, S., Duys, D., Larson, K., & Sarvela, P. (2002). Rural elementary students', parents', and teachers' perceptions of bullying. *American Journal of Health Behavior, 26,* 266–277.

Swearer, S.M., & Doll, B. (2001). Bullying in schools: An ecological framework. *Journal of Emotional Abuse, 2,* 7–23.

Swearer, S.M., Espelage, D.L., & Napolitano, S.A. (2009). *Bullying prevention and intervention: Realistic strategies for schools.* New York, NY: Guilford Press

Ttofi, M.M., Farrington, D.P., & Baldry, A.C. (2008). *Effectiveness of programmes to reduce school bullying: A systematic review.* Retrieved from the Swedish National Council for Crime Prevention website www.bra.se/extra/measurepoint/?module_instance=4&name=Effectiveness_of_programmes_to_reduce_school_bullying_webb.pdf&url=/dynamaster/file_archive/081023/04395cbc57201c39fa6c7f78319ea2ab/Effectiveness%255fof%255fprogrammes%255fto%255freduce%255fschool%255fbullying%255fwebb.pdf.

Whitaker, D.J., Rosenbluth, B., Valle, L.A., & Sanchez, E. (2004). Expect Respect: A school-based intervention to promote awareness and effective responses to bullying and sexual harassment. In D.L. Espelage & S.M. Swearer (Eds.), *Bullying in American schools: A social-ecological perspective on prevention and intervention* (pp. 327–350). Hillsdale, NJ: Lawrence Erlbaum Associates, Inc.

22

IMPLEMENTATION OF THE OLWEUS BULLYING PREVENTION PROGRAM IN AMERICAN SCHOOLS

Lessons Learned from the Field

SUSAN P. LIMBER

Attention to bullying problems among children and youth has increased dramatically in the last decade with American educators, the press, and the general public. Whereas bullying had been the focus of wide public concern in Scandinavia since the early 1980s (Olweus, 1993), and while school-based interventions were being tested in England in the early 1990s, bullying was not on the radar screens of most Americans until several years later. In the mid-1990s, stories of bullying experiences began to appear in the national news media (ABC News, 1995) and school-based bullying prevention programs first emerged in American schools (e.g., Garrity, Jens, Porter, Sager, & Short-Camilli, 1994; South Carolina Educational Television, 1995; Sjostrom & Stein, 1996). Today, a conservative count yields at least 40 different school-based programs (including both curricula and comprehensive approaches) that focus significantly on bullying and that are in use in elementary, middle, and high schools in the United States. This estimate includes only those programs that focus to a significant extent on bullying and involve more than a minimal time commitment from school staff. The number of additional materials available to educators, parents, and others (e.g., books, multimedia resources, posters, gamers, booklets) is tremendous.[1]

This dramatic increase in bullying prevention programs in American schools may be attributed to several factors. First, the research base upon which programs may be built has become significantly stronger in recent years as research on the nature and prevalence of bullying has dramatically increased in the United States and abroad. A search of the PsycINFO database[2] revealed only four books, journal articles, chapters, or dissertations on the topic of bullying in 1988. By 2001, there were 123, and there have been more than 150 published each year since 2004.

Second, interest in preventing aggressive and violent behavior among children has naturally led us to look for early indices of such behavior in children. Educators have correctly recognized that behaviors that are entrenched in middle or high school may be significantly more malleable in early elementary grades. Since bullying may be viewed as an early sign of trouble in some children, attention has rightly turned to its prevention in early grades. Third, media attention to research findings on bullying and to tragic events linked to bullying (such as suicides and the shootings at Columbine High School and several other schools) have kept bullying on the minds of Americans. As Smith and Morita (1999) noted,

> It appears to be a combination of sound research and media interest ... which leads to governmental response and opportunities for funding and intervention work. Research on its own may just gather dust on library shelves; media interest on its own may just generate temporary concerns lacking a knowledge base for action. But an encouraging phenomenon ... has been how at times this combination of research and concerned publicity ... can lead to resources being devoted to tackle the problem seriously. (p. 3)

Fourth, there has been a dramatic increase in state legislative activity around bullying in schools. In 1999, there were no state laws addressing bullying. Within three years, there were 15, and currently there are 41.3 Although these laws vary in their definitions and requirements, most require that school districts develop policies about bullying among students (Alley & Limber, 2009).

School-based bullying prevention interventions vary considerably in their approach. Some are purely curricular programs, while others provide tips and strategies for teachers to address and prevent bullying within their classrooms. Still others are more comprehensive in approach and focus on changing the school climate and norms with regard to bullying.

To date, one of the best-researched and most widely used interventions is the Olweus Bullying Prevention Program (OBPP). In this chapter, I will provide a brief overview of this comprehensive program, including its history, its use in other countries, and findings from research on its effectiveness. I will discuss in some detail the use of this Norwegian program in U.S. schools and will conclude by highlighting some of the major challenges and benefits that I perceive in the implementation of comprehensive bullying prevention programs in U.S. schools.

OVERVIEW OF THE OLWEUS BULLYING PREVENTION PROGRAM

The OBPP was developed by Dan Olweus, a psychologist at the University of Bergen in Bergen, Norway. The program was first implemented and evaluated in 42 schools in Bergen, Norway, as part of a national campaign against bully–victim problems that was launched by the Norwegian Ministry of Education in 1983 (Olweus, 1993; Olweus & Limber, 2010a, b ; Olweus, Limber, & Mihalic, 1999). The primary impetus for the national campaign was a widely read newspaper account in 1982 of three boys who had apparently committed suicide as a result of severe bullying by their peers (Olweus, 1993).

Goals and Principles of the OBPP

The goals of the program are to:

- reduce existing bully–victim problems among elementary, middle, and junior high school students;

- prevent the development of new bully–victim problems;
- improve peer relations at the school (Olweus et al., 2007).

The program is designed to counteract known risk factors for bullying behaviors, which include a lack of parental warmth and involvement, a lack of supervision, a lack of clear and consistent rules to govern children's behavior, and harsh or corporal punishment (Olweus, 1993; Olweus, Limber, & Mihalic, 1999; Olweus et al., 2007). Thus, the program was developed on the following four principles. Adults at school (and ideally at home) should:

1. Show warmth and positive interest in students.
2. Set firm limits to unacceptable behavior.
3. Consistently use non-corporal, non-hostile consequences when rules for inappropriate behavior are not followed.
4. Function as authorities and positive role models.

Distinguishing Characteristics of the Program

There are several important characteristics of the program that distinguish it from many other bullying prevention programs. First, the program is universal in that it represents a school-wide effort involving all adults within the school environment (i.e., administrators, teachers, parents, and non-teaching staff) as well as students. Second, the program is both systems-oriented and individual-oriented. It is focused on altering the school environment as a whole, as well as addressing issues with individual students. Third, as will be discussed in some detail below, the Olweus program is research based. Finally, the program is not time-limited—there are no end dates for the program. Rather, the program requires systematic efforts over time and is intended to become woven into the fabric of the school.

Program Interventions

The goals, principles, and approach of the OBPP in the United States have remained true to the original model, although a number of cultural adaptations have been made to fit the American context. In the United States, OBPP program components are implemented at four levels: the school-wide level, the classroom level, the individual level, and the community level.

School-wide interventions include the following (Olweus et al., 2007):

- Formation of a Bullying Prevention Coordinating Committee (a representative team from the school) to plan and coordinate all aspects of the school's violence prevention activities, including the Olweus Bullying Prevention Program.
- Intensive training (two days) for members of the Bullying Prevention Coordinating Committee, and at least one day of training for all school staff.
- Administration of the Olweus Bullying Questionnaire (Olweus, 1997), an anonymous questionnaire which assesses the students' experiences with and attitudes about bullying at the school.
- Formation of staff discussion groups to provide opportunities for school staff to learn more about bullying issues, share program successes and concerns.

- Introduction of school-wide rules against bullying and use of appropriate positive and negative consequences for students who follow/do not follow the school rules.
- Refinement of a school's supervisory system (including developing strategies to increase adult supervision of students, particularly at "hot-spots" for bullying, developing means of tracking and reporting bullying, assessing the skills and attitudes of supervising adults, and evaluating the physical design of the school).
- A school-wide kick-off event to introduce the program to students.
- Engagement of parents around the school's bullying prevention efforts.

A primary focus of classroom-level interventions involves regular (weekly) classroom meetings to discuss issues related to bullying and peer relations. The meetings are intended to improve class cohesion and community, provide a forum for discussing rules about bullying, and problem-solve strategies to address bullying. They also give the teacher an opportunity to stay abreast of social issues of concern to students. Required program materials (*Teacher Guide* and CD-ROM/DVD (Olweus & Limber, 2007)) and recommended supplemental materials may be used by teachers to help facilitate discussions among students.

At the individual level, staff members are encouraged to increase student supervision, particularly in identified "hot spots" for bullying. In addition, all staff members are trained to intervene on the spot when they observe bullying. Procedures also have been developed to guide staff to react appropriately when bullying has been identified or is suspected. These procedures include meetings with a child who is suspected of being bullied and his or her parents, and, subsequently, meetings with a child who is suspected of bullying and his or her parents. Finally, school personnel are encouraged to work with parents and mental health professionals to develop individualized plans, whenever appropriate, to support students who have been bullied and to change the behavior of students who bully.

Community-level interventions are also important, as bullying does not stop at the school-house doors (Olweus & Limber, 2010a). In this regard, members of a schools' Bullying Prevention Coordinating Committee are encouraged to involve at least one community member of the committee, look for ways that community members can support the school's efforts, and collaborate to spread bullying prevention messages and strategies into community settings where children and youth are engaged.

RESEARCH FINDINGS

The OBPP has been evaluated in several large-scale studies in Norway and also in the United States. Major findings will be discussed briefly.

Norwegian Evaluations

The initial evaluation of the Olweus Bullying Prevention Program in Bergen, Norway, targeting 2,500 5th to 8th graders over a period of two-and-a-half years, found significant reductions in self-reported bullying and victimization (by approximately 50%), reductions in teachers' and students' ratings of bullying behavior among children in the classroom, reductions in self-reported antisocial behavior (such as vandalism, theft, and truancy), and increases in students' perceptions of positive school climate (including students' satisfaction with school, and improved order and discipline (Olweus, 1991, 1993, 1994, 2005; Olweus & Limber, 2010a, b). A dosage-response relationship was observed, whereby those classes that had implemented essential program components (class rules against bullying, role playing, class meetings), experienced the greatest reduction in bullying (Olweus & Alsaker, 1991).

Subsequent to the initial evaluation of the program, six follow-up outcome evaluations of the OBPP have been conducted in Norway, involving more than 20,000 students from more than 150 schools. Studies focused on students in grades 4–7 have produced consistently positive results (Olweus & Limber, 2010b). Included in these studies is a long-term study of 14 schools in Oslo indicating that these reductions were retained after five years. Positive results also have been found with Norwegian students in grades 8–10, although less consistently and with somewhat weaker effects (Olweus & Limber, 2010b).

Based on the success of early evaluations of the OBPP in Norway, several school-based anti-bullying programs inspired by the OBPP have been implemented and evaluated in a variety of countries including Belgium (Stevens, de Bourdeaudhuij, & Van Oost, 2000; Stevens, Van Oost, & de Bourdeaudhuij, 2004), Canada (Pepler, Craig, Ziegler, & Charach, 1994; Pepler, Craig, O'Connell, Atlas, & Charach, 2004), Germany (Hanewinkel, 2004), and the United Kingdom (Whitney, Rivers, Smith, & Sharp, 1994; Eslea & Smith, 1998; Smith, Sharp, Eslea, & Thompson, 2004). These studies are not replications of the OBPP, as the programs as implemented have deviated considerably from the OBPP in their program components and model of implementation (Olweus & Limber, 2010b).

Evaluations in the United States

The first evaluation of the OBPP in the United States took place in the mid-1990s and involved elementary and middle schools in six primarily rural school districts in South Carolina (Limber, Nation, Tracy, Melton & Flerx, 2004; Melton et al., 1998; Olweus & Limber, 2010b). The sample was largely African American and of low socioeconomic status. After seven months of program implementation, significant reductions in bullying rates were documented among students in the intervention schools, compared to the comparison schools. For example, in intervention schools, there was a 16% decrease in the percentages of students who indicated they had bullied others several times or more often within the school term, whereas there was a 12% increase in rates of bullying among students in comparison schools, resulting in an overall relative reduction of approximately 28%. There also was an increase over time in the frequency of self-reported antisocial behavior among students in comparison schools, while for students in intervention schools there was either no increase or a slower rate of increase with regard to measures of general delinquency, vandalism, school misbehavior, and sanctions for school misbehavior. Results suggested that the program slowed the age-related rate of increase in students' involvement in antisocial behavior. There were no significant changes in the frequency with which students reported being bullied. The program continued one additional year, but it unfortunately was implemented with such low degrees of fidelity that it no longer could be considered a faithful implementation of the program (an issue we will return to below).

Black and Jackson (2007) evaluated the effectiveness of the OBPP in six large elementary and middle schools in inner-city Philadelphia, over four years of implementation. Using an observational measure to assess Bullying Incident Density (a checklist of bullying behaviors that included physical, verbal, and emotional bullying) during recess and lunch, researchers documented reductions in bullying incident density of 45% over the course of four years—from 65 incidents at baseline to 36 incidents per 100 student hours.

Bauer, Lozano & Rivara (2007) evaluated the OBPP using a non-randomized controlled study with ten middle schools (seven interventions, three control) in Washington state. Using the Olweus Bully/Victim Questionnaire, researchers found significant program effects for relational victimization and physical victimization among white students but not among other races or ethnicities. They also observed overall positive program effects with regard to students' perceptions that other students actively intervened in bullying incidents.

Pagliocca, Limber, & Hashima (2007) evaluated the effectiveness of the OBPP in three elementary schools in a suburban community in southern California, surveying students and teachers. Using a selection of cohorts design to assess program effects over a three-year period, researchers documented reductions in self-reports of being bullied decreased 21% after one year and 14% after two years. Self-reports of bullying others decreased 8% after one year and 17% after two years. Other findings of note included increases in bullied students' propensities to tell a teacher about their bullying, students' perceptions that teachers and other adults try to stop bullying, teachers' perceptions that there were clear rules about bullying, and teachers' beliefs that they knew how to respond to bullying. There also were marked increases in teachers' perceptions that bullying policies had been clearly communicated to students, parents, teachers, non-teaching staff, and parents.

In sum, the U.S. evaluations are clearly promising. Current U.S. research (planned and underway) will provide a more nuanced picture of the effectiveness of the program with different populations, a more detailed analysis of the effectiveness of particular program elements, and an assessment of the conditions under which the program may have the greatest effects (Olweus & Limber, 2010b).

IMPLEMENTATION OF THE OBPP IN THE UNITED STATES

These promising findings from studies in the United States and abroad have led to recognition of the program by a number of governmental agencies and organizations. It has been designated as one of 11 Blueprints for Violence Prevention (Center for the Study and Prevention of Violence), recognized as a model program by the Substance Abuse and Mental Health Services Administration, selected as an effective program by the Office of Juvenile Justice and Delinquency Prevention, and designated as a Level 2 Program[4] by the U.S. Department of Education.

To support implementation of the OBPP in the United States, faculty and staff affiliated with Clemson University's Institute on Family and Neighborhood Life have worked to disseminate the model widely to interested schools in North America. At the same time, they have strived to put in place reasonable training and consultation processes and resources to help ensure high fidelity. Emphasis has been placed on building local capacity to implement the program. Training-of-trainer (TOT) events have been held at national, state, and local levels, and more than 400 trainers from 42 states (plus the District of Columbia, Canada, the Dominican Republic, and Puerto Rico) have been certified to provide training in the model (Olweus & Limber, 2010a).

American Experiences and Adaptations

As previously emphasized, the goals and general approach of the Olweus program in the United States have remained true to those of the original Norwegian model. However, several themes are emerging from the collective experiences of American trainers and staff in U.S. schools regarding experiences and adaptations that may be unique to American schools.

Importance of a committee to coordinate school-wide policies and activities. The Bullying Prevention Coordinating Committee appears to serve particularly important coordinating functions within American schools and to be critical to the success of most programs. As mentioned above, the Bullying Prevention Coordinating Committee is a representative team from the school whose job is to plan and coordinate all aspects of the school's bullying prevention and violence prevention activities (Olweus et al., 2007). Membership typically consists of 8 to 15 members, and includes an administrator, a teacher from each grade, a school counselor and/or other school-based mental health professional, a member of the non-teaching staff (e.g., a bus driver, cafeteria worker, custodian), one or two parents, a representative from the community (e.g., staff from an after-school program or youth organization), and other key personnel (e.g., Title IX representative, nurse, school resource officer). Together, this team receives intensive training in the program, develops a plan for implementing the program in their school, introduces the program to other members of the school staff, and meets regularly throughout the school year to ensure effective implementation of the program and coordination with other school activities. Some middle school committees have included one or more student representatives, to help ensure student input into the planning of the OBPP; others have formed special student advisory committees who meet periodically with the adult committee. All schools are encouraged to find developmentally appropriate ways to meaningfully involve students in the ongoing efforts of the OBPP.

There are several possible reasons why the work of this committee is so critical in American schools. First, the structure and size of American schools is somewhat different from that of our Norwegian counterparts. Students in most American middle schools change classes throughout the day and typically have four or five teachers, whereas Norwegian school children in similar grades generally have a single teacher with whom they spend the entire school day. Moreover, most American schools are significantly larger than those in Norway and frequently have multiple prevention and intervention initiatives in place at any given time. The size and complexity of most American middle schools and the volume of prevention and intervention initiatives demand particularly tight coordination. From experience, the Bullying Prevention Coordinating Committee serves these coordination purposes well.

A second reason why the Bullying Prevention Coordinating Committee may have taken on particular importance in American schools is that it assumes some of the coordinating functions that our Norwegian counterparts have largely granted to another program component—staff discussion groups. Olweus has encouraged schools to set aside at least one hour every several weeks for teachers to participate in staff discussion groups in order to learn about the program in detail, discuss implementation challenges that may arise, and maintain enthusiasm for the program (Olweus et al., 1999). Administrators in most American schools have found it difficult to arrange for all staff to meet with such frequency. Instead, staff discussion groups typically meet approximately once per month (Olweus et al., 2007). Between these meetings, staff members are kept abreast of interim developments with the program by members of the Bullying Prevention Coordinating Committee.

Classroom meetings with students. Teachers in American schools also have experienced some challenges in holding classroom meetings—a critical component of the Olweus Bullying Prevention Program. One difficulty experienced by many middle or junior high school teachers has been reserving a consistent time during the school week to focus on issues of bullying and peer relations. Over the last several years, teachers have been under mounting pressure to prepare students for standardized tests and cover required academic material. As a result, some middle school (and even elementary school) teachers report that they do not have time during the week to hold a classroom meeting in which students can discuss issues of bullying and peer relations, role play possible resolutions to bullying situations, or share their thoughts about ways to make the school safer or more humane.

Experience in implementing the Olweus program suggests that consistent use of classroom meetings tends to be more challenging in a middle school or junior high school environment, where children change classes and have multiple teachers, than in an elementary school setting, where students spend the vast majority of the school day with one teacher. Elementary school teachers frequently have flexibility to arrange their own weekly schedules to accommodate classroom meetings, while staff in middle or junior high schools typically must confer with fellow grade-level teachers and administrators to designate an appropriate day and time each week to hold such meetings.

Administrator support appears to be important to the success of classroom meetings as a technique for bullying prevention, particularly in middle school and junior high school environments. Classroom meetings are more likely to be held (and used effectively) in schools where administrators champion the use of classroom meetings, actively work to schedule time in the weekly calendar for meetings, and support teachers in developing skills to facilitate meetings.

To conduct effective classroom meetings, teachers must be skilled in facilitating discussion about social issues and relationships. Without training and practice, some teachers are understandably uncomfortable stepping outside their traditional academic roles to explore such difficult issues with their students. Implementation of the Olweus program in American schools frequently has involved extra training for teachers in the use of classroom meetings. School counselors and teachers more experienced in conducting classroom meetings also have been enlisted to mentor less experienced teachers in using classroom meetings effectively. Optional program resources have recently been developed to help teachers conduct class meetings effectively, including a DVD, which provides examples of class meeting discussions about bullying within elementary and middle school settings (Olweus et al., 2008), and numerous developmentally appropriate activities that may be used as part of OBPP class meetings (Flerx et al., 2009a, 2009b; Limber, Agatston, & Kowalski, 2008a, 2008b).

Community involvement. The original OBPP model did not include a community component. However, within the American context, we have long recognized the importance of involving community members in their bullying prevention efforts (Olweus et al., 2007). Although activities vary among communities, they typically have involved efforts to:

- inform residents in the local community about the program (e. g., convening meetings with leaders of the community in order to discuss the school's program, encouraging local media coverage of the school's efforts);

- engage community members in the school's bullying prevention activities (e.g., involving community members on the Bullying Prevention Coordinating Committee; engage community members as playground, bus, or cafeteria aids to watch for bullying behavior; solicit material assistance from local businesses to support aspects of the program);
- engage community members, students, and school staff in anti-bullying efforts within the broader community (e.g., introducing messages and core components of the program into after-school activities, camp experiences, or youth gatherings within faith-based organization).

Such efforts may not only strengthen the school's program but also influence attitudes and norms of the broader community of children, youth, and adults regarding the acceptance of bullying.

TRANSLATING RESEARCH INTO PRACTICE: IMPLICATIONS FOR BULLYING PREVENTION AND INTERVENTION PROGRAMS

Comprehensive bullying prevention programs hold significant promise for reducing bullying within a school environment and sustaining effects over time (Limber, 2002; see also Mulvey & Caufman, 2001, for a discussion of the importance of comprehensive approaches in violence prevention programs). As noted above, the adoption of such models has increased significantly in U.S. schools in recent years. However, perhaps not surprisingly, educators, parents, and others seeking to introduce comprehensive bullying prevention programs such as the OBPP into American schools have faced (and likely will continue to face) some common challenges, most of which relate to schools' readiness to implement the program and their ability to do so with fidelity (Olweus & Limber, 2010a).

Resistance on the Part of Staff and Parents

One of the biggest barriers to the successful adoption of comprehensive bullying prevention efforts is resistance on the part of some school staff and parents. Although the increased national attention to bullying likely has reduced the numbers of skeptics, it still is not uncommon to find at least a handful of staff or parents at any given school who believe that bullying is not a concern. Some adults seriously underestimate its frequency. Others acknowledge the presence in all schools but view the experience of bullying as a rite of passage or even a positive learning experience for children. ("Kids will be kids," "It's a normal part of growing up," "Kids need to learn to deal with bullying on their own"). These adults misjudge the significant social, emotional, and academic costs of bullying for victimized children (Chase, 2001) and overestimate the ability of victimized children to stop bullying without the assistance of adults. As a young child explained to a colleague, "If I thought I could deal with bullying on my own, why would I have told an adult?"

Some adult attitudes may be changed (or at least softened) with education. Indeed, appropriate education of staff and parents is a critical component of any bullying prevention effort. Findings should be shared with school staff and parents regarding the prevalence of bullying among children and its harmful effects on victims, bystanders, and the entire school community. Data from surveys of students within a given school may be particularly compelling and may help to persuade skeptical adults that bullying is not only present in their school, but is also an issue of concern for many students.

Although it is not uncommon to find a handful of naysayers at any given school, efforts to introduce and sustain a comprehensive bullying prevention program may be doomed if a majority of the school staff do not believe that bullying is a serious issue. Indeed, Olweus (Olweus, 1993; Olweus et al., 2007; Olweus et al., 1999) argues that two important prerequisites to the successful implementation of the Olweus Bullying Prevention Program are: (1) awareness of a majority of school staff regarding problems of bullying, and (2) commitment of a majority of the staff to its prevention.

The attitudes of building-level administrators toward bullying prevention efforts are particularly important to the success of a school-wide program. Without the active support of the principal, a program may flounder. Staff may not feel supported in efforts to discipline children for bullying behavior or develop safety plans for victimized children; teachers may be reluctant to spend class time focusing on bullying prevention; and students, parents, and staff may accurately perceive that bullying prevention is not a priority at the school. In sum, it is difficult to change the climate of a school without the support of the school's natural leader.

Desires for Simple, Short-term Solutions to Bullying

As educators and members of the public are increasingly recognizing the need to focus on prevention of bullying, many are, understandably, seeking simple, short-term interventions to address bullying problems in their schools (Limber, 2002). Not uncommonly, school administrators and their staff adopt a piecemeal approach to bullying prevention. Bullying may be the topic of a staff in-service training, a PTA meeting, a school-wide assembly, or lessons taught by individual teachers. Few state laws encourage more comprehensive bullying prevention approaches (Alley & Limber, 2009). Although such individual efforts may represent important initial steps in the adoption of a comprehensive bullying prevention strategy, they cannot be expected to significantly reduce bullying problems. As Bob Chase, President of the National Education Association noted, "a single school assembly won't solve the problem" (2001). Nor will a curriculum that is taught for two weeks by the 6th grade health teacher. What is required to reduce the prevalence of bullying is nothing less than a change in the school climate and in the norms for behavior (Limber, 2002). Research on the effectiveness of school-based violence prevention and intervention programs lends support for this conclusion (Mulvey & Cauffman, 2001). A study of elementary school-based violence interventions found that those schools that focused on the broader school environment, as opposed to more narrow curricular strategies, appeared more successful in altering students' violent behavior (Howard, Flora, & Griffin, 1999). Similarly, a meta-analysis of bullying prevention programs by Ttofi, Farrington, and Baldry (2008) found that those programs with more program elements and greater duration and intensity had greater effects on bullying. As noted above, effecting changes in the climate of a school requires a comprehensive, school-wide effort involving the entire school community. Unfortunately, many schools elect less time-consuming and ultimately less effective strategies.

Implementation without Fidelity

Another challenge experienced in the dissemination of the OBPP (as well as numerous other prevention programs) is the tendency of school personnel to "cherry pick" program elements that are perceived as easier to implement, while failing to implement those that pose bigger challenges (Olweus & Limber, 2010a).

As noted above, a critical element of the OBPP involves holding regular classroom meetings with students to discuss bullying and peer relations. Olweus has recommend holding class meetings weekly throughout the course of the school year (Olweus et al., 2007; Olweus et al., 1999) and found that those classrooms that held regular classroom meetings had significantly greater reductions in reports of bullying than those that did not (Olweus, 1993). With increasing pressures on educators to cover required academic material and to adequately prepare students for yearly standardized tests, many administrators and teachers are understandably reluctant to set aside even 20 to 30 minutes per week for class meetings. Some opt, instead, to integrate anti-bullying themes into language arts, social studies, and other academic subjects. Lessons about bullying can and should be effectively woven throughout the elementary, middle school, and even high school curriculum (Flerx et al., 2009a, b). However, such opportunities do not replace the need for a regularly scheduled classroom meeting, during which students may freely express ideas and concerns that they may have about bullying and peer relations, teachers can better keep their fingers on the pulse of students' concerns, and teachers and students together can work to build a sense of caring and community within the classroom setting.

Anecdotal evidence suggests that schools that have successfully implemented classroom meetings have been able to show that such activities are a good investment of teachers' time. By setting aside 20–30 minutes once or twice per week to discuss issues related to bullying and peer relations within a classroom, teachers may actually spend less time in dealing with such issues as they arise throughout the school week.

Use of Mediation and/or Conflict Resolution Techniques to Address Bullying Incidents

Other challenges to the implementation of comprehensive bullying prevention programs relate to schools' use of competing or contradictory strategies, including conflict resolution, peer mediation, group treatment for children who bully, and zero tolerance (student exclusion) strategies.

Both peer mediation and conflict resolution strategies are commonly used in American schools. Although these techniques may be effective in cases of conflict between students of relatively equal power, they may be detrimental in bullying situations and should be discouraged (Cohen, 2002; Limber, 2002). Bullying is a form of victimization and should be considered no more a "conflict" than domestic violence or child abuse. Consequently, the messages that mediation likely sends to both parties are inappropriate ("You both are partly right and partly wrong," "We need to work out this conflict between you"). The appropriate message to a child who bullies should be that his or her behavior is wrong and that it will not be tolerated. The appropriate message to children who are bullied should be that they do not deserve to be bullied and that the adults at the school will do everything they can to see that it comes to an end. Not only may mediation send inappropriate messages to children who bully and their victims, but it may also further victimize a child who has been bullied and/or lead to retaliation. Because of the imbalance of power that exists in bullying situations, children who have been bullied may find it extremely distressing to face their tormentors. Mediation should only be considered in bullying incidents if a bullied child asks to confront his or her tormentor, if he or she is adequately prepared to do so, and if a qualified adult supervises the interaction.

Given the pervasiveness of conflict resolution and peer mediation strategies in many school systems, staff must be trained to better recognize the differences between bullying and conflict among students and efforts must be made to triage suspected cases of bullying so that they are not dealt with inappropriately.

Group Treatment for Children Who Bully

Another strategy that some schools utilize to address bullying behavior involves group therapeutic treatment for children who bully. Such treatment may focus on anger management, skill-building, empathy-building, or the enhancement of self-esteem (Limber, 2002). Although well intentioned, such strategies may be counter-productive, even with skillful adult facilitators. In some instances, students' behavior may further deteriorate, as group members tend to serve as role models and reinforcers for each other's antisocial and bullying behavior. Moreover, therapeutic efforts designed to boost the self-esteem of children who bully (whether done in group or in individual sessions) likely will be ineffective in reducing children's bullying behavior (Limber, 2002). Such efforts are premised on the assumption that low self-esteem is at the root of bullying behavior. Most evidence suggests that although victims of bullying and bully-victims (children who are bullied and who also bully others) tend to have low self-esteem, children who bully typically do not (Andreou, 2000; Kokkinos & Panayioto, 2004; Marini, Dane, Bosacki, & YLC-CURA, 2006; Olweus, 1993; Salmivali, Kaukiainen, Kaistaniemi, & Lagerspetz, 1999).

Zero Tolerance (Student Exclusion) for Bullying

Other approaches to bullying prevention and intervention have focused on removing students who bully from the school setting. In recent years, a number of schools and school districts have adopted zero tolerance policies for aggressive, violent, or potentially violent behavior, including bullying. Specific policies vary widely with regard to those behaviors that trigger zero tolerance policies and the consequences for violating such policies. A number of schools and districts require suspension or expulsion for children who physically bully their peers. The state of Georgia requires by law that each local board of education detail a procedure by which any student in grades 6–12 who has committed an offense of physical bullying for the third time in a school year be assigned to an alternative school (Ga. Code Ann, 2001).

Such policies raise several concerns and may actually be detrimental to a community's bullying prevention efforts (Limber, 2002). First, they cast a wide net. Approximately one in five students report that they have bullied their peers at least several times within a school term (Nansel et al., 2001). Even if zero tolerance policies focus only on physical bullying, there is a potential for numerous students to be affected.

Second, such policies may harm, rather than improve, the social environment of the school and academic outcomes. The APA Task Force on Zero Tolerance (2008) carefully reviewed the research literature and concluded:

schools with higher rates of school suspension and expulsion appear to have *less* satisfactory ratings of school climate, less satisfactory school governance structures, and to spend a disproportionate amount of time on disciplinary matters. Perhaps more importantly, recent research indicates a negative relationship between the use of school suspension and expulsion and school-wide academic achievement.(p. 855, citations excluded)

These policies also run counter to the goal of most bullying prevention programs to encourage students to report known or suspected bullying. Severe punishments for bullying, such as school exclusion, may have a chilling effect on students' (and staff members') willingness to come forward with concerns about the behaviors of their peers (Mulvey & Caufman, 2001).

Third, children who bully their peers with some frequency are at higher risk for engaging in other antisocial behaviors such as truancy, fighting, theft, and vandalism (Olweus, 1993). If unchecked, these behaviors may escalate. Children who bully are in need of positive, pro-social role models, including adults and students in their regular school. Removal of children from such positive influences may be detrimental (see also Conoley, Hindmand, Jacobs, & Gagnon, 1997). As the APA Zero Tolerance Task Force noted in its comprehensive review of data on zero tolerance policies, "school suspension in general appears to predict higher future rates of misbehavior and suspension among those students who are suspended" (2008, p. 854). In rare cases, public safety may demand that a child be removed from his or her public school environment. However, student exclusion as a broad-based bullying prevention and intervention policy is ill-advised and may seriously undermine other positive bullying prevention efforts.

REASONS FOR OPTIMISM

Recent heightened public attention to bullying among children and youth and the increase in relevant research present an important opportunity for the implementation of sound, research-based prevention programs in schools. Unfortunately, the proliferation of "simple solutions" to bullying prevention have the potential to overwhelm educators and distract them from strategies that are more likely to reap results. Key to the success of bullying prevention efforts will be:

- commitment to changing the school environment and norms with regard to bullying;
- support from administrators, teachers, and parents for adopting comprehensive approaches to bullying prevention, as opposed to simpler solutions;
- recognition that bullying prevention efforts must not be time-limited, but rather sustained over time and woven into the fabric of the school environment.

NOTES

1. For a partial listing of such resources appropriate for a tween audience (i.e., children and youth aged 9–13), see www.stopbullyingnow.hrsa.gov/adults/catalog-of-resources.aspx.
2. The search used "bully*" as a search term within keywords of journals, books, reviews, and dissertations.

3. For a current listing of state laws addressing bullying, visit www.stopbullyingnow.hrsa.gov/adults/state-laws.aspx.

4. "Level 2" programs have been scientifically demonstrated to prevent delinquency or reduce risk and enhance protection for delinquency and other child and youth problems using either an experimental or quasi-experimental research design with a comparison group.

REFERENCES

ABC News (1995). *Teased, taunted, and bullied.*

Alley, R., & Limber, S.P. (2009). Legal issues for school personnel. In S. M. Swearer, D. L. Espelage, & S. A. Napolitano (Eds.), *Bullying prevention and intervention: Realistic strategies for schools* (pp. 53–73). New York, NY: Guilford.

Andreou, E. (2000). Bully/victim problems and their association with psychological constructs in 8- to 12-year old Greek schoolchildren. *Aggressive Behavior, 26,* 49–56.

APA Zero Tolerance Task Force (2008). Are zero tolerance policies effective in the schools? An evidentiary review and recommendations. *American Psychologist, 63,* 852–862.

Bauer, N., Lozano, P., & Rivara, F.P. (2007). The effectiveness of the Olweus Bullying Prevention Program in Public Middle Schools: A controlled trial. *Journal of Adolescent Health, 40,* 266–274.

Black, S.A., & Jackson, E. (2007). Using bullying incident density to evaluate the Olweus Bullying Prevention Programme. *School Psychology International, 28,* 623–638.

Chase, B. (2001). *Bullyproofing our schools: To eliminate bullying, first we must agree to not tolerate it.* Newspaper Editorial. From http://www.suburbanramseyfamilycollaborative.org/bullyproofing.html.

Cohen, R. (2002, February). Stop mediating these conflicts now! *The School Mediator: Peer Mediation Insights from the Desk of Richard Cohen.* http://schoolmediation.com/newsletters/2002/2_02.html.

Conoley, J.C., Hindmand, R., Jacobs, Y., & Gagnon, W. (1997). How schools promote violence. *Family Futures, 1,* 8–11.

Eslea, M., & Smith, P.K. (1998). The long-term effectiveness of anti-bullying work in primary schools. *Educational Research, 40,* 203–218.

Flerx, V., Limber, S.P., Mullin, N., Riese, J., Snyder, M., & Olweus, D. (2009a). *Class meetings that matter: A year's worth of resources for grades K–5.* Center City, MN: Hazeldon.

Flerx, V., Limber, S.P., Mullin, N., Riese, J., Snyder, M., & Olweus, D. (2009b). *Class meetings that matter: A year's worth of resources for grades 6–8.* Center City, MN: Hazeldon.

Garrity, C., Jens, K., Porter, W., Sager, N., & Short-Camilli, C. (1994). *Bully-proofing your school: A comprehensive approach.* Longmont, CO: Sopris West. Ga. Code Ann. sec. 20–2-145 (2001).

Hanewinkel, R. (2004). Prevention of bullying in German schools: An evaluation of an anti-bullying approach. In P.K. Smith, D. Pepler, & K. Rigby (Eds.), *Bullying in schools: How successful can interventions be?* (pp. 81–97). Cambridge, UK: Cambridge University Press.

Howard, K.A., Flora, J., & Griffin, M. (1999). Violence-prevention programs in schools: State of the science and implications for future research. *Applied & Preventive Psychology, 8,* 197–215.

Kokkinos, C.M., & Panayiotou, G. (2004). Predicting bullying and victimization among early adolescents: Associations with disruptive behavior disorders. *Aggressive Behavior, 30,* 520–533.

Limber, S.P. (2002). *Addressing youth bullying behaviors.* Proceedings from the American Medical Association Educational Forum on Adolescent Health: Youth Bullying. Chicago, IL: American Medical Association.

Limber, S.P., Agatston, P.W., & Kowalski, R.M. (2008a). *Cyberbullying: A prevention curriculum for grades 3–5.* Center City, MN: Hazelden.

Limber, S.P., Agatston, P.W., & Kowalski, R.M. (2008b). *Cyberbullying: A prevention curriculum for grades 6–12.* Center City, MN: Hazelden.

Limber, S.P., Nation, M., Tracy, A.J., Melton, G.B., & Flerx, V. (2004). Implementation of the Olweus Bullying Prevention Program in the Southeastern United States. In P.K. Smith, D. Pepler, & K. Rigby (Eds.), *Bullying in schools: How successful can interventions be?* (pp. 55–79). Cambridge, UK: Cambridge University Press.

Marini, Z.A., Dane, A.V., Bosacki, S.L., & YLC-CURA (2006). Direct and indirect bully-victims: Differential psychosocial risk factors associated with adolescents involved in bullying and victimization. *Aggressive Behavior, 32,* 551–569.

Melton, G.B., Limber, S.P., Cunningham, P., Osgood, D.W., Chambers, J., Flerx, V., et al. (1998). *Violence among rural youth. Final report.* Washington, DC: Office of Juvenile Justice and Delinquency Prevention.

Mulvey, E.P., & Cauffman, E. (2001). The inherent limits of predicting school violence. *American Psychologist, 56,* 797–802.

Nansel, T. R., Overpeck, M., Pilla, R. S., Ruan, W. J., Simmons-Morton, B., & Scheidt, P. (2001). Bullying behavior among U.S. youth: Prevalence and association with psychosocial adjustment. *Journal of the American Medical Association, 285,* 2094–2100.

Olweus, D. (1991). Bully/Victim problems among schoolchildren: Basic facts and effects of a school based intervention program. In D.J. Pepler & K.H. Rubin (Eds.), *The development and treatment of childhood aggression* (pp. 411–448). Hillsdale, NJ: Lawrence Erlbaum.

Olweus, D. (1993). *Bullying at school: what we know and what we can do.* New York, NY: Blackwell.

Olweus, D. (1994). Annotation: Bullying at school: Basic facts and effects of a school based intervention program. *Journal of Children Psychology and Psychiatry, 7,* 1171–1190.

Olweus, D. (1997). *Olweus bullying questionnaire.* Center City, MN: Hazelden

Olweus, D. (2005). A useful evaluation design and effects of the Olweus Bullying Prevention Program. *Psychology, Crime & Law, 11,* 389–402.

Olweus, D., & Alsaker, F.D. (1991). Assessing change in a cohort longitudinal study with hierarchical data. In D. Magnusson, L.R. Bergman, G. Rudinger, & B. Torestad (Eds.), *Problems and methods in longitudinal research* (pp. 107–132). New York, NY: Cambridge University Press.

Olweus, D., & Limber, S.P. (2007). *Olweus Bullying Prevention Program teacher guide.* Center City, MN: Hazelden.

Olweus, D., & Limber, S.P. (2010a). Bullying in school: Evaluation and dissemination of the Olweus Bullying Prevention Program. *American Journal of Orthopsychiatry, 80,* 120–129.

Olweus, D., & Limber, S.P. (2010b). The Olweus Bullying Prevention Program: Implementation and evaluation over two decades. In S.R. Jimerson, S.M. Swearer, & D.L. Espelage (Eds.), *Handbook of bullying in school: An international perspective* (pp. 377–401). New York, NY: Routledge.

Olweus, D., Limber, S., & Mihalic, S. (1999). *The bullying prevention program: Blueprints for violence prevention.* Boulder, CO: Center for the Study and Prevention of Violence.

Olweus, D., Limber, S.P., Flerx, V., Mullin, N., Riese, J., & Snyder. M. (2007). *Olweus Bullying Prevention Program schoolwide guide.* Center City, MN: Hazelden.

Olweus, D., Limber, S.P., Flerx, V., Mullin, N., Riese, J., & Snyder, M. (2008). *Class meetings and individual interventions.* Center City, MN: Hazelden.

Pagliocca, P.M., Limber, S.P., & Hashima, P. (2007). *Evaluation report for the Chula Vista Olweus Bullying Prevention Program.* Final report prepared for the Chula Vista Police Department.

Pepler, D.J., Craig, W., Ziegler, S., & Charach, A. (1994). An evaluation of an anti-bullying intervention in Toronto schools. *Canadian Journal of Community Mental Health, 13,* 95–110.

Pepler, D.J., Craig, W.M., O'Connell, P., Atlas, R., & Charach, A. (2004). Making a difference in bullying: Evaluation of a systemic school-based programme in Canada. In P.K. Smith, D. Pepler, & K. Rigby (Eds.), *Bullying in schools: How successful can interventions be?* (pp. 125–139). Cambridge, UK: Cambridge University Press.

Salmivalli, C., Kaukiainen, A., Kaistaniemi, L., & Lagerspetz, K.M.J. (1999). Self-evaluated self-esteem, peer-evaluated self-esteem, and defensive egotism as predictors of adolescents' participation in bullying situations. *Personality and Social Psychology Bulletin, 25,* 1268–1278.

Sjostrom, L., & Stein, N. (1996). *Bullyproof: A teacher's guide on teasing and bullying.* Wellesley, MA: Wellesley College Center for Research on Women.

Smith, P.K., & Morita, Y. (1999). Introduction. In P.K. Smith, Y. Morita, J. Junger-Tas, D. Olweus, R. Catalano, & P. Slee (Eds.), *The nature of school bullying* (pp. 1–4). New York, NY: Routledge.

Smith, P.K., Sharp, S., Eslea, M., & Thompson, D. (2004). England: the Sheffield project. In P.K. Smith, D. Pepler, & K. Rigby (Eds.), *Bullying in schools: How successful can interventions be?* (pp. 99–123). Cambridge, UK: Cambridge University Press.

South Carolina Educational Television (1995). *Bullying.* Columbia, SC: Author.

Stevens, V., De Bourdeaudhuij, I., & Van Oost, P. (2000). Bullying in Flemish schools: An evaluation of anti-bullying intervention in primary and secondary schools. *British Journal of Educational Psychology, 70,* 195–210.

Stevens, V., Van Oost, P., & De Bourdeaudhuij, I. (2004). Interventions against bullying in Flemish schools: Programme development and evaluation. In P.K. Smith, D. Pepler, & K. Rigby (Eds.), *Bullying in schools: How successful can interventions be?* (pp. 141–165). New York, NY: Cambridge University Press.

Ttofi, M.M., Farrington, D.P., & Baldry, A.C. (2008). *Effectiveness of Programmes to Reduce Bullying.* Stockholm, Sweden: Swedish National Council for Crime Prevention.

Whitney, I., Rivers, I., Smith, P.K., & Sharp, S. (1994). The Sheffield Project: Methodology and findings. In P.K. Smith & S. Sharp (Eds.), *School Bullying: Insights and Perspectives* (pp. 20–56). New York, NY: Routledge.

INDEX